D. W. Davies (Ed.)

Advances in Cryptology– EUROCRYPT '91

Workshop on the Theory and Application
of Cryptographic Techniques
Brighton, UK, April 8-11, 1991
Proceedings

Springer-Verlag
Berlin Heidelberg New York
London Paris Tokyo
Hong Kong Barcelona
Budapest

Series Editors

Gerhard Goos
GMD Forschungsstelle
Universität Karlsruhe
Vincenz-Priessnitz-Straße 1
W-7500 Karlsruhe, FRG

Juris Hartmanis
Department of Computer Science
Cornell University
Upson Hall
Ithaca, NY 14853, USA

Volume Editor

Donald W. Davies
Royal Holloway and Bedford New College, Univ. of London
Egham Hill, Surrey TW 20 0EX, UK

CR Subject Classification (1991): E.3-4, D.4.6, H.2.0, G.2.1

ISBN 3-540-54620-0 Springer-Verlag Berlin Heidelberg New York
ISBN 0-387-54620-0 Springer-Verlag New York Berlin Heidelberg

© Springer-Verlag Berlin Heidelberg 1991
Printed in Germany

Typesetting: Camera ready by author
Printing and binding: Druckhaus Beltz, Hemsbach/Bergstr.
45/3140-543210 - Printed on acid-free paper

Preface

A series of open workshops devoted to modern cryptology began in Santa Barbara, California in 1981 and was followed in 1982 by a European counterpart in Burg Feurstein, Germany. The series has been maintained with summer meetings in Santa Barbara and spring meetings somewhere in Europe. At the 1983 meeting in Santa Barbara the International Association for Cryptologic Research was launched and it now sponsors all the meetings of the series.

Following the tradition of the series, papers were invited in the form of extended abstracts and were reviewed by the programme committee, which selected those to be presented. After the meeting, full papers were produced, in some cases with improvements and corrections. These papers form the main part of the present volume. They are placed in the same order that they took at the meeting and under the same headings, for ease of reference by those who attended. The classification under these headings was a little arbitrary, needing to fit the timing of the day's activities, but it makes a workable method of arrangement.

Also following tradition, a "rump session" was held during one evening, under the effective chairmanship of John Gordon. These were short presentations and those present found them to have some real interest, therefore we have taken the unusual step of including short papers contributed by the rump session speakers at the end of this volume, with a necessarily simplified review process.

There was no attempt by the programme committee to guide the programme towards particular themes, though the interests of the committee members may have influeced the shape of the meeting. In our admittedly rough classification the biggest group was about sequences, the term interpreted rather widely. The next biggest group concerned cryptanalysis, which was welcomed because cryptanalysis is the criterion by which algorithms and protocols in cryptography must be judged.

Zero-knowledge interactive protocols figured less this year than at earlier meetings - a consequence of the submissions we received, not of policy.

Smaller groups of papers dealt with S-box criteria, signatures and new ideas in public key cryptography. Then there were many papers placed into sessions labelled "theory" and "applications".

My task as programme chair was made easier by the high quality of papers we received, though we regretted having to reject some of the papers because of time limitations. I would like to thank the programme committee for its hard work of reviewing papers and the organizing committee for ensuring that everything ran smoothly, including the social events. Then, of course, the authors deserve many thanks for favouring Eurocrypt '91 with the publication of their excellent work and for preparing their final papers with (in most cases) admirable despatch.

London, August 1991   Donald W. Davies

EUROCRYPT '91

General Chairman:
Andrew J. Clark
(Logica Aerospace and Defence Ltd.)

Organizing Committee:
Keith Martin
(Royal Holloway and Bedford New College, Univ. of London)
Martin Meikle-Small (Aspen Consultants)
Ben Meisner (RHBNC)
Kathleen Quinn (RHBNC)
Matthew Robshaw (RHBNC)

Program Chairman:
Donald W. Davies (RBHNC)

Program Committee:
Thomas Beth (Univ. of Karlsruhe)
Colin Boyd (Univ. of Manchester)
Norbert Cot (EHEI Université, Paris)
Viveke Fåk (Linköping University)
John Gordon (Cybermation Limited)
Siegfried Herda (GMD, Germany)
Arjen Lenstra (Bellcore, NJ)
Tsutomu Matsumoto (Yokohama National Univ.)
Fred Piper (RHBNC)
Claus Schnorr (Universität Frankfurt)

EUROCRYPT '91 was sponsored by:
International Association for Cryptologic Research (IACR)
in association with:
Logica Aerospace and Defence Limited
ABN Bank
Coopers and Lybrand Deloitte
Northern Telecom
with additional support from:
Computer Security Limited
IBM United Kingdom Limited

Contents

Differential Cryptanalysis of Feal and N-Hash

Eli Biham   *Adi Shamir*

The Weizmann Institute of Science
Department of Applied Mathematics and Computer Science
Rehovot 76100, Israel

Abstract

In [1,2] we introduced the notion of differential cryptanalysis and described its application to DES[8] and several of its variants. In this paper we show the applicability of differential cryptanalysis to the Feal family of encryption algorithms and to the N-Hash hash function.

1   Introduction

Feal is a family of encryption algorithms, which are designed to have simple and efficient software implementations on 8-bit microprocessors. The original member of this family, called Feal-4[10], had four rounds. This version was broken by Den Boer[3] using a chosen plaintext attack with 100 to 10000 ciphertexts.

The designers of Feal reacted by creating a second version, called Feal-8[9,7]. This version used the same F function as Feal-4, but increased the number of rounds to eight.

Feal-8 was broken by the chosen plaintext differential cryptanalytic attack described in this paper. As a result, two new versions were added to the family: Feal-N[4] with any even number N of rounds, and Feal-NX[5] with an extended 128-bit key. In addition, The designers proposed a more complex eight-round version called N-Hash[6] as a cryptographically strong hash function which maps arbitrarily long inputs into 128-bit values.

The main results reported in this paper are as follows: Feal-8 is breakable under a chosen plaintext attack with 2000 ciphertexts. Feal-N can be broken faster than via exhaustive search for any $N \leq 31$ rounds, and Feal-NX is just as easy to break as Feal-N for any value of N. The chosen plaintext differential cryptanalytic attacks can be transformed into known plaintext attacks, and can be applied even in the CBC mode of operation, provided we have sufficiently many known plaintext/ciphertext pairs (about 2^{38} in the case of Feal-8). Variants of N-Hash with up to 12 rounds can be broken faster than via the birthday paradox, but for technical reasons we can apply this attack only when the number of rounds is divisible by three. In the full paper we also show that Feal-4 is trivially breakable with eight chosen plaintexts or via a non-differential attack with about 100000 known plaintexts.

2 Differential Cryptanalysis of Feal

The notion of differential cryptanalysis and its application to DES-like cryptosystems are described in [1,2]. Due to space limitations, we can only give a high level description of such an attack in this extended abstract.

The basic tool of differential cryptanalytic attacks is a pair of ciphertexts whose corresponding plaintexts have a particular difference. The method analyses many pairs with the same difference and locates the most probable key. For Feal the difference is chosen as a particular XORed value of the two plaintexts.

The following notation is used in this paper:

n_x: An hexadecimal number is denoted by a subscript x (i.e., $10_x = 16$).

X^*, X': At any intermediate point during the encryption of pairs of messages, X and X^* are the corresponding intermediate values of the two executions of the algorithm, and X' is defined to be $X' = X \oplus X^*$.

P: The plaintext. P^* is the other plaintext in the pair and $P' = P \oplus P^*$ is the plaintexts XOR.

T: The ciphertexts of the corresponding plaintexts P, P^* are denoted by T and T^*. $T' = T \oplus T^*$ is the ciphertexts XOR.

(l, r): The left and right halves of the ciphertext T are denoted by l and r respectively.

$a, \ldots, h$: The 32 bit inputs of the F function in the various rounds. See figure 1.

$A, \ldots, H$: The 32 bit outputs of the F function in the various rounds. See figure 1.

ROL2(X): Rotation of the byte X by two bits to the left.

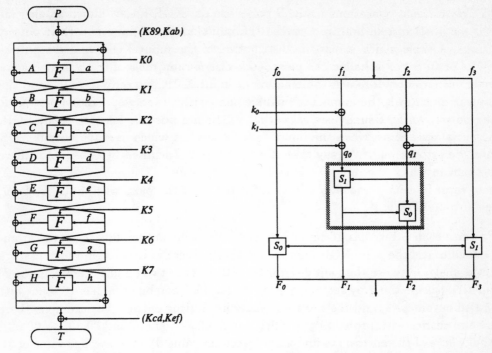

Figure 1: The structure and the F function of Feal-8

$S_i(x, y)$: The Feal S boxes: $S_i(x, y) = \mathrm{ROL2}(x + y + i \pmod{256})$.

q_i^x: The value inside the F function, with input x (one of h, g, ...). Used as q_i for anonymous input and as q^x for the 16-bit value. See figure 1.

X_i: The ith byte of X (for 16, 32 or 64-bit X).

$X_{i,j}$: The jth bit of X_i (where 0 is the least significant bit).

$\#X$: The number of bits set to 1 in the lower seven bits of byte X.

$|$: The logical-or operator.

The structure of Feal (see figure 1) is similar to the structure of DES with a new F function and modified initial and final transformations. The F function of Feal contains two new operations: byte rotation which is XOR-linear and byte addition which is not XOR-linear. The byte addition operation is the only non linear operation in Feal and therefore the strength of Feal crucially depends on its non-linearity. At the beginning and at the end of the encryption process the right half of the data is XORed with the left half of the data and the whole data is XORed with additional subkeys, rather than permuted as in DES. Due to their linearity, these XORs pose only minor difficulty to our attacks.

The addition operations in the S boxes are not XOR-linear. However, there is still a statistical relationship between the input XORs of pairs and their output XORs. A table which shows the distribution of the input XORs and the output XORs of an S box is called the *pairs XOR distribution table* of the S box. Such a table has an entry for each combination of input XOR and output XOR, and the value of an entry is the number of possible pairs with the corresponding input XOR and output XOR. Usually several output XORs are possible for each input XOR. A special case arises when the input XOR is zero, in which case the output XOR must be zero as well. We say that X *may cause* Y (denoted by $X \to Y$) if there is a pair in which the input XOR is X and the output XOR is Y. We say that X *may cause* Y *with probability* p if for a fraction p of the pairs with input XOR X, the output XOR is Y.

Since each S box has 16 input bits and only eight output bits it is not recommended to use the pairs XOR distribution tables directly. Instead, in the first stage of the analysis we use the joint distribution table of the two middle S boxes in the F function (inside the gray rectangle in figure 1). This combination has 16 input bits and 16 output bits, and the table has many interesting entries. For example, there are two entries with probability 1 which are $00\ 00_x \to 00\ 00_x$ and $80\ 80_x \to 00\ 02_x$. About 98% of the entries are impossible (contain value 0). The average value of all the entries is 1, but the average value of the possible entries is about 50. In the full paper we describe how we can easily decide if $X \to Y$ or not for given XOR values X and Y without consulting the table.

The S boxes also have the following properties with respect to pairs: Let $Z = S_i(X, Y)$. If $X' = 80_x$ and $Y' = 80_x$ then $Z' = 00_x$ always. If $X' = 80_x$ and $Y' = 00_x$ then $Z' = 02_x$ always. For any input XORs X' and Y' of the S boxes the resultant output XOR $Z' = \mathrm{ROL2}(X' \oplus Y')$ is obtained with probability about $\frac{1}{2^{\#(X'|Y')}}$. This happens because each bit which is different in the pairs (X and X^*, or Y and Y^*) gives rise to a different carry with probability close to $\frac{1}{2}$. If all the carries happen at the same bits in the pair then the equation is satisfied.

The final XOR of the subkeys with the ciphertexts is significant when we look for the subkeys. The input of the F function in the last round is a function of the ciphertext XORed with an additional subkey of the final transformation rather than just a function of the ciphertext (as in DES). Therefore, the counting scheme finds a XOR combination of the subkey of the last round and the additional subkey, rather than the subkey of the last round itself.

Definition 1 *The actual XOR combinations of subkeys which are found by the attack are called* **actual subkeys**. *The actual subkey of round* $i + 1$ *is denoted by* AKi. *The 16-bit XOR combinations* $(AKi_0 \oplus AKi_1, AKi_2 \oplus AKi_3)$ *are called* **16-bit actual subkeys**. *The actual subkey of the last round of a cryptosystem is called the* **last actual subkey**.

Example 1 *The actual subkeys of Feal-8 in the even rounds $i + 1$ are the 32 bit values*

$$AKi = Kcd \oplus Kef \oplus \mathrm{am}(Ki)$$

where $\mathrm{am}(Ki)$ *is the 32-bit value* $(0, Ki_0, Ki_1, 0)$. *The actual subkeys in the odd rounds are the 32 bit values*

$$AKi = Kcd \oplus \mathrm{am}(Ki).$$

A tool which pushes the knowledge of the XORs of pairs as many rounds as possible is called a *characteristic*. An *n-round characteristic* Ω starts with an input XOR value Ω_P and assigns a probability in which the data XOR after n rounds becomes Ω_T. Two characteristics Ω^1 and Ω^2 can be concatenated to form a longer characteristic whenever Ω_T^1 equals the swapped value of the two halves of Ω_P^2, and the probability of Ω is the product of the probabilities of Ω^1 and Ω^2. A pair whose intermediate XORs equal the values specified by a characteristic is called a *right pair* with respect to the characteristic. Any other pair is called a *wrong pair* with respect to the characteristic. Note that in Feal, the plaintext XOR P' is different from the input XOR of the characteristic Ω_P due to the initial and final transformations.

Given a sufficiently long characteristic and a right pair we can calculate the output XOR of F function in the last round. The inputs themselves of this F function are known from the ciphertexts up to a XOR with subkeys. For any possible value of the last actual subkey, we count the number of possible pairs for which the output XOR is as expected. Every right pair suggests the right value of the actual subkey. The wrong pairs suggest random values. Since the right pairs occur with the characteristic's probability, the right value of the actual subkey should be counted more often than any other value. Therefore, it can be identified.

The simplest example of a one-round characteristic with probability 1 is:

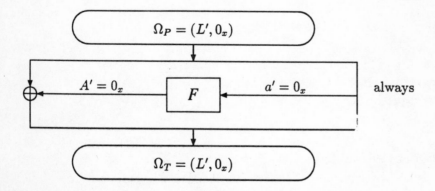

There are three other one-round characteristics with probability 1. A typical one is:

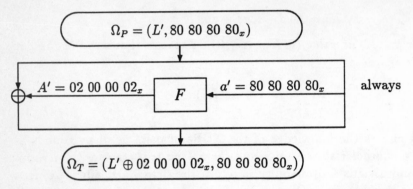

Three non trivial three-round characteristics with probability 1 also exist.

A five-round characteristic with probability $\frac{1}{16}$, a six-round characteristic with probability $\frac{1}{128}$ and an iterative characteristic with probability $\frac{1}{4}$ per round are described later in this extended abstract.

3 Cryptanalysis of Feal-8

In this section we describe a differential cryptanalytic attack on Feal-8 which uses about 1000 pairs of ciphertexts whose corresponding plaintexts are chosen at random satisfying

$$P' = A2\ 00\ 80\ 00\ 22\ 80\ 80\ 00_x.$$

The plaintext XOR is motivated by the following six round characteristic whose probability is 1/128:

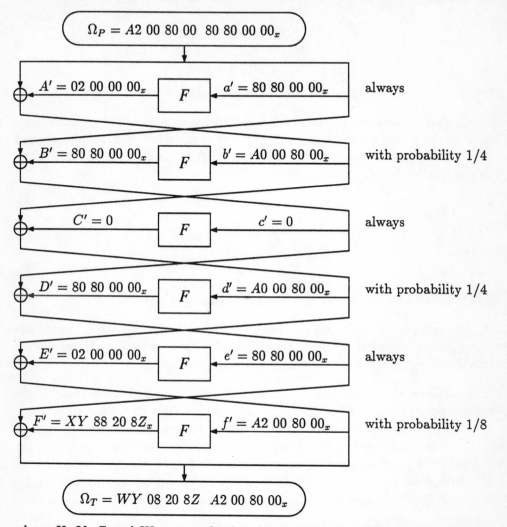

where X, Y, Z and W are not fixed and can range (for different right pairs) over $X \in \{5, 6, 7, 9, A, B, D, E, F\}$, $Y \in \{9, A, B\}$, $Z \in \{0, 1, 3\}$ and $W = X \oplus 8$.

In order to find the last actual subkey we do the following. Given the ciphertexts T and T^* of a right pair, we can deduce:

$$
\begin{aligned}
g' &= WY\ 08\ 20\ 8Z_x \\
h' &= l' \oplus r' \\
G' &= f' \oplus h' = A2\ 00\ 80\ 00_x \oplus l' \oplus r' \\
H' &= l' \oplus g' = l' \oplus WY\ 08\ 20\ 8Z_x.
\end{aligned}
$$

Therefore, all the bits of h' and G' and 24 bits of each of g' and H' are known.

The counting method is used to find the 16-bit last actual subkey. Filtering can be done by the knowledge of bits in the other two bytes of H' and in the seventh round. Assuming $g' \to G'$ we can reverse calculate the values of $g'_{i,0}$ from G' by

$$
\begin{aligned}
g'_{0,0} &= G'_{0,2} \oplus G'_{1,0} \\
g'_{3,0} &= G'_{3,2} \oplus G'_{2,0} \\
g'_{2,0} &= G'_{2,2} \oplus G'_{1,0} \oplus g'_{3,0} \\
g'_{1,0} &= G'_{1,2} \oplus g'_{0,0} \oplus g'_{2,0} \oplus g'_{3,0}
\end{aligned}
$$

and verify that the two known bits $g'_{1,0}$ and $g'_{2,0}$ from the characteristic are the same. About $\frac{3}{4}$ of the wrong pairs are discarded by this verification. We can also discard about $\frac{4}{5}$ of the other wrong pairs for which $g' \not\to G'$. Assuming $h' \to H'$ we can verify the four bits of $H'_{i,2}$ by

$$
\begin{aligned}
H'_{0,2} &= H'_{1,0} \oplus h'_{0,0} \\
H'_{1,2} &= h'_{0,0} \oplus h'_{1,0} \oplus h'_{2,0} \oplus h'_{3,0} \\
H'_{2,2} &= H'_{1,0} \oplus h'_{2,0} \oplus h'_{3,0} \\
H'_{3,2} &= H'_{2,0} \oplus h'_{3,0}.
\end{aligned}
$$

This verification discards about $\frac{15}{16}$ of the remaining wrong pairs.

All the right pairs must be verified correctly. Only $\frac{1}{4} \cdot \frac{1}{5} \cdot \frac{1}{16} = \frac{1}{320}$ of the wrong pairs should pass the three filters. Since the right pairs occur with the characteristic's probability of $\frac{1}{128}$, most of the remaining pairs are right pairs.

The counting scheme counts the number of pairs for which each value of the 16-bit last actual subkey is possible. Our calculations show that the right value is about 2^{15} times more likely to be counted than a random value. This ratio is so high that only eight right pairs are typically needed for the attack, and thus the total number of pairs we have to examine is about $8 \cdot 128 \approx 1000$. Note that we cannot distinguish between the right value of the actual subkey and the same value XORed with 80 80_x. Therefore, we find two possibilities for the 16-bit actual subkey.

Given the last 16-bit actual subkey it is possible to extend it to the full last actual subkey and then find the previous actual subkeys using similar approaches with shorter characteristics whose probabilities are much higher. Once the last actual subkey is found, we can partially decrypt the ciphertexts and proceed to find the previous five actual subkeys from which we can derive the following values:

$$
\begin{aligned}
&K5 \oplus K7 \\
&K4 \oplus K6 \\
&K3 \oplus K5 \\
&K2 \oplus K4 \\
&K1 \oplus K3.
\end{aligned}
$$

Using these values we can easily derive the value of the key itself by analyzing the structure of the key processing algorithm.

This attack was implemented on a COMPAQ personal computer. It finds the key in less than two minutes using 1000 pairs with more than 95% success rate. Using 2000 pairs it finds the key with almost 100% success rate. The program uses 280K bytes of memory.

4 Cryptanalysis of Feal-N and Feal-NX with $N \leq$ 31 rounds

Feal-N[4] was suggested as an N-round extension of Feal-8 after our attack on Feal-8 was announced. Feal-NX[5] is similar to Feal-N but uses a longer 128-bit key and a different key processing algorithm. Since our attack ignores the key processing and finds the actual subkeys, we can apply it to both Feal-N and Feal-NX with identical complexity and performance.

The attack on Feal with an arbitrary number of rounds is based on the following iterative characteristic:

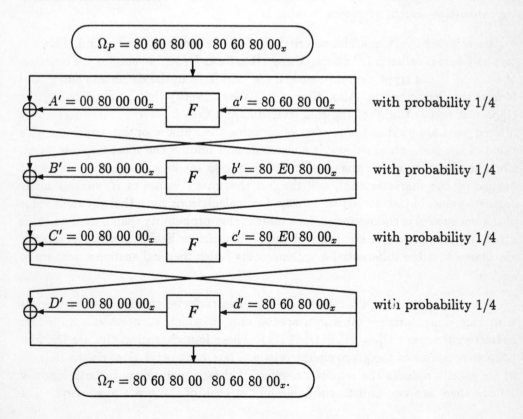

$$\Omega_P = 80\ 60\ 80\ 00\ \ 80\ 60\ 80\ 00_x$$

$A' = 00\ 80\ 00\ 00_x$ F $a' = 80\ 60\ 80\ 00_x$ with probability 1/4

$B' = 00\ 80\ 00\ 00_x$ F $b' = 80\ E0\ 80\ 00_x$ with probability 1/4

$C' = 00\ 80\ 00\ 00_x$ F $c' = 80\ E0\ 80\ 00_x$ with probability 1/4

$D' = 00\ 80\ 00\ 00_x$ F $d' = 80\ 60\ 80\ 00_x$ with probability 1/4

$$\Omega_T = 80\ 60\ 80\ 00\ \ 80\ 60\ 80\ 00_x.$$

The probability of each round of this characteristic is 1/4, and it can be concatenated to itself any number of times since the swapped value of the two halves of Ω_P equals Ω_T. Thus, an n-round characteristic with probability $\frac{1}{4^n} = 2^{-2n}$ can be obtained.

An attack based on a characteristic which is shorter by two rounds than the cryptosystem is called a *2R-attack*. In this case, we know the ciphertext XOR T' and the input XOR of the last round (w.l.g. we employ the notation of an eight-round cryptosystem) h' by the ciphertext, and f' and g' by the characteristic. Thus, $G' = f' \oplus h'$ and $H' = g' \oplus l'$. Each pair is verified to have $g' \to G'$ and $h' \to H'$ and the resultant pairs are used in the process of counting the possibilities in order to find the last actual subkey. The counting is done in two steps. In the first step we find the 16-bit last actual subkey. In the second step we find the two other eight-bit values of the last actual subkey. Two of the bits of the last actual subkey are indistinguishable. Therefore, we must try the following steps in parallel for the four possibilities of these two bits. The verification of $g' \to G'$ leaves only 2^{-19} of the pairs (since for either $g' = 80\ 60\ 80\ 00_x$ or $g' = 80\ E0\ 80\ 00_x$ there are only about 2^{13} possible output XORs G'). The verification of $h' \to H'$ leaves 2^{-11} of the pairs (the fraction of the possible entries in the pairs XORs distribution table of the F function). Our calculations show that the right value of the last subkey is counted with a detectably higher probability than a random value up to $N \leq 28$ rounds, and thus we can break Feal-N with 2R-attacks for any $N \leq 28$ rounds, faster than via exhaustive search, as shown in table 1.

An attack based on a characteristic which is shorter by one round than the cryptosystem is called a *1R-attack*. Using 1R-attacks (w.l.g. we employ the notation of an eight-round cryptosystem), we know T' and h' from the ciphertext and g' and h' from the characteristic. Also, $H' = g' \oplus l'$. We can verify that h' calculated by the ciphertext equals the h' of the characteristic, and that $h' \to H'$. The successfully filtered pairs are used in the process of counting the number of times each possible value of the last actual subkey is suggested, and finding the most popular value. Complicating factors are the small number of bits set in h' (which is a constant defined by the characteristic), and the fact that many values of H' suggest many common values of the last actual subkey. Our calculations show that the right value of the last subkey is counted with detectably higher probability than a random value up to $N \leq 31$ rounds. A summary of the 1R-attacks on Feal-N appears in table 1, and shows that the differential cryptanalysis is faster than exhaustive search up to $N \leq 31$.

Note that in both the 1R-attacks and the 2R-attacks we use eight-message octets with four characteristics (this is a special case in which an octet can have four characteristics since $\Omega_P^4 = \Omega_P^1 \oplus \Omega_P^2 \oplus \Omega_P^3$). These four characteristics are the four possible rotations of the given characteristic. Thus, each octet gives rise to 16 pairs which greatly reduces the required number of chosen plaintexts. In both kinds of attacks there are two indistinguishable bits at each of the last two subkeys. The

N	2R-attack			1R-attack		
	Prob	Pairs	Data	Prob	Pairs	Data
8	2^{-12}	2^{14}	2^{13}	2^{-14}	2^{17}	2^{16}
9	2^{-14}	2^{16}	2^{15}	2^{-16}	2^{19}	2^{18}
10	2^{-16}	2^{18}	2^{17}	2^{-18}	2^{21}	2^{20}
11	2^{-18}	2^{20}	2^{19}	2^{-20}	2^{23}	2^{22}
12	2^{-20}	2^{22}	2^{21}	2^{-22}	2^{25}	2^{24}
13	2^{-22}	2^{24}	2^{23}	2^{-24}	2^{27}	2^{26}
14	2^{-24}	2^{26}	2^{25}	2^{-26}	2^{29}	2^{28}
15	2^{-26}	2^{28}	2^{27}	2^{-28}	2^{31}	2^{30}
16	2^{-28}	2^{30}	2^{29}	2^{-30}	2^{33}	2^{32}
17	2^{-30}	2^{32}	2^{31}	2^{-32}	2^{35}	2^{34}
18	2^{-32}	2^{34}	2^{33}	2^{-34}	2^{37}	2^{36}
19	2^{-34}	2^{36}	2^{35}	2^{-36}	2^{39}	2^{38}
20	2^{-36}	2^{38}	2^{37}	2^{-38}	2^{41}	2^{40}
21	2^{-38}	2^{40}	2^{39}	2^{-40}	2^{43}	2^{42}
22	2^{-40}	2^{42}	2^{41}	2^{-42}	2^{45}	2^{44}
23	2^{-42}	2^{44}	2^{43}	2^{-44}	2^{47}	2^{46}
24	2^{-44}	2^{46}	2^{45}	2^{-46}	2^{49}	2^{48}
25	2^{-46}	2^{49}	2^{48}	2^{-48}	2^{51}	2^{50}
26	2^{-48}	2^{52}	2^{51}	2^{-50}	2^{53}	2^{52}
27	2^{-50}	2^{55}	2^{54}	2^{-52}	2^{55}	2^{54}
28	2^{-52}	2^{58}	2^{57}	2^{-54}	2^{57}	2^{56}
29	2^{-54}			2^{-56}	2^{59}	2^{58}
30	2^{-56}			2^{-58}	2^{61}	2^{60}
31	2^{-58}			2^{-60}	2^{64}	$\underline{2^{63}}$
32	2^{-60}			2^{-62}	2^{67}	$\underline{2^{66}}$

Table 1: Attacks on Feal-N

attacking program should try all the 16 possible values of these bits when analyzing the earlier subkeys.

5 Known Plaintext Differential Cryptanalytic Attacks

Differential cryptanalytic attacks are chosen plaintext attacks in which the plaintext pairs can be chosen at random as long as they satisfy the plaintext XOR condition. Unlike other chosen plaintext attacks, differential cryptanalytic attacks can be easily converted to known plaintext attacks by the following observation.

Assume that the chosen plaintext differential cryptanalytic attack needs m pairs, and that we are given $2^{32} \cdot \sqrt{2m}$ random known plaintexts and their corresponding ciphertexts. Consider all the $\frac{\left(2^{32} \cdot \sqrt{2m}\right)^2}{2} = 2^{64} \cdot m$ possible pairs of plaintexts they can form. Each pair has a plaintext XOR which can be easily calculated. Since the block size is 64 bits, there are only 2^{64} possible plaintext XOR values, and thus there are about $\frac{2^{64} \cdot m}{2^{64}} = m$ pairs creating each plaintext XOR value. In particular, with high probability there are about m pairs with each one of the several plaintext XOR values needed for differential cryptanalysis.

The known plaintext attack is not limited to the electronic code book (ECB) mode of operation. In particular, the cipher block chaining (CBC) mode can also be broken by this attack since when the plaintexts and the ciphertexts are known, it is easy to calculate the real input of the encryption function.

Table 2 summarizes the resultant known plaintext differential cryptanalytic attacks on Feal and DES. For each of the listed cryptosystems with the listed number of rounds, the table describes the number of pairs of each characteristic and the total number of random plaintexts needed for the chosen plaintext attack and for the known plaintext attack. These results hold even for the variants with independent subkeys.

6 Cryptanalysis of N-Hash

N-Hash[6] is a cryptographically strong hash function which hashes messages of arbitrary length to 128-bit values. The messages are divided into 128-bit blocks, and each block is mixed with the hashed value computed so far by a randomizing function g. The new hashed value is the XOR of the output of the g-function with the block itself and with the old hashed value. The g-function contains eight randomizing rounds, and each one of them calls the F function (similar to the one

Cryptosystem	Number of pairs of one char	Number of chosen plaintexts	Number of known plaintexts
Feal-4	4	8	$2^{33.5}$
Feal-8	1000	2000	$2^{37.5}$
Feal-16	2^{28}	2^{29}	$2^{46.5}$
Feal-24	2^{44}	2^{45}	$2^{54.5}$
Feal-30	2^{59}	2^{60}	2^{62}
Feal-31	2^{62}	2^{63}	$2^{63.5}$
DES-6	120	240	2^{36}
DES-8	25000	50000	2^{40}
DES-13	2^{43}	2^{44}	2^{54}
DES-14	2^{50}	2^{51}	$2^{57.5}$
DES-15	2^{51}	2^{52}	2^{58}
DES-16	2^{57}	2^{61}	2^{61}

Table 2: Known plaintext attacks on Feal and DES

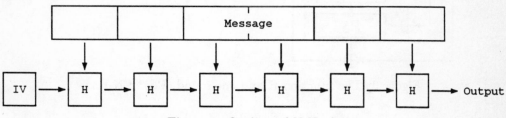

Figure 2: Outline of N-Hash

of Feal) four times. A graphic description of N-Hash is given in figures 2, 3, and 4.

Breaking a cryptographically strong hash function means finding two different messages which hash to the same value. In particular, we break N-Hash by finding two different 128-bit messages which are hashed to the same 128-bit value. Since the output of the g-function is XORed with its input in order to form the hashed value, it suffices to find a right pair for a characteristic of the g-function in which $\Omega_P = \Omega_T$. After XORing the input with the output of the g-function, the hashed value XOR becomes zero and thus the two messages have the same hashed value.

The following characteristic is a three round iterative characteristic with probability 2^{-16} (N-Hash does not swap the two halves after each round since the swap operation is part of the round itself. Therefore, the concatenation of the characteristic Ω^1 with the characteristic Ω^2 is possible whenever $\Omega_T^1 = \Omega_P^2$ without swapping). In the description of this characteristic we refer to the value 80 60 80 00$_x$ as ψ and

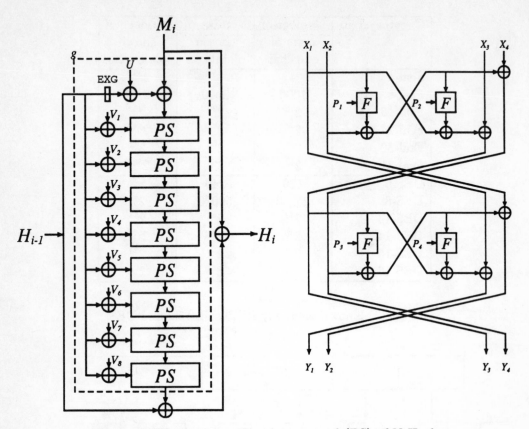

Figure 3: The function H and one round (PS) of N-Hash

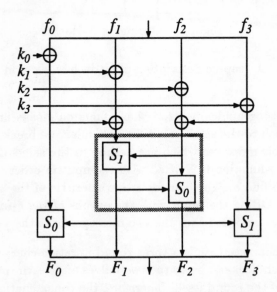

Figure 4: The F function of N-Hash

Number of Rounds	Complexity
3	2^8
6	2^{24}
9	2^{40}
12	2^{56}
15	2^{72}

Table 3: Results of the attack on N-Hash

to the value 80 E0 80 00$_x$ as φ. Note that both $\psi \to (\psi \oplus \varphi)$ and $\varphi \to (\psi \oplus \varphi)$ with probability $\frac{1}{4}$ by the F function. The behavior of the XORs in the F function in this characteristic is similar to their behavior in the iterative characteristic of Feal. The characteristic itself is based on the input XOR:

$$\Omega_P = (\psi, \psi, 0, 0).$$

With probability $\frac{1}{256}$ the data XOR after the first round is

$$(0, 0, \varphi, \varphi).$$

With probability $\frac{1}{256}$ the data XOR after the second round is

$$(\psi, \psi, \varphi, \varphi).$$

The data after the third round is always

$$\Omega_T = \Omega_P = (\psi, \psi, 0, 0).$$

Therefore, the probability of the characteristic is 2^{-16}.

A pair of messages whose XOR equals Ω_P has probability $(2^{-16})^2 = 2^{-32}$ to have Ω_T as its output XOR after the sixth round of the g-function, and thus to have the same hashed value after their inputs and outputs are XORed by the six-round variant of N-Hash. Instead of trying about 2^{32} random pairs of messages we can choose only pairs from a smaller set in which the characteristic is guaranteed to be satisfied in the four F functions in the first round. The probability in this set is increased by a factor of 256, and thus only about 2^{24} such pairs have to be tested in order to find a pair of messages which hash to the same value.

This specific attack works only for variants of N-Hash whose number of rounds is divisible by three. Table 3 describes the results of this attack. We can see from the table that this attack is faster than the birthday attack (whose complexity is 2^{64}) for variants of N-Hash with up to 12 rounds.

The attack on N-Hash with six rounds was implemented on a personal computer and the following pairs of messages were found within about two hours:

- − CAECE595 127ABF3C 1ADE09C8 1F9AD8C2
  − 4A8C6595 921A3F3C 1ADE09C8 1F9AD8C2
  − Common hash value: 12B931A6 399776B7 640B9289 36C2EF1D

- − 5878BE49 F2962D67 30661E17 0C38F35E
  − D8183E49 72F6AD67 30661E17 0C38F35E
  − Common hash value: 29B0FE97 3D179E0E 5B147598 137D28CF.

References

[1] Eli Biham, Adi Shamir, *Differential Cryptanalysis of DES-like Cryptosystems (extended abstract)*, Advances in cryptology, proceedings of CRYPTO 90, 1990.

[2] Eli Biham, Adi Shamir, *Differential Cryptanalysis of DES-like Cryptosystems*, accepted by the Journal of Cryptology, 1990.

[3] Bert Den Boer, *Cryptanalysis of F.E.A.L.*, Advances in cryptology, proceedings of EUROCRYPT 88, 1988.

[4] Shoji Miyaguchi, *Feal-N specifications*.

[5] Shoji Miyaguchi, News on Feal cipher, talk at the RUMP session at CRYPTO 90, 1990.

[6] S. Miyaguchi, K. Ohta, M. Iwata, *128-bit hash function (N-Hash)*, proceedings of SECURICOM 90, pp. 123–137, March 1990.

[7] Shoji Miyaguchi, Akira Shiraishi, Akihiro Shimizu, *Fast Data Encryption Algorithm Feal-8*, Review of electrical communications laboratories, Vol. 36, No. 4, 1988.

[8] National Bureau of Standards, *Data Encryption Standard*, U.S. Department of Commerce, FIPS pub. 46, January 1977.

[9] Akihiro Shimizu, Shoji Miyaguchi, *Fast Data Encryption Algorithm Feal*, Advances in cryptology, proceedings of EUROCRYPT 87, pp. 267, 1987.

[10] Akihiro Shimizu, Shoji Miyaguchi, *Fast Data Encryption Algorithm Feal*, Abstracts of EUROCRYPT 87, Amsterdam, April 1987.

Markov Ciphers
and
Differential Cryptanalysis

Xuejia Lai   James L. Massey

Institute for Signal and Information Processing
Swiss Federal Institute of Technology
CH–8092 Zürich, Switzerland

Sean Murphy
Royal Holloway & Bedford New College
University of London, Egham, Surrey TW20 0EX

Abstract

This paper considers the security of iterated block ciphers against the differential crypt-analysis introduced by Biham and Shamir. Differential cryptanalysis is a chosen-plaintext attack on secret-key block ciphers that are based on iterating a cryptographically weak function r times (e.g., the 16-round Data Encryption Standard (DES)). It is shown that the success of such attacks on an r-round cipher depends on the existence of (r-1)-round differentials that have high probabilities, where an i-round differential is defined as a cou-ple (α, β) such that a pair of distinct plaintexts with difference α can result in a pair of i-th round outputs that have difference β, for an appropriate notion of "difference". The probabilities of such differentials can be used to determine a lower bound on the com-plexity of a differential cryptanalysis attack and to show when an r-round cipher is not vulnerable to such attacks. The concept of "Markov ciphers" is introduced for iterated ciphers because of its significance in differential cryptanalysis. If an iterated cipher is Markov and its round subkeys are independent, then the sequence of differences at each round output forms a Markov chain. It follows from a result of Biham and Shamir that DES is a Markov cipher. It is shown that, for the appropriate notion of "difference", the Proposed Encryption Standard (PES) of Lai and Massey, which is an 8-round iterated cipher, is a Markov cipher, as are also the mini-version of PES with block length 8, 16 and 32 bits. It is shown that PES(8) and PES(16) are immune to differential cryptanalysis after sufficiently many rounds. A detailed cryptanalysis of the full-size PES is given and shows that the very plausibly most probable 7-round differential has a probability about 2^{-58}. A differential cryptanalysis attack of PES(64) based on this differential is shown to require all 2^{64} possible encryptions. This cryptanalysis of PES suggested a new design principle for Markov ciphers, viz., that their transition probability matrices should not be symmetric. A minor modification of PES, consistent with all the original design principles, is proposed that satisfies this new design criterion. This modified cipher, called Improved PES (IPES), is described and shown to be highly resistant to differential cryptanalysis.

1. Introduction

Many secret-key block ciphers are cryptosystems based on iterating a cryptographically weak function several times. Each iteration is called a round. The output of each round is a function of the output of the previous round and of a subkey derived from the full secret key by a key-schedule algorithm. Such a secret-key block cipher with r-iterations is called an r-round iterated cipher. For example, the well-known Data Encryption Standard (DES) is a 16-round iterated cipher.

Differential cryptanalysis, introduced by Biham and Shamir in [1], is a chosen-plaintext attack to find the secret key of an iterated ciphers. It analyzes the effect of the "difference" of a pair of plaintexts on the "difference" of succeeding round outputs in an r-round iterated cipher. In Section 2, we describe differential cryptanalysis of a general r-round iterated cipher in terms of (r-1)-round "differentials" instead of in terms of the "i-round characteristics" used in [1]. The hypothesis of stochastic equivalence, which has been implicitly assumed in differential cryptanalysis, is explicitly formulated in Section 2. It is pointed out that one of the two prerequisites for differential cryptanalysis to succeed on an r-round cipher is the existence of an (r-1)-round differential with high probability, and it is shown that a lower bound on the complexity of differential cryptanalysis can be obtained from the maximum differential probability.

In Section 3, Markov ciphers are defined as iterated ciphers whose round functions satisfy the condition that the differential probability is independent of the choice of one of the component plaintexts under an appropriate definition of difference. It is shown that, for a Markov cipher with independent subkeys, the sequence of round differences forms a Markov chain. It follows from a result of Biham and Shamir [1] that DES is a Markov cipher. The study of differential cryptanalysis for an r-round Markov cipher is reduced to the study of the transition probabilities created by its round function. In particular, Markov chain techniques can be used to show whether the cipher is secure against differential cryptanalysis after sufficiently many rounds.

At Eurocrypt'90, a new iterated cipher, the Proposed Encryption Standard (PES) was introduced by Lai and Massey [2]. The PES contains 8 rounds plus an output transformation. In Section 4, standard PES with block length 64 bits and mini-versions of PES with block length 8, 16 and 32 are considered. These are all shown to be Markov ciphers. The ciphers PES(8) and PES(16) are shown to be immune to differential cryptanalysis after sufficiently many rounds. A detailed cryptanalysis of PES(64), given in the Appendix, shows that the very plausibly most likely one-round differential has probability

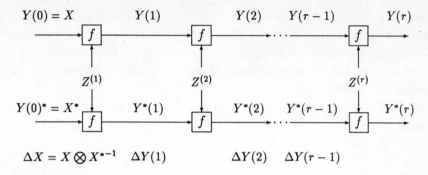

Figure 1: Encrypting a pair of plaintexts with an r-round iterated cipher

about 2^{-9}, which leads to a 7-round differential with probability about 2^{-58}. Differential cryptanalysis of PES(64) based on this differential requires the cryptanalyst to perform all 2^{64} possible encryptions. The attacker thus obtains the secret key after 2^{64} encryptions, which is much less than the 2^{128} encryptions of an exhaustive key search; however, the 2^{64} encryptions specify the entire mapping from plaintext to ciphertext determined by the secret key and hence the attacker has no need to find the actual secret key.

The cryptanalysis of PES shows that the symmetry of transition probability matrix of its Markov chain is responsible for the "undesirably large" probability of its most probable 7-round differential. This suggests a new design principle for Markov ciphers, viz., that their transition probability matrices should not be symmetric. A minor modification of PES, called Improved PES (IPES), was suggested by this new design principle and is described in Section 5. It is shown that this modification substantially improves the security of PES without violating any of the earlier design principles used for PES.

2. Differential Cryptanalysis of Iterated Ciphers

Throughout this paper, we consider the encryption of a pair of *distinct* plaintexts by an r-round iterated cipher as shown schematically in Fig.1. In this figure, the round function $Y = f(X, Z)$ is such that, for every round subkey Z, $f(\cdot, Z)$ establishes a one-to-one correspondence between the round input X and the round output Y. Let the "difference" ΔX between two plaintexts (or two ciphertexts) X and X^* be defined as

$$\Delta X = X \otimes X^{*-1},$$

where $\otimes$ denotes a specified group operation on the set of plaintexts (= set of ciphertexts) and X^{*-1} denotes the inverse of the element X^* in the group. The round function $Y = f(X, Z)$ is said to be *cryptographically weak* if, given a few triples $(\Delta X, Y, Y^*)$, it is feasible (in most cases) to determine the subkey Z.

From the pair of encryptions, one obtains the sequence of differences $\Delta Y(0), \Delta Y(1), ...,$ $\Delta Y(r)$ where $Y(0) = X$ and $Y^*(0) = X^*$ denote the plaintext pair [so that $\Delta Y(0) = \Delta X$]

and where $Y(i)$ and $Y^*(i)$ for $(0 < i < r)$ are the outputs of the i-th round, which are also the inputs to the (i+1)-th round. The subkey for the i-th round is denoted as $Z^{(i)}$. In the following discussion, we always assume that $X \neq X^*$ because, when $X = X^*$, all $\Delta Y(i)$ would equal the *neutral* element e of the group, which case is of no interest for differential cryptanalysis.

Differential cryptanalysis exploits the fact that the round function f in an iterated cipher is usually cryptographically weak. Thus, if the ciphertext pair is known and the difference of the pair of inputs to the last round can somehow be obtained, then it is possible to determine (some substantial part of) the subkey of the last round. In differential cryptanalysis, this is achieved by *choosing* plaintext pairs (X, X^*) with a specified difference α such that the difference $\Delta Y(r-1)$ of the pair of inputs to the last round will take on a particular value β with high probability. Based on this idea, we make the following definition.

Definition. An *i-round differential* is a couple (α, β), where α is the difference of a pair of distinct plaintexts X and X^* and where β is a possible difference for the resulting i-th round outputs $Y(i)$ and $Y^*(i)$. The *probability of an i-round differential* (α, β) is the conditional probability that β is the difference $\Delta Y(i)$ of the ciphertext pair after i rounds given that the plaintext pair (X, X^*) has difference $\Delta X = \alpha$ *when the plaintext* X *and the subkeys* $Z^{(1)}, ..., Z^{(i)}$ *are independent and uniformly random.* We denote this differential probability by $P(\Delta Y(i) = \beta | \Delta X = \alpha)$.

The basic procedure of a differential cryptanalysis *attack* on an r-round iterated cipher can be summarized as follows:

1) Find an (r-1)-round differential (α, β) such that $P(\Delta Y(r-1) = \beta | \Delta X = \alpha)$ has maximum, or nearly maximum, probability.

2) Choose a plaintext X uniformly at random and compute X^* so that the difference ΔX between X and X^* is α. Submit X and X^* for encryption under the actual key Z. From the resultant ciphertexts $Y(r)$ and $Y^*(r)$, find every possible value (if any) of the subkey $Z^{(r)}$ of the last round corresponding to the anticipated difference $\Delta Y(r-1) = \beta$. Add one to the count of the number of appearances of each such value of the subkey $Z^{(r)}$.

3) Repeat 2) until one or more values of the subkey $Z^{(r)}$ are counted significantly more often than the others. Take this most-often-counted subkey, or this small set of such subkeys, as the cryptanalyst's decision for the actual subkey $Z^{(r)}$.

Note that, in a differential cryptanalysis attack, all the subkeys are *fixed* and only the plaintext can be randomly chosen. In the computation of a differential probability, however, the plaintext and all subkeys are independent and uniformly random. In preparing a differential cryptanalysis attack, one uses the computed differential probabilities to determine which differential to use in the attack; hence, one is tacitly making the following hypothesis.

Hypothesis of Stochastic Equivalence.   For an (r-1)-round differential (α, β),

$$P(\Delta Y(r-1) = \beta | \Delta X = \alpha) \approx P(\Delta Y(r-1) = \beta | \Delta X = \alpha, Z^{(1)} = \omega_1, ..., Z^{(r-1)} = \omega_{r-1})$$

for almost all subkey values $(\omega_1, ..., \omega_{r-1})$.

From the above description of a differential cryptanalysis attack and from the fact that there are $2^m - 1$ possible values of $\Delta Y(r-1)$, one deduces the following result.

Suppose the hypothesis of stochastic equivalence is true, then an r-round cipher with independent subkeys is vulnerable to differential cryptanalysis if and only if the round function is weak and there exists an (r-1)-round differential (α, β) such that $P(\Delta Y(r-1) = \beta | \Delta X = \alpha) \gg 2^{-m}$, where m is the block length of the cipher.

Let $Comp(r)$ denote the *complexity* of differential cryptanalysis of an r-round cipher which, following [1], is defined as the number of encryptions used.

Theorem 1.   *(Lower bound on the complexity of a differential cryptanalysis attack on an r-round iterated cipher.)*
Suppose the hypothesis of stochastic equivalence is true, then, in an attack by differential cryptanalysis,

$$Comp(r) \geq 2/(p_{max} - \frac{1}{2^m - 1}) \text{ where } p_{max} = \max_\alpha \max_\beta P(\Delta Y(r-1) = \beta | \Delta X = \alpha),$$

and where m is the block length of the plaintext In particular, if $p_{max} \approx \frac{1}{2^m-1}$, then a differential cryptanalysis attack will not succeed.

Proof.   Note that the anticipated value β of the difference $\Delta Y(r-1)$ must certainly be taken on at least once more on the average than a randomly chosen value β' if differential cryptanalysis is to succeed. Thus, $Tp_{max} \geq \frac{T}{2^m-1} + 1$ is a necessary condition for success in T trials, where each trial consists in choosing a pair of plaintexts with the specified difference α.

Remark. In [1], differential cryptanalysis of DES was described in terms of "i-round characteristics". In our notation, an i-round characteristic as defined in [1] is an $(i+1)$-tuple $(\alpha, \beta_1, ..., \beta_i)$ considered as a possible value of $(\Delta X, \Delta Y(1), ..., \Delta Y(i))$. Thus, a one-round characteristic coincides with a one-round differential and an i-round characteristic determines a sequence of i differentials, $(\Delta X, \Delta Y(j)) = (\alpha, \beta_j)$. The probability of an i-round characteristic is defined in [1] as

$$P(\Delta Y(1) = \beta_1, \Delta Y(2) = \beta_2, .., \Delta Y(i) = \beta_i | \Delta X = \alpha)$$

where the plaintext X and the subkeys $Z^{(1)}, ..., Z^{(i)}$ are independent and uniformly random. We use the notion of differentials rather than characteristics because, in the differential cryptanalysis of an r-round cipher, only the knowledge of $\Delta Y(r-1)$ is required for determining the subkey $Z^{(r)}$, no matter what the intermediate differences

$\Delta Y(j), 1 \leq j < r - 1$, may be. The most probable differential will have in general a probability greater than that of the most probable characteristic (although for DES with a small number of rounds, the two probabilities are roughly the same). Thus, by using differential probabilities rather than characteristic probabilities, we consider in fact the true probability that differential cryptanalysis will succeed, not just a lower bound on this probability. This is why we were able to derive a *lower bound* on the complexity of a differential cryptanalysis attack from the probability of differentials.

3. Markov Ciphers

In this section, a class of iterated ciphers that are especially interesting for differential cryptanalysis will be considered. For such a cipher, the sequence $\Delta Y(0), \Delta Y(1), ..., \Delta Y(r)$ forms a Markov chain. Recall that a sequence of discrete random variables $v_0, v_1, ..., v_r$ is a *Markov chain* if, for $0 \leq i < r$ (where $r = \infty$ is allowed),

$$P(v_{i+1} = \beta_{i+1} | v_i = \beta_i, v_{i-1} = \beta_{i-1}, ..., v_0 = \beta_0) = P(v_{i+1} = \beta_{i+1} | v_i = \beta_i).$$

A Markov chain is called *homogeneous* if $P(v_{i+1} = \beta | v_i = \alpha)$ is independent of i for all α and β. [In what follows, we always assume that the plaintext X is independent of the subkeys $Z^{(1)}, ..., Z^{(r)}$.]

Definition. An iterated cipher with round function $Y = f(X, Z)$ is a *Markov cipher* if there is a group operation $\otimes$ for defining differences such that, for all choices of α ($\alpha \neq e$) and β ($\beta \neq e$),

$$P(\Delta Y = \beta | \Delta X = \alpha, X = \gamma)$$

is independent of γ when the subkey Z is uniformly random, or, equivalently, if

$$P(\Delta Y = \beta | \Delta X = \alpha, X = \gamma) = P(\Delta Y(1) = \beta_1 | \Delta X = \alpha)$$

for all choices of γ when the subkey Z is uniformly random.

The following crucial theorem explains the terminology "Markov cipher".

Theorem 2. *If an r-round iterated cipher is a Markov cipher and the r round keys are independent and uniformly random, then the sequence of differences $\Delta X = \Delta Y(0)$, $\Delta Y(1), ..., \Delta Y(r)$ is a homogeneous Markov chain. Moreover, this Markov chain is stationary if ΔX is uniformly distributed over the non-neutral elements of the group.*

Proof. To show that the sequence $\Delta X, \Delta Y(1), ..., \Delta Y(r)$ is a Markov chain, it is sufficient to show for the second round that

$$P(\Delta Y(2) = \beta_2 | \Delta Y(1) = \beta_1, \Delta X = \alpha) = P(\Delta Y(2) = \beta_2 | \Delta Y(1) = \beta_1).$$

To show this, we note that

$$P(\Delta Y(2) = \beta_2 | \Delta Y(1) = \beta_1, \Delta X = \alpha)$$
$$= \sum_\gamma P(Y(1) = \gamma, \Delta Y(2) = \beta_2 | \Delta Y(1) = \beta_1, \Delta X = \alpha)$$
$$= \sum_\gamma P(Y(1) = \gamma | \Delta Y(1) = \beta_1, \Delta X = \alpha) P(\Delta Y(2) = \beta_2 | \Delta Y(1) = \beta_1, Y(1) = \gamma, \Delta X = \alpha)$$
$$= \sum_\gamma P(Y(1) = \gamma | \Delta Y(1) = \beta_1, \Delta X = \alpha) P(\Delta Y(2) = \beta_2 | \Delta Y(1) = \beta_1, Y(1) = \gamma)$$
$$= \sum_\gamma P(Y(1) = \gamma | \Delta Y(1) = \beta_1, \Delta X = \alpha) P(\Delta Y(2) = \beta_2 | \Delta Y(1) = \beta_1)$$
$$= P(\Delta Y(2) = \beta_2 | \Delta Y(1) = \beta_1),$$

where the third equality comes from the fact that $Y(1)$ and $\Delta Y(1)$ together determine both $Y(1)$ and $Y(1)^*$ so that $\Delta Y(2)$ has no further dependence on ΔX when $Y(1)$ and $\Delta Y(1)$ are specified. Because the same round function is used in each round, this Markov chain is homogeneous. For any key $Z = z$, the round function $f(\cdot, z)$ is a bijective mapping from the set of plaintexts to the set of ciphertexts. This bijection induces a bijection from pairs of distinct plaintexts (X, X^*) to pairs of distinct ciphertexts $(Y, Y^*) = (f(X, z), f(X^*, z))$. The fact that X and $\Delta X (\neq e)$ are independent and uniformly distributed implies that (X, X^*) is uniformly distributed over pairs of distinct plaintexts. Thus, (Y, Y^*) is also uniformly distributed over pairs of distinct ciphertexts and hence $\Delta Y (\neq e)$ is also uniformly distributed. Thus the uniform distribution is a stationary distribution for this Markov chain.

Example 1. *DES is a Markov cipher under the definition of difference as $\Delta X = X \oplus X^*$ where $\oplus$ denotes bitwise XOR. (This is just a restatement of Lemma 1 in [1].)*

For a Markov cipher with independent and uniformly random round subkeys, the probability of an r-round characteristic is given by the Chapman-Kolmogorov equation for a Markov chain as

$$P(\Delta Y(1) = \beta_1, \Delta Y(2) = \beta_2, .., \Delta Y(r) = \beta_r | \Delta X = \beta_0) = \prod_{i=1}^r P(\Delta Y(1) = \beta_i | \Delta X = \beta_{i-1}).$$

It follows that the probability of an r-round differential (β_0, β_r) is

$$P(\Delta Y(r) = \beta_r | \Delta X = \beta_0) = \sum_{\beta_1} \sum_{\beta_2} \cdots \sum_{\beta_{r-1}} \prod_{i=1}^r P(\Delta Y(1) = \beta_i | \Delta X = \beta_{i-1})$$

where the sums are over all possible values of differences between distinct elements, i.e., over all group elements excepting the neutral element e.

For any Markov cipher, let Π denote the *transition probability matrix* of the homogeneous Markov chain $\Delta X = \Delta Y(0), \Delta Y(1), ..., \Delta Y(r)$. The (i, j) entry in Π is

$P(\Delta Y(1) = \alpha_j | \Delta X = \alpha_i)$ where $\alpha_1, \alpha_2, ..., \alpha_M$ is some agreed-upon ordering of the M possible values of ΔX and $M = 2^m - 1$ for an m-bit cipher. Then, for any r, the (i,j) entry in Π^r, $p_{ij}^{(r)}$, equals $P(\Delta Y(r) = \alpha_j | \Delta X = \alpha_i)$, i.e., $p_{ij}^{(r)}$ is just the probability of the r-round differential (α_i, α_j).

The security of iterated cryptosystems is based on the belief that a cryptographically "strong" function can be obtained by iterating a cryptographically "weak" function enough times. For Markov ciphers, one has the following fact.

Theorem 3. *For a Markov cipher of block length m with independent and uniformly random round subkeys, if the semi-infinite Markov chain $\Delta X = \Delta Y(0), \Delta Y(1), ...$ has a "steady-state probability" distribution, i.e., if there is a probability vector $(p_1, p_2, .., p_M)$, such that, for all α_i, $\lim_{r \to \infty} P(\Delta Y(r) = \alpha_j | \Delta X = \alpha_i) = p_j$, then this steady state distribution must be the uniform distribution $(1/M, 1/M, ..., 1/M)$, i.e., $\lim_{r \to \infty} P(\Delta Y(r) = \beta | \Delta X = \alpha) = \frac{1}{2^m - 1}$ for every differential (α, β), so that every differential will be roughly equally likely after sufficiently many rounds. If we assume additionally that the hypothesis of stochastic equivalence holds for this Markov cipher, then, for almost all subkeys, this cipher is secure against a differential cryptanalysis attack after sufficiently many rounds.*

Proof. The theorem follows from the facts that the existence of a steady-state probability distribution implies that a homogeneous Markov chain has a unique stationary distribution, which is the steady-state distribution, and that, according to Theorem 2, the uniform distribution is a stationary distribution.

4. Analysis of the block cipher PES

The block cipher PES, proposed by Lai and Massey in [2], is an iterated block cipher based on three group operations on 16-bit subblocks, namely, bitwise-XOR, denoted as $\oplus$; addition modulo 2^{16} of integers represented by 16-bit subblocks, denoted as $\boxplus$; and multiplication modulo $2^{16} + 1$ (with the all-zero 16-bit subblock considered as representing 2^{16}), denoted as $\odot$. The encryption process of PES is shown in Fig.2. In order to consider differential cryptanalysis of PES, we must first define "difference".

The encryption of a plaintext pair by an r-round PES can be described as shown in Fig. 3, where X_i and $Z_j^{(i)}$ denote 16-bit subblocks, where $X = (X_1, X_2, X_3, X_4)$, where $Z_A^{(i)} = (Z_1^{(i)}, Z_2^{(i)}, Z_3^{(i)}, Z_4^{(i)})$, where $Z_B^{(i)} = (Z_5^{(i)}, Z_6^{(i)})$, and where we introduce an operation $\otimes$ defined on 64-bit blocks by

$$X \otimes Z_A^{(i)} = (X_1 \odot Z_1^{(i)}, X_2 \odot Z_2^{(i)}, X_3 \boxplus Z_3^{(i)}, X_4 \boxplus Z_4^{(i)}). \tag{1}$$

Under the operation $\otimes$, the set of all 64-bit blocks forms a group. Let X^{-1} be the inverse of X in this group. Then, for PES, we define the *difference* of two distinct 64-bit blocks X and X^* as $\Delta X = X \otimes X^{*-1}$. The appropriateness of this definition stems from the following fact:

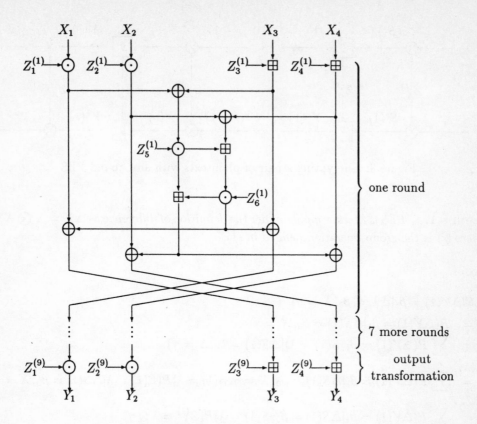

X_i : 16-bit plaintext subblock
Y_i : 16-bit ciphertext subblock
$Z_i^{(r)}$: 16-bit key subblock
$\oplus$: bit-by-bit exclusive-OR of 16-bit subblocks
$\boxplus$: addition modulo 2^{16} of 16-bit integers
$\odot$: multiplication modulo $2^{16} + 1$ of 16-bit integers
     with the zero subblock corresponding to 2^{16}

Figure 2: The encryption process of the block cipher PES.

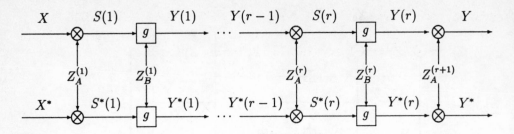

Figure 3: Encrypting a pair of plaintexts with an r-round PES

Lemma 1. *PES is Markov cipher under the definition of difference as* $\Delta X = X \otimes X^{*-1}$, *where* $\otimes$ *is the group operation defined in (1).*

Proof.

$$P(\Delta Y(1) = \beta_1 | \Delta X = \beta_0, X = \gamma)$$
$$= P(\Delta Y(1) = \beta_1 | \Delta S(1) = \beta_0, X = \gamma)$$
$$= \sum_\lambda P(\Delta Y(1) = \beta_1, S(1) = \lambda) | \Delta S(1) = \beta_0, X = \gamma)$$
$$= \sum_\lambda P(\Delta Y(1) = \beta_1 | \Delta S(1) = \beta_0, X = \gamma, S(1) = \lambda) P(S(1) = \lambda | \Delta S(1) = \beta_0, X = \gamma)$$
$$= \sum_\lambda P(\Delta Y(1) = \beta_1 | \Delta S(1) = \beta_0, S(1) = \lambda) P(Z_A^{(1)} = \lambda \otimes \gamma^{-1})$$
$$= 2^{-64} \sum_\lambda P(\Delta Y(1) = \beta_1 | \Delta S(1) = \beta_0, S(1) = \lambda),$$

which is independent of γ, where we have used the facts that $\Delta S(1) = \Delta X$ since $S(1) = X \otimes Z_A^{(1)}$ and that

$$P(S(1) = \lambda | \Delta S(1) = \beta_0, X = \gamma) = P(S(1) = \lambda | X = \gamma) = P(Z_A^{(1)} = \lambda \otimes \gamma^{-1}).$$

The regular structure of PES makes it possible, and insightful, to consider "mini" PES ciphers with shorter block length. A mini PES has the same computational graph as the standard PES shown in Fig.2, but the subblocks are only n bits long (n=2, 4 or 8) rather than 16, and the operations $\oplus, \boxplus$ and $\odot$ are then the corresponding bitwise XOR, addition modulo 2^n, and multiplication modulo $2^n + 1$. Note that for n=2, 4 and 8, these three operations are still group operations. Thus, the resulting mini PES is a Markov cipher with block length $4n$, by the same argument as for PES(64).

We have been able to prove that, for PES(8) and PES(16), the uniform distribution is indeed the steady-state probability of the sequence of differences. Thus, PES(8) and

PES(16) with sufficiently many rounds are guaranteed secure against differential crypt-analysis. We conjecture that PES(32) and PES(64) also have the uniform distribution as the steady-state probability distribution for their sequences of differences.

In order to find the one-round differential with highest probability, an exhaustive search was performed for the mini ciphers PES(8) and PES(16). The most likely one-round differentials $(\Delta X, \Delta Y(1))$ for PES(8) and PES(16) are:

$$\Delta Y(1) = \Delta X = (\Delta X_1, \Delta X_2, \Delta X_3, \Delta X_4) = (0, 1, odd, 0), \qquad odd \in \{1, 3, .., 2^n - 1\},$$

and each has a probability approximately $2^{-(2n-2)}$. The i-round differentials $(\Delta X, \Delta Y(i))$ that take on these same values also have the greatest probabilities for small $i > 1$. The probabilities of the above i-round differentials for PES(8) and PES(16) are shown in Table 1.

p_{df}	8-bit	16-bit
1-round	1.25×2^{-2}	1.13×2^{-6}
2-round	1.62×2^{-3}	1.47×2^{-10}
3-round	1.07×2^{-3}	1.03×2^{-13}†
4-round	1.43×2^{-4}	1.6×2^{-16}†
5-round	0.97×2^{-4}	*†

Table 1: The probabilities of the (estimated or proved) most probable i-round differentials for PES(8) and PES(16). (* : statistically indistinguishable from 2^{-4n}; † : estimated by statistical test.)

For PES(64), a detailed cryptanalysis (see the Appendix) strongly suggests that the most probable one-round differentials correspond to eight values of ΔX, namely $\alpha_i = (0, 0, 0, \gamma_i)$ (i=1,2,...,8) where $\gamma_1 = 2^{16} - 1$, $\gamma_2 = 1$, $\gamma_3 = 2^{16} - 3$, $\gamma_4 = 3$, $\gamma_5 = 2^{16} - 5$, $\gamma_6 = 5$, $\gamma_7 = 2^{16} - 7$, and $\gamma_8 = 7$. The 8×8 submatrix of the transition probability matrix Π corresponding to these values is shown in the Appendix to be well-approximated by

$$T = 10^{-7} \begin{pmatrix} 0 & 25460 & 12556 & 0 & 0 & 9417 & 698 & 0 \\ 25460 & 0 & 0 & 12556 & 9417 & 0 & 0 & 698 \\ 12556 & 0 & 0 & 0 & 6278 & 0 & 0 & 3139 \\ 0 & 12556 & 0 & 0 & 0 & 6278 & 3139 & 0 \\ 0 & 9417 & 6278 & 0 & 0 & 0 & 0 & 0 \\ 9417 & 0 & 0 & 6278 & 0 & 0 & 0 & 0 \\ 698 & 0 & 0 & 3139 & 0 & 0 & 0 & 0 \\ 0 & 698 & 3139 & 0 & 0 & 0 & 0 & 0 \end{pmatrix}.$$

Note that the (i, j) entry in T^k is just

$$P(\Delta Y(k) = \alpha_j, \Delta Y(k-1) \in A, \cdots, \Delta Y(1) \in A, |\Delta X = \alpha_i)$$

where $A = \{\alpha_1, \alpha_2, ..., \alpha_8\}$, which is a lower bound on the (i,j) entry of Π^k. One obtains

$$T^7 = 2^{-58} \begin{pmatrix} 0 & 1.22 & 0.53 & 0 & 0 & 0.43 & 0.07 & 0 \\ 1.22 & 0 & 0 & 0.53 & 0.43 & 0 & 0 & 0.07 \\ 0.53 & 0 & 0 & 0.23 & 0.19 & 0 & 0 & 0.03 \\ 0 & 0.53 & 0.23 & 0 & 0 & 0.19 & 0.03 & 0 \\ 0 & 0.43 & 0.19 & 0 & 0 & 0.15 & 0.03 & 0 \\ 0.43 & 0 & 0 & 0.19 & 0.15 & 0 & 0 & 0.03 \\ 0.07 & 0 & 0 & 0.03 & 0.03 & 0 & 0 & 0 \\ 0 & 0.07 & 0.03 & 0 & 0 & 0.03 & 0 & 0 \end{pmatrix}$$

which is a lower bound on, and a plausibly good approximation to, the probabilities of the 7-round differential (α_i, α_j). One sees that the differential (α_1, α_2) has probability about 1.22×2^{-58} and appears to be the largest 7-round differential probability. Our lower bound on the complexity of differential cryptanalysis shows then that at least 2^{59} encryptions will be required. The detailed cryptanalysis given in the Appendix shows that in fact the differential cryptanalysis attack will require all 2^{64} possible encryptions.

5. Improved PES

PES can be modified to improve its security without violating the design principles [2] used for PES. The resulting modified cipher will be called Improved PES and denoted as IPES. The only essential modification is that *a different (and simpler) permutation of subblocks is used at the end of each of the first 7 rounds.* The software implementation of IPES is in fact more efficient than that of PES.

The computational graph of the encryption process of IPES is shown in Fig.4. Note that the permutation before the output transformation "undoes" the permutation at the end of 8-th round, i.e., at the end of 8-th round, the subblocks are *not* in fact permuted.

The key schedule used to generate the encryption key subblocks for IPES is the same as for PES (see [2]).

The decryption key DK for IPES is computed from the encryption key Z as follows,

for $r = 2, .., 8$: $(DK_1^{(r)}, DK_2^{(r)}, DK_3^{(r)}, DK_4^{(r)}) = (Z_1^{(10-r)^{-1}}, -Z_3^{(10-r)}, -Z_2^{(10-r)}, Z_4^{(10-r)^{-1}})$

for $r = 1, 9$: $(DK_1^{(r)}, DK_2^{(r)}, DK_3^{(r)}, DK_4^{(r)}) = (Z_1^{(10-r)^{-1}}, -Z_2^{(10-r)}, -Z_3^{(10-r)}, Z_4^{(10-r)^{-1}})$

for $r = 1, .., 8$: $(DK_5^{(r)}, DK_6^{(r)}) = (Z_5^{(9-r)}, Z_6^{(9-r)})$,

where Z^{-1} denotes the multiplicative inverse (modulo $2^{16} + 1$) of Z, i.e., $Z \odot Z^{-1} = 1$ and where $-Z$ denotes the additive inverse (modulo 2^{16}) of Z, i.e., $-Z \boxplus Z = 0$. Thus, symmetry of encryption and decryption, which was one of the design principles of PES, is maintained in the sense that $IPES(IPES(X,Z), DK) = X$.

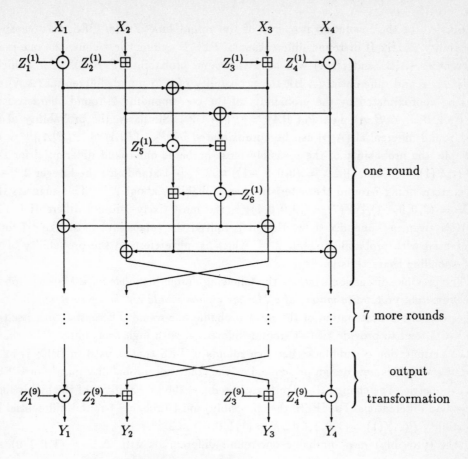

X_i : 16-bit plaintext subblock

Y_i : 16-bit ciphertext subblock

$Z_i^{(r)}$: 16-bit key subblock

$\oplus$: bit-by-bit exclusive-OR of 16-bit subblocks

$\boxplus$: addition modulo 2^{16} of 16-bit integers

$\odot$: multiplication modulo $2^{16}+1$ of 16-bit integers
with the zero subblock corresponding to 2^{16}

Figure 4: Encryption process of IPES.

Because of the involution property of the round function for PES, the transition probability matrix Π of round differentials of PES is symmetric. Thus, the one-round differentials (A,B) and (B,A) will have the same probability $P(B|A)$. For a highly likely one-round differential (A,B), the probability of a 2i-round differential (A,A) can thus be approximated by the probability of the corresponding 2i-round characteristics $(A, B, A, B, ..., A, B, A)$, i.e., $P_{2i}(A|A) \approx [P(B|A)]^{2i}$. Similarly, the probability of the 2i+1 round differential (A,B) can be approximated by $P_{2i+1}(B|A) \approx [P(B|A)]^{2i+1}$. For example, the probability of the plausibly most probable one-round differential for PES is $P(\Delta Y(1) = (0,0,0,1)|\Delta X = (0,0,0,-1)) \approx 2^{-9}$, [$-1$ stands for the integer $2^{16} - 1$,] the corresponding 7-round characteristics has probability about 2^{-61}. This suggests that $(\Delta X = (0,0,0,-1), \Delta Y(7) = (0,0,0,1))$ is the most likely 7-round differential. The analysis given in Appendix shows that it is indeed the (plausibly) most likely 7-round differential with probability about 2^{-58}, which is quite close to the probability of the corresponding characteristic.

The previous discussion suggests the following *design principle* for a Markov cipher: *The transition probability matrix of a Markov cipher should not be symmetric.* Otherwise, the concatenation of the most probable one-round differential with itself r-1 times will tend to provide an (r-1)-round differential with high probability. The change of the permutation of subblocks between rounds of PES that is used in IPES is in accordance with this new design principle, i.e., the transition probability matrix of IPES is not symmetric. The change also significantly reduces the probabilities of the highly likely one-round differentials. For IPES, the (plausibly) most probable 1-round differential has probability $P(\Delta Y(1) = (1,0,1,0)|\Delta X = (1,1,0,0)) \approx 2^{-18}$, and the (provably) most probable one-round differentials with $\Delta X = (1,0,1,0)$ and $\Delta X = (1,1,-1,1)$ are

$P(\Delta Y(1) = (1,1,-1,1)|\Delta X = (1,0,1,0)) \approx 2^{-34}$, and
$P(\Delta Y(1) = (1,1,0,0)|\Delta X = (1,1,-1,1)) \approx 2^{-34}$.

These figures imply that the corresponding 3-round characteristic $((1,1,0,0), (1,0,1,0), (1,1,-1,1), (1,1,0,0))$ has probability about 2^{-86}. This suggests that the probability of the 3-round differential $(\Delta X = (1,1,0,0), \Delta Y(3) = (1,1,0,0))$ should not be significantly larger than the average value, 2^{-64}. Other known one-round differentials for IPES with high probabilities are

$P(\Delta Y(1) = (1,H,0,3)|\Delta X = (1,H,H,1)) \approx 2^{-30}$,
$P(\Delta Y(1) = (1,0,H,3)|\Delta X = (1,H,0,3)) \approx 2^{-30}$,
$P(\Delta Y(1) = (1,H,H,1)|\Delta X = (1,0,H,3)) \approx 2^{-30}$,

where H stands for the integer 2^{15} whose corresponding 16-bit subblock is $(1,\overbrace{0,..,0,0}^{15 bits})$. To date, we have found no evidence that there are any 3-round differentials for IPES whose probabilities are significantly larger than $2^{-m} = 2^{-64}$.

Finally, we remark that if one uses the difference defined as $DX = X_1 \bigoplus X_2$, then the most probable differentials (that we have found) for IPES become

$P(DY(1) = (0, H, 0, H)|DX = (0, H, H, 0)) = P(Z_5^{(1)} \in \{0, 1\}) = 2^{-15},$
$P(DY(1) = (0, 0, H, H)|DX = (0, H, 0, H)) = P(Z_4^{(1)} \in \{0, 1\}) = 2^{-15},$ and
$P(DY(1) = (0, H, H, 0)|DX = (0, 0, H, H)) = P(Z_4^{(1)} \in \{0, 1\}, Z_5^{(1)} \in \{0, 1\}) = 2^{-30}.$
However, IPES is not a Markov cipher for this notion of difference. If DX is used as the definition of difference, the hypothesis of stochastic equivalence does not hold at all for IPES so that the differential probabilities computed for this notion of difference have no relation to an attack by differential cryptanalysis. The fact that the 3-round differential $(DX = (0, H, H, 0), DY(3) = (0, H, H, 0))$ for the difference DX has probability much larger than 3-round differentials for the "appropriate" difference ΔX used above has thus no significance for differential cryptanalysis.

Appendix: Detailed Differential Cryptanalysis of PES

1. Some One Round Differentials for PES

We first calculate the probabilities of certain one-round differentials for PES for pairs of input blocks that differ by a given value. This will enable us to calculate the probability of a $7\frac{1}{2}$-round differential from which it is usually possible to find the sub-key used in the last round.

Clearly a 16-bit number is its own inverse under the group operation $\oplus$. Let $-z$ denote the inverse of z under $\boxplus$, and z^{-1} the inverse of z under $\odot$. For any n-bit number z, let z' denote the n-bit complement of z. We also introduce some notation for the difference of two 16-bit numbers z_1, z_2 under the group operations $\odot$ and $\boxplus$. Let δ denote the difference under $\odot$ and ∂ denote the difference under $\boxplus$, i.e.,

$$\delta z = z_1 \odot z_2^{-1}, \qquad \partial z = z_1 \boxplus - z_2.$$

Then, for any 16-bit number k,

$$(z_1 \odot k) \odot (z_2 \odot k)^{-1} = \delta z, \qquad (z_1 \boxplus k) \boxplus - (z_2 \boxplus k) = \partial z.$$

Suppose $\delta z = z_1 \odot z_2^{-1} = 0$, where we recall that 2^{16} is represented by the integer 0 for the operation $\odot$. Then for $z_1, z_2 \notin \{0, 1\}$,

$$z_1 = 2^{16} z_2 = (2^{16} + 1)z_2 - z_2 = -z_2 \pmod{2^{16} + 1}, \quad \text{so} \quad z_1 + z_2 = 0 \pmod{2^{16} + 1.}$$

Because z_1 and z_2 are positive 16-bit numbers, we have $z_1 + z_2 = 2^{16} + 1$. If $z_1 = 0$, then $z_2 = 1$, so in either case $z_1 + z_2 = 1 \pmod{2^{16}}$. Clearly, the converse also holds and so we have

$$\delta z = 0 \iff z_1 + z_2 = 1 \pmod{2^{16}}. \tag{A.1}$$

Consider the MA-box, as defined in [2] and shown within the dashed lines in Figure 5. Suppose we have inputs (p_1, q_1) and (p_2, q_2) with outputs (t_1, u_1) and (t_2, u_2) respectively. The notion of the other 16-bit subblocks within the MA-box are defined in Figure 5. Suppose further that

$$p_1 + p_2 = 1 \pmod{2^{16}}, \qquad q_1 + q_2 = 0 \pmod{2^{16}}.$$

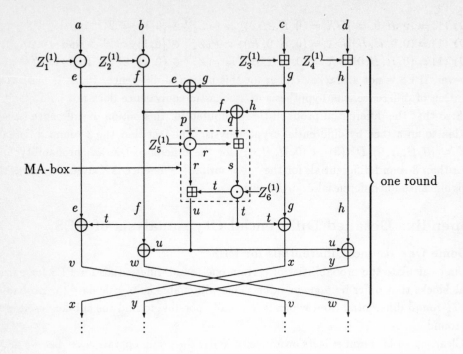

$\oplus$: bit-by-bit exclusive-OR of 16-bit subblocks
$\boxplus$: addition modulo 2^{16} of 16-bit integers
$\odot$: multiplication modulo $2^{16}+1$ of 16-bit integers
with the zero subblock corresponding to 2^{16}

Figure 5: The first round of PES and the notation used for differential cryptanalysis

Then $\delta p = 0$, so $\delta r = 0$ and hence $r_1 + r_2 = 1 \pmod{2^{16}}$. Thus,

$$s_1 + s_2 = (r_1 \boxplus q_1) + (r_2 \boxplus q_2) = r_1 + r_2 + q_1 + q_2 = 1 \pmod{2^{16}},$$

and hence $\delta s = 0$. Therefore $\delta t = 0$ so that $t_1 + t_2 = 1 \pmod{2^{16}}$ and hence

$$u_1 + u_2 = (r_1 \boxplus t_1) + (r_2 \boxplus t_2) = r_1 + r_2 + t_1 + t_2 = 2 \pmod{2^{16}}.$$

Thus, we have shown the following relationship between a pair of inputs and a pair of outputs of the MA-box,

$$p_1 + p_2 = 1, \quad q_1 + q_2 = 0 \pmod{2^{16}} \quad \Rightarrow \quad t_1 + t_2 = 1, \quad u_1 + u_2 = 2 \pmod{2^{16}}. \quad (A.2)$$

Consider one round of the cipher, as shown in Figure 5, where (a, b, c, d) are input subblocks and (x, y, v, w) the output subblocks. The intermediate results are defined in Figure 5. Suppose we have a pair of inputs with

$$(\delta a, \delta b, \delta c, \delta d) = (0, 0, 0, n) \quad \text{where } n \in S = \{\pm 1, \pm 3, \pm 5, \pm 7\}.$$

Then trivially we have $(\delta e, \delta g, \partial f, \partial h) = (0, 0, 0, n)$. Apart from the MA-box, an encryption round separates into two parts, and we consider first the half starting with (a, c). Suppose that

$$e_1 = (\alpha, 10...0, \theta)$$

for some $[16 - (l + 1)]$-bit number α, where $l \in \{0, \cdots, 15\}$ and $\theta \in \{0, 1\}$, so there are $(l - 1)$ consecutive zeros before θ. Such an e_1 has probability 2^{-l}. From $(A.1)$, we know that, since $\delta e = 0$, $\quad e_1 + e_2 = 1 \pmod{2^{16}}$, and thus

$$e_2 = (\alpha', 10...0, \theta').$$

Now we can write g_i as

$$g_1 = g_2 = (\beta, 00...0, \phi),$$

where β is a $[16 - (l + 1)]$-bit number and $\phi \in \{0, 1\}$. For a given l such an e_2 occurs with probability 2^{-l}. Then we have

$$\begin{aligned} p_1 &= e_1 \oplus g_1 = (\alpha \oplus \beta, 10...0, \theta \oplus \phi) \\ p_2 &= e_2 \oplus g_2 = (\alpha' \oplus \beta, 10...0, \theta' \oplus \phi) \end{aligned}$$

and thus $p_1 + p_2 = 1 \pmod{2^{16}}$. From the MA-box result $(A.2)$, it follows that

$$q_1 + q_2 = 0 \pmod{2^{16}} \quad \Rightarrow \quad t_1 + t_2 = 1 \pmod{2^{16}}.$$

Thus, with probability 2^{-l},

$$t_1 = (\gamma, 10...0, \rho), \qquad t_2 = (\gamma', 10...0, \rho'),$$

for some $[16 - (l + 1)]$-bit number γ and $\rho \in \{0, 1\}$. Thus, for a given l, e_i, g_i and t_i all have the forms specified above with probability 2^{-3l}. Hence, e_i, g_i and t_i all have the forms specified above for some l with probability

$$\sum_{l=1}^{15} 2^{-3l} \approx \frac{1}{7}.$$

Thus, with probability $\frac{1}{7}$, we simultaneously obtain two results. Firstly, we have

$$\begin{aligned} v_1 &= e_1 \oplus t_1 = (\alpha \oplus \gamma, 00...0, \theta \oplus \rho) \\ v_2 &= e_2 \oplus t_2 = (\alpha \oplus \gamma, 00...0, \theta \oplus \rho) \end{aligned}$$

so that $v_1 = v_2$ and hence $\partial v = 0$. Secondly,

$$\begin{aligned} x_1 &= g_1 \oplus t_1 = (\beta \oplus \gamma, 10...0, \phi \oplus \rho) \\ x_2 &= g_2 \oplus t_2 = (\beta \oplus \gamma', 10...0, \phi \oplus \rho') \end{aligned}$$

so that $\quad x_1 + x_2 = 1 \pmod{2^{16}}$ and hence $\delta x = 0$. Thus, we have shown that if $q_1 + q_2 = 0 \pmod{2^{16}}$, then

$$(\delta a, \partial c) = (0, 0) \Rightarrow (\delta x, \partial v) = (0, 0) \quad \text{with probability} \approx \frac{1}{7}.$$

For the other half of the encryption process, we have $\delta f = 0$ and $\partial h \in S$. If we can find f and h such that $q_1 + q_2 = 0 \pmod{2^{16}}$, then, provided $\delta p = 0$, we have $u_1 + u_2 = 2 \pmod{2^{16}}$. In order to find a differential with high probability, we need to find such (u_1, u_2) with $\delta y = 0$ and $\partial w \in S$, where

$$y_i = h_i \oplus u_i, \qquad w_i = f_i \oplus u_i.$$

Thus, we need to find f, h and u, where

$$f_1 + f_2 = 1 \pmod{2^{16}}, \quad h_1 - h_2 \in S, \quad u_1 + u_2 = 2 \pmod{2^{16}}, \qquad (A.3)$$

that satisfy, for q, w and y defined as above,

$$q_1 + q_2 = 0 \pmod{2^{16}}, \quad w_1 - w_2 \in S, \quad y_1 + y_2 = 1 \pmod{2^{16}}. \qquad (A.4)$$

We can find most of the possible solutions fairly easily. Suppose

$$
\begin{aligned}
f_1 &= (\alpha, \theta_1), & f_2 &= (\alpha', \theta_2), \\
h_1 &= (\beta, \phi_1), & h_2 &= (\beta, \phi_2), \\
u_1 &= (\gamma, \rho_1), & u_2 &= (\gamma', \rho_2),
\end{aligned}
$$

for 12-bit numbers α, β, γ, and 4-bit numbers θ_i, ϕ_i, ρ_i. Then, from (A.3), we have

$$\theta_1 + \theta_2 = 17, \quad \phi_1 - \phi_2 \in S, \quad \rho_1 + \rho_2 = 18. \qquad (A.5)$$

Now, by definition,

$$
\begin{aligned}
q_1 &= (\alpha \oplus \beta, \theta_1 \oplus \phi_1), & q_2 &= (\alpha' \oplus \beta, \theta_2 \oplus \phi_2), \\
y_1 &= (\beta \oplus \gamma, \phi_1 \oplus \rho_1), & y_2 &= (\beta \oplus \gamma', \phi_2 \oplus \rho_2), \\
w_1 &= (\alpha \oplus \gamma, \theta_1 \oplus \rho_1), & w_2 &= (\alpha \oplus \gamma, \theta_2 \oplus \rho_2),
\end{aligned}
$$

and thus (A.4) requires us to find solutions to

$$
\begin{aligned}
(\theta_1 \oplus \phi_1) + (\theta_2 \oplus \phi_2) &= 16 \\
(\phi_1 \oplus \rho_1) + (\phi_2 \oplus \rho_2) &= 17 \\
(\theta_1 \oplus \rho_1) - (\theta_2 \oplus \rho_2) &\in S.
\end{aligned}
\qquad (A.6)
$$

There are 514 triplets of 4-bit numbers satisfying (A.5) and (A.6). The numbers of solutions that correspond to each pair of elements of S are given in the matrix M below, where the rows and columns are in the order $\{-1, 1, -3, 3, -5, 5, -7, 7\}$,

$$
M = \begin{pmatrix}
0 & 73 & 36 & 0 & 0 & 27 & 2 & 0 \\
73 & 0 & 0 & 36 & 27 & 0 & 0 & 2 \\
36 & 0 & 0 & 0 & 18 & 0 & 0 & 9 \\
0 & 36 & 0 & 0 & 0 & 18 & 9 & 0 \\
0 & 27 & 18 & 0 & 0 & 0 & 0 & 0 \\
27 & 0 & 0 & 18 & 0 & 0 & 0 & 0 \\
2 & 0 & 0 & 9 & 0 & 0 & 0 & 0 \\
0 & 2 & 9 & 0 & 0 & 0 & 0 & 0
\end{pmatrix}.
$$

This gives a matrix of transition probabilities, $T_{b,d} = 2^{-12}M$, where

$$T_{b,d} = 10^{-7} \begin{pmatrix} 0 & 178223 & 87891 & 0 & 0 & 65918 & 4882 & 0 \\ 178223 & 0 & 0 & 87891 & 65918 & 0 & 0 & 4882 \\ 87891 & 0 & 0 & 0 & 43945 & 0 & 0 & 21973 \\ 0 & 87891 & 0 & 0 & 0 & 43945 & 21973 & 0 \\ 0 & 65918 & 43945 & 0 & 0 & 0 & 0 & 0 \\ 65918 & 0 & 0 & 43945 & 0 & 0 & 0 & 0 \\ 4882 & 0 & 0 & 21973 & 0 & 0 & 0 & 0 \\ 0 & 4882 & 21973 & 0 & 0 & 0 & 0 & 0 \end{pmatrix}.$$

We can now make a similar statement to the one above for the other half of the cipher. Given $p_1 + p_2 = 1 \pmod{2^{16}}$, $(\delta b, \partial d) = (0, n_1) \Rightarrow (\delta y, \partial w) = (0, n_2)$ for $n_1, n_2 \in S$ with probability given by the appropriate entry of $T_{b,d}$.

We can now calculate some approximate 1-round differential probabilities for PES. These are given by the transition matrix $T_{a,b,c,d} = \frac{1}{7}T_{b,d}$. Therefore,

$$T_{a,b,c,d} = 10^{-7} \begin{pmatrix} 0 & 25460 & 12556 & 0 & 0 & 9417 & 698 & 0 \\ 25460 & 0 & 0 & 12556 & 9417 & 0 & 0 & 698 \\ 12556 & 0 & 0 & 0 & 6278 & 0 & 0 & 3139 \\ 0 & 12556 & 0 & 0 & 0 & 6278 & 3139 & 0 \\ 0 & 9417 & 6278 & 0 & 0 & 0 & 0 & 0 \\ 9417 & 0 & 0 & 6278 & 0 & 0 & 0 & 0 \\ 698 & 0 & 0 & 3139 & 0 & 0 & 0 & 0 \\ 0 & 698 & 3139 & 0 & 0 & 0 & 0 & 0 \end{pmatrix},$$

and hence

$$(\delta a, \delta b, \partial c, \partial d) = (0, 0, 0, n_1) \Rightarrow (\delta x, \delta y, \partial v, \partial w) = (0, 0, 0, n_2) \quad \text{for } n_1, n_2 \in S$$

with probability given by the appropriate entry of $T_{a,b,c,d}$.

It is of interest to know how accurate our approximation is. For purposes of comparison, the differential probabilities were calculated by simulation. The results, based on 10,000,000 randomly chosen input pairs for each element of S, are given in the matrix $\hat{T}$ given below:

$$\hat{T} = 10^{-7} \begin{pmatrix} 0 & 25291 & 12891 & 0 & 0 & 9755 & 817 & 0 \\ 25691 & 0 & 0 & 12769 & 9509 & 0 & 0 & 807 \\ 12712 & 0 & 0 & 0 & 6353 & 0 & 0 & 3154 \\ 0 & 12800 & 0 & 0 & 0 & 6324 & 3050 & 0 \\ 0 & 9482 & 6422 & 0 & 0 & 0 & 0 & 0 \\ 9396 & 0 & 0 & 6329 & 0 & 0 & 0 & 0 \\ 770 & 0 & 0 & 3148 & 0 & 0 & 0 & 0 \\ 0 & 757 & 3173 & 0 & 0 & 0 & 0 & 0 \end{pmatrix}.$$

3. A Possible Cryptanalysis of the PES

We can now calculate a 7-round transition matrix, whose entries give the probability that, given that the input pair to the first round differ by a given value, then the ouput differences of the seventh round and the input differences to all the intermediate rounds are all of the required form. We denote this matrix by $T7_{a,b,c,d}$. It is easily calculated since

$$T7_{a,b,c,d} = T^7_{a,b,c,d} = 2^{-12 \times 7} 7^{-7} M^7.$$

The calculation gives the following matrix:

$$T7_{a,b,c,d} = \begin{pmatrix} 1.22 \times 2^{-58} & 1.06 \times 2^{-59} & 0.86 \times 2^{-59} & 1.12 \times 2^{-62} \\ 1.06 \times 2^{-59} & 0.92 \times 2^{-60} & 1.52 \times 2^{-61} & 0.96 \times 2^{-63} \\ 0.86 \times 2^{-59} & 1.52 \times 2^{-61} & 1.21 \times 2^{-61} & 0.96 \times 2^{-63} \\ 1.12 \times 2^{-62} & 0.96 \times 2^{-63} & 0.96 \times 2^{-63} & 1.76 \times 2^{-65} \end{pmatrix}$$

where the (i, j) entry of the matrix gives a plausibly good approximation of the probability of the 7-round differentials of the form

$$(\delta a^1, \delta b^1, \partial c^1, \partial d^1) = (0, 0, 0, \pm(2i - 1)), \quad (\delta a^7, \delta b^7, \partial c^7, \partial d^7) = (0, 0, 0, \mp(-1)^{i+j}(2j - 1))$$

where the superscript indicates the round index.

We can now obtain the key as follows. Suppose initially we choose $(\delta a^1, \delta b^1, \partial c^1, \partial d^1) = (0, 0, 0, 1)$, then we know that after 7 encryption rounds that

$$(\delta a^8, \delta b^8, \partial c^8, \partial d^8) = (\delta e^8, \delta f^8, \partial g^8, \partial h^8) = (0, 0, 0, -1)$$

with probability 1.22×2^{-58}. From our earlier arguments on the (a, c) half of the cipher, it follows that $(\delta a, \partial c) = (0, 0) \Rightarrow \delta p = 0$ with probability $\approx \frac{1}{3}$, and, by an argument similar to one given above of searching all the 4-bit numbers, we can show that

$$(\delta b, \partial d) = (0, 1) \Rightarrow q_1 + q_2 = 0 \quad (\text{mod } 2^{16})$$

with probability $\approx \frac{42}{256}$. Hence we have

$$t_1 + t_2 = 1 \quad (\text{mod } 2^{16}), \quad u_1 + u_2 = 2 \quad (\text{mod } 2^{16}),$$

with probability $\approx \frac{14}{256} = 1.75 \times 2^{-5}$. After 7 rounds, we have

$$(\delta e^8, \delta f^8, \partial g^8, \partial h^8) = (0, 0, 0, -1)$$
$$p_1^8 + p_2^8 = 1, \quad q_1^8 + q_2^8 = 0, \quad t_1^8 + t_2^8 = 1, \quad u_1^8 + u_2^8 = 2$$

with probability 1.07×2^{-62}.

We can now determine the 96 key bits that are used from this stage to the ciphertext in the following way. If we denote the ciphertext as $(e_i^9, f_i^9, g_i^9, h_i^9)$, then observing one ciphertext pair gives us

$$(\delta e^9, \delta f^9, \partial g^9, \partial h^9) = (\delta x^8, \delta y^8, \partial v^8, \partial w^8).$$

As before, we divide the encryption round into two halves and we consider first the half ending with (x, v). For a given $(\delta x^8, \partial v^8)$, each 48-bit triplet (t_1^8, x_1^8, v_1^8) determines all the other quantities in that half of the cipher outside the MA-box. We have additionally to satisfy three 16-bit constraints in order to satisfy the conditions for the $7\frac{1}{2}$-round characteristics given above. Hence, for a given $(\delta x^8, \partial v^8)$, there will on the average be one 48-bit triplet (t_1^8, x_1^8, v_1^8) and hence also one possible value for the key blocks $Z_1^{(9)}$ and $Z_3^{(9)}$ (in the notation of Figure 2). However, some values of $(\delta x^8, \partial v^8)$ will give considerably more triplets (t_1^8, x_1^8, v_1^8). For example, if $(\delta x^8, \partial v^8) = (0, 0)$, the differential ouput, then one seventh of all triplets (t_1^8, x_1^8, v_1^8) will be possible. Such differences do occur infrequently, (the one given above with probability 2^{-32}) and do not significantly affect the argument given below. Note that these 48-bit triplets and two 16-bit key blocks can be pre-calculated for each value of $(\delta e^9, \partial g^9)$. A similar result obviously holds for $(\delta f^9, \partial h^9)$. Combining the two results, we can see that, for each value of $(\delta e^9, \delta f^9, \partial g^9, \partial h^9)$, we obtain on the average one value for $(p_1^8, q_1^8, t_1^8, u_1^8)$, and from inverting the MA-box, we then obtain on average one value for the key blocks $Z_5^{(8)}$ and $Z_6^{(8)}$. Hence, for each plaintext-ciphertext pair, we obtain on the average one possible value for 96 key bits, that is to say, a particular value for the 96 key bits occurs with a probability of 2^{-96} per encryption pair.

If a key occurs with probability p, then in 2^N encryption pairs, the key occurs k times with probability

$$\binom{2^N}{k} p^k (1 - p)^{2^N - k} \approx \frac{(2^N p)^k}{k!} e^{-2^N p}.$$

Thus, in 2^N encryption pairs, an incorrect key will occur two or more times with probability $\frac{1}{2} \times 2^{2(N-96)}$. If we encrypt the whole message space ($N = 64, 2^N p = 2^{-32}$), then a wrong key will occur two or more times with probability

$$1 - P(\text{wrong key occurs 0 or 1 time}) = 1 - exp(-2^{-32}) - 2^{-32} exp(-2^{-32}) \approx \frac{1}{2} 2^{-64},$$

so this event will happen for 2^{31} of the 96-bit keys. The correct key, however, occurs with this probability whenever the $7\frac{1}{2}$-round differential does not occur, and with probability $p = 1.07 \times 2^{-62}$ when the differential does occur. Thus in 2^{64} encryption pairs ($2^N p = 4.28$), the correct key will occur less than twice with probability

$$exp(-4.28) + 4.28 exp(-4.28) \approx 0.073,$$

so the correct key is highly likely to occur more than once (about 93% of the time). To find the key, we can then just try all the 96-bit keys that occur more than once in this procedure, there are approximately 2^{31} such keys. However, since the subkeys are determined by 128-bit key, there are 2^{32} keys that give rise to each last round 96-bit subkey, so there are 2^{63} keys that give last round subkeys occurring more than once. We therefore have a reduced key search of about 2^{63} after all the encryptions have taken place. Since the true key occurs with a much larger probability than any of the false subkeys, we would expect to deal with it before we had tried too many false keys. In that way, we should have to try only the 2^{32} keys that give the correct 96-bit subkey, and a few other subkeys perhaps. Thus, the key search will in practice be reduced to almost 2^{32}.

4. Conclusions

The cryptanalysis of PES given above is, of course, computationally infeasible, but it does illustrate some interesting points. The first is that the true strength of the standard PES algorithm is of the order 2^{64} encryptions, a considerable reduction from the work that a cryptanalyst would expected in an exhaustive key search for the 128-bit key. Second, it shows that a chosen plaintext attack would be computationally possible on a reduced round standard PES. It can be seen that the attack outlined above works on an m-round PES with roughly 2^{8m} encryption pairs. Thus a 4-round PES could be broken with roughly 2^{32} encryption pairs. These conclusions of course do not apply to the modified PES, called IPES and described in this paper; IPES appears to be invulnerable to differential cryptanalysis for the reason given in Section 5.

Acknowledgements

The authors are grateful to Prof. Hans Bühlmann of the ETH Zürich for a helpful suggestion. This research was supported by the Swiss Commission for the Advancement of Scientific Research, Research Grant KWF 2146.1, and by the British Science and Engineering Research Council, Research Grant GR/E 64640.

References

[1] E.Biham and A.Shamir, "Differential Cryptanalysis of DES–like Cryptosystems", to appear in Journal of Cryptology, Vol.4, No.1, 1991.

[2] X.Lai and J.L.Massey, "A Proposal for a New Block Encryption Standard", Advances in Cryptology-EUROCRYPT'90, Springer-Verlag, Berlin 1991, pp. 389-404.

The Knapsack Hash Function proposed at Crypto'89 can be broken

Paul Camion   Jacques Patarin

INRIA, B.P. 105, Domaine de Voluceau – Rocquencourt, 78153 Le Chesnay Cedex – France

EUROCRYPT'91, Brighton, England.

Abstract

Ivan Damgård [4] suggested at Crypto'89 concrete examples of hash functions among which a knapsack scheme. We will here show that a probabilistic algorithm can break this scheme with a number in the region of 2^{32} computations. That number of operations is feasible in realistic time with modern computers. Thus the proposed hash function is not very secure. Among those computations a substantial number can be performed once for all. A faster result can be obtained since parallelism is easy. Moreover, ways to extend the present algorithm to other knapsacks than the present (256, 128) suggested by Damgård are investigated.

The proposed knapsack

Let $a_1, \ldots, a_s$ be fixed integers of A binary digits, randomly selected. If T is a plaintext of s binary symbols, $T = x_1 \ldots x_s$, then $b = \sum_{i=1}^{s} x_i a_i$ will be the proposed hashed value. The values assigned are 256 for s and 120 for A. Thus b has at most $120 + 8 = 128$ binary digits. Thus roughly the probability that a random $256 - bit$ string be a solution is 2^{-128}. We will see that it is somewhat larger. Here a probabilistic algorithm is however designed which solves the problem.

We nevertheless must emphasize that breaking that primitive (the proposed knapsack) does not allow us to break the hash function $h : \{0,1\}^* \to \{0,1\}^t$ whose construction is described in Theorem 3.1 of [4]. See also [7] for an improvement of that construction. We only show that the family $\mathcal{F}$ of functions defined by the proposed knapsack for $m = 256$ and $t(m) = 128$ is not collision free and hence does not satisfy the hypothesis of Theorem 3.1 of [4].

1 The general scheme of our algorithm

1.1 Description

<u>Aim:</u> Given b, find a binary sequence $x_1, x_2, \ldots, x_s$ such that $\sum_{i=1}^{256} x_i a_i = b$.

This is a Knapsack problem, which has an expected high number of solutions, i.e at first sight $\simeq \dfrac{2^{256}}{2^{128}}$ and we will show a way to find one of those solutions.

Step 0 : We choose integers m, m_1, m_2, m_3, m_4 such that

a) $m = m_1 m_2 m_3 m_4 > 2^{128}$

b) The m_i are pairwise coprime, and $m_i \simeq 2^{32}$, $i = 1, 2, 3, 4$.

Let b_i be the residue of b modulo m_i, $i = 1, 2, 3, 4$. By the chinese remainder theorem we have that $x = b$ is the only integer such that

1. $x \equiv b_i \, [m_i], i = 1, 2, 3, 4$.

2. $0 \le x < m$.

Here is a diagram of the sequence of operations that is considered. Let us sketch the meaning of the diagram before going into details.
Each black point represents a step resulting in an estimated 2^{32} binary sequences. The length of those sequences is 64 for steps 1, 2, 3, 4. It is 128 for steps 5 and 6 and finally step 7 produces about 2^{32} sequences of length 256 among which test modulo m_4 selects a solution with probability close to 1.

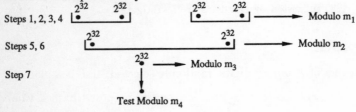

We now go through each step in detail.

Step 1 : We find all sequences (x_i), $1 \le i \le 64$, $x_i = 0$ or 1, such that

$$\sum_{i=1}^{64} x_i a_i \equiv b_1 \, [m_1].$$

We will find about 2^{32} such sequences because there are 2^{64} sequences (x_i) of 64 bits, and m_1 is close to 2^{32}. In fact, we will examine in Section 2 what is the expected number of solutions to be obtained when the algorithm is brought to completion.

Important remark. Finding sequences (x_i) such that $\sum_{i=1}^{64} x_i a_i \equiv b_1 \ [m_1]$ needs a number in the region of 2^{32} operations, if a memory with sufficient size is available.

Indeed, we just have to do the following.

a) compute and store all values of $b_1 - \sum_{i=1}^{32} x_i a_i$ modulo m_1.

b) compute and store all values of $\sum_{i=33}^{64} x_i a_i$ modulo m_1.

c) keep all pairs of sequences (x_i) which give the same value modulo m_1 in a) and b).

More details. In Section 3 we give more details about operations a), b), c), about the memory needed and about the number of solutions to be found.

Step 2 : The same way, we find about 2^{32} binary sequences (x_i) such that $\sum_{i=65}^{128} x_i a_i \equiv 0 \ [m_1]$.

Step 3 : The same way, we find about 2^{32} binary sequences (x_i) such that $\sum_{i=129}^{192} x_i a_i \equiv 0 \ [m_1]$.

Step 4 : The same way, we find about 2^{32} binary sequences (x_i) such that $\sum_{i=193}^{256} x_i a_i \equiv 0 \ [m_1]$.

Step 5 : We denote $\sum_{i=1}^{64} x_i a_i$ by s_1 and $\sum_{i=65}^{128} x_i a_i$ by s_2.

From the sequences (x_i) found at Steps 1 and 2, and using the procedure a) b) c) above, we find about 2^{32} sequences (x_i), $1 \le i \le 128$ such that $s_1 + s_2 \equiv b_2 \ [m_2]$. For there are about $2^{32} \times 2^{32} = 2^{64}$ sequences (x_i), $1 \le i \le 128$ such that $(x_1, \ldots, x_{64})$ is a solution in Step 1 and $(x_{65}, \ldots, x_{128})$ is a solution in Step 2. So if the numbers $s_1 + s_2$ are about equally distributed modulo $m_2, m_2 \simeq 2^{32}$, we find about $\dfrac{2^{64}}{2^{32}} = 2^{32}$ among those sequences such that $s_1 + s_2 \equiv b_2 \ [m_2]$. If we find noticeably less than 2^{32} such solutions, we will see at the end of this Section 1 what to do.

All sequences (x_i) to be found in Step 5 also have the following property:

$$s_1 + s_2 \equiv b_2 \ [m_2] \text{ and } s_1 + s_2 \equiv b_1 \ [m_1].$$

This is because $s_1 \equiv b_1 \ [m_1]$ and $s_2 \equiv 0 \ [m_1]$.

Remark Step 5 also uses a number in the region of 2^{32} operations. The computer problem is the same as for step 1. Details will be given in Section 3. We essentially have two sets E and F of about 2^{32} elements, and we want to find all possible couples (a, b), $a \in E$, $b \in F$, such that $a = b \equiv k \ [m_i]$, where k is a fixed value and m_i is close to 2^{32}.

Step 6 : The same way, from the sequences (x_i) found at Steps 3 and 4, we find about 2^{32} sequences (x_i), $129 \leq i \leq 256$, such that

$$\text{if } s_3 = \sum_{i=129}^{192} x_i a_i \text{ and } s_4 = \sum_{i=193}^{256} x_i a_i, \text{ we have that } s_3 + s_4 \equiv 0 \ [m_2].$$

Moreover $s_3 + s_4 \equiv 0 \ [m_1]$, since $s_3 \equiv 0 \ [m_1]$ and $s_4 \equiv 0 \ [m_1]$.

Step 7 : The same way, but now from the sequences (x_i) found at the Steps 5 and 6, we find about 2^{32} sequences (x_i), $1 \leq i \leq 256$ such that $(s_1 + s_2) + (s_3 + s_4) \equiv b_3 \ [m_3]$.

By construction, we also have that

$$s_1 + s_2 + s_3 + s_4 \equiv b_1 \ [m_1] \text{ and } s_1 + s_2 + s_3 + s_4 \equiv b_2 \ [m_2].$$

Modulo m_4, we have about 2^{32} possible values, indeed $m_4 \simeq 2^{32}$. Since we found 2^{32} sequences (x_i), there is a high probability that at least one of these sequences is such that $s_1 + s_2 + s_3 + s_4 \equiv b_4 \ [m_4]$. We will see in section 2 that we generally find more than one such sequence. We will see at the end of this section what to do if we don't find any such sequence.

Now, suppose that we have such a sequence.

$$s_1 + s_2 + s_3 + s_4 = \sum_{j=1}^{256} x_j a_j.$$

That sequence (x_i) is such that

1. $\sum_{j=1}^{256} x_j a_j \equiv b_i \ [m_i], i = 1, 2, 3, 4.$

2. $0 \leq \sum_{j=1}^{256} x_j a_j \leq 256 \cdot 2^{120} = 2^{128}.$

Thus by a) and b) in Step 0, we finally found a sequence (x_i) such that $\sum_{j=1}^{256} x_j a_j = b$, as desired.

A careful justification of the fact that an average number of 2^{32} solutions are to be found in step 7 is a consequence of corollary 1 in section 2.3. It essentially relies on the fact that the sum of two mutually independent uniformly distributed random variables (m.i.u.d.r.v.) over an abelian group is itself a m.i.u.d.r.v..

Remark What are we going to do if at any a step we have got much less than 2^{32} solutions, or if at the end we don't find any solution such that $s_1 + s_2 + s_3 + s_4 \equiv b_4 \ [m_i], i = 1, 2, 3, 4$?

Then it is possible to use the algorithm again, but with new chosen values. For example we can replace b_1 by $s_1 \equiv b_1 - \lambda \ [m_1]$ at Step 1, and 0 by $s_2 \equiv \lambda \ [m_1]$ at Step 2, where λ is any fixed integer in $[0, m_1 - 1]$.

Or we can even just permute the a_i's.

At each try, we will have a high probability of success, so the probability of success after a few tries can be as close to 1 as desired.

2 Proof

2.1 The collision free functions family

In this section the given sequence element from $[0, 2^{120}[^n$, is denoted by $a^* = \{a_1^*, a_2^*, \ldots, a_n^*\}$ and the value for which a collision is searched is denoted by b^*.

Let us recall what we need form the definition in [5] of a **collision free function family** $\mathcal{F}$. Such a family is given by an infinite family of finite sets $\{F_n\}_{n=1}^\infty$, and a function $t : \mathbb{N} \to \mathbb{N}$, such that $t(n) < n$ for all $n \in \mathbb{N}$.

Now a member of F_n here is a function

$$f_a : \{0,1\}^n \to \{0,1\}^t$$

defined by

$$x \rightsquigarrow \sum_{i=1}^n x_i a_i$$

where $a = (a_1, \ldots, a_n)$ belongs to the product $\mathcal{A} = [0, 2^\ell[^n$ of n intervals of integers, for $\ell = t - \log n$.

Integer $\sum_{i=1}^n x_i a_i$ is considered a binary sequence which is its writing in the radix two. Function f_a is called an instance of $\mathcal{F}$ of size n.

We here consider the set F_n for which $n = 256$ and $t(n) = 128$. However the argument here does not generally depend on specifie values of n or other parameters but if so we will point it out.

2.2 Some questions to be replied

The particular function f_a that will be analyzed is given by an a randomly selected from $\mathcal{A}$.

The set $\mathcal{A}$ is thus made a sample space.

For this specific application it has the **equally likely probability measure** but our argument can be exploited in more general situations.

To clarify, let us state one of the problems we will be faced with. Let q be an integer (q is large but small compared to 2^ℓ).

Given b in $[0, 2^t[$, the following expectation will be estimated

$$e(b) = \sum_{a \in \mathcal{A}} p(a)|\{x | x \in \{0,1\}^n, f_a(x) \equiv b \ [q]\}| \tag{1}$$

where p is the probability measure on $\mathcal{A}$.

Other expectations are needed as the following

$$e_j(b) = \sum_{a \in \mathcal{A}} p(a)|\{x | x \in \{0,1\}^n, f_a(x) \equiv b \ [q] \quad \text{and} \quad |s(x)| = j\}|, \ j = 0, \ldots, n,$$

where the **support** $s(x)$ of x is defined as

$$s(x) = \{i | x_i = 1\}.$$

We will in particular observe that those expectations don't depend on a particular choice of a non zero b, for a non zero j.

2.3 Random variables

The boolean function ϕ(statement) takes the value 1 if "statement" is true and 0 otherwise. We here introduce **random variables** (briefly r.v.) defined on $\mathcal{A}$ and **with values in an abelian group**.
Let q be an integer relatively small compared to 2^ℓ. The additive group $(\mathbb{Z}/q\mathbb{Z}, +)$ of integers modulo q is the abelian group denoted by G_q. Let $I = [0, 2^\ell[$ be a sample space with the equally likely probability measure.
Then the mapping

$$\theta : I \to G_q \tag{2}$$

defines a r.v. which may be considered **uniformly distributed** since q is negligeable compared to $\dfrac{2^\ell}{q}$.
Moreover we will consider sums of mutually independent (briefly m.i.) r.v. identical to θ and it is not difficult to prove that for whatever probability distribution, (briefly p.d.) at the only condition that the considered random variable with values in an abelian group has a positive probability on each element of a set of generators of that group, then the p.d. of the sum of a large number of m.i.r.v. identical to the given one approaches a uniform distribution.
To every subset J of $[1, n]$ corresponds a random variable $\theta_J : \mathcal{A} \to G_q$ defined by

$$\forall a \in \mathcal{A} : \theta_J(a) = \sum_{j \in J} a_j \in G_q$$

and we thus have

$$P_r\{\theta_J = b\} = \sum_{a \in \mathcal{A}, \theta_J(a) = b} P(a).$$

For convenience we also define $\theta_\emptyset$ by

$$\forall a \in \mathcal{A} : \theta_\emptyset(a) = 0 \in G_q$$

Clearly θ_J is a sum of $|J|$ m.i.r.v. identical to θ and $\theta_{J_1} = \theta_{J_2}$ for $|J_1| = |J_2|$. We thus denote by θ_j the common r.v. θ_J with $|J| = j$ and $\theta_\emptyset$ is denoted by θ_0.

We then have that

$$P_r\{\theta_\emptyset = b\} = \phi(b = 0).$$

We now classically have the

Theorem 1 *Given b, then the expectation $e(b)$ is worth*

$$\sum_{a \in \mathcal{A}} p(a) |\{x | x \in \{0,1\}^n, f_a(x) \equiv b \ [q]\}| = \sum_{x \in \{0,1\}^n} P_r\{\theta_{s(x)} = b\}. \tag{3}$$

Proof

The L.H.S. is worth

$$\sum_{(a,x)\in\mathcal{A}\times\{0,1\}^n} p(a)\,\phi\left(\sum_{i=1}^{n}x_ia_i \equiv b\ [q]\right)$$

$$= \sum_{x\in\{0,1\}^n} \quad \sum_{a\in\mathcal{A},\sum_{i=1}^{n}x_ia_i\equiv b\ [q]} p(a),$$

which is nothing but the R.H.S.

Corollary 1 *If θ is a uniformly distributed random variable (briefly u.d.r.v.) then the expectation considered in Theorem 1 is worth*

$$(2^n-1)/q + \phi(b=0).$$

Corollary 2 *Given an integer $j, 0 \leq j \leq m$, the expectation*

$$e_j(b) = \sum_{a\in\mathcal{A}}p(a)|\{x|x\in\{0,1\}^n, f_a(x) \equiv b\ [q] \quad and\ |s(x)| = j\}$$

is worth

$$\binom{n}{j} P_r\{\theta_j = b\}.$$

If θ is a u.d.r.v., then this is $\binom{n}{j}/q$ for $j > 0$ and $\phi(b=0)$ for $j=0$.

2.4 The expected weight distribution in the sample to be scanned

2.4.1 The expected number of collisions

Let m_1, m_2, m_3, m_4 be the integers given in section 1 and take $q = m_1m_2m_3$. Since $q \simeq 2^{96} < b^*$ then the set

$$R = \{x \in \{0,1\}^n, f_{a'}(x) \equiv b^*\ [q]\}$$

contains the set M of all x in $\{0,1\}$ such that $f_{a'}(x) = b^*$ from which we have to exhibit a member, among other $0-1$ sequences. By Theorem 1 we can assess that the expected size $e(b^*)$ of R is $2^n/q = 2^{160}$.

By Corollary 2, the weight ratio distribution in R is the same as is $\{0,1\}^n$ i.e.

$$\left(\frac{\binom{n}{j}}{2^n}\right)^n_{j=0}$$

The size of M may be in its turn assessed.

The set $\{0,1\}^n$ being assumed to have the equally likely probability measure we have that

$$P_r\{np - t \leq \sum_{i=1}^{n} x_i \leq np + t\} = \sum_{np-t \leq i \leq np+t} \binom{n}{i} p^i q^{n-i}.$$

For $n = 256, p = q = \dfrac{1}{2}$ and $t = 20$, this is worth 0.9897. This means that in most cases, b will lie in the interval $[108.2^{119}, 148.2^{119}]$, so that there are about $41.2^{119} \simeq 2^{124.35}$ possible values for b. Thus when a value b^* is assigned to b in that range then the size of M is in the region of $2^{256-124.35} = 2^{131.64}$.

Now M is contained in R.

This means that the probability to obtain a collision when drawing an element from R at random is $2^{131.64-160} = 2^{-28.35}$.

If we could operate such drawings about 2^{32} times, then the expected number of collisions obtained would be $2^{-28.35} \times 2^{32} = 2^{3.64} > 12$.

Actually our algorithm consists in constructing a subset S of R the expected size of which is 2^{32} in which the expected number of collisions is still $2^{3.64}$.

2.4.2 A suitable partition of the set R

Given a partition $E_1 \cup E_2 \cup E_3 \cup E_4$ of $[1, n]$ with $|E_i| = n/4, i = 1, \ldots, 4$ we define a partition $\{S_\gamma\}_{\gamma \in \Gamma}$ of R, where $\Gamma = G_{m_1} \times G_{m_1} \times G_{m_1} \times G_{m_2}, \gamma$ being a quadruple (c_1, c_2, c_3, d_1).

The set S_γ is defined as

$$\{x | x \in R, \sum_{i \in E_j} x_i a_i^* \equiv c_j \, [m_1], j = 1, 2, 3, \sum_{i \in F_1} x_i a_i^* \equiv d_1 \, [m_2]\},$$

where $F_1 = E_1 \cup E_2$. Also $F_2 = E_3 \cup E_4$.

Notice that for x in S_γ, since $S_\gamma \subset R$, we necessarily have that

$$\sum_{i \in E_4} x_i a_i^* \equiv b^* - c_1 - c_2 - c_3 \, [m_1], \quad \sum_{i \in F_2} x_i a_i^* \equiv b^* - d_1 \, [m_2] \text{ and } \sum_{i=1}^{n} x_i a_i^* \equiv b^* [m_3].$$

Clearly by the general property of θ defined in (2.3) the conditional probability

$$P_r\{x \in S_\gamma | x \in R\}$$

is very close to $1/m_1^3 m_2$ and thus Theorem 1 entails that the expected size of S_γ is $|R|/m_1^3 m_2$ which in the example dealt with is 2^{32}.

Notice that in the description of the algorithm, c_1 was chosen to be equal to $b^* \bmod m$, and $c_2 \equiv c_3 \equiv 0 \, [m]$, also $d_1 \equiv b^* \, [m_2]$. **We next give evidence that the expected size of $S_\gamma \cap M$ does not depend on a particular choice of γ.**

We will need a corollary to corollary 2 of Theorem 1.

Corollary 3 *For any $\gamma \in \Gamma$, the weight ratio distribution in S_γ is very close to*

$$\left(\frac{\binom{n}{j}}{2^n} \right)^n_{j=0}$$

Indeed for every J for which $J \cap E_i \neq \emptyset$, $i = 1, 2, 3, 4$, we have that

$$P_r(x \in S_\gamma \quad \text{and} \quad s(x) = J)$$

$$= \prod_{j=1}^4 P_r \left(\sum_{i \in J \cap E_j} x_i a_i \equiv c_j \, [m_1] \right) \prod_{j=1}^2 \left(\sum_{i \in J \cap F_j} x_i a_i \equiv d_j \, [m_2] \right) P_r \left(\sum_{i=1}^n x_i a_i \equiv b \, [m_3] \right)$$

$= 1/m_1^4 m_2^2 m_3$, where $\gamma = (c_1, c_2, c_3, d_1)$ and $c_4 \equiv b - c_1 - c_2 - c_3 \, [m_1]$, $d_2 \equiv b - d \, [m_2]$.
Moreover the contribution of the sets J, such that $J \cap E_i = \emptyset$ for some i, to the expectation

$$\sum_{a \in \mathcal{A}} p(a) |\{x | x \in S_\gamma, |s(x)| = j\}|$$

being negligeable for the relevant sizes of j, then a similar argument as the one used for proving corollary 2 proves the thesis.

2.5 Sums of random variables with integer values

The expected size of M, given b, is

$$\sum_{a \in \mathcal{A}} P(a) \left| \left\{ x | x \in \{0,1\}^n, \sum_{i=1}^n x_i a_i = b \right\} \right|.$$

A random variable $\omega_J : a \rightsquigarrow \sum_{i \in J} a_i$ mapping $\mathcal{A}$ into $[0, 2^t[$ corresponds to each subset J of $[1, n]$. Notice that $P_r\{\omega_J = b\}$ here depends on b and J when $\mathcal{A}$ has the equally likely probability measure. But by symmetry, for any b, $P_r\{\omega_J = b\}$ only depends on the size of J.
By the same argument as for Theorem 1 we have that the expected size of M is

$$\sum_{J \subset [1,n]} P_r\{\omega_J = b\}.$$

We now consider any partition $H_1 \cup H_2 = [1, n]$. To obtain the evidence claimed in section 2.4.2, we need to show that given q small and any $J \subset [1, n]$ such that $J \cap H_1 \neq \emptyset$, we have that

$$P_r \left\{ \sum_{i \in H_1 \cap J} x_i a_i \equiv c \, [q] \, |x \in M \right\}$$

very slightly depend on the choice of c. Thus the expected size of $M \cap S_\gamma$ will only slightly depend on the choice of γ.
We have that

$$\omega_J(a) = \sum_{i \in J \cap H_1} a_i + \sum_{i \in J \cap H_2} a_i$$

and for $\omega_J(a) = b$, then if $J \cap H_1$ is not empty, $\sum_{i \in J \cap H_1} a_i$ takes all integer values from 0 to b, as a runs over $\mathcal{A}$. We will observe on some numerical values that over q successive values $v_1, \ldots, v_1 + q - 1$ taken by v in $[0, b]$ then the variation of $P_r\{\omega_{J \cap H_1} = v\}$ is negligeable. Now in view of corollary 3, for a given partition $H_1 \cup H_2 = [1, n]$ where the smallest size of H_i is 64, $i = 1, 2$ then the contribution to

$$P_r\left\{\sum_{i \in H_1} x_i a_i \equiv c\,[q]\,|x \in M\right\}$$

of x's such that $s(x) \cap H_1 = \emptyset$ is negligeable since most of the weights of x's in S_γ are in the interval $[118, 148]$, by corollary 3, and

$$\binom{256 - 64}{118} \Big/ \binom{256}{118} = 8.65\ 10^{-22}.$$

We use the following result on the probability distribution of the sum of j m.i.u.d.r.v. with values in the interval of integers $[0, h[$.
([4] page 52).
Let c be in $[0, jh[$. As c and h grow indefinitely, their ratio $\frac{c}{h}$ approaching ξ which is a real number in $[0, j[$, then the probability distribution

$$a_{j,c} = P_r\{X_1 + X_2 + \ldots + X_j < c\}$$

tends to

$$F(\xi) = \lim_{\frac{c}{h} \to \xi} a_{j,c} = \frac{1}{j!} \sum_{\nu < \xi} \binom{j}{\nu} (\xi - \nu)^j.$$

We compute $F(\xi)$ and $F(\xi + \varepsilon)$ for $\varepsilon = \frac{q}{h} = \frac{2^{32}}{2^{120}} = 2^{-88}$ and for a few values of j and x. Since $F(\xi)$ is increasing we only have to notice that $F(\xi + \varepsilon)$ is very close to $F(\xi)$ to be convinced of the claim in 2.4.2. We also compute some values for $\varepsilon = 2^{-10}$ to show that for q in the region of 2^{110} we would move away from our assumption.

j	ξ	ε	$F(\xi)$	$F(\xi + \varepsilon) - F(\xi)$	Ratio
32	15	2^{-88}	$2.7\ 10^{-1}$	$6.53\ 10^{-28}$	$2.41\ 10^{-27}$
32	5	2^{-88}	$8.62\ 10^{-14}$	$1.77\ 10^{-39}$	$2.05\ 10^{-26}$
15	7	2^{-88}	$3.28\ 10^{-1}$	$1.04\ 10^{-27}$	$3.15\ 10^{-27}$
15	3	2^{-88}	$1.06\ 10^{-5}$	$1.68\ 10^{-31}$	$1.59\ 10^{-26}$
32	15	2^{-10}	$2.71\ 10^{-1}$	$1.97\ 10^{-4}$	$7.29\ 10^{-4}$
32	5	2^{-10}	$8.62\ 10^{-14}$	$2.17\ 10^{-15}$	$2.51\ 10^{-2}$
15	7	2^{-10}	$3.29\ 10^{-1}$	$3.13\ 10^{-4}$	$9.53\ 10^{-4}$
15	3	2^{-10}	$1.06\ 10^{-5}$	$5.09\ 10^{-8}$	$4.8\ 10^{-3}$

3 More details about the algorithm

3.1 About 2^{32} operations and 64 Gigabytes of memory

At several steps of the algorithm, we are faced with the following problem. We have to find all binary sequences (x_i), $1 \leq i \leq 64$, such that $\sum_{i=1}^{64} x_i a_i \equiv b_1 \ [m_1]$, where $m_1 \simeq 2^{32}$, and where b_1 is a fixed value. We here show in detail how to do this in about 2^{32} operations and we estimate the needed size of memory.

Implementation 1 Let R be a file that can contain 2^{32} words of 32 bits, and let S be a file that can contain 2^{32} words of 64 bits. We store in the file R intermediate results and S will be the file of solutions (x_i).

Step a : For each $(x_1, \ldots, x_{32})$ we compute $k = b_1 - \sum_{i=1}^{32} x_i a_i$ modulo m_1 and store $(x_1, \ldots, x_{32})$ in file R at address k. If a solution $(x'_1, \ldots, x'_{32})$ was already introduced at that address, then $(x_1, \ldots, x_{32})$ is dropped. In implementation 2 however all intermediate results will be stored. This **step a** needs about 2^{32} operations since there are 2^{32} sequences $(x_1, \ldots, x_{32})$.

Step b : For each $(x_{33}, \ldots, x_{64})$ then $k' \equiv \sum_{i=33}^{64} x_i a_i$ modulo m_1 is computed.

First case: The register at address k' in file R contains a sequence $(x_1, \ldots x_{32})$. Then $(x_1, \ldots, x_{32}, x_{33}, \ldots x_{64})$ is stored in S because then $k' \equiv \sum_{i=33}^{64} x_i a_i \ [m_1] \equiv b_1 - \sum_{i=1}^{32} x_i a_i \ [m_1]$, which entails $\sum_{i=1}^{64} x_i a_i \equiv b_1 \ [m_1]$.

Second case: The register at address k' in file R is empty. Here the following $(x_{33}, \ldots, x_{64})$ is considered. This **step b** also needs about 2^{32} operations.

Hence after **a** and **b** we will have a solution (x_i) for each value k' such that $\sum_{i=1}^{64} x_i a_i \equiv b_1 \ [m_1]$ and $\sum_{i=33}^{64} x_i a_i = k'$.

Implementation 2 It is possible to improve implementation 1 in order to obtain all solutions $(x_1, \ldots, x_{64})$ still in about 2^{32} operations and with about $4 \cdot 2^{32} \cdot 32$ bits of memory. Let X be a new file for 2^{32} words of 32 bits.

Step a If the register with address k computed from $(x_1, \ldots, x_{32})$ already contains the intermediate result $(x'_1, \ldots, x'_{32})$, then shift $(x'_1, \ldots, x'_{32})$ to the address $(x_1, \ldots, x_{32})$ of X, and introduce $(x_1, \ldots, x_{32})$ in the register with address k of file R.

Step b We only have to consider the first case. Sequence $(x_1, \ldots, x_{32})$ is found at address k' in file R. Then $(x'_1, \ldots, x'_{32})$ if any is found at address $(x_1, \ldots, x_{32})$ of X. Next $(x''_1, \ldots, x''_{32})$ if any is found at address $(x'_1, \ldots, x'_{32})$ of X and so on untill an empty register appears. In file S are stored successively $(x_1, \ldots, x_{32}, x_{33}, \ldots, x_{64}), (x'_1, \ldots, x_{32}, x_{33}, \ldots, x_{64})$, $(x''_1, \ldots, x''_{32}, x_{33}, \ldots, x_{64}) \ldots$. That way all solutions are exhibited and stored in S in about 2.2^{32} operations.

Size of memory We need about $4 \cdot 2^{32}.32$ bits $= 64$ Gigabytes and 1.4 Gigabytes Disks are available today. The size of memory needed is thus high but not unrealistic.

3.2 Some steps can be done once for all

In our algorithm, Steps 2, 3, 4, and 6 do not depend on the value of b. The numbers a_i being publicly disclosed, computations in those steps can be performed once for all.

4 Generalizations of our algorithm to other sizes of Knapsacks

The problem. Let $a_1, \ldots, a_s$, be fixed integers of A binary digits. If T is a plaintext of s binary symbols, i.e. $T = x_1 \ldots x_s$, then $b = \sum_{i=1}^{s} x_i a_i$ is the proposed hashed value. The integer b has B binary digits i.e. $B \simeq A + \log_2 s$.

We have seen in Section 1 that it is possible to find a sequence (x_i) such that $\sum_{i=1}^{s} x_i a_i = b$, when b is given, in about 2^{32} operations, when $s = 256$ and $B = 128$. We will now consider some other values for s and B.

Case $s = 512$ and $B = 160$. It is still possible to find a sequence (x_i) when $s = 512$ and $b = 160$ in about 2^{32} operations: we will just have to add a stage in our algorithm. Schematically we will then have the following. Notice that 2^{32} is the evaluation of the number of solutions.

Explanation of the scheme: m_1, m_2, m_3, m_4, m_5 are pairwise coprime integers such that $m_i \simeq 2^{32}$, $i = 1, 2, 3, 4$, or 5, and $m_1 m_2 m_3 m_4 m_5 > 2^{160}$.

Let b_i be the residue of b modulo m_i.

- At Stage (1), we find about 2^{32} solutions (x_i) such that $\sum_{i=1}^{64} x_i a_i \equiv b_1 \; [m_1]$, about 2^{32} solution (x_i) such that $\sum_{i=65}^{128} x_i a_i \equiv 0 \; [m_1], \ldots$, about 2^{32} solutions (x_i) such that $\sum_{i=449}^{512} x_i a_i \equiv 0 \; [m_1]$.

- At Stage (2), we regroup in pairs the solutions found at Stage (1) to find about 2^{32} solutions (x_i) such that $\sum_{i=1}^{128} x_i a_i \equiv b_2 \; [m_2], \ldots$, about 2^{32} solutions (x_i) such that $\sum_{i=385}^{512} x_i a_i \equiv 0 \; [m_2]$. Notice that these sequences (x_i) also verify $\sum_{i=1}^{128} x_i a_i \equiv b_1 + 0 \; [m_1], \ldots$, and $\sum_{i=385}^{512} x_i a_i \equiv 0 + 0 \; [m_1]$.

- At Stage (3), we regroup in pairs the solutions of Stage (2) to find about 2^{32} solutions (x_i) such that $\sum_{i=1}^{256} x_i a_i \equiv b_3 \; [m_3]$ and 2^{32} solutions (x_i) such that $\sum_{i=257}^{512} x_i a_i \equiv 0 \; [m_3]$. Then at Stage (4) we regroup these solutions to finally find a solution (x_i) at Stage (5) such that $\sum_{i=1}^{512} x_i a_i \equiv b_i \; [m_i]$, $i = 1, 2, 3, 4$ or 5.

By the chinese remainder theorem, we then found a sequence (x_i) such that $\sum_{i=1}^{512} x_i a_i = b$, as wanted.

Other Generalizations. With the same technique, by using one, two, etc. more stages, and still with about 2^{32} operations, we can solve the cases where $b = 192$ and $s = 1024$, or $b = 224$ and $s = 2048$ etc.

So, our algorithm can solve these cases in about 2^{32} operations:

Upper bound for # binary digits t of b	Lower bound for # binary symbols s of plaintext T.
96	128
128	256
160	512
192	1024
224	2048
etc.	

If $b = 64$ and $s = 128$, using the same process, a sequence (x_i) will be found in about 2^{16} operations. Schematically:

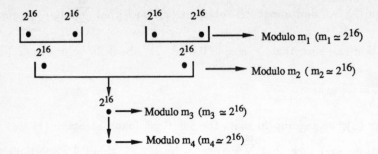

5   Optimality

5.1   A slight improvement

In section 2.4.1, we have seen that the expected number of collisions obtained is at least 12. If the expected size of S_γ defined in 2.4.2 would be 2^{30} instead of 2^{32}, we would have an expected number of at least $2^{16} > 3$ collisions which is a satisfactory prospect.
Let $m_1 = 2^t, m_2 = 2^u, m_3 = 2^v$ and $m^4 = 2^w$. Setting t to 32, u to 31 and v to 32, then by corollary 1, the expected size of S_γ becomes $2^{256-4t-2u-v} = 2^{30}$.

5.2   The designed sizes are best possible. Needlessness of an extra stage

We first point out that if separating step 7 in section 1.1 from the final scanning of S_γ modulo m_4 helps assessing the expectations in section 2, however the result of all computations is the same if we directly compute modulo $m_3\, m_4$ in step 4. Disregarding the refinement above and considering that $2^v = m_3\, m_4$, we have that at the end of the process the expected number of solutions is 2^r with $r = 256 - 4t - 2u - v$.
The first constraints are thus $t \geq 0, u \geq 0, v \geq 0$ and

$$(1) \qquad 256 - 4t - 2u - v \geq 0$$

But we need that $m_1 m_2 m_3 m_4 \geq b$ for relations 1 and 2 of section 1.1 :

$$(2) \qquad t + u + v \geq 128.$$

Now the expected sizes of the sets we have to deal with are

$$2^{64-t} \quad \text{and} \quad 2^{128-2t-u}.$$

The maximum of these numbers is to be as small as possible and we thus have that

$$(3) \qquad 64 - t = 128 - 2t - u.$$

Adding (1) and (2) we get

$$128 - t - u \geq 2t,$$

and since by (3) we have that $t + u = 64$, we obtain $0 \leq t \leq 32$. We thus minimize 2^{64-t} by setting $t = 32$ and thus $u = 32, v = 64$ which were the selected values. With one more stage, the sizes of the sets to be recorder would be $2^{32-t}, 2^{64-2t-u}, 2^{128-4t-2u-v}$ where $m_1 = 2^t, m_2 = 2^u, m_3 = 2^v, m_4 = 2^w$.

We here have the constraints $t + u + v + w \geq 128$ and $256 - 8t - 4u - 2v - w \geq 0$, from which $128 - 4t - 2u - v \geq 3t + u$. If we attempt to obtain a smaller size than previously, we need that $3t + u \leq 128 - 4t - 2u - v \leq 32$ and $64 - 2t - u \leq 32$, which implies $t \leq 0$. Since $2^t = m_1$ we must have $t = 0$. This means that the considered extra stage is useless.

6   Conclusion

The technique is very efficient for a lot of values of s and t. With the values sugested by I. Damgård, we can find a sequence (x_i) using a number in the region of 2^{32} operations and about 60 Gigabytes of memory. This is high, but not impracticable. Still, if $t = 256$ and $s = 512$ for example, finding a sequence (x_i) in a number in the region of 2^{32} operations remains an open problem.

References

[1] P. Camion, *Can a Fast signature Scheme Without Secret Key be Secure?*, in AAECC-2, Lecture Notes in Computer Science n° 228, Springer-Verlag.

[2] P. Camion and Ph. Godlewski, *Manipulation and Errors, Localization and Detection*, Proceedings of EuroCrypt'88, Lecture Notes in Computer Science n° 330, Springer-Verlag.

[3] M. Campana and M. Girault, *How to Use Compressed Encoding Mechanisms in Data Protection*, Securicom 88, March 15–17, pp. 91–110.

[4] D. Dacunha-Castelle and D. Revuz, *Recueil de problèmes de calcul des probabilités*, Masson et Cie, Paris, 1970.

[5] I. Damgård, *Design Principles for Hash Functions*, Proceedings of Crypto'89, Springer-Verlag.

[6] D.W. Davis and W.L. Price, *Security for computer Networks*, John Wiley and Sons, Chichester 1984.

[7] M. Girault, *Hash Functions Using Modulo-n Operations*, Proceedings of EuroCrypt'87, Springer-Verlag.

[8] J.K. Gibson, *Some comments on Damgard's hashing principle*, Electronic letters 19th July 1990, Vol. 26 n° 15.

An Improved Low-Density Subset Sum Algorithm

M. J. Coster [†]
B. A. LaMacchia [‡]
A. M. Odlyzko

AT&T Bell Laboratories
Murray Hill, New Jersey 07974

C. P. Schnorr

Universität Frankfurt
Fachbereich Mathematik/Informatik
Postfach 11 19 32
6000 Frankfurt am Main
Germany

ABSTRACT

The general subset sum problem is NP-complete. However, there are two algorithms, one due to Brickell and the other to Lagarias and Odlyzko, which in polynomial time solve almost all subset sum problems of sufficiently low density. Both methods rely on basis reduction algorithms to find short non-zero vectors in special lattices. The Lagarias-Odlyzko algorithm would solve almost all subset sum problems of density $< 0.6463\ldots$ in polynomial time if it could invoke a polynomial-time algorithm for finding the shortest non-zero vector in a lattice. This note shows that a simple modification of that algorithm would solve almost all problems of density $< 0.9408\ldots$ if it could find shortest non-zero vectors in lattices. This modification also yields dramatic improvements in practice when it is combined with known lattice basis reduction algorithms.

1. Introduction

The *knapsack* or *subset sum* problem is to find, given positive integers $a_1, \ldots, a_n$ (the weights) and s, some subset of the a_i that sum to s, or equivalently to find variables $e_1, \ldots, e_n$, with

---

[†] Visit to AT&T Bell Laboratories supported by a Fulbright scholarship.
[‡] Present address: MIT, Cambridge, MA 02139.

$e_i \in \{0.1\}$, such that

$$\sum_{i=1}^{n} e_i a_i = s. \tag{1.1}$$

This problem is known to be NP-complete [9] (in its feasibility recognition form), and so is thought to be very hard in general. This has led to the invention of several public-key cryptosystems based on the knapsack problem. Almost all of these have been broken by now, however. (See [2, 3, 5, 16] for surveys of this field.) Most of the attacks exploited specific constructions of the relevant cryptosystems. In addition, two algorithms have been proposed, one by Brickell [1] and the other by Lagarias and Odlyzko [12] which show that almost all low-density subset sum problems can be solved in polynomial time. The *density* of a set of weights $a_1, \ldots, a_n$ is defined by

$$d = \frac{n}{\log_2 \max_{1 \le i \le n} a_i}. \tag{1.2}$$

The interesting case is $d \le 1$, since for $d > 1$ there will in general be many subsets of weights with the same sum, and so such sets of weights could not be used for transmitting information. The Brickell and Lagarias-Odlyzko algorithms solve almost all subset sum problems with d sufficiently small.

Both the Brickell and Lagarias-Odlyzko algorithms reduce the subset sum problem to that of finding a short vector in a lattice. The exact complexity of finding short vectors in lattices is not known, and expert opinion appears to be divided as to whether this problem is polynomial or not. At the moment, the best known polynomial time method in this area is the L^3 lattice basis reduction algorithm of Lenstra, Lenstra, and Lovász [14], which is only guaranteed to find a non-zero vector in an n-dimensional lattice that is at most an exponential times the length of the shortest non-zero vector in that lattice. If one uses that algorithm, the Lagarias-Odlyzko method can be shown rigorously to solve almost all subset sum problems of density $< c/n$ for large n and for a fixed constant c, as is done in [12]. (See [7] for a simplified analysis of the algorithm.) Using more recent algorithms of Schnorr [20], one can improve the cutoff bound to c'/n for arbitrarily small constants $c' > 0$, but at the cost of increasing the degree of the polynomial that bounds the running time.

Finding short vectors in lattices may be very hard in general. On the other hand, published algorithms, such as the L^3 one, perform much be.ter in practice than is guaranteed by their worst case bounds, especially when they are modified [12, 13, 18], and new algorithms are being invented [19, 20, 22]. Thus it is possible that on average, the problem of finding short vectors in lattices is easy, even if it is hard in the worst case. Therefore it seems worthwhile to separate the issues of efficiency of lattice basis reduction algorithms from the question of how well the subset sum problem can be reduced to that of finding a short vector in a lattice. (Note that Paz and Schnorr [17] have shown that the general problem of finding the shortest non-zero vector in a lattice is reducible to that of solving some subset sum problem, but with some loss of efficiency.)

Consider a *lattice oracle* that, given a basis for a lattice, with high probability yields in polynomial time the shortest non-zero vector in that lattice. We do not know how to construct such an oracle, but it might be possible to do so, and in any case in relatively low dimensions, known polynomial time algorithms act like such an oracle. The analysis of [12] showed that availability of such an oracle would let the Lagarias-Odlyzko algorithm solve almost all subset sum problems of density $< 0.6463\ldots$, but not higher than that. (Similar analyses are not available for the Brickell algorithm [1], although it seems to require even lower densities. See also [8].)

In this note we analyze a simple modification of the part of the Lagarias-Odlyzko algorithm that reduces the subset sum problem to a short vector in a lattice problem. We show that with this modification, a single call to a lattice oracle would lead to polynomial time solutions of almost all problems of density $< 0.9408\ldots$. Empirical tests show that this modification also leads to dramatic improvement in the performance of practical algorithms. We present some results on this in Section 4. More data and fuller comparisons will be given in [13].

In Section 2 we derive the Lagarias-Odlyzko bound using the approach in [7]. We show in Section 3 that this bound may be increased to $0.9408\ldots$ using a simple modification of the Lagarias-Odlyzko attack. Finally, Section 4 discusses possible improvements on the new bound and practical results.

Joux and Stern [11] have found another modification of the Lagarias-Odlyzko algorithm. While the lattice they use is very different from ours, they obtain the same $0.9408\ldots$ density bound.

2. Previous results

In [12], Lagarias and Odlyzko show that if the density is bounded by $0.6463\ldots$, the lattice oracle is guaranteed to find the solution vector with high probability. This section derives the $0.6463\ldots$ bound using simpler techniques due to Frieze [7]. Our presentation differs from that of [7] in a few technical details.

Let A be a positive integer and let $a_1, \ldots a_n$ be random integers with $0 < a_i \leq A$ for $1 \leq i \leq n$. Let $\mathbf{e} = (e_1, \ldots, e_n) \in \{0,1\}^n$, $\mathbf{e} \neq (0, 0, \ldots, 0)$ depending only on n, be fixed and let

$$s = \sum_{i=1}^{n} e_i a_i, \qquad\qquad t = \sum_{i=1}^{n} a_i.$$

We may assume that $s \geq t/n$, since if $s < t/n$ any $a_i \geq t/n$ cannot be in the subset, and may be removed from consideration. Similarly, $s \leq (1-(1/n))t$, otherwise any $a_i \leq (1-(1/n))t$ may be removed from consideration. Thus,

$$\frac{1}{n}t \leq s \leq \frac{n-1}{n}t. \qquad (2.1)$$

We recall the Lagarias-Odlyzko attack on low-density subset sum problems. Define the vectors $\mathbf{b_1}, \ldots, \mathbf{b_{n+1}}$ as follows:

$$\mathbf{b_1} = (1.0.\ldots, 0, Na_1),$$
$$\mathbf{b_2} = (0.1.\ldots, 0, Na_2),$$
$$\vdots$$
$$\mathbf{b_n} = (0.0.\ldots, 1, Na_n),$$
$$\mathbf{b_{n+1}} = (0.0.\ldots, 0, Ns),$$

where N is a positive integer which will be chosen later. Let L be the lattice spanned by the vectors $\mathbf{b_1}, \ldots, \mathbf{b_{n+1}}$ (i.e. $L = \{\sum_{i=1}^{n+1} z_i \mathbf{b_i} : z_i \in \mathbb{Z} \quad \text{for } 1 \leq i \leq n+1\}$).

Notice that the solution vector $\hat{\mathbf{e}} = (e_1.\ldots.e_n, 0)$ is in L. Following the proof in [7] we are interested in vectors $\hat{\mathbf{x}} = (x_1, x_2, \ldots, x_{n+1})$ which satisfy:

$$\|\hat{\mathbf{x}}\| \leq \|\hat{\mathbf{e}}\|.$$
$$\hat{\mathbf{x}} \in L. \qquad (2.2)$$
$$\hat{\mathbf{x}} \notin \{0.\hat{\mathbf{e}}, -\hat{\mathbf{e}}\}.$$

We may assume that

$$\sum_{i=1}^{n} e_i \leq \tfrac{1}{2}n, \qquad (2.3)$$

(i.e. the subset contains at most one-half of the a_i's). If $\sum_{i=1}^{n} e_i > \frac{1}{2}n$, we may replace s by $t - s$, $\mathbf{b_{n+1}}$ by $\mathbf{b'_{n+1}} = (0, \ldots, 0, N(t-s))$, and $\hat{\mathbf{e}}$ by $\hat{\mathbf{e}}' = (1 - e_1, 1 - e_2, \ldots 1 - e_n, 0)$. Solving this problem is equivalent to solving the given problem, $\sum_{i=1}^{n}(1 - e_i) \leq \frac{1}{2}n$, and $s' = t - s \geq t/n$. (To be fully rigorous, we actually apply the basic method to two problems, at least one of which is covered by the condition $\sum_{i=1}^{n} e_i \leq \frac{1}{2}n$, and our analysis below applies to this case.)

Choose $N > \sqrt{n}$. It is clear that $\hat{\mathbf{x}}$ satisfies Equation 2.2 only if $x_{n+1} = 0$. (Otherwise, $\|\hat{\mathbf{x}}\| \geq |x_{n+1}| \geq N > \sqrt{n} \geq \|\hat{\mathbf{e}}\|$, which contradicts Equation 2.2.) Let y be defined by

$$ys = \sum_{i=1}^{n} x_i a_i, \tag{2.4}$$

and deduce that

$$|y|s = \left| \sum_{i=1}^{n} x_i a_i \right| \leq \|\hat{\mathbf{x}}\| \left| \sum_{i=1}^{n} a_i \right| \leq t\sqrt{\tfrac{1}{2}n}. \tag{2.5}$$

Hence, using Equation 2.1 above,

$$|y| \leq n\sqrt{\tfrac{1}{2}n}. \tag{2.6}$$

Note that since $-y$ is the coefficient of $\mathbf{b}_{n+1}$ in the expansion of $\hat{\mathbf{x}}$ in terms of the basis vectors, $y \in \mathbb{Z}$.

We will show that the probability P — that a lattice L contains a short vector which satisfies Equation 2.2 — is:

$$P = \Pr(\exists \, \hat{\mathbf{x}} \text{ which satisfies Equation 2.2})$$

$$\leq n \left(2n\sqrt{\tfrac{1}{2}n} + 1 \right) \frac{2^{c_0 n}}{A}, \quad \text{for } c_0 = 1.54724\ldots \tag{2.7}$$

This implies that, if $A = 2^{cn}$ with $c > c_0$, $\lim_{n \to \infty} P = 0$. If the density of a subset sum problem is less than $0.6463\ldots$, then

$$\frac{n}{\log_2 \max_{1 \leq i \leq n} a_i} < 0.6463\ldots \implies \max_{1 \leq i \leq n} a_i > 2^{n/0.6463\ldots}$$

$$\implies A > 2^{c_0 n}.$$

Thus, all subset sum problems with density $< 0.6463\ldots$ could be solved in polynomial time, given the existence of a lattice oracle.

We will now prove Equation 2.7. Let $\mathbf{x} = (x_1, \ldots, x_n)$ denote an element of $\mathbb{Z}^n$. (Note that if $\hat{\mathbf{x}} = (x_1, \ldots, x_n, 0)$, then $\|\hat{\mathbf{x}}\| = \|\mathbf{x}\|$ and as a special case we have $\|\hat{\mathbf{e}}\| = \|\mathbf{e}\|$.) First we estimate the probability P by

$$P \leq \Pr(\exists \, \mathbf{x}, y \text{ s.t. } \|\mathbf{x}\| \leq \|\mathbf{e}\|, |y| \leq n\sqrt{\tfrac{1}{2}n}, \mathbf{x} \notin \{\mathbf{0}, \mathbf{e}, -\mathbf{e}\}, \sum_{i=1}^{n} x_i a_i = ys),$$

$$\leq \Pr\left(\sum_{i=1}^{n} a_i x_i = ys : 0 < \|\mathbf{x}\| \leq \|\mathbf{e}\|, |y| \leq n\sqrt{\tfrac{1}{2}n}, \mathbf{x} \notin \{\mathbf{0}, \mathbf{e}, -\mathbf{e}\} \right)$$

$$\cdot |\{\mathbf{x} \colon \|\mathbf{x}\| \leq \|\mathbf{e}\|\}| \cdot \left| \left\{ y \colon |y| \leq n\sqrt{\tfrac{1}{2}n} \right\} \right|. \tag{2.8}$$

We have to estimate three factors in the right side of Equation 2.8. For the first factor of Equation 2.8 we may rewrite $\sum_{i=1}^{n} a_i x_i = ys$ as:

$$\sum_{i=1}^{n} a_i z_i = 0. \quad \text{where } z_i = x_i - y e_i.$$

Since $\mathbf{x}$ is non-zero and $\|\mathbf{x}\| \le \|\mathbf{e}\|$, we have $\mathbf{z} = (z_1, \ldots, z_n) \ne \mathbf{0}$, and so we may assume without loss of generality (by increasing the bound for the probability by a factor of at most n) that $z_1 \ne 0$. If z' is defined as $-(\sum_{i=2}^{n} a_i z_i / z_1)$, then

$$\Pr\left(\sum_{i=1}^{n} a_i z_i = 0\right) = \Pr(a_1 = z').$$

$$= \sum_{j=1}^{A} \Pr(a_1 = z' | z' = j) \Pr(z' = j),$$

$$= \sum_{j=1}^{A} \Pr(a_1 = z') \Pr(z' = j), \quad (a_1 \text{ and } j \text{ are independent}),$$

$$= \sum_{j=1}^{A} \frac{1}{A} \Pr(z' = j),$$

$$\le \frac{1}{A}.$$

Now we consider the second factor of Equation 2.8. From [12] (which borrowed the technique from [15]) we know that

$$|\{\mathbf{x} \colon \|\mathbf{x}\| \le \|\mathbf{e}\|\}| \le \left|\left\{\mathbf{x} \colon \|\mathbf{x}\| \le \sqrt{\tfrac{1}{2}n}\right\}\right| \le 2^{c_0 n}, \quad \text{where } c_0 = 1.54724\ldots \quad (2.9)$$

It is clear that the last factor of Equation 2.8 can be estimated by $2n\sqrt{\tfrac{1}{2}n} + 1$. This proves Equation 2.7.

3. A new, improved bound on the density

The main result of this note is an improvement in the maximum density of subset sum problems which can "almost always" be solved:

Theorem. *Let A be a positive integer, and let $a_1, \ldots, a_n$ be random integers with $0 < a_i \le A$ for $1 \le i \le n$. Let $\mathbf{e} = (e_1, \ldots, e_n) \in \{0, 1\}^n$ be arbitrary, and let $s = \sum_{i=1}^{n} e_i a_i$. If the density $d < 0.9408\ldots$, then the subset sum problem defined by $a_1, \ldots, a_n$ and s may "almost always" be solved in polynomial time with a single call to a lattice oracle.*

Proof. We need to make only minor changes to the proof presented in Section 2. As above, A is a fixed positive integer and $a_1, \ldots, a_n$ are random integers with $0 < a_i \leq A$ for $1 \leq i \leq n$. Let $\mathbf{e} = (e_1, \ldots, e_n) \in \{0, 1\}^n$ be fixed, let $s = \sum_{i=1}^n e_i a_i$, and let $t = \sum_{i=1}^n a_i$. Vectors $\mathbf{b_1}, \ldots, \mathbf{b_n}$ are defined as in Section 2. Vector $\mathbf{b_{n+1}}$ is replaced, however. by

$$\mathbf{b'_{n+1}} = (\tfrac{1}{2}, \tfrac{1}{2}, \ldots, \tfrac{1}{2}, Ns).$$

Let L' be the lattice spanned by the vectors $\mathbf{b_1}, \ldots, \mathbf{b_n}, \mathbf{b'_{n+1}}$.

In Section 2, we knew that the vector $\hat{\mathbf{e}} = (e_1, \ldots, e_n, 0)$ was in the lattice L. Notice that the new lattice L' does not contain $\hat{\mathbf{e}}$ but instead contains the vector $\hat{\mathbf{e}}'$:

$$\hat{\mathbf{e}}' = (e'_1, \ldots, e'_n, 0), \quad \text{where } e'_i = e_i - \tfrac{1}{2}.$$

Since $e_i \in \{0, 1\}$ for $1 \leq i \leq n$, we know that $e'_i \in \{-\tfrac{1}{2}, \tfrac{1}{2}\}$ for $1 \leq i \leq n$. Notice that $\|\hat{\mathbf{e}}'\|^2 \leq \tfrac{1}{4}n$ independent of the number of e_i's which are equal to 1.

Again, we are interested in the number of vectors $\hat{\mathbf{x}}$ which satisfy conditions similar to Equation 2.2:

$$\begin{aligned} &\|\hat{\mathbf{x}}\| \leq \|\hat{\mathbf{e}}'\|, \\ &\hat{\mathbf{x}} \in L', \\ &\hat{\mathbf{x}} \notin \{\mathbf{0}, \hat{\mathbf{e}}', -\hat{\mathbf{e}}'\}. \end{aligned} \tag{3.1}$$

Setting $N > \tfrac{1}{2}\sqrt{n}$ implies that $x_{n+1} = 0$ for any $\hat{\mathbf{x}}$ which satisfies Equation 3.1. Suppose that $\hat{\mathbf{x}} = \sum_{i=1}^n y_i \mathbf{b_i} + y \mathbf{b'_{n+1}}$ satisfies Equation 3.1, then we can express x_i in terms of y_i and y in the following way

$$x_i = y_i + \tfrac{1}{2}y, \quad \text{for } 1 \leq i \leq n,$$

$$0 = x_{n+1} = N \cdot \left\{ \sum_{i=1}^n a_i y_i + ys \right\}.$$

This implies that

$$\sum_{i=1}^n a_i y_i = -ys.$$

Therefore, Equation 2.4 can be replaced by:

$$\sum_{i=1}^n x_i a_i = \tfrac{1}{2}y(t - 2s), \tag{3.2}$$

since $(\sum_{i=1}^n \mathbf{b_i}) - 2\mathbf{b'_{n+1}} = (0, 0, \ldots, 0, N(t - 2s))$.

We now establish a bound on the size of $|y|$. From above,

$$|y(t - 2s)| = 2 \left| \sum_{i=1}^{n} x_i a_i \right|$$

$$\leq n\alpha\sqrt{n}, \quad \text{where } \alpha = \max_{1 \leq i \leq n} a_i. \quad (3.3)$$

If $|t - 2s| \geq \frac{1}{2}\alpha$, then $|y||t - 2s| \geq |y|\alpha$, and

$$|y| \leq 2n\sqrt{n}. \quad (3.4)$$

by Equation 3.3. If $|t - 2s| < \frac{1}{2}\alpha$, then we can solve two problems: one where α is assumed to be part of the subset which sums to s, and one where α is assumed to be part of the subset which sums to $t - s$. In the first case, the new problem has $s' = s - \alpha, t' = t - \alpha$, and

$$|t' - 2s'| = |t - \alpha - 2s + 2\alpha| = |t - 2s + \alpha| \geq \frac{1}{2}\alpha. \quad (3.5)$$

For the second case, the new problem has $s' = s, t' = t - \alpha$, and

$$|t' - 2s'| = |t - 2s - \alpha| \geq \frac{1}{2}\alpha. \quad (3.6)$$

Thus we may always assume $|t - 2s| \geq \frac{1}{2}\alpha$ and that the bound in Equation 3.4 holds.

We may now calculate the bound on probability P that there exists a vector $\hat{x}$ which satisfies Equation 3.1. We now let $\mathbf{x} = (x_1, \ldots, x_n)$ be any vector such that $2 \mathbf{x} \in \mathbb{Z}^n$. We obtain the following bound, similar to Equation 2.8:

$$P \leq \Pr\left(\sum_{i=1}^{n} a_i x_i = \frac{1}{2}y(t - 2s) \right) \cdot \left| \left\{ \mathbf{x} \colon \|\mathbf{x}\| \leq \frac{1}{2}\sqrt{n} \right\} \right| \cdot n \left(4n\sqrt{n} + 1 \right). \quad (3.7)$$

As in Section 2, $\Pr(\sum_{i=1}^{n} a_i x_i = \frac{1}{2}y(t - 2s)) \leq 1/A$. To estimate the number of vectors $\mathbf{x}$ with $\|\mathbf{x}\| \leq \frac{1}{2}\sqrt{n}$, we again use the technique in [12, 15], but in a more complicated way. The number of $\mathbf{x}$ with $\|\mathbf{x}\| \leq \sqrt{n}/2$ is bounded above by

$$\left| \left\{ \mathbf{w} = (w_1, \ldots, w_n) : w_i \in \mathbb{Z} \quad \text{for all } i, \|\mathbf{w}\| \leq \frac{1}{2}\sqrt{n} \right\} \right|$$
$$+ \left| \left\{ \mathbf{w} = (w_1, \ldots, w_n) : w_i \in \mathbb{Z} \quad \text{for all } i. \|\mathbf{w} - (\frac{1}{2}, \frac{1}{2}, \ldots, \frac{1}{2})\| \leq \frac{1}{2}\sqrt{n} \right\} \right|. \quad (3.8)$$

In [15] it is shown that for n sufficiently large, the second summand in Equation 3.8 above is smaller than the first summand by a factor that is exponential in n. In any case, the second summand equals 2^n. By the method of [12, 15], the first summand is bounded, for every $u > 0$, by

$$2^{(\log_2 e)\delta(u)n}.$$

where

$$\delta(u) = \tfrac{1}{4}u + \ln \theta(e^{-u}), \quad \text{for } \theta(z) = 1 + 2\sum_{k=1}^{\infty} z^{k^2}.$$

Numerically, we may calculate the minimum value of $\delta(u)$, and obtain

$$\delta(u) \geq \delta(u_0) = 0.7367\ldots, \qquad\qquad \text{for } u_0 = 1.8132\ldots$$

Thus, for large n, we have

$$\left|\left\{\mathbf{x}\colon \|\mathbf{x}\| \leq \tfrac{1}{2}\sqrt{n}\right\}\right| \leq 2^{c_0' n}, \qquad\qquad \text{for } c_0' = 1.0628\ldots,$$

$$P \leq n\left(4n\sqrt{n}+1\right)\frac{2^{c_0' n}}{A}.$$

Thus, any subset sum problem with density $d < 1/c_0' = 0.9408\ldots$ may be solved in polynomial time, given the existence of a lattice oracle. ∎

4. Discussion

The analysis above shows that it is possible to improve the density bound from $0.6463\ldots$ to $0.9408\ldots$ by modifying one vector in the lattice basis. We now consider the possibilities of improving on this bound.

Solving subset sum problems with basis reduction is closely connected to lattice covering problems. In particular, we want to cover the vertices of the n-cube (representing the possible e solution vectors) with a polynomial number of n-spheres of radius $\sqrt{\alpha n}$. Lagarias and Odlyzko showed that it was possible to cover the n-cube with two n-spheres of radius $\sqrt{\tfrac{1}{2}n}$. The two spheres (centered at $(0, 0, \ldots . 0)$ and $(1, 1, \ldots, 1))$ correspond to the two basis reduction problems which must be solved for any given subset sum problem. Our analysis above uses one n-sphere of radius $\tfrac{1}{2}\sqrt{n}$ centered at $(\tfrac{1}{2}, \tfrac{1}{2}, \ldots, \tfrac{1}{2})$ to cover all the points.

One way to improve the bound presented above would be to show that it is possible to cover the vertices of the n-cube with a polynomial number of n-spheres of radius $\sqrt{\alpha n}$ with $\alpha < \tfrac{1}{4}$. We show that this is not possible, and that the asymptotic bound of $0.9408\ldots$ cannot be improved in this way. The following proposition shows that any n-sphere of radius $\sqrt{\alpha n}$ with $\alpha < \tfrac{1}{4}$ can cover only an exponentially small fraction of the vertices of the n-cube. Thus, no polynomial collection of such spheres can satisfy our requirements.

Proposition. *Any sphere of radius $\sqrt{\alpha n}, \alpha < \tfrac{1}{4}$, in $\mathbb{R}^n$ contains at most $(2 - \delta)^n$ points of $\{0, 1\}^n$, for some $\delta = \delta(\alpha) > 0$.*

Proof. Suppose that the n-sphere is centered at the point $\mathbf{c} = (c_1, \ldots, c_n)$. We are interested in the number of points $\mathbf{e} \in \{0, 1\}^n$ for which $\|\mathbf{c} - \mathbf{e}\|^2 \leq \alpha n$. Using the upper bound technique of [15], we show that N, the number of points in $\{0, 1\}^n$ inside the sphere, is bounded by

$$N \leq e^{\alpha n} \prod_{i=1}^{n} (e^{-c_i^2} + e^{-(c_i - 1)^2}). \tag{4.1}$$

If the point $\mathbf{e} = (e_1, \ldots, e_n)$ is inside the sphere, then $\|\mathbf{c} - \mathbf{e}\|^2 = \sum_{i=1}^{n} (c_i - e_i)^2 \leq \alpha n$, and after expanding the right side, Equation 4.1 contains a term of the form

$$\exp\left(\alpha n - \sum_{i=1}^{n} (c_i - e_i)^2\right) \geq 1,$$

for each such point $\mathbf{e}$, which proves Equation 4.1 since all terms in the expansion are nonnegative.

Since the terms in the product in Equation 4.1 are independent, we know that the value of N is bounded by

$$e^{\alpha n} \max_{\mathbf{c} \in \mathcal{R}^n} \prod_{i=1}^{n} \left(e^{-c_i^2} + e^{-(c_i - 1)^2}\right) \leq e^{\alpha n} (2 e^{-1/4})^n.$$

(It is easy to show that the maximum value of $f(z) = e^{-z^2} + e^{-(z-1)^2}$ is $2 e^{-1/4}$.) Thus,

$$N \leq e^{n\alpha} 2^n e^{(-1/4)n} = 2^n e^{n(\alpha - 1/4)}$$

$$= (2 - \delta(\alpha))^n, \quad \text{for } \delta(\alpha) = 2(1 - e^{\alpha - 1/4})$$

For all $\alpha < \frac{1}{4}$, $\delta(\alpha) > 0$, which proves the proposition. ∎

As $n \to \infty$, any n-sphere with radius $\sqrt{\alpha n}$, $\alpha < \frac{1}{4}$, will contain at most $(2 - \delta(\alpha))^n$ points in $\{0, 1\}^n$. Thus, any polynomial-sized collection of spheres cannot contain all the points in $\{0, 1\}^n$. Thus we cannot hope to asymptotically improve the $0.9408\ldots$ bound by reducing a polynomial number of bases with different $\mathbf{b_{n+1}}$ vectors. However, for small dimensions it might be possible to improve the bound, even though any such advantage will disappear as n grows.

In cases where the subset sum problem (Equation 1.1) to be solved is known to have $\sum e_i$ small (as occurs in some knapsack cryptosystems, such as the Chor-Rivest one [4], which has still not been broken), it is possible to again improve on the results of [12] by our approach. For example, if we know that

$$\sum_{i=1}^{n} e_i = \beta n.$$

we can replace the vector $\mathbf{b_{n+1}}$ in the basis of L by

$$\mathbf{b''_{n+1}} = (\beta, \beta, \ldots, \beta, Ns),$$

and then the lattice L will contain a vector of length $\sqrt{n\beta(1-\beta)}$, and our analysis shows that in this case it then becomes possible to solve most problems with even smaller weights a_i. However, it appears that there are choices for parameters in the Chor-Rivest knapsack that would resist even this attack.

When we consider the L_∞ or sup-norm,

$$\|(x_1, \ldots, x_n)\|_\infty = \max_{1 \le j \le n} |x_j|,$$

then we find that the vector $\hat{e}'$ has norm $1/2$. Since there are at most 2^n non-zero vectors in L' of norm $\le 1/2$, we can solve almost all subset sum problems of any density < 1 if we have a lattice oracle for the sup-norm. Formally, we may make the following proposition:

Proposition. *Let A be a positive integer, and let $a_1, \ldots, a_n$ be random integers with $0 < a_i \le A$ for $1 \le i \le n$. Let $\mathbf{e} = (e_1, \ldots, e_n) \in \{0,1\}^n$ be arbitrary, and let $s = \sum_{i=1}^{n} e_i a_i$. If the density $d < 1$, then the subset sum problem defined by $a_1, \ldots, a_n$ and s may "almost always" be solved in polynomial time, given the existence of a sup-norm lattice oracle.*

The general sup-norm shortest vector problem is known to be NP-complete [6]; the complexity of the square-norm shortest vector problem is an open problem. That a sup-norm lattice oracle yields a better density bound than a square-norm lattice oracle suggests that the shortest vector problem for the sup-norm might be harder than for the square-norm.

Sections 3 and 4 presented theoretical results that assume the availability of an efficient method for finding the shortest non-zero vector in a lattice. When one uses known algorithms for lattice basis reduction, applying them to lattice L' instead of lattice L also yields dramatic improvements, although the results are not as good as they would be in the presence of a lattice oracle. For example, Table 1 presents the comparison obtained in one particular set of experiments. The lattices used were not exactly L and L', and the reduction algorithm used a combination of ideas from several sources. More extensive data sets and details of the computations are presented in [13]. For each entry in Table 1, n denotes the number of items, and b the number of bits (chosen at random) for each item. For each $(n.b)$ combination, 20 problems were attempted, where in each case $e_i = 1$ for exactly $n/2$ of the items. The entries for the L and L' column indicate what fraction of the 20 problems were solved in each case. Combining the improved lattice of this paper with variants of the algorithms of [19] leads to solutions of subset sum problems of even higher densities, as is shown in [21].

Table 1: Fraction of random subset sum problems solved by a particular reduction algorithm applied to bases L and L', respectively

n	b	L	L'
50	50	0.05	1.00
50	60	0.55	1.00
50	75	1.00	–
66	76	–	0.25
66	84	–	0.80
66	92	–	0.95
66	100	–	1.00
66	104	0.30	1.00
66	108	0.55	1.00
66	112	0.60	1.00
66	116	1.00	–

References

[1] E. F. Brickell, Solving low density knapsacks. *Advances in Cryptology, Proceedings of Crypto '83*, Plenum Press. New York (1984), 25-37.

[2] E. F. Brickell, The cryptanalysis of knapsack cryptosystems. *Applications of Discrete Mathematics*, R. D. Ringeisen and F. S. Roberts, eds., SIAM (1988), 3-23.

[3] E. F. Brickell and A. M. Odlyzko, Cryptanalysis: a survey of recent results, *Proc. IEEE* **76** (1988), 578-593.

[4] B. Chor and R. Rivest, A knapsack-type public key cryptosystem based on arithmetic in finite fields, *IEEE Trans. Information Theory* **IT-34** (1988), 901-909.

[5] Y. Desmedt, What happened with knapsack cryptographic schemes?, *Performance Limits in Communication, Theory and Practice*, J. K. Skwirzynski, ed., Kluwer (1988), 113-134.

[6] P. van Emde Boas, Another NP-complete partition problem and the complexity of computing short vectors in a lattice, Rept. 81-04, Dept. of Mathematics, Univ. of Amsterdam, 1981.

[7] A. M. Frieze, On the Lagarias-Odlyzko algorithm for the subset sum problem, *SIAM J. Comput.* **15(2)** (May 1986), 536-539.

[8] M. L. Furst and R. Kannan, Succinct certificates for almost all subset sum problems, *SIAM J. Comput.* **18** (1989), 550-558.

[9] M. R. Garey and D. S. Johnson, *Computers and Intractability: A Guide to the Theory of NP-Completeness*, W. H. Freeman and Company (1979).

[10] J. Hastad, B. Just, J. C. Lagarias, and C. P. Schnorr, Polynomial time algorithms for finding integer relations among real numbers, *SIAM J. Comput.* **18(5)** (October 1989), 859-881.

[11] A. Joux and J. Stern, Improving the critical density of the Lagarias-Odlyzko attack against subset sum problems, *Proceedings of Fundamentals of Computation Theory '91*, to be published.

[12] J. C. Lagarias and A. M. Odlyzko, Solving low-density subset sum problems, *J. Assoc. Comp. Mach.* **32(1)** (January 1985), 229-246.

[13] B. A. LaMacchia, *Basis Reduction Algorithms and Subset Sum Problems*, SM Thesis, Dept. of Elect. Eng. and Comp. Sci., Massachusetts Institute of Technology, Cambridge, MA (1991).

[14] A. K. Lenstra, H. W. Lenstra, and L. Lovász, Factoring polynomials with rational coefficients, *Math. Ann.* **261** (1982), 515-534.

[15] J. E. Mazo and A. M. Odlyzko, Lattice points in high-dimensional spheres, *Monatsh. Math.* **110** (1990), 47-61.

[16] A. M. Odlyzko, The rise and fall of knapsack cryptosystems, *Cryptology and Computational Number Theory*, C. Pomerance, ed., Am. Math. Soc., Proc. Symp. Appl. Math. **42** (1990), 75-88.

[17] A. Paz and C. P. Schnorr, Approximating integer lattices by lattices with cyclic factor groups, *Automata, Languages, and Programming:* 14th *ICALP, Lecture Notes in Computer Science* **267**, Springer-Verlag, NY (1987), 386-393.

[18] S. Radziszowski and D. Kreher, Solving subset sum problems with the L^3 algorithm, *J. Combin. Math. Combin. Comput.* **3** (1988), 49-63.

[19] C. P. Schnorr, A hierarchy of polynomial time lattice basis reduction algorithms, *Theoretical Computer Science* **53** (1987), 201-224.

[20] C. P. Schnorr, A more efficient algorithm for lattice basis reduction, *J. Algorithms* **9** (1988), 47-62.

[21] C. P. Schnorr and M. Euchner, Lattice Basis Reduction: Improved Practical Algorithms and Solving Subset Sum Problems, *Proceedings of Fundamentals of Computation Theory '91*, to be published.

[22] M. Seysen, Simultaneous reduction of a lattice basis and its reciprocal basis, *Combinatorica*, to appear.

Cryptanalysis of McEliece's Public-Key Cryptosystem

Valery I. Korzhik
Department of Communication Theory
Leningrad Electroengineering Institute of Communications
Mojka 66
Leningrad, 191065, USSR

and

Andrey I. Turkin
Computer Department
Gorky Polytechnical Institute
Nizhnii Novgorod, USSR

Abstract: An approach is proposed for the cryptanalysis of the well-known version of McEliece's public-key cryptosystem that is based on a new iterative optimization algorithm for decoding an arbitrary linear code. The algorithm provides guaranteed correction of all error patterns with Hamming weight less than d/2, where d is the minimum distance of the code, and has time complexity about $O(n^3)$ where n is the block length. The approach is illustrated by the cryptanalysis of McEliece's system when a (63, 36) binary code with d = 11 is the underlying linear code.

1. INTRODUCTION

We consider the well-known version [1] of McEliece's public-key cryptosystem. This cryptosystem is based on the generator matrix G of an (n, k) linear error-correcting code with minimum distance d having an efficient decoding algorithm that corrects all patterns of [(d -- 1)/2] or fewer errors (e. g., a Goppa code). In McEliece's system, a k-bit plaintext message **m** is transformed to a binary cryptogram **c** as

$$c = m \, G' + e$$

where + denotes bitwise modulo-two addition, The k × n matrix G' is obtained from G in the manner

$$G' = S \, G \, P,$$

where S is a nonsingular k × k binary matrix and P is an n × n permutation matrix. The binary n-tuple **e** is an "error pattern" of Hamming weight at most [(d -- 1)/2] that is randomly chosen for each message **m** that is encrypted. Knowledge of the individual matrices S, G and P allows the intended recipient to compute

$$c\, P^{-1^{\bullet}} = (m\, S)\, G + e\, P^{-1},$$

then to recover the code word (m S) by use of the decoding algorithm, and finally to complete the decryption by computing (m S) S^{-1} = **m**. However, if the individual matrices S, G and P are not known but only their product G' is known, as is the case for the cryptanalyst, then the crucial difficulty is to determine the error pattern **e**.

2. A NEW APPROACH TO CRYPTANALYSIS OF McELIECE'S SYSTEM

One approach open to the cryptanalyst of the McEliece system is to find k coordinates in which the matrix G' contains a nonsingular k × k matrix and where **e** contains only zeroes. In [1] it is shown how to choose the parameters k and t for a Goppa code of given length n to maximize the cryptanalyst's effort for this attack.

A second approach for the cryptanalyst is to exploit the fact that the matrix G' may itself turn out to be equivalent to the generator matrix of another Goppa code, in which case knowledge of this matrix alone suffices to permit correction of the error pattern **e**. The probability of such a "fortunate event" (from the cryptanalyst's standpoint) is calculated in [1] and shown to be negligibly small.

We propose a third approach for the cryptanalyst based on the iterative optimization algorithm reported in [2]. This algorithm results in guaranteed correction of error patterns with weight at most [(d - 1)/2] for an arbitrary linear code with minimum distance d. The cryptanalyst can use this algorithm on the cryptogram **c** to obtain the code word **m** G', after which he simply recovers the message **m** by inverting any k columns of G' that contain a nonsingular matrix.

The main features of this efficient (i.e., polynomial time) algorithm for decoding an arbitrary linear code up to its guaranteed error-correcting limit are the following:
(1) the embedding of a discrete set of binary-valued vectors into the continuous vector space R^n;
(2) the reduction of the decoding problem to the problem of finding extrema in R^n under the constraints determined by the code; and
(3) an iterative procedure for finding the desired extremum when the Hamming weight of the error pattern is at most [(d - 1)/2].
We remark that the existence of this efficient iterative decoding algorithm, a complete description and proof of which will be given in [2], does not

contradict the fact that the problem of decoding an arbitrarily given binary word to the nearest code word in an arbitrary linear code is known to be NP-complete [3], because the mentioned algorithm requires that the given binary word be at distance at most $[(d - 1)/2]$ from a code word in order to guarantee decoding to the nearest code word. We remark also that this algorithm does not give a solution to the related NP-complete problem of integer programming.

3. CRYPTANALYSIS FOR THE (63, 26) CODE

To show the applicability of the iterative decoding algorithm to cryptanalysis does not require that its general capabilities be proved; it suffices to show that cryptanalysis based upon it succeeds in many cases. To show this for McEliece's system, we considered the case where G is the generator matrix of a (63, 36) Bose-Chaudhuri-Hocquenghem (BCH) code with minimum distance d = 11. This matrix was transformed into G' by means of a randomly chosen 36×36 nonsingular matrix S and a 63×63 randomly chosen permutation matrix P. The error pattern **e** was a randomly selected 63-tuple of Hamming weight 5. In 100 trials of the cryptanalytic procedure described above, the correct message **m** was found every time. The cryptanalysis required about 10^6 operations, compared to the approximately $5 \cdot 10^6$ operations that would be required in an exhaustive attack.

In general, for an arbitrary (n, k) code, the attack reported here requires about $20 \cdot n^3$ operations. In particular, for the (1024, 654) BCH code with d = 65 that was recommended in [1], cryptanalysis on an IBM PC requires about 60 hours. The conclusion in [1] about the excellent security afforded by this system appears now to have been premature.

(During Eurocrypt '91, the above described cryptanalytic attack on the McEliece public-key cryptosystem was demonstrated on an IBM PC.)

REFERENCES

[1] C. M. Adams and H. Meijer, *Security-related comments regarding McEliece's public-key cryptosystem*, **IEEE Trans. Info. Th.**, vol. IT-35, pp. 454-457, March 1989.

[2] A. I. Turkin and V. I. Korzhik, *The practically-optimal decoding algorithm for arbitrary linear codes over a BSC with polynomial time complexity*, to be presented at the IEEE Intl. Symp. Info. Th., Budapest, June 1991.

[3] E. R. Berlekamp, R. J. McEliece and H. C. A. van Tilborg, *On the inherent intractability of certain coding problems*, **IEEE Trans. Info. Th.**, vol. IT-24, pp. 384-386, May 1978.

On the Security of the Schnorr Scheme using Preprocessing

Peter de Rooij
PTT Research*

Abstract

In this paper, it is shown that the Schnorr scheme with preprocessing as proposed in [4] leaks too much information. An attack based on this information leakage is presented that retrieves the secret key. The complexity of this attack is upper bounded by $2k \cdot k^{3(d-2)}$ steps, and the expected required number of signatures is less than $2k \cdot (\frac{k}{2})^{d-2}$, where k is a security parameter. This complexity is significantly lower than the $k^{k(d-2)}$ steps, conjectured in [4]. For example, for the security parameters that are proposed in [4], the secret key can on average be found in $2^{37.5}$ steps, instead of in 2^{72} steps. This shows that it is inevitable to either modify the preprocessing algorithm, or choose the values of the security parameters larger than proposed in [4].

Finally, we briefly discuss the possibility of averting the proposed attack by modifying the preprocessing algorithm.

1   Introduction

The Schnorr scheme [4] comprises an interactive identification protocol based on the discrete logarithm problem and a related signature scheme. In addition, a preprocessing algorithm that substantially speeds up the calculations of the prover/signer in the scheme is proposed. This preprocessing algorithm can be useful in any protocol where modular exponentiations are used.

In this paper, an attack based on the use of this preprocessing algorithm is presented. This attack shows that the values of the security parameters should be chosen larger than proposed in [4], in order to reach the designated level of security. Alternatively, the preprocessing algorithm itself can be modified.

This paper is organized as follows. In Section 2, the Schnorr scheme and the preprocessing algorithm are briefly introduced. In Section 3, an 'information leak' in the preprocessing is pointed out and an attack based on this leak is presented in Section 4. In Section 5 the possibility of averting the attack by changing the preprocessing algorithm is briefly investigated. Section 6 gives the conclusions.

---

*P.O. Box 421, 2260 AK Leidschendam, The Netherlands; E-mail P_dRooij@pttrnl.nl

2   The scheme and the preprocessing algorithm

The identification protocol in the Schnorr scheme [4] is based on the Chaum-Evertse-van de Graaf-protocol [1]. Essentially, it condenses this protocol into one single round. Furthermore, a signature scheme, based on the identification protocol, is given. We briefly describe both the identification protocol and the signature scheme as far as relevant to this paper. For details, see [4].

2.1   Preliminaries

The following parameters are chosen once and for all, and are known to all users: a large prime p, a prime q that divides $p-1$, a primitive qth root of unity $\alpha \in Z_p$ and a security parameter t. In [4], it is proposed to take p and q in the order of 512 bits and 140 bits respectively, and $t = 72$.

Each user chooses a secret key $s \in Z_q^*$. The corresponding public key is $v = \alpha^{-s} \bmod p$. A key authentication center signs, for each user, a string (I, v), consisting of the identity I and the public key v of the user. This signature is used to authenticate the public key, but since this is of no relevance to this paper, we will disregard this aspect from now on.

2.2   The Identification Protocol

Suppose *prover* A wants to prove his identity to *verifier* B. First, A picks a random number $r \in Z_q^*$ and sends the *initial commitment* $x = \alpha^r \bmod p$ to B. Then B returns a random number $e \in \{0, \ldots, 2^t - 1\}$, called the *challenge*, to A. Finally, A sends $y = r + se \bmod q$ to B. B checks A's proof of identity by calculating $\overline{x} = \alpha^y v^e \bmod p$. B will accept the proof if and only if $\overline{x} = x$.

In the rest of this paper, all calculations will be modulo q, except where indicated otherwise.

2.3   The Signature Scheme

The signature scheme is an extension of the identification protocol analogous to the extensions of the Fiat-Shamir and Guillou-Quisquater ID protocols [2, 3]. That is, a t-bit hash value of the initial commitment x and the message m to be signed replaces the challenge. The signature consists of this hash value and of y as in the identification protocol.

Let h denote the hash function that is used to compute the hash value. A message m is signed by *signer* A as follows. First, A picks a random number $r \in Z_q^*$ and calculates $x = \alpha^r \bmod p$; from this $e = h(x, m)$ and $y = r + se$ are computed. The signature consists of the pair (y, e).

The signature of A on m can be checked as follows. Compute $\overline{x} = \alpha^y v^e \bmod p$ and $\overline{e} = h(\overline{x}, m)$. The signature will be accepted if and only if $\overline{e} = e$.

In the sequel, a pair (y, e) is called a signature, even if it is made by the identification protocol. The attack that will be proposed later on, is based on the assumption that p, q, α, t, and a sufficient number of correct signatures are available. The verifier, for example, possesses this information.

2.4 The preprocessing

The aim of the preprocessing is to reduce the computational effort of the prover/signer. This effort is determined by the modular exponentiation $\alpha^r \bmod p$. The preprocessing essentially enables the performance of this exponentiation with the effort of a few multiplications only. This is achieved by taking, instead of a random r, a linear combination of several random numbers $r_i \in Z_q{}^*$ for which $x_i = \alpha^{r_i} \bmod p$ are precomputed.

Therefore, each user initially stores a collection of k pairs (r_i, x_i), $0 \leq i < k$, such that $x_i = \alpha^{r_i} \bmod p$. Here k is a security parameter. Furthermore, the r_i's are independently and randomly chosen from $Z_q{}^*$. Then, for each signature, the pair (r, x) is chosen as a combination of these pairs (r_i, x_i). Subsequently, the collection of pairs is 'rejuvenated' by replacing one of the pairs (r_i, x_i) by a similar combination. The first time, (r_0, x_0) is replaced by a combination of the pairs (r_i, x_i) for $0 \leq i < k$. This new pair is denoted (r_k, x_k). The next time, (r_{k+1}, x_{k+1}) replaces (r_1, x_1), and so on. A security parameter d determines the number of pairs used in these combinations. As both the new and the original pairs (r_i, x_i) will be used, we will, in contrast to [4], not reduce the indices modulo k. Clearly, this does not alter the preprocessing itself.

Denote the value of r used in the ith initial commitment by r_i^*, and the initial commitment itself by x_i^*. We start numbering from k, for then the index of the initial commitment is the same as the index of the corresponding new r_i. Then this index can be used as a sequential number of the signatures. Denote this sequential number by ν. We now give the preprocessing algorithm in detail.

The Preprocessing Algorithm

0. *Initialization.* Load k pairs (r_i, x_i) as above, $0 \leq i < k$;
   $\nu := k$;

1. Pick random numbers $a(0; \nu), \ldots, a(d - 3; \nu) \in \{\nu - k, \ldots, \nu - 1\}$;
   $a(d - 2; \nu) := \nu - 1$; $a(d - 1; \nu) := \nu - k$; $a(d; \nu) := \nu - 1$;

2. $r_\nu := \sum_{i=0}^{d} 2^i r_{a(i;\nu)} \bmod q$; $x_\nu := \prod_{i=0}^{d} \left(x_{a(i;\nu)} \right)^{2^i} \bmod p$;
   $r_\nu^* := r_{\nu-k} + 2r_{\nu-1} \bmod q$; $x_\nu^* := x_{\nu-k} \cdot x_{\nu-1}^2 \bmod p$;

3. Keep the pair (r_ν^*, x_ν^*) ready for the next signature;
   replace the pair $(r_{\nu-k}, x_{\nu-k})$ by the new pair (r_ν, x_ν);

4. $\nu := \nu + 1$;
   goto 1 for the next signature.

In [4], an algorithm for the computations in step 2 is given that requires d multiplications and d squarings modulo p, d additions modulo q and d bitshifts on q-bit numbers.

In the sequel, it is assumed that the $a(j;\nu)$ in the preprocessing algorithm are chosen independently from a uniform distribution. It seems reasonable to assume this, as any dependence or non-uniformity can be exploited by an attack.

3 The preprocessing leaks information

In [4], a number of possible attacks on the preprocessing in the Schnorr scheme are considered. Subsequently, values for the security parameters k and d are suggested that make those attacks infeasible. In this section, we will look at the preprocessing from another point of view. Instead of considering all possibilities for the $a(i;\nu)$ or the most likely ones, as is done in [4], we consider a special case only. This special case has a relatively low probability of occurrence, but it provides a much higher amount of information about the secret key.

The special case we will consider is the event 'for all i, $0 \le i \le d$, $a(i;\nu)$ takes on one of the values $\nu - 1$ and $\nu - k$'. If this happens, r_ν is a linear combination of $r_{\nu-1}$ and $r_{\nu-k}$ only. Now, in some cases, only three occurrences of this special case are needed to find the secret key with high probability, as the following lemma shows.

Lemma 3.1 Let $0 < a < b$. Suppose that $a(j;\nu) = \nu - 1$ or $a(j;\nu) = \nu - k$ for the three values $\nu = i$, $\nu = i + a(k-1)$ and $\nu = i + b(k-1)$, and for $0 \le j \le d$.

If the signatures with indices $i, i+k-1, \ldots, i+(b-1)(k-1)$, and $i+k, i+2k-1, \ldots, i+(b-1)(k-1)+1$ are available, then the secret key s can be determined with high probability by solving a system of three equations in three unknowns.

Proof: Note that r_i, $r_{i+a\cdot(k-1)}$ and $r_{i+b\cdot(k-1)}$, can be written as

$$r_i = \lambda r_{i-1} + \mu r_{i-k}, \tag{1}$$

$$r_{i+a\cdot(k-1)} = \lambda' r_{i-1+a\cdot(k-1)} + \mu' r_{i-1+(a-1)\cdot(k-1)}, \tag{2}$$

$$r_{i+b\cdot(k-1)} = \lambda'' r_{i-1+b\cdot(k-1)} + \mu'' r_{i-1+(b-1)\cdot(k-1)}, \tag{3}$$

yielding three equations in nine unknowns (the r_j's). We will collect a number of additional equations that link those r_j's and s. The *linking equations* will be provided by the signatures as follows. Since, by definition, $r_j^* = r_{j-k} + 2r_{j-1}$ and $y_j = r_j^* + se_j$ for all j, it follows that

$$r_{j-1} = 2^{-1} \cdot (y_j - se_j - r_{j-k}). \tag{4}$$

Repeated use of these linking equations enables us to write an arbitrary $r_{j+c(k-1)}$, $c \in \mathbb{N}$, as a linear combination of y_j, se_j and r_j. More precisely,

$$
\begin{aligned}
r_{j+c(k-1)} &= 2^{-1}(y_{j+c(k-1)+1} - se_{j+c(k-1)+1} - r_{j+(c-1)(k-1)}) \\
&= 2^{-1}\Big(y_{j+c(k-1)+1} - se_{j+c(k-1)+1} + \\
&\qquad -2^{-1}(y_{j+(c-1)(k-1)+1} - se_{j+(c-1)(k-1)+1} - r_{j+(c-2)(k-1)})\Big) \\
&\;\;\vdots \\
&= (-1)^c 2^{-c} r_j + \sum_{l=1}^{c}(-1)^{l-c}2^{l-c-1}\Big(y_{j+l(k-1)+1} - se_{j+l(k-1)+1}\Big) \tag{5}
\end{aligned}
$$

for all positive integers c.

With this equality, we can rewrite the Equations (1)–(3). The right-hand sides can be rewritten to linear combinations of s, r_{i-k} and known constants, provided the signatures (y_j, e_j) are available for $j = i, i+k-1, \ldots, i+b(k-1)$. Furthermore, if the signatures (y_j, e_j) for $j = i+k, \ldots, i+b(k-1)+1$ are available, the lefthand sides can be rewritten to linear combinations of s, r_i and known constants. Then we find three equations in the three unknowns s, r_i and r_{i-k}. These equations are independent with high probability, see Appendix A. □

4   An attack

From the previous section, it can be concluded that a small number of signatures yield sufficient information to recover the secret key s, provided some of the corresponding r_i's satisfy certain conditions. These conditions are stated concisely by the following definition.

Definition 4.1 *A set $C = \{i, i+a(k-1), i+b(k-1)\}$ of indices will be called a candidate. A candidate C will be said to fit if for $\nu \in C$ we have that $a(j; \nu) \in \{\nu - 1, \nu - k\}$ for all j, $0 \le j \le d$. Likewise, a signature with sequential number ν will be said to fit if $a(j; \nu) \in \{\nu - 1, \nu - k\}$ for all j, $0 \le j \le d$.*

So, if a fitting candidate C and signatures as indicated in Lemma 3.1 are available, then the secret key s can be calculated with high probability. Note that there are several possible values of λ, λ', λ'', μ, μ' and μ'' in (1)–(3), corresponding to different choices $a(j; \nu) = \nu - 1$ or $\nu - k$ for all j and for $\nu \in C$. Obviously one must know or guess these values in order to perform the calculations.

This leads us to the following idea for an attack. Consider a (large) number of candidates. Then, for all possible ways in which they can fit, do the following. First, calculate the solution $\hat{s}$ of the corresponding set of equations (1)–(3) using the appropriate linking equations, and subsequently check this solution by calculating $\alpha^{-\hat{s}} \bmod p$. We have found the secret key if $v = \alpha^{-\hat{s}}$.

The proposed attack

```
for (all possible candidates) do {
    for (all possible fittings for this candidate) do {
        calculate the corresponding solution ŝ;
        v̂ = α⁻ˢ mod p;
        if (v̂ = v)
            stop;      /* we have found the secret key now!  */
    }
}
```

Note that the order in which the candidates are tried does not matter, for each candidate has the same probability of fitting. In the proofs in the sequel it is assumed for simplicity that they are tried in order of their largest index.

Call the calculation of one estimate s plus the corresponding $\hat{v}$ a *try*. The calculations for one try comprise a few modular multiplications and additions modulo q for the calculation of s, the calculation of $\hat{v}$ requires a full exponentiation modulo p, albeit with a $\log q$-bit exponent only (which is in the order of $\log p / \log q$ times as fast as one with a $\log p$-bit exponent). Therefore, this exponentiation determines the workload of one try.

The following lemma gives the probability that an arbitrary candidate fits.

Lemma 4.2 *The probability that a single arbitrary signature fits is $\left(\frac{2}{k}\right)^{d-2}$. The probability that an arbitrary candidate $\{i, i + a(k-1), i + b(k-1)\}$ fits, is*

$$\mathrm{P}(success) = \left(\frac{2}{k}\right)^{3 \cdot (d-2)}.$$

Proof: There are $d - 2$ values of j for which the $a(j; \nu)$ are chosen at random. Each of these $a(j; \nu)$'s must take on one of two values out of the k possible values, in order to provide a fitting signature. The result follows from the fact that the $a(j; \nu)$ are chosen independently from a uniform distribution. □

With the aid of the above lemma, the required number of signatures can be calculated.

Lemma 4.3 *The expected number of signatures N required to obtain exactly one fitting candidate is less than $(2k - 1) \cdot \left(\frac{k}{2}\right)^{d-2}$.*

Proof: We prove this lemma in two steps. First, the expected number of signatures needed to have l fitting signatures is calculated, for general l. Then the probability that the lth fitting signature completes the first fitting candidate is calculated.

Suppose a large set of consecutive signatures is available. The probability that the mth element in the sequence is the lth fitting one, is (cf. Lemma 4.2)

$$p(m, l) = \binom{m - 1}{l - 1} \left(\left(\frac{2}{k}\right)^{d-2}\right)^{l} \left(1 - \left(\frac{2}{k}\right)^{d-2}\right)^{m-l}.$$

Therefore, the expected position in the sequence of the lth fitting signature is

$$\sum_{m=l}^{\infty} m \cdot p(m, l) = l \sum_{m=l}^{\infty} \binom{m}{l} \left(\left(\frac{2}{k}\right)^{d-2}\right)^{l} \left(1 - \left(\frac{2}{k}\right)^{d-2}\right)^{m-l} = l \cdot \left(\frac{k}{2}\right)^{d-2}.$$

Denote the probability that the lth fitting signature completes the first candidate in the sequence by $\mathrm{P}(l = l)$. Since the the probability that a signature fits is independent of its index, the fitting signatures are uniformly distributed over the indices modulo $k - 1$. We see that $\mathrm{P}(l = l)$ is the probability that the lth signature that fits is the third one for its index mod $k-1$, and no other index mod $k-1$ has occurred three times yet. Therefore, trivially $P(l=l)=0$ if $l<3$ or $l>2k-1$. In general, the related expectation $E_l l$ is hard to evaluate, but obviously $E_l l < 2k-1$.

It is easy to see that the expected required number of signatures N, necessary to obtain exactly one fitting candidate, equals $N=(\frac{k}{2})^{d-2}\cdot E_l l$, from which the result follows.

$\square$

From this, the number of signatures required for an attack can be calculated. This is done in the next theorem.

Theorem 4.4 *If $k<2^{2(d-2)}$, then the expected number of consecutive signatures N', necessary for a successful attack is less than $2k\cdot(\frac{k}{2})^{d-2}$.*

Proof: N' is smaller than N times the expected number of fitting candidates that provides an independent system of equations, for this is the required number if we would start all over in case of a dependent system. (In that case we 'loose' all fitting signatures encountered so far.) That is, $N' < N/P$, where $P=P(\text{independent})$, see Appendix A. The result follows.

$\square$

This theorem, finally, enables the calculation of the workload.

Theorem 4.5 *The expected number of steps of the proposed attack is less than*

$$\frac{k^{3(d-2)}}{(k-1)^2}\cdot E_l\binom{l+2}{3} < 2k\cdot k^{3(d-2)}$$

for $k \geq 6$.

Proof: We calculate the number of steps in the attack, given that n' signatures are required to complete the attack. The set of the n' signatures used in the attack is partitioned into $k-1$ subsets according to the index of the signature mod $k-1$. These subsets have size approximately $n'/(k-1)$. For each triple of signatures in each of these subsets, we have checked whether this triple is a fitting candidate. So the number of candidates we tried before we had a fitting signature is

$$(k-1)\cdot\binom{\frac{n'}{k-1}}{3} \lesssim \frac{n'^3}{6(k-1)^2},$$

see Theorem 4.4. Hence the expected number T of candidates tried before the attack is successful is upper bounded by

$$
\begin{aligned}
T &= \sum_{n'=3}^{\infty}\frac{n'^3}{6(k-1)^2}\sum_{l=3}^{2k-1}p(n',l)\cdot P(l=l)\\
&= \frac{1}{6(k-1)^2}\sum_{l=3}^{2k-1}P(l=l)\cdot\sum_{n'=3}^{\infty}n'^3 p(n',l)
\end{aligned}
$$

$$= \frac{1}{(k-1)^2} \sum_{l=3}^{2k-1} \binom{l+2}{3} P(l=l) \cdot \sum_{n'=l}^{\infty} \binom{n'+2}{l+2} \left(\left(\frac{2}{k}\right)^{d-2}\right)^l \left(1 - \left(\frac{2}{k}\right)^{d-2}\right)^{n'-l}$$

$$= \frac{1}{(k-1)^2} \left(\frac{k}{2}\right)^{3(d-2)} \sum_{l=3}^{2k-1} \binom{l+2}{3} P(l=l)$$

$$= \frac{1}{(k-1)^2} \left(\frac{k}{2}\right)^{3(d-2)} E_l \binom{l+2}{3}$$

$$< 2k \cdot \left(\frac{k}{2}\right)^{3(d-2)},$$

for $k \leq 6$. (Use $P(l=l) = 0$ for $l > 2k-1$.)

There are $2^{3(d-2)}$ possible ways for a candidate to fit. At least 2^{d-2} of those possibilities provide a dependent system of equations, see Appendix A and Lemma 3.1. Therefore, we perform $2^{3(d-2)} - 2^{d-2}$ tries per candidate in the attack. From this the result follows. $\square$

The proposed attack requires an expected number of signatures less than $2k \cdot \left(\frac{k}{2}\right)^{d-2}$ signatures, and an expected number of steps less than $2k \cdot k^{3(d-2)}$. For the parameters proposed in [4], these quantities can be calculated explicitly.

Corollary 4.6 For $k = 8$, $d = 6$, the parameters proposed in [4], the number of signatures required to have one fitting candidate is $N \approx 2034$, the expected number of signatures in the proposed attack is $N' < 2043$ and the expected number of steps $\approx 2^{37.5} = 2.0 \cdot 10^{11}$.

Proof: The result follows from the fact that $E_l l = 7.95 \cdots$ and $E_l \binom{l+2}{3} \approx 143$ for $k = 8$ (the expectations can be evaluated explicitly by hand) and the proofs of Lemma 4.3 and Theorem 4.4 and 4.5. $\square$

Hence, this attack shows that these parameters are not sufficient to reach the designated level of security: in [4] it is conjectured that an attack will take $\mathcal{O}(2^{72})$ with the suggested parameters, or in general $\mathcal{O}(k^{k(d-1)})$ steps.

Remark Comparing the proposed attack with those considered in [4], one might say that the low probability of a fitting candidate $((2/k)^{d-2}$ instead of $1)$ is 'cancelled out' by a proportionally lower number of tries per candidate (2^{d-2} instead of k^{d-2}). The gain of the proposed attack is a consequence of the fact that only three fitting signatures are needed, instead of k or $k+1$.

5   Conclusions

The idea of preprocessing [4] is interesting, because by using a preprocessing algorithm, an exponentiation can be performed with the effort of a few multiplications only. However, one must be careful using preprocessing algorithms, for these leak information. When used in the Schnorr scheme, the preprocessing algorithm, as proposed in [4], leaks too much information, for the attack presented in this paper enables retrieving the secret key from on average two thousand signatures in on average $2^{37.5}$ steps. Since the calculations for this attack can be performed in parallel to a large extent, the attack does not seem infeasible.

The proposed attack exploits the following properties of the preprocessing algorithm from [4], and seems to depend on them.

- There exists a kind of dependence —the fitting candidates— that occurs with small but nonnegligible probability.

- The required linking equations are provided by the signatures, and have nonnegligible probability of occurrence (in fact they occur with probability 1).

This suggests that the attack will become infeasible, if one of the mentioned probabilities is made substantially smaller. It seems possible to do so, even if one takes the security and efficiency requirements from [4] into account. The design of such an algorithm falls outside the scope of this paper, however —the aim of this discussion is to indicate the possibility of doing so.

We conclude that more research is needed before one can safely use this kind of preprocessing algorithm. It seems possible to design efficient preprocessing algorithms for the Schnorr scheme that avert the attack.

Acknowledgements

The author would like to thank Jean-Paul Boly and Johan van Tilburg for their constructive comments on earlier versions of this paper.

References

[1] D. Chaum, J. H. Evertse and J. van de Graaf, 'An improved protocol for demonstration possession of discrete logarithms and some generalizations', *Proc. Eurocrypt'87*, Lecture Notes in Computer Science vol. **304**, pp. 127–141, Springer Verlag, Berlin, 1988.

[2] U. Feige, A. Fiat and A. Shamir, 'Zero knowledge proofs of identity', *Proc. of STOC 1987*, pp. 210–217.

[3] J. J. Quisquater and L. S. Guillou, 'A practical zero-knowledge protocol fitted to security microprocessor minimizing both transmission and memory', *Proc. Eurocrypt'88*, Lecture Notes in Computer Science vol. **330**, pp. 123–128, Springer Verlag, Berlin, 1988.

[4] C. P. Schnorr, 'Efficient identification and signatures for smart cards', *Proc. CRYPTO'89*, Lecture Notes in Computer Science vol. **435**, pp. 239–251, Springer Verlag, Berlin, 1990.

A Independence of equations in the attack

The attack presented in this paper is based on the possibility of solving the set of equations we obtain from Equations (1)–(3) by means of the linking equations, see Lemma 3.1. By tedious but elementary calculations, the set of equations given below is found.

$$\begin{cases} \frac{1}{2}\lambda y_i &= (\frac{1}{2}\lambda - \mu)r_{i-k} &+ r_i &+ \frac{1}{2}\lambda e_i s \\ C_a &= (\frac{1}{2}\lambda' - \mu')(-2)^{-a}r_{i-k} &+ (-2)^{-a}r_i &+ E_a s \\ C_b &= (\frac{1}{2}\lambda'' - \mu'')(-2)^{-b}r_{i-k} &+ (-2)^{-b}r_i &+ E_b s \end{cases} \quad (6)$$

where

$$C_a = \tfrac{1}{2}\lambda' y_{i+a(k-1)} + (\tfrac{1}{2}\lambda' - \mu') \sum_{l=1}^{a}(-2)^{l-a-1}y_{i+(l-1)(k-1)} + \sum_{l=1}^{a}(-2)^{l-a-1}y_{i+l(k-1)+1},$$

$$C_b = \tfrac{1}{2}\lambda'' y_{i+b(k-1)} + (\tfrac{1}{2}\lambda'' - \mu'') \sum_{l=1}^{b}(-2)^{l-b-1}y_{i+(l-1)(k-1)} + \sum_{l=1}^{b}(-2)^{l-b-1}y_{i+l(k-1)+1},$$

and

$$E_a = \tfrac{1}{2}\lambda' e_{i+a(k-1)} + (\tfrac{1}{2}\lambda' - \mu') \sum_{l=1}^{a}(-2)^{l-a-1}e_{i+(l-1)(k-1)},$$

$$E_b = \{\tfrac{1}{2}\lambda'' e_{i+b(k-1)} + (\tfrac{1}{2}\lambda'' - \mu'') \sum_{l=1}^{b}(-2)^{l-b-1}e_{i+(l-1)(k-1)}.$$

The probability that these equations are independent is the probability that the first two columns are different times the probability that the third column is not a linear combination of the first two columns, given that those are different. This latter probability follows from the fact that for any choice of λ, E_a, λ'', μ'' and $e_{i+c(k-1)}$ for $c < b$ there is exactly one $e_{i+b(k-1)} \in Z_q{}^*$ that makes the third column a linear combination of the first two columns (for there is one value of E_b that does so). Since we also have $e_{i+b(k-1)} < 2^t$, the probability that this happens is certainly less than 2^{-t}.

Hence we have

$$P \doteq \mathrm{P}(\text{independence}) > \left(1 - \mathrm{P}(\tfrac{1}{2}\lambda - \mu = \tfrac{1}{2}\lambda' - \mu' = \tfrac{1}{2}\lambda'' - \mu'')\right) \cdot (1 - 2^{-t})$$

and

$$P < 1 - \mathrm{P}(\tfrac{1}{2}\lambda - \mu = \tfrac{1}{2}\lambda' - \mu' = \tfrac{1}{2}\lambda'' - \mu'').$$

Now λ is the sum of the powers 2^j over those j for which $a(j;i) = i - 1$, and μ is the sum of the other powers 2^j with $0 \le j \le d$. Therefore, it is not hard to see that every choice of the $a(j;i)$'s yields a unique value of $\frac{1}{2}\lambda - \mu$. Thus it holds that $\frac{1}{2}\lambda - \mu = \frac{1}{2}\lambda' - \mu' = \frac{1}{2}\lambda'' - \mu''$ if and only if $a(j;i) = a(j;i+a(k-1)) = a(j;i+b(k-1))$ (which happens with probability one quarter) for all j. From this it follows that

$$(1 - (\tfrac{1}{2})^{2(d-2)}) \cdot (1 - 2^{-t}) < P < (1 - (\tfrac{1}{2})^{2(d-2)}).$$

For $d = 6$ and $t = 72$, we have $P \approx \frac{255}{256}$.

BROADCAST INTERACTIVE PROOFS

(Extended Abstract)

Mike Burmester*
Dept. of Mathematics
RHBNC - University of London
Egham, Surrey TW20 OEX
U.K.

Yvo Desmedt[†]
Dept. of EE & CS
P.O.Box 784
WI 53201 Milwaukee
U.S.A.

Abstract

In this paper we extend the notion of (single-verifier) interactive zero-knowledge proofs to (multi-verifier) broadcast proofs. In our scheme the prover broadcasts messages to many verifiers simultaneously. We consider two cases: one for which the number of rounds of messages exchanged is unbounded (as a function of the length of the common input x), and one for which it is constant. Compared to repeated single-verifier proofs (one proof for each verifier), the saving in broadcast bits is of the order of the number of verifiers in the first case, provided there are enough verifiers. More precisely, if the number of verifiers exceeds $\log |x|$ then there is "practically" no extra cost in broadcast bits by further increasing the number of verifiers. In the second case the saving in the number of rounds is "practically" $|x|/\log |x|$. An added feature of broadcast proofs of the second type is that they are *sabotage-free*.

Our scheme makes use of a *network* which directs the messages of the verifiers to the prover. The universality of the scheme derives from the way in which the network handles collisions.

*Supported by SERC grant GR/F 57700.
[†]Research is being supported by NSF grant NCR-9106327

1 Introduction

Suppose that an authority (say the president of the U.S.A.) wants to prove something to a large number of verifiers. The proof can be related, for example, to a command or some action. One obvious solution would be to prove it separately to each verifier, sequentially. This solution however could be very time consuming, certainly when the number of verifiers is large. Another solution is to perform all the proofs in parallel. However in both cases the number of bits communicated could be enormous. Our solution is completely different. The prover will use a broadcast station and the verifiers will call in their questions. We shall take into account aspects such as the time it will take to run the protocol and the *bandwidth*, and the total number of bits that must be broadcast, which must be small. For us broadcasting is expensive and phone calls are cheap. Furthermore we shall use a network which reduces substantially the number of operators required to answer incoming calls.

When the same message is sent to many receivers broadcasting is the logical solution. Recently broadcast has been receiving a lot of attention in the research on cryptography. Fiat discussed the protection of privacy and selective broadcast [7] and Desmedt-Yung discussed the issue of authenticating broadcasted messages [6]. In this paper we discuss how broadcasting can simplify the prover's effort when multi verifiers want to check interactively a zero-knowledge proof.

In our model the prover is P and the verifiers are $V_1, \ldots, V_v$. P broadcasts to all the verifiers. Each V_i has a one-directional line to a (telephone) network W. P has n incoming lines originating from W. These lines are "read-only". The prover P communicates his messages to the V_i by broadcasting them, whereas the V_i will "phone-in" their "queries" through the network W. Each verifier selects a particular line of the prover. W directs incoming calls to P on a "first-come/first-serve" basis (and chooses randomly if there is a collision).

Our proof is a *multi-verifier* interactive zero-knowledge proof. Multi-prover interactive proofs were introduced in [3] in a theoretical context. We are mainly concerned here with practical aspects, and our approach is completely different. Multi-language zero-knowledge proofs were recently discussed in [12].

We remark that existing non-interactive zero-knowledge proofs, such as [4, 5], are not practical and many signature schemes are not zero-knowledge.

This note is organized as follows. In Section 2 we consider a formal setting for broadcast proofs. *We recommend that the reader who is satisfied with the informal model above should omit this section in a first reading.* In Section 3 we present a "sequential" broadcast zero-knowledge proof. In Section 4 we present a constant-round zero-knowledge broadcast proof. which is sabotage-free.

2 A formal setting: definitions and notations

For a formal setting we use the framework in [9, pp. 4–10].

Definition 1 A Turing machine which is equipped with a read-only input tape, a work tape, a random tape, a history tape, i read-only communication tapes and j write-only communication tapes, is called an (i,j)-*interactive Turing machine.*

Observe that the interactive Turing machines in [9] have *one* read-only communication tape and *one* write-only communication tape. Below we use the abbreviations, ITM for an "interactive probabilistic Turing machine", and MITM for an (i,j)-interactive probabilistic Turing machine, when there is no ambiguity about i and j.

Definition 2 A *broadcast interactive protocol* $(P, W, V_1, \ldots, V_v)$ consists of v ITM's $V_1, \ldots, V_v$, one $(n,1)$-ITM and one (v,n)-ITM, denoted by P and W respectively, which are such that:

- P and $V_1, \ldots, V_v$ share a common communication tape which is write-only for P and read-only for all the V_i. When P writes a string on this tape, we say that P *broadcasts* that string.

- P and W share n communication tapes which are read-only for P and write-only for W. We call these tapes: *incoming phone lines.*

- W and $V_1, \ldots V_v$ share v communication tapes which are read-only for W and write-only for $V_1, \ldots, V_v$. We call these: *outgoing phone lines*.

W is the network. Its purpose is to direct incoming calls from the V_i to P and to prevent "collisions": if more than one call is addressed to any particular line, then W selects randomly which verifier receives the line.

Let $(P, W, V_1, \ldots, V_v)$ be a broadcast interactive protocol, x be the input, and σ be the concatenation of the strings written on the communication tapes by $P, W, V_1, \ldots, V_v$ and the random coin tosses of $V_1, \ldots, V_v$. We say that $(P, W, V_1, \ldots, V_v)$ outputs σ on input x. $(P, W, V_1, \ldots, V_v)(x)$ is the probability space which assigns to σ the probability that $(P, W, V_1, \ldots, V_v)$ outputs σ on input x. Joint-View$_{(P,W,V_1,\ldots,V_v)}(x)$, is the joint probability space generated by $(P, W, V_1, \ldots, V_v)(x)$. Below we will use the notation $\tilde{P}$ or $\tilde{V}_i$ to indicate that P or V_i do not necessarily adhere to the program of $(P, W, V_1, \ldots, V_v)$. We use the notation P, V_i only for participants who adhere to the program. We call such participants *honest*. We shall assume that the network W is *not corrupted*. In other words, the *anonymity* of the callers is guaranteed. So a dishonest prover cannot single out a particular verifier.

Definition 3 Let $L \subset \{0,1\}^*$ be a language, $(P, W, V_1, \ldots, V_v)$ a broadcast interactive protocol, x the common input. We say that $(P, W, V_1, \ldots, V_v)$ is a *broadcast proof* for L if,

- *Completeness* (If $x \in L$ and if all the verifiers are honest then every verifier will accept the proof.) For any c, for all sufficiently large x, if $x \in L$ then $\forall i : \mathrm{Prob}(V_i \text{ accepts } x) \geq 1 - |x|^{-c}$ (overwhelming).

- *Soundness* (If $x \notin L$ then an honest verifier will not accept.) For any c, for all sufficiently large x, for any dishonest proof system $(\tilde{P}, W, \tilde{V}_1, \ldots, \tilde{V}_v)$: if $x \notin L$ then for each *honest* $\tilde{V}_j$: $\mathrm{Prob}(\tilde{V}_j \text{ accepts } x) \leq |x|^{-c}$ (negligible).

Definition 4 A broadcast proof $(P, W, V_1, \ldots, V_v)$ for L is *zero-knowledge* if it is possible to simulate the joint-view of the verifiers when $x \in L$. Formally, for any $x \in L$, for any ITM's $\tilde{V}_1, \ldots, \tilde{V}_v$ (possibly cheating), for any "histories" $\widetilde{H}_1, \ldots, \widetilde{H}_v$, there exist a probabilistic Turing machine M running in expected polynomial time, such that the family of probability spaces $\{M(x; \widetilde{H}_1, \ldots, \widetilde{H}_v)\}$ is indistinguishable from the family of probability spaces $\{\text{Joint-View}_{(P,W,\widetilde{V}_1,\ldots,\widetilde{V}_v)}(x; \widetilde{H}_1, \ldots, \widetilde{H}_v)\}$. As in the case of single verifier proofs we have *perfect, statistical, computational* zero-knowledge proofs corresponding to the level of distinguishability [9].

Definition 5 Let $(P, W, V_1, \ldots, V_v)$ be broadcast proof for L. It is *sabotage-free* if

- For any c, for all sufficiently large x, for any dishonest proof system $(\widetilde{P}, W, \widetilde{V}_1, \ldots, \widetilde{V}_v)$, with $\widetilde{P} = P$: if $x \in L$ then for every *honest* $\widetilde{V}_j$: $\text{Prob}(\widetilde{V}_j \text{ accepts } x) \geq 1 - |x|^{-c}$.

Remarks

(i) For us, v and n are functions of the input length $|x|$, and v is polynomially bounded. Our formal model does not allow for this. In the final paper we will present a model which solves this problem.

(ii) One may wonder why we have introduced the sabotage-free aspect. Completenes implies that if $x \in L$, V_j accepts x *only* if all the other verifiers are honest. Because of the way our network is set up, it is not excluded that an honest prover will fail. When $x \in L$, dishonest verifiers could conspire against a honest verifier such that the last one will never accept.

(iii) Our model implicitly assumes that a dishonest verifier cannot eavesdrop on the questions asked by honest verifiers. To enforce this, privacy protection could be used when necessary.

(iv) We have avoided to use a model which is too restrictive. On the n phone lines at the prover's premises many phone calls could be received before the prover answers, or the prover could just answer the first one, or he could wait a certain time and then answer when no further calls are received. Our model allows for this.

3 Broadcast proofs: A first approach

3.1 An introduction

We first present a new "single-verifier" zero-knowledge proof on which we will build our scheme. This proof is based on concepts proposed by Fiat-Shamir [8] and Guillou-Quisquater [10].

Let a, b, be constants, $0 < a < b$. The common input is $x = (I, u, N)$, where N be the product of large prime numbers, $I \in Z_N^*$, and u is a prime with $|N|^a \leq u \leq |N|^b$, where $|N|$ is the binary length of N. Observe that $|N| = \Theta(|x|)$. The prover proves that there exists an s such that: $I s^u \equiv 1 (\bmod N)$. We call s the "secret". Let $n = \lfloor \log_2 u \rfloor$ and $s_1 = s$, $s_2 = s^2$, $\ldots$, $s_n = s^{2^{n-1}}$, $I_1 = I$, $I_2 = I^2$, $\ldots$, $I_n = I^{2^{n-1}}$. We assume that P and V have calculated all the I_j from I and N before the protocol starts.

Observe that one generally assumes that it is hard to decide if a number I has a u-th root modulo N [1]. No correlation between the complexity of this problem and the choice for u have been found so far. Therefore it is reasonable to restrict u to be a prime with $|N|^a \leq u \leq |N|^b$. In the final paper we shall exhibit a protocol for a more general setting.

The protocol[1] has as follows.

First V verifies if u is a prime and if $|N|^a \leq u \leq |N|^b$. Then, repeat $t = |x|$ times:

Step 1 P sends V the number $z \equiv r^u (\bmod N)$ where $r \in_R Z_N^*$.

Step 2 V sends P the bit string $(b_1, \ldots, b_n) \in_R \{0, 1\}^n$ as a query.

Step 3 P halts the protocol if the query is not of the correct form; otherwise P sends V the number $y \equiv r \cdot \prod_{b_j=1} s_j \ (\bmod N)$.

Step 4 The verifier V checks that $y \in Z_N^*$ and that $z \equiv y^u \cdot \prod_{b_j=1} I_j \ (\bmod N)$.

If this is not so the protocol is halted.

If V has not halted the protocol then V accepts x.

---

[1]In the protocol, "$\in_R$" indicates a random selection with uniform distribution, independently of earlier choices.

Lemma 1 *The protocol above defines a zero-knowledge proof of membership for the language* $L = \{(I, u, N) \mid u \text{ is a prime}, |N|^a \leq u \leq |N|^b, I \in (Z_N^*)^u\}$.

Proof. The proof is straightforward and will be given in the final paper.
□

3.2 A broadcast proof

We will use the protocol above to describe a broadcast proof. The main difference is that we assign to each s_j one incoming phone line. We assume that P and all the V_i have calculated the I_j from I and N before the protocol starts. The network in this case operates, essentially, on a "first-come/first-serve" basis. However the caller does not know if his call has been accepted. The prover allows some time between broadcasts for the verifiers to make their calls. The broadcast protocol has as follows.
Repeat T times:

Step 1 P sets $f_i^J = 0$ for $i = 0, 1$ and $J = 1, \ldots, n$. P broadcasts the number $z \equiv r^u \pmod{N}$ where $r \in_R Z_N^*$.

Step 2 Each V_i, $i = 1, \ldots, v$, sends: W a line number $J_i \in_R \{1, \ldots, n\}$ and P (via W) the query $b_{J_i} \in_R \{0, 1\}$. P reads (simultaneously during this step) the incoming queries (scanning line after line). If on some line J, the incoming query $q \notin \{0, 1\}$ then P ignores it, else $f_q^J = f_q^J + 1$.

Step 3 P broadcasts the number $y \equiv r \cdot \prod_{\bar{b}_j = 1} s_j \pmod{N}$ where $\bar{b}_j$ have been randomly selected by P such that $\text{Prob}(\bar{b}_j \text{ is selected}) = f_{\bar{b}_j}^j / (f_0^j + f_1^j)$ and in case that both f_0^j and f_1^j are zero $\bar{b}_j$ is chosen randomly with uniform probability distribution.

Step 4 Each V_i checks that $y \in Z_N^*$ and $z \equiv y^u \cdot I_1^{b_1} \cdots I_{J_i}^{b_{J_i}} \cdots I_n^{b_n} \pmod{N}$, by using his own b_{J_i} and by allowing all possible values for the other queries $b_j \in \{0, 1\}$ (this requires only $2^{n-1} < u \leq |N|^b = \Theta(|x|^b)$ operations). If one of these verifications is successful, then the verifier V_i performs: **success:=success+1**.

Regardless of the outcome, the protocol is repeated for a maximum of T times. At the end of the protocol a verifier will accept if and only if **success** $\geq t$, where $t = |x|$ is the number of iterations of the single verifier protocol.

3.3 Theorem and proof

Theorem 1 *Suppose that:*

(i) $n = O(\log |x|)$,

(ii) $d \geq n/v \geq b > 0$, *where* $d = O(\log |N|)$ *and* $b = 8 \cdot |x|^{-\frac{1}{4}}$.

(iii) $T = t/(p(1-c))$ *is an integer, where* $p = 1/2 + b(1 - e^{-1})/2$ *and* c *is such that* $c > t^{-\frac{1}{4}}$ *and*

$$2p(1 - 2c) > 1. \tag{1}$$

If the number of iterations of the broadcast protocol is (precisely) T, then $(P, W, V_1, \ldots, V_v)$ is a zero-knowledge broadcast proof for the language $L = \{(I, u, N) \mid u$ is a prime, $|N|^a \leq u \leq |N|^b, I \in (Z_N^*)^u\}$.

Remarks

(i) A crude approximation for T is $2t$. So the honest prover can prove that $x \in L$ by "running twice" the single-verifier protocol, "irrespectively" of the number of verifiers.

(ii) Observe that for the broadcast proof of Section 3.2 *each* verifier asks only a *one* bit question, while in the single-verifier proof of Section 3.1 *the* verifier asks an n-bit question.

(iii) In the final paper we will generalize Theorem 1. The main difference is that the queries b_i of the verifiers V_i are selected from a set $\{1, \ldots, q\}$, where $q \geq 2$.

Proof of Theorem 1. (It is suggested to skip this in a first reading.)

We shall require the following lemmas:

Lemma 2 *If the prover P is honest and if all the verifiers are honest, then the probability that the query of a verifier will be answered correctly is*

$$\bar{p} = \frac{1}{2} + \frac{n}{2v}\left(1 - (1 - n^{-1})^v\right). \tag{2}$$

Proof. Will be given in the full paper. $\square$

Lemma 3 $\bar{p} \geq p$.

Proof. Will be given in the full paper. $\square$

Lemma 4 *Suppose that $x \notin L$. If the honest verifier V_i asks the query b_i, then the probability $\tilde{p}$ that a (cheating) prover $\tilde{P}$ (any $\tilde{P}$) can answer this query correctly is no better than $1/2$.*

Proof. Will be given in the full paper. $\square$

Lemma 5 *We can choose the c in (1) and in such a way that $c > t^{-\frac{1}{4}}$ and $T = t/(p(1-c))$ is an integer.*

Proof. Will be given in the full paper. $\square$

We can now prove the main theorem.

Completeness (*When all the verifiers are honest, the honest prover will answer correctly every verifier, for at least t iterations out of T, with overwhelming probability.*) We shall use Okamoto's bound [11, p. 69] for the tail probabilities of the binomial distribution. Let $\bar{z}$ be the number of times in T iterations that the honest prover P will answer correctly the query of an honest verifier V. Then $\bar{p}$ is the expected value of $\bar{z}/T$ and,

$$\text{Prob}\{\mid \bar{z}/T - \bar{p} \mid \geq \varepsilon\} < \exp[-2T\varepsilon^2], \text{ for any } \varepsilon > 0. \tag{3}$$

We take $\varepsilon = cp$. By Lemma 5, $T\varepsilon^2 = tc^2p/(1-c) \geq wt^{\frac{1}{2}}$, w a constant, since $p > 1/2$. We are assuming that $t = |x|$, so e^{-t} is negligible. Thus $\exp[-2T\varepsilon^2]$ is negligible, and from (3), $\text{Prob}\{\bar{z} \leq \bar{p}T - \varepsilon T\}$ is negligible. By Lemma 5, $t = pT(1 - c) = pT - cpT = pT - \varepsilon T \leq \bar{p}T - \varepsilon T$, since $\bar{p} \geq p$ by Lemma 3. So $\text{Prob}\{\bar{z} \leq t\}$ is negligible, and therefore $\text{Prob}\{\bar{z} \geq t\}$ is overwhelming.

Soundness (*The probability that a dishonest prover will answer correctly for t or more iterations out of T is negligible.*) In this case $x \notin L$, but the prover $\tilde{P}$ wants to make an honest verifier V accept the proof. From Lemma 4 the probability $\tilde{p}$ that $\tilde{P}$ will succeed in having success=1 after the first round is at most $1/2$. If $\tilde{z}$ is the number of times out of T that $\tilde{P}$ will increase success then, as in the previous case, $\text{Prob}\{\tilde{z}/T - \tilde{p} \geq \varepsilon\} = \text{Prob}\{\tilde{z} \geq \tilde{p}T + \varepsilon T\}$ is negligible for $\varepsilon = cp$. Indeed, $\tilde{p}T + \varepsilon T = \tilde{p}T + cpT \leq (\frac{1}{2} + cp)T < p(1-c)T = t$, by (1). So $\text{Prob}\{\tilde{z} \geq t\}$ is negligible.

Zero-Knowledge (*If the prover is honest then it is possible to simulate the joint-view of all the verifiers.*) This is straightforward, since the number of queries is polynomially bounded. Indeed, $2^n < u \leq |N|^b = \Theta(|x|^b)$. $\qquad\square$

Remark

The number of users v of the broadcast proof can be as much as $nb^{-1} = \frac{1}{8}|x|^{\frac{1}{4}}\log|x|$. We can get v to be linear in $|x|$ if we take the number of rounds to be $t = c(|x|/\log|x|)^4$, c a constant.

4 A broadcast proof based on the constant round proof of Bellare-Micali-Ostrovsky

4.1 Introduction

Recently Bellare, Micali and Ostrovsky proposed a 5 step perfect zero-knowledge proof for graph isomorphism [2]. Their protocol can be used to design a sabotage-free broadcast proof. Below we present a variation of this protocol. This is a 5 step zero-know- ledge proof for quadratic residuocity[2]. The common input is $x = (I; N)$, where $Is^2 \equiv 1 \pmod{N}$ and N is the product of two large primes. We define $I_i \equiv I \pmod{N}$ and $s_i \equiv s \pmod{N}$, $i = 1, \ldots, k$. Here $k = |x|$.

---

[2]Bellare–Micali–Ostrowski [2] mention that they have a 5 step perfect zero knowledge interactive proof for quadratic residuocity, but do not describe their protocol. We presume that it is similar to the one given here.

4.2 A 5 step zero-knowledge interactive proof for quadratic residuocity

Step 1 P sends V the number $\chi \equiv \rho^2 (\mathrm{mod} N)$ where $\rho \in_R Z_N^*$.

Step 2 V sends P the numbers $\beta_i \equiv \mu_i^2 \chi^{q_i} (\mathrm{mod} N)$ where $\mu_i \in_R Z_N^*$ and $q_i \in_R \{0,1\}$, $i = 1, \ldots, k$.

Step 3 P sends V the numbers $z_i \equiv r_i^2 (\mathrm{mod} N)$ where $r_i \in_R Z_N^*$, $i = 1, \ldots, k$.

Step 4 V sends P the bits q_i and the numbers μ_i for $i = 1, \ldots, k$.

Step 5 P checks that the q_i are bits, that $\mu_i \in Z_N^*$, and that $\beta_i \equiv \mu_i^2 \chi^{q_i}$ $(\mathrm{mod} N)$ for $i = 1, \ldots, k$. The protocol is halted if this is not so. Otherwise P sends V the numbers ρ and $y_i \equiv r_i s_i^{q_i} (\mathrm{mod} N)$, for $i = 1, \ldots, k$.

Step 5' V checks that the ρ and y_i belong to Z_N^*, that $\chi \equiv \rho^2 (\mathrm{mod} N)$, and that $z_i \equiv y_i^2 I_i^{q_i} (\mathrm{mod} N)$ for all $i = 1, \ldots, k$. If this is the case he accepts, otherwise he rejects. (V did **not** sent).

4.3 A 5 step zero-knowledge sabotage-free broadcast proof for quadratic residuocity

The broadcast proof is essentially a parallelized version of the Fiat-Shamir scheme, but its novelty is that it is zero-knowledge in 5 rounds. (In the final paper we will present an adjusted version for which there is a substantial saving in broadcast bits.) Below we use the notation $g(|x|) \prec h(|x|)$ to indicate that the functions g, h of $|x|$ are bounded by $\lim_{|x| \to \infty} g(|x|) / h(|x|) = 0$.

Let h be such that $\log |x| \prec h \prec |x| / \log |x|$ and let $n = k/h$. (The case when h is *not* a factor of $|x|$ can be easily accomodated by taking $k = \Theta(|x|)$; we shall do this in the final paper.) We partition the secrets into subsets

$$(s_{11}, \ldots, s_{1h}), \ldots, (s_{i1}, \ldots, s_{ih}), \ldots, (s_{n1}, \ldots, s_{nh}).$$

Each subset is assigned to an incoming phone line. So the number of queries per line, $q = 2^h$, is superpolynomial. Then the probability with which a dishonest prover can "guess" the correct answer, $1/q$, is negligible. The public numbers are

$$(I_{11}, \ldots, I_{1h}), \ldots, (I_{i1}, \ldots, I_{ih}), \ldots, (I_{n1}, \ldots, I_{nh}).$$

For the broadcast protocol we use a "first-come, first-serve" network. In this case the *lines are exclusive and the verifiers know when their call is selected.* In what follows we only consider verifiers which know that they have been selected. So our network model is different from the one we used earlier. We assume that if a verifier's call is selected in Step 2, then the line is reserved for the remaining 3 steps. The protocol has as follows:

Step 1 P sends all the V_i, $i = 1, \ldots, v$, the number $\chi \equiv \rho^2 (\mathrm{mod}\, N)$ where $\rho \in_R Z_N^*$.

Step 2 Each V_i sends: W the line-number $J_i \in_R \{1, \ldots, n\}$, and P (via W) $\beta_{J_i 1}, \ldots, \beta_{J_i n} (\mathrm{mod}\, N)$, where $\beta_{J_i m} \equiv \mu_{J_i m}^2 \chi^{q_{J_i m}} (\mathrm{mod}\, N)$ with $\mu_{J_i m} \in_R Z_N^*$ and $q_{J_i m} \in_R \{0, 1\}$, $m = 1, \ldots, h$.

Step 3 For each line $J \in \{1, \ldots, n\}$, P selects a verifier $V_l \in_R \{V_j \mid V_j \text{ has selected line } J\}$ and broadcasts all these l. Then P broadcasts the numbers $z_i \equiv r_i^2 (\mathrm{mod}\, N)$ where $r_i \in_R Z_N^*$, $i = 11, \ldots, nh$.

Step 4 Each acknowledged V_l sends P the bits $q_{J_l 1}, \ldots, q_{J_l h}$ and the numbers $\mu_{J_l 1}, \ldots, \mu_{J_l h}$.

Step 5 P checks that the q_j are bits, that $\mu_j \in Z_N^*$ and that $\beta_j \equiv \mu_j^2 \chi^{q_j} (\mathrm{mod}\, N)$, $j = 11, \ldots, nh$. P broadcasts ρ and Y_j where: $Y_{J_i 1} = 0, \ldots, Y_{J_i h} = 0$ if any one of these checks has failed for $j = J_i m$; otherwise $Y_j \equiv r_j s_j^{q_j} (\mathrm{mod}\, N)$.

Step 5' Each acknowledged V_i checks that the ρ and $Y_{J_i m}$ belong to Z_N^*, that $\chi \equiv \rho^2 (\mathrm{mod}\, N)$, and that $z_{J_i m} \equiv Y_{J_i m}^2 \cdot I_{J_i m}^{q_{J_i m}} (\mathrm{mod}\, N)$, $m = 1, \ldots h$. If this is the case he accepts, otherwise he rejects.

Theorem 2 *The protocol described above defines a 1-call sabotage-free broadcast zero-knowledge proof $(P, W, V_1, \ldots, V_v)$ for quadratic residuocity.*

Proof. **Completeness** (*The honest prover will answer correctly, with overwhelming probability, the first call of every verifier, even when all the* *other verifiers cheat.*) This follows directly from the completeness of the single verifier protocol.

Soundness (*The probability that a dishonest prover will answer correctly a single call of any honest verifier is negligible.*) This follows from the fact that the number of queries per line is superpolynomial. Consequently a dishonest prover can only guess the answer with a negligible probability of success.

Zero-Knowledge (*If the prover is honest then it is possible to simulate the joint-view of all the verifiers.*) This follows immediately from the fact that the single-verifier proof is zero-knowledge. □

5 Conclusion

Broadcast protocols are more efficient and have lower bandwidth require-ments than repeated single-verifier proofs. (In the final paper we will discuss the bandwidth needed for these proofs.) We have assumed throughout that the network is honest (the telephone companies should be pleased!).

Acknowledgement

We acknowledge G. Beaumont for general discussions about probability the-ory and for mentioning Okamoto's bound.

REFERENCES

[1] L. M. Adleman and K. S. McCurley. Open problems in number theoretic complexity. In D. Johnson, T. Nishizeki, A. Nozaki, and H. Wilf, edi-tors, *Discrete Algorithms and Complexity, Proceedings of the Japan-US Joint Seminar (Perspective in Computing series, Vol. 15)*, pp. 263–286. Academic Press Inc., Orlando, Florida, June 4–6, Kyoto, Japan 1986.

[2] M. Bellare, S. Micali, and R. Ostrovsky. Perfect zero-knowledge in con-stant rounds. In *Proceedings of the twenty second annual ACM Symp. Theory of Computing, STOC*, pp. 482–493, May 14–16, 1990.

[3] M. Ben-Or, S. Goldwasser, J. Kilian, and A. Wigderson. Multi-prover interactive proofs: How to remove intractability assumptions. In *Proceedings of the twentieth annual ACM Symp. Theory of Computing, STOC*, pp. 113–131, May 2–4, 1988.

[4] M. Blum, A. De Santis, S. Micali, and G. Persiano. Non-interactive zero-knowledge, December 20, 1989.

[5] A. De Santis, S. Micali, and G. Persiano. Non-interactive zero-knowledge with preprocessing. In S. Goldwasser, editor, *Advances in Cryptology — Crypto '88, Proceedings (Lecture Notes in Computer Science 403)*, pp. 269–282. Springer-Verlag, 1990.

[6] Y. Desmedt and M. Yung. Arbitrated unconditionally secure authentication can be unconditionally protected against arbiter's attacks. Presented at Crypto '90, August 12–15, 1990, Santa Barbara, California, U.S.A., to appear in: Advances in Cryptology, Proc. of Crypto '90 (Lecture Notes in Computer Science), Springer-Verlag.

[7] A. Fiat. Broadcast encryption issues. Presented at the rump session of Crypto '90, August 12–15, 1990, Santa Barbara, California, U.S.A., 1990.

[8] A. Fiat and A. Shamir. How to prove yourself: Practical solutions to identification and signature problems. In A. Odlyzko, editor, *Advances in Cryptology, Proc. of Crypto '86 (Lecture Notes in Computer Science 263)*, pp. 186–194. Springer-Verlag, 1987.

[9] S. Goldwasser, S. Micali, and C. Rackoff. The knowledge complexity of interactive proof systems. *Siam J. Comput.*, 18(1), pp. 186–208, February 1989.

[10] L.C. Guillou and J.-J. Quisquater. A practical zero-knowledge protocol fitted to security microprocessor minimizing both transmission and

memory. In C. G. Günther, editor, *Advances in Cryptology, Proc. of Eurocrypt '88 (Lecture Notes in Computer Science 330)*, Springer-Verlag (1988), pp. 123–128.

[11] N. L. Johnson and S. Kotz. *Discrete distributions*. John Wiley, New York, 1969.

[12] K. Kurosawa and S. Tsujii. Multi-language zero-knowledge interactive proof system. Presented at Crypto '90, August 12–15, 1990, Santa Barbara, California, U.S.A., to appear in: Advances in Cryptology, Proc. of Crypto '90 (Lecture Notes in Computer Science), Springer-Verlag.

Direct Zero Knowledge Proofs of Computational Power in Five Rounds

Tatsuaki Okamoto[†]   David Chaum[‡]   Kazuo Ohta[†]

†NTT Laboratories
Nippon Telegraph and Telephone Corporation
1-2356, Take, Yokosuka-shi, Kanagawa-ken, 238-03 Japan

‡Centre for Mathematics and Computer Science
Kruislaan 413, 1098SJ, Amsterdam, Netherlands

Abstract

Zero-knowledge proofs of *computational power* have been proposed by Yung and others. In this paper, we propose an *efficient (direct) and constant round (five round)* construction of zero knowledge proofs of computational power. To formulate the classes that can be applied to these efficient protocols, we introduce a class of invulnerable problems, $FewPR$ and $FewPR_U$. We show that any invulnerable problem in $FewPR$ and $FewPR_U$ has an efficient and constant round zero knowledge proof of computational power, assuming the existence of a one-way function. We discuss some applications of these zero-knowledge proofs of computational power.

1. Introduction

Zero knowledge interactive proofs that were originally introduced by Goldwasser, Micali, and Rackoff [GMR] were defined for "membership" problems, in which the membership of an instance in language L is demonstrated. On the other hand, two other types of (zero-knowledge) interactive proofs have been proposed; one is proofs of "knowledge" [FFS, TW], in which prover's possession of knowledge is demonstrated, and the other is proofs of "computational power"[Y, K, OkOh, BDLP], in which prover's computational power or ability of solving a problem is demonstrated.

In many cases, a protocol constructed for a zero-knowledge proof of "membership" is also a protocol for a zero-knowledge proof of "knowledge", if the infinite power prover in the former one can be replaced by a poly-time bounded prover with an auxiliary input in the latter one. On the other hand, zero-knowledge proofs of "computational power" are quite different from zero-knowledge proofs of "membership". For example, a protocol of a zero-knowledge proof of "membership" usually cannot be a protocol for a zero-knowledge proof of "computational power", although the former can be used for constructing the latter as a subprotocol.

Similar to the relationship between zero-knowledge proofs of "membership" and "knowledge", there is also a relationship between zero-knowledge proofs of "computational power" and "knowledge". Note that, therefore, we have two types of zero-knowledge proofs of "knowledge"; one is related to "membership" zero-knowledge proofs (where knowledge is a "witness of the related language") and the other is related to "computational power" zero-knowledge proofs (where knowledge is a "key of the related trapdoor function").

Regarding zero-knowledge proofs of "membership" and its related proofs of "knowledge", some efficient and constant round (five or four round)[1] constructions have been proposed [BMO, FFS, FeS, TW]. However, these results do not imply that we can also construct an efficient zero-knowledge proofs of "computational power", since, as mentioned above, zero-knowledge proofs of "computational power" are quite different from those of "membership". Actually, the previously proposed zero-knowledge proofs of "computational power" [Y, K] are very inefficient, because these proofs use some zero-knowledge proofs of knowledge as subprotocols repeated polynomially many times. Moreover, no direct construction of the zero-knowledge proof of knowledge used as sub-protocol in these zero-knowledge proofs is given, since its construction is only guaranteed by an inefficient (even though polynomial-time) reduction to a zero-knowledge proof for an NP-complete predicate. On the other hand, zero-knowledge proofs of "computational power" by [OkOh, BDLP] need specific and strong cryptographic assumptions, although they are efficient ([OkOh] is three rounds, and [BDLP] is four rounds).

In this paper, we propose *efficient (direct) and constant round (five round)* zero knowledge interactive proofs of "computational power" assuming the existence of a secure bit-commitment (or of a one-way function [H, ILL, N]). In order to formulate the classes that can be applied to these efficient proofs, we introduce the class of invulnerable problems, $FewPR$ and $FewPR_U$. We show that any invulnerable problem in $FewPR$ and $FewPR_U$ has an efficient (direct) and constant round (five round) zero knowledge proof of computational power, assuming the existence of a secure bit-commitment.

As an application of this efficient zero knowledge proof of "computational power", we show an efficient zero knowledge proof of "knowledge", in which prover's possession of knowledge (a key of the related trapdoor function) is demonstrated. As a typical example of this application, we show a zero-knowledge proof of possessing prime factors of a composite number, which is much more efficient than the previously proposed protocol in [TW]. We also discuss another application for an identification scheme.

2. Notations

$\nu(n)$ denotes a function vanishing faster than the inverse of any polynomial. Formally,
$$\forall c > 0 \ \exists d > 0 \ \forall n > d \qquad \nu(n) < 1/n^c.$$

Negligible probability is the probability that behaves as $\nu(n)$, and overwhelming probability is probablity behaves as $1 - \nu(n)$. When S is a set, $\| S \|$ denotes the number of elements in the set S. $\oplus$ denotes the exclusive-or.

(P, V) is an interactive pair of Turing machines, where P is the prover, and V is the verifier [GMR, TM]. Let $T \in \{P, V\}$. $T(s)$ denotes T begun with s on its input work tape. $(P, V)(x)$ refers to the probability space that assigns to the string σ the probability that (P, V), on input x, outputs σ.

---

[1] Here, one "round" means one message transmission. Note that "round" is used as a couple of message transmissions (send and return) in [FeS].

3. Invulnerable Problems

In this section, we define the problems whose instance-witness pairs are efficiently generated. These are variants of the *invulnerable* problems introduced by Abadi, Allender, Broder, Feigenbaum, and Hemachandra [AABFH].

Definition 1: R denotes a *predicate* that can be computed in polynomial time by a deterministic algorithm.

$$\mathcal{S}_R = \{(x, w) \mid R(x, w)\},$$

$$\mathcal{X}_R = \{x \mid \exists w \ R(x, w)\},$$

$$\mathcal{W}_R(x) = \{w \mid R(x, w)\},$$

$$FewPR = \{R \mid \exists c > 0 \ \forall x \in \mathcal{X}_R \ \| \mathcal{W}_R(x) \| \leq |x|^c\},$$

R_U denotes a *predicate with an auxiliary witness* that can be computed in polynomial time by a deterministic algorithm with an auxiliary witness.

$$\mathcal{S}_{R_U} = \{(x, w, u) \mid R_u(x, w)\},$$

$$\mathcal{X}_{R_U} = \{x \mid \exists w \ \exists u \ R_u(x, w)\},$$

$$\mathcal{W}_{R_U}(x) = \{w \mid R_u(x, w)\},$$

$$FewPR_U = \{R_u \mid \exists c > 0 \ \forall x \in \mathcal{X}_{R_U} \ \| \mathcal{W}_{R_U}(x) \| \leq |x|^c\},$$

Note: In our definition, when $R \in FewPR$ (or $R_U \in FewPR_U$) is determined, the size of $x \in \mathcal{X}_R$ (or $x \in \mathcal{X}_{R_U}$) is fixed. In other words, R is defined for each size of $x \in \mathcal{X}_R$. We write $|R|$ as $|x|$ $(x \in \mathcal{X}_R)$.

Definition 2: The *uniform generation scheme* for $R \in FewPR$, which we denote G_R, is a polynomial-time algorithm that, on R, obtains an output string y. If y is $(x, w) \in \mathcal{S}_R$ with uniform probability, where $R(x, w)$, then G_R outputs (x, w); otherwise, it outputs Λ. G_R is α-*invulnerable*, if the probability that there exists a polynomial-time algorithm computing w from x for nonnegligible fraction of $x \in \mathcal{X}_R$ or G_R outputs Λ is at most $1 - \alpha$.

The *uniform generation scheme* for $R_U \in FewPR_U$, which we denote G_{R_U}, is a polynomial time algorithm that, on input R_U, obtains an output string y. If y is $(x, w, u) \in \mathcal{S}_{R_U}$ with uniform probability, where $R_u(x, w)$, then G_{R_U} outputs (x, w, u); otherwise, it outputs Λ. G_{R_U} is α-*invulnerable*, if the probability that there exists a polynomial-time algorithm computing w from x and R_U for nonnegligible fraction of $x \in \mathcal{X}_{R_U}$ or G_{R_U} outputs Λ is at most $1 - \alpha$.

R or R_U is α-invulnerable, if there exists an α-invulnerable uniform generation scheme. A subset $\mathcal{C} \subset FewPR$ is α-invulnerable, if any $R \in \mathcal{C}$ is α-invulnerable. A subset $\mathcal{C} \subset FewPR_U$ is α-invulnerable, if any $R_U \in \mathcal{C}$ is α-invulnerable. When $1 - \alpha$ is negligible, α-*invulnerable* is refered to simply as *invulnerable*.

Example 1: (Invulnerable problem in $FewPR$)

$$R(x, w) : x = E(w),$$

where E is a one-way function (e.g., an encryption function).

Example 2: (Invulnerable problem in $FewPR$)

$$R(x, w) : x = w^e \bmod n,$$

where $n = p \cdot q$ (p, q: prime), e is coprime to $p - 1$ and $q - 1$. If breaking the RSA scheme is hard, then this is an invulnerable problem in $FewPR$.

Example 3: (Invulnerable problem in $FewPR_U$)

$$R_u(x, w) : x = g^u \bmod p, \quad w = b^u \bmod p,$$

where p is prime, g is a primitive element of $GF(p)$, and b is an element in $GF(p)$ ($b = g^a \bmod p$). If breaking the DH scheme is hard, then this is an invulnerable problem in $FewPR_U$.

Remark: Hereafter, we will only talk about $FewPR$ and omit $FewPR_U$, because they are almost same.

4. Interactive Proofs of Computational Power

In this section, we introduce the formal definition of interactive proofs of computational power.

Definition 3: (P, V) is an interactive proof that the prover P has the computational power to solve the invulnerable problem $\mathcal{C} \subset FewPR$, if and only if it satisfies the following two conditions
- Completeness:
  For any $R \in \mathcal{C}$,

$$\Pr\{(P, V) \text{ accepts } R\} > 1 - \nu(|R|).$$

The probability is taken over the coin tosses of P and V.
- Soundness:
  For any $c > 0$, there exists a polynomial-time probabilistic algorithm M (with complete control over P^*) such that, for any machine P^* acting as a prover, and any sufficiently large $R \in \mathcal{C}$,

$$\Pr\{(P^*, V) \text{ accepts } R\} > 1/|R|^c \quad \rightarrow \quad \Pr\{M(x) = \mathcal{W}_R(x), \ x \in \mathcal{D}_R\} > 1 - \nu(|R|),$$

where $\mathcal{D}_R \subset \mathcal{X}_R$, $\| \mathcal{D}_R \| < |R|^{c'}$ for a constant c', and $\mathcal{D}_R$ is randomly selected from $\mathcal{X}_R$ with the same distribution as generated by verifier V. The probability is taken over the coin tosses of P^*, M, V, and the distribution of $\mathcal{D}_R$.

5. Efficient Zero Knowledge Interactive Proof of Computational Power to Solve an Invulnerable Problem in FewPR

In this section, we show that any invulnerable problem in $FewPR$ (and $FewPR_U$) has an efficient (direct) and constant round (five round) zero-knowledge interactive proof of computational power assuming the existence of a secure bit-commitment (or of a one-way function).

First, before describing the construction of zero-knowledge proofs of computational power, we roughly introduce the notion of the bit-commitment (see the formal definition in [N]). The bit-commitment protocol between Alice (committer) and Bob (verifier) consists of two stages; the *commit stage* and the *revealing stage*. In the commit stage, after their exchanging messages, Bob has some information that represents Alice's secret bit b. In the revealing stage, Bob knows b. Roughly, after the commit stage, Bob cannot guess b, and Alice can reveal only one possible value. Here, when the protocol needs k rounds in the commit stage, we call it k *round* bit-commitment. We can construct *one round* bit-commitment using probabilistic encryption [GM], and *two round* bit-commitment using any one-way function [H, ILL, N]. In the commit stage of one round bit-commiment, Alice generates a random number r and sends $BC(b, r)$ to Bob, where BC is a bit-commit function. When Alice wishes to commit l bits, $b_1, b_2, \ldots, b_l$, she sends $BC(b_1, r_1)$, $\ldots$, $BC(b_l, r_l)$ to Bob. Hereafter, we will simply write $BC(\overline{b}, \overline{r})$ as $(BC(b_1, r_1), \ldots, BC(b_l, r_l))$, where $\overline{b} = (b_1, \ldots, b_l)$ and $\overline{r} = (r_1, \ldots, r_l)$.

Next, we show the protocol of an efficient (direct) and constant round (five round) zero-knowledge interactive proof of computational power.

Protocol A

Let $\mathcal{C} \subset FewPR$ be an invulnerable problem. The following (P, V) protocol on input $R \in \mathcal{C}$ should be repeated $m = O(|R|)$ times.

(i) P generates random bit strings r_i and t_i $(i = 1, 2, \ldots, I)$, and calculates bit-commitment $v_i = BC(r_i, t_i)$ $(i = 1, 2, \ldots, I)$, where BC is a bit-commitment function, and t_i is a random bit string to commit r_i. Here, I is the maximum number of witnesses of R with $|R|$.

(ii) V randomly generates $(x, w) \in \mathcal{S}_R$ using G_R, and sends x to P. If G_R does not output anything, V sends *terminate* to P and halts.

(iii) P generates random bit strings s_i, and calculates $u_i = s_i \oplus r_i$ $(i = 1, 2, \ldots, I)$. P computes $\{w_i \mid R(x, w_i), i = 1, 2, \ldots, I\}$ from x using P's computational power, and calculates $z_i = BC(w_i, s_i)$ $(i = 1, 2, \ldots, I)$. (When the number of the witnesses of x is less than I, P set any values as the dummy witnesses.) If P cannot find any witness w_i, then P sends *terminate* to V and halts. Otherwise, P sends u_i, z_i $(i = 1, 2, \ldots, I)$ to V.

(iv) V sends w to P.

(v) P checks whether there exists j such that $w = w_j$. If j exists, V sends j, r_j and t_j, otherwise P halts.

(vi) V checks whether $v_j = BC(r_j, t_j)$ and $z_j = BC(w, (u_j \oplus r_j))$ hold or not. If they hold, V continues the protocol, otherwise rejects and halts.

After m repetitions of this protocol, if V has not rejected it, V accepts and halts.

Remark: If Naor's bit-commitment scheme [N] is used, V also sends random bits for P's bit-commitment before steps (i) and (iii). Note that if probabilistic encryption or blob is used as a bit-commitment, V does not need to send any information for P's bit-commitment.

Theorem 1: If there exists a secure (one round) bit-commitment, then Protocol A is a computational zero knowledge interactive proof that the prover has the computational power to solve $R \in \mathcal{C}$.

(Proof)

(Completeness)

Since P has the power of computing $\{w_i \mid R(x, w_i), i = 1, 2, \ldots, I\}$, then clearly P can be proven valid with probability 1.

(Soundness)

Here, for any $c > 0$, we construct a polynomial time algorithm M such that when for any sufficiently large $R \in \mathcal{C}$

$$\Pr\{(P^*, V) \text{ accepts } R\} > 1/|R|^c,$$

then

$$\Pr\{M(x) = \mathcal{W}_R(x), \ x \in \mathcal{D}_R\} > 1 - \nu(|R|).$$

This algorithm consists of two phases. In the first phase, M executes protocol A with P^* by simulating the honest verifier, and obtains the values of random numbers t_i, and r_i generated by P^* with nonnegligible probability. By repeating polynomially many times this procedure with fixing the random tape of P^*, M obtains all t_i, and r_i that are used for commiting true witnesses but dummy witnesses.

In the second phase, M resets P^*, and also executes protocol A, where M does not simulate the honest verifier, but sends $x \in \mathcal{D}_R$ to P^* in step (ii). In step (iii), P^* outputs z_i. Because in step (iv) M cannot send a valid w, then P^* halts in step (v). However, since, in the first phase, M knows all t_i and r_i, then M can obtain all w_i from u_i, z_i, t_i, and r_i with nonnegligible probability, because the same random tape of P^* is used in the first and second phases.

Thus, we can extract all w_i from $x \in \mathcal{D}_R$ with overwhelming probability by repeating the above procedure polynomially many times.

(Zero knowledgeness)

Let V^* be any polynomial time algorithm for the verifier.

The simulator M can simulate the history, $(P, V^*)(R)$, by using V^* as a black-box as follows:

The following procedure should be repeated $m = O(|R|)$ times.

(1) M generates prover's first message, $\{v_i'; i = 1, 2, \ldots, I\}$, by using the same procedure as honest prover's, where $v_i' = BC(r_i', t_i')$.

(2) M gives $\{v_i'; i = 1, 2, \ldots, I\}$ to V^* as prover's first message and runs V^*, which outputs x' as verifier's first message.

(3) M generates random numbers $\{w_i'\}$, $\{s_i'\}$ and computes $\{u_i' = s_i' \oplus r_i'\}$, $\{z_i' = BC(w_i', s_i')\}$, where $i = 1, 2, \ldots, I$.

(4) M gives $\{u_i', z_i'; i = 1, 2, \ldots, I\}$ to V^* as prover's second message and runs V^*, which outputs w' as verifier's second message.

(5) M checks whether $R(x', w')$ holds or not. If $R(x', w')$ does not hold, then M outputs $(\{v_i'; \ i = 1, 2, \ldots, I\}, \ x', \ \{u_i', z_i'; i = 1, 2, \ldots, I\}, w')$, and halts. If it holds, then go to step (6).

(6) M resets V^*, and repeats the exact same procedure of steps (1) and (2) with the same ramdom tapes.

(7) M randomly generates $j \in \{1, \ldots, I\}$, s_i'' $(i = 1, \ldots, I)$ and w_i'' for $i = 1, \ldots, j - 1, j+1, \ldots, I$. M sets $w_j'' = w'$, and computes $u_i'' = s_i'' \oplus r_i'$, $z_i'' = BC(w_i'', s_i'')$ $(i = 1, \ldots, I)$.

(8) M gives $\{u_i'', z_i''; i = 1, \ldots, I\}$ to V^* as prover's second message, and runs V^*, which outputs w'' as verifier's second message.

(9) M checks whether $w'' = w'$ or not. If it holds, M outputs $(\{v_i'; i = 1, \ldots, I\}, x', \{u_i'', z_i''; i = 1, \ldots, I\}, w', (j, t_j', r_j'))$ as the history. Otherwise, M returns to step (6).

First, the real history H_0 of $(\{v_i; i = 1, \ldots, I\}, x, \{u_i, z_i; i = 1, \ldots, I\}, w)$ is computationally indistinguishable from the first-stage simulated history H_1 of $(\{v_i'; i = 1, \ldots, I\}, x', \{u_i', z_i'; i = 1, \ldots, I\}, w')$. This is because if there exists a distinguisher D that distinguishes H_0 and H_1, then we can use D to extract one committed bit of the bit-commitment scheme with nonnegligible probability. This contradicts the definition of bit-commitment, since V^* and M are polynomial-time bounded and D is nonuniformly polynomial-time bounded.

Similarly, the first-stage simulated history H_1 is computationally indistinguishable from the final-stage simulated history H_2 of $(\{v_i'; i = 1, \ldots, I\}, x', \{u_i'', z_i''; i = 1, \ldots, I\}, w')$. This is because H_1 is computationally indistinguishable from $H_1' = (\{v_i'; i = 1, \ldots, I\}, x', \{R_i, z_i'; i = 1, \ldots, I\}, w')$, H_2 is computationally indistinguishable from $H_2' = (\{v_i'; i = 1, \ldots, I\}, x', \{R_i, z_i''; i = 1, \ldots, I\}, w')$, and H_1' and H_2' are computationally indistinguishable, where R_i is a real random string.

Thus, the output of M is computationally indistinguishable from the real history, since H_2 is computationally indistinguishable from H_0.

Then, we show that the running time of M is polynomial time with overwhelming probability. Suppose that p_i is the probability that V^* outputs w_i as w' on input $(\{v_i'; i = 1, \ldots, I\}, x', \{u_i', z_i'; i = 1, \ldots, I\})$ and p_i' is the probability that V^* outputs w_i as w' on input $(\{v_i'; i = 1, \ldots, I\}, x', \{u_i'', z_i''; i = 1, \ldots, I\})$. The expected repetition number from step (6) to (9) is $\sum_i p_i/p_i'$. From the property of the bit-commitment, $\varepsilon = |p_i - p_i'| < \nu(|R|)$. If there exists c_0 for sufficient large $|R|$ such that $p_i > 1/|R|^{c_0}$, then $|1 - p_i'/p_i| \leq \varepsilon/p_i < \nu(|R|)$. Hence, $\sum_i p_i/p_i' < I + \nu(|R|)$. If $p_i < \nu(|R|)$, then we can neglect the history with w_i, since the probability of the history is negligible and the history without w_i is statistically indistinguishable from the real history. Thus, the running time of the simulation is polynomial time with overwhelming probability.

(QED)

Notes:

(1) In the above protocol, the prover shows his power to compute all witnesses, $w_1, \ldots, w_I$, from instance x. Definition 3 and this protocol can be easily modified to those in which the prover shows his power to compute a subset of $\{w_1, \ldots, w_I\}$ from x. In the modified protocol, the verifier accepts the proof if the ratio of the number of the accepted cycles to the total cycle number is greater than a predetermined value (e.g., $1/(I - c)$; c is an arbitrary constant), where a"cycle" means step (i) to (vi) in Protocol A.

(2) The zero-knowledge protocol in the case of example 1 demonstrates that the prover can calculate E^{-1}.

(3) The zero-knowledge protocol in the case of example 2 demonstrates that the prover can decrypt an RSA ciphertext.

(4) The zero-knowledge protocol in the case of example 3 demonstrates that, given p, g, b, the prover can generate $b^u \bmod p$ from $g^u \bmod p$ without knowing u.

Corollary 1: Let $C \subset FewPR$ or $FewPR_U$ be an invulnerable problem. If there exists a secure (one round) bit-commitment, then there exists a constant round (five round) computational zero knowledge interactive proof that the prover has the computational power to solve $R \in C$.

(Proof Sketch)

Clearly, the parallel version of Protocol A satisfies the completeness and soundness conditions.

To prove the zero-knowledgeness, first, simulator M of this protocol executes the parallel version of steps (1) and (2) of simulator's procedure in Theorem 1's proof. Here, V^* outputs m instances, $x'_1, \ldots, x'_m$, as verifier's first messages. Then, M obtains witnesses of each instance x_k ($k = 1, \ldots, m$) that V^* outputs nonnegligibly as verifier's second message, by repeating the parallel version of steps (6) through (9) of simulator's procedure in Theorem 1's proof. (Here, w''_j can be a random string in step (7).) The expected repetition number is polynomial in $|R|$. Then, M puts all obtained witnesses in z''_i (which corresponds to step (7)), and executes the procedure which corresponds to steps (8) and (9) of simulator's procedure in Theorem 1's proof.

Therefore, The running time of M is polynomial time with overwhelming probability, and the output of M is computationally indistinguishable from the real history.

(QED)

Corollary 2: Let $C \subset FewPR$ or $FewPR_U$ be an invulnerable problem. If there exists a secure blob (chameleon bit-commitment [BCC]), then there exists a *perfect* zero knowledge *argument* that the prover has the computational power to solve $R \in C$.

(Proof Sketch) If we use the same simulator M as that of Theorem 1, the output of M is perfectly indistinguishable to the real history of (P, V^*). The expected running time of M is $\sum_i p_i / p_i \leq I$.

(QED)

Corollary 3: Let $C \subset FewPR$ or $FewPR_U$ be an invulnerable problem. If there exists a secure (one round) blob (chameleon bit-commitment [BCC]), then there exists a constant round (five round) *statistical* zero knowledge *argument* that the prover has the computational power to solve $R \in C$.

(Proof Sketch) If we use the same simulator M as that of Corollary 1, the output of M is statistically indistinguishable to the real history of (P, V^*). The expected running time of M is polynomial time with overwhelming probability.

(QED)

Corollary 4: Let $C \subset FewPR$ or $FewPR_U$ be an invulnerable problem. If there exists a one-way function, then there exists a constant round (six round) computational zero knowledge interactive proof that the prover has the computational power to solve $R \in C$.

6. Applications

6.1 Zero-Knowledge Proofs for Possession of Knowledge

In this subsection, we show an efficient zero knowledge proof of "knowledge", based on our zero-knowledge proof of "computational power".

When the power of the prover's ability is bounded in polynomial-time, protocol A for example 2 (Section 3) becomes a zero knowledge proof of "knowledge", which demonstrates that the prover has a secret key or algorithm for decrypting an RSA ciphertext. In the same situation, protocol A for example 3 demonstrates that the prover has a secret key or algorithm for computing b^u mod p from g^u mod p, g, b, and p. Here, note that we need another definition of interactive proofs of "knowledge" than that by [FFS, TW].

Simialrly, when E in example 1 is the Rabin scheme, we can construct a zero-knowledge proof of possessing prime factors of a composite number. Note that this protocol is a zero knowledge proof of "knowledge" in the sense of [FFS, TW]. Clearly, this protocol is much more efficient than the previously proposed protocol in [TW].

6.2 Identification Schemes

The zero-knowledge proofs of computational power can be applied to identification schemes. In the above-mentioned zero-knowledge proofs, we assume that the prover has infinite power. When we apply the zero-knowledge proofs to identification schemes, we must assume that the power of a prover is bounded in polynomial-time, and that the prover possesses a secret auxiliary input. Then, we use a trapdoor one-way function (public-key encryption) (E, d), where E is a function, and d is a secret key for the trapdoor (in other words, the inverse of E can be efficiently computed using d.) By using this trapdoor function, we can construct an invulnerable problem $R \in FewPR$ such that

$$R(x, w) : x = E(w),$$

and there exists a polynomial-time algorithm D_d, where $x = E(D_d(x))$. The identification scheme is as follows:

(Key generation)
First, prover P randomly generates (E, d), and publishes E as his public key (d is his secret key).

(Identification) P proves to a verifier that P has the power to compute the inverse of E through Protocol A.

Thus, we can construct an identification scheme if there exists a trapdoor one-way function.

7. Conclusion

In this paper, we have proposed an *efficient (direct) and constant round (five round)* construction of zero knowledge proofs of computational power. We have shown that any invulnerable problem in $FewPR$ and $FewPR_U$ has an efficient and constant round zero knowledge proof of computational power, assuming the existence of a one-way function.

We have discussed some applications of these zero-knowledge proofs of computational power.

Acknowledgements: We would like to thank Toshiya Itoh and Kouichi Sakurai for their invaluable discussions on the preliminary manuscript. We would also like to thank Ivan Damgård for his pointing out an error in the proof of Theorem 1 in the preliminary manuscript.

References

[AABFH] M.Abadi, E.Allender, A.Broder, F.Feigenbaum, and L.Hemachandra, "On Generating Solved Instances of Computational Problems," the Proceedings of Crypto (1988)

[BDLP] J.Brandt, I.Damgård, P.Landrock, T.Pedersen, "Zero-Knowledge Authentication Scheme with Secret Key Exchange," (Preprint)

[BMO] M.Bellare, S.Micali, and R.Ostrovsky, "Perfect Zero-Knowledge in Constant Rounds," the Proceedings of STOC, pp.482-493 (1990)

[FeS] U.Feige, A.Shamir, "Zero-Knowledge Proofs of Knowledge in Two Rounds," the Proceedings of Crypto'89, pp.526-544 (1989)

[FFS] U.Feige, A.Fiat and A.Shamir, "Zero Knowledge Proofs of Identity," the Proceedings of STOC, pp.210-217 (1987)

[FiS] A.Fiat and A.Shamir, "How to Prove Yourself," the Proceedings of Crypto (1986)

[GM] S.Goldwasser, S.Micali, "Probabilistic Encryption," Journal of Computer and System Science, pp270-299 (1984)

[GMR] S.Goldwasser, S.Micali, and C.Rackoff, "Knowledge Complexity of Interactive Proofs," the Proceedings of STOC, pp291-304 (1985)

[GMW] O.Goldreich, S.Micali, and A.Wigderson, "Proofs that Yield Nothing But their Validity and a Methodology of Cryptographic Protocol Design," the Proceedings of FOCS, pp.174-187 (1986)

[H] J.Håstad, "Pseudo-Random Generators under Uniform Assumptions," the Proceedings of STOC, pp.395-404 (1990)

[ILL] R.Impagliazzo, L.Levin, M.Luby "Pseudo-Random Number Generation from One-Way Functions," the Proceedings of STOC, pp.12-24 (1989)

[K] K.Kurosawa, "Dual Zero Knowledge Interactive Proof Systems," Technical Report of the IEICE. Japan, ISEC88-33 (1988)

[OkOh] T.Okamoto, and K.Ohta, "Zero Knowledge Proofs for Possession of Black-boxes," SCIS'89 (in Japan) (1989)

[N] M.Naor, "Bit Commitment Using Pseudo-Randomness," the Proceedings of Crypto'89 (1989)

[TW] M.Tompa and H.Woll, "Random Self-Reducibility and Zero Knowledge Interactive Proofs of Possession of Information," the Proceedings of FOCS, pp.472-482 (1987)

[Y] M.Yung, "Zero-Knowledge Profs of Computational Power," the Proceedings of Eurocrypt'89, (1989)

On the Reversibility of Oblivious Transfer *

Claude Crépeau [†]   Miklós Sántha [‡]

Laboratoire de Recherche en Informatique

Université de Paris-Sud

Bâtiment 490

91405 Orsay FRANCE

Abstract

A $\binom{2}{1}$-OT$_2$ (one-out-of-two Bit Oblivious Transfer) is a technique by which a party S owning two secret bits b_0, b_1, can transfer one of them b_c to another party R, who chooses c. This is done in a way that does not release any bias about $b_{\bar{c}}$ to R nor any bias about c to S. How can one build a $_2$TO-$\binom{2}{1}$ ($\binom{2}{1}$-OT$_2$ from R to S) given a $\binom{2}{1}$-OT$_2$ (from S to R)? This question is interesting because in many scenarios, one of the two parties will be much more powerful than the other.

In the current paper we answer this question and show a number of related extensions. One interesting extension of this transfer is the $\binom{2}{1}$-OT$_2^k$ (one-out-of-two String O.T.) in which the two secrets q_0, q_1 are elements of $GF^k(2)$ instead of bits. We show that $\frac{k}{2}$TO-$\binom{2}{1}$ can be obtained at about the same cost as $\binom{2}{1}$-OT$_2^k$, in terms of number of calls to $\binom{2}{1}$-OT$_2$.

1 Introduction

A $\binom{2}{1}$-OT$_2$ (one-out-of-two Bit Oblivious Transfer) is a technique by which a party S owning two secret bits b_0, b_1, can transfer one of them b_c to another party R, who chooses c. This is done in a way that does not release any bias about $b_{\bar{c}}$ to R nor any bias about c to S. This primitive was first introduced in [EGL83] with application to contract signing protocols. A natural and interesting extension of this transfer is the $\binom{2}{1}$-OT$_2^k$ (one-out-of-two String Oblivious Transfer, know as ANNBP in [BCR86]) in which the two secrets q_0, q_1 are elements of $GF^k(2)$ instead of bits. One can find in [CS] a reduction of $\binom{2}{1}$-OT$_2^k$ to $\binom{2}{1}$-OT$_2$, i.e. an efficient two-party protocol to achieve $\binom{2}{1}$-OT$_2^k$ based on the assumption of the existence of a protocol for $\binom{2}{1}$-OT$_2$. This reduction uses essentially $9k$ calls to $\binom{2}{1}$-OT$_2$ to perform one $\binom{2}{1}$-OT$_2^k$.

Assume now that we are in a scenario where one party is much more powerful in terms of computational power or simply in terms of technology than the other party. In such a setting it is likely that $\binom{2}{1}$-OT$_2$ can be implemented in one direction but not the other. In particular one can make a computational assumption of the "weaker" party but not of the other. This scenario was also studied by Ostrovsky, Venkatesan and Yung in [OVY91] where they independently give a reduction similar to 2.1. Also if quantum technology is used [Cre90,BC91] it might be the case that one party is limited in the equipment it can carry (especially if one participant sits on a smart card!). Therefore a fundamental question is: **"Can we reverse $\binom{2}{1}$-OT$_2$?"**.

---

*This work was performed while the authors were visiting the Universität des Saarlandes, Saarbrücken.

[†]Supported in part by an NSERC Postdoctorate Scholarship.

[‡]Supported in part by an Alexander von Humboldt Fellowship.

Let's call $_2\text{TO-}_1$ and $_2\text{TO-}_1$ the reversed versions of $_1\text{-OT}_2$ and $_1\text{-OT}_2$. As we shall see in section 2 we can achieve $_2\text{TO-}\binom{2}{1}$ from $\binom{2}{1}\text{-OT}_2$ at the cost of using $\binom{2}{1}\text{-OT}_2$ many times (not necessarily constant) to perform a single $_2\text{TO-}\binom{2}{1}$. On the other hand, we show in section 3 that if we wish to perform many $_2\text{TO-}\binom{2}{1}$ simultaneously (to perform $_2^k\text{TO-}\binom{2}{1}$ for instance) it is possible to reduce the marginal cost to a constant number of calls to $\binom{2}{1}\text{-OT}_2$ per $_2\text{TO-}\binom{2}{1}$.

2 Reversing $\binom{2}{1}\text{-OT}_2$

To start with, consider the following reduction that constitutes our first attempt to build a $_2\text{TO-}\binom{2}{1}$ from $\binom{2}{1}\text{-OT}_2$.

Reduction 2.1 ($_2\text{TO-}\binom{2}{1}(c, (b_0, b_1))$ from $\binom{2}{1}\text{-OT}_2$)

1: S finds a random bit-matrix $C = \begin{pmatrix} C_{00} & C_{01} \\ C_{10} & C_{11} \end{pmatrix}$
   such that $C_{00} \oplus C_{01} = \bar{c}$ and $C_{10} \oplus C_{11} = c$.

2: S runs $\binom{2}{1}\text{-OT}_2((C_{00}, C_{01}), b_0)$ and $\binom{2}{1}\text{-OT}_2((C_{10}, C_{11}), b_1)$ with $\mathcal{R}$.

3: $\mathcal{R}$ computes $b \leftarrow C_{0b_0} \oplus C_{1b_1}$ and sends b to S.

4: S computes $out \leftarrow C_{00} \oplus C_{10} \oplus b$ and outputs out.

Theorem 2.1 *If S and $\mathcal{R}$ follow honestly the reduction 2.1 then S's output value will be b_c.*

Proof. We make use of the following trivial Lemma:

Lemma 2.2 $\forall b, c_0, c_1 \; [c_0 \oplus c_b = b \wedge (c_0 \oplus c_1)]$.

We have the following equalities

$$
\begin{aligned}
out &= C_{00} \oplus C_{10} \oplus b \\
    &= (C_{00} \oplus C_{0b_0}) \oplus (C_{10} \oplus C_{1b_1}) \\
    &= (b_0 \wedge (C_{00} \oplus C_{01})) \oplus (b_1 \wedge (C_{10} \oplus C_{11})) \quad \text{by Lemma 2.2} \\
    &= (b_0 \wedge \bar{c}) \oplus (b_1 \wedge c) \\
    &= b_c
\end{aligned}
$$

∎

Unfortunately, this reduction does not provide a full solution to our problem because i. is clear that S can "cheat" this reduction in the sense that he can get $b_0 \oplus b_1$ by picking a matrix C such that $C_{00} \oplus C_{01} = C_{10} \oplus C_{11} = 1$. Indeed what the above reduction achieves is not really a $_2\text{TO-}\binom{2}{1}$ but something weaker that can be described in terms of a scalar product. Consider the following reduction **ralacs** that returns the scalar product $(c_0, c_1) \cdot (b_0, b_1)$ to S on respective inputs (c_0, c_1) and (b_0, b_1).

Reduction 2.2 (ralacs$((c_0, c_1), (b_0, b_1))$ from $\binom{2}{1}$–OT$_2$)

1: S finds a random bit-matrix $C = \begin{pmatrix} C_{00} & C_{01} \\ C_{10} & C_{11} \end{pmatrix}$
   such that $C_{00} \oplus C_{01} = c_0$ and $C_{10} \oplus C_{11} = c_1$.

2: S runs $\binom{2}{1}$–OT$_2((C_{00}, C_{01}), b_0)$ and $\binom{2}{1}$–OT$_2((C_{10}, C_{11}), b_1)$ with $\mathcal{R}$.

3: $\mathcal{R}$ computes $b \leftarrow C_{0b_0} \oplus C_{1b_1}$ and sends b to S.

4: S computes $out \leftarrow C_{00} \oplus C_{10} \oplus b$ and outputs out.

The proof of the correctness of this reduction can be obtained in a way similar to that of theorem 2.1. Notice that in fact the reduction 2.1 is nothing more than reduction 2.2 performed with arguments $((\bar{c}, c), (b_0, b_1))$. Thus we have

Theorem 2.3 *If S and $\mathcal{R}$ follow honestly the reduction 2.2 then S's output value will be $(c_0, c_1) \cdot (b_0, b_1)$.*

But this time, the reduction we get is also "private". The notion of privacy expresses the fact that all the actions that a cheating participant could take are of no advantage over being honest (in the sense that whatever a cheater gets by cheating he could get by behaving honestly using a different input). For a precise definition of this notion we refer the reader to [Cre90,CM91].

Theorem 2.4 *The reduction 2.2 is both $\mathcal{R}$-private and S-private.*

Proof. The $\mathcal{R}$-privacy of this reduction is simple to prove since all the information $\mathcal{R}$ may get (one bit in each line of C) is purely random. The S-privacy is due to the fact that any choice of C defines some legitimate values for c_0 and c_1 that could be used honestly in the reduction (this was not the case with reduction 2.1). ∎

For sake of simplicity, we present the following reduction **scalar**, dual to **ralacs**, with exactly the same properties except that $\mathcal{R}$ gets the output from **scalar** instead of S in **ralacs**.

Reduction 2.3 (scalar$((b_0, b_1), (c_0, c_1))$ from $\binom{2}{1}$–OT$_2$)

1: S finds a random bit-matrix $B = \begin{pmatrix} B_{00} & B_{01} \\ B_{10} & B_{11} \end{pmatrix}$
   such that $B_{00} \oplus B_{01} = b_0$ and $B_{10} \oplus B_{11} = b_1$.

2: S runs $\binom{2}{1}$–OT$_2((B_{00}, B_{01}), c_0)$ and $\binom{2}{1}$–OT$_2((B_{10}, B_{11}), c_1)$ with $\mathcal{R}$.

3: S computes $b \leftarrow B_{00} \oplus B_{10}$ and sends b to $\mathcal{R}$.

4: $\mathcal{R}$ computes $out \leftarrow B_{0c_0} \oplus B_{1c_1} \oplus b$ and outputs out.

We study **scalar** instead of **ralacs** in the rest of the paper in order to be able to define reductions in the "forward" direction, that is with information flowing from S to $\mathcal{R}$. The reader should keep in mind that the constructions based on **scalar** can be achieved in the "reverse" direction by switching S and $\mathcal{R}$ and using **ralacs** instead.

The reader may observe that indeed **scalar** is nothing else but a specific implementation of a primitive known as $2BP$ defined in [BCR86]. In a computational model, a similar idea is implicitly used to solve the problem of computing scalar products in full generality in [GV88]. In [BCR86] it is shown that given any primitive that transfers either b_0, b_1 or any one bit of information about b_0, b_1, it is possible to construct a protocol statistically indistinguishable from $\binom{2}{1}$-OT_2. Since reduction 2.3 enables an adversary to get either b_0, b_1, $b_0 \oplus b_1$ or no information at all (!!), it is clear that we can apply their solution.

Their solution requires a blow up in the number of times the primitive is used. In fact, in order to get a protocol that will be exponentially close to $\binom{2}{1}$-OT_2 (in some parameter s) their approach requires $\Theta(s)$ calls to **scalar**.

Combining the two ideas, the final resulting reduction is

Reduction 2.4 ($\binom{2}{1}$-$OT_2((b_0, b_1), c)$ from scalar)

    1: S chooses random bits $b_0^1, ..., b_0^s$ and $b_1^1, ..., b_1^s$

       such that $\bigoplus_{i=1}^{s} b_0^i = b_0$ and $\bigoplus_{i=1}^{s} b_1^i = b_1$.

    2: S chooses $3s$ random bits $\pi_1, ..., \pi_s, ⓪_0^1, ..., ⓪_0^s, ⓪_1^1, ..., ⓪_1^s$.

    3: $\overset{s}{\underset{i=1}{\text{DO}}}$ IF $\pi_i = 0$ THEN

       execute $a_0^i \leftarrow$ **scalar**$((b_0^i, ⓪_1^i), (\bar{c}, c))$ and $a_1^i \leftarrow$ **scalar**$((⓪_0^i, b_1^i), (\bar{c}, c))$

       ELSE

       execute $a_0^i \leftarrow$ **scalar**$((⓪_0^i, b_1^i), (\bar{c}, c))$ and $a_1^i \leftarrow$ **scalar**$((b_0^i, ⓪_1^i), (\bar{c}, c))$.

    4: S reveals $\pi_1, \pi_2, ..., \pi_s$ to $\mathcal{R}$.

    5: $\mathcal{R}$ computes $out \leftarrow \bigoplus_{i=1}^{s} a_{c \oplus \pi_i}^i$ and outputs out.

Theorem 2.5 *The reduction 2.4 is a correct and statistically private reduction of $\binom{2}{1}$-OT_2 to* **scalar***.*

In other words, if both parties behave honestly then the reduction 2.4 implements a $\binom{2}{1}$-OT_2 using calls to **scalar**. In all cases, S will gain no information whatsoever about $\mathcal{R}$'s input, while $\mathcal{R}$ may learn information about both b_0, b_1 but only with probability 2^{-s}. The formal proof of these statements will appear in the final paper.

3 Achieving $\binom{2}{1}$-OT_2^k from scalar

Assume S and $\mathcal{R}$ have a mean of accomplishing $\binom{2}{1}$-OT_2 and that they wish to perform a $\frac{k}{2}$TO-$\binom{2}{1}$ over the two k-bit strings q_0, q_1. For any string x, let x^i denote the ith bit of x. For a set of indices $I = \{i_1, i_2, ..., i_m\}$, we define x^I to be the concatenation $x^{i_1} x^{i_2} ... x^{i_m}$, the indices taken in increasing order.

As mentioned earlier, there is a reduction from $\binom{2}{1}$-OT_2^k to $\binom{2}{1}$-OT_2, therefore we could apply this reduction to obtain $\binom{2}{1}$-OT_2^k from **scalar**. Unfortunately, this solution will significantly increase the number of call to **scalar** necessary to implement $\binom{2}{1}$-OT_2^k. In [CS] an almost optimal reduction from $\binom{2}{1}$-OT_2^k to $\binom{2}{1}$-OT_2 requires about $9k$ calls to $\binom{2}{1}$-OT_2. If we combine this with our reduction 2.4 we get a total expansion factor in $\Theta(k(s + \log k))$ calls to **scalar** in order to achieve a protocol exponentially close (in s) to $\binom{2}{1}$-OT_2^k. The purpose of this section is to design a better reduction that achieves $\binom{2}{1}$-OT_2^k with only $O(s + k)$ calls to **scalar**.

3.1   Main Tool

Consider a function $f : GF^n(2) \to GF^k(2)$ with the nice property that for every input string x and every I such that $\#I < d$, seeing the bits x^I releases no information about $f(x)$. Let us be more precise about this.

Definition 3.1 A subset $I \subseteq \{1, 2, ..., n\}$ *biases* a function $f : GF^n(2) \to GF^k(2)$ if

$$\exists q_0, q_1, x \; \left[\#\{z | z^I = x^I, \, f(z) = q_0\} \neq \#\{z | z^I = x^I, \, f(z) = q_1\} \right]$$

such an x^I is said to *release information* about $f(x)$.

Definition 3.2 A (n, k, d)-*function* is a function $f : GF^n(2) \to GF^k(2)$ such that

$$\forall I \subseteq \{1, 2, ..., n\}, \#I < d \; [I \text{ does not bias } f].$$

We seek (n, k, d)-*functions* that are easily computable and for which random inverses can be easily computed. If we choose f to be a linear function $f(x) = Mx$ we get that f is an $(n, k, d)-$ *function* if and only if M is the generator matrix of an (n, k, d) binary linear code. The proof of this fact can be found in [BBR88,CGH*85].

Our main idea is the following. To transfer one of q_0, q_1, S picks at random two bit strings x_0, x_1 such that $q_0 = f(x_0)$ and $q_1 = f(x_1)$. Then using the protocol **scalar** the bits of x_0, x_1 are transferred to $\mathcal{R}$ in a way that an honest $\mathcal{R}$ will be able to get exactly x_c and compute $q_c = f(x_c)$, while a cheating $\mathcal{R}$ would get less than d bits of at least one of x_0, x_1 and therefore no information about one of q_0 or q_1.

3.2   New Reduction

First we present a new reduction from $\binom{2}{1}$-OT_2^k to $\binom{2}{1}$-OT_2 that uses the (n, k, d)-functions and from which the reduction from $\binom{2}{1}$-OT_2^k to **scalar** will be deduced. Assume that we define f from a $(n, Rn, \delta n)$ binary linear code, we do the following:

Reduction 3.1 ($\binom{2}{1}$-$OT_2^{Rn}((q_0, q_1), c)$ from $\binom{2}{1}$-OT_2)

1: S finds random x_0, x_1 such that $f(x_0) = q_0$ and $f(x_1) = q_1$.

2: S finds random y_0, y_1 such that $\mid y_0 \mid = \mid y_1 \mid = en$ and such

that $\displaystyle\bigoplus_{m=(i-1)e+1}^{ie} y_0^m = x_0^i$ and $\displaystyle\bigoplus_{m=(i-1)e+1}^{ie} y_1^m = x_1^i$, for $1 \leq i \leq n$.

3: S finds a random permutation σ of $\{1, 2, ..., en\}$.

4: $\displaystyle\mathop{DO}_{i=1}^{en}$ execute $a^i \leftarrow \binom{2}{1}$-$OT_2((y_0^{\sigma(i)}, y_1^{\sigma(i)}), c)$.

5: S reveals σ to $\mathcal{R}$.

6: $\displaystyle\mathop{DO}_{i=1}^{n}$ $\mathcal{R}$ computes $z^i \leftarrow \displaystyle\bigoplus_{m=(i-1)e+1}^{ie} a^{\sigma^{-1}(m)}$.

7: $\mathcal{R}$ computes $out \leftarrow f(z)$ and outputs out.

Theorem 3.3 *If S and $\mathcal{R}$ follow honestly the reduction 3.1 then $\mathcal{R}$'s output value will be q_c.*

Proof. By definition of the y_i's, it is clear that the value of z computed at step 6 is indeed x_c. It follows from the definition of f that the output is therefore correct.

∎

On the other hand, the only significant way $\mathcal{R}$ could cheat this reduction is by using values of c that are not the same all the time at step 4. Name for $1 \leq i \leq en$, c^i the value of c used by $\mathcal{R}$ at step 4. Name c^* the less frequent value among the c^i's. Let

$$\xi_0^i = \begin{cases} 1 & \text{if } \mathcal{R} \text{ got } y_0^{(i-1)e+1}, ..., y_0^{ie} \\ 0 & \text{otherwise} \end{cases}$$

be the indicator random variable of x_0^i (with value 1 if and only if $\mathcal{R}$ can compute x_0^i) and define similarly ξ_1^i. We claim that the expected number of $x_{c^*}^i$ that $\mathcal{R}$ can compute will not exceed δn with very high probability (if e is big enough). This implies that he cannot get any information about q_{c^*}, because f is a $(n, Rn, \delta n)$-function.

Claim 3.4 *If for $\epsilon > 0$ we have $e > -(1 + \epsilon) \log \delta$ then*

$$\text{Prob} \left(\sum_{i=1}^n \xi_{c^*}^i > \delta n \right) < \alpha^n$$

for some constant $0 < \alpha < 1$.

The proof of this claim can be obtain by extension of Chernoff's bound [Chv84].

What we seek now is to minimize the number of $\binom{2}{1}$-OT_2 used. If we start with string of length Rn, this reduction uses en calls to $\binom{2}{1}$-OT_2, thus the expansion factor to be minimized is e/R under the conditions that

- e is a positive integer,

- $e > -(1 + \epsilon) \log \delta$,

- we most be able to obtain a $(n, Rn, \delta n)$ binary linear code.

It is known that a random $Rn \times (1 + \epsilon)n$ binary matrix generates a $((1 + \epsilon)n, Rn, \delta n)$ binary linear code such that $R \approx 1 - H(\delta)$ with probability essentially 1, where $H(x)$ is the entropy function $H(x) = x \log x + (1 - x) \log(1 - x)$ (consult [MS77]).

If we put all these facts together we get that the optimal value occurs around $e = 4$. This leads us to values of $\delta \approx 0.06$ and $R \approx \frac{2}{3}$. Thus a total expansion factor of about $e/R \approx 6$. This is not bad at all considering that the best know reduction from $\binom{2}{1}$-OT_2^k to $\binom{2}{1}$-OT_2 gives an expansion factor of about 5 (consult [CS]). Also, any family of codes with better parameter than those given by the Varshamov-Gilbert curve [MS77] will reduce the ratio e/R even more.

3.3 Switching to scalar

What we described in subsection 3.2 is a technique to perform $\binom{2}{1}$-OT_2^k from $\binom{2}{1}$-OT_2. The reason for this is that we can easily extend the above reduction to a reduction for $\binom{2}{1}$-OT_2^k based on **scalar** with an expansion factor twice bigger. The idea is simply to combine the reductions 3.1 and 2.4.

Reduction 3.2 ($\binom{2}{1}$-$\mathbf{OT}_2^{Rn}((q_0, q_1), c)$ **from scalar**)

1: S finds random x_0, x_1 such that $f(x_0) = q_0$ and $f(x_1) = q_1$.

2: S finds random y_0, y_1 such that $\mid y_0 \mid = \mid y_1 \mid = en$ and such

that $\displaystyle\bigoplus_{m=(i-1)e+1}^{ie} y_0^m = x_0^i$ and $\displaystyle\bigoplus_{m=(i-1)e+1}^{ie} y_1^m = x_1^i$, for $1 \le i \le n$.

3: S finds a random permutation σ of $\{1, 2, ..., en\}$.

4: S chooses $3en$ random bits $\pi_1, ..., \pi_{en}, \textcircled{+}_0^1, ..., \textcircled{+}_0^{en}, \textcircled{+}_1^1, ..., \textcircled{+}_1^{en}$.

5: $\displaystyle\mathop{\mathrm{DO}}_{i=1}^{en}$ IF $\pi_i = 0$ THEN

   run $a_0^i \leftarrow$ **scalar**$((y_0^{\sigma(i)}, \textcircled{+}_1^i), (\bar{c}, c))$ and $a_1^i \leftarrow$ **scalar**$((\textcircled{+}_0^i, y_1^{\sigma(i)}), (\bar{c}, c))$

   ELSE

   run $a_0^i \leftarrow$ **scalar**$((\textcircled{+}_0^i, y_1^{\sigma(i)}), (\bar{c}, c))$ and $a_1^i \leftarrow$ **scalar**$((y_0^{\sigma(i)}, \textcircled{+}_1^i), (\bar{c}, c))$.

6: S reveals σ and $\pi_1, \pi_2, ..., \pi_s$ to $\mathcal{R}$.

7: $\displaystyle\mathop{\mathrm{DO}}_{i=1}^{n}$ $\mathcal{R}$ computes $z^i \leftarrow \displaystyle\bigoplus_{m=(i-1)e+1}^{ie} a_{c \oplus \pi_{\sigma^{-1}(m)}}^{\sigma^{-1}(m)}$.

8: $\mathcal{R}$ computes $out \leftarrow f(z)$ and outputs out.

Without entering into too many details, this reduction is clearly correct by construction. Again in this case the only significant way $\mathcal{R}$ could "cheat" is by using different values of c at step 5. Replacing $\binom{2}{1}$-OT_2 by **scalar** *does not change* the expected number of x_0^i's and x_1^i's received by $\mathcal{R}$. The analysis is therefore the same as for reduction 3.1. The cost of reduction 3.2 in terms of the number of calls to **scalar** is twice the cost of reduction 3.1 in terms of calls to $\binom{2}{1}$-OT_2. This leaves us with a total expansion factor of about 12 for reduction 3.2.

3.4 $\frac{k}{2}$TO-$\binom{2}{1}$ from $\binom{2}{1}$-OT_2

Let's not forget our final goal which was to accomplish a $\frac{k}{2}$TO-$\binom{2}{1}$ with a minimum number of $\binom{2}{1}$-OT_2. The reduction 3.2, when the roles of S and $\mathcal{R}$ are reversed and **ralacs** is used instead of **scalar**, leads us to a solution for $\frac{k}{2}$TO-$\binom{2}{1}$ using roughly $12k$ calls to **ralacs**. Combining with reduction 2.2 we get a correct and statistically private reduction of $\frac{k}{2}$TO-$\binom{2}{1}$ to $\binom{2}{1}$-OT_2 using roughly $24k$ such calls. This compares reasonably with the result in the forward direction using $9k$ calls [CS].

If one wishes to accomplish an approximation to $\frac{k}{2}$TO-$\binom{2}{1}$ where all the probabilities involved may differ of at most 2^{-s}, then running reduction 3.2 to accomplish $\frac{l}{2}$TO-$\binom{2}{1}$, for $l \in O(s + k)$ will reduce all the probabilities below that limit. The initial strings q_0, q_1 of length k can be arbitrarily padded to length l. The total cost in terms in $\binom{2}{1}$-OT_2 will be in $O(s + k)$.

Acknowledgements

We would like to thank Gilles Brassard and Johannes Buchmann, for their help, comments, and support.

References

[BBR88]   C. H. Bennett, G. Brassard, and J.-M. Robert. Privacy amplification by public discussion. *SIAM J. Computing*, 17(2):210–229, April 1988.

[BC91]   G. Brassard and C. Crépeau. Quantum bit commitment and coin tossing protocols. In S. Vanstone, editor, *Advances in Cryptology: Proceedings of Crypto '90*, Springer-Verlag, 1991. to appear.

[BCR86]   G. Brassard, C. Crépeau, and J.-M. Robert. Information theoretic reductions among disclosure problems. In 27th *Symp. of Found. of Computer Sci.*, pages 168–173, IEEE, 1986.

[CGH*85] B. Chor, O. Goldreich, J. Hastad, J. Friedmann, S. Rudich, and R. Smolensky. The bit extraction problem or t-resilient functions. In *Proceedings of the 26th IEEE Symposium on Foundations of Computer Science*, pages 396–407, IEEE, Portland, 1985.

[Chv84]   V. Chvatal. Probabilistic methods in graph theory. *Annals of Operations Research*, 1:171–182, 1984.

[CM91]   C. Crépeau and S. Micali. Secure two-party protocols. 1991. in preparation.

[Cre90]   C. Crépeau. *Correct and Private Reductions among Oblivious Transfers*. PhD thesis, Department of Elec. Eng. and Computer Science, Massachusetts Institute of Technology, 1990. Supervised by Silvio Micali.

[CS]   C. Crépeau and M. Sántha. Efficient reductions among oblivious transfer protocols. submitted to STOC 91.

[EGL83]   S. Even, O. Goldreich, and A. Lempel. A randomized protocol for signing contracts. In R. L. Rivest, A. Sherman, and D. Chaum, editors, *Proceedings CRYPTO 82*, pages 205–210, Plenum Press, New York, 1983.

[GV88]   O. Goldreich and R. Vainish. How to solve any protocol problem-an efficiency improvement (extended abstract). In C. Pomerance, editor, *Advances in Cryptology: Proceedings of Crypto '87*, pages 73–86. Springer-Verlag, 1988.

[MS77]   F.J. MacWilliams and N.J.A. Sloane. *The Theory of Error-Correcting Codes*. North-Holland, 1977.

[OVY91]   R. Ostrovsky, R. Venkatesan, and M. Yung. On the complexity of asymmetric games. In *Proceedings of Sequences '91*, 1991. to appear. This work was first presented at the DIMACS workshop on cryptography, October 1990.

Ziv-Lempel Complexity for Periodic Sequences and its Cryptographic Application

Sibylle Mund
Siemens AG
ZFE IS KOM4
Otto-Hahn-Ring 6
8000 München 83
West Germany

Abstract

The Ziv-Lempel complexity is a well-known complexity measure. In our paper we consider the Ziv-Lempel complexity for periodic sequences as well as for pseudorandom number sequences. Further on, we will look at its crypto-graphic significance and compare it with other complexity measures such as the linear complexity.

1 Introduction

In the last couple of years several different complexity measures were used to examine pseudorandom number sequences in cryptography. Examples for such complexity measures are the linear complexity which is defined in Rueppel [Ruep 86] or the maximal-order complexity which was introduced by Jansen [Jans 89]. Both complexity measures can be used to test pseudorandom number sequences against the qualities of random number sequences has and therefore to distinguish between pseudorandom number sequences with good qualities and those with bad qualities.

Another complexity measure for sequences was defined by Ziv and Lempel in 1976 [Lemp 76]. This complexity measure is a measure of the rate at which new patterns emerge as we move along the sequence. Until now the Ziv-Lempel complexity was mainly used in connection with the Ziv-Lempel algorithm for data compression. In cryptography it was applied by Leung and Tavares [Leun 85] for testing block ciphers. In his PhD. thesis [Wan 88] M. Wang mentions some of the properties of the Ziv-Lempel complexity which are also part of the work in this paper but he does not prove this properties.

In our paper we will consider minimal and maximal values of the Ziv-Lempel complexity. After that we will have a closer look at the Ziv-Lempel complexity for periodic pseudorandom number sequences. Particularly, we will see that the Ziv-Lempel complexity of these sequences depends on the start position s_j where the computation of the complexity has started and that the Ziv-Lempel complexity for such a sequence has a constant value after maximal $2p - 1$ positions of the sequence have been considered (p denotes the period of the sequence). After that we will consider the Ziv-Lempel complexity for arbitrary pseudorandom number sequences. Finally, the Ziv-Lempel complexity will be compared with other well-known cryptographic complexity measures such as the linear complexity or the maximal-order complexity. Here, we will mainly consider the question whether it is necessary to examine pseudorandom number sequences using the Ziv-Lempel complexity or whether it is enough to use only the linear complexity.

2 Definition and Computation of the Ziv-Lempel complexity

As we mentioned above Ziv and Lempel introduced a complexity measure for finite sequences in 1976. Intuitively, this complexity is a measure of the rate at which new patterns emerge as we move along the sequence. We refer the reader to [Lem 76] for the formal description. In this paper we will only provide a short description as it is given in [Ziv 78].

Let $S = s_1...s_n$ be a sequence of length n then the following rules can be used to obtain the Ziv-Lempel complexity of the sequence S:

1) A slash is inserted following s_1

2) Assume that the i-th slash comes after the letter s_{k_i}, $1 \leq k_i \leq n - 1$. The next slash will be inserted after the letter $s_{k_{i+1}}$ where $k_{i+1} = k_i + L_i + 1 \leq n$ and L_i is the maximal length of a substring $s_{k_i+1}...s_{k_i+L_i}$ such that there exists an integer p_i (where $1 \leq p_i \leq k_i$) for which $s_{p_i}...s_{p_i+L_i-1} = s_{k_i+1}...s_{k_i+L_i}$.

If s_n is followed by a slash the Ziv-Lempel complexity is equal to the number of slashes, otherwise the Ziv-Lempel complexity is equal to the number of slashes plus one.

To illustrate the mechanism for the computation of the Ziv-Lempel complexity we will use the following example: let $X = 1001101110000111$ be a binary sequence then we can insert slashes into the sequence X using the two rules and we will obtain the sequence X with the following partition $X = 1|0|01|101|1100|00111|$. X is now devided into six patterns and therefore the Ziv-Lempel complexity C for the sequence X is equal to 6.

In the next step we will present an algorithm for the computation of the Ziv-Lempel complexity. To compute the Ziv-Lempel complexity we have to define an algorithm for the execution of rule 2. Rule 2 can be executed using the following two steps:

a) Initialization: Let $n + 1$ be the sequence position where the computation of a new pattern starts, let J contain all positions j for which $s_j = s_{n+1}$ $(1 \leq j \leq n)$ and let $l = 2$.

b) Repeat the following step until J is empty: delete all $j \in J$ for which $s_{j+l-1} \neq s_{n+l}$ and increase l by 1 if J is not empty. Otherwise l is the length of the new pattern which is defined by $s_{n+1}...s_{n+l}$.

These two steps enable us to compute the patterns of a sequence S and therefore also the Ziv-Lempel complexity of the sequence.

To improve the computational complexity of the computation of the Ziv-Lempel complexity pattern recognition algorithms such as the algorithm of Blumer, Blumer, Ehrenfeucht, Haussler and McConnel [Blu 83] can be used.

3 Minimal and Maximal value of the Ziv-Lempel complexity

In this section we consider a binary sequence $S = s_1..s_n$ of length n which consists of k ones and n - k zeros $(0 \leq k \leq n)$. Our aim is to examine the minimal resp. maximal value of the Ziv-Lempel complexity of this sequence.

For the minimal value of the Ziv-Lempel complexity we obtain the following Theorem.

Theorem 1: The minimal value of the Ziv-Lempel complexity C_{min} of a sequence $S = s_1...s_n$ is

$$C_{min} = \begin{cases} 2 & \text{if } k = 0 \text{ or } k = 1 \text{ or } k = n \text{ or } k = n-1 \\ \\ 3 & \text{in all the other cases} \end{cases}$$

Proof: Computing the Ziv-Lempel complexity for a sequence S we have to use s_1 as the first pattern. To get now a minimal Ziv-Lempel complexity $C_{min} = 2$ we have to use $s_2...s_n$ as a second pattern. This is only possible if the positions s_j, $2 \leq j \leq n-1$, have the same value as position s_1. If the value of position of s_n is different to the value of position s_1 we get an unique pattern $s_2...s_n$, otherwise the pattern will not be unique. Depending on the way how s_1 was chosen there will be $k = 0, k = 1, k = n-1$ or $k = n$ ones in the sequence.

For any other choice of k at least three patterns have to be used to get the Ziv-Lempel complexity of the sequence and therefore the possible minimal value of the Ziv-Lempel complexity C_{min} is 3. To obtain now a sequence with minimal Ziv-Lempel complexity the sequence can be constructed in the following way: Under the assumption that s_1 is equal to 1 the first pattern p_1 is again equal to s_1, the second pattern p_2 is equal to a $(k-1)$-times repetition of p_1 followed by the inverse value of p_1 and the third pattern p_3 consists only of a $(n - k)$-times repetition of the inverse value of p_1. If s_1 is equal to 0 the same procedure can be done but p_2 contains then $(n - k - 1)$ repetitions of p_1 and p_3 $(k -1)$. This is only one principle to construct such sequences. It is also possible to have one 1 as value of the final position of pattern p_3 and therefore to reduce the numbers of ones in pattern p_2 by 1. The same principle can also be applied to the zeroes, if the sequence starts with a zero. ∎

For a further construction principle of sequences with C_{min} = 3 let l_1 = 1 be the length of pattern p_1, l_2 the length of pattern p_2 and l_3 = $n - l_1 - l_2$ the length of pattern p_3 and $k < n/2$. Furthermore let p_1 = 0, p_2 = 0...01 and p_3 be a repetition of the final l positions of p_2 for $(m -1)$-times followed by zeros or for $(m - 2)$-times where the last position has the value 1, then we obtain additional sequences with C_{min} = 3 if for l_1, l_2 and l_3 the following equation holds:

$$(m - 2) \cdot l + 1 \leqq n - l_1 - l_2 \leqq m \cdot l, \qquad l \leqq l_2$$

The following sequences are examples which are constructed using these three principles:

S = 11.....10 which has Ziv-Lempel complexity C = 2.
S = 11...100...0 which has Ziv-Lempel complexity C = 3.
S = 00...011..10 which has the Ziv-Lempel complexity C = 3.
S = 000...001001....00100 which has the Ziv-Lempel complexity C = 3.

After having considered the minimal value of the Ziv-Lempel complexity for a sequence S, in a next step we will now examine its maximal value.

Whereas it is possible to make some assumptions about the minimal value of the Ziv-Lempel complexity for any k, $1 \leqq k \leqq n$, this is not possible in the case of the maximal value of the Ziv-Lempel complexity. Here we can only give the maximal value of the Ziv-Lempel complexity for some certain values of k.

Lemma 1: Let n be the sequence length and

$$n = \sum_{\substack{i = 0 \\ i \text{ even}}}^{k} l_i + l_{i + 1} + r \quad (1)$$

with $l_0 = l_1 = 1$, $l_i = l_{i-2} + l_{i-1}$ and $l_{i + 1} = l_{i-2} + l_{i-1} + 1$ for $2 \leqq i \leqq k$ and $0 \leqq r < l_{k + 2} + l_{k + 3}$ then the maximal value of the Ziv-Lempel complexity C_{max} is

$$C_{max} = \begin{cases} k & \text{for} \quad r = 0 \\ k + 1 & \text{for} \quad 1 \leq r \leq l_{k+2} \\ k + 2 & \text{for} \quad l_{k+2} \leq r \leq l_{k+2} + l_{k+3} \end{cases}$$

if the number of ones or zeros in the sequence is equal to $k/2$.

Proof: Using formula (1) we get a construction criterion for a sequence of length n which contains $k/2$ ones and has Ziv-Lempel complexity C_{max}. If the patterns p_i (i even) of length l_i only consist of zeros and the patterns p_{i+1} of length l_{i+1} have the form 00..001, then each of these patterns defines a unique pattern as it is necessary to get the Ziv-Lempel complexity and the Ziv-Lempel complexity of the sequence is equal to C_{max}.

It is not possible to obtain a Ziv-Lempel complexity C which is greater than C_{max} under the assumption that the sequence length is equal to n and that the number of ones which the sequence contains is equal to $k/2$; because the number of patterns used to compute the Ziv-Lempel complexity will be maximal if each one appears in a different pattern and if each of the patterns containing a single one is followed by a pattern containing no one. After the rules for the construction of the patterns a pattern containing no one has to be followed by a pattern containing a single one and therefore it is not possible to have more than k patterns without a single one. ∎

If the number of ones in the sequence is less than $k/2$ the maximal Ziv-Lempel complexity can be obtained using the same construction method.

4 Ziv-Lempel complexity for periodic sequences

In this section we consider the Ziv-Lempel complexity for periodic sequences $s_1...s_{p-1}s_p s_{p+1}...$ where p is the period of the sequence and $s_{p+i} = s_i$ for $0 < i \leq p$. This type of sequence is often generated by pseudorandom number generators but can also be obtained if we consider message files which consist of a repetition of one message for a certain number of times. In our theorems we will obtain the maximal length l of a periodic sequence which is needed to compute the Ziv-Lempel complexity for the sequence of any length greater than l.

In the following we will start with the consideration of a special case of sequences and then continue our examination with the general case of periodic sequences. We assume for our first theorem that the sequence $s_1....s_p$ has Ziv-Lempel complexity C and the sequence $s_1....s_{p+1}$ has Ziv-Lempel complexity C + 1. Using this condition we see that one period of the sequence finishes with a complete pattern as it is defined by the Ziv-Lempel complexity. Then we obtain the following theorem.

Lemma 2: If S is a periodic sequence where $s_1...s_p$ has the Ziv-Lempel complexity C and $s_1...s_{p+1}$ has the Ziv-Lempel complexity C + 1 then for $l \geq q = p + 1$, the sequence $s_1...s_l$ will have the Ziv-Lempel complexity C + 1.

Proof: Because of the period of the sequence s_{p+i} has the same value as s_i for $i \geq 1$ and because of the start of a new pattern at position p + 1 the pattern given by $s_{p+1}...s_{p+j}$ can allways be found as $s_1...s_j$ for $j \geq 1$ in the sequence. Therefore for any $j \geq 1$ the increase of j by one does not define a new pattern and therfore the Ziv-Lempel complexity can never be greater than C + 1 for $j \geq 1.$ ∎

Now we will consider the more general case where it is only known that the sequence S has a period p.

Lemma 3: If S is a sequence with period p, Ziv-Lempel complexity C for $s_1...s_{p-k}$ and Ziv-Lempel complexity C + 1 for $s_1...s_{p+1}$ then there exists a q such that the sequence $s_1...s_j$ has the Ziv-Lempel complexity C + 1 for $p - k < j \leq q$ and the Ziv-Lempel complexity C + 2 for $j > q$. $(k > 0)$

Proof: Because of the period of the sequence the pattern starting at position p - k + 1 cannot be of infinite length. Therefore a position q = p + l must exist in such a way that $s_{p-k+1}...s_{p+l}$ defines a unique pattern. All sequences $s_1...s_j$ have the same Ziv-Lempel complexity C + 1 for $p - k + 1 \leq j \leq p + l = q$.

Because of the period of the sequence the pattern starting at position p + l + 1 can also be found with starting position l + 1. Because of the periodicity of the sequences this is true for every pattern length $j \geq 1$. Therefore all these sequences have the same Ziv-Lempel complexity C + 2. ∎

In our next two lemmas we will determine a maximum for the pattern length of the pattern $s_{p-k+1}...s_{p+l}$ and using this maximum we can provide an upper bound of the sequence length which has to be examined in the case of periodic sequences to obtain the Ziv-Lempel complexity of the sequence.

Lemma 4: Using the assumptions of lemma 2 the maximum length m for the pattern $s_{p-k+1}...s_{p+l}$ is p - k.

Proof: The following equitation has to be true to obtain a pattern

$$s_{p-k+1} \neq s_{j+1}$$

and

$$s_{p-k+m} = s_{j+m} \quad \text{for } 0 < m < l$$

where j is called the starting point of the existing pattern $s_j...s_l$. Now let us assume $l > p - k$ then we obtain the following additional equation

$$s_{j+l} = s_{j+l-p+k}$$

which itself provides us a new equation

$$s_{j+l-p+k} = s_{p+j+l-p+k} = s_{j+l+k}$$

because of the period p of the sequence. Starting with s_{j+l+k} we obtain

$$s_{j+l+k} = s_{j+l-p+k+k} = s_{p+j+l-p+2k} = s_{2j+2k+l}$$

Continuing this chain we obtain

$$s_{j+k+l} = s_{2j+2k+l} = \cdots = s_{xj+xk+l} \qquad \text{for } x > 0$$

Now we have to consider

$$s_{p-k+l} \neq s_{xj+xk+l}$$

In a first step we will show that for fixed $l > p - k$ and certain choices of j and k the two values are equal and therefore it is not possible to have a pattern length $l > p - k$. For simplification let us only write i when we actually mean s_i.

$$p - k + l = xj + xk + l$$

If for some $y > 0, \underline{x} > 0$:

$$yp - k + l = \underline{x}j + \underline{x}k + l$$

because we have a periodic function. We obtain now

$$yp = \underline{x}j + (\underline{x} + 1)k \leftrightarrow \underline{x} = (yp - k)/(j * k) \qquad (1.1)$$

So if there exists y for p and k such that the value of the fraction (1.1) is an integer, $p - k + l$ can never be chosen different from $j + l$, and therefore it is not possible to have a pattern length greater than $p - k$.

Let us now consider the case in which (1.1) has no integer solution. Because of the definition of the Ziv-Lempel complexity and the period of the sequence we get the following additional equitations:

$$s_1 = s_{p+1} = s_{j+k+1} = s_{p+j+k+1} = s_{2j+2k+1} = \cdots = s_{xj+xk+1}$$

$$s_2 = s_{p+2} = s_{j+k+2} = \cdots = s_{xj+xk+2}$$

Continuation leads to

$$s_{k+j} = s_{p+k+j} = s_{j+j+k+k} = \cdots = s_{xj+xk}$$

$$s_{k+j+1} = s_{p+k+j+1} = s_{j+j+k+k+1} = \cdots = s_{xj+xk+1}$$

therefore we would only obtain a sequence with period $j + k$ instead of period p. It is not possible to have a patternlength $l > p - k$ and period p. ∎

Lemma 5: $q \leq 2p - 2$ under the assumption made in lemma 3.

Proof: Follows from lemma 3 using $k = 1$ which is the maximum pattern length l. ∎

Now we examine at which position j the pattern $s_{p-k+1}...s_{p+l}$ starts in the part $s_1...s_{p+k}$ of the sequence. We see, the number of j's will be limited and will depend on the value of k and the length of the pattern l.

Lemma 6: Using the assumption made in lemma 3 for fixed k and $l \leq p - k$, j has to be chosen in such a way that $j + l \leq p - k$.

Proof: The same proof construction as in lemma 3 can be used if the assumption $l > p - k$ is replaced by the assumption $j + l > p - k$. ∎

Using lemma 5 we get the number of sequences with period p and $q = 2p - 2$. For $l = p - k = p - 1$, j has to be equal to 0 and therefore we can obtain exactly 2 sequences for this condition:

$$S1 = 0|0...01|00...0|10 \quad \text{where the 1 is at position } p - 1$$

$$S2 = 1|1...10|11...1|01 \quad \text{where the 0 is at position } p - 1$$

S2 is the complement sequence to S1. For both sequences C is equal to 3.

Theorem 2: In a sequence with period p the Ziv-Lempel complexity C has a constant value after maximal $2p - 1$ positions of the sequence have been considered.

Proof: Follows immediately from lemma 1 - 5. ∎

Theorem 2 shows that it is sufficient to use $2p - 1$ positions of a periodic sequence for the computation of the Ziv-Lempel complexity.

We will now undertake a closer examination of the starting points for the computation of the Ziv-Lempel complexity. We will see that the Ziv-Lempel complexity for a periodic sequence depends on the starting point and that therefore we can obtain different values for the Ziv-Lempel complexity for different starting points.

Lemma 7: Let S be a periodic sequence with period p, let C_1 be the Ziv-Lempel complexity of the sequence computed with start position s_i and C_2 be the Ziv-Lempel complexity of the sequence computed with start position s_{i+1} then C_1 and C_2 can be different.

Proof: In our proof we show only one possible situation where C_1 and C_2 will be different. Let S_1 be the periodic sequence used to compute C1 with $s_1 \neq s_2$ and $s_2 = s_3$, then we obtain a pattern $p_1 = s_1$, a pattern $p_2 = s_2$ and further patterns p_i for which we assume that $p_i = s_i...s_{i+k}$ and $s_i...s_{i+k-1}$ is equal $s_j...s_{j+k-1}$ for $j > 1$ ($i > 2$, $k > 0$) or in words no pattern should be built using a already existing pattern starting at position 1 of the sequence S_1. C_2 will now be computed using starting position s_2.Therefore we loose the pattern $p_1 = s_1$. Under the assumption that for the last limited pattern of S_1 $p_{C_1-1} = s_{p-k}\cdot ...s_{p+j}$ a similar pattern can be found in S_2 which has the form $s_{p-k-1}\cdot ...s_p s_{p+1}...s_{p+j}$

$(k, j, \underline{i} > 0)$. We actually reduce the number of patterns in S_2 by one because we lost the inital pattern p_1. Therefore the Ziv-Lempel complexity C_2 is equal to $C_1 - 1$ and therefore C_2 is not equal to C_1.∎

This result shows us a great difference between the behaviour of the Ziv-Lempel complexity and of other complexity measures such as the linear complexity for sequences or the maximum order complexity.

Now we will look at the Ziv-Lempel complexity values C_i computed for a periodic sequence where C_i is computed using start position s_i $(1 \leq i < p)$. We see that the values C_i are distributed around the average value $\underline{C} = 1/n \, (C_1 + \ldots + C_{p-1})$. Examing the value C_i we get with the highest probability the value $\underline{C}$ and with exponentially decreasing probabilities the complexity values $\underline{C} - j$ and $\underline{C} + j$ $(j > 0)$. We also see that $\underline{C} - j$ is bounded by a value C_{min} called minimal Ziv-Lempel complexity of the periodic sequence and $\underline{C} + j$ by a value C_{max} called maximal Ziv-Lempel complexity of the periodic sequence. Having $\underline{C}$ fixed C_{min} and C_{max} will also be fixed because of the structure of the sequence defined by C.

5 Ziv-Lempel complexity for binary pseudorandom number sequences

The Ziv-Lempel complexity can be used to examine pseudorandom number sequences. In the following let us assume $p(s_j = 1) = p(s_j = 0) = 0.5$.

In a first step we will examine the average length of a pattern which starts at position s_{n+1}.

Lemma 8: Under the assumption that each position of the sequence can be computed independently of any previous position the average length of a pattern starting at position s_{n+1} is $p_a = \lfloor \log_2 n \rfloor + k$ where $\lfloor x \rfloor$ denotes the integer part of x and k is equal to $k = ((1 - c_0 \cdot 1 + c_0 \cdot 2^{-1} \cdot 2 + c_0 \cdot 2^{-2} \cdot 3 + \ldots) / (1 - c_0 + c_0 \cdot 2^{-1} + c_0 \cdot 2^{-2} + \ldots)$ and c_0 can be computed using the following formula: $c_0 = n$; for $j = 1$ to $\lfloor \log_2 n \rfloor + 1$ do $c_0 = c_0 / 2$.

Proof: The average length of a pattern is equal to the number of steps which are needed on average until the set J is empty. Under the assumption that the probability $p(s_j = 1) = p(s_j = 0) = 0.5$ we obtain on average $n/2$ values $j \in J$ in step a) of the algorithm given in section 2. As long as there are 2 or more elementes in J in step b) of this algorithm the number of j's $\in$ J will be halved on average if I is increased by 1. This is the case for $\lfloor \log_2 n \rfloor$ steps. If J contains for the first time less than two positions a new pattern exists in a certain number of cases. The number is $1 - c_0$ where c_0 is computed by the formula given above. After that in each round r we will obtain new patterns with length $\lfloor \log 2 n \rfloor + r + 1$ in $c_0 \cdot 2^{-r}$ cases where $0 < r$. On average k rounds are needed until a new pattern is obtained. Therefore the pattern length of the new pattern starting at position $n + 1$ will have on average the length $\lfloor \log_2 n \rfloor + k$. ∎

Remark: $2 \leq k < 3$

For $n = 2^{-m} (0 < m)$ we obtain $c_0 = 0.5$ and therefore $(\sum\limits_{k=1}^{\infty} 2^{-k} \cdot k) / \sum\limits_{k=1}^{\infty} 2^{-k}$

If $c_o \rightarrow 0$ we obtain $\lim ((1-c_0) \cdot 1 + c_0 \cdot 2^{-1} \cdot 2 + c_0 \cdot 2^{-2} \cdot 3 + ...) / (1 - c_0 + c_0 \cdot 2^{-1}$

$+ c_0 \cdot 2^{-2} + ...) = (\sum\limits_{k=1}^{\infty} 2^{-k} \cdot (k+1)) / \sum\limits_{k=1}^{\infty} 2^{-k} = 3$

Having an estimation of the average pattern length for a pattern starting at position j, $1 \leq j \leq n$ we can now give an estimation of the average Ziv-Lempel complexity Ca for a sequence of length n under the assumption that each pattern of the sequence is computed independently of the former patterns. The estimation can be given using the following induction:

1) For $j := 1$: $C_a := 1$ and $j_0 := 1$
2) For $j := 2...n$: if $j = j_0 + \lfloor \log_2 j_0 \rfloor + k$ then $C_a := C_a + 1$ and $j_0 := j$

Both measures the Ziv-Lempel complexity C_a and the pattern length pa can be used to examine pseudorandom number sequences. We would expect that a good pseudorandom number sequence has a Ziv-Lempel complexity which is close to the value C_a and that each pattern of the sequence has a length p_i which is close to the corresponding p_{a_i}. If the Ziv-Lempel complexity of the sequence is much smaller than the Ziv-Lempel complexity C_a then the sequence will have at least one multiple repetition of a sequence pattern and therefore there exists at least one pattern length p_i such that p_i is much greater than p_{a_i}. The pattern i will be a repetition of already existing patterns. This should be avoided for two reasons:

1) Often the pattern i might repeat a pattern which does not include the same number of ones and zeros for several times and therefore the ones and zeros might locally not be randomly distributed with $p(s_j = 1) = p(s_j = 0) = 0.5$

2) The multiple repetition of a pattern can also be a disadvantage if the pseudorandom number sequence is used in a stream cipher. If not only the pseudorandom number sequence has a multiple repetition of patterns but also the plaintext, the corresponding ciphertext might also have a multiple repetition of patterns.

Therefore the pattern length p_i and the Ziv-Lempel complexity can be used to indicate pseudorandom number sequences which are not desirable.

124

6 Ziv-Lempel complexity and other cryptographic complexity measures

In this paper we only want to compare the Ziv-Lempel complexity with the linear complexity. A comparision of the Ziv-Lempel complexity with the maximal-order complexity would have a similar effect.

Looking only at the linear complexity we see the sequence can have a great linear complexity which is suitable but on the other side the same sequence can have a small value for the Ziv-Lempel complexity which is not desirable. An example would be the sequence $S = 00...001$. Therefore the value for the linear complexity alone does not say much about the quality of the sequence. But considering also the Ziv-Lempel complexity for this kind of sequences the value for the Ziv-Lempel complexity will be close to the minimal Ziv-Lempel complexity and therefore the sequence would not be suitable.

If the linear complexity profile is considered instead of the linear complexity we obtain much better statements about the quality of the sequence and the Ziv-Lempel complexity can be seen as an additional measure providing us with some more information about repetitions of patterns in the sequence. Particularly, the Ziv-Lempel complexity can be used to detect repetitions of patterns.

Let us now consider the case of R repetitions of a pattern in the sequence $S = s_1...s_k$ and let us define the complexity length for the linear complexity. If s_i is the first position in the sequence with linear complexity C_i and if s_j is the first position with linear complexity $C_i + 1$ then $j - i$ will be considered as the complexity length.

Now we consider a sequence $S = s_1...s_k$ which has the following Ziv-Lempel complexity $S = s_1|s_2...|s_i...s_k|$ where $s_i...s_k$ consists of $R > 1$ repetitions of a pattern $s_j...s_{i-1}$ where $1 \leq j \leq i - 1$. Let us consider the linear complexity and therefore the complexity length of this sequence. If $s_i...s_k$ is equal to $s_1...s_{i-1} s_1...s_{i-1}...s_1...s_{i-1}s_k$ then there exists an $\underline{i}$ where $i < \underline{i} < 2i$ according to the well-known results for the linear complexity in periodic sequences such that the linear complexity C_l is the same for $s_1...s_j$, $\underline{i} \leq j \leq k$. The complexity length $k - \underline{i}$ will then indicate that there is an unregularity in the sequence because $k - \underline{i}$ will be large in comparision to the other complexity lergths in the squence.

If $s_i...s_k$ is equal to $s_j...s_{i-1}s_j...s_{i-1}...s_j...s_{i-1}...s_k$ then the theorems about periodic sequences and the linear complexity canot be used and the linear complexity for the sequence $s_1...s_k$ will normally increase in such a form that there is no indication that the pattern $s_j...s_{i-1}$ is repeated for R times.

Considering these two cases we see the linear complexity and the complexity length alone are not enough to discover all kinds of repetitions of patterns which are possible in a sequence. Therefore we need an additional complexity measure which enables us to detect other kind of repetitions of patterns which do not influence the linear complexity. The Ziv-Lempel complexity together with the pattern length can be used as such a complexity measure.

7 Conclusions

In cryptanalysis it should be possible to use a complexity measure for several different tasks such as the examination of pseudorandom number sequences or the identification of a period in a sequence. Therefore it is necessary to determine requirements which help to identify complexity measures which are good for all these different tasks. In the following we will present four points which we think a complexity measure should fullfil:

1) Indication and identification of a period in a sequence: The complexity measure should be able to detect a period in a sequence and to identify its starting point and its length.

2) Independence of the complexity value in a periodic sequence from the position where the computation had started: If in a periodic sequence the complexity value is computed using different start positions, the result should be the same after a certain number of positions had been considered.

3) Examination of pseudorandom number sequences: It should be possible to use the complexity measure to examine pseudorandom number sequences and to compare the results against results obtained from random sequences.

4) Computation of the sequence: Knowing the complexity of the sequence it should be possible in an easy and efficient way to compute the sequence.

If we now look at the Ziv-Lempel complexity and compare our results with this four points we see that the Ziv-Lempel complexity fullfils some of these points but that there are still some points with great difficulties. For example, the Ziv-Lempel complexity does not fullfil points 2) and 4). However, the Ziv-Lempel complexity can be used to indicate a period in a sequence and it can be used to examine pseudorandom number sequences. Here there are still some problems to be solved because it is far from clear how the distribution of Ziv-Lempel complexity behaves for a certain sequence length.Therefore, additional examinations of the Ziv-Lempel complexity measure in cryptography are necessary.

Nevertheless, the Ziv-Lempel complexity is usefull in cryptography because as it is shown in section 6, it can detect weaknesses in a sequence which can not be detected by the linear complexity.

8 References

[Blu 83]   A. Blumer, J. Blumer, A. Ehrenfeucht, D. Haussler, R. McConnel: Linear Size Finite Automata for the Set of all Subwords of a Word, An Outline of Results, Bul. Eur. Assoc. Theor. Comp. Sci., No. 21, 1983, pp. 12-20

[Jans 89]   C. Jansen: Investigations On Nonlinear Streamcipher Systems: Construction and Evaluation Methods, PhD. Thesis

[Lemp 76]   A. Lempel, J. Ziv: On the Complexity of Finite Sequences, IEEE Transaction on Information Theory, IT-22, No.1

[Leun 85]   A. Leung, S. Tavares: Sequence Complexity as aTest for Cryptographic Systems, Advances in Cryptology - Crypto 84, lecture Notes in Computer Science, springer Verlag, Heidelberg, 1985

[Ruep 86]   R. Rueppel: Analysis and Design of Stream Ciphers, Springer Verlag, Berlin, 1986

[Wan 88]   M. Wang: Cryptographic Aspects of Sequence Complexity Measures, PhD. Thesis, ETH Zürich, 1988

[Ziv 78]   J. Ziv: Coding Theorems for Individual Sequences, IEEE Transaaction on Information Theory, IT-24, No. 4

A Secret Key Cryptosystem by Iterating a Chaotic Map

Toshiki Habutsu

Yoshifumi Nishio

Iwao Sasase

Shinsaku Mori

Department of Electrical Engineering, Keio University

3-14-1 Hiyoshi, Kohoku-ku, Yokohama 223 JAPAN

Tel. +81-45-563-1141 Ext. 3319

Fax. +81-45-563-3421

Abstract

Chaos is introduced to cryptology. As an example of the applications, a secret key cryptosystem by iterating a one dimensional chaotic map is proposed. This system is based on the characteristics of chaos, which are sensitivity of parameters, sensitivity of initial points, and randomness of sequences obtained by iterating a chaotic map. A ciphertext is obtained by the iteration of a inverse chaotic map from an initial point, which denotes a plaintext. If the times of the iteration is large enough, the randomness of the encryption and the decryption function is so large that attackers cannot break this cryptosystem by statistic characteristics. In addition to the security of the statistical point, even if the cryptosystem is composed by a tent map, which is one of the simplest chaotic maps, setting a finite computation size avoids a ciphertext only attack. The most attractive point of the cryptosystem is that the cryptosystem is composed by only iterating a simple calculations though the information rate of the cryptosystem is about 0.5.

1 Introduction

Random oscillation of the solutions in deterministic systems described as differential or difference equations, is called chaos [1]. Recently many types of chaos-generating systems have been proposed and analyzed in various fields. Especially, chaotic behavior of solutions in some types of one-dimensional difference equations

$$X_{n+1} = F(X_n) \qquad X_n \in [0, 1] \tag{1}$$

is investigated in detail [2]. One-dimensional discrete maps F generating chaotic solutions are called chaotic maps.

Chaotic solutions have the following features.

1. Sensitivity of parameters. – If a parameter (the shape of F) varies slightly, two sequences obtained from repeated calculations on a chaotic map from an initial point, eventually become quite different.

2. Sensitivity of initial points. – If an initial point X_0 varies slightly, two sequences obtained from repeated calculations on a chaotic map with a parameter, eventually become quite different.

3. Randomness. – Solutions starting from almost all X_0 in $[0,1]$ wander in $[0,1]$ at random and their distribution is uniform.

Therefore, if one doesn't know both the exact parameter and the exact initial point, he cannot expect the motion of the chaotic solution.

In this paper, we propose a secret key cryptosystem by iterating a one-dimensional map F generating chaos. This system is based on repeated calculations on a chaotic map as $X_n = F^n(X_0)$. We use the parameter α of the map for a secret key, and a point p in an interval $[0,1]$ for plaintext. Encryption function is n-times composite of F^{-1} and decryption function is n-times composite of F. Therefore, encryption and decryption are achieved by only repeating a very simple calculation.

Generally, because F is m to one map, one plaintext has m^n ciphertexts and any one of m^n ciphertexts can be deciphered only using the secret key. Therefore, senders can select the ciphertexts by any arbitrary random generator. We determine the parameter sizes to prevent statistic attacks. If the times of composite is large enough, it is expected that ciphertext variations act at random and are independent of key variations, because of the characteristics of chaotic maps.

We also discuss about a ciphertext only attack. In the following section, we explain our cryptosystem by iterating a tent map. Although tent map has linearity, we can prevent the ciphertext only attack from breaking our cryptosystem by setting finite computation size.

2 A Secret Key Cryptosystem by Iterating a Tent Map

In this section, we explain our cryptosystem. As an example of chaotic maps, we use tent map which is one of the most popular and the simplest chaotic maps.

2.1 Preliminaries

Tent map is a one-dimensional and piecewise linear map. Figures 1(a) and 1(b) show a tent map and its inverse map. These maps transform an interval $[0,1]$ onto itself and contain only one parameter α, which represents the location of the top of the tent. These maps are described as follows.

$$F : \begin{cases} X_{k+1} = \dfrac{X_k}{\alpha} & (0 \le X_k \le \alpha) \\ X_{k+1} = \dfrac{X_k - 1}{\alpha - 1} & (\alpha < X_k \le 1). \end{cases} \tag{2}$$

$$F^{-1} : \begin{cases} X_{k-1} = \alpha X_k \\ \quad\text{or} \\ X_{k-1} = (\alpha - 1)X_k + 1. \end{cases} \tag{3}$$

Sequences calculated from arbitrary initial point with iterating F act chaotically because the function F is expansionary everywhere in the interval $[0,1]$. Such the sequences obtained by iterating a tent map distribute in uniform $U(0,1)$ [3].

F is two to one map and F^{-1} is one to two map. Therefore, F^n is 2^n to one map and F^{-n} is one to 2^n map. Since $X = F(F^{-1}(X))$ is always satisfied, $X = F^n(F^{-n}(X))$ is also satisfied.

2.2 Cryptosystem

(1) Secret Key

A parameter α denotes a secret key. If a sender and a receiver have a secret key, they are able to calculate the function F accurately.

(2) Encryption

i) — Set an initial point as a plaintext p, where $0 < p < 1$.

ii) — Calculate n-times composite of the inverse map $F^{-n}(p)$ by calculating F^{-1} repeatedly.

$$C = F^{-1}(F^{-1}(\cdots F^{-1}(p) \cdots)) = F^{-n}(p). \tag{4}$$

On each calculation, select one of two equations of F^{-1} in eq. (3) in any arbitrary way. This means that one plaintext has 2^n ciphertexts and one of 2^n ciphertexts is sent to the receiver. Finally, send the value C to the receiver.

(3) Decryption

Calculate n-times composite of the map $F^n(C)$ by calculating F repeatedly and recover the plaintext p.

$$p = F(F(\cdots F(C) \cdots)) = F^n(C) = F^n(F^{-n}(p)). \tag{5}$$

Note that only α is required for this computation. The information about which of two equations is used for each encryption process (F^{-1}), is not necessary for the decryption process. Any one of 2^n ciphertexts, even when the coin-flipping is used in the encryption process, is deciphered without fail.

Figure 2 visualizes an encryption and a decryption. Firstly, a sender sets an initial point p as a plaintext. On the first step of the encryption, he chooses right or left. If he chooses right, p is mapped to X^{-1} in the figure. The sender repeats this n times. The receiver only has to do is to trace inversely. The plaintext p which is exactly equal to α, is not a singular point. It is easy to confirm that the plaintext is enciphered similar to another plain texts: simply choose right or left side as the other plaintexts.

The encryption and the decryption are achieved by repeating a simple calculation. They require n times multiplications. On the each calculation, it is necessary to set a computation size. There are two reasons to set it. The first reason is that memory size of computer is finite. The second reason is about security of our cryptosystem. Because tent map is piecewise linear, our cryptosystem also has linearity. If ciphertext is described with the whole size digits, there exists a ciphertext only attack to our cryptosystem because of its linearity. We discuss about this problem in the following section.

3 Discussions

In this section, we discuss about the security and performances of our cryptosystem. Firstly, we determine the size of the parameters to prevent statistical attack and step-by-step attack. Secondly, we discuss about the size of ciphertexts to prevent failing decryption. Thirdly, we discuss about the ciphertext only attack. And finally, we discuss about the other chaotic maps to increase the security.

3.1 Requirements of the Parameters

3.1.1 Secret Key and Plaintext Size

Figures 3(a) and 3(b) show the distribution of the ciphertexts for different parameters. When α is close to 0, the distribution of ciphertexts is narrow as in figure 3(a) and eavesdroppers have larger probability of the achievement of attacking the key. Similarly, α must not be near 1. However when α is around 0.5 as in figure 3(b), the distribution of the ciphertexts is uniform enough. Therefore, we assume that α should be between 0.4 and 0.6.

The key space size and the plaintext size are required 64 bits against step-by-step attack. If they are described with 20 digits, both of the key space size and the plaintext size are about 64 bits.

3.1.2 The Times of Mapping : n

If a ciphertext is deciphered with two keys which are slightly different, the sequences are separating as n is getting larger, and eventually they become independent. Therefore, we determine n so as to satisfy the following two conditions.

i) By selecting some keys and computing plaintexts by deciphering a ciphertext, the distribution of the plaintexts for respective keys is uniform distribution $U(0, 1)$.

ii) Changing the keys chosen in i) slightly makes the distribution independence from the distribution in i).

If these two conditions are satisfied, attackers cannot expect the plaintext from the ciphertext, as far as they do not know the accurate key.

Figure 4 shows the distribution of plaintexts obtained from a ciphertext with 1000 keys, where $n = 75$. It is shown that the distribution is consistent with uniform distribution $U(0, 1)$. Therefore, condition i) is satisfied.

In order to test the condition ii), we use χ^2 test. The concept of the methods is as follows. Further details about the test of independence are in [4].

i) Divide the interval $[0, 1]$ into l class intervals.

ii) Compute the N pairs of $F_\alpha{}^n(C)$ and $F_{\alpha+\Delta\alpha}{}^n(C)$, and make $l \times l$ contingency table (frequency $= k_{ij}$).

iii) Compute

$$\chi^2 = N(\sum_{i=1}^{l}\sum_{j=1}^{l} \frac{k_{ij}^2}{\sum_{j=1}^{l} k_{ij} \cdot \sum_{i=1}^{l} k_{ij}} - 1). \tag{6}$$

If this value is smaller than the upper 5% point of χ^2 of which the number of the degrees of freedom is $(l-1) \times (l-1)$, the independence is not rejected using the level of significance 0.05.

Figure 5 shows times of mapping n versus χ^2, where $l = 11$, $N = 1000$ and $\Delta\alpha = 10^{-20}$. Because the upper 5% point of χ_{100}^2 is 124.3, the independence is not rejected when $n \geq 73$.

Leaving a safety margin, we determine that the times of mapping n is 75.

3.2 Ciphertext Size

Ciphertext size is equal to calculation size. If we have a computer with infinite memory, it is clear that the decryption process has no error. However, digital computer's memory is finite, so calculation error always exist. For this reason, we determine the size S not to occur any calculation error.

Firstly, we discuss about error in encryption process. Encryption function is contractional and its coefficient is about 0.5. At worst, error is 0.5×10^{-S} on each step of encryption and it is accumulated. Consequently, the error in encryption process is at worst

$$E_e = 0.5 \times 10^{-S} \times \sum_{k=0}^{n-2}(\frac{1}{2})^k = 10^{-S}(1 - (\frac{1}{2})^{n-1}). \tag{7}$$

Secondly, we discuss about error in decryption process. Decryption function is expansionary and its coefficient is about 2. Consequently, the error in decryption process is at worst

$$E_d = 0.5 \times 10^{-S} \times \sum_{k=0}^{n-1} 2^k. \tag{8}$$

Totally, computation error is at worst

$$E = 2^n \times E_e + E_d = 3 \times 2^{n-1} \times 10^{-S}. \tag{9}$$

If this error is smaller than 0.5×10^{-20}, plaintext is always recovered. Consequently, calculation size should be

$$S > n\log_{10}2 + \log_{10}3 + 20 = 43.05. \tag{10}$$

Figure 6 shows the rate of the correct decryption versus the significant digits obtained by a computer experiment. Since the times of composite of inverse map is 75, the size of ciphertext space is 20 digits +75 bits ($= 42.58$ digits). Actually, some more digits are required because computation error is accumulated by each step. As a result, if 44 digits is taken for the computation size, the decryption process is always correct.

We briefly discuss about the information rate of the cryptosystem. The information rate R is

$$R = \frac{\text{plaintext size}}{\text{ciphertext size}} = \frac{20}{44} \sim 0.5. \tag{11}$$

If you use FEAL or DES, for example, with a 32 bits message and a 32 bits random number, this system is similar to our cryptosystem, because its information rate is 0.5 and one message has 2^{32} ciphertexts, which all can be deciphered with the same decryption key. However, our cryptosystem is only composed of an easy function, which is an interesting point of our cryptosystem.

3.3 Ciphertext Only Attack

Because tent map is piecewise linear, n-times composite of tent map is also piecewise linear. Therefore, our cryptosystem has also linearity. If computation size is infinite, our cryptosystem is attacked because of its linearity. First we show the ciphertext only attack, and then we show why this attack does not succeed to break our cryptosystem.

From the encryption function eq. (3), almost all X_k are divided into the following two states, and thus almost all ciphertexts are divided into these states.

State 1 : a multiple of α

State 2 : 1+ a multiple of α.

[Proof]

i) First, we think the case when X_k is in state 1. If the sender chooses the left side of the tent map at this step, X_{k-1}, which is the next X_k, is in the state 1 because

$$X_{k-1} = \alpha(\alpha A_1), \tag{12}$$

where $X_k = \alpha A_1$. If the sender chooses the right side of the tent map at this step, X_{k-1} is in state 2 because

$$X_{k-1} = (\alpha - 1)\alpha A_2 + 1 = \alpha(\alpha - 1)A_2 + 1, \tag{13}$$

where $X_k = \alpha A_2$.

ii) Second, we think the case when X_k is in state 2. Whichever the sender chooses, X_{k-1} is in state 1 because

$$X_{k-1} = \alpha(\alpha A_3 + 1), \tag{14}$$

where $X_k = \alpha A_3 + 1$, and

$$\begin{aligned} X_{k-1} &= (\alpha - 1)(\alpha A_4 + 1) + 1 \\ &= \alpha(\alpha A_4 - A_4 + 1), \end{aligned} \tag{15}$$

where $X_k = \alpha A_4 + 1$.

iii) Finally, we think the first step of the encryption. Whatever plaintext p is, just after the sender chooses the left side of the tent map, X_k is in state 1. After this state, X_k is in state 1 or state 2 as we mentioned above. The only one case which X_k is never in these two states is that the sender chooses the right side of the tent map during all the encryption steps. If the sender chooses the side randomly, the provability of this is 2^{-75}. Consequently, almost all ciphertexts are divided into these states.

This fact enables attackers the following attack. If an attacker can eavesdrop two ciphertexts C_0 and C_1, he can obtain the key α after at most four times tests like

$$\gcd(|\,(C_0 - b_0)\,|\,10^{20\times(n+1)}, |\,(C_1 - b_1)\,|\,10^{20\times(n+1)}) = \text{a multiple of } \alpha \times 10^{20}, \qquad (16)$$

where b_0 and b_1 are 1 or 0. This is the ciphertext only attack.

Next we show why this attack does not succeed to break our cryptosystem if we set computation size. If a sender calculated a ciphertext whose size was infinite, it is described by

$$\text{key size} \times n + \text{plaintext size} = 1520 \text{ digits} \qquad (17)$$

because key size and plaintext size are both 20 digits, and $n = 75$. If he sent the ciphertext of this size to receiver and an attacker could eavesdrop it, the attacker can obtain the key α because the linearity of our cryptosystem still exists. However, ciphertext can be described by only 44 digits. This means that the attacker lacks the information to succeed the attack. In other words, although our cryptosystem is described by linear functions, setting computation size saves our cryptosystem from the attack.

3.4 Other Chaotic Maps

As we mentioned above, the ciphertext only attack is avoided by the setting computation size but the tent map cryptosystem still has linearity. There will exist other types of attacks such as chosen plaintext attack, known plaintext attack, and so on. We expect that these attack will be based on the characteristics of the linearity. We recommend other chaotic maps to avoid these attacks. For example, a certain of non-linear one-dimensional chaotic map meets this condition. Further research is necessary for this aspect.

4 Conclusions

We have proposed a new secret key cryptosystem by iterating a chaotic map. In the case that we use a tent map as a chaotic map, we determine the parameter sizes to prevent statistic attacks by χ^2 test, whose result is that the times of mapping should be larger than 73 if the key size and the plaintext size are both 20digits. We verify that correct decryption is achieved if the computation size is larger than 44 digits. We also verify that the computation size prevent the ciphertext only attack from breaking our cryptosystem. In the proposed system, a plaintext has 2^n ciphertexts and one of 2^n ciphertexts is sent to the receiver. Even if the ciphertext is chosen by any arbitrary way, the receiver can obtain the plaintext only using the secret key.

Acknowledgement

The authors wish to thank Dr. Tsutomu Matsumoto at Yokohama National University for his valuable suggestions and all the participants of EUROCRYPT 91 for their useful discussions.

References

[1] J. M. T. Thompson and H. B. Stewart: "Nonlinear Dynamics and Chaos", John Wiley and Sons, Chichester, 1986.

[2] P. Collet and J. P. Eckmann: "Iterated Maps on the Interval as Dynamical Systems", Birkhäuser, Boston, 1980.

[3] S. Oishi and H. Inoue: "Pseudo-Random Number Generators and Chaos", Trans. IECE Japan, E65, 9, pp.534-541 (Sept. 1982)

[4] G. K. Bhattacharyya and R. A. Johnson: "Statistical Concepts and Methods", John Wiley and Sons, Tronto, 1977.

[5] T. Habutsu, Y. Nishio, I. Sasase, and S. Mori: "A Secret Key Cryptosystem Using a Chaotic Map", Trans. IEICE Japan, E73,7, pp.1041-1044 (July 1990)

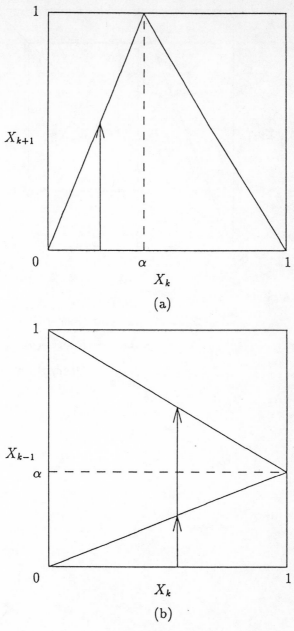

Fig.1 (a) Tent map.
    (b) Inverse tent map.

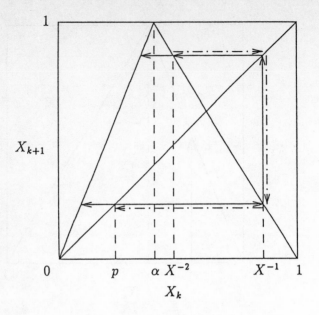

Fig.2 Encryption and Decryption.

$\longrightarrow$: Encryption

$- \cdot \succ$: Decryption

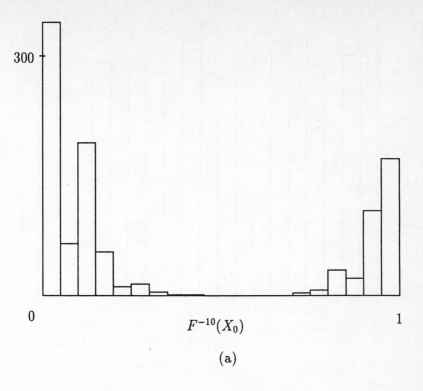

$$F^{-10}(X_0)$$

(a)

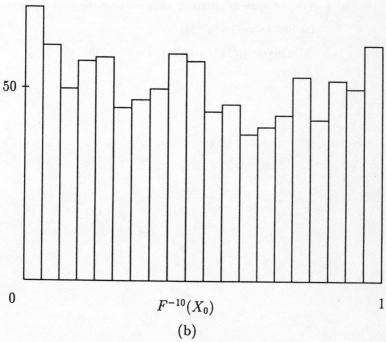

$$F^{-10}(X_0)$$

(b)

Fig. 3 The histogram of $F^{-10}(X_0)$

in 20 intervals $[i/20, (i+1)/20)$, $i = 0, \cdots, 19$.

(a) $\alpha = 0.11$ $X_0 = 0.2356$

(b) $\alpha = 0.46$ $X_0 = 0.2356$

138

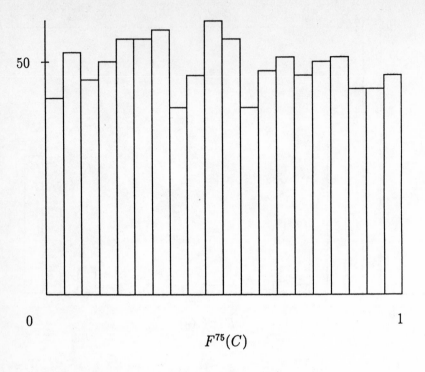

$F^{75}(C)$

Fig. 4 The histogram of plaintexts obtained from the same ciphertext
for 1000 keys $(C = 0.3987)$
:20 intervals $[i/20, (i+1)/20)$, $i = 0, \cdots, 19$.

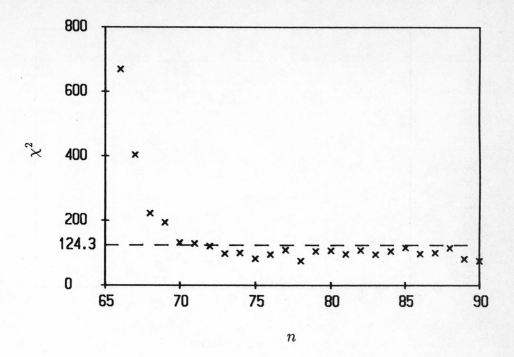

Fig. 5 The results of χ^2 test.

$(\chi^2_{100}(0.05) = 124.3)$

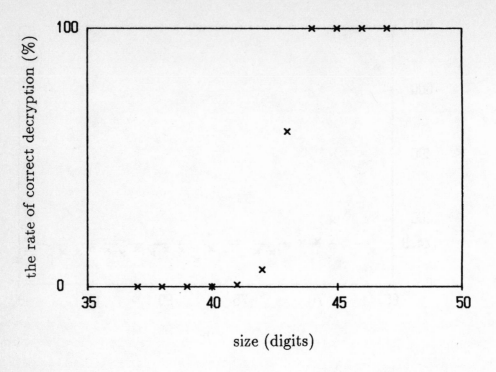

Fig. 6   The rate of correct decryption.

(Computer simulation : 1000 samples)

Boolean Functions Satisfying
Higher Order Propagation Criteria

B. Preneel,* René Govaerts and Joos Vandewalle

Katholieke Universiteit Leuven, Laboratorium ESAT,
Kardinaal Mercierlaan, 94, B–3001 Heverlee, Belgium.

Abstract

Boolean functions that satisfy higher order propagation criteria are studied. A complete characterization is given of the autocorrelation function and Walsh spectrum of second order functions. The number of second order functions satisfying $PC(k)$ is related to a problem in coding theory and can be computed explicitly for $k = 1, n - 1$ and n. A new interpretation of the number of balanced second order functions is given and a class of functions showing interesting properties is discussed.

1 Definitions

1.1 Boolean functions

A Boolean function $f(\underline{x})$ is a function whose domain is the vector space $\mathbb{Z}_2^n$ of binary n-tuples $(x_1, x_2, \ldots, x_n)$ that takes the values 0 and 1. In some cases it will be more convenient to work with functions that take the values $\{-1, 1\}$. The functions $\hat{f}(\underline{x})$ is defined as $\hat{f}(\underline{x}) = 1 - 2 \cdot f(\underline{x})$. The Hamming weight hwt of an element of $\mathbb{Z}_2^n$ is the number of components equal to 1.

A Boolean function is said to be linear if there exists a $\underline{w} \in \mathbb{Z}_2^n$ such that it can be written as $L_{\underline{w}}(\underline{x}) = \underline{x} \cdot \underline{w}$ or $\hat{L}_{\underline{w}}(\underline{x}) = (-1)^{\underline{x} \cdot \underline{w}}$. Here $\underline{x} \cdot \underline{w}$ denotes the dot product of $\underline{x}$ and $\underline{w}$, defined as $\underline{x} \cdot \underline{w} = x_1 w_1 \oplus x_2 w_2 \oplus \ldots \oplus x_n w_n$. The set of affine functions is the union of the set of the linear functions and their complement.

Definition 1 *Let $f(\underline{x})$ be any real-valued function with domain the vector space*

---

*NFWO aspirant navorser, sponsored by the National Fund for Scientific Research (Belgium).

$\mathbb{Z}_2^n$. The **Walsh transform** of $f(\underline{x})$ is the real-valued function over the vector space $\mathbb{Z}_2^n$ defined as

$$F(\underline{w}) = \sum_{\underline{x}} f(\underline{x}) \cdot (-1)^{\underline{x} \cdot \underline{w}},$$

where $\sum_{\underline{x}}$ denotes the sum over all 2^n elements of $\mathbb{Z}_2^n$.

The relationship between the Walsh transform of $f(\underline{x})$ and $\hat{f}(\underline{x})$ is given by [For88]

$$\hat{F}(\underline{w}) = -2F(\underline{w}) + 2^n\,\delta(\underline{w}) \quad \text{and} \quad F(\underline{w}) = -\frac{1}{2}\hat{F}(\underline{w}) + 2^{n-1}\,\delta(\underline{w}),$$

where $\delta(\underline{w})$ denotes the Kronecker delta $(\delta(\underline{0}) = 1, \delta(\underline{k}) = 0 \;\; \forall \underline{k} \neq \underline{0})$.

Definition 2 *The* **autocorrelation function** $\hat{r}(\underline{s})$ *is defined as*

$$\hat{r}(\underline{s}) = \sum_{\underline{x}} \hat{f}(\underline{x}) \cdot \hat{f}(\underline{x} \oplus \underline{s}).$$

Note that $\hat{r}(\underline{0})$ equals 2^n.

It can also be of interest to write a Boolean function as the sum of all products of the variables:

$$f(\underline{x}) = a_0 \oplus \bigoplus_{1 \le i \le n} a_i x_i \;\oplus\; \bigoplus_{1 \le i < j \le n} a_{ij} x_i x_j \;\oplus \ldots \oplus\; a_{12\ldots n} x_1 x_2 \cdots x_n.$$

This form is called the algebraic normal form of a Boolean function f and the corresponding transformation is called the algebraic normal transform.

Definition 3 *The* **non-linear order** *of a Boolean function (notation:* $\mathrm{ord}\,(f)$*) is defined as the degree of the highest order term in the algebraic normal form.*

The affine Boolean functions are the functions with non-linear order < 2.

1.2 Properties of Boolean Functions

A Boolean function is said to be **balanced** if its truth table contains as many 0 as 1 entries. It is easy to show that this is equivalent to $\hat{F}(\underline{0}) = 0$.

A Boolean function is said to be **mth order correlation immune** if $f(\underline{x})$ is statistically independent of any subset of m input variables [Sie84, XM88]. This can be shown to be equivalent to

$$\hat{F}(\underline{w}) = 0 \quad 1 \le hwt(\underline{w}) \le m,$$

and a necessary condition is $\mathrm{ord}(f) \le n - m$. If f is also balanced, this upper bound can be improved to $n - m - 1$, unless $m = n - 1$.

A Boolean function $f(\underline{x})$ satisfies the **propagation criterion of degree k** **($PC(k)$)** if $f(\underline{x})$ changes with a probability of one half whenever i $(1 \leq i \leq k)$ bits of $\underline{x}$ are complemented [PVV90]:

$$\hat{r}(\underline{s}) = 0 \text{ for } 1 \leq hwt(\underline{s}) \leq k.$$

Note that the Strict Avalanche Criterion (SAC) is equivalent to $PC(1)$ and perfect non-linear is $PC(n)$.

A Boolean function $f(\underline{x})$ of n variables satisfies the **propagation criterion of degree k and order m ($PC(k)$ of order m)** if any function obtained from $f(\underline{x})$ by keeping m input bits constant satisfies $PC(k)$.

The **propagation matrix N_n** for all Boolean functions of n variables is the $n \times n$ matrix: $N_n(k,m) = \#\{f \mid f$ satisfies $PC(k)$ of order $m\}/2^{n+1}$, with $k + m \leq n$. The division by 2^{n+1} implies that abstraction is made of linear and constant terms, that have no influence on propagation properties. The propagation matrix for all second order Boolean functions of three to seven bits is given in table 1. In this paper, we will explain most numbers in this table and, if possible, generalize certain properties for arbitrary n.

k \ m	0	1	2
1	4	1	0
2	1	1	–
3	0	–	–

k \ m	0	1	2	3
1	41	10	1	0
2	28	1	1	–
3	28	0	–	–
4	28	–	–	–

k \ m	0	1	2	3	4
1	768	253	26	1	0
2	448	28	1	1	–
3	168	28	0	–	–
4	28	28	–	–	–
5	0	–	–	–	–

k \ m	0	1	2	3	4	5
1	27449	12068	1858	76	1	0
2	18788	3188	1	1	1	–
3	14308	421	1	0	–	–
4	13888	1	1	–	–	–
5	13888	0	–	–	–	–
6	13888	–	–	–	–	–

k \ m	0	1	2	3	4	5	6
1	1887284	1052793	236926	15796	232	1	0
2	1419852	237048	4901	1	1	1	–
3	889672	17668	841	1	0	–	–
4	402752	13888	1	1	–	–	–
5	111104	13888	0	–	–	–	–
6	13888	13888	–	–	–	–	–
7	0	–	–	–	–	–	–

Table 1: The matrices $N_3(k,m)$, $N_4(k,m)$, $N_5(k,m)$, $N_6(k,m)$ and $N_7(k,m)$ for second order functions.

2 Propagation characteristics of second order functions

Second order functions have been studied intensively to derive properties of the second order Reed-Muller codes. For the study of second order functions, it is useful to write the second order coefficients of the algebraic normal form in a binary symmetric matrix with zero diagonal: $[b_{ij}] = [a_{ij}]$, where $a_{ii} = 0$. This is called a **symplectic matrix**. The number of second order coefficients equals $\frac{n \cdot (n-1)}{2}$ and will be denoted with $\Delta(n)$. The second order functions can be reduced with an equivalence transform to a canonical form based on Dickson's theorem.

Theorem 1 (Dickson's theorem) *If B is a symplectic $n \times n$ matrix of rank $2h$, then there exists an invertible binary matrix R such that RBR^T has zeroes everywhere except on the two diagonals immediately above and below the main diagonal, and there has $1010 \ldots 100 \ldots 0$ with h ones.*
Every second order Boolean function can by an affine transformation of variables be reduced to $\bigoplus_{i=1}^{h} x_{2i-1} x_{2i} \oplus \epsilon$, with ϵ an affine function of x_{2h+1} through x_n.

The rank of the $2^{\Delta(n)}$ symplectic matrices is given by following theorem [MWS77]:

Lemma 1 *The number of symplectic $n \times n$ matrices over $\mathbb{Z}_2$ of rank $2h$ equals*

$$M(n, 2h) = \begin{bmatrix} n \\ 2h \end{bmatrix} \cdot M(2h, 2h).$$

Here $\begin{bmatrix} n \\ k \end{bmatrix}$ denotes the binary Gaussian binomial coefficient, defined for all non-negative integers k by

$$\begin{bmatrix} n \\ 0 \end{bmatrix} = 1, \quad \begin{bmatrix} n \\ k \end{bmatrix} = \begin{bmatrix} n-1 \\ k-1 \end{bmatrix} + 2^k \begin{bmatrix} n-1 \\ k \end{bmatrix}$$

and $M(2h, 2h) = (2^{2h-1} - 1)2^{2h-2} \cdots (2^3 - 1)2^2$.

In [MWS77] it is shown that in case n is even the functions of n bits satisfying $PC(n)$ (bent functions) are the functions for which the corresponding matrix B has full rank. The number of these functions is given by $M(n, n)$.

For n odd, the highest criterion that can be satisfied is $PC(n-1)$. The previous result can be extended for n odd.

Theorem 2 *Let f be a Boolean function of n variables, $n > 2$ and odd.*
Then f satisfies $PC(n - 1)$ of order 0 and 1 iff f is obtained with following construction:

1. *Let f' be a function of $n - 1$ variables satisfying $PC(n - 1)$ with algebraic normal form coefficients equal to a'_{ij}.*

2. *Define $a_{ij} = a'_{ij}$ for $1 \leq i < j \leq n - 1$ and*

$$a_{in} = \bigoplus_{j=0, j \neq i}^{n-1} a_{ij} \quad for \ 1 \leq i \leq n - 1.$$

The number of functions satisfying $PC(n-1)$ of order 0 and 1 is given by $M(n-1, n-1)$.

Proof: The first part of the proof consists of showing that every function satisfying $PC(n-1)$ of order 0 satisfies $PC(n-1)$ of order 1. This part is a simple corollary of theorem 5 (cfr. infra). To characterize the functions satisfying $PC(n-1)$ of order 1, it is recalled that every function f^* obtained from f by fixing one input bit should satisfy $PC(n-1)$. This can be restated with the symplectic matrices B and B^* that correspond to f and f^* respectively: every matrix B^* obtained from B by deleting one column and the corresponding row should have full rank $n-1$. As the rank of a symplectic matrix is always even, this implies that B has necessarily rank $n-1$ and that any column (row) can be written as a linear combination of the other columns (rows). Any symplectic matrix B^* of rank $n-1$ can be extended in 2^{n-1} ways to a matrix B. However, if any matrix obtained from deleting one column and the corresponding row in B should have rank $n-1$, the only solution is that the added column (row) is the sum of all other columns (rows). This can be shown as follows: if a particular column and row are not selected in the sum, the deletion of this column and row from B will result in a singular matrix B^*, contradicting the requirement. ∎

Theorem 11 in [PVV90] states that a second order function satisfies $PC(1)$ or SAC if and only if every variable occurs at least once in the second order terms of the algebraic normal form. This makes it possible to compute the number of second order functions satisfying $PC(1)$.

Theorem 3 *The number of second order n-bit functions satisfying $PC(1)$ is given by*

$$N_n(1,0) = \sum_{k=1}^{n-1} (-1)^{n-k-1} \binom{n-1}{k} 2^{\Delta(k)} (2^k - 1).$$

Proof: This follows from the observation that the second order functions satisfying $PC(1)$ correspond to the undirected simple graphs with n vertices with minimal degree equal to 1. The degree of a vertex is equal to the number of edges incident to that vertex, and the minimal degree of a graph is the minimum of the set consisting of the degrees of the vertices. It is easily seen that the number of these graphs is given by following recursive equation (for $n > 1$):

$$N_n(1,0) = 2^{\Delta(n)} - 1 - \sum_{k=2}^{n-1} \binom{n}{k} N_k(1,0).$$

The theorem follows from the solution of this equation. ∎

3   Autocorrelation function properties

In [PVV90] it was shown that the non-linear order of functions satisfying $PC(1)$ is bounded by $n - 1$. A well known result is that the non-linear order of functions satisfying $PC(n)$ (n even and > 2) is bounded by $n/2$, and for functions satisfying $PC(n - 1)$ (n odd and > 2) the corresponding upper bound is $\lceil n/2 \rceil$.

An extension of this result for functions satisfying $PC(k)$ is non-trivial, because k depends on both the number of zeroes of the autocorrelation function as well as on the position of these zeroes. Hence $PC(k)$ is not invariant under affine transformations, where the non-linear order clearly is. The way to proceed is first to study a number that is invariant under affine transformations, namely the number of zeroes of the autocorrelation function (denoted by $N_{\hat{r}}$) and then to apply the results to $PC(k)$.

The upper bound on the non-linear order for functions satisfying $PC(1)$ can be improved as follows: even if the autocorrelation function has one zero, the function can not have maximal non-linear order.

Theorem 4 *Let f be a Boolean function of n variables with $n > 2$.*
If $N_{\hat{r}} > 0$ then $\operatorname{ord}(f) \leq n - 1$.

Proof: It is sufficient to show that the Hamming weight of f is even. Let $\underline{s}$ be the value for which $\hat{r}(\underline{s}) = 0$ or $r(\underline{s}) = 2^{n-1}$. Then

$$
\begin{aligned}
hwt(f) &= \sum_{\underline{x}} f(\underline{x}) \bmod 2 \\
&= \sum_{\underline{x}} f(\underline{x} \oplus \underline{s}) \bmod 2 \\
&= \frac{1}{2} \sum_{\underline{x}} f(\underline{x}) \oplus f(\underline{x} \oplus \underline{s}) \bmod 2 \\
&= \frac{1}{2} r(\underline{s}) \bmod 2 = 2^{n-2} \bmod 2.
\end{aligned}
$$

If $n > 2$, the theorem follows.   ∎

A second result for second order functions is based on Dickson's theorem and Lemma 1.

Theorem 5 *The autocorrelation function of second order functions takes the values 0 and $\pm 2^n$. The number of zeroes is given by $N_{\hat{r}} = 2^n - 2^{n-2h}$ for $1 \leq h \leq \lfloor \frac{n}{2} \rfloor$. The number of functions with this number of zeroes equals $M(n, 2h)$. There are $\begin{bmatrix} n \\ 2h \end{bmatrix}$ possible patterns for these zeroes and to every pattern correspond exactly $M(2h, 2h)$ functions.*

The coordinates where $\hat{r}(\underline{s}) \neq 0$ form a $n - 2h$ dimensional subspace of $\mathbb{Z}_2^n$.

Proof: For the canonical second order function:

$$f(\underline{x}) = \bigoplus_{i=1}^{h} x_{2i-1}x_{2i},$$

the autocorrelation function can be written as follows:

$$r(\underline{s}) = \sum_{\underline{x}} \left(\bigoplus_{i=1}^{h} s_{2i-1}s_{2i} \oplus \bigoplus_{i=1}^{h}(x_{2i-1}s_i \oplus x_{2i}s_{2i-1}) \right).$$

Note that the affine function ϵ can be omitted because affine terms have no influence on the autocorrelation function. In case $r(\underline{s}) = 2^{n-1}$, corresponding to $\hat{r}(\underline{s}) = 0$, the first part of the sum has no influence on the result. It is easily seen that $r(\underline{s})$ will be equal to 2^{n-1} if there exists at least one $s_i \neq 0$, with $1 \leq i \leq 2h$. Hence the number of non-zeroes of $\hat{r}(\underline{s})$ equals 2^{n-2h}, corresponding to the vectors $\underline{s}$ with $s_i = 0$, for $1 \leq i \leq 2h$. It is clear that these vectors form a subspace of $\mathbb{Z}_2^n$ of dimension $n - 2h$. The number of distinct subspaces of dimension $n - 2h$ corresponds to the number of $[n, n - 2h]$ codes and equals $\begin{bmatrix} n \\ 2h \end{bmatrix}$ [MWS77]. ∎

The last part of Theorem 5 makes it in principle possible to compute the number of second order functions satisfying $PC(k)$.

Corollary 1 *The number of second order functions of n variables satisfying $PC(k)$ is given by*

$$\sum_{h=1}^{\lfloor \frac{n}{2} \rfloor} L(n, n - 2h, k)M(2h, 2h),$$

where $L(n, r, k)$ denotes the number of linear $[n, r, d]$ codes with minimum distance $d > k$.

Proof: This follows from the observation that a function will satisfy $PC(k)$ if the non-zeroes of r, that form a subspace of dimension $n - 2h$, occur at positions with Hamming weight $> k$. This is equivalent to the statement that the non-zeroes should form a linear code with length n, dimension $n - 2h$ and minimum distance $d > k$. ∎

Because of the Singleton bound ($d \leq n - r + 1$) [MWS77] the lower limit of this sum can be increased to $\lfloor \frac{k+1}{2} \rfloor$. However, the computation of $L(n, r, k)$ even for small values of n is a difficult problem. Even the maximal d for given n and r (notation $d_{max}(n, r)$) remains an open problem except for $r \leq 5$ and $d \leq 3$. In [HeSt73] a table of known bounds $d_{max}(n, r)$ is listed for $n \leq 127$. A small relevant part is reproduced in table 2. In case $n = 6$, $1 \leq h \leq 3$, the autocorrelation

r n	1	2	3	4	5
4	4	2	2	1	5
5	5	3	2	2	1
6	6	4	3	2	2
7	7	4	4	3	3

Table 2: Upper bound on the minimum distance d for linear $[n, r, d]$ codes.

functions has 1, 4 or 16 non-zeroes and the number of corresponding functions is 13888 (bent functions), 18228 and 651. In case of 4 non-zeroes, $r = 2$ and from table 2 one finds $d_{max}(6, 2) = 4$. Hence the bent functions are the only functions satisfying $PC(4)$, $PC(5)$ and $PC(6)$. The number of $[6, 2, 4]$, $[6, 2, 3]$, $[6, 2, 2]$ and $[6, 2, 1]$ codes is 15, 160, 305 and 171 respectively. With every code correspond 28 functions, resulting in 420, 4480, 8540 and 4788 functions for every class. In case of 16 non-zeroes, every code corresponds to exactly one function. The number of $[6, 4, 2]$ and $[6, 4, 1]$ codes is given by 121 and 530. The number of 6-bit functions satisfying $PC(3)$ equals $13888 + 420 = 14308$, the number of functions satisfying $PC(2)$ equals $13888 + 420 + 4480 = 18788$, and the number of functions satisfying $PC(1)$ equals $18788 + 8540 + 121 = 27449$. This last result can also be obtained with theorem 3.

The number of $[n, 1, d]$ codes equals $\binom{n}{d}$ and hence for n odd the functions satisfying $PC(k)$ with $d_{max}(n, 3) \leq k \leq n - 1$ is given by

$$M(n - 1, n - 1) \sum_{i=k+1}^{n} \binom{n}{i},$$

for which no closed form exists.

4 Walsh transform and balancedness

It has been shown in [PVV90] that dyadic shifts in the Walsh spectrum modify only linear and constant terms and that the propagation characteristics remain unaffected. A corollary of this observation is that adding the right linear terms to a function with at least one zero in the Walsh spectrum will result in a balanced function with the same propagation properties. If the image of the other zeroes of the spectrum under the same transformation is the set of vectors with low Hamming weight, the corresponding function will also be correlation immune. This indicates that the number of zeroes of the Walsh spectrum is a relevant property.

The weight distribution of functions with $ord \leq 2$ is known from the study of Reed-Muller codes [MWS77].

Theorem 6 *Let A_i be the number of functions with* $ord \leq 2$ *and Hamming weight i. Then $A_i = 0$ unless $i = 2^{n-1}$ or $i = 2^{n-1} \pm 2^{n-1-h}$ for some h, $0 \leq h \leq \lfloor \frac{n}{2} \rfloor$. Also $A_0 = A_{2^n} = 1$ and*

$$A_{2^{n-1} \pm 2^{n-1-h}} = 2^{h(h+1)} \cdot \frac{(2^n - 1)(2^{n-1} - 1) \cdots (2^{n-2h+1} - 1)}{(2^{2h} - 1)(2^{2h-2} - 1) \cdots (2^2 - 1)} \quad for \; 1 \leq h \leq \lfloor \frac{n}{2} \rfloor.$$

$A_{2^{n-1}}$ can be evaluated because all A_i sum to $2^{1+n+\Delta(n)}$.

Based on Dickson's theorem, the number of zeroes of the Walsh spectrum of a second order function can be calculated.

Theorem 7 *The number of zeroes of the Walsh transform of a second order function is given by $N_{\hat{F}} = 2^n - 2^{2h}$ for $1 \leq h \leq \lfloor \frac{n}{2} \rfloor$. The number of functions with this number of zeroes equals $M(n, 2h)$. If $\hat{F}(\underline{w}) \neq 0$, then $| \hat{F}(\underline{w}) | = 2^{n-h}$.*

Proof: It will be shown that $\hat{F}(\underline{w})$, the Walsh transform of

$$f(\underline{x}) = \bigoplus_{i=1}^{h} x_{2i-1} x_{2i}$$

is equal in absolute value to 2^{n-h} for $w_i = 0$, $2h + 1 \leq i \leq n$ and equal to zero elsewhere. The theorem then follows from the application of Dickson's theorem and from the observation that the addition of the affine term ϵ only causes a dyadic shift of the Walsh spectrum. The Walsh transform of f can be written as:

$$\hat{F}(\underline{w}) = \sum_{\underline{x}} (-1)^{\bigoplus_{i=1}^{h} x_{2i-1} x_{2i}} \cdot (-1)^{\bigoplus_{i=1}^{n} x_i w_i}.$$

Here we assume that $2h < n$. In case $h = 2n$, f is a bent function and the theorem is clearly true.

- In case $w_i = 0$, $2h+1 \leq i \leq n$, the expression for the Walsh transform reduces to

$$\hat{F}(\underline{w}) = \sum_{\underline{x}} (-1)^{\bigoplus_{i=1}^{h} x_{2i-1} x_{2i}} \cdot (-1)^{\bigoplus_{i=1}^{2h} x_i w_i}.$$

As the variables x_{2h+1} through x_n do not occur in this sum, it can be simplified to

$$\hat{F}(\underline{w}) = 2^{n-2h} \cdot \sum_{\underline{x}'} (-1)^{\bigoplus_{i=1}^{h} x_{2i-1} x_{2i}} \cdot (-1)^{\bigoplus_{i=1}^{2h} x_i w_i},$$

where $\underline{x}'$ denotes $[x_1 \ldots x_{2h}]$. By observing that the remaining sum corresponds to the Walsh transform of a bent function of $2h$ variables, it follows that its absolute value equals 2^h.

- In the other case, let U denote the set of indices $\{i_1, i_2, \ldots, i_k\}$ in the interval $[2h+1, n]$ for which $w_{i_j} = 1$. The Walsh transform can then be written as

$$\hat{F}(\underline{w}) = \sum_{\underline{x}'} (-1)^{\bigoplus_{i=1}^{h} x_{2i-1}x_{2i}} \cdot (-1)^{\bigoplus_{i=1}^{2h} x_i w_i} \cdot \sum_{\underline{x}''} (-1)^{\bigoplus_{i,j \in U} x_{i_j}},$$

where $\underline{x}'$ denotes $[x_1 \ldots x_{2h}]$ and $\underline{x}''$ denotes $[x_{2h} \ldots x_n]$. It is easily seen that the second sum vanishes, and hence $\hat{F}(\underline{w})$ equals zero.

∎

From the proof it follows that the coordinates were $\hat{F}(\underline{w}) \neq 0$ will form a subspace of $\mathbb{Z}_2^n$ of dimension $2h$ if and only if the affine function ϵ is constant. If this condition is not satisfied, the non-zeroes will be a dyadic shift of a subspace.

Theorem 7 results in a new interpretation of the number of balanced functions with $ord \leq 2$. There are $2(2^n - 1)$ balanced linear functions and every second order function with q zeroes in the Walsh spectrum corresponds to $2q$ balanced functions through addition of affine terms. Hence the total number of balanced functions with $ord \leq 2$ can also be written as

$$A_{2^{n-1}} = 2(2^n - 1) + 2 \left(\sum_{h=1}^{\lfloor \frac{n}{2} \rfloor - 1} (2^n - 2^{2h}) M(n, 2h) \right).$$

For bent functions it is already known that the autocorrelation function has only one non-zero element and the Walsh spectrum has no zeroes. Following corollary, resulting from the combination of Theorem 5 and Theorem 7, gives the relation between the number of non-zeroes of the autocorrelation function and the Walsh spectrum for second order functions.

Corollary 2 *Let f be a Boolean function of n variables with* $ord(f) \leq 2$. *Then*

$$(2^n - N_{\hat{r}}) \cdot (2^n - N_{\hat{F}}) = 2^n.$$

Note that if $ord(f) = n$, $N_{\hat{r}} = 0$ (theorem 4) and $N_{\hat{F}} = 0$ (because $hwt(f)$ is always odd) and this expression reaches its maximal value 2^{2n}. We conjecture that if $ord(f) > 2$, $(2^n - N_{\hat{r}}) \cdot (2^n - N_{\hat{F}}) \geq 2^n$, and equality holds only for functions satisfying $PC(n)$ or $PC(n-1)$.

5 A special class of functions

For $n = 5$ there exist 192 4th order functions satisfying $PC(2)$. The non-zeroes of the autocorrelation function have all absolute value 8. The zeroes of the autocorrelation function form the set of all 15 vectors with Hamming weight 1 or 2. An example of this class is

$$f_1(\underline{x}) = x_1x_2x_3x_4 \oplus x_1x_2x_3x_5 \oplus x_1x_2x_4x_5 \oplus x_1x_3x_4x_5 \oplus x_2x_3x_4x_5$$
$$\oplus x_1x_4 \oplus x_1x_5 \oplus x_2x_3 \oplus x_2x_5 \oplus x_3x_4.$$

The value distribution of the Walsh spectrum (table 3) shows that this function is correlation immune of order 1. A related function f_2 can be defined as

$$f_2(\underline{x}) = f_1(\underline{x}) \oplus x_1 \oplus x_2 \oplus x_3 \oplus x_4 \oplus x_5.$$

The Walsh spectrum of f_2 is obtained by a dyadic shift over [11111] of the Walsh spectrum of f_1, resulting in a balanced function satisfying $PC(2)$ (table 3). Note that it is not possible to obtain from f_1 through an affine transformation of variables a function that is balanced and correlation immune of order 1, as this requires the vanishing of all coefficients of order 4 [XM88].

$hwt(\underline{w})$	0	1	2	3	4	5
$\mid \hat{F}_1(\underline{w}) \mid$	12	0	4	8	4	0
$\mid \hat{F}_2(\underline{w}) \mid$	0	4	8	4	0	12

$hwt(\underline{s})$	0	1	2	3	4	5
$\hat{r}_1(\underline{s})$	32	0	0	8	8	−8
$\hat{r}_2(\underline{s})$	32	0	4	−8	8	8

Table 3: Value distribution of the Walsh spectrum and the autocorrelation function for the functions f_1 and f_2.

6 Summary

The distribution of the autocorrelation function and Walsh transform is invariant under affine transformations and can be computed for second order functions based on Dickson's theorem. In case of second order functions, a relation between the distribution of the autocorrelation function and the number of functions satisfying $PC(k)$ has been established and the study of the Walsh transform gives a new interpretation to the number of balanced second order functions. Finally a special class of functions of 5 bits combining interesting properties have been introduced. An interesting open problem is to generalize this class for arbitrary n.

References

[For88]   R. Forré, "The strict avalanche criterion: spectral properties of Boolean functions and an extended definition", *Advances in Cryptology, Proc. Crypto 88*, Springer Verlag, 1990, p. 450–468.

[HeSt73] H.J. Helgert and R.D. Stinaff, "Minimum-Distance bounds for binary linear codes", *IEEE Trans. Inform. Theory*, Vol. IT-19, p. 344–356, May 1973.

[MWS77]   F.J. MacWilliams and N.J.A. Sloane, *"The theory of error-correcting codes"*, North-Holland Publishing Company, Amsterdam, 1977.

[MS89]   W. Meier and O. Staffelbach, "Nonlinearity criteria for cryptographic functions", *Advances in Cryptology, Proc. Eurocrypt 89*, Springer Verlag, 1990, pp. 549–562.

[PVV90]   B. Preneel, W. Van Leekwijck, L. Van Linden, R. Govaerts and J. Vandewalle, "Propagation Characteristics of Boolean Functions", *Advances in Cryptology, Proc. Eurocrypt 90, Lecture Notes in Computer Science 473*, Springer Verlag, 1991, pp. 161–173.

[Ruep90] R.A. Rueppel, "Stream Ciphers", in *Contemporary Cryptology: The Science of Information Integrity*, G. Simmons, ed., IEEE Press, to appear.

[Sie84]   T. Siegenthaler, "Correlation immunity of non-linear combining functions for cryptographic applications", *IEEE Trans. Inform. Theory*, Vol. IT-30, p. 776–780, Oct. 1984.

[VV90]   W. Van Leekwijck and L. Van Linden, *"Cryptographic properties of Boolean functions – in Dutch, Cryptografische eigenschappen van Booleaanse functies"*, ESAT Katholieke Universiteit Leuven, Thesis grad. eng., 1990.

[XM88]   G.-Z. Xiao and J.L. Massey, "A spectral characterization of correlation-immune combining functions", *IEEE Trans. Inform. Theory*, Vol. IT-34, p. 569–571, May 1988.

The Maximum Order Complexity of Sequence Ensembles

CEES J.A. JANSEN

Philips Crypto B.V.

Abstract

In this paper we extend the theory of maximum order complexity from a single sequence to an ensemble of sequences. In particular, the maximum order complexity of an ensemble of sequences is defined and its properties discussed. Also, an algorithm is given to determine the maximum order complexity of an ensemble of sequences linear in time and memory. It is also shown how to determine the maximum order feedback shift register equivalent of a given ensmble of sequences, i.e. including a feedback function. Hence, the problem of finding the absolutely shortest (possibly nonlinear) feedback shift register, that can generate two or more given sequences with characters from some arbitrary finite alphabet, is solved. Finally, the consequences for sequence prediction based on the minimum number of observations are discussed.

1 Introduction

The notion of maximum order complexity of sequences was introduced in [8] as the length of the shortest feedback shift register that can generate a given (part of a) sequence, where the feedback function may be any function, mapping states onto characters. The import of maximum order complexity is that it tells exactly how many keystream characters have to be observed at least, in order to be able to generate the entire sequence by means of a feedback shift register of that length. Also maximum order complexity can be viewed as an additional figure of merit to judge the randomness of sequences.

We recall a number of results as given in [8, 9, 10]:

- the typical complexity profile closely follows the $2 \log l$ curve

- there exists a linear time and memory algorithm to determine the maximum order complexity profile of a given sequence; this algorithm in fact builds a directed acyclic word graph (DAWG) from the sequence

- generally, there exists a class of feedback functions which all give rise to one and the same sequence (even for periodic sequences)

- determining the maximum order feedback shift register equivalent of a given sequence of length l has an expected order of $2l^2 \log l$, where the feedback function is given by its algebraic normal form, however for DeBruijn sequences the order is $l \log l$

- the DAWG can efficiently be used for predicting successive characters of a given sequence after the least number of observations.

In this paper we consider the following problem. Suppose that a number of sequences with characters from some finite alphabet are given. What is the shortest feedback shift register that can generate all the given sequences, i.e. one FSR with one fixed, possibly nonlinear feedback function? To this end, the theory of maximum order complexity is generalized to include the multiple sequence case. In particular, the maximum order complexity of an ensemble of sequences is defined and its properties examined in Section 2. Section 3 deals with a multiple sequence DAWG to determine the ensemble complexity. Finally, in Section 4 it is considered how to determine the maximum order FSR equivalent of an ensemble of sequences, and how to resynthesize sequences with the DAWG.

2   The Maximum Order Complexity of an Ensemble of Sequences

Let $\mathcal{Z}$ denote an ensemble of N sequences $z_i = (\alpha_{0,i}, \alpha_{1,i}, \ldots, \alpha_{l_i-1,i})$ of lengths l_i, $1 \le i \le N$, with characters $\alpha_{j,i} \in \mathcal{A}$, where the alphabet $\mathcal{A}$ is some finite set. How many sections (i.e. memory cells) should a feedback shift register at least have in order to generate all N sequences of $\mathcal{Z}$? So regardless of what the (memoryless) feedback function would have to be, linear or nonlinear. Analogous to the single sequence situation, the following definition of maximum order complexity is proposed:

Definition 1 *The maximum order complexity $c(\mathcal{Z})$ of an ensemble $\mathcal{Z}$ containing N sequences $z_i = (\alpha_{0,i}, \alpha_{1,i}, \ldots, \alpha_{l_i-1,i})$ of lengths l_i, $1 \le i \le N$, with characters $\alpha_{j,i} \in \mathcal{A}$, where the alphabet $\mathcal{A}$ is some finite set, is defined to be the length L of the shortest feedback shift register for which there exists a memoryless feedback mapping, such that the FSR can generate all N sequences of $\mathcal{Z}$.*

This definition clearly implies that all the sequences of $\mathcal{Z}$ are uniquely identified by their first $c(\mathcal{Z})$ characters, assuming that all sequences of $\mathcal{Z}$ are distinct. In the case that only periodic sequences are considered, clearly any consecutive $c(\mathcal{Z})$ characters uniquely identify any of the sequences of $\mathcal{Z}$. The periodic case is in fact more general, as it also covers the situation that an observed sequence does not necessarily start with the first character of a given sequence. These observations and the fact that one can easily construct an example in which two sequences can be identified by a subsequence of length much shorter than $c(\mathcal{Z})$ characters, are the motivation for the following definition:

Definition 2 *The ensemble complexity of an ensemble $\mathcal{Z}$ containing N sequences $z_i = (\alpha_{0,i}, \alpha_{1,i}, \ldots, \alpha_{l_i-1,i})$, of lengths l_i, $1 \leq i \leq N$, with characters $\alpha_{j,i} \in \mathcal{A}$, where the alphabet $\mathcal{A}$ is some finite set, denoted by $c_{\mathcal{E}}(\mathcal{Z})$, is defined as the shortest length ℓ, such that any subsequence of length ℓ uniquely identifies each of the N sequences $z_i \in \mathcal{Z}$.*

Definition 2 has a clear Information Theoretic significance, as shown in [8, Ch. 7], i.e. it tells how many characters have to be observed, in order to know exactly to which sequence these characters belong.

One can easily see that the following inequalities hold for the ensemble complexity:

$$\log|\mathcal{Z}| \leq c_{\mathcal{E}}(\mathcal{Z}) \leq \max_i l_i, \quad \text{and} \tag{1}$$

$$\log|\mathcal{Z}| \leq c_{\mathcal{E}}(\mathcal{Z}) \leq \max_i p_i, \quad \text{for periodic sequences.} \tag{2}$$

Now let $\hat{c}(\mathcal{Z})$ denote the maximum of all the individual maximum order complexities, i.e.:

$$\hat{c}(\mathcal{Z}) := \max_{z_i \in \mathcal{Z}} c(z_i). \tag{3}$$

The relation between $c(\mathcal{Z})$, $c_{\mathcal{E}}$ and $\hat{c}$ is given in the next proposition.

Proposition 1 *Let $c(\mathcal{Z})$, $c_{\mathcal{E}}(\mathcal{Z})$ and $\hat{c}(\mathcal{Z})$ be as defined before. Then the inequality $\hat{c}(\mathcal{Z}) \leq c(\mathcal{Z}) \leq \max(\hat{c}(\mathcal{Z}), c_{\mathcal{E}}(\mathcal{Z}))$ holds for any ensemble $\mathcal{Z}$.*

The proof is easily obtained by using the definitions. A direct consequence of Proposition 1 is that, if $c_{\mathcal{E}} < \hat{c}$, then $c(\mathcal{Z}) = \hat{c}$. For the special case of periodic sequences it can easily be shown that $c(\mathcal{Z}) = \max(\hat{c}(\mathcal{Z}), c_{\mathcal{E}}(\mathcal{Z}))$.

Note that from the definition of maximum order complexity it can be seen that the highest value in the auto- or crosscorrelation function of one or two sequences is lowerbounded by the maximum order complexity of the sequence or the ensemble of two sequences.

Typical Complexities

Let us consider an ensmble of randomly chosen sequences. From the results of Arratia et al. [1, 2, 3] we know that the length of the longest subsequence which is common to all sequences in the ensemble tends towards $\sum_i \log l_i/(N-1)$. This value can therefore be seen as a lowerbound to the expected ensemble complexity. However, $c_{\mathcal{E}}$ does not deal with the longest common subsequence, but rather with the shortest length such that all subsequences uniquely identify all sequences. Hence, for $N = 2$ the lowerbound is significant, but for $N > 2$ it is not.

An obvious lowerbound for the expected value of $\hat{c}$ is the expected complexity of the longest sequence in the ensemble, i.e. $2\max_i \log l_i$.

An upperbound to all complexities is obtained by considering all sequences in the ensemble as constituting one sequence of length $\sum l_i$, i.e. $2\log\sum_i l_i$.

Statistical experiments seem to indicate that indeed all complexities are close to the upperbound.

The Class of Feedback Functions

In the case of an ensemble of sequences $\mathcal{Z}$ the maximum order feedback shift register equivalent is defined as the FSR of length $c(\mathcal{Z})$ and a feedback function such that the FSR can generate all the sequences $z_i \in \mathcal{Z}$. As usual we restrict ourselves to periodic sequences of characters which are elements from some finite field $GF(q)$. This situation is typical for nonsingular nonlinear feedback shift registers, which may have a cycle structure with many distinct cycles

For finite field sequences it is customary to use the truth table to derive an analytical expression for the feedback function. The memory cells of the FSR provide for the argument values and hence the truth table is determined by all the occurring FSR states or equivalently all sequences $z_i \in \mathcal{Z}$.

In general not all q^c possible FSR states occur in a particular ensemble. Consequently, there exists a class $\Phi_{\mathcal{Z}}$ of feedback functions which all give rise to the same ensemble of sequences $\mathcal{Z}$. The number of feedback functions in this class is given by the following proposition:

Proposition 2 *Let $\Phi_{\mathcal{Z}}$ denote the class of feedback functions of the maximum order feedback shift register equivalent of the ensemble $\mathcal{Z}$ of periodic sequences z_i over $GF(q)$, where $\mathcal{Z}$ has maximum order complexity c and the z_i are periodic with periods p_i. Then the number $|\Phi_{\mathcal{Z}}|$ of functions in the class $\Phi_{\mathcal{Z}}$ satisfies:*

$$|\Phi_{\mathcal{Z}}| = q^{q^c - \sum p_i}.$$

This result is in contrast with linear complexity where the feedback function is unique for periodic sequences. Hence, $\Phi_{\mathcal{Z}}$ in general contains more than one function and one is able to search for functions exhibiting certain properties such as nonsingularity, the least order product function or the function with the least number of terms.

Proposition 2 also confirms that $c(\mathcal{Z}) \geq \log_q \sum p_i$. For an ensemble, containing only dual sequences ([8, pg. 44]) $\Phi_{\mathcal{Z}}$ contains exactly one feedback function.

The above considerations have an interesting impact on generators, capable of generating a number of N binary periodic sequences of period 2^n, such as DeBruijn sequences [6] and Run Permuted sequences [8, 11]. To generate an ensemble $\mathcal{B}$ of these sequences, a FSR of length $c(\mathcal{B})$ is needed, with

$$c(\mathcal{B}) \geq n + \log N. \tag{4}$$

Inequality (4) shows that for DeBruijn sequences the FSR length increases with at least one bit each time the number of sequences is doubled. However, for an ensemble of Run Permuted sequences of equal complexities, the complexity of the ensemble could be equal to the complexities of the individual sequences.

To generate an ensemble $\mathcal{D}$ of all $2^{2^{n-1}-n}$ DeBruijn sequences of order n requires a FSR of length at least 2^{n-1} according to (4). However, it can be shown that $c(\mathcal{D}) = 2^n - 2$, which makes it infeasible to generate $\mathcal{D}$ by means of one FSR.

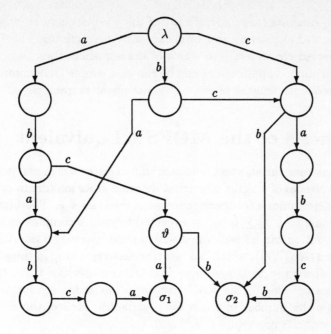

Figure 1: DAWG of *ababca* and *bcabcb*.

3 A Multiple Sequence DAWG

In [4] Blumer et al. describe a linear-time and -memory algorithm to build a *Directed Acyclic Word Graph* (DAWG) from a given string of letters, using a mechanism of suffixpointers. This DAWG is then used to recognize all substrings (or words) in the string. In [9, 10] it was shown how to use this algorithm for determining the maximum order complexity profile of a single given sequence.

Blumer et al. generalized their algorithm to build a DAWG from two or more given strings of letters, as described in [5]. We have subsequently adapted Blumer's algorithm to determine $c(\mathcal{Z})$ and $c_{\mathcal{E}}(\mathcal{Z})$ – in fact their profiles – linear in time and memory.

Example 1 Consider the following two sequences over $\{a, b, c\}$: $z_1 = (a, b, a, b, c, a)$ and $z_2 = (b, c, a, b, c, b)$.
Their respective MOC profiles are (0,1,1,1,3,3) and (0,1,1,1,1,3). The profile of $c(z_1 \cup z_2)$ is (0,1,1,1,3,3,3,3,3,3,3,4), whereas the $c_{\mathcal{E}}(z_1 \cup z_2)$ profile is (2,3,4,4,4,4). The corresponding DAWG (without the suffix pointers) is depicted in Figure 1. The profile of $c(z_1|z_2)$ is (0,1,1,1,3,3,3,3,3,3,3,7), where $z_1|z_2$ denotes the concatenation of z_1 and z_2.

As for the single sequence case, Blumer's algorithm can be used for various other purposes by postprocessing the DAWG. For example, to find a subsequence in any of the given sequences is an operation which is linear in the subsequence length. It is also possible to generate (any part of) any of the given sequences, based on the least number of observed characters and simultaneously determining – also after the least number of observed characters – to which of the sequences the characters belong.

The aforementioned applications can be run on a simple DOS compatible personal computer for sequence lengths of several thousands of characters.

4 Synthesis of the MOFSR Equivalent

To actually construct the shortest feedback shift register which can generates a given ensemble of sequences of lengths l_i one first determines its maximum order complexity and then one determines a feedback function in the class Φ_Z. The first operation has order proportional to $L := \sum l_i$ and is expected to yield a complexity value of $2 \log L$. The second operation can be performed with a technique called the Algebraic Normal Form Transform (see [7, 8]), which is a fast transform resulting in the algebraic normal form of the feedback function, assuming that the non-specified truth table entries are either all zeroes or ones. This ANF transform has order $c2^c$ for the binary case, where c denotes the number of truth table variables. Hence, the expected order of the MOFSR synthesis procedure is $L^2 \log L$.

Example 2 Consider the ensemble S of the two dual sequences $\underline{s}_1 = (11010)^\infty$ and $\underline{s}_2 = (11110010000)^\infty$. In this case $c(S) = 4$ and the truth table is completely specified. The feedback function is $F(x_0, x_1, x_2, x_3) = 1 + x_0 + x_1 + x_2 + x_1 x_3 + x_2 x_3$.

5 Conclusions

We have generalized the theory of maximum order complexity to the case of multiple sequence ensembles. To this end, new definitions of maximum order complexity and ensemble complexity were introduced and the consequences for some special sequence sets, such as DeBruijn sequences and Run Permuted sequences, examined. The described results provide a better understanding of nonlinear feedback shift registers and the complexity of sequences.

The practical import of this theory has been enhanced by the adaptation of Blumer's generalized algorithm, which allows for an efficient determination of the complexity of a given ensemble of sequences, and can be applied for sequence prediction.

References

[1] R. Arratia and M. S. Waterman. "Critical Phenomena in Sequence Matching", *The Annals of Probability*, vol. 13, no. 4, pp. 1236–1249, 1985.

[2] R. Arratia and M. S. Waterman. "An Erdös–Rényi Law with Shifts", *Adv. in Math.*, vol. 55, pp. 13–23, 1985.

[3] R. Arratia, L. Gordon and M. S. Waterman. "An Extreme Value Theory for Sequence Matching", *The Annals of Statistics*, vol. 14, no. 3, pp. 971–993, 1986.

[4] A. Blumer, J. Blumer, A. Ehrenfeucht, D. Haussler and R. McConnell. "Linear Size Finite Automata for the Set of all Subwords of a Word: An Outline of Results", *Bul. Eur. Assoc. Theor. Comp. Sci.*, no. 21, pp. 12–20, 1983.

[5] A. Blumer, J. Blumer, D. Haussler, R. McConnell and A. Ehrenfeucht. "Complete Inverted Files for Efficient Text Retrieval and Analysis", *JACM*, vol. 34, no. 3, pp. 578–595, July 1987.

[6] H. Fredricksen. "A survey of full-length nonlinear shift register cycle algorithms", *SIAM Rev.*, vol. 24, pp. 195–221, April 1982.

[7] C. J. A. Jansen and D. E. Boekee. "The Algebraic Normal Form of Arbitrary Functions of Finite Fields", *Proceedings of the Eighth Symposium on Information Theory in the Benelux, Deventer, The Netherlands*, pp. 69–76, May 1987.

[8] C. J. A. Jansen. *Investigations On Nonlinear Streamcipher Systems: Construction and Evaluation Methods*, PhD. Thesis, Technical University of Delft, Delft, 1989.

[9] C. J. A. Jansen and D. E. Boekee. "The Shortest Feedback Shift Register That Can Generate A Given Sequence", *Proceedings of Crypto '89, Santa Barbara, USA*.

[10] C. J. A. Jansen and D. E. Boekee. "On the Significance of the Directed Acyclic Word Graph in Cryptology", *Proceedings of Auscrypt '90, Sydney, Australia*.

[11] C. J. A. Jansen "On the Construction of Run Permuted Sequences", *proceedings of Eurocrypt '90, Århus, Denmark*.

THE NUMBER OF OUTPUT SEQUENCES OF A BINARY SEQUENCE GENERATOR

Jovan Dj. Golić

Institute of Applied Mathematics and Electronics, Belgrade
School of Electrical Engineering, University of Belgrade,
Yugoslavia

Abstract: In this paper, a number of output sequences is proposed as a characteristic of binary sequence generators for cryptographic applications. Sufficient conditions for a variable-memory binary sequence generator to produce maximum possible number of output sequences are derived.

I. INTRODUCTION

An important characteristic of every binary sequence generator (BSG) for cryptographic or spread-spectrum applications is the number of output sequences it can produce for all the permitted initial states. A natural requirement is that different initial states give rise to different output sequences. For almost all the BSG's known in the cryptographic literature, this property has not been analyzed.

In this paper, we analyze the number of output sequences of a recently proposed [1] nonlinear BSG consisting of three linear feedback shift registers (LFSR's) and a variable memory (MEM-BSG). It is shown in [1] that MEM-BSG is suitable for generating fast binary sequences of large period and linear complexity and with good correlation properties. A number of output sequences of a well-known nonlinear BSG [2] with two LFSR's and a multiplexer (MUX-BSG) is also determined.

II. MEM-BSG

In this section we provide a short description of a MEM-BSG [1], shown in Fig. 1.

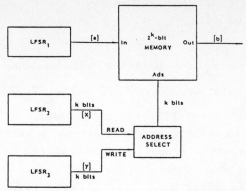

Fig. 1. Variable-memory binary sequence generator (MEM-BSG).

$LFSR_i$ of length m_i has a primitive characteristic polynomial $f_i(x)$, $i=1,2,3$. All the LFSR's are clocked by the same clock and have nonnull initial states, thus generating maximum-length pseudonoise (PN) sequences of periods $P_i=2^{m_i}-1$, $i=1,2,3$, respectively. The initial content of the 2^k bit memory is arbitrary. The read and write addresses are the binary k-tuples taken from any k stages of $LFSR_2$ and $LFSR_3$, respectively, whereas the binary output of $LFSR_1$ is used to load the memory. At any time $t=0,1,2,\ldots$ the following two operations are carried out. First, the output bit $b(t)$ is read out of the memory location addressed by the read address $X(t)$. Second, the output bit $a(t)$ of $LFSR_1$ is written into the memory location addressed by the write address $Y(t)$. The BSG just described will be referred to as a MEM-BSG. It implements a time-varying nonlinear function of the phase shifts of a maximum-length sequence.

The output sequences of a MEM-BSG need not be periodic, because of the initial memory content. To make them periodic and independent of the initial memory content, in all that follows we assume $t=P_3$ is the initial time, that is, we set $t-P_3 \to t$.

III. ANALYSIS

In order to establish large enough lower bounds on the linear complexity and period of the output sequences of a MEM-BSG, it was assumed in [1] that

$$1 \leq k < \min\{m_2, m_3\}. \tag{1}$$

$$2^{m_3}-1 \leq m_1,\tag{2}$$

that m_1, m_2, and m_3 are pairwise coprime, and that the k address stages of $LFSR_2$ are equidistant if $3 \leq k \leq m_2-2$. Hovever, our objective here is to obtain the sufficient conditions, as general as possible, for a MEM-BSG to generate the maximum possible number of output sequences, for all the nonnull initial states of the LFSR's. To this end, instead of the four conditions given above, we shall here maintain only the first two, (1) and (2), generalize the third one, and drop the fourth one.

We start from a suitable expression for the MEM-BSG output sequence [b], derived in [1]:

$$b(t) = \sum_{s=0}^{P_3-1} C_s(t) \, V_s(t), \qquad t=0,1,2,\ldots\tag{3}$$

where

$$C_s(t) = \begin{cases} 1, & t-s=0 \bmod P_3 \\ 0, & t-s \neq 0 \bmod P_3 \end{cases}, \qquad s=0,1,\ldots, P_3-1\tag{4}$$

$$V_s(t) = a(t-\phi_s(X_t)), \quad t=0,1,2,\ldots, \qquad s=0,1,\ldots, P_3-1,\tag{5}$$

X_t, $t=0,1,2,\ldots$, is the read address sequence, of period P_2, taking values in the set $\underset{\sim}{K} = \{0,1\}^k$, and for each $s=0,1,\ldots, P_3-1$, $\phi_s(\underset{\sim}{j})$, $\underset{\sim}{j} \epsilon \underset{\sim}{K}$, is an injective mapping $\underset{\sim}{K} \to \{1,\ldots, P_3\}$ which is defined in [1] in terms of the write address sequence. This definition is not needed here, but only the fact that

$$P_3 = \text{lcm } \{M_{\underset{\sim}{j}} : \underset{\sim}{j} \epsilon \underset{\sim}{K}\}\tag{6}$$

where for each $\underset{\sim}{j} \epsilon \underset{\sim}{K}$, $M_{\underset{\sim}{j}}$ denotes the period of the periodic extension

sequence $\phi_t(\underset{\sim}{j}) = \phi_{t \bmod P_3}(\underset{\sim}{j})$, $t=0,1,2,\ldots$. Note that (3) actually means that [b] consists of P_3 interleaved sequences $[V_s(P_3 t+s)]$, $s=0,1,\ldots,$

P_3-1, which are the decimated versions of $[V_s(t+s)]$, $s=0,1,\ldots, P_3-1$.

We now state and prove a theorem that gives the sufficient conditions for a MEM-BSG to produce the maximum possible number of output sequences.

Theorem: If the conditions (1) and (2) are satisfied and

$$\gcd (m_1, m_2) \neq m_1 \tag{7}$$

$$\gcd \left(P_2, \frac{P_1}{\gcd(P_1,P_2)}\right) = 1 \tag{8}$$

$$\gcd (P_3, P_1 P_2) = 1, \tag{9}$$

then the MEM-BSG generates $P_1 P_2 P_3$ different output sequences, for all the nonnull initial states of LFSR_i, $i=1,2,3$.

Proof: First note that (1) and (2) imply that m_2, $m_3 \geq 2$ and $m_1 \geq 3$. Since each LFSR_i generates cyclic shifts of the corresponding maximum-length sequence, the set of all the output sequences of the MEM-BSG is determined by:

$$b_{ijn}(t) = \sum_{s=0}^{P_3-1} C_s(t) \, a_0(t+i-\phi^0_{s+n}(X^0_{t+j})), \quad t=0,1,2,\ldots \tag{10}$$

for $i=0,\ldots, P_1-1$, $j=0,\ldots, P_2-1$, $n=0,\ldots, P_3-1$, where the sequences $[a_0(t)]$, $[X^0_t]$, and $[\phi^0_t(j)]$, $j\epsilon K$, correspond to arbitrarily chosen initial states of LFSR_i, $i=1,2,3$, respectively. We should prove that $b_{ijn}(t)=b_{i'j'n'}(t)$, $t=0,1,2,\ldots$, which is equivalent to

$$a_0(P_3 t+s+i-\phi^0_{s+n}(X^0_{P_3 t+s+j})) = a_0(P_3 t+s+i'-\phi^0_{s+n'}(X^0_{P_3 t+s+j'})),$$

$$s=0,\ldots, P_3-1, \quad t=0,1,2,\ldots \tag{11}$$

implies that $(i',j',n')=(i,j,n)$, for all admitted (i,j,n) and (i',j',n'). Since the periods of the sequences $[X^0_t]$ and $[a_0(t)]$ are P_2 and P_1, respectively, the periods of $[a_0(t+s+i-\phi^0_{s+n}(X^0_{t+s+j}))]$ and

$[a_0(t+s+i'-\phi^0_{s+n}\cdot(X^0_{t+s+j'})]$ both divide P_1P_2, for each $s=0,\ldots,P_3-1$. In view of (9) it then follows that (11) involves a proper decimation by P_3 of the corresponding sequences. Employing the fact that a proper decimation is an one-to-one correspondence (see [2], for example), we obtain that (11) is equivalent to

$$a_0(t+s+i-\phi^0_{s+n}(X^0_{t+s+j})) = a_0(t+s+i'-\phi^0_{s+n}\cdot(X^0_{t+s+j'})),$$
$$s=0,\ldots,P_3-1, \quad t=0,1,2,\ldots. \tag{12}$$

Further, setting $t \to P_2t+r$, (12) becomes

$$a_0(P_2t+r+s+i-\phi^0_{s+n}(X^0_{r+s+j})) = a_0(P_2t+r+s+i'-\phi^0_{s+n}\cdot(X^0_{r+s+j'})),$$
$$r=0,\ldots,P_2-1, \quad s=0,\ldots,P_3-1, \quad t=0,1,2,\ldots, \tag{13}$$

because $[X^0_t]$ has period P_2. In (13) we deal with a decimation by P_2 of the corresponding cyclic shifts of $[a^0_t]$. This decimation need not be proper. Nevertheless, on the condition (7), the decimation does not change the linear complexity [2, Lemma 2.2.8], and, hence, is an one-to-one correspondence of all the cyclic shifts of $[a_0(t)]$. Accordingly, (13) is equivalent to

$$[i - \phi^0_{s+n}(X^0_{r+s+j}) = i' - \phi^0_{s+n}\cdot(X^0_{r+s+j'})] \bmod P_1,$$
$$r=0,\ldots,P_2-1, \quad s=0,\ldots,P_3-1. \tag{14}$$

Considering the periodicity of the sequences $[X^0_t]$ and $[\phi^0_t(\underset{\sim}{j})]$, $\underset{\sim}{j} \epsilon \underset{\sim}{K}$, (14) reduces to

$$[\phi^0_{(s+n-n')\bmod P_3}(X^0_{(r+j-j')\bmod P_2}) = \phi^0_s(X^0_r)+i'-i] \bmod P_1,$$
$$r=0,\ldots,P_2-1, \quad s=0,\ldots,P_3-1. \tag{15}$$

With the notation $P'_1=P_1/\gcd(P_1, (i'-i)\bmod P_1)$, (15) gives rise to

$$[\phi^0_{(s+(n-n')P'_1)\bmod P_3}(X^0_{(r+(j-j')P'_1)\bmod P_2}) =$$

$$= \phi_s^0(X_r^0) + lcm(P_1, (i'-i)modP_1) = \phi_s^0(X_r^0)] \mod P_1,$$

$$r=0, \ldots, P_2-1, \quad s=0, \ldots, P_3-1, \tag{16}$$

i.e.,

$$[\phi_{(s+(n-n')P_1^{\cdot}t)modP_3}^0(X_{(r+(j-j')P_1^{\cdot}t)modP_2}^0) = \phi_s^0(X_r^0)] \mod P_1,$$

$$r=0, \ldots, P_2-1, \quad s=0, \ldots, P_3-1, \quad t=0,1,2,\ldots . \tag{17}$$

Setting $t=P_2$, (17) becomes

$$[\phi_{(s+(n-n')P_1^{\cdot}P_2)modP_3}^0(X_r^0) = \phi_s^0(X_r^0)] \mod P_1,$$

$$r=0, \ldots, P_2-1, \quad s=0, \ldots, P_3-1, \tag{18}$$

i.e.,

$$[\phi_{(s+(n-n')P_1^{\cdot}P_2)modP_3}^0(\underset{\sim}{j}) = \phi_s^0(\underset{\sim}{j}), \quad \underset{\sim}{j}\epsilon K, \quad s=0, \ldots, P_3-1, \tag{19}$$

where in (19), instead of the equality modulo P_1, we have the ordinary equality, because (2) implies that $1 \leq \phi_s^0(\underset{\sim}{j}) \leq P_3 \leq m_1 \langle 2^{m_1}-1=P_1$, for any $m_1 \geq 3$, $\underset{\sim}{j} \epsilon \underset{\sim}{K}$, and $s=0, \ldots, P_3-1$. Further, recalling that the period of $[\phi_t^0(\underset{\sim}{j})]$ denoted by $M_{\underset{\sim}{j}}$ satisfies $M_{\underset{\sim}{j}}|P_3$, for each $\underset{\sim}{j} \epsilon \underset{\sim}{K}$, from (19) we obtain

$$M_{\underset{\sim}{j}}|[(n-n')P_1^{\cdot}P_2]modP_3, \quad \underset{\sim}{j}\epsilon \underset{\sim}{K}, \tag{20}$$

which in view of (6) leads to

$$P_3|[(n-n') \frac{P_1 P_2}{gcd(P_1, (i'-i)modP_1)}]modP_3, \tag{21}$$

i.e.,

$$[(n-n') \frac{P_1 P_2}{gcd(P_1, (i'-i)modP_1)}]modP_3 = 0. \tag{22}$$

Finally, (9) and (22) imply that n'=n.

Having proved that (11) results in n'=n, we now turn back to (15). With n'=n it becomes

$$[\phi_s^0(X_{(r+(j-j'))\bmod P_2}^0) = \phi_s^0(X_r^0)+i'-i]\bmod P_1,$$

$$r=0,\ldots,\ P_2-1,\quad s=0,\ldots,\ P_3-1, \tag{23}$$

which yields

$$[\phi_s^0(X_{(r+(j-j'))\bmod P_2}^0) = \phi_s^0(X_r^0)+i'-i]\bmod P,$$

$$r=0,\ldots,\ P_2-1,\quad s=0,\ldots,\ P_3-1, \tag{24}$$

where $P=P_1/\gcd(P_1,P_2)$. In a similar way as (15) implies (16), (24) implies

$$[\phi_s^0(X_{(r+(j-j')P')\bmod P_2}^0) = \phi_s^0(X_r^0)]\bmod P,$$

$$r=0,\ldots,\ P_2-1,\quad s=0,\ldots,\ P_3-1, \tag{25}$$

where $P'=P/\gcd(P,\ (i'-i)\bmod P)$. On the other hand, from (7) we obtain

$$P = \frac{P_1}{\gcd(P_1,P_2)} = \frac{2^{m_1}-1}{2^{\gcd(m_1,m_2)}-1} \geq \frac{2^{m_1}-1}{2^{m_1/2}-1} =$$

$$2^{m_1/2}+1 > m_1,\ m_1\geq 3. \tag{26}$$

which together with (2) yields $1\leq\phi_s^0(j)\leq P_3\leq m_1 < P,\ m_1\geq 3$, for each $j\in K$ and $s=0,\ldots,\ P_3-1$. Consequently, (25) remains true if the modulo P equality is replaced by the ordinary one. For each $s=0,\ldots,\ P_3-1$, the period of $[\phi_s^0(X_t^0)]$ is P_2 since $\phi_s^0(j)$, $j\in K$, is an injection. Therefore, from (25) it follows that

$$P_2\left|\left[(j-j')\frac{P}{\gcd(P,(i'-i)\bmod P)}\right]\bmod P_2\right. \tag{27}$$

i.e.,

$$\left[(j-j')\frac{P}{\gcd(P,(i'-i)\bmod P)}\right]\bmod P_2 = 0, \tag{28}$$

which in view of (8) results in $j'=j$.

Now we turn to (23). With $j'=j$ it reduces to $[i'=i]\bmod P_1$, that is, to $i'=i$. We have thus proved that from (11) it follows that $(i',j',n')=(i,j,n)$, for all admitted (i,j,n) and (i',j',n'). Q.E.D.

Note that the case $\gcd(m_1, m_2)=1$, which was considered in [1], is a special case of (7) and (8), meaning that the theorem remains true if (7) and (8) are replaced by $\gcd(m_1, m_2)=1$.

Finally, we analyze a well-known BSG [2] with two LFSR's and a multiplexer (MUX-BSG). Consider a MUX-BSG obtained from a MEM-BSG by substituting a k-bit address multiplexer for a 2^k-bit memory and LFSR$_3$. The multiplexer k-bit address is generated in the same way as the read address in the MEM-BSG, while the 2^k multiplexer inputs are taken from any 2^k stages of LFSR$_1$. It is shown in [1] that there is a strong connection between the MEM-BSG and the so-defined MUX-BSG. Accordingly, in a similar way one can prove that on the conditions (7) and (8) the MUX-BSG generates $P_1 P_2$ different output sequences for all the nonnull initial states of LFSR$_1$ and LFSR$_2$. This fact was not revealed in [2].

IV. CONCLUSION

As a characteristic of binary sequence generators (BSG's) for cryptographic applications, the number of output sequences they can generate for all the permitted initial states is proposed. A natural cryptographic criterion is that this number be maximum possible. It is shown that this property can be analyzed for some types of the BSG's. It is proved that under certain conditions the recently defined MEM-BSG [1] and the well-known MUX-BSG [2] both produce maximum possible number of output sequences.

V. REFERENCES

[1] Jovan Dj. Golić, Miodrag M. Mihaljević, "Minimal linear equivalent analysis of a variable-memory binary sequence generator" IEEE Trans. Inform. Theory, vol. IT-36, pp. 190-192, Jan. 1990.

[2] S.M. Jennings, "A special class of binary sequences", Ph.D. thesis, Westfield College, London University, 1980.

Linear Complexity of Periodically Repeated Random Sequences

Zong-Duo Dai *
Dept. of Math., RHBNC, University of London,
Egham Hill, Egham, Surrey, TW20 0EX, U.K.

Jun-Hui Yang
Computing Center, Academia Sinica,
P.O.Box 2719, 100080, Beijing, China

Abstract

On the linear complexity $\Lambda(\tilde{z})$ of a periodically repeated random bit sequence $\tilde{z}$, R. Rueppel proved that, for two extreme cases of the period T, the expected linear complexity $E[\Lambda(\tilde{z})]$ is almost equal to T, and suggested that $E[\Lambda(\tilde{z})]$ would be close to T in general [6, pp. 33-52] [7, 8]. In this note we obtain bounds of $E[\Lambda(\tilde{z})]$, as well as bounds of the variance $Var[\Lambda(\tilde{z})]$, both for the general case of T, and we estimate the probability distribution of $\Lambda(\tilde{z})$. Our results on $E[\Lambda(\tilde{z})]$ quantify the closeness of $E[\Lambda(\tilde{z})]$ and T, in particular, formally confirm R. Rueppel's suggestion.

Keywords: Linear Complexity, Random Sequences.

1 Introduction

The linear complexity [8, p. 32] (or linear equivalence [1, p.199]) of a sequence is the length of the shortest linear shift register (LFSR) by which the given

---

*On leave from Graduate School, Academia Sinica, 100039-08, Beijing, China, with this work supported by SERC grant GR/F 72727.

sequence could be generated. Since there exists an efficient algorithm for finding the shortest LFSR which generates a given sequence (the Berlekamp-Massey LFSR synthesis algorithm [5]), the linear complexity is particularly important as a measure of the unpredictability of sequences. The statistical properties of the linear complexity of a periodically repeated random bit string are of considerable practical interest [6, pp. 33-52] [7, 8], since deterministically generated key streams in cipher systems must be ultimately periodic.

Given T, let $z^T = z_0, z_1, \ldots, z_{T-1}$ be a binary sequence where z_i ($0 \leq i \leq T-1$) is selected according to a fair coin tossing experiment, and let $\tilde{z}$ be the semi-infinite sequence by periodically repeating the random bit string z^T. Let $\mathcal{Z}$ be the sample space consisting of all the possible semi-infinite periodically repeated random sequences $\tilde{z}$. The elements in $\mathcal{Z}$ are equiprobable. Since $|\mathcal{Z}| = 2^T$, where $|\mathcal{Z}|$ denote the size of $\mathcal{Z}$, so the probability of the occurrence of each $\tilde{z}$ is equal to $1/|\mathcal{Z}| = 2^{-T}$. Let $\Lambda(\tilde{z})$ denote the linear complexity of $\tilde{z}$, then $\Lambda(\tilde{z})$ is a random variable on the sample space $\mathcal{Z}$. Let $E[\Lambda(\tilde{z})]$ be the expected linear complexity of $\tilde{z}$, and $Var[\Lambda(\tilde{z})]$ the variance of the linear complexity $\Lambda(\tilde{z})$.

R. Rueppel computed $E[\Lambda(\tilde{z})]$ in two extreme cases: when $T = 2^n - 1$ (any prime n) and when $T = 2^m$ (any m) [6, pp. 33-52] [7, 8]. In both cases he proved that $E[\Lambda(\tilde{z})]$ is almost equal to T, or more precisely, $E[\Lambda(\tilde{z})] \geq\simeq e^{-1/n}(2^n - 3/2)$ when $T = 2^n - 1$, and

$$E[\Lambda(\tilde{z})] = 2^m - 1 + 2^{-2^m} \tag{1}$$

when $T = 2^m$, and suggested that in the general case $E[\Lambda(\tilde{z})]$ would be close to T.

D. Gollmann [2] proved that, when $T = p^n$, $p > 2$ prime, and p^2 is not a factor of $2^{p-1} - 1$,

$$E[\Lambda(\tilde{z})] = p^n - \frac{1}{2} - (p-1) \sum_{i=0}^{n-1} p^i 2^{-n_p p^i}, \tag{2}$$

where n_p is the degree of the irreducible polynomials with period p over $GF(2)$.

In this note we consider $E[\Lambda(\tilde{z})]$, as well as $Var[\Lambda(\tilde{z})]$, both for the general case. We obtain expressions for $E[\Lambda(\tilde{z})]$ and for $Var[\Lambda(\tilde{z})]$, and we bound $E[\Lambda(\tilde{z})]$ and $Var[\Lambda(\tilde{z})]$ in terms of the arithmetic function $d(T)$, and then we bound $E[\Lambda(\tilde{z})]$ and $Var[\Lambda(\tilde{z})]$ in terms of analytic functions, or more precisely, we show that for any $\varepsilon > 0$, (i) $E[\Lambda(\tilde{z})] > T - T^{\varepsilon}$ and $Var[\Lambda(\tilde{z})] < T^{\varepsilon}$, provided T is large enough, (ii) $E[\Lambda(\tilde{z})] > T - T^{(1+\varepsilon)\log 2/\log\log T}$ and $Var[\Lambda(\tilde{z})] < T^{(1+\varepsilon)\log 2/\log\log T}$, provided T is large enough, and (iii) $E[\Lambda(\tilde{z})] > T - (\log T)^{(1+\varepsilon)\log 2}$ and $Var[\Lambda(\tilde{z})] < \log_2(1 + T)(\log T)^{(1+\varepsilon)\log 2}$ for almost all T (see Remark 1 in section 4). We also estimate the probability distribution of $\Lambda(\tilde{z})$, for any $\varepsilon > \delta > 0$ we get that $Prob.(\Lambda(\tilde{z}) > T - T^{\varepsilon}) > 1 - T^{-2\varepsilon+\delta}$ for large enough T. Our results on $E[\Lambda(\tilde{z})]$ quantify the closeness of $E[\Lambda(\tilde{z})]$ and T, and in particular formally confirm R. Rueppel's suggestion.

In this paper the base of the logarithms is e, $i.e.$, $\log = \log_e$, unless indicated otherwise.

2   Expressions for $E[\Lambda(\tilde{z})]$ and $Var[\Lambda(\tilde{z})]$

We identify the sequence $\tilde{z}$ with its generating function $\tilde{z}(x)$, defined over the binary field $GF(2)$, as $\tilde{z}(x) = \sum_{j=0}^{\infty} z_j x^j$. It is known that $\tilde{z}(x)$ is equal to a rational fraction $\tilde{z}(x) = z^*(x)/(1 - x^T) = P(\tilde{z}, x)/C(\tilde{z}, x)$, where $z^*(x) = \sum_{j=0}^{T-1} z_j x^j$, $P(\tilde{z}, x)$ and $C(\tilde{z}, x)$ are coprime to each other. It is also known that $C(\tilde{z}, x)$ is the minimal polynomial [1, p.201][8, p. 26] of $\tilde{z}$, and $\Lambda(\tilde{z}) = degC(\tilde{z}, x)$, where $degC(\tilde{z}, x)$ is the degree of $C(\tilde{z}, x)$.

The range of $C(\tilde{z}, x)$ depends on the factorization of $1 - x^T$. If $T = 2^m T_1$, $\gcd(2, T_1) = 1$, it is known [4, pp. 64-65] that $1 - x^T = \prod_{d|T_1} \prod_{j=1}^{\phi(d)/n_d} C_{d,j}^{2^m}(x)$, where for any given d, $C_{d,j}(x)$ ($0 \le j \le \phi(d)/n_d$) are all the distinct monic irreducible polynomials with period d over $GF(2)$, and of the same degree n_d, where n_d is the order of 2 modulo d, ($i.e.$, the least positive integer such that $2^{n_d} = 1 \pmod d$), $\phi(d)$ is the Euler's function, ($i.e.$, the number of the integers $i, 1 \le i \le d$, coprime to d). As a factor of $1 - x^T$, $C(\tilde{z}, x)$ must be of the form $C(\tilde{z}, x) = \prod_{d|T_1} \prod_{j=1}^{\phi(d)/n_d} C_{d,j}^{e_{d,j}(\tilde{z})}(x)$, $0 \le e_{d,j}(\tilde{z}) \le 2^m$. The exponent $e_{d,j}(\tilde{z})$ is a random variable defined on $\mathcal{Z}$ with range $[0, 2^m]$. Now we have $\Lambda(\tilde{z}) = \sum_{d|T_1} \sum_{j=1}^{\phi(d)/n_d} n_d e_{d,j}(\tilde{z})$.

Lemma 1 .

1.   The random variable $e_{d,j}(\tilde{z})$ has the following probability density function

$$Prob.(e_{d,j}(\tilde{z}) = e) = \begin{cases} 2^{-n_d 2^m} & e = 0, \\ 2^{-n_d 2^m}(2^{n_d e} - 2^{n_d(e-1)}) & e > 0. \end{cases}$$

2.   All the random variables $e_{d,j}(\tilde{z})$, $d \mid T_1$, $1 \leq j \leq \phi(d)/n_d$, are mutually independent.

Observe that the probability density function of $e_{d,j}(\tilde{z})$ is not dependent on the parameter j, we denote by E_d the expected value of $e_{d,j}(\tilde{z})$, and by V_d the variance of $e_{d,j}(\tilde{z})$.

Lemma 2

$$E_d = 2^m - \frac{2^{n_d 2^m} - 1}{2^{n_d 2^m}(2^{n_d} - 1)},$$

and

$$V_d = \frac{2^{n_d(2^{m+1}+1)} - (2^{m+1} + 1)(2^{n_d(2^m+1)} - 2^{n_d 2^m}) - 1}{2^{n_d 2^{m+1}}(2^{n_d} - 1)^2}.$$

Theorem 1 (Expressions) *Let $T = 2^m T_1$, $\gcd(2, T_1) = 1$. Then*

$$E[\Lambda(\tilde{z})] = T - \sum_{d \mid T_1} \frac{\phi(d)(2^{n_d 2^m} - 1)}{2^{n_d 2^m}(2^{n_d} - 1)},$$

and

$$Var[\Lambda(\tilde{z})] = \sum_{d \mid T_1} \frac{\phi(d)n_d[2^{n_d(2^{m+1}+1)} - (2^{m+1} + 1)(2^{n_d(2^m+1)} - 2^{n_d 2^m}) - 1]}{2^{n_d 2^{m+1}}(2^{n_d} - 1)^2}.$$

Theorem 1 gives a way to calculate $E[\Lambda(\tilde{z})]$ and $Var[\Lambda(\tilde{z})]$ based on the factorization of T case by case. In the special case when $T = 2^m$ this is straightforward. Both of the summations in Theorem 1 contain only one term with $d = 1$, from which one obtains (1), as well as

$$Var[\Lambda(\tilde{z})] = \frac{2^{2^{m+1}+1} - (2^{m+1} + 1)(2^{(2^m+1)} - 2^{2^m}) - 1}{2^{2^{m+1}}} < 2 .$$

For another exampe, when $T = p^n$, $p > 2$ prime, and p^2 is not a factor of $2^{p-1} - 1$, from $E[\Lambda(\tilde{z})]$'s expression, in which the summation contains $n + 1$ terms with $d = p^i, 0 \leq i \leq n$, and $n_{p^i} = n_p p^{i-1}, 1 \leq i \leq n$, one obtains (2). But the real significance of Theorem 1 is that from it one may bound $E[\Lambda(\tilde{z})]$ and $Var[\Lambda(\tilde{z})]$ in terms of the arithmetic function $d(n)$, which is defined to be the number of all possible positive factors of n, i.e., $d(n) = \sum_{d|n} 1$.

3 Bounds for $E[\Lambda(\tilde{z})]$ and $Var[\Lambda(\tilde{z})]$ by $d(n)$

Theorem 2 *Let* $T = 2^m T_1$, $\gcd(2, T_1) = 1$. *Then*

$$E[\Lambda(\tilde{z})] > T - d(T_1) \geq T - d(T),$$

and

$$Var[\Lambda(\tilde{z})] < d(T_1)(1 + \log_2(1 + T_1)) \leq d(T)(1 + \log_2(1 + T)).$$

With Theorem 2 and the factorization of T, the evaluation for both of $E[\Lambda(\tilde{z})]$ and $Var[\Lambda(\tilde{z})]$ becomes easier. In fact, if $T_1 = \prod_{i=1}^{s} p_i^{e_i}$, where $p_i, 1 \leq i \leq s$, are distinct prime factors, then $d(T_1) = \prod_{i=1}^{s}(1 + e_i)$ [2, p. 238]. Hence $E[\Lambda(\tilde{z})] > T - \prod_{i=1}^{s}(1 + e_i)$ and $Var[\Lambda(\tilde{z})] < (1 + \log_2(1 + T_1)) \prod_{i=1}^{s}(1 + e_i)$. What is more interesting is that from Theorem 2 we shall get analytic bounds for $E[\Lambda(\tilde{z})]$ and $Var[\Lambda(\tilde{z})]$ based on the orders of $d(n)$.

4 Bounds for $E[\Lambda(\tilde{z})]$ and $Var[\Lambda(\tilde{z})]$ by Analytic Functions

Lemma 3 [2, pp. 259-261, p. 361] *If* $\varepsilon > 0$, *then we have*

1. $d(n) < n^\varepsilon$ *for all* $n > n_\varepsilon$, *where* n_ε *depends on* ε.

2. $d(n) < n^{(1+\varepsilon)\log 2/\log\log n}$ *for all* $n > n_\varepsilon$, *where* n_ε *depends on* ε.

3. $d(n) < (\log n)^{(1+\varepsilon)\log 2}$ *for almost all numbers* n.

Remark 1 A property P of positive integers n is said to be true for **almost all numbers** if $\lim_{x \to \infty} N(x)/x = 1$, where $N(x)$ is the number of positive integers less than x which satisfy P.

Remark 2 Lemma 3 provides three kinds of bounds for $d(n)$. The bounds given in item *1* and item *2* hold for large enough n. The bound given in item *2*, a kind of power of n with the exponent tending slowly to zero when n goes to infinity, is tighter than the bound given in item *1*, but the latter looks much simpler. The bound given in item *3* is the tightest one, but it holds only for almost all n.

From Theorem 2 and Lemma 3 we may obtain immediately three kinds of bounds for $E[\Lambda(\tilde{z})]$.

Theorem 3 (Bounds for $E[\Lambda(\tilde{z})]$) *If $\varepsilon > 0$, then we have*

1. $E[\Lambda(\tilde{z})] > T - T^{\varepsilon}$ *for all $T > T_\varepsilon$, where T_ε depends on ε.*

2. $E[\Lambda(\tilde{z})] > T - T^{(1+\varepsilon)\log 2/\log\log T}$ *for all $T > T_\varepsilon$, where T_ε depends on ε.*

3. $E[\Lambda(\tilde{z})] > T - (\log T)^{(1+\varepsilon)\log 2}$ *for almost-all T.*

Remark 3 The bounds on $E[\Lambda(\tilde{z})]$ shown in Theorem 3 quantify the closeness of $E[\Lambda(\tilde{z})]$ and T, and in particular, the expected linear complexity $E[\Lambda(\tilde{z})]$ and the period T are of the same asymptotical order, *i.e.*, $\lim_{T \to \infty} E[\Lambda(\tilde{z})]/T = 1$, hence formally confirm R. Rueppel's suggestion.

Theorem 4 (Bounds for $Var[\Lambda(\tilde{z})]$) *If $\varepsilon > 0$, then we have*

1. $Var[\Lambda(\tilde{z})] < T^{\varepsilon}$, *for all $T > T_\varepsilon$, where T_ε depends on ε.*

2. $Var[\Lambda(\tilde{z})] < T^{(1+\varepsilon)\log 2/\log\log T}$, *for all $T > T_\varepsilon$, where T_ε depends on ε.*

3. $Var[\Lambda(\tilde{z})] < (\log T)^{(1+\varepsilon)\log 2} \log_2(1 + T)$, *for almost-all T.*

5   Probability Distribution of $\Lambda(\tilde{z})$

Based on the knowlege on $E[\Lambda(\tilde{z})]$ and $Var[\Lambda(\tilde{z})]$, we prove that the linear complexity $\Lambda(\tilde{z})$ distributes very close to the length T with a probability almost equal to 1, provided T is large enough, as shown in the following theorem.

Theorem 5 *If $\varepsilon > \delta > 0$, then for large enough T we have*

$$Prob.(\Lambda(\tilde{z}) > T - T^{\varepsilon}) > 1 - T^{-2\varepsilon + \delta}$$

6   From GF(2) to GF(q)

With the same arguments the results above can be generalized to the semi-infinite periodically repeated random sequences over any given finite field $GF(q)$, $q = p^m$, p prime,

Given T, let $z^T = z_0, z_1, \ldots, z_{T-1}$ be a random sequence of length T over $GF(q)$, and $\tilde{z}$ the semi-infinite sequence by periodically repeating z^T. Let $\mathcal{Z}$ be the sample space consisting of all the possible semi-infinite periodically repeated random sequences $\tilde{z}$, then $|\mathcal{Z}| = q^T$. We assume the elements in $\mathcal{Z}$ are equiprobable, *i.e.*, the probability of the occurrence of each $\tilde{z}$ is equal to q^{-T}. Now let n_d denote the order of q modulo d, then Theorem 1 extends to

Theorem 6 *Let $T = p^m T_1$, $\gcd(p, T_1) = 1$. Then*

$$E[\Lambda(\tilde{z})] = T - \sum_{d|T_1} \frac{\phi(d)(q^{n_d p^m} - 1)}{q^{n_d p^m}(q^{n_d} - 1)},$$

and

$$Var[\Lambda(\tilde{z})] = \sum_{d|T_1} \frac{\phi(d)n_d[q^{n_d(2p^m+1)} - (2p^m + 1)(q^{n_d(p^m+1)} - q^{n_d p^m}) - 1]}{q^{2n_d p^m}(q^{n_d} - 1)^2}.$$

And Theorem 2 extends to

Theorem 7 *Let $T = p^m T_1$, $\gcd(p, T_1) = 1$. Then*

$$E[\Lambda(\tilde{z})] > T - d(T_1) \geq T - d(T),$$

and

$$Var[\Lambda(\tilde{z})] < d(T_1)(1 + \log_q(1 + T_1)) \leq d(T)(1 + \log_q(1 + T)).$$

Hence all the other theorems over $GF(2)$ above can be extended to over $GF(q)$.

175

Acknowledgement

The authors are very grateful to Fred Piper for his invitation of visiting RHBNC, University of London, and for his valuable comments and suggestions about this work. The authors would like to thank the hospitality of the Department of Mathematics, RHBNC, University of London, where some of this work was undertaken. Thanks are also due to Mike Burmester for his help in improving the English of this paper.

References

[1] H. Beker and F. Piper, "Ciper Systems", Northwood Books, London, 1982.

[2] D. Gollman, "Linear Complexity of Sequences with Period p^n", Eurocrypt'86, A Workshop on the Theory and Application of Chryptographic Techniques, May 20-22, 1986, in Linkoping, Sweden, pp. 3.2-3.3.

[3] G. H. Hardy and E. M. Wright, "An Introduction To The Theory of Numbers", Oxford, The Clarendon Press, 1938.

[4] R. Lidl and H. Niederreiter, "Finite Fields", *Encyclopaedia of Mathematics and its Applications* **20**, Reading, Mass, Addison-Wesley, 1983.

[5] J. L. Massey, "Shift-Register Synthesis and BCH decoding", IEEE Trans. on Info. Theory, Vol. IT-15, pp. 122-127, Jan. 1969.

[6] R. A. Rueppel, "New Approaches to Stream Ciphers", Ph.D.dissertation, Inst. of Telecommunications, Swiss Federal Inst. of Technol., Zurich, Dec. 1984.

[7] R. A. Rueppel, "Linear Complexity and Random Sequences", Presented at Eurocrypt'85

[8] R. A. Rueppel, "Analysis and Design of Stream Ciphers", Springer, Berlin-Heidelberg-New York-London-Paris-Tokyo: Springer-Verlag. 1986.

On A Fast Correlation Attack
on
Certain Stream Ciphers

Vladimir Chepyzhov
Institute for Problems of Information
Transmission
USSR Academy of Sciences
Ermolovoy 19, Moscow GSP-4, USSR

Ben Smeets
Department of Information Theory
Lund University
Box 118
S-221 00 Lund, Sweden

Abstract—In this paper we present a new algorithm for the recovery of the initial state of a linear feedback shift register when a noisy output sequence is given. Our work is focussed on the investigation of the asymptotical behaviour of the recovery process rather than on the construction of an optimal recovery procedure. Our results show the importance of low-weight checks and show also that the complexity of the recovery problem grows less than exponentially with the length of the shift register, even if the number of taps grows linearly with the register length. Our procedure works for shift register with arbitrary feedback polynomial.

1 Introduction

It was observed by Siegenthaler [1] that if the key generator used in a stream cipher is correlated to a linear feedback shift (LFSR) sequence with a probability that exceeds 0.5, then it is possible possible to reconstruct the initial state of the shift register. In the traditional setting it is assumed that the feedback connections of the LFSR are known to the cryptanalyst and that only the initial state is unkown to him. In the correlation attack as it originally was desribed by Siegenthaler, one uses an exhaustive search through the state space of the shift register. Such a search is not very realistic when the degree r (= length of the LFSR) of the feedback polynomial of the LFSR exceeds 60, especially when this task has to be performed frequently. Recently it was shown by Meier and Staffelbach [2] that in certain cases one can avoid this exhaustive search. In particular they showed that if the number t of feedback taps is small, then it is possible to restore the initial state by an iterative procedure with much less complexity than exhaustive search. Using the same idea, several others authors proposed iterative improvement algorithms, see for example [3]. Unfortunately the

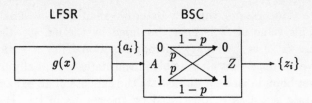

Figure 1: The correlation attack model for initial state recovery problem.

length of the key sequence that must be available to the cryptanalyst may be forbidding large. The algorithm of Meier and Staffelbach has asymptotical complexity $O(r)$ when the number of taps t is fixed. However, if t grows linearly with r, then the complexity of their algorithm is exponential in r.

In this paper we present another procedure for finding the initial state of the LFSR. The algorithm is divided into two stages; the first stage is the search for low-weight checks and the second is the iterative improvement procedure for restoring the initial state. Also in the algorithm of Meier and Staffelbach (and others too) there are two stages but there the required checks are obtained by a simple algebraic procedure. Their procedure, albeit very fast, uses the available key stream not very efficiently and thus forces the cryptanalyst to exhibit long key stream subsequences. Our algorithm is using the key stream almost as efficiently as possible at the expense of an increase of the complexity of the first stage. Our algorithm that we use for the first stage is derived from efficient algorithms for finding the non-zero codeword of lowest weight in a linear code, [4], [5]. The second stage of our algorithm is almost identical to Gallager's algorithm for the decoding of low-density parity-check codes [6].

2 The cryptanalyst's problem and definitions

Our attack is like in [1] and [2] based on the model shown in Figure 1. The (observed) output sequence $\{z_i\}$ is regarded as a corrupted version of the LFSR output sequence $\{a_i\}$. It is assumed that the value of z_i only depends on the input a_i and the observation at time i. For this model it is natural to say that the symbol a_i is passed through an (observation) channel whose output z_i we can observe. The model of this channel we just described is also known as the Binary (Memoryless) Symmetric Channel, BSC. The probability $q = 1 - p$ is also known as the correlation probability since $P(a_i = z_i) = q$. The cryptanalyst's problem can now be formulated as follows:

Statement of the problem: Let $p < 0.5$ an let the (primitive)[1] feedback polynomial of the LFSR, denoted by $g(x)$, be of degree r. The problem is to restore the linear feedback shift register subsequence $\{a_i\}_{i=0}^{N-1}$ from the observed subsequence $\{z_i\}_{i=0}^{N-1}$, where $r < N << 2^r - 1$. The value of N should be as small as possible.

---

[1] For simplicity the reader can think of primitive feedback polynomial. However, mutatis mutandis, everything is valid for arbitrary feedback polynomials.

We fix N to some value greater than r. Later we shall see how small a value of N can be chosen. This value of N is lower bounded by the unicity distance given by $r/(1 - H(p))$, where $H(x)$ is the binary entropy function $H(x) = -x \log_2 x - (1 - x) \log_2(1-x)$. Here we assumed that all possible initial states are equally likely. Values of N close to this lower bound can be obtained att the expense of an exhaustive search through the initial state space as is illustrated by the results in [1]. But this gives an exponential growth (with r) in complexity of the recovery procedure. We want to avoid such a growth in complexity.

Before we start with the discussion of our procedure, we give some definitions. As in [2] the following polynomials play an essential role:

Definition 1: Let $h(x)$ be a polynomial of degree $\geq r = \deg g(x)$, with $h_0 = h(0) = 1$ such that for any sequence $\{a_i\}$ (whose formal power series we denote by $a(x)$) generated by the LFSR with feedback polynomial $g(x)$ we have $h(x) \cdot a(x)$ is a polynomial of degree $< \deg h(x)$. Then the polynomial $h(x)$ is called *a check* (polynomial of the LFSR).

From shift register theory we know that whenever the polynomial $h(x)$ is a check, then $g(x)$ divides $h(x)$. From another point of view we can regard the checks of degree less than n as the codewords of the $(n, n - r)$ linear code generated by the polynomial $g(x)$. This code has rate $R = \frac{n-r}{n}$ and redundancy r. To simplify the exposition of our attack we assume the we already obtained a set of M checks $\{h^{(i)}(x)\}_{i=1}^{M}$.

Definition 2: Let the set $\{h^{(i)}(x)\}_{i=1}^{M}$ be a set of checks and let the coefficients $h_j^{(i)}$ be determined from $h^{(i)}(x) = \sum_{j=0}^{\infty} h_j^{(i)} x^j$. This set is called *a set of M checks of length L with at most t taps* if:

1. $\forall i = 1, \ldots, M, \quad h_0^{(i)} = 1$, and $\deg h^{(i)} < L$,
2. $\forall h^{(i)}(x), \quad \# \left\{ h_j^{(i)} ; h_j^{(i)} \neq 0, j \geq 1 \right\} \leq t$,
3. $\forall \ell_1, \ell_2 : \ell_1 \neq \ell_2, \quad \left\{ j ; h_j^{(\ell_1)} \neq 1 \right\} \cap \left\{ j ; h_j^{(\ell_2)} \neq 1 \right\} = \emptyset$.

In words this means that the Hamming weight of the polynomials in the set of checks is not more than $t + 1$ and that two different checks have different non-zero coefficients except for their constant term.

Example: The following polynomials are independent checks of length L with at most t taps in the case $g(x) = 1 + x$, $t = 3$ and $L = 8$.

$$h^{(1)}(x) = 1 + x + x^5 + x^7,$$
$$h^{(2)}(x) = 1 + x^2 + x^3 + x^4,$$
$$h^{(3)}(x) = 1 + x^6.$$

3 Iterative improvement

Let us consider some symbol a_i from the sequence $\{a_i\}$. If $h(x) = \sum_{j=0}^{L-1} h_j x^j$ is a check, then

$$a_i = \sum_{j \geq 1, h_j = 1} a_{i-j} = a_{i_1} + a_{i_2} + \ldots + a_{i_t},$$

where the i_k's denote the value of the indices $i - j$ when $h_j = 1$. If we have a set of M independent checks $\{h^{(i)}\}_{i=1}^M$, then we have for this symbol a_i;

$$
\begin{aligned}
a_i + a_{i_1^{(1)}} + a_{i_2^{(1)}} + \cdots + a_{i_t^{(1)}} &= 0 \\
a_i + a_{i_1^{(2)}} + a_{i_2^{(2)}} + \cdots + a_{i_t^{(2)}} &= 0 \\
\vdots \qquad \vdots \qquad\qquad \vdots & \\
a_i + a_{i_1^{(M)}} + a_{i_2^{(M)}} + \cdots + a_{i_t^{(M)}} &= 0.
\end{aligned}
\tag{1}
$$

We note that all the indices $i_j^{(\ell)}$ are different. It is easy to see that these equations can be applied to every symbol a_i as long as $i - L > 0$. If we replace in equation (1) the values of a_i and $a_{i_j^{(\ell)}}$ by the corresponding values of z_i and $z_{i_j^{(\ell)}}$, then maybe not all the equations hold because the a_i's are not necessarily equal to the corresponding z_i's.

Using these (check) equations it is possible to compute a new value $\tilde{z}_i^{(1)}$ of z_i such that $P(\tilde{z}_i^{(1)} = a_i) > q$ using the ideas of Gallager for the decoding of low-density parity-check codes. We compute for every index i a new value of z_i and we obtain the (sub)sequence $\{\widetilde{z^{(1)}}_i\}_{i=0}^{N-1}$. Using the procedure again on this sequence we can get the sequence $\{\widetilde{z^{(2)}}_i\}_{i=0}^{N-1}$ in such a manner that the number of disagreements between $\{\widetilde{z^{(s)}}_i\}_{i=0}^{N-1}$ and $\{z_i\}_{i=0}^{N-1}$ vanishes as s increases. Our procedure obviously works under the conditions that the first step must lead to a smaller number of expected disagreements. Hence the first step deserves our special attention.

In what follows we consider the noisy output symbols as random variables, conveniently denoted by Z_i, $i \geq 0$. We define the random variable

$$
\tilde{Z}_i \overset{\text{def}}{=} \sum_{j=1}^t h_j Z_{i-j}.
\tag{2}
$$

When no errors occur, then $Z_i = \tilde{Z}_i = a_i$. Therefore we also consider the random variable

$$
Y_i \overset{\text{def}}{=} Z_i + \tilde{Z}_i,
\tag{3}
$$

and we note that $Y_i = 0$ when $Z_i = a_i$ for all i. The probability $P(Z_i = a_i) = q = 1 - p > 0.5$. The probability that $\tilde{Z}_i = a_i$ is given by

$$
\begin{aligned}
P(\tilde{Z}_i = a_i) &= P(\#\text{symbol changes is even}) \\
&= \sum_{i=0, i \text{ even}}^t \binom{t}{i} p^i q^{t-i} = 1 - \sum_{i=0, i \text{ odd}}^t \binom{t}{i} p^i q^{t-i} \\
&= \frac{1}{2}\left[\sum_{i=0}^t \binom{t}{i} p^i q^{t-i} - \sum_{i=0}^t \binom{t}{i} (-p)^i q^{t-i} \right] \\
&= \frac{1}{2}[1 + (2\varepsilon)^t].
\end{aligned}
\tag{4}
$$

Let

$$
Q \overset{\text{def}}{=} P(\tilde{Z}_i = a_i).
\tag{5}
$$

Let D (random variable !) denote the number of non zeros in $\{Y_i\}_{i=0}^{N-1}$. In the first correction step we determine the sequence $\{s^{(1)}_i\}$ defined by

$$z_i^{(1)} = \begin{cases} z_i, & \text{when } D < T \\ z_i + 1, & \text{when } D \geq T. \end{cases}$$

We now compute the probabilities $P(z_i^{(1)} = a_i)$ after the first correction of $\{z_i\}$. then

$$P(z_i^{(1)} = a_i) = P(z_i^{(1)} = a_i, D < T) + P(z_i^{(1)} = a_i, D \geq T),$$

where T is some fixed integer value in the range $[0, M]$ to be chosen later. Since

$$P(z_i^{(1)} = a_i, D < T) = P(z_i^{(0)} = z_i = a_i, D < T)$$

$$= q \sum_{d=0}^{T-1} \binom{M}{d} (1 - Q)^d Q^{M-d}, \tag{6}$$

and, similarly,

$$P(z_i^{(1)} = a_i, D \geq T) = p \sum_{d=T}^{M} \binom{M}{d} Q^d (1 - Q)^{M-d}. \tag{7}$$

Combining these two results gives

$$P(z_i^{(1)} = a_i) = q + \sum_{d=T}^{M} \binom{M}{d} (Q(1 - Q))^{M-d} \left[pQ^{2d-M} - q(1 - Q)^{2d-M} \right]. \tag{8}$$

We get on the average more correct symbols after the first step if

$$\tilde{Q} \stackrel{\text{def}}{=} P(z_i^{(1)} = a_i) \geq q = P(z_i = a_i). \tag{9}$$

By inspection of equation (8) it follows that if

$$pQ^{2T-M} - q(1 - Q)^{2T-M} > 0,$$

then for all $i \geq T$

$$pQ^{2i-M} - q(1 - Q)^{2i-M} > 0.$$

Thus we have the following Lemma:

Lemma 1: Let Q and $\tilde{Q}$ be defined by equation (5), resp. equation (9). Furthermore, let

$$T = \max\left\{ d \in [0..M] ; \left(\frac{Q}{1 - Q} \right)^{M-2d} > \frac{q}{1 - q} \right\}, \tag{10a}$$

then

$$\tilde{Q} > Q \quad \text{if and only if} \quad \left(\frac{Q}{1 - Q} \right)^{M} > \frac{q}{1 - q}. \tag{10b}$$

∎

From this we have the following important result:

Theorem 2: For convergence of the iterative improvement procedure to the correct (sub)sequence $\{a_i\}$ we need at least

$$M = \frac{\log \frac{q}{1-q}}{\log \frac{Q}{1-Q}} \tag{11}$$

independent checks. ◼

We have the corollary:

Corollary 3: Let $q = 1/2 + \varepsilon$ and $Q = \frac{1}{2}(1 + (2\varepsilon)^t)$, then we need

$$M_0 = O\left(\left(\frac{1}{2\varepsilon}\right)^{t-1}\right) \quad \text{checks.}$$

◼

When the conditions for convergence are satisfied we know from [6] that the required number of iterations is normally very small. Hence, by ensuring that we meet the conditions of convergence with some additional safety margin, the iterative improvement process has roughly the complexity $C_{it} = O(MN)$ since for all the N symbols we have to evaluate the M check equations. Summarizing we see that the fewer the taps t, the fewer checks we need.

4 Finding low-weight checks

The value of N that can be chosen is related with the problem of how many symbols of $\{z_i\}$ we need for obtaining the set of M independent checks. This brings us back to the first stage of our attack procedure: the search of non-zero codewords of low (Hamming) weight. If these codewords have large degrees, then we need also a large N because we want only those codewords which give independent checks.

Recall that the linear code we have to investigate has length n, informativity $n-r$, and redundancy r. We want a fast algorithm that will find the non-zero codewords of small weight, possibly the lowest. This algorithm should be applicable to any linear code and should have small complexity for almost all linear codes. The following lemma is important:

Lemma 4: For virtually all linear (n,k) codes having a minimum distance at most d, the minimum weight codeword ($\neq 0$) can be found in

$$O\left(2^{H(\frac{d}{n})k}\right) \quad \text{steps}$$

using the algorithm described below. ◼

By virtually we mean that the result holds for all but a fraction of codes which vanishes when n goes to infinity.

The lemma follows from the results in [4] and [5]. We give a sketch of the proof using some probabilistic argument.

Sketch of the proof: Let us consider a linear binary (n, k) code with generating matrix G. Note that this is an $n \times k$ binary matrix. Let us also consider a fixed information set of k digits of this code. (An information set is a set of indices of k columns of G that have full rank k.) If the minimum codeword has weight d, then with high probability the informational part of this word has weight at most $d \cdot \frac{k}{n}$. To find this word we have to try all possible patterns of weight at most $d \cdot \frac{k}{n}$ as the informational part. Each of these patterns has a corresponding redundancy part (of the codeword). For each pattern we check whether the sum of the weights of the informational and redundancy parts is at most d. We continue with this process until we find a minimal codeword. The complexity of this algorithm is of the same order as the number of patterns of length k and of weight at most $d\frac{k}{n}$. i.e.,

$$\sum_{0 \leq i < d\frac{k}{n}} \binom{k}{i} \leq 2^{H(\frac{d}{n})k}.$$

Using Gray codes this trial process can be implemented efficiently. □

Remark: By using at most n different informational sets we can avoid the probabilistic nature of the proof. The extra cost of this has no influence on our final result.

From coding theory we know that virtually all linear (n, k) codes of fixed rate $R = k/n$ satisfy the Varshamov-Gilbert bound: $d = n \cdot H^{-1}(1-R) + o(n)$. Thus we can expect that the complexity of finding a codeword of weight $d = n \cdot H^{-1}(1-R) + o(n)$ has order $O(2^{(1-R)k}) = O(2^{(1-\frac{r}{n})r})$. Combining all this we arrive at the following result.

Lemma 5: The complexity of finding a set of M independent checks with at most $d - 1$ taps and length $(d - 1)M + n$ is of order

$$\mathcal{C}_{chk} = M \times O(2^{(1-\frac{r}{n})r}),$$

where $d = n \cdot H^{-1}(1 - R) + o(n)$. ■

Proof: The cost of finding the first check of length at most n is $O(2^{(1-\frac{r}{n})r})$. For the second check we have to cancel the $d - 1$ coefficient positions occupied by the first check. In order to search again among n possible positions we add $d - 1$ to the allowed length of the second check. Hence, after M checks we have a length that is not more than $M(d - 1) + n$. The search complexity for every check is essentially the same. Thus the total cost is $M \times O(2^{(1-\frac{r}{n})r})$. □

We are now ready to formulate the main result:

Theorem 6: Let $p = \mathrm{P}(Z_i \neq a_i)$, $p = \frac{1}{2} - \varepsilon < \frac{1}{2}$, and let us fix $n > r$ and $d = n \cdot H^{-1}(1 - R) + o(n)$. To break the system we need to observe a segment of length N of $\{z_i\}$, where

$$N = 2((d - 1)M + n). \tag{12a}$$

Furthermore, we need

$$M = O\left(\left(\frac{1}{2\varepsilon}\right)^d\right), \quad \left(M \approx 2M_0, \text{ where } M_0 = \left(\frac{1}{2\varepsilon}\right)^{d-2}\right). \tag{12b}$$

The first stage of the algorithm has complexity

$$C_{chk} = O\left(\left(\frac{1}{2\varepsilon}\right)^d \cdot 2^{(1-\frac{r}{n})r}\right) \tag{13a}$$

and the second stage for recovering the initial state has complexity

$$C_{it} = O\left(d\left(\frac{1}{2\varepsilon}\right)^{2d}\right). \tag{13b}$$

∎

Proof: In order to break the system we determine first twice as many checks than is given by Corallary 3. The maximal length of this set is given by Lemma 5 and is not more than $(d-1)M + n$. With this set we can perform the first step on the first halve of the known $2((d-1)M + n)$ z_i symbols. The second halve of the symbols are dealt with by using the reciprocals (or reversed forms) of the polynomials in the set. Thus we can carry out the first step if we have $2((d-1)M + n)$ symbols of $\{z_i\}$. Convergence in the first and subsequent iteration is guaranteed by Theorem 2. The results on the complexities are immediate from the previous results. □

The total work load is of course the sum $C_{alg} = C_{chk} + C_{it}$ and we have to choose the parameters n and d in such a way that we minimize C_{alg}. For this purpose fix $\rho = \frac{r}{n}$ and let r go to infinity. Then $\delta \stackrel{\text{def}}{=} \lim_{r\to\infty} \frac{d}{r} = \frac{H^{-1}(\rho)}{\rho}$, i.e., $H(\delta\rho) = \rho$. We introduce

$$\alpha(\rho) \stackrel{\text{def}}{=} \lim_{r\to\infty} \frac{\log_2 C_{chk}}{r} = 1 - \rho + L\delta, \tag{14a}$$

$$\beta(\rho) \stackrel{\text{def}}{=} \lim_{r\to\infty} \frac{\log_2 C_{it}}{r} = 2L\delta, \tag{14b}$$

where $L = -\log_2(2\varepsilon)$. Furthermore,

$$\gamma(\rho) \stackrel{\text{def}}{=} \lim_{r\to\infty} \frac{\log_2(C_{chk} + C_{it})}{r} = \max(\alpha(\rho), \beta(\rho)). \tag{14c}$$

For the optimal algorithm we have

$$\gamma_{opt}(\varepsilon) = \min_{0<\rho<1} \gamma(\rho).$$

Thus we obtain the following corollary to the previous theorem:

Corollary 7: The complexity to break the system has order $O\left(2^{\gamma_{opt}(\varepsilon)r}\right).$ ∎

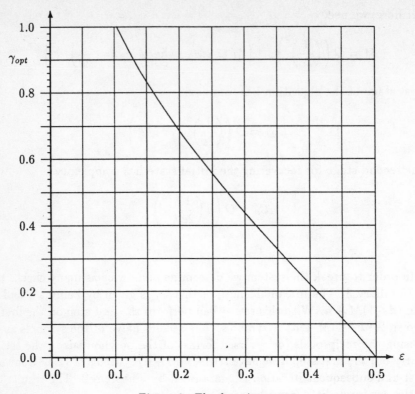

Figure 2: The function γ_{opt}.

In Figure 2 we show γ_{opt} as a function of ε. We see that our algorithm has a complexity less than $O(2^r)$ for $\varepsilon > 0.10$. In Reference [5] another algorithm is described for finding the minimal weight codeword(s). Using this algorithm we obtain that the overall complexity is less than $O(2^r)$ for all ε. However the result in [5] relies on the ability to solve a combinatorial problem for which a complexity bound can be derived but for which the corresponding algorithm is missing. For this reason we paid only attention to our simple algorithm. In any case, using the algorithm we have described, we find that $\gamma_{opt} = 0.56$ when $p = 0.25$ which we have for the generators of Geffe, Pless and Bruer.

5   Conclusion

Summarizing, we have obtained a new algorithm for breaking stream ciphers and we have given a detailed asymptotical analysis. It is important to mention that we deliberately avoided to use more clever iterative improvement schemes like the ones discussed in [2], [3], and [6], since this would make the asymptotic analysis harder, maybe impossible, and in any case less transparent. The analysis clearly shows the importance of checks of (a) low-weight and (b) of low degree. Property (a) leads to a smaller number of required checks and property (b) leads to a smaller demand of the number of known (or observed) symbols. The analysis also shows that the complexity of the algorithm is less than exhaustive search even when t grows linearly with the length of the shift register.

We have verified our analysis through simulations. Since the second stage of the algorithm has been verified through the works of [2] and [6] we concentrated our simulations on the first stage. Our results show that we indeed obtain the required number of checks with an amount of work (=time) that is in accordance with Theorem 6. In addition we observed that we can get a set of M independent checks which is "dense". By this we mean that $|\{j\,;\,h_j^{(i)}, i = 1, 2, \ldots, M\}|$ / $\max_i \deg h^{(i)}(x) \approx 1$, or, in words, for almost all indices $j = 0, 1, \ldots, L - 1$, L the length of the set of checks, there is a polynomial $h^{(i)}(x)$ with a coefficient that checks z_j.

6 Acknowledgement

The first author would like to thank the USSR Academy of Sciences, the Royal Swedish Academy of Sciences, and the Department of Information Theory in Lund for their support and making this work possible.

References

[1] T. Siegenthaler, "Decrypting a class of stream ciphers using ciphertext only", IEEE Trans. Comput., Vol. C-34, 1985, pp. 81-85.

[2] W. Meier, and O. Staffelbach, "Fast correlation attacks on certain stream ciphers", J. Cryptology, 1989, pp. 159-176.

[3] M. Mihaljevic, and J. Golic, "A fast iterative algorithm for a shift register initial state reconstruction given the noisy output sequence", *Proc. Auscrypt 1990*, pp. 165-175.

[4] G. S. Evseev, "Complexity of decoding for linear codes", Probl. Peredach. Inform., Vol. 19, 1983, pp. 3-8.

[5] J. T. Coffey, and R. M. Goodman, "The complexity of information set decoding", IEEE Trans. Inform. Theory, Vol. IT-36, 1990, pp. 1031-1037.

[6] R. G. Gallager, *Low-Density Parity-Check Codes*, MIT Press, Cambridge, MA, 1963.

Analysis of Pseudo Random Sequences Generated by Cellular Automata

Willi Meier [1]   Othmar Staffelbach [2]

[1] HTL Brugg-Windisch
CH-5200 Windisch, Switzerland

[2] GRETAG, Althardstrasse 70
CH-8105 Regensdorf, Switzerland

Abstract

The security of cellular automata for stream cipher applications is investigated. A cryptanalytic algorithm is developed for a known plaintext attack where the plaintext is assumed to be known up to the unicity distance. The algorithm is shown to be successful on small computers for key sizes up to N between 300 and 500 bits. For a cellular automaton to be secure against more powerful adversaries it is concluded that the key size N needs to be about 1000 bits.

The cryptanalytic algorithm takes advantage of an equivalent description of the cryptosystem in which the keys are not equiprobable. It is shown that key search can be reduced considerably if one is contented to succeed only with a certain success probability. This is established by an information theoretic analysis of arbitrary key sources with non-uniform probability distribution.

1   Introduction

In [7],[8] S. Wolfram introduced cellular automata for pseudo random sequence generation with possible application for stream ciphers. Another application is suggested in [1], which uses pseudo random sequences produced by cellular automata for constructing collision free hash functions.

A one-dimensional cellular automaton consists of a (possibly infinite) line of sites with values $s_i \in GF(2)$. These values are updated in parallel (synchronously) in discrete time steps according to a fixed rule of the form

$$s'_i = \Phi(s_{i-r}, s_{i-r+1}, \ldots, s_{i+r}). \tag{1}$$

Practical implementations of cellular automata must contain a finite number of sites N. These are arranged in a circular register, so as to have periodic boundary conditions.

Cellular automata have been investigated in studies of the origins of randomness and chaos in physical systems ([6], [7]). As pointed out in [2], cellular automata differ from cryptographic mechanisms such as feedback shift registers in that, even if they are invertible, it is not possible to calculate the predecessor of an arbitrary state by simply reversing the rule for finding the successor. It is suggested in [7] that the problem of deducing the initial configuration from partial output is equivalent to the general problem of solving Boolean equations, which is NP-complete.

The investigations in [7] concentrate on rules (1) with 3 arguments, i.e., $r = 1$. The two rules that seem best as random sequence generators are nonlinear, and are given by

$$s_i' = s_{i-1} \text{ XOR } (s_i \text{ OR } s_{i+1}) \tag{2}$$

or equivalently, $s_i' = s_{i-1} + s_i + s_{i+1} + s_i s_{i+1} \bmod 2$, and

$$s_i' = s_{i-1} \text{ XOR } (s_i \text{ OR } (\text{NOT } s_{i+1})) \tag{3}$$

or equivalently, $s_i' = 1 + s_{i-1} + s_{i+1} + s_i s_{i+1} \bmod 2$. It is indicated in [7] that, with respect to certain measures, rule (2) appears to be more favourable than rule (3). For stream cipher applications the values $s_i(t)$ attained by a particular site i through time serve as pseudo random bits in a key stream sequence. The initial state of the register is used as the seed, or the secret key.

In view of the period of the output sequences, practical implementations with key size $N = 127$ have been suggested in [7]. In this paper we address the question whether this key size is sufficient to withstand cryptanalysis. To this end a cryptanalytic algorithm is developed in Section 2 which appears to be successful on a PC for key sizes up to N between 300 and 500 bits (depending on the updating rule). Using large parallel computers with special hardware, it is conceivable that cryptanalysis is possible up to a key size of about 1000 bits.

In this cryptanalysis a known plaintext attack is assumed where the plaintext is known up to the unicity distance. It is shown that there is an equivalent cryptosystem, such that the problem of deducing the original key can be reduced to finding the key in the equivalent system. It turns out that the number of keys in the equivalent system is much smaller. Thus a search for the equivalent key is much more efficient than a search for the original key.

Moreover the equivalent system has another property which is favourable for cryptanalysis, namely that certain keys have much higher probability than others. It turns out that in this situation the cost of a cryptanalytic attack is considerably reduced if one is contented to succeed only with a certain success probability δ (e.g., $\delta = 0.5$). In this respect, the efficiency of our cryptanalytic algorithm has been determined by numerous experiments for different key sizes.

The results of Section 3 show that the security of the cellular automaton for rule (2) is in fact quite low for key sizes $N \le 300$. As an example we mention that, for key size $N = 200$ and success probability $\delta = 0.5$, the average number of trials μ necessary to find the key was obtained to be about 23,000. Thus the effective key size can be estimated as $\log_2 \mu = 14.5$ bits. For larger N we can extrapolate from the experiments that, for the cellular automaton (with rule (2)) to be secure, one needs the key size of about 1000 bits, as mentioned above.

If our cryptanalytic algorithm is applied to cellular automata satisfying rule (3), it turns out that cryptanalysis is much easier than for rule (2). In fact, for the average number of trials μ, the effective key size $\log_2 \mu$ is roughly half of the corresponding value for rule (2), e.g., for $N = 400$ we have obtained $\log_2 \mu = 13.8$ bits. Therefore, our cryptanalysis confirms to prefer rule (2) over rule (3).

The equivalent cryptosystem used in our attack implements a key source with a strongly non-uniform, but not explicitly known probability distribution. In general, for a given cryptosystem, knowledge of additional information (e.g., part of the plaintext) may result in an equivalent description of the cryptosystem where the keys in the equivalent system are no longer equiprobable. Therefore, an analysis of an "exhaustive search" for key sources with non-uniform probability distribution is of independent interest. Since by assumption one does not know the most probable keys, which would be tried first in an optimum search, the best one can do is to generate the trial keys according to the original probability distribution of the key source until the correct key has been found.

Suppose that the cryptanalyst performs m different attacks on m keys chosen by the cryptographer, and that the required numbers of trials are listed in ascending order $T_1 \leq T_2 \leq \ldots \leq T_m$. Then the mean value

$$\mu(m, \delta) = \frac{1}{\lceil \delta m \rceil} \sum_{i=1}^{\lceil \delta m \rceil} T_i$$

is an empirical value for the average number of trials to a given success probability δ.

In Section 4 lower and upper bounds for the expected value of $\mu(m, \delta)$ are derived for any key source. The natural question arises how $\mu(m, \delta)$ is related to the entropy of the key source. For stationary ergodic key sources with finite memory (as considered in [4]), it is shown that the expected value of μ satisfies

$$\lim_{N \to \infty} \liminf_{m \to \infty} \frac{\log_2 E[\mu(m, \delta)]}{N} = \lim_{N \to \infty} \limsup_{m \to \infty} \frac{\log_2 E[\mu(m, \delta)]}{N} = H_S,$$

where H_S denotes the per bit entropy of the key source S (as introduced by Shannon [5]). Although the key source considered in our analysis of cellular automata does not completely fit into the model of an ergodic source, one suspects that $E[\mu(m, \delta)]$ is related to the entropy. Therefore the experimental results in Sections 2 and 3 (notably Table 1) may also be applied to estimate the entropy of sequences produced by cellular automata (see [7], [3]).

2　Cryptanalysis on Cellular Automata

By (2) the values of the sites determined by a site vector $S(t) = (s_{i-n}(t), \ldots, s_i(t), \ldots, s_{i+n}(t))$ form a triangle as shown in Figure 1. The sequence $\{s_i(t)\}$ in the middle column is called the *temporal* sequence (at site i). The security of a stream cipher based on cellular automata relies on the difficulty of determining the seed from the given temporal sequence. In an exhaustive search one would try all possible seeds until the correct temporal sequence is produced.

$$s_{i-n}(t) \quad * \quad \ldots \quad * \quad s_{i-1}(t) \quad s_i(t) \quad s_{i+1}(t) \quad * \quad \ldots \quad * \quad s_{i+n}(t)$$

$$* \quad \ldots \quad * \quad s_{i-1}(t+1) \quad s_i(t+1) \quad s_{i+1}(t+1) \quad * \quad \ldots \quad *$$

$$* \quad \vdots \quad \vdots \quad \vdots \quad *$$

$$* \quad * \quad *$$

$$s_i(t+n)$$

Figure 1: Triangle determined by $s_{i-n}(t), \ldots, s_{i+n}(t)$.

In this section we develop a different approach which finds the seed using the partial linearity of (2) by writing it in the form

$$s_{i-1}(t) = s_i(t+1) \text{ XOR } (s_i(t) \text{ OR } s_{i+1}(t)). \tag{4}$$

Given the values of the cells in two adjacent columns, this allows the values of all cells in a triangle to the left of the temporal sequence to be reconstructed. This process will be called *completion backwards*. By completion backwards, $N-1$ digits of the temporal sequence $\{s_i(t)\}$ and $N-2$ digits of its right adjacent sequence $\{s_{i+1}(t)\}$ determine the seed. Similarly the seed may also be reconstructed from $N-2$ digits of the temporal sequence and $N-1$ digits of its left adjacent sequence $\{s_{i-1}(t)\}$.

Thus if $N-1$ digits of the temporal sequence are given, knowledge of the seed is equivalent to knowledge of one of its adjacent sequences. In view of this equivalence an adjacent sequence can be considered as a key which determines the remainder of the temporal sequence. In a known plaintext attack only (a portion of) the temporal sequence is known, but neither of its adjacent sequences. Our aim is to search for a correct (right or left) adjacent sequence and to determine the seed by completion backwards. In fact it turns out that this search can be done much faster than a direct exhaustive search over the original seed.

In constructing adjacent sequences, which are consistent with a given temporal sequence, there is an essential difference between left and right adjacent sequences. We explain this difference for a general cellular automaton of width $2n+1$ where the sites $s_{i-n}(t), \ldots, s_{i+n}(t)$ are not restricted by periodic boundary conditions.

Suppose we are given a temporal sequence $s_i(t), \ldots, s_i(t+n)$. Referring to Figure 1, the problem of finding the left adjacent sequence is equivalent to completing the triangle consistently to the left of the temporal sequence. By (2), knowledge of $s_{i-n}(t), \ldots, s_{i-1}(t)$ together with the temporal sequence is sufficient to determine the triangle to the left. However the sites $s_{i-n}(t), \ldots, s_{i-1}(t)$ cannot be chosen arbitrarily. For example, in the case $s_i(t) = 1$ we must have $s_{i-1}(t) = s_i(t+1) + 1$, and there are similar restrictions at any site in the process of extending to the left.

On the other hand, for triangles to the right any choice of the sites $s_{i+1}(t), \ldots, s_{i+n}(t)$ has a completion consistent with the given temporal sequence. This follows from the fact that, by (4), for any right adjacent $s_{i+1}(t)$ there is a left adjacent $s_{i-1}(t)$ consistent with the next digit $s_i(t+1)$ of the temporal sequence. Furthermore, according to (2), any choice of $s_{i+2}(t), \ldots, s_{i+n}(t)$ has a consistent extension to

$s_{i+1}(t + 1)$, ..., $s_{i+n-1}(t + 1)$. Iteration of this construction leads to the desired completion of the triangle to the right. This process will be called *completion forwards* which, for any choice of the sites $s_{i+1}(t)$, ..., $s_{i+n}(t)$ constructs a right adjacent sequence consistent with the given temporal sequence.

Now suppose that the cellular automaton satisfies periodic boundary conditions with period N. This means that the indices are calculated modulo N. For illustration consider Figure 1 where $n = N - 1$ and $s_{i-1}(t) = s_{i+N-1}(t), \ldots, s_{i-N+1}(t) = s_{i+1}(t)$. Thus to determine the seed we can either compute $(s_i(t), \ldots, s_{i+N-1}(t))$ or $(s_{i-N+1}(t), \ldots, s_i(t))$. For $t' \geq t$, the right adjacent $s_{i+1}(t')$ may not be chosen arbitrarily to be consistent with the next digit $s_i(t' + 1)$ of the temporal sequence, as the left adjacent $s_{i-1}(t')$ may be restricted by the boundary conditions. Nevertheless, by neglecting the boundary conditions, for any choice of the values $s_{i+1}(t), \ldots, s_{i+N-1}(t)$, completion forwards yields a consistent triangle to the right, and one obtains a possible candidate for the right adjacent sequence. In fact, if $s_{i+1}(t), \ldots, s_{i+N-1}(t)$ coincide with the original seed, the correct right adjacent sequence will be produced. Surprisingly, it turns out that there are many (incorrect) seeds leading to the correct right adjacent sequence which, by completion backwards, determines the correct seed. This phenomenon is the basis of our cryptanalytic algorithm which, for given digits $s_i(t), \ldots, s_i(t + N - 1)$ of the temporal sequence, determines the seed.

Algorithm.

1. Generate a random seed $s_{i+1}(t), \ldots, s_{i+N-1}(t)$.

2. Complete forwards, i.e. determine the right adjacent sequence by executing

   FOR $k := 1$ TO $N - 2$ DO FOR $j := 1$ TO $N - k - 1$ DO
   $s_{i+j}(t+k) := s_{i+j-1}(t+k-1)$ XOR $(s_{i+j}(t+k-1)$ OR $s_{i+j+1}(t+k-1))$

3. Complete backwards, i.e. determine the seed $s_{i-N+1}(t), \ldots s_{i-1}(t)$ by executing

   FOR $j := 1$ TO $N - 1$ DO FOR $k := N - 1 - j$ DOWNTO 0 DO
   $s_{i-j}(t+k) := s_{i-j+1}(t+k+1)$ XOR $(s_{i-j+1}(t+k)$ OR $s_{i-j+2}(t+k))$

4. Load the cellular automaton with the computed seed and produce the output sequence up to the length according to the unicity distance. Terminate if the produced sequence coincides with the given temporal sequence else go to step 1.

The algorithm is illustrated by an example with $N = 5$ as shown in Figure 2. Let the seed be $(s_i, \ldots, s_{i+4}) = (0, 1, 0, 1, 1)$. Then, by the boundary conditions, $(s_{i-4}, \ldots, s_{i-1}) = (1, 0, 1, 1)$, and the resulting temporal sequence is obtained as $(0, 0, 1, 0, 0)$. According to step 1 of the algorithm the digits $s_{i+1}, \ldots, s_{i+4}$ are chosen randomly. If s_{i+1} happens to be 1, then by rule (2) the right adjacent sequence produced turns out to be independent of the choice of s_{i+2}, s_{i+3} and s_{i+4}. (Therefore these digits are marked by $\star$ in Figure 2.) Thus there is only one right adjacent sequence with $s_{i+1} = 1$. As one can see from Figure 2, this right adjacent sequence is in fact correct. Thus with probability 1/2 the correct seed is found in the first trial.

s_{i-4}	s_{i-3}	s_{i-2}	s_{i-1}	s_i	s_{i+1}	s_{i+2}	s_{i+3}	s_{i+4}
1	0	1	1	[0]	[1]	[0]	[1]	[1]
	0	1	0	0	1	0	1	
		1	1	1	1	0		
			0	0	0			
				0				

Generation of temporal sequence.

s_{i-4}	s_{i-3}	s_{i-2}	s_{i-1}	s_i	s_{i+1}	s_{i+2}	s_{i+3}	s_{i+4}
[1]	[0]	[1]	[1]	[0]	1	⋆	⋆	⋆
	0	1	0	0	1	⋆	⋆	
		1	1	1	1	⋆		
			0	0	0			
				0				

Determination of the seed by completion backwards.

Figure 2: Cryptanalysis—a small example.

The example shows that for a given temporal sequence there may be only few right adjacent sequences, and that some of these occur with high probability, e.g., for the temporal sequence $(0,0,1,0,0)$ the sequence $(1,1,1,0)$ is generated with probability $1/2$ as right adjacent sequence. The phenomenon as observed in the example also arises in a general automaton with arbitrary N. This is based on the fact that some changes in right-hand initial sites have no effect on the given part of the temporal sequence or its right adjacent sequence. In fact it has been observed in [7] that the effect of a bit change propagates to the left with speed rougly $1/4$. By the partial linearity of (2) the speed of propagation to the right is 1. This further justifies to search for right adjacent rather than for left adjacent sequences.

In general, a temporal sequence $s_i(t), \ldots, s_i(t+n-1)$ of length n together with the values of $n+1$ sites $s_{i+1}(t), \ldots, s_{i+n+1}(t)$ determines a right adjacent sequence $s_{i+1}(t), \ldots, s_{i+1}(t+n)$ of length $n+1$. It appears that the number of right adjacent sequences strongly depends on the given temporal sequence. In fact for some temporal sequences there remain only very few possibilities for the right adjacent sequence. Suppose for example that the temporal sequence consists of n consecutive digits 0, i.e., $s_i(t) = s_i(t+1) = \ldots = s_i(t+n-1) = 0$. Let k be the smallest non-negative integer with $s_{i+1}(t+k) = 1$. Then rule (2) implies that $s_{i+1}(t+k) = s_{i+1}(t+k+1) = \cdots = s_{i+1}(t+n) = 1$. Thus the right adjacent sequence $s_{i+1}(t), \ldots, s_{i+1}(t+n)$ can only consist of k digits 0 followed by $n-k+1$ digits 1. Hence in this case the number of possible right adjacent sequences grows only linearly in the length n of the temporal sequence. By slightly different arguments one can show that a similar result holds for temporal sequences consisting of n consecutive digits 1.

For arbitrary temporal sequences statistical experiments show that also in general there are only few possibilities for the right adjacent sequence. In Table 1, for every N, $2 \leq N \leq 17$, samples of 100 temporal sequences of length $N - 1$ have been generated. For any of these temporal sequences the number of all possible right adjacent sequences have been determined by an exhaustive search over all 2^N seeds. As a result, for each sample the mean value μ and standard deviation σ are listed in Table 1. Note for example that for $N = 17$, in the average, there are only about 42 right adjacent sequences compared to all $2^{17} = 131,072$ possible sequences of length 17.

N	μ	σ	N	μ	σ
2	3.00	0.00	3	4.00	0.00
4	5.00	0.00	5	6.29	0.46
6	7.73	0.81	7	9.59	1.21
8	11.47	1.67	9	13.90	2.38
10	15.78	2.85	11	18.36	3.67
12	21.64	4.45	13	24.95	5.57
14	28.18	7.03	15	32.86	7.72
16	37.49	9.71	17	41.86	10.63

Table 1: Statistics on the number of right adjacent sequences.

3 Experimental results

In this section we report on the results of extensive experiments concerning our cryptanalytic algorithm. In these experiments we simulate a known plaintext attack where the keys are chosen with uniform probability as seed of the cellular automaton of size N (i.e., the size of the keys is N). The problem of cryptanalysis consists in determining the seed (or the key) from the produced output sequence, which is assumed to be known up to the unicity distance.

It turns out that the efficiency of our cryptanalytic algorithm strongly depends on properties of the known output sequence, i.e., on the chosen key. In fact, the algorithm is much more efficient for those keys whose corresponding output sequences (or temporal sequences) turn out to have only few right adjacent sequences. As pointed out in Section 2, for a cellular automaton with known output sequence the search for the original key K_s (the seed) is equivalent to finding the correct right adjacent sequence. Therefore we consider the right adjacent sequence as an equivalent key, denoted by K_r. By completion forwards there is a mapping

$$F : \{K_s\} \longrightarrow \{K_r\}. \tag{5}$$

By assumption, the keys K_s are equiprobable, whereas the keys K_r turn out to have a non-uniform probability distribution determined by the mapping F,

$$P(K_r) = \frac{1}{2^N} |\{K_s \,|\, F(K_s) = K_r\}|. \tag{6}$$

For the cellular automaton to be secure, the mapping F is supposed to be complex and involved. Thus it has to be assumed that the probability distribution (6) is not explicitly known, neither to the cryptographer nor to the cryptanalyst. In particular one does not know the most probable keys which in an optimum search would be tried first. Therefore the best one can do is to generate the keys K_r according to the probability distribution (6). This is done by choosing K_s randomly according to the uniform distribution and to generate the key K_r as the corresponding right adjacent sequence. Then the expected number of trials T for finding a particular key K_r can be computed as

$$E[T|K_r] = \frac{1}{P(K_r)} \tag{7}$$

which in fact is lowest for the most probable keys. If the cryptanalytic attack is required to be successful on every key, the expected number of trials is

$$E[T] = \sum_{K_r} E[T|K_r] \, P(K_r) = \sum_{K_r} \frac{1}{P(K_r)} P(K_r) = |\{K_r\}|. \tag{8}$$

In the average this is much smaller than the number of trials necessary for an exhaustive search over K_s, as $|\{K_r\}| \ll 2^N$ (e.g., see Table 1). Nevertheless for large N it may become infeasible to find the key in every case, as $|\{K_r\}|$ may be too large. However it turns out that certain keys K_r appear with high probability $P(K_r)$ (i.e., are accidentially generated by the cryptographer with high probability). By (7), the expected number of trials for finding such keys may be much smaller than the average expected number as obtained in (8). Thus we are in the situation that the algorithm may not be able to find the key in every case, but may succeed with a certain success probability δ, say $\delta = 0.5$. In order to obtain an estimate of the complexity of the attack to a given success probability δ, we set up our experiments as follows.

1. Simulate the cryptographer by choosing a random key K_s as seed of the cellular automaton.

2. Simulate a known plaintext situation by generating the output sequence (or the temporal sequence) up to the unicity distance.

3. Apply the cryptanalytic algorithm of Section 2 in order to determine the key K_r (or K_s respectively) and count the number T of trials that have been necessary.

These steps are repeated a certain number of times m, and the required numbers of trials are listed in ascending order, $T_1 \leq T_2 \leq \ldots \leq T_m$. To obtain an empirical value for the average number of trials for success probability δ we compute the mean value

$$\mu = \frac{1}{\lceil \delta m \rceil} \sum_{i=1}^{\lceil \delta m \rceil} T_i. \tag{9}$$

In Table 2 the results of $m = 100$ experiments are listed for each key size $N = 10, 20, \ldots, 300$, as indicated. The success probability has been chosen to be $\delta = 0.5$. The value $\log_2 \mu$ as given in the third and sixth column indicates the *effective key size* with respect to this success probability δ.

Key size	μ	$\log_2 \mu$	Key size	μ	$\log_2 \mu$
10	2.9	1.5	20	5.5	2.4
30	10.2	3.4	40	23.0	4.5
50	23.9	4.6	60	73.7	6.2
70	102.6	6.7	80	178.9	7.5
90	270.5	8.1	100	334.1	8.4
110	687.5	9.4	120	1,696.3	10.7
130	1,626.0	10.7	140	1,956.8	10.9
150	2,740.3	11.4	160	4,131.3	12.0
170	9,267.8	13.2	180	10,206.1	13.3
190	14,876.0	13.9	200	23,367.5	14.5
250	97,583.1	16.6	300	272,195.6	18.1

Table 2: Complexity of the attack with success probability $\delta = 0.5$ for rule (2). (For technical reasons the entry for $N = 250$ corresponds to $\delta = 0.44$ and for $N = 300$ to $\delta = 0.27$.)

The results of our experiments allow to estimate the security of the cellular automaton for stream cipher applications. In this respect Table 2 shows that the security is quite low for key sizes $N \leq 300$. For larger key size we have to extrapolate the average complexity of the attack from the values μ obtained for $N \leq 300$. For this purpose we observe that the number of right adjacent sequences grows at most exponentially in the length n of the sequence, i.e.,

$$f_r(m + n) \leq f_r(m) f_r(n) \tag{10}$$

where $f_r(n)$ denotes the number of all possible length n right adjacent sequences corresponding to a given temporal sequence. Then (10) implies that the complexity of the attack also grows at most exponentially in the length N of the key.

The derivation of (10) is explained in Figure 3. Let $\mathcal{A}$ be the set of all possible right adjacent sequences $(s_{i+1}(t), \ldots, s_{i+1}(t+m-1))$ of length m, let $\mathcal{B}$ be the set of all possible right adjacent sequences $(s_{i+1}(t+m), \ldots, s_{i+1}(t+m+n-1))$ of length n, and let $\mathcal{C}$ be the set of all possible right adjacent sequences $(s_{i+1}(t), \ldots, s_{i+1}(t+m+n-1))$ of length $m+n$. Then for any right adjacent sequence $\{s_{i+1}\}$ in $\mathcal{C}$, the sequence $\{s'_{i+1}\}$ formed by the first m digits of $\{s_{i+1}\}$ lies in $\mathcal{A}$, and the sequence $\{s''_{i+1}\}$ formed by the last n digits of $\{s_{i+1}\}$ lies in $\mathcal{B}$. Therefore we have $|\mathcal{C}| \leq |\mathcal{A}| \cdot |\mathcal{B}|$, which proves (10). Inequality usually holds in (10), since the site values $s_{i+1}(t+m), \ldots, s_{i+m}(t+m)$ can be chosen arbitrarily in generating the set $\mathcal{B}$ whereas, in generating the set $\mathcal{C}$, they are restricted to conditions caused by the cellular automaton rule (2). Thus there may exist pairs $(\{s'_{i+1}\}, \{s''_{i+1}\})$ in $\mathcal{A} \times \mathcal{B}$ whose concatenation is not a right adjacent sequence of length $m + n$.

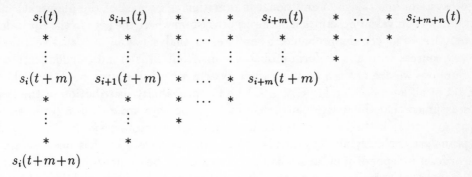

Figure 3: Generation of right adjacent sequences.

A subexponential growth of the average complexity of the attack is also suggested by Table 2, e.g., for $N = 200$ we have $\log_2 \mu = 14.5$ which is less than the double of $\log_2 \mu = 8.4$ for $N = 100$. Therefore, from the results for $N = 250$ or $N = 300$ we extrapolate values of N for which the attack requires approximately 2^{50} trials. These values lie in the range between $N = 750$ and $N = 900$. Therefore, using large parallel computers with special hardware, it is conceivable that cryptanalysis is possible up to a key size of about 1000 bits.

Our cryptanalytic algorithm also applies to cellular automata satisfying other rules, e.g., rule (3). It turns out that the algorithm for rule (3) is much more efficient than for rule (2). In Table 3 the results of $m = 100$ experiments are listed for each key size $N = 50, 100, \ldots, 400$ and for success probability $\delta = 0.5$. The results show that the effective key size $\log_2 \mu$ for rule (3) is roughly half of the effective key size for rule (2).

Key size	μ	$\log_2 \mu$	Key size	μ	$\log_2 \mu$
50	22.8	4.5	100	82.8	6.4
150	206.2	7.7	200	423.3	8.7
250	1,396.3	10.4	300	2,559.3	11.3
350	5,457.6	12.4	400	14,400.5	13.8

Table 3: Complexity of the attack with success probability $\delta = 0.5$ for rule (3).

4 Key Search for Key Sources with Non-uniform Probability Distribution

In Sections 2 and 3 the search for the seed K_s of a cellular automaton to a given output sequence was reduced to finding the correct right adjacent sequence. In this equivalent description the right adjacent sequence was considered as a key K_r which turned out to have a non-uniform probability distribution. In general, for a given cryptosystem, knowledge of additional information (e.g., part of the plaintext) may result in an equivalent description of the cryptosystem where the keys in the equivalent system are no longer equiprobable. Therefore, an analysis of an "exhaustive search" for key sources with non-uniform probability distribution is of independent interest.

Suppose we are given a cryptographic system with key source S. Denote by $\mathcal{K}$ the set of all keys and let $\{P(k), k \in \mathcal{K}\}$ be the probability distribution of the keys. It is assumed that the individual probabilities of the keys are *unknown* (even to the cryptographer). If the keys are available in an ordered list $\mathcal{K} = \{k_1, k_2, \ldots, k_M\}$ the cryptanalyst could try all keys in this order until the correct key has been found. If this order is independent of the probability distribution, he cannot take any advantage of the fact that some keys are more probable than others. An *optimum search* would be to try the keys in the order of decreasing probabilities. Since by assumption this order is unknown, the best one can do is to generate the keys by the original key source S according to the probability distribution P. Then the expected number of trials T for finding a particular key k can be computed as

$$E[T|k] = \frac{1}{P(k)} \tag{11}$$

which implies that the most probable keys are easiest to find. However, over all keys the cryptographer may choose, the expected number of trials is

$$E[T] = \sum_{k \in \mathcal{K}} E[T|k]\, P(k) = \sum_{k \in \mathcal{K}} \frac{1}{P(k)} P(k) = |\mathcal{K}|. \tag{12}$$

This means that in the average, or in long terms, cryptanalysis cannot take advantage of the fact that the probability distribution of the keys is not uniform. However the situation turns out to be different if the cryptanalyst is contented with finding the key only with a certain success probability δ, e.g. $\delta = 0.5$.

As in our experiments in Section 3 suppose that the cryptanalyst performs m different attacks on m keys chosen by the cryptographer according to the probability distribution P of the key source S. The required number of trials are listed in ascending order $T_1 \leq T_2 \leq \ldots \leq T_m$. Then the mean value

$$\mu(m, \delta) = \frac{1}{\lceil \delta m \rceil} \sum_{i=1}^{\lceil \delta m \rceil} T_i \tag{13}$$

is an empirical value for the average number of trials to a given success probability δ. Our aim is to establish a relationship between the expected value of $\mu(m, \delta)$ in (13) and the entropy of the key source S.

Let $A \subset \mathcal{K}$ be a subset of keys. Then a key k produced by the source S accidentally lies in A with probability

$$P(A) = \sum_{k \in A} P(k). \tag{14}$$

The expected number of trials T conditioned on the event that the key, chosen by the cryptographer, lies in A is given by

$$E[T \mid k \in A] = \sum_{k \in A} E[T|k] \frac{P(k)}{P(A)} = \sum_{k \in A} \frac{1}{P(k)} \cdot \frac{P(k)}{P(A)} = \frac{|A|}{P(A)}. \tag{15}$$

Lemma 1 *For any δ, $0 < \delta < 1$, and any subset $A \subset \mathcal{K}$ with $P(A) > \delta$,*

$$\limsup_{m \to \infty} E[\mu(m, \delta)] \leq \frac{|A|}{P(A)}. \tag{16}$$

Proof. Let B denote the event that at least $\lceil \delta m \rceil$ keys, out of the m keys chosen by the cryptographer, lie in A. Then the expected value of $\mu(m, \delta)$, conditioned on the event B, satisfies the inequality

$$E[\mu(m, \delta) \mid B] \leq E[T \mid k \in A] = \frac{|A|}{P(A)}. \tag{17}$$

On the other hand the expected value of $\mu(m, \delta)$, conditioned on the complementary event of B (denoted by B^c), satisfies the inequality

$$E[\mu(m, \delta) \mid B^c] \leq \max\left(\frac{|A|}{P(A)}, \frac{M - |A|}{1 - P(A)}\right). \tag{18}$$

Since $P(A) > \delta$, by the law of large numbers, for any $\varepsilon > 0$ there is an integer m_0 such that for all $m \geq m_0$, the event B has probability $\lambda = P(B) > 1 - \varepsilon$. Thus

$$\begin{aligned} E[\mu(m, \delta)] &= E[\mu(m, \delta) \mid B] \, P(B) + E[\mu(m, \delta) \mid B^c] \, P(B^c) \\ &\lambda \, E[\mu(m, \delta) \mid B] + (1 - \lambda) \, E[\mu(m, \delta) \mid B^c] \end{aligned} \tag{19}$$

The first term in (19) is bounded by (17), whereas the second term is of the form $(1 - \lambda)K$ where K is bounded by (18). Since the bound (18) is independent of m, by choosing ε sufficiently small (or equivalently, by choosing m sufficiently large), the second term in (19) can be made arbitrarily small. $\square$

Lemma 2 *For any δ, $0 < \delta < 1$, and any subset $A \subset \mathcal{K}$ with $\varepsilon = 1 - P(A) < \delta$,*

$$\liminf_{m \to \infty} E[\mu(m, \delta)] \geq \frac{\alpha}{p_a}, \tag{20}$$

where p_a denotes the probability of the most probable key in A, and where $\alpha = (\delta - \varepsilon)^2/(4\delta)$.

Proof. Let $k \in \mathcal{K}$ and $p = P(k)$. For $0 < \beta < 1$, let $P(T < (\beta/p) \mid k)$ denote the probability of $T < \beta/p$, conditioned on the event that the cryptographer has chosen key k. Then by Bernoulli's inequality we have

$$P(T < (\beta/p) \mid k) = 1 - (1 - p)^{\lfloor \beta/p \rfloor} < 1 - (1 - \lfloor \beta/p \rfloor p) = \lfloor \beta/p \rfloor p \leq \beta.$$

Thus for any key in A,

$$P(T < (\beta/p_a) \mid k) \le P(T < (\beta/p) \mid k) < \beta, \tag{21}$$

which can be applied to estimate

$$P(T < \beta/p_a) = \sum_{k \in A} P(T < (\beta/p_a) \mid k) \, P(k) + \sum_{k \in \mathcal{K}-A} P(T < (\beta/p_a) \mid k) \, P(k). \tag{22}$$

According to (21), the first term in (22) is bounded by $\beta(1 - \varepsilon) < \beta$, whereas the second term is trivially bounded by $P(\mathcal{K} - A) = \varepsilon$. Hence

$$P(T < \beta/p_a) < \beta + \varepsilon. \tag{23}$$

Let $\delta_1 = P(T < \beta/p_a)$ and $\delta_2 = \beta + \varepsilon$. Since $\varepsilon < \delta$, it is possible to choose β such that $\delta_2 < \delta$. We will make the choice $\delta_2 = (\delta + \varepsilon)/2$. Let B denote the event that at most $\delta_2 m$ numbers T among $T_1, \ldots, T_m$ are below β/p_a. Then the expected value of $\mu(m, \delta)$ conditioned on B satisfies

$$E[\mu(m, \delta) \mid B] \ge \frac{(\delta - \delta_2)}{\delta} \cdot \frac{\beta}{p_a} = \frac{(\delta - \delta_2)(\delta_2 - \varepsilon)}{\delta p_a} = \frac{(\delta - \varepsilon)^2}{4 \delta p_a}. \tag{24}$$

Since by (23), $\delta_1 = P(T < \beta/p_a) < \delta_2$, it follows, by the law of large numbers, that for any $\eta > 0$ there is an integer m_0 (depending on δ_1, δ_2 and η, only) such that for all $m > m_0$ the event B has probabilty $P(B) > 1 - \eta$. Hence

$$E[\mu(m, \delta] \ge E[\mu(m, \delta) \mid B] \, P(B) \ge \frac{(\delta - \varepsilon)^2}{4 \delta p_a} (1 - \eta). \tag{25}$$

By choosing m sufficiently large, η can be made arbitrarily small. This implies that (20) is satisfied with $\alpha = (\delta - \varepsilon)^2/(4\delta)$. $\square$

Now we consider the case where the keys produced by the source S are bit strings of length N, i.e., $M = 2^N$. We assume that S is a stationary ergodic source with a finite memory according to the model considered in [4]. In this model the state of the source is given by the k preceeding output bits $(u_{n-1}, \ldots, u_{n-k})$. Therefore any state has only two possible successors, namely $(u_n, \ldots, u_{n-k+1})$ with $u_n = 0$, or with $u_n = 1$. It follows that there is a one-to-one correspondence between the state sequence of the source and its output sequence. Therefore the entropy per symbol (or state) H_S, as introduced by Shannon in [5], can be considered as the entropy per ouput bit of the key source (see [4]). As a consequence, Shannon's Theorem 3 in [5] can be applied, which is stated here as follows.

Theorem 3 (Shannon) *For any $\varepsilon > 0$ and $\eta > 0$ there exists an integer N_0 such that for all $N \ge N_0$, there is a set $A \subset \mathcal{K}$ with probability $P(A) > 1 - \varepsilon$ such that the probability of any element in A lies within the bounds*

$$2^{-(H_S+\eta)N} \le p \le 2^{-(H_S-\eta)N}. \tag{26}$$

As a consequence the cardinality of A lies within the bounds

$$2^{(H_S-\eta)N} \le |A| \le 2^{(H_S+\eta)N}. \tag{27}$$

In Theorem 3 we may choose $\varepsilon < \min(\delta, 1 - \delta)$ in order to apply Lemma 1 and Lemma 2, and thus we obtain

$$\alpha \, 2^{(H_S - \eta)N} \leq \liminf_{m \to \infty} E[\mu(m, \delta)] \leq \limsup_{m \to \infty} E[\mu(m, \delta)] \leq \frac{1}{1 - \varepsilon} 2^{(H_S + \eta)N},$$

or by taking logarithms and dividing by N,

$$\begin{aligned}
\frac{\log_2 \alpha}{N} + (H_S - \eta) &\leq \liminf_{m \to \infty} \frac{\log_2 E[\mu(m, \delta)]}{N} \\
&\leq \limsup_{m \to \infty} \frac{\log_2 E[\mu(m, \delta)]}{N} \leq (H_S + \eta) - \frac{\log_2(1 - \varepsilon)}{N}.
\end{aligned}$$

By choosing N sufficiently large, ε and η can be made arbitrarily small. At the same time α approaches the value $\delta/4$. Thus we have proved the following theorem. □

Theorem 4 *An ergodic stationary key source S with a finite memory satisfies*

$$\lim_{N \to \infty} \liminf_{m \to \infty} \frac{\log_2 E[\mu(m, \delta)]}{N} = \lim_{N \to \infty} \limsup_{m \to \infty} \frac{\log_2 E[\mu(m, \delta)]}{N} = H_S. \tag{28}$$

References

[1] I. Damgård, *A Design Principle for Hash Functions*, Advances in Cryptology— Crypto'89, Proceedings, pp. 416–427, Springer-Verlag, 1990.

[2] W. Diffie, *The First Ten Years of Public-Key Cryptography*, Proceedings of the IEEE, pp. 560–577, 1988.

[3] P. Grassberger, *Toward a Quantitative Theory of Self-Generated Complexity*, International Journal of Theoretical Physics, Vol. 25, pp. 907–938, 1986.

[4] U. Maurer, *A Universal Statistical Test for Random Bit Generators*, Proceedings of Crypto'90, Springer-Verlag, to appear.

[5] C.E. Shannon, *A Mathematical Theory of Communication*, Bell Syst. Tech. Journal, Vol. 27, pp. 379–423, 623–656, 1948.

[6] S. Wolfram, *Origins of Randomness in Physical Systems*, Physical Review Letters, Vol. 55, pp. 449–452, 1985.

[7] S. Wolfram, *Random Sequence Generation by Cellular Automata*, Advances in Applied Mathematics 7, pp. 123–169, 1986.

[8] S. Wolfram, *Cryptography with Cellular Automata*, Advances in Cryptology— Crypto'85, Proceedings, pp. 429–432, Springer-Verlag, 1986.

ON BINARY SEQUENCES FROM RECURSIONS "modulo 2^e" MADE NON-LINEAR BY THE BIT-BY-BIT "XOR" FUNCTION

W.G.CHAMBERS

Department of Electronic and Electrical Engineering, King's College London, Strand, London WC2R 2LS, UK

Z.D.DAI

Mathematics Department, Royal Holloway and Bedford New College (University of London), Egham, Surrey, UK. On leave from the Graduate School, Academia Sinica, Beijing, People's Republic of China; supported by SERC grant GR/F72727

Abstract: We consider binary sequences obtained by choosing the the most significant bit of each element in a sequence obtained from a feedback shift register of length n operating over the ring $Z/2^e$, that is with arithmetic carried out modulo 2^e. The feedback has been made non-linear by using the bit-by-bit exclusive-or function as well as the linear operation of addition. This should increase the cryptologic strength without greatly increasing the computing overheads. The periods and linear equivalences are discussed. Provided certain conditions are met it is easy to check that the period achieves its maximal value.

1) Introduction: For e a positive integer let $Z/2^e$ denote the ring of integers $\{0,\ldots,2^e-1\}$ with addition, subtraction, and multiplication carried out "mod 2^e". (In other words if the result of the arithmetic operation gives a value outside the ring, then it is brought back by adding or subtracting a suitable multiple of 2^e.) We start by considering linear recursions of the form

$$a_{t+n} = \sum_{j=0}^{n-1} c_j a_{t+j} \bmod 2^e \quad \text{for} \quad t = 0,1,2,\ldots \tag{1}$$

with $a_0, a_1, \ldots, a_{n-1}$ specifying the initial conditions. At least one of these values is odd. Here a_t and c_j belong to $Z/2^e$. Here and throughout this presentation for a, p integer with $p > 1$ we define $a \bmod p$ as that integer $\in \{0,1,\ldots,p-1\}$ obtained by adding (subtracting) the appropriate integer multiple of p to (from) a. (The operator "mod" will be taken as binding more loosely than arithmetic operators such as "+", but more tightly than "=", so that for instance $a = b + c \bmod p$ means $a = ((b+c) \bmod p)$.) We may then derive a binary output by picking the most significant bit of each a_t. This can provide a convenient way of generating pseudo-random binary sequences on general-purpose microprocessors, in which case e would typically be the number of bits in a computer-word. It should be a particularly convenient technique on some digital signal processors which have high-speed facilities for multiply-accumulation. Now as regards the cryptologic security: The generator is a linear congruential generator and cryptanalytic techniques are available at least when the coefficients are known [1]. These techniques suppose that the output sequence is truncated down to the several most significant bits and it seems unlikely that they are practicable when only the most significant bit of each output is available. Nonetheless it seems reasonable to increase the security. One way is to make the coefficients F_j key-dependent and to use some kind of non-linear output filtering. We discuss instead what should be an even better possibility, the use of the bit-by-bit exclusive-or function as a source of non-linearity *inside* the recursion. Non-linearity should be cryptographically more effective here than when used in filtering the output. Moreover the exclusive-or function is a fast operation readily available on most microprocessors and digital signal processors and it is non-linear in $Z/2^e$ for $e > 1$.

The exclusive-or function (denoted by $\oplus$) is defined as follows: For a, b non-negative integers with $a = \sum_{k=0}^{\infty} a_k 2^k$ and $b = \sum_{k=0}^{\infty} b_k 2^k$ (with $a_k, b_k \in \{0,1\}$) we set

$$a \oplus b = \sum_{k=0}^{\infty} ((a_k + b_k) \bmod 2) 2^k.$$

To make the discussion definite we consider a recursion of the form

$$a_t = (\sum_{j=0}^{n-1} c_j a_{t+j} \bmod 2^e) \oplus (\sum_{j=0}^{n-1} d_j a_{t+j} \bmod 2^e) \quad \text{for} \quad t = 0, 1, 2, \ldots \qquad (2)$$

Here at least one of the d_j is non-zero, and at least two of the c_j are odd to guarantee a proper non-linear carry. Moreover the *base polynomial*

$$h(x) = x^n + \sum_{j=0}^{n-1} (c_j + d_j) x^j \bmod 2 \qquad (3)$$

is a primitive binary polynomial. (The operation "mod p" applied to a polynomial expression signifies that the coefficients are to be evaluated "mod p".)

The period of the generator (1) has been investigated long ago by Ward [2]; more recent work concerns the period and upper and lower bounds on the linear equivalence of the binary sequences produced by taking the bit of a given order of significance from each a_t [3], [4], [5], [6]. Let a_t have the binary decomposition $a_t = \sum_{i=0}^{e-1} a_{t,i} 2^i$ with $a_{t,i} \in \{0,1\}$. Denote the sequence $\{a_0, a_1, a_2, \ldots\}$ by α and the binary sequences $\{a_{0,i}, a_{1,i}, a_{2,i}, \ldots\}$ by α_i. We quote the following results: If the base polynomial $h(x)$ is a primitive binary polynomial of degree n, the possible periods of α_i are $2^k (2^n - 1)$ with $k = 0, 1, \ldots, i$. Moreover for any i satisfying $1 < i < e$ and with $h(x) = x^n + f(x) \bmod 2$ a specified primitive polynomial and with α_0 not identically zero, all but a fraction $2/2^n$ of the possible connection polynomials $f(x) = \sum_{i=0}^{n-1} c_i x^i$ give α_i the maximal period $(2^n - 1)2^i$. From the practical point of view this means that provided we keep n reasonably large, say > 40, there is not much risk of obtaining a short-period sequence. There are also "fast" tests for checking that the period is maximal [3], [4], [7].

Unless we have some understanding about the periods of sequences generated by (2) there is always the worry that we may obtain a dangerously short period for some initial conditions and/or choices of connection polynomial. This is·the standard objection to the use of non-linear recursions which otherwise would seem to be an attractive proposition in cryptography. The results stated in the last paragraph were derived using the linearity of (1). What can be said about the periods of sequences generated by (2) depends very much on the d_j. If any of the d_j are odd we can say very little definitely apart from the fact that the period is a factor of $(2^n - 1)2^{e-1}$. Much more definite conclusions apply if all the d_j are even, and for the rest of this presentation we concentrate on this case. There may be a price to pay for this increased understanding in that the generator may not be quite as strong cryptologically as in the general case.

We shall present (for the case when all the d_j are even) a "fast" test to check whether the period is maximal, and the probability of the period's not being maximal if the coefficients are chosen at random. We shall also present expressions for characteristic polynomials from which upper bounds to the linear equivalence may be found; computer results demonstrate that these are tight in simple cases.

2) **Test for maximal period**: Tests for maximal period in the outputs from (1) have been discussed in [4] and [7]. We now describe a test for the generator (2), in the case when all the d_j are even.

Let any quantity that takes only the values 0 and 1 be called *binary-valued*. Similarly designate a polynomial (sequence) as *binary-valued* if all its coefficients (elements) are binary-valued. Put $f(x) = \sum_{i=0}^{n-1} c_i x^i$, $g(x) = \sum_{i=0}^{n-1} d_i x^i$. Then set

$$f(x) = \sum_{k=0}^{e-1} f_k(x) 2^k, \quad g(x) = \sum_{k=0}^{e-1} g_k(x) 2^k, \quad \alpha = \sum_{k=0}^{e-1} \alpha_k 2^k,$$

with $f_k(x)$ and $g_k(x)$ binary-valued polynomials, and with the α_k binary-valued sequences.

Let

$$g_0(x) = 0$$

and let the base polynomial (3)

$$h(x) = \sum_0^n h_i x^i = x^n + f(x) \bmod 2$$

be a primitive binary polynomial, with binary valued coefficients h_i. Moreover let at least one of the initial settings $a_0, a_1, \ldots, a_{n-1}$ be odd. These are the conditions for the theorem. Next let θ denote a root of $h(x)$ (in GF(2^n)), and set

$$\Phi = \sum_{0 \le i < j < n} h_i h_j \theta^{i+j}, \quad \kappa = \sum_{i=1,3,5,\ldots}^n h_i \theta^i.$$

Also define v_1, v_2, v_3 by

$$v_1 = \Phi + (f_1(\theta))^2 + (g_1(\theta))^2,$$

$$v_2 = v_1(v_1^2 + \kappa^4) + (g_1(\theta))^2 \theta^{2n} \kappa^2,$$

$$v_3 = \kappa^4 v_2 + (g_1(\theta))^4 \theta^{4n} v_1.$$

All these quantities are in GF(2^n). Then we have

Theorem 1: With the conditions just stated, the period of α_1 has the maximal value $2(2^n - 1)$ if and only if $v_1 \neq 0$, the period of α_2 has the maximal value $4(2^n - 1)$ if and only if $v_1v_2 \neq 0$, and for $k \geq 3$ the period of α_k has the maximal value $2^k(2^n - 1)$ if and only if $v_1v_2v_3 \neq 0$.

We make the following remarks:

1) The period does not depend on $f_i(x)$ or $g_i(x)$ for $i \geq 2$.

2) If $g_1(x) = 0$ (as well as $g_0(x) = 0$), then the results depend only on $f_1(x)$ and we may equivalently use alternative methods [4], [7] for testing the period of the generator (1) obtained by setting $g(x) = 0$.

3) An alternative is to test the period of α_3 for shortness, but this needs of the order of 2^n steps.

4) Computations in $\mathrm{GF}(2^n)$ are equivalent to computations with binary polynomials "modulo" the base polynomial $h(x)$. The root θ is represented by the polynomial x. The coefficients g_{ij} in the binary polynomial $\sum_{i=0}^{n-1} g_{ij}x^j$ obtained as the remainder when x^i is divided by $h(x)$ are precomputed for $i = 0, 1, 2, \ldots, 2n - 2$, and are used to find products. Each multiplication or squaring then requires of the order of n^2 operations.

We also have

Theorem 2: If (with $h(x)$ a fixed primitive polynomial) we choose $f_1(x)$ and $g_1(x)$ at random, then for $k \geq 3$ the probability that α_k has a short period is $4/2^n - 4/4^n$; if we set $g_1(x) = 0$ and choose $f_1(x)$ at random, then the probability is $2/2^n$.

3) Upper bounds on the minimal polynomial: We define the shift operator x acting on a sequence by $x\alpha = \{a_1, a_2, a_3, \ldots\}$ where α is the sequence $\{a_0, a_1, a_2, \ldots\}$. More generally with $f(x) = \sum c_i x^i$ we define $f(x)\alpha$ as the sequence with its t-th element equal to $\sum c_i a_{t+i}$. We call the binary polynomial $f(x)$ a *characteristic polynomial* of the binary sequence α if $f(x)\alpha \bmod 2 = 0$. Evidently with $g(x)$ any polynomial we have that $f(x)g(x) \bmod 2$ is also a characteristic polynomial of α, so that a characteristic polynomial of a given sequence is by no means unique. However there is only one characteristic polynomial of least degree which we shall call the minimal polynomial, and its degree is called the *linear equivalence*. Thus the degree of any characteristic polynomial provides an upper bound on the linear equivalence of a sequence. Moreover the minimal polynomial is a factor of every characteristic polynomial and so in terms of the partial ordering defined by divisibility characteristic polynomials provide *upper bounds* on the minimal polynomial. We present the following formulae for characteristic polynomials of the binary sequences described above. Computer studies have encouraged us to believe that these are of degree not much greater than the degree of the minimal polynomial and therefore that they as it were provide a close upper bound.

Let θ denote a specifically chosen root of the base polynomial $h(x)$, a primitive element in $\mathrm{GF}(2^n)$, since $h(x)$ is a primitive binary polynomial of degree n. For any non-negative integer i let $w(i)$ denote the number of 1's in the base-2 expression of i. Then for $s > 0$ define the (binary) polynomials

$$g_s(x) = \prod_{0 < i \leq T: \, w(i) \leq s} (x - \theta^i),$$

where $T = 2^n - 1$. (Note that $g_1(x) = h(x)$, and that $g_s(x) = (1 - x^T)$ for $s \geq n$.) Then it can be shown that

$$T_k(x) = g_1(x) \cdot \prod_{0 \leq j < 2^{k-1}} g_{k+1+2j-w(j)}(x)$$

is a characteristic polynomial of α_k in all cases [3]. For $k \geq n - 1$ we have the simple formula

$$T_k(x) = h(x) \cdot (1 - x^T)^{2^{k-1}}.$$

When $g_0(x) = 0$ but $g_1(x) \neq 0$, so that $g(x)$ is a multiple of 2 but not of 4, then

$$T_k'(x) = g_1(x) \cdot g_5(x) \cdot g_6(x) \cdot \prod_{2 \leq j < 2^{k-1}} g_{\Delta(k,j)}(x)$$

with

$$\Delta(k, j) = k + 1 + 2j - w(j) - \max(0, k - 3 - \lfloor \log_2 j \rfloor)$$

is a characteristic polynomial of α_k; it is a factor of $T_k(x)$ for $k \geq 4$. Finally when $g(x)$ is a multiple of 4, then

$$T_k''(x) = g_1(x) \cdot g_4(x) \cdot \prod_{1 \leq j < 2^{k-1}} g_{\Delta(k,j)}(x)$$

is a characteristic polynomial of α_k; it is a factor of $T_k'(x)$ for $k \geq 2$ and of $T_k(x)$ for $k \geq 3$. This result is just the generalization of the result for (1) given in [3] and [5]. Computer studies demonstrate that for values of n and k up to 12 these characteristic polynomials are minimal in many cases; thus they should provide reasonably tight bounds on the linear equivalence, even in the general case. In any practical case with n and k fairly large the ratio of the upper bound provided by T_k with that provided by T_k' or T_k'' is very close to unity.

REFERENCES

[1] A M Frieze, J Hastad, R Kannan, J C Lagarias, A Shamir, "Reconstructing truncated integer variables satisfying linear congruences", *SIAM J. Comput.*, **17**, 262-280 (1988)

[2] M Ward, "The arithmetical theory of linear recurring series", Transactions of the American Mathematical Society, **35**, 600-628 (July 1933)

[3] Z D Dai, "Binary Sequences Derived from Maximal Length Linear Sequences over Integral Residue Rings", *Proceedings of the Workshop on Stream Ciphers*, eds. T Beth, D Gollmann, F Piper, P Wild, Report 89/1, Europäisches Institut für Systemsicherheit, Universität Karlsruhe, D-7500 Karlsruhe 1.

[4] Z D Dai, M Q Huang, "A Criterion for Primitiveness of Polynomials over $Z/(2^d)$", Kexue Tongbao, to be published

[5] Z D Dai, "Binary Sequences Derived from Sequences over the Integral Residue Rings: (I) Periods and Minimal Polynomials", to be submitted

[6] Z D Dai, T Beth, D Gollmann, "Lower Bounds for the Linear Complexity of Binary Sequences derived from Sequences over Residue Rings", Proceedings of Eurocrypt-90

[7] W G Chambers, Z D Dai, "A simple but effective modification to a multiplicative congruential random-number generator", to be published in IEE Proc E

WEAKNESSES OF UNDENIABLE SIGNATURE SCHEMES

(Extended Abstract)

Yvo Desmedt*
Dept. of EE & CS
P.O.Box 784
Milwaukee, WI 53201
U.S.A.

Moti Yung
IBM T. J. Watson Research Center
P.O. Box 218
Yorktown Heights, NY 10598
U.S.A.

Abstract

The nice concept of undeniable signatures was presented by Chaum and van Antwerpen [10]. In [7] Chaum mentioned that "with undeniable signatures only paying customers are able to verify the signature." Using methods based on "divertible zero-knowledge proofs" and "distributed secure *mental* games played among cooperating users", we show that in certain contexts *non*-paying verifiers can check the signature as well, thus demonstrating that the applicability of undeniable signatures is somewhat restricted and must rely on the physical (or other) isolation of the verifying customer. In addition, we show that the first undeniable signature schemes suffer from certain security problems due to their multiplicative nature (similar to problems the RSA signature scheme has).

1   Introduction

Undeniable signatures were introduced in [10], further work on the subject is given in [7, 21, 2]. Unlike digital signatures, undeniable signatures cannot be verified without cooperation of the signer. This means that in an initial "commitment phase" the signer sends a message together with a commitment information.

---

*This research has been partially supported by NSF Grant NCR-9004879.

Later (*e.g.*, one year later), in the "verification phase", the signer will prove that this commitment corresponds to a signature; such verification proofs can be zero-knowledge as presented at Eurocrypt '90 [7]. Chaum [7] (and later also in [2]) mentioned that "undeniable signatures are preferable to digital signatures for many upcoming applications." The following (and other) applications which exemplify the potential of the notion of "undeniable signature" were given:

- "Consider ... the signature a software supplier issues on its software, which allows customers to check that the software is genuine and unmodified. With undeniable signatures, *only paying customers are able to verify the signature*, and they are still ensured that the supplier is accountable for the software.

- "All manner of inter-organizational messages ... are a natural candidate for signatures that provide for dispute resolution. But self-authentication would greatly increase the illicit salability of such information."

In this paper we demonstrate that, in fact, the signer in the verification phase *cannot* restrict the recipients of his proof of signature validity in scenarios where the set of users can communicate with each other (such as in public networks). In other words, while the prover thinks that he is proving the validity of his signature to a specific person, he could *without his knowledge be proving it to a large group of people, convincing all of them simultaneously*. Thus, in the case of signing software releases, a dishonest customer could buy the software and sell it to a group of users at half the price. Then, when these customers want to check the validity of the signature the customer will help the others in checking the validity of their copies, as we will discuss in Section 3. Observe that when the group of users is afraid that the above customer is a crook (a computer hacker), they can still be convinced of the validity (invalidity) of the software release.[1] In addition, we show how to use divertible zero-knowledge to attack the original undeniable signature scheme, in which one of the verifiers can be fooled to believe he is running a legal protocol, while actually he is talking with an intermediate cheating party.

---

[1] Due to initial remarks of [5] following the initial presentation of these paper's ideas, and in order to clarify any possible confusion, we will discuss this last aspect in sufficient details in Section 3.2.

In the final version of this paper we will present certain settings in which under additional assumptions about the context, the problems presented can be reduced.

The first undeniable signatures schemes suffer from similar problems as the RSA signature scheme does. While it was proven secure with respect to key-only attacks[2] [7], an eavesdropper/ active eavesdropper can, during the commitment phase, modify commitments for signatures into ones for other messages. In particular, the scheme is insecure with respect to an "existential chosen plaintext attack": agreeing to sign and verify a randomly looking message chosen by the verifier, may imply that the signer is actually committed to another "meaningful message he has no information about". In Section 4 we explain how this and more can be achieved.

We first overview Chaum's zero-knowledge undeniable signature scheme.

2   The undeniable signature scheme

We review the undeniable signature scheme in which all users know G and g, where G is a group which order is p, a prime, and g is a generator. Each user announces g^x as public key and keeps his own x secret. To commit to a signature for the message m, the sender sends: (m, m^x) in the commitment phase. Let us denote $z = m^x$.

When asked to validate the signature (during the verification phase) the following *confirmation* protocol[3] is executed as in Figure 1.
When the receiver's checking returns correctly, he accepts the confirmation of the message as being valid. Observe that if the *signer has committed to more than one message the verifier must provide m.*

Chaum also discusses a *disavowal* protocol. If the receiver has received for the message $m \neq 1$ a commitment $z = m^{x'}$, (note that each element of the group, can be written in such a form because the order of the group is a prime, so each element but the identity is a generator) where $x' \neq x$, then the sender can prove that z is not of the proper form. Since this protocol is almost irrelevant in our context we do *not* discuss it in detail.

---

[2] when the attacker tries to forge, solely based on the availability of the public keys.

[3] Choosing a in the set A with uniform probability distribution and independently of other events is denote as $a \in_R A$.

Signer   Verifier

$$a \in_R Z_p,$$
$$b \in_R Z_p$$

$$\xleftarrow{\quad r = m^a g^b \quad}$$

$$q \in_R Z_p$$
$$s_1 := r \cdot g^q,$$
$$s_2 := g^{qx} r^x$$

$$\xrightarrow{\quad s_1, s_2 \quad}$$

$$\xleftarrow{\quad a, b \quad}$$

Checks $r = m^a g^b$

$$\xrightarrow{\quad q \quad}$$

Checks
$$s_1 = r \cdot g^q,$$
$$s_2 = (g^x)^{b+q} \cdot z^a$$

Figure 1: Chaum's zero-knowledge confirmation scheme.

The scheme works since for a forger, using the public-key directory (the sender's public-key), the probability of coming up with a pair which is a message and a commitment to its signature and cannot be successfully disavowed is negligible for large enough values of p (assuming discrete logarithm mod p is hard). So, the scheme is secure with respect to key-only attack.

3   Verification by multiple unknown verifiers is possible

In this section we show that in *any* undeniable signature scheme the signer has no control on how many verifiers he confirms the validity of the signature to. To this end, the verifiers collaborate using the concept of secure function evaluations knows also as "Mental Games" [20, 19, 9]. Mental games allow n players to play any partial-information game over the telephone (using a conference call) following the specified rules of the game such that no one can cheat, assuming that half of the players are honest. (The last result even guarantees that one player in the game is unconditionally secure). (The game can be played over secure physical lines assuming two thirds are honest as, for example, in [8]). It enables secure distributed computing of a function where the players compute together the result of a function correctly, based on their private inputs while maintaining the secrecy of their inputs.

In the honest case the sender validates the signature to a verifier. Now, we replace this one verifier by a group of verifiers. The rules of the game are that *all* the verifiers get convinced of the validity of the commitment once the protocol is finished. We now distinguish two cases: the group of users trust that one individual, called the trusted party, will not impersonate the signer or will attempt to give fraudulent zero-knowledge proofs. In the second case we do not make this assumption.

3.1 All verifiers trust one of them

This simpler scenario was raised in [5] and is similar to a possible scenario mentioned in [7] (see remark 1 at the end of this section). It is actually a methodological way to approach the general setting of the next subsection. In this case we do not have to use the full power of the mental games and the protocol is very simple. The protocol runs in the background by the collaborating parties and relies on zero-knowledge and bit-commitment protocols.

The technical details, in general, are as following. The collaborating verifiers generate a random string of bits to be used in the validation protocol (for example, they generate the required bits for each step) executed with the sender. To do this, the verifier's work together in a sub-protocol hidden from the sender. The verifiers all commit to random bits (using the simple bit commitment protocol due to Blum [1], they can initially commit to many bits and then open them as needed and fast). When they open these commitments these private bits are exclusive-ored together. This gives the result of the sub-protocol which is a common string of random bits to be used as the randomness in the interactive step with the sender in the validation stage. This randomness is trusted by all verifiers, even when they do not trust each other. Thus, this random string is fed into a trusted box which executes the protocol as an actual verifier with the sender and all verifiers having access to the transcript of the validation are simultaneously convinced. The on-line opening of commitments and ex-oring is a very simple computation, thus this scenario is important and enables one trusted simple device to serve many verifiers at the same time (while paying only once) even when the random number generator in that simple device and many of the verifiers are possibly unreliable or predictable.

Even when the sender requires that the verifier (to whom, for example, he sold his software release) uses some adaptation such as (for example) forcing the verifier to use a public key to encrypt a message, all the other verifiers can be convinced even without learning the key used (since instead of opening the key, the actual verifier can convince the rest of the players in a zero-knowledge fashion that the key was used to encrypt data based on their common random data, this validation proof can even be executed in an off-line fashion after the completion of the protocol).

As a conclusion, one can see that in an environment where the verifier is not physically isolated, it is always possible for him (using the sender) to convince others of the validity of a signature, without assuming that the others "fully trust" the actual verifier (this opens a possibility of "validation piracy").

3.2   No verifier is trusted by the others

We now discuss the case that no verifier is trusted and that verifiers are afraid that the one who is communicating with the prover (signer) will reveal something to him to allow him to give a fraudulent proof. More they are afraid that one verifier himself will attempt to give a false proof to all other verifiers. We can view this case as a fault-tolerant extension of the previous case, and in this case the verifiers use the full power of mental games.

Mental games allow many individuals to securely compute the output of a multiple input algorithm such that none of the other individuals will know the inputs used by the others. It has been proven that any such algorithm can be securely executed (guaranteeing privacy of inputs) provided that half of the participants are honest [20, 19, 9]. So the following holds:

Theorem 1 *No undeniable signature scheme is secure against a multi-verifier* *attack provided that half of the verifiers are honest.*

Proof.   The proof relies on [20]. Suppose that a confirmation protocol of an undeniable signature scheme, in which there is one prover and one verifier, is given. We call this scheme "the game". We now modify the game into what we call the "modified game". Assume that the verifier has to compute (at some stage) some $A(x, y, s)$ (where x is public, y is an information which is secret, but $E(y)$, is a public encryption of y (for example a signature or an encryption key) which is encrypted in public so that validation based on y can be executed, and s is secret but known to the verifier), and send the result to the prover. Then we modify this into a computation of $A'(x, y, s_1, s_2, \ldots, s_m)$, where m is the number of multi-verifiers and s_i is secret but known to verifier i. Now this A' is computed using the concept of mental game and the output is sent to the prover. All the verifiers are convinced during the game that indeed the right y key corresponding to $E(y)$ is used as an additional input of the actual verifier. For example, in the case that s corresponds to a (uniformly) randomly chosen string, $A'(x, y, s_1, s_2, \ldots, s_m) = A(x, y, s_1 \oplus s_2 \oplus \cdots \oplus s_m)$. (A more formal proof will be given in the final paper.) $\square$

It is clear from the proof that the approach in this case is almost identical to the one given in Section 3.1, but that the calculation of what has to be sent to the prover is done using mental games. Recently Ohta–Okamoto–Fujioka have given as open problem the question of the existence of "an equivalent condition that plural verifiers can not be convinced of the validity of a signature." The above answers in the negative this question, (and thus, physical assumptions such as isolation or other contextual constraints are necessary).

3.3   Using divertible zero-knowledge

Now, we discuss a worse scenario which applies to undeniable signatures of the type of [7]. Let us illustrate the scenario. Alice wants to buy a nice software release, but she is a software pirate (with a scul of a businesswoman). She convinces Bob that she is a representative of the software company, so Bob pays her to buy the software. Alice does this, and then continues to sell it to colleague pirates, without paying the company. When Bob wants his software validated he plays the confirmation protocol with Alice. Alice then plays *simultaneously* the protocol with the software company. She may also, at the same time, convince all her colleagues of the validity of her software, for reduced fees.

Figure 2 explains the technical details, which are based on "divertible zero-knowledge proofs" [16, 23] where the verifier in the middle diverts the exchanged messages.

Observe that at the end both verifiers are completely convinced of the validity of the commitment.

The verifier in the above protocol can be replaced by a chain of verifiers in which Alice, in the above example, is communicating with the sender, the other cooperating pirates are in the middle between Alice and Bob, and Bob (the victimized customer) is at the end of the chain. The cooperating (but not trusting) colleagues in the middle are all (but the honest Bob) aware of the diversion and are taking part in it (multi-step diversion, each diverting the previously given information). Once the protocol is successfully terminated, they are all simultaneously convinced.

Remark 1 David Chaum has communicated to us the following three points [6] which we present (based on our understanding). The first point is that the exact use of mental games, mentioned in the pre-proceedings version of this work, was not clear; we hope the above clarifies it. Second, he pointed out that there are other means of isolation of the verifier (rather then only physical) which help in prevention of collaborations, he suggests exploiting the fact that, currently, mental games require a certain amount of computational time, and thus, imposing temporal restriction on the verifier's responses may effectively isolate the verifier. This was discussed in [5] and for the technique and details see Chaum's paper based on his presentation. Finally, Chaum's third point is that he was aware of possible covert cooperation of many verifiers (perhaps similar to the case of subsection 3.1) and had mentioned in the *recent works* section of his Eurocrypt-90 paper [7] (on page 463) a solution to such attacks by applying a *verifier commit protocol* (which may possibly be the protocol relying on temporal constraints which was suggested in the discussion of the previous point).

We would like to say that it is only natural (in a cryptologic setting) that we try to point out a broad range of weaknesses while David tries to point out as broader as possible scenario in which the weaknesses do not apply. We view the remarks and the discussion as a healthy exchange and thank him for his remarks.

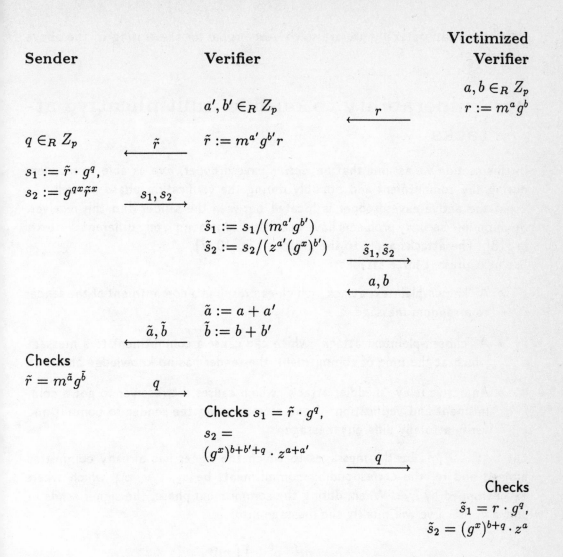

Figure 2: Attack based on divertible zero-knowledge

(We note that, naturally, we are solely responsible for the writing of the above remark).

4 Vulnerability to on-line multiplicative attacks

In this section we assume that an *active* eavesdropper, Eve, is able to interfere during the commitment and possibly during the verification phase as well. As usual the active eavesdropper is located between the sender and the receiver. Such on-line security problems have been studied in completely different contexts in [18]. The attacks apply to the protocols in [10, 7].
We next present three attacks:

- A "known-plaintext attack" which can result in a commitment of the sender to a random message.

- A "chosen-plaintext attack" which can cause a commitment to a message which at the time of commitment, the sender has no knowledge about.

- An active relay "meddler attack" which causes the receiver to get a commitment and verification of one message, and the sender to commit and verify a totally different message.

Let m_1, ..., m_c be the messages to which the signer has already committed himself and let the corresponding commitments be z_1, ..., z_c, which where eavesdropped by Eve. When, during the commitment phase, the signer sends m and $z = m^x$, Eve will modify the message into:

$$\tilde{m} = m^f \cdot g^{e_0} \cdot \prod_{i=1}^{c} m_i^{e_i}$$

and the commitment into:

$$\tilde{z} = z^f \cdot (g^x)^{e_0} \cdot \prod_{i=1}^{c} z_i^{e_i}$$

by choosing (arbitrary) f, e_i, and sending $\tilde{m}, \tilde{z}$ to the receiver. Observe that if all the z_i and z were proper commitments for m_i and respectively m, then $\tilde{z}$ is a valid commitment for $\tilde{m}$. When the verification phase starts and the receiver (of the commitment) sends $\tilde{m}$ and $\tilde{z}$ for validation, Eve will forward those. At this stage the sender of the commitment is in a position that he could determine that he never committed to this message, *i.e.*, by having stored all the messages to which he ever committed. However, the disavowal protocol does not allow him to deny having committed to this signature, which is due to the above observation. (Recall that when m and z are given, such that $z = m^x$, the sender cannot execute a disavowal protocol for the fact of not sending m.) So no choice is left for him but to participate in the confirmation protocol and there is no need for Eve to interact in this protocol. This is a known plaintext attack where Eve is able to generate a set of random signatures.

Now we allow the m_i to be chosen by Eve, instead of by the sender. This is the chosen plaintext attack. This attack is very similar to the chosen plaintext attacks proposed against RSA. Similar techniques as discussed in [11, 14, 15, 12, 17, 13, 22] can also be used here for this purpose. The chosen plaintext attacks allow Eve to generate commitments for any message of her choice, by adapting her attack to this message and the signer has no information about the message he is committing himself to (since the message signed directly is random). It was noticed by Chaum that "blinding" is possible in the setting of the undeniable signature protocol, which implies that random messages will be signed. In fact, the attack above exploits exactly the possibility of "blinding" which is very dangerous (a double-ended sword) in this setting, once it is combined with chosen-plaintext.

We now present a variant of our attack which we call the "meddler attack". It applies to the protocol in [7]. In this new attack Eve will actively (with the help of the sender) convince the receiver that $\hat{m}$ is a valid message in such a way that the sender does not know $\hat{m}$! During the commitment phase Eve acts as a meddler and replaces m and z respectively by $\hat{m} = m^f \cdot g^e$ and $\hat{z} = z^f \cdot (g^x)^e$. When the verification phase starts and the receiver sends $\hat{m}$ and $\hat{z}$ to the sender, Eve will replace them by m and z. So the sender "believes" that he is confirming the validity of z as an undeniable signature for m, but he will (due to Eve) in fact convince the receiver that $\hat{z}$ is a valid undeniable signature for $\hat{m}$. The sender serves as an oracle for Eve to compute a commitment for one (say, what he believes to be a randomly looking) message, while in the process the sender commits to a totally different (possibly meaningful and harmful) message. Eve's interaction is explained in Figure 3.

Sender	Eve	Receiver

$$\text{Receiver: } a \in_R Z_p,$$
$$b \in_R Z_p$$

$$\xleftarrow{\quad r = \hat{m}^a g^b \quad}$$

$$q \in_R Z_p$$

$$\xleftarrow{\quad r \quad}$$

$$s_1 =: r \cdot g^q,$$
$$s_2 := g^{qx} r^x$$

$$\xrightarrow{\quad s_1, s_2 \quad}$$

$$\xrightarrow{\quad s_1, s_2 \quad}$$

$$\xleftarrow{\quad a, b \quad}$$

$$\hat{a} := f \cdot a \pmod{p}$$
$$\hat{b} := e \cdot a + b$$
$$\pmod{p}$$

$$\xleftarrow{\quad \hat{a}, \hat{b} \quad}$$

Checks

$$r = m^{\hat{a}} g^{\hat{b}}$$

$$\xrightarrow{\quad q \quad}$$

$$\xrightarrow{\quad q \quad}$$

Checks

$$s_1 = r \cdot g^q,$$
$$s_2 = (g^x)^{b+q} \cdot \hat{z}^a$$

Figure 3: The meddler's, Eve's, interaction

5   Conclusions

We have presented certain scenarios in which carefulness is required when applying undeniable signatures. As with any other cryptographic primitive it is important to clarify and better understand the exact setting in which undeniable signature applies.

First we have observed that a verifier who behaves as an active relay-station provides an anonymous way of verifying the validity of the commitment to a multitude of verifiers. This demonstrates that the concept of anonymity, studied by Chaum [3, 4] is indeed very powerful and can also be used for cryptanalytic purposes. In particular, in protocols like "undeniable signature" where the protocol goals includes restriction to a "specified receiver", anonymous channels violate the goals and should be detected. Even when the channel is not anonymous, but relies on information which the verifier is committed to (for possible verification by a judge), exclusive use of the channel cannot be assured. Mental games play an important role in this context.

Secondly, we have demonstrated that multiplicative undeniable signature schemes suffer from weaknesses similar in nature to the RSA signature scheme. The proven secure non-multiplicative versions [21, 2] of the notion do not suffer from this disadvantage.

In the final version we will explain how the problem of multitude of unknown verifiers can be reduced by providing personalized commitments to signatures. This applies to such applications such as software validation, in settings where there exists an active authority that probes the software users.

Acknowledgement

We acknowledge Mike Burmester for having presented this paper and for useful discussions, Gus Simmons for his comments, and David Chaum for his remarks.

REFERENCES

[1] M. Blum. Coin flipping by telephone — a protocol for solving impossible problems. In *digest of papers COMPCON82*, pp. 133–137. IEEE Computer Society, February 1982.

[2] J. Boyar, D. Chaum, I. Damgard, and T. Pedersen. Convertible undeniable signatures. Presented at Crypto '90, August 12–15, 1990, Santa Barbara, California, U.S.A., to appear in: Advances in Cryptology. Proc. of Crypto '90 (Lecture Notes in Computer Science), Springer-Verlag, 1990.

[3] D. Chaum. Untraceable electronic mail, return addresses, and digital pseudonyms. *Commun. ACM*, 24(2), pp. 84–88, February 1981.

[4] D. Chaum. The dining cryptographers problem: unconditional sender and recipient untraceability. *Journal of Cryptology*, 1(1), pp. 65–75, 1988.

[5] D. Chaum. On weaknesses of 'weaknesses of undeniable signatures'. Presented at the rump session of Eurocrypt '91, Brighton, U.K., April (Communicated to us by Gus Simmons.) 1991.

[6] D. Chaum. Personal Communication (over the phone, no coin flipping!).

[7] D. Chaum. Zero-knowledge undeniable signatures. In I. Damgård, editor, *Advances in Cryptology, Proc. of Eurocrypt '90 (Lecture Notes in Computer Science 473)*, pp. 458–464. Springer-Verlag, 1991. Åarhus, Denmark, May 21–24.

[8] D. Chaum, C. Crépeau, and I. Damgård. Multiparty unconditionally secure protocols. In *Proceedings of the twentieth annual ACM Symp. Theory of Computing, STOC*, pp. 11–19, May 2–4, 1988.

[9] D. Chaum, I. Damgård, and J. van de Graaf. Multiparty computations ensuring privacy of each party's input and correctness of the result. In C. Pomerance, editor, *Advances in Cryptology, Proc. of Crypto '87 (Lecture Notes in Computer Science 293)*, pp. 87–119. Springer-Verlag, 1988. Santa Barbara, Ca., August 16-20, 1987.

[10] D. Chaum and H. van Antwerpen. Undeniable signatures. In G. Brassard, editor, *Advances in Cryptology — Crypto '89, Proceedings (Lecture Notes in Computer Science 435)*, pp. 212–216. Springer-Verlag, 1990. Santa Barbara, California, U.S.A., August 20–24.

[11] G. I. Davida. Chosen signature cryptanalysis of the RSA (MIT) public key cryptosystem. Tech. Report TR-CS-82-2, University of Wisconsin-Milwaukee, October 1982.

[12] W. de Jonge and D. Chaum. Attacks on some RSA signatures. In *Advances in Cryptology: Crypto '85, Proceedings (Lecture Notes in Computer Science 218)*, pp. 18–27. Springer-Verlag, New York, 1986. Santa Barbara, California, U.S.A., August 18–22, 1985.

[13] W. de Jonge and D. Chaum. Some variations on RSA signatures & their security. In A. Odlyzko, editor, *Advances in Cryptology, Proc. of Crypto '86 (Lecture Notes in Computer Science 263)*, pp. 49–59. Springer-Verlag, 1987. Santa Barbara, California, U. S. A., August 11–15.

[14] R. A. DeMilo, and M. J. Merritt Chosen signature cryptanalysis of public key cryptosystems. Technical Memorandum, Georgia Institute of Technology, October 1982.

[15] D. E. R. Denning. Digital signatures with RSA and other public-key cryptosystems. *Comm. ACM 27*, pp. 388–392, 1984.

[16] Y. Desmedt, C. Goutier, and S. Bengio. Special uses and abuses of the Fiat-Shamir passport protocol. In C. Pomerance, editor, *Advances in Cryptology, Proc. of Crypto '87 (Lecture Notes in Computer Science 293)*, pp. 21–39. Springer-Verlag, 1988. Santa Barbara, California, U.S.A., August 16–20.

[17] Y. Desmedt and A. Odlyzko. A chosen text attack on the RSA cryptosystem and some discrete logarithm schemes. In Hugh C. Williams, editor, *Advances in Cryptology: Crypto '85, Proceedings (Lecture Notes in Computer Science 218)*, pp. 516–522. Springer-Verlag, 1986. Santa Barbara, California, U.S.A., August 18–20.

[18] O. Dolev and A. Yao. On the security of public key cryptography. *IEEE Trans. Inform. Theory*, 29, pp. 198–208, March 1983.

[19] Z. Galil, S. Haber, and M. Yung. Cryptographic computations: secure fault-tolerant protocols and the public-key model In C. Pomerance, editor,

Advances in Cryptology, Proc. of Crypto '87 (Lecture Notes in Computer Science 293), pp. 135–155. Springer-Verlag, 1988. Santa Barbara, Ca., August 16-20, 1987.

[20] O. Goldreich, S. Micali, and A. Wigderson. How to play any mental game. In *Proceedings of the Nineteenth annual ACM Symp. Theory of Computing, STOC*, pp. 218–229, May 25–27, 1987.

[21] S. Micali. Public announcement at Crypto '89.

[22] J. H. Moore. Protocol failures in cryptosystems. *Proc. IEEE*, 76(5), pp. 594–602, May 1988.

[23] T. Okamoto and K. Ohta. Divertible zero knowledge interactive proofs and commutative random self-reducibility. In J.-J. Quisquater and J. Vandewalle, editors, *Advances in Cryptology, Proc. of Eurocrypt '89 (Lecture Notes in Computer Science 434)*, pp. 134–149. Springer-Verlag, 1990. Houthalen, Belgium, April 10–13.

Distributed Provers with Applications to Undeniable Signatures

Torben Pryds Pedersen

Aarhus University, Computer Science Department

Ny Munkegade, DK-8000 Århus C, Denmark

Abstract

This paper introduces distributed prover protocols. Such a protocol is a proof system in which a polynomially bounded prover is replaced by many provers each having partial information about the witness owned by the original prover. As an application of this concept, it is shown how the signer of undeniable signatures can distribute part of his secret key to n agents such that any k of these can verify a signature. This facility is useful in most applications of undeniable signatures, and as the proposed protocols are practical, the results in this paper makes undeniable signatures more useful. The first part of the paper describes a method for verifiable secret sharing, which allows non-interactive verification of the shares and is as secure as the Shamir secret sharing scheme in the proposed applications.

1 Introduction

Undeniable signatures were introduced in [CvA90]. Briefly, an undeniable signature is a signature which cannot be verified without the help of the signer (see [CvA90] and [Cha91]). They are therefore less personal than ordinary signatures in the sense that a signature cannot be related to the signer without his help. On the other hand, the signer can only repudiate an alleged signature by proving that it is incorrect.

A manufacturer can use undeniable signatures to sign his products, such that someone who wants to verify the genuineness of a given product has to contact the manufacturer. This way the manufacturer can control the usage of his products.

Convertible undeniable signatures are undeniable signatures with the added property that the signer can convert all the undeniable signatures to ordinary signatures by releasing a part of the secret key, and selectively convertible undeniable signatures allow the signer to convert single signatures to ordinary signatures without affecting other undeniable signatures (see [BCDP90]).

In almost all applications of undeniable signatures that one can imagine, it might be a problem that only the signer can verify the signatures, because this requires that he can always be reached. Since an undeniable signature does not prove anything in itself, it is very reasonable that a receiver of a signature demands that either the signer or an agent authorized by the signer is always willing to verify signatures. Such an agent can also be a big help to the signer, since a person signing many messages quite rapidly can be overburdened verifying signatures.

With convertible undeniable signatures it is possible for the signer to authorize an agent who can verify all signatures, and if the signatures are selectively convertible, agents can be authorized to verify single signatures. However, this requires that the signer trusts the agents completely.

If the signer does not (want to) trust single persons, he may want to authorize n agents such that verification requires at least k of these to cooperate. This facility was proposed by David Chaum and this paper shows how it can be achieved. The construction falls in two parts. First it is described how the signer can distribute the keys such that each agent can verify that he has received correct shares, and then it is shown how the agents can verify or deny signatures.

In Section 3 we present a scheme for distributing a secret s which uses the fact that information about s is known beforehand through a public key. This scheme is based on the secret sharing scheme by Shamir, which is shortly described in Section 2. After a short description of the undeniable signature scheme from [BCDP90] in Section 4, Section 5 shows how a number of agents can verify these signatures, and Section 6 discusses the possibility of using agents to deny signatures.

2   The Shamir Scheme

In this section the Shamir secret sharing scheme is briefly described and the properties needed in the following sections are summarized (see also [Sha79]).

A (k, n)-threshold secret sharing scheme is a protocol between $n + 1$ players in which the *dealer* distributes partial information (*share* or *shadow*) about a *secret* (or *key*) to n participants such that

- Any group of fewer than k participants cannot obtain any information about the secret.

- Any group of at least k participants can compute the secret in polynomial time.

Consider a field $I\!F$ and let the secret, s, be an element of $I\!F$. In order to distribute s among $P_1, \ldots, P_n$ (where $n < |I\!F|$) the dealer chooses a polynomial $f \in I\!F[x]$ of degree at most $k - 1$ satisfying $f(0) = s$. Participant P_i receives $s_i = f(x_i)$ as his private share, where $x_i \in I\!F \setminus \{0\}$ is public information about P_i ($x_i \neq x_j$ for $i \neq j$).

Due to the fact that there is one and only one polynomial of degree at most $k - 1$ satisfying $f(x_i) = s_i$ for k values of i, the Shamir scheme satisfies the definition of a (k, n)-threshold scheme. Any k persons $(P_{i_1}, \ldots, P_{i_k})$ can find f by the formula:

$$f(x) = \sum_{l=1}^{k}(\prod_{h\neq l} \frac{x - x_{i_h}}{x_{i_l} - x_{i_h}})f(x_{i_l})$$

$$= \sum_{l=1}^{k}(\prod_{h\neq l} \frac{x - x_{i_h}}{x_{i_l} - x_{i_h}})s_{i_l} \qquad (1)$$

Thus

$$s = \sum_{j=1}^{k} a_j s_{i_j},$$

where $a_1, \ldots, a_k$ are given by

$$a_j = \prod_{h\neq j} \frac{x_{i_h}}{x_{i_h} - x_{i_j}}.$$

Thus each a_i is non-zero and can easily be computed from the public information.

3   Verifiable Secret Sharing

Now the Shamir scheme is applied in a setting where the secret is given as a discrete logarithm. The resulting scheme has the advantage that each participant can verify his share. In [P.F87] Feldman obtained a verifiable secret sharing scheme from the Shamir secret sharing scheme by broadcasting probabilistic encryptions of the polynomial used to generate the shares. Under the assumption that the encryption function is a "homomorphism" it was possible for each shareholder to verify his share without communicating with the other participants.

The scheme suggested by Feldman aims at hiding the secret to be distributed in a very strong sense. However this is not necessary if some information about the secret is known beforehand. We now present a scheme very similar to [P.F87] which is somewhat simpler due to the fact that the public information about the secret is used in the verification of the shares.

3.1   Verification using Discrete Logarithms

Throughout this paper p and q are large primes such that q divides $p-1$, and g generates the subgroup, G_q, of $\mathbb{Z}_p$ of order q. It is assumed that p, q and g are publicly known.

Assume the dealer has a secret $s \in \mathbb{Z}_q$ and is committed to s through a public key $h = g^s$. This secret can be distributed to $P_1, \ldots, P_n$, as follows:

PROTOCOL DISTRIBUTE

1. Compute shares s_i using the Shamir secret sharing scheme in the field $\mathbb{F} = \mathbb{Z}_q$ by first choosing a polynomial $f = f_0 + f_1 x + \ldots + f_{k-1} x^{k-1}$ over $\mathbb{Z}_q$ of degree $k - 1$ satisfying $f(0) = s$ and then computing

$$s_i = f(x_i).$$

Here x_i is public information about P_i as described above.

2. Send s_i *secretly* to P_i, and *broadcast* $(g^{f_i})_{i=1,\ldots,k-1}$ to all n participants.

Thus the dealer has to broadcast $k - 1$ elements in G_q and to send secretly n elements in $\mathbb{Z}_q$.

The public information corresponding to the share s_i is denoted $h_i = g^{s_i}$. Thus h_i depends on s_i in the same way that h depends on s. A participant not knowing s_i can compute h_i as $(g^{f_0} = h)$

$$h_i = \prod_{j=0}^{k-1} (g^{f_j})^{x_i^j}.$$

When all shares have been distributed each participant verifies his share as follows

PROTOCOL VERIFY SHARE (at P_i)

1. Compute $h_l = \prod_{j=0}^{k-1} (g^{f_j})^{x_l^j}$ for all $l = 1, \ldots, n$.
2. Verify, that $h_i = g^{s_i}$.
3. If this is false broadcast s_i and stop.
   Otherwise accept the share.

The signer can always detect, if P_i falsely claims to have received a wrong share, and in that case he should start all over discarding P_i from future protocols.

If the signer follows the protocol, all honest agents will accept their shares, and $h_i = g^{s_i}$ will be publicly known for $i = 1, \ldots, n$. The next proposition shows, that no matter how the dealer computes the shares, any k participants who have accepted their shares can find s.

Proposition 3.1
Any k participants, who have followed PROTOCOL VERIFY SHARE and accepted, can find s.

Proof
Assume that the k participants are $P_1, \ldots, P_k$. It is sufficient to show that the unique polynomial f' of degree at most $k - 1$ satisfying

$$f'(x_i) = s_i \qquad \text{for } i = 1, \ldots, k$$

also satisfies $f'(0) = s$. But

$$\prod_{j=0}^{k-1} (g^{f_j})^{x_i^j} = h_i = g^{s_i} = g^{f'(x_i)}$$

implies

$$\sum_{j=0}^{k-1} f_j x_i^j = f'(x_i) \bmod q$$

and the uniqueness of f' implies that $f'(0) = f(0) = s$. ∎

Theorem 3.2 below shows that any number of participants can simulate the dealer perfectly no matter what shares they get. Thus fewer than k participants do not get any information about s which allows them to compute something that they could not have computed before the secret was distributed.

Theorem 3.2

Any l participants having shares $(s_{i_j})_{j=1,\ldots,l}$ can find $(g^{f_j})_{j=0,\ldots,k-1}$, such that

$$f'(x) = f'_0 + f'_1 x + \ldots + f'_{k-1} x^{k-1}$$

is a random polynomial of degree at most $k-1$ satisfying

$$\begin{aligned}
f'(0) &= s \\
f'(x_{i_j}) &= s_{i_j}, \qquad j = 1, \ldots, l.
\end{aligned}$$

Proof

If $l \geq k$ the proposition is trivial as any k agents can find the polynomial used by the signer.

Now assume that $1 \leq l < k$ and let the l agents in question be $P_1, \ldots, P_l$. The l participants generate f' as follows:

1. Choose $k - 1 - l$ random "shares" $s_{l+1}, \ldots, s_{k-1}$ corresponding to the public information $x_{l+1}, \ldots, x_{k-1}$.

2. Find g^{f_i} for $i = 0, \ldots, k-1$, where the polynomial $f'(x) = f'_0 + \ldots + f'_{k-1} x^{k-1}$ satisfies $f'(x_i) = s_i$ for $i = 1, \ldots, k-1$ and $f'(0) = s$ (see below).

As $s_{l+1}, \ldots, s_{k-1}$ were chosen at random the (unknown) polynomial f' generated this way is completely random such that

$$\begin{aligned}
f'(0) &= s \\
f'(x_j) &= s_j, \qquad j = 1, \ldots, l.
\end{aligned}$$

It only remains to show how $(g^{f_i})_i$ are found. The polynomial f' is going to satisfy $(s_0 = s, x_0 = 0)$:

$$
\begin{pmatrix}
1 & x_0 & x_0^2 & \cdots & x_0^{k-1} \\
1 & x_1 & x_1^2 & \cdots & x_1^{k-1} \\
\vdots & \vdots & \vdots & & \vdots \\
1 & x_{k-1} & x_{k-1}^2 & \cdots & x_{k-1}^{k-1}
\end{pmatrix}
\begin{pmatrix}
f_0' \\
f_1' \\
\vdots \\
f_{k-1}'
\end{pmatrix}
=
\begin{pmatrix}
s_0 \\
s_1 \\
\vdots \\
s_{k-1}
\end{pmatrix}
$$

This $k \times k$ matrix is a Van der Monde matrix, and it has an inverse, A, as $x_i \neq 0$ and $x_i \neq x_j$ for $i \neq j$. Thus

$$
A
\begin{pmatrix}
s_0 \\
s_1 \\
\vdots \\
s_{k-1}
\end{pmatrix}
=
\begin{pmatrix}
f_0' \\
f_1' \\
\vdots \\
f_{k-1}'
\end{pmatrix}.
$$

Let

$$
A =
\begin{pmatrix}
a_{00} & a_{01} & a_{02} & \cdots & a_{0,k-1} \\
a_{10} & a_{11} & a_{12} & \cdots & a_{1,k-1} \\
\vdots & \vdots & \vdots & & \vdots \\
a_{k-1,0} & a_{k-1,1} & a_{k-1,2} & \cdots & a_{k-1,k-1}
\end{pmatrix}
$$

and note that $P_1, \ldots, P_l$ can find each a_{ij}. Thus g^{f_i} can be computed for $i = 0, \ldots, k-1$ by the formula ($g^{s_0} = $ h is known)

$$
\prod_{j=0}^{k-1} g^{s_j a_{ij}} = g^{f_i}.
$$

This proves the theorem. ∎

4 Convertible Undeniable Signatures

This section contains a short description of the selectively convertible undeniable signature scheme from [BCDP90].

Let p, q and g be as above. For all a and b in G_q with $b \neq 1$ the discrete logarithm of a to the base b is defined and denoted $\log_b(a)$. The simultaneous discrete logarithm problem is to decide given four elements a, b, c and d if $\log_b(a)$ equals $\log_d(c)$.

The private keys in the scheme are

$$KS1 = x \text{ and } KS2 = z, \quad 1 < x, z < q$$

and the public key is

$$KP = (p, q, g, y, u), \text{ where } y = g^x \text{ and } u = g^z.$$

Any receiver of the public key can easily verify that y and u generate G_q.

The signature on the message m is $sign(m) = (g^t, r, s)$, where (r, s) is the El Gamal signature on $M = g^t t z m \bmod q$ (in this product g^t is considered an element in $\mathbb{Z}_q$). That is

$$g^M = y^r r^s \bmod p.$$

As noted in [BCDP90] m should be hashed before signing, but the hash function is omitted here.

Given m and (T, r, s) both the signer and the verifier can compute $w = T^{Tm}$ and $v = y^r r^s$. The signer can prove that (T, r, s) is (not) a signature on m by proving that $\log_w(v) = \log_g(u)$ ($\log_w(v) \neq \log_g(u)$). The protocol in figure 1 is a variant of the proof system for simultaneous discrete logarithm in [Cha91] and shows how the signer can verify a signature.

P		V
		Choose $a, b \in \mathbb{Z}$ and compute $ch = w^a g^b$
	$\xleftarrow{\quad ch \quad}$	
Choose $r \in \mathbb{Z}$ and compute $h_1 = ch^r$ and $h_2 = h_1^z$		
	$\xrightarrow{\quad (h_1, h_2) \quad}$	
	$\xleftarrow{\quad (a, b) \quad}$	
Verify that $ch = w^a g^b$		
	$\xrightarrow{\quad r \quad}$	
		Verify, that $h_1 = (w^a g^b)^r$ and $h_2 = (v^a u^b)^r$

Figure 1: Proof that $\log_w(v) = \log_g(u)(= z)$.

The signer can convert all his signatures to ordinary signatures by releasing z. Alternatively, a signature (T, r, s) on the message m can be converted to a digital signature by releasing t such that $T = g^t$. Given t, a signature can be verified as follows:

1. Verify, that $T = g^t$.

2. Verify, that $(u^{mT})^t = y^r r^s$.

Anyone, who can solve the simultaneous discrete logarithm problem can obviously recognize valid signatures. In [BCDP90] it is argued that it is hard to verify a signature without the aid of the signer even if the signer verifies other signatures.

5 Distributed Prover Protocols

If the signer in an undeniable signature scheme is going away for a while, the receivers of signatures might request that a trusted third person gets the secret key of the scheme such that this person can verify signatures during the signer's absence. If the signer doesn't want to give away the secret, an obvious solution is to distribute it to n persons (agents) with a (k, n)-secret sharing scheme. When a verifier wants a signature to be verified or denied, he can ask k of these n persons for assistance.

Such an $(k+1)$-party protocol between the verifier and k agents will in general be called a *distributed prover protocol* (a distributed prover protocol differs from a multi-prover proof system (see [BOGKW88]) as the provers may have unlimited computing power in the latter case).

These k persons can help the verifier by first finding the secret and subsequently one of them can execute the usual verification/denial protocol. However, this would be against the intentions of the signer, because in that case the secret could just as well have been given to one person in the first place.

In this section we construct protocols that allow k persons to verify signatures *without* finding the secret. From a theoretical point of view it is possible to solve this problem, if the agents are allowed to talk with each other (for instance by using the techniques in [CDvdG88]). However, the distributed verification protocol presented in Section 5.2 is very efficient, and it does not require interaction between the agents. Thus secret communication is only needed in the setup phase when the secret key is distributed.

First the model is presented and a definition of security of a distributed prover protocol is given.

5.1 The Model

It is assumed that the n agents are selected such that at most $k - 1$ of them will ever deviate from the prescribed protocols and try to find the secret key.

Each agent is modeled by a probabilistic polynomial time Turing machine having in addition to a computation tape and a random tape

- a tape for broadcasting messages (can be read by all other participants);
- a tape for common input (shared by all users);
- a tape for auxiliary input (can only be read by the owner);
- a tape for receiving secret messages from the signer (read only).

A cryptographic protocol is secure, if any polynomial (in a security parameter) number of executions of it does not enable one of the parties to do a computation afterwards, that he could not have done beforehand.

As a polynomial number of polynomial time Turing machines can be simulated by a single polynomial time Turing machine, it can be assumed that the verifier is the same in all executions of the protocol (although the verifier may behave differently in each execution). This automatically handles the situation where different verifiers cooperate.

Definition 5.1
An agent is *honest* if it follows the protocol in all executions. An agent who is not honest is called *dishonest*.

For any verifier and any set of dishonest agents consider the following protocol:

1. Distribute the secret.

2. Repeat a polynomial number of times: The verifier and the dishonest agents select an input to the distributed protocol and a set of agents with whom the protocol is executed.

Following the ideas of [CDvdG88], where the security of general multi-party protocols is defined, we say

Definition 5.2
Let K_P be the public key of the original prover.
A distributed prover protocol is secure, if for every set of dishonest agents and every verifier, V^*, for every set of auxiliary inputs to the verifiers and the dishonest agents, there exists a probabilistic polynomial time machine, M, such that the output of M on input K_p is polynomially indistinguishable from the transcript of an execution of the above protocol.

This definition allows that an execution of the distributed protocol reveals some information about the shares of the honest agents as long as this information cannot be used to obtain new information about the original prover's secret key or the signatures.

5.2 Distributed Verification

Consider the case where the signer, S, has signed the message, m, using the random exponent, t. Thus $sign(m) = (T, r, s)$ where $T = g^t$ and (r, s) is the El Gamal signature on the product $Ttzm$ modulo q. S distributes the ability to verify this signature to n agents ($P_1, \ldots, P_n$ with corresponding public keys $x_1, \ldots, x_n$) by distributing t. As $T = g^t$ is part of the signature (and therefore not secret), the secret sharing scheme from Section 3 can be used:

PROTOCOL DISTRIBUTE SINGLE SIGNATURE

1. S broadcasts T to the n agents.

2. S distributes t using PROTOCOL DISTRIBUTE in section 3. Thus P_i gets the share $t_i = f(x_i)$, where f is a polynomial over $\mathbb{Z}_q$ of degree $k - 1$ such that $f(0) = t$.

3. Each agent P_i executes PROTOCOL VERIFY SHARE from section 3.

4. S sends $H(m, r, s)$ to each agent, where H is a collision-free hash function.

After the execution of this protocol each P_i has a secret share t_i with corresponding public information $h_i = g^{t_i}$. In addition to these values each agent has a hash value of the signature and the signed message, which is used to decide if a signature should be verified.

When a person, V, asks k agents (say $P_1, \ldots, P_k$) to verify a signature (T', r', s') on a message m', the agents first have to make sure that they *are able to* verify it and then decide if the signature is correct. Let $a_1, \ldots, a_k$ be elements in $\mathbb{Z}_q$ such that

$$\sum_{i=1}^{k} t_i a_i = t.$$

As mentioned in Section 3, each a_i can be computed from $(x_i)_{i=1,\ldots,k}$.

PROTOCOL DECIDE

1. V and each P_i verify that $T' = \prod_1^k h_i^{a_i}$.
   If this is not the case, the agents can neither verify nor deny the signature.

2. Each P_i verifies that the signer has sent $H(m', r', s')$. If this is true, the agents agree to verify the signature and otherwise they tell V that they are not able to verify it.

The result of PROTOCOL DECIDE is *not* a proof that the signature is correct/false, because the decision is based on values that anyone could have produced.

$P_1, \ldots, P_k$ can verify a signature by executing (now $T' = T$)

PROTOCOL DISTRIBUTED VERIFICATION

1. P_i and V compute $w = u^{Tm'}$ and $v = y^{r'} r'^{s'}$.

2. $P_1, \ldots, P_k$ proves that $\log_w(v) = \log_g(T)$ as shown in figure 2.

3. V accepts the signature if and only if it accepts the proof.

An honest agent reveals w^{t_i} in an execution of the protocol, as it can be computed from $ch^{r_i t_i}$ when r_i is known. The following theorem shows, that an honest agent does not reveal more than this, and it is shown that the agents cannot verify an invalid signature.

231

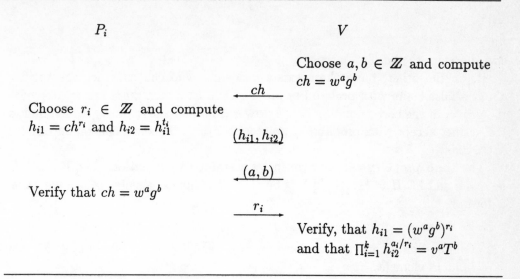

P_i V

Choose $a, b \in \mathbb{Z}$ and compute
$ch = w^a g^b$

$\xleftarrow{\quad ch \quad}$

Choose $r_i \in \mathbb{Z}$ and compute
$h_{i1} = ch^{r_i}$ and $h_{i2} = h_{i1}^{t_i}$

$\xrightarrow{\quad (h_{i1}, h_{i2}) \quad}$

$\xleftarrow{\quad (a, b) \quad}$

Verify that $ch = w^a g^b$

$\xrightarrow{\quad r_i \quad}$

Verify, that $h_{i1} = (w^a g^b)^{r_i}$
and that $\prod_{i=1}^{k} h_{i2}^{a_i/r_i} = v^a T^b$

Figure 2: Distributed proof that $\log_w(v) = \log_g(T)(= \sum a_i t_i)$.

Theorem 5.3
The protocol in figure 2 satisfies

1. If $v = w^t$, the verifier accepts with probability 1.
2. If $v \neq w^t$, the verifier accepts with probability at most $\frac{1}{q}$ – even if the agents have unlimited computing power.
3. For any probabilistic polynomial time verifier V^* and for any set $D \subseteq \{1, \ldots, k\}$ of dishonest agents there is a machine $M_{V^*, D}$ running in expected polynomial time such that $M_{V^*, D}$ given
   - the common input (p, q, g, T, w, v), where $\log_g(T) = \log_w(v)$;
   - the auxiliary input of V^* (aux_{V^*});
   - the auxiliary input of the dishonest agents $((aux_i)_{i \in D})$; and
   - $(w^{t_i})_{i \in H}$ where $H = \{1, \ldots, k\} \setminus D$

   outputs a conversation having the same distribution as in real executions of the protocol.

Proof
If $v = w^t$ and the provers follow the protocol then

$$\prod_{i=1}^{k} h_{i2}^{a_i/r_i} = \prod_{i=1}^{k} (ch^{r_i t_i})^{a_i/r_i}$$
$$= \prod_{i=1}^{k} ch^{t_i a_i}$$

$$= ch^t$$
$$= v^a T^b.$$

and therefore the verifier accepts.

If, on the other, hand there exists k agents, who can convince the verifier about a false claim with probability greater than q^{-1}, then there is a strategy for the prover in the corresponding single prover protocol (see figure 1), which makes the verifier accept with probability greater than q^{-1}. This is a contradiction (see [BCDP90]).

The third property can be proven by a standard simulation. Let V^* and D be given and let $H = \{1, \ldots, k\} \setminus D$ be the set of honest agents. $M_{V^*, D}$ works as follows

1. V^* produces a challenge ch.

2. For the honest provers compute $h_{i1} = g^{e_i}$ and $h_{i2} = h_i^{e_i}$ where $e_i \in \mathbb{Z}_q$ is a random element.
   For the dishonest provers (h_{i1}, h_{i2}) is computed as in the protocol.

3. Get (a, b) from the verifier.
   If $ch \neq w^a g^b$ stop.

4. Rewind V^* and the provers in D to after ch was sent.

5. For $i \in H$ compute $h_{i1} = ch^{r_i}$ and $h_{i2} = ((w^{t_i})^a h_i^b)^{r_i}$.
   The dishonest provers compute (h_{i1}, h_{i2}) as usual.

6. Get (a', b') from the verifier.
   If $ch \neq w^{a'} g^{b'}$: goto (4).
   If $(a', b') \neq (a, b)$: find $\log_g(w) = \frac{b'-b}{a-a'} \bmod q$, simulate the honest provers perfectly and then stop.
   If $(a', b') = (a, b)$: give r_i to the verifier for $i \in H$, and for $i \in D$ compute r_i as usual. Then stop.

This machine runs in expected polynomial time, and its output has the same distribution as the conversations of a real execution, because the pairs (h_{i1}, h_{i2}) always have the same distribution as in real executions. ∎

As the verifier may execute the protocol several times on input, (w, v), the verifier may learn (w^{t_i}) for all $i \in H$, where $H = \{1, \ldots, n\} \setminus D$ denotes the set of honest agents. The following theorem shows that as long as the honest agents get randomly chosen shares, then no matter what secret shares the dishonest agents get, this information is completely useless with respect to any polynomial time computation of the verifier and the dishonest agents.

This is proven by giving for any verifier, V^* and any set of dishonest agents, D, a polynomial time machine, which on input $g, h, (t_i)_{i \in D}$ simulates the following perfectly (see Section 5.1):

1. The signer chooses random shares for $i \in H$ with the property that any k agents in $H \cup D$ can find t and publishes $h_i \in G_q$ for $i \in H$.

2. A polynomial (in $|q|$) number of times, V^* and the agents in D, choose a set of k agents among $H \cup D$. Then these k agents execute the protocol with V^* on input (w, v).

Note, that we have assumed that the same input will be used in all executions. The distributed protocol is secure, even if the agents get different inputs in each execution, but in the proposed application, the input will always be the same unless a collision of the hash-function has been found.

Theorem 5.4
For any probabilistic polynomial time verifier, V^*, and all sets of dishonest agents, D, all sets of shares, $(t_i)_{i \in D}$, there exists a probabilistic expected polynomial time machine, $M_{V^*, D}$, which on input $(p, q, g, h, (t_i)_{i \in D})$ and the auxiliary inputs of V^* and the dishonest agents simulates the above scheme perfectly.

Proof sketch
If $|D| \geq k$, the theorem is obviously true.

For $|D| < k$ the simulator is based on the same principles as the proof of Theorem 3.2 and works as follows:

1. Choose a subset $H' \subseteq H$, such that $|H' \cup D| = k - 1$.
   Choose random shares $t_i \in \mathbb{Z}_q$ for $i \in H'$ and let $h_i = g^{t_i}$ and $v_i = w^{t_i}$.

2. As in the proof of Theorem 3.2 compute g^{f_j} and w^{f_j} for $j = 0, \ldots, k - 1$, where the polynomial

$$f(x) = f_0 + \ldots + f_{k-1} x^{k-1}$$

satisfies

$$f(0) = t$$
$$f(x_i) = t_i \qquad \text{for } i \in H' \cup D$$

3. Compute for $i \in H \setminus H'$ the public information

$$h_i = g^{f(x_i)} = \prod_{j=0}^{k-1} (g^{f_j})^{x_i^j}$$

and

$$v_i = w^{f(x_i)} = \prod_{j=0}^{k-1} (w^{f_j})^{x_i^j}$$

Let $t_i = f(x_i)$ (t_i is not known for $i \in H \setminus H'$).

4. Run V^* and the dishonest agents to choose a set of agents to execute the protocol.

5. Run the simulator from the proof of Theorem 5.3 giving it v_i for $i \in H$ as input.

6. Run V^* and the dishonest agents in order to decide whether to go to 4) or to stop.

By assumption the protocol is only executed a polynomial number of times and thus $M_{V^*,D}$ stops in expected polynomial time.

Furthermore, the output of $M_{V^*,D}$ has the same distribution as a a real execution of the protocol described above Theorem 5.4, because the h_i's and v_i's have the correct distribution and the simulation in the proof of Theorem 5.3 is perfect. ∎

It has silently been assumed that all executions of the protocol are done sequentially. Due to the fact that the protocol in figure 1 is also perfect zero-knowledge when executed many times with different verifiers simultaneously, the distributed protocol is also secure, when executed in parallel (with different sets of agents).

In particular this implies that the verifier cannot use a transcript of an execution of PROTOCOL DISTRIBUTED VERIFICATION as a proof of the validity of a signature.

5.3 Generalizations

The simulator in the proof of Theorem 5.4 can be modified to handle different inputs to each execution of the protocol by computing the v_i's in step 5. By distributing z, the signer can therefore authorize agents, that are able to verify all the signatures.

This facility, however, requires that the agents are able to decide whether a given triple (T, r, s) is a signature on m or not. They can do this by performing a multi-party computation, whose output says if the signature is valid or not. In this case, care must be taken to prevent that a dishonest agent convinces the verifier of the result of this computation.

Alternatively, the signer could give the agents a list of hash values of signatures and then the agents make their decision based on this list. This requires, that the signer updates this list every time a new message is signed.

6 Distributed Denial

This section investigates the possibility of using the agents to deny signatures. It can be argued that this facility is not necessary, since denial of signatures is not expected to take place as often as verification. Furthermore, it is likely, that denial will take place in court, and in that case it is more reasonable that the signer or a single agent authorized by the signer is present.

In spite of this, the following section suggests how a number of agents can prove that an alleged signature is false. Suppose (T, r, s) is a legal signature on m which has been distributed to the n agents as described above. Thus $t = \log_g T$ has been distributed to n agents and at some point k of these are asked to prove that a given triple (T', r', s') is not a signature on m', where T equals T'.

As the signer only uses T in one signature the agents know that the signature is invalid if $T' = T$ and the signer did not send $H(m', r', s')$ when the correct signature was distributed (see Section 5.2).

Using the techniques described below, agents sharing z can deny any (false) signature, but as discussed in Section 5.3 this requires that they are able to decide whether an arbitrary signature is correct or not.

6.1   Denial by the Agents

Assume that the signer has distributed T to $P_1, \ldots, P_n$ as described in Section 5.2. $P_1, \ldots, P_k$ can prove that (T, r, s) is not a signature on m as follows:

PROTOCOL DISTRIBUTED DENIAL

1. P_i and V compute $w = u^{Tm}$ and $v = y^r r^s$.

2. $P_1, \ldots, P_k$ proves that $\log_w(v) \neq \log_g(T)$ as shown in figure 3.

3. V accepts that the signature is false if and only if he accepts the proof.

Figure 3 shows how the agents can prove inequality of discrete logarithms. All participants in this protocol get p, q, g, T, $(h_1, \ldots, h_k)$ and (v, w) as common input, and the i'th prover gets $t_i = \log_g h_i$ as auxiliary input. The keys to the commitment scheme should be supplied by a trusted key authentication center.

Theorem 6.1
The protocol in figure 3 satisfies

1. If $\log_w(v) \neq \log_g(T)$ then V accepts with probability $1 - \frac{1}{q}$, if the agents follow the protocol.

2. If $\log_w(v) = \log_g(T)$ then no matter what k agents with unlimited computing power does, V accepts with probability at most $\frac{1}{q}$.

Proof
For $e \neq 0 \bmod q$

$$w_2 = v_1 \iff v^e = (w^e)^x$$
$$\iff v = w^t.$$

P_i	V
Choose $e_i \in \mathbb{Z}_q$ and $r_i \in \{0,1\}^*$. Compute $w_{1i} = w^{e_i}$ and $\beta_i = E(w_{1i}, r_i)$.	

$$\xrightarrow{\quad \beta_i \quad}$$

When everybody has sent β_i, the commitments are opened.

$$\xrightarrow{\quad r_i \quad}$$

P_i	V
Find all w_{1i} and compute $w_1 = \prod_1^k w_{1i}$ If $w_1 = 1$ stop. Compute $v_{1i} = v^{e_i}$	Find all w_{1i} and compute $w_1 = \prod_1^k w_{1i}$. If $w_1 = 1$ stop and reject the proof.

$$\xrightarrow{\quad v_{1i} \quad}$$

P_i	V
Prove to V that $\log_v(v_{1i}) = \log_w(w_{1i})$ as in figure 1	Execute the proof in figure 1 with P_i and verify that $\log_v(v_{1i}) = \log_w(w_{1i})$
Compute $v_1 = \prod_1^k v_{1i}$ Compute, $w_{2i} = w_1^{t_i}$	Compute $v_1 = \prod_1^k v_{1i}$

$$\xrightarrow{\quad w_{2i} \quad}$$

P_i	V
Prove that $\log_{w_1}(w_{2i}) = \log_g(h_i)$ as in figure 1 Compute $w_2 = \prod_1^k w_{1i}^{a_i}$	Compute $w_2 = \prod_1^k w_{1i}^{a_i}$ If one of the proofs is not accepted, stop. Otherwise: accept, if $w_2 \neq v_1$ and reject, if $w_2 = v_1$.

Figure 3: Distributed proof that $\log_w(v) \neq \log_g(T)$, where $T = \prod h_i^{a_i}$ and $h_i = g^{t_i}$. $E(\alpha, r)$ denotes a commitment to α using the random string $r \in \{0,1\}^*$.

Therefore the first claim follows from the fact that V accepts the proof if $w_1 \neq 1$, which happens with probability $1 - \frac{1}{q}$.

The second claim follows from the fact that a cheater in the proof system in figure 1 will succeed with probability at most $\frac{1}{q}$. ∎

The proof system in figure 3 is probably *not* auxiliary input zero-knowledge, because if the verifier does not cooperate with any provers, each P_i reveals

$$(v_1, w_1, w_{2i}) = (v^e, w^e, w_1^{t_i}),$$

which presumably cannot be constructed by a polynomial time machine which gets v and w as input (here $e = \sum_1^k e_i$, is unknown).

Despite this the following shows that it is very hard for the verifier to obtain any advantage by executing the protocol.

First notice, that the verifier cannot choose v and w freely, but they must be chosen on the form

$$v = y^r r^s \qquad \text{and} \qquad w = u^{TH(m)}$$

where H is a hash-function. Under the assumption that the image of m under H looks like a random string of bits, w looks like a random element of G_q. Furthermore, if the ElGamal scheme is secure, then v is the image of r and s under a one-way function, and thus it is hard for the verifier to control v and w. In Appendix A, it is argued that if the verifier cannot choose v and w better than at random, then the protocol is secure.

As it also seems to be very hard to exploit the knowledge of r, s, m and T, the only possibility for a cheating verifier is to execute the protocol several times with the same v and/or w (perhaps with different sets of agents). But due to the fact that w_1 is chosen (almost) at random in each execution, it seems hard to obtain any information by comparing different executions of the protocol.

7 Conclusion

This paper has introduced distributed prover protocols. This notion has many potential applications, and here we have shown how the signer of undeniable signatures can use it to authorize agents, such that any k of these agents can verify an undeniable signature without being able to sign new messages. Furthermore, it is shown that the agents can be authorized to verify either a single signature or all signatures produced by the signer.

In order to distribute the secret key to the agents, a variation of the verifiable secret sharing scheme proposed by Feldman has been presented. The resulting scheme is designed for situations where the secret key is "known" as the discrete logarithm and is optimal with respect to the secrecy of the key. We have mainly focused on the application of this scheme in distributed prover protocols, but it can be used in any multi-party computation in which the secret input of each player (x_i) can be recognized through the public information (g^{x_i}, g).

Finally it has been shown how the agents can deny false signatures.

Acknowledgements

I wish to thank David Chaum for suggesting this problem and Ivan Damgård for many discussions about the proposed methods.

References

[BCDP90]   J. Boyar, D. Chaum, I. Damgård, and T. Pedersen. Convertible undeniable signatures, 1990. To appear in the proceedings of Crypto'90.

[BOGKW88] M. Ben-Or, S. Goldwasser, J. Kilian, and A. Wigderson. Multiprover interactive proofs: How to remove intractability. In *Proceedings of the 20th Annual ACM Symposium on the Theory of Computing*, pages 113 – 131, 1988.

[CDvdG88] D. Chaum, I. Damgård, and J. van de Graaf. Multiparty computations ensuring privacy of each party's input and correctness of the result. In *Advances in Cryptology - proceedings of CRYPTO 87*, Lecture Notes in Computer Science, pages 87–119. Springer-Verlag, 1988.

[Cha91]   D. Chaum. Zero-knowledge undeniable signatures. In *Advances in Cryptology - proceedings of EUROCRYPT 90*, Lecture Notes in Computer Science, pages 458 – 464. Springer Verlag, 1991.

[CvA90]   D. Chaum and H. van Antwerpen. Undeniable signatures. In *Advances in Cryptology - proceedings of CRYPTO 89*, Lecture Notes in Computer Science. Springer Verlag, 1990.

[P.F87]   P.Feldman. A practical scheme for non-interactive verifiable secret sharing. In *Proceedings of the 28th IEEE Symposium on the Foundations of Computer Science*, pages 427 – 437, 1987.

[Sha79]   A. Shamir. How to share a secret. *CACM*, 22:612–613, 1979.

A The Distributed Proof of Different Discrete Logarithms

This appendix contains an analysis of the protocol in figure 3. An honest prover in a single execution of the protocol will be simulated by generating

$$v_{1i} = v^{e_i}$$
$$w_{1i} = w^{e_i}$$
$$w_{2i} : \text{ a random element of } G_q$$

where e is chosen at random in $\mathbb{Z}_q$. This simulation does not work against a verifier who (for example) knows a and b such that

$$v = h_i^b \qquad \text{and} \qquad w = g^a$$

because then w_{2i} must satisfy (remember $h_i = g^{t_i}$)

$$w_{2i}^{b/a} = w_1^{t_i b/a} = v_1$$

but this is very unlikely for a randomly chosen w_{2i}. However, as noted in Section 6.1 it is very hard for the verifier to choose such a pair (v, w) in PROTOCOL DISTRIBUTED DENIAL.

In the following it is therefore assumed that v and w are chosen uniformly at random in G_q. Consider an execution of the protocol between $P_1, \ldots, P_k$ and a verifier V^*, and assume that $D \subset \{P_1, \ldots, P_k\}$ is the set of dishonest provers. Let ci denote the common input to the protocol (omitting p, q and g). Then ci is on the form

$$(T, h_1, \ldots, h_k, v, w).$$

where

$$T = \prod_{i=1}^{k} h_i^{a_i} \qquad \text{and} \qquad \log_w v \neq \log_g T.$$

A polynomially bounded machine, $M_{V^*,D}$, with access to the dishonest provers and V^* simulates an honest prover as following on input ci:

1. Choose e_i at random and compute β_i.

2. Open β_i and when all k values of w_{1j} are known, compute w_1 as their product.

3. Compute $v_{1i} = v^{e_i}$ and when all k values of v_{1i} are known, prove that $\log_v(v_{1i})$ is equal to $\log_w(w_{1i})$. Finally compute $v_1 = \prod_{j=1}^{k} v_{1j}$.

4. Choose w_{2i} at random.

5. Simulate the "proof" that $\log_{w_1}(w_{2i}) = \log_g(h_i)$.

In step 5) the simulator is going to simulate a "proof" of a false claim as it is very unlikely that w_{2i} equals $w_1^{t_i}$. Lemma A.1 below shows that it is possible to simulate the proof system for equality of discrete logarithms in such a way that the simulator always stops in expected polynomial time (this is not the case for the "obvious" simulator). Furthermore, if the input to the simulator is correct, then the output of the simulator is statistically indistinguishable from executions of the protocol in figure 1.

$M_{V^*,D}$ generates (v_{1i}, w_{1i}) with the same distribution as executions of the protocol. The only difference between a simulated conversation and a transcript of a real execution of the protocol is that the simulator chooses w_{2i} at random. If this random w_{2i} cannot be distinguished from $w_1^{t_i}$ then the the simulation of the "proof" that $\log_{w_1} w_{2i} = \log_g h_i$ cannot be distinguished from an execution of a correct proof.

However, in order for the signature scheme to be undeniable it must be infeasible to decide if $\log_g T$ equals $\log_w v$ for randomly chosen v and w. As v, w and w_1 are chosen at random (almost) it is reasonable to assume that w_{2i} cannot be distinguished from $w_1^{t_i}$, and thus the simulations can not be distinguished from real executions.

Lemma A.1

Consider the proof-system in figure 1.
For any probabilistic polynomial time verifier V^* there is a machine M_{V^*} running in expected polynomial time on all inputs (p, q, g, u, v, w). If $\log_g(u) = \log_w(v)$, the output of M_{V^*} is statistically indistinguishable from a transcript of an execution of the protocol.

Proof

Let V^* be a polynomial time verifier. M_{V^*} does the following: (remember that $u = g^z$)

1. V^* produces a challenge ch.

2. Compute $h_1 = g^e$ and $h_2 = u^e$ where $e \in \mathbb{Z}_q$ is a random element.

3. Get (a, b) from the verifier.
   If $ch \neq w^a g^b$ stop.

4. Alternately execute one round of procedure A and B below until one of them stops:
   Procedure A:

   (a) Rewind V^* to after ch was sent.

   (b) Compute $h_1 = ch^r$ and $h_2 = (v^a u^b)^r$.

   (c) Get (a', b') from the verifier.
   If $ch \neq w^{a'} g^{b'}$: goto (a).
   If $(a', b') \neq (a, b)$: find $\log_g(w) = \frac{b - b'}{a' - a}$, simulate the protocol perfectly

and then stop.

If $(a', b') = (a, b)$: give r to the verifier and stop.

Procedure B:

(a) $count := 0$.

(b) Rewind V^* to after ch was sent.

(c) Compute $h_1 = g^e$ and $h_2 = u^e$, where $e \in \mathbb{Z}_q$ is chosen at random.

(d) Get (a', b') from the verifier.

(e) If $ch = w^{a'}g^{b'}$: $count := count + 1$.

(f) If $count < |q|$: goto (b);

Otherwise: stop.

Let $P(ch)$ be the probability that V^* sends (a, b) such that $ch = w^a g^b$ when given random pairs (h_1, h_2) satisfying $h_1^z = h_2$.

To show that M_{V^*} runs in expected polynomial time it is sufficient to show that the expected number of iterations of procedure B is polynomial. As each round of B is run independently of previous rounds, this number is

$$P(ch)\frac{|q|}{P(ch)} = |q|$$

Next it will be shown that the output of the simulator is statistically indistinguishable from executions of the protocol whenever the input satisfies $\log_g(u) = \log_w(v)$. If M_{V^*} stops in step 3, the generated output has the correct distribution.

If M_{V^*} stops, because procedure A stops before procedure B, there are two possibilities:

- The simulator has found $(a, b) \neq (a', b')$ such that $ch = w^a g^b = w^{a'} g^{b'}$. In this case the simulation is perfect.

- The simulator has generated the messages

$$h_1 = ch^r, \ h_2 = (v^a u^b)^r \text{ and } r \text{ randomly chosen.}$$

These messages have the same distribution as the messages in real executions.

Finally there is the possibility, that procedure B stops before A, in which case the output of the simulator differs from executions of the protocol. It will now be shown that this happens with negligible probability.

We say that A has success in a round, if it stops. Similarly B has success in one round if the verifier sends (a', b') such that $ch = w^{a'} g^{b'}$. A wins as soon as it has one success, and B wins if it has $|q|$ successes before A has had any. Let the outcome of one execution of a round of A and B be $(P = P(ch))$

- α, if A has success. $Prob[\alpha] = P$.

- β, if B has success and A has not. $Prob[\beta] = P(1 - P)$.

- $discard$, if neither A nor B has success.

By performing many (independent) experiments with outcomes and probabilities as above and by removing all occurrences of *discard* we get a list of α and β. The probability that β occurs at a given place in the list is ($P > 0$ as the protocol did not stop in step 3)

$$P_\beta = \frac{P(1-P)}{P + P(1-P)} < \frac{1}{2}.$$

B only wins if the first $|q|$ elements in the list are β:

$$Prob[B \text{ wins}] = P_\beta^{|q|} < 2^{-|q|}$$

Thus a simulated conversation has the same distribution as in a real execution of the proof system except with probability less than $2^{-|q|}$. ∎

Interactive Bi-Proof Systems
and Undeniable Signature Schemes

Atsushi Fujioka   Tatsuaki Okamoto   Kazuo Ohta

NTT Laboratories

Nippon Telegraph and Telephone Corporation

1-2356, Take, Yokosuka-shi, Kanagawa-ken, 238-03 Japan

Abstract

This paper proposes a new construction of the *minimum knowledge undeniable signature scheme* which solves a problem inherent in Chaum's scheme. We formulate a new proof system, the *minimum knowledge interactive bi-proof system*, and a pair of languages, the *common witness problem*, based on the random self-reducible problem. And we show that any common witness problem has the minimum knowledge interactive bi-proof system. A practical construction for undeniable signature schemes is proposed based on such a proof system. These schemes assure signature confirmation and disavowal with the same protocol (or at the same time).

1 Introduction

Digital signatures [DH] are one of the most important concepts of modern cryptography, and have many applications in information security systems.

A new paradigm of signature schemes, *undeniable signatures*, was recently proposed by Chaum *et al.* [CA, Ch], and its properties are different from those of digital signatures. Although an undeniable signature is similar to a digital signature in that it is a number issued by a signer that is related to the signer's public-key and his message, the difference is that an undeniable signature cannot be verified without the cooperation of the signer.

Undeniable signature schemes [CA, Ch] consist of two parts, a confirmation protocol and a disavowal protocol. In the confirmation protocol, a verifier can verify the validity of a signature by interacting with the signer, and there is no chance that the signer can falsely represent the validity of an invalid signature. If the validity test fails, the verifier can determine if the signature is invalid or the signer is false by the disavowal protocol.

Chaum's scheme [Ch] has a problem, in which two different protocols are necessary for the confirmation and disavowal of the signature. If a dishonest prover, say, Alice claims that her valid signature is not valid, then first the verifier, say, Bob must execute the disavowal protocol to check her claim, then knows that her claim is not true. However, Bob cannot believe that her signature is valid just from this negative result of the disavowal protocol, because Alice may not follow the valid disavowal protocol. So, Bob must execute the confirmation protocol to determine that her signature is valid. Therefore, in the above case, Bob must execute the both protocols to confirm the validity of her signature.

This paper proposes a new undeniable signature scheme which solves the above problem of Chaum's scheme. That is, our scheme assures signature confirmation and disavowal with the same protocol. In other words, executing our scheme once is equivalent to executing both confirmation and disavowal protocols at the same time. Hence, without regard to signer's claim, the verifier can always determine whether a signature is valid or invalid, through executing our scheme only once.

First, in order to construct our undeniable signature scheme, we formulate a class of new proof systems, the *interactive bi-proof systems*, which can exactly determine which of $x \in L_1$ or $x \in L_2$ is a true theorem where L_1 and L_2 are disjoint languages. Roughly speaking, when $x \in L_1$, a prover can prove "x is in L_1", however no prover can prove "x is in L_1" when $x \notin L_1$. On the other hand, when $x \in L_2$, the prover can prove "x is in L_2" with the same protocol, however no prover can prove "x is in L_2" when $x \notin L_2$.

Next, based on the *random self-reducible* problem [TW], we introduce a pair of languages, the *common witness problem*, and show that any common witness problem has the minimum knowledge interactive bi-proof system. Here, the minimum knowledge [GHY] is a variant of zero-knowledge. For example, in a zero-knowledge proof, the prover releases the knowledge such as "$x \in L$", while in a minimum knowledge proof, the prover releases the knowledge such as which one is correct, "$x \in L_1$" or "$x \in L_2$".

Finally, we propose new undeniable signature schemes, which solve the above-mentioned problem of Chaum's scheme, by using these minimum knowledge interactive bi-proof systems for a common witness problem. In addition, several variations of our scheme are discussed in terms of increasing efficiency and useful applications.

2   Interactive Bi-Proof System

First we formulate a new proof system for our undeniable signature scheme.

In interactive proof systems [GMR], a prover has infinite power while the verifier is restricted to probabilistic polynomial time bounded. They interact to perform a proof '$x \in L$' for a language L. When $x \in L$, the proof is accomplished; however, when $x \notin L$, no prover can claim that "x is in L" and such proof is rejected.

This property approximates that of signature schemes. That is, when a signature is valid, the signer can prove it. When, however, the signature is not valid, no signer can prove its validity.

To construct an undeniable signature scheme, we must add a new requirement to the interactive proof system: the verifier can distinguish between $x \notin L$ and the falseness of the signer. The existing interactive proof system does not ensure that the verifier can distinguish between them when proof is rejected. We have, therefore, defined a new proof system, the *interactive bi-proof system*, for a pair of disjoint languages, L_1 and L_2. When $x \in L_1$, a prover can show that "x is in L_1", and when $x \in L_2$, then "x is in L_2". However, no prover can prove that "x is in L_1" when $x \notin L_1$ or "x is in L_2" when $x \notin L_2$.

Definition 2.1 *Let L_1 and L_2 be disjoint languages over $\{0,1\}^*$. Let (P,V) be an interactive protocol. We say that (P,V) is an interactive bi-proof system for (L_1, L_2) if we have the following:*

- *Completeness*

  - *For each k, for sufficiently large $x \in L_1$ given as input to (P,V), V halts and accepts x as "x is in L_1" with a probability of at least $1 - |x|^{-k}$.*

  - *For each k, for sufficiently large $x \in L_2$ given as input to (P,V), V halts and accepts x as "x is in L_2" with a probability of at least $1 - |x|^{-k}$.*

    (The probabilities here are taken over the coin tosses of P and V.)

- *Soundness*

  - *For each k, for sufficiently large $x \notin L_1$, for any ITM P', on input x to (P',V), V halts and accepts x as "x is in L_1" with a probability of at most $|x|^{-k}$.*

  - *For each k, for sufficiently large $x \notin L_2$, for any ITM P', on input x to (P',V), V halts and accepts x as "x is in L_2" with a probability of at most $|x|^{-k}$.*

(The probabilities here are taken over the coin tosses of P' and V.)

Next we define the *minimum knowledgeness* of this proof system.

Definition 2.2 *Let (P,V) be an interactive bi-proof system for (L_1, L_2). We say that (P,V) is minimum knowledge if, given any expected polynomial time probabilistic Turing machine V', there exists another probabilistic Turing machine $M_{V'}$, running in expected polynomial time, such that for all $x \in L_1 \cup L_2$:*

- *$B(x)$ is a probability distribution where $B(x)$ is the output of interactive protocol (P,V) and the distribution probability are taken over the coin tosses of P and V.*

- *$M_{V'}$ has one-time access to an oracle, as follows. Given any input x and auxiliary input h, $M_{V'}$ queries the oracle with input x; the oracle returns a value distributed according $B(x)$.*

- *The ensembles*

$$\left\{ M_{V'}[x, h] \mid x \in L_1 \cup L_2, h \in \{0,1\}^{poly(|x|)} \right\}$$

and

$$\left\{ VIEW_{V'}\{(P, V')[x, h]\} \mid x \in L_1 \cup L_2, h \in \{0,1\}^{poly(|x|)} \right\}$$

are indistinguishable.

(If the ensembles are identical, we say that the bi-proof system is *perfectly* minimum knowledge.)

See [GMR, GHY] for the definitions of *interactive protocol*, *ITM*, *minimum knowledgeness*, *VIEW*, and *indistinguishability*.

3 Interactive Bi-Proof System and Random Self-Reducibility

In this section, we show the essential conditions of the interactive bi-proof system.

First, we explain random self-reducibility [TW].

Definition 3.1 *Let $\mathcal{N}$ be a countably infinite set. For any $N \in \mathcal{N}$, let $|N|$ denotes the length of a suitable representation of N. For any $N \in \mathcal{N}$, let X_N, Y_N be finite sets, and $R_N \subseteq X_N \times Y_N$ be a relation. Let*

$$dom\ R_N = \left\{ x \in X_N \mid (x,y) \in R_N \text{ for some } y \in Y_N \right\}$$

denote the domain of R_N,

$$R_N(x) = \{y \mid (x, y) \in R_N\}$$

the image of $x \in X_N$, and

$$R_N(X_N) = \{y \mid (x, y) \in R_N, \ x \in X_N\}$$

the image of R_N. R is *random self-reducible* if and only if there is a *polynomial time algorithm A that, given any inputs $N \in \mathcal{N}$, $x \in dom\, R_N$, and $r \in \{0,1\}^{\omega}$, outputs $x' = A(N, x, r) \in dom\, R_N$ satisfying the following three properties.*

R1. *If the bits of r are random, uniform and independent, then x' is uniformly distributed over $dom\, R_N$.*

R2. *There is a polynomial time algorithm that, given $N, x, \bar{r}$, and any $y' \in R_N(x')$, outputs $y \in R_N(x)$. Here $\bar{r}$ is the finite prefix of r consumed in computing $x' = A(N, x, r)$.*

R3. *There is a polynomial time algorithm that, given N, x, r, and any $y \in R_N(x)$, outputs some $y' \in R_N(x')$. If, in addition, the bits of r are random, uniform, and independent, then y' is uniformly distributed on $R_N(x')$.*

Based on the above problem, we define the following problem.

Definition 3.2 *Let the relation $R_{(1)}$ and $R_{(2)}$ be random self-reducible. The following pair of languages (L_R, L_C),*

$$L_R = \{(x_1, x_2) \mid \exists y \, [(x_1, y) \in R_{(1),N} \ \wedge \ (x_2, y) \in R_{(2),N}]\},$$

$$L_P = \{(x_1, x_2) \mid \exists y \, [(x_1, y) \in R_{(1),N}]\},$$

$$L_C = \overline{L_R} \cap L_P,$$

are called the common witness problem.

(Note that in this case, L_R and L_C are disjoint, and $L_R \cap L_P = L_R$.)

Now we can obtain the following theorem about the relation of the interactive bi-proof system and the common witness problem.

Theorem 3.3 *Let the relation $R_{(1)}$ and $R_{(2)}$ be random self-reducible and satisfy the following conditions:*

T1. For any $y \in R_{(i),N}(X_{(i),N})$, the number of x satisfying $(x, y) \in R_{(i),N}$ is one, and there are probabilistic polynomial time algorithms $B_{(i)}$ that, given N, y, output x satisfying $(x, y) \in R_{(i),N}$ where $i = 1$ and 2.

T2. There are probabilistic polynomial time algorithms that, given N, output random pairs $(x, y) \in R_{(i),N}$ with x uniformly distributed over $dom\ R_{(i),N}$ and y uniformly distributed over $R_{(i),N}(x)$ where $i = 1$ and 2.

T3. If $(x, y) \notin R_{(i),N}$, then for any r, $(x', y') \notin R_{(i),N}$ ($i = 1$ and 2) where x' is created from x and r, and y' is created from y and r.

T4. $R_{(1),N}(X_{(1),N}) = R_{(2),N}(X_{(2),N})$, and any y' created from y and r on $R_{(1),N}$ is equal to the one created from y and r on $R_{(2),N}$.

T5. $\exists y\ [(x_1, y) \in R_{(1),N} \wedge (x_2, y) \in R_{(2),N}] \Rightarrow \forall y\ [(x_1, y) \in R_{(1),N} \Rightarrow (x_2, y) \in R_{(2),N}]$. Let set $F(x_1, x_2, x_1')$ be $\{x_2' \mid \exists r[x_1' = A_{(1)}(N, x_1, r) \wedge x_2' = A_{(2)}(N, x_2, r)]\}$. Then, for any x_1, x_2, and x_1', the number of elements of set $F(x_1, x_2, x_1')$ is at most 1.

T6. If there exists a probabilistic polynomial time algorithm that, given x_1, x_2, x_1', x_2' ($x_i \in dom\ R_{(i),N}, i = 1, 2$), determines whether $\exists r\ [x_1' = A_{(1)}(N, x_1, r) \wedge x_2' = A_{(2)}(N, x_2, r)]$ with non-negligible probability, then there exists a probabilistic polynomial time algorithm that, given $(x_1, x_2) \in (L_R, L_C)$, determines $(x_1, x_2) \in L_R$ or $(x_1, x_2) \in L_C$ with overwhelming probability.

Then, on inputs N and $x = (x_1, x_2)$, there is a *minimum knowledge interactive bi-proof system* (P, V) for any common witness problem (L_R, L_C).

Sketch of Proof:

We consider the following protocol. Without loss of generality, there exists $(x_1, y_1) \in R_{(1),N}$ from the definition of L_P.

Protocol:

Step 1 Repeat t times from **Step 2** to **Step 7** where $t = O(|x|)$.

Step 2 P generates random numbers r, a, v ($|v| = |x_2| = n$), and calculates X_1, Z,

$$X_1 = A_{(1)}(N, x_1, r),$$

$$Z = BC(v, a).$$

And P sends X_1, Z to V. Here, BC is a bit-commitment function [Na], v is committed bits, and a is random bits used for concealing v. (For simplicity, we write $BC(v, a)$ as $BC(v_1, a_1)\| \cdots \|BC(v_n, a_n)$, where $v = v_1\| \cdots \|v_n$, $a = a_1\| \cdots \|a_n$, and $\|$ denotes concatenation.)

Step 3 V generates random number u ($|u| = |x_2| = n$), and sends u to P.

Step 4 P calculates $q = u \oplus v$ and X_2,

$$X_2 = h_q(A_{(2)}(N, x_2, r)).$$

And P sends X_2 and a, v to V. Here, function h_q is a hard-core predicate or hard-core function shown in Definitions 2 and 3 of [GL], where $|q| = \left| A_{(2)}(N, x_2, r) \right|$ when h_q is a hard-core predicate, and $|q| = 2 \left| A_{(2)}(N, x_2, r) \right|$ when h_q is a hard-core function. Hereafter, for simplicity, we will consider h_q a hard-core predicate. Then, $h_q(w) = \sum_{i=1}^{n} w_i q_i \bmod 2$, where $w = w_1 \| \cdots \| w_n$, $q = q_1 \| \cdots \| q_n$, and $|w_i| = |q_i| = 1$ ($i = 1, \ldots, n$).

Step 5 V checks whether $BC(v, a)$ holds. If it does not hold, V rejects the proof. Otherwise, V calculates $q = u \oplus v$, generates random bit e, and sends it to P.

Step 6 P calculates Y.

$$\begin{cases} Y = r & \text{if } e = 0, \\ Y = y_1' & \text{if } e = 1. \end{cases}$$

Here $y_1' \in R_{(1),N}(x_1')$ ($x_1' = A_{(1)}(N, x_1, r)$) is created from y_1 and r. And P sends it to V.

Step 7 V checks as follows:

- When $e = 0$, V checks the following equations

$$X_1 \overset{?}{=} A_{(1)}(N, x_1, Y),$$

$$X_2 \overset{?}{=} h_q(A_{(2)}(N, x_2, Y)).$$

If both tests succeed, set this round as "honest" and continue the protocol.

Otherwise V rejects the proof.

- When $e = 1$, V checks the following equations

$$(X_1, Y) \overset{?}{\in} R_{(1),N},$$

$$X_2 \overset{?}{=} h_q(B_{(2)}(N, Y)).$$

If both tests succeed, set this round as "L_R" and continue the protocol. If only first test succeeds, set this round as "L_C" and continue the protocol.

Otherwise V rejects the proof.

Step 8 After t rounds, V determines the proof as follows:

- If every round is either "L_R" or "honest", then V accepts as "$x \in L_R$".

- If every round of $e = 0$ is "honest" and $R > 1/3$, then V accepts as "$x \in L_C$", where $R = \#\{\text{"}L_C\text{" round}\}/\#\{\text{"}e = 1\text{" round}\}$. ($\#S$ denotes the number of elements of set S.)

- Otherwise V rejects the proof.

Remark:

hen h_q is a hard-core function (or $|X_2| > 1$), V determines the proof as "$x \in L_C$" as follows: When $|X_2|$ is $O(|x|)$, if every round is either "L_C" or "honest", then V accepts as "$x \in L_C$". When $|X_2|$ is $c = O(1)$, if every round of $e = 0$ is "honest" and $R > 1 - 1/2^c - d$, then V accepts as "$x \in L_C$", where d is a constant.

Consider the completeness and soundness conditions.

- *Completeness*

  o In the case of $x \in L_R$, there exists some y, such that $(x_1, y) \in R_{(1),N} \wedge (x_2, y) \in R_{(2),N}$. Then, it is clear that if P follows the protocol, then both checks in **Step 7** are accomplished. So V accepts as "x is in L_R" with probability 1.

  o On the other hand, when $x \in L_C$, y where $(x_1, y) \in R_{(1),N}$ does not satisfy $(x_2, y) \in R_{(2),N}$. Condition T3 directly implies that P's response Y, cannot satisfy $X_2 = h_q(B_{(2)}(N, Y))$ in **Step 7** with probability $1/2$ in each round. So V accepts as "x is in L_C" with overwhelming probability after t rounds repetition.

- *Soundness*

  o In the case of $x \notin L_R$, to cheat V with non-negligible probability, P' must create the messages X_1, X_2 and Y which satisfy both tests in **Step 7**, i.e., $e = 0$ and $e = 1$. When $x \notin L_R$, two cases are considered, $x \in L_C$ or $x \notin L_P$. First we consider $x \in L_C$. In this case, for all y where $(x_1, y) \in R_{(1),N}$, this y must not satisfy $(x_2, y) \in R_{(2),N}$ from the definition of L_C and condition T5. To cheat V, Y that is created from y and r, however, must satisfy $X_2 = h_q(B_{(2)}(N, Y))$ with probability 1. For this, $(X_2, Y) \in R_{(2),N}$ must be satisfied, since q is randomly generated after r is determined. This contradicts condition T3.

On the other hand, when $x \notin L_P$, there is no y where $(x_1, y) \in R_{(1),N}$. So if Y satisfies $(X_1, Y) \in R_{(1),N}$, this contradicts condition T3.

o In the case of $x \notin L_C$, to cheat V with non-negligible probability, P' must create the messages X_1, X_2 and Y which satisfy only first side of tests in **Step 7-2** ($e = 1$) and both tests in **Step 7-1** ($e = 0$). In this case, two cases are also considered, $x \in L_R$ or $x \notin L_P$.

First we consider $x \in L_R$. In this case, for all y where $(x_1, y) \in R_{(1),N}$, this y must satisfy $(x_2, y) \in R_{(2),N}$ from the definition of L_R and condition T5. To cheat V, Y that is created from y and r, however, must not satisfy $X_2 = h_q(B_{(2)}(N, Y))$ with probability $1/2$ in each round. For this, $(X_2, Y) \in R_{(2),N}$ must not be satisfied with at least non-negligible probability. This contradicts the condition T5.

On the other hand, when $x \notin L_P$, there is no y where $(x_1, y) \in R_{(1),N}$. So if Y satisfies $(X_1, Y) \in R_{(1),N}$, this contradicts condition T3.

- *Minimum knowledgeness*

Then we prove the minimum knowledgeness. First, on input $x \in L_R \cup L_C$, the simulator accesses to an oracle and knows $x \in L_R$ or $x \in L_C$. After that it simulates the view of the history by the 'standard guessing' algorithm.

When $x \in L_R$, it is clear that the simulator can perfectly simulate the view, or that this protocol satisfies perfect minimum knowledgeness.

When $x \notin L_C$, to prove that this protocol is (computationally) minimum knowledge, we must show that (X_1, X_2, q) is (computationally) indistinguishable from (X_1, a, q), where a is a real random number. If BC is a secure bit-commitment function and the prover is honest, then q is a random number. If the common witness problem is not $\mathcal{BPP}$, then a bit-commitment function BC exists [Na, ILL]. From condition T6 and Lemma 1 of [GL], if the common witness problem to be proven in this bi-proof system is not in $\mathcal{BPP}$, then (X_1, X_2) is computationally indistinguishable from (X_1, a). Then, this protocol is (computationally) minimum knowledge. If the common witness problem is in $\mathcal{BPP}$, this protocol is trivially (perfectly) minimum knowledge.

¶

Remark 1:

If the common witness problem is defined over the discrete logarithm problem, then condition T6 holds, because the problem, given g^x, m^x, to check $\exists r \, [\, g^{x+r} \, \wedge \, m^{x+r}]$ is equivalent to the problem to check $\exists x \, [\, g^x \, \wedge \, m^x]$.

Remark 2:

In the above protocol (sequential version), q is generated in each round. However, in the parallel (five round) version of the above protocol [FFS, BMO], the same q is commonly used by all t round messages. So, the communication amount of these parallel versions is much reduced than that of the sequential version.

Remark 3:

The *discrete logarithm* problem and the *graph isomorphism* problem are good examples of problems that satisfy the above conditions.

4 Application to Undeniable Signature Schemes

4.1 Proposed Undeniable Signature Schemes

We apply the interactive bi-proof system directly to an undeniable signature scheme.

From **Theorem 3.3**, if a random self-reducible problem exists, then there exists an interactive bi-proof system. The definition of the interactive bi-proof system is suitable for undeniable signature schemes, so there exists an undeniable signature scheme based on the random self-reducible problem.

We consider the discrete logarithms problem similar to those in [CA, Ch].

- **Center Key Generation**

  - Center generates a large prime number p and selects a primitive root g of field $GF(p)$.

- **Signer Key generation**

  - Signer generates his secret key x, and computes y $(= g^x \bmod p)$. He publishes y as his public key.

- **Signature generation**

  o Signer generates signature s of a message m from p and his secret key x, $s = m^x \bmod p$.

- **Signature confirmation and disavowal**

  o Repeat the following procedure t times where $t = O(|x|)$.

  o Signer generates random numbers r, a, v ($|v| = |x_2|$), and calculates

  $$X_1 = g^r \cdot y \bmod p,$$

  $$Z = BC(v, a).$$

  and sends (X_1, Z) to verifier.

  o Verifier generates random number u ($|u| = |x_2|$), and sends u to the prover.

  o Prover calculates $q = u \oplus v$ and

  $$X_2 = h_q(m^r \cdot s \bmod p),$$

  and sends X_2 and a, v to the verifier.

  o Verifier checks whether $BC(v, a)$ holds. If it does not hold, verifier rejects the protocol. Otherwise, verifier calculates $q = u \oplus v$, generates $e \in_R \{0, 1\}$ and sends it to the signer.

  o Signer computes Y ($= r + ex \bmod p - 1$) and sends it to the verifier.

  o Verifier checks as follows:

    * When $e = 0$, verifier checks the following equations

    $$X_1 \stackrel{?}{=} g^Y \cdot y \bmod p,$$

    $$X_2 \stackrel{?}{=} h_q(m^Y \cdot s \bmod p).$$

    If both tests succeed, set this round as "honest" and continue the protocol.
    Otherwise verifier rejects the protocol.

    * When $e = 1$, verifier checks the following equations

    $$X_1 \stackrel{?}{=} g^Y \bmod p,$$

    $$X_2 \stackrel{?}{=} h_q(m^Y \bmod p).$$

If both tests succeed, set this round as "valid" and continue the protocol. If only first test succeeds, set this round as "invalid" and continue the protocol.

Otherwise verifier rejects the protocol.

o After t rounds, verifier determines the validity of (m, s) as follows:

* If every round is either "valid" or "honest", then verifier accepts as "s is the valid signature of m".

* If every round of $e = 0$ is "honest" and $R > 1/3$, then verifier accepts as "s is the invalid signature of m", where $R = \#\{$"invalid" round$\}/\#\{$"$e = 1$" round$\}$.

* Otherwise verifier rejects the protocol.

This protocol satisfies minimum knowledge interactive bi-proof system.

Remark:

haum's confirmation and disavowal protocols are called *zero* knowledge; however, our protocol is called *minimum* knowledge. In both schemes, these words mean that each protocol releases no additional knowledge except that which the prover wants to release. The different point is as follows:

In Chaum's scheme, to prove the validity of a signature, signer Alice claims the validity/invalidity of her signature before using the confirmation/disavowal protocol. To support her claim she then uses the appropriate protocol. In this sequence, the protocols release no additional bit than her claim, so each confirmation/disavowal protocol of his scheme is zero knowledge.

However in our scheme, regardless of the signature's claim, a signer executes the same protocol. Our protocol releases one bit, i.e., the validity or invalidity, so our scheme is minimum knowledge.

4.2 Efficiency

Our scheme is more efficient than Chaum's because our scheme consists of only one protocol. It implies that when this scheme is implemented, the confirmation and disavowal protocol can be done with the same equipment. Furthermore, in this protocol, the number of powering and multiplication operations are smaller than that of the disavowal protocol in Chaum's scheme [Ch].

For even more efficiency, we are proposing two enhancements, one is the *higher degree version* and another is the *parallel version*. Unfortunately these protocols cannot be proven to satisfy minimum knowledgeness, however, both can decrease the amount of transmission overhead.

To satisfy minimum knowledgeness in the parallel version, the constant round zero knowledge technique shown in [BMO] can be applied to our scheme. This can reduce the round number of the protocol. Moreover, as described in **Remark 2** of **Theorem 3.3**, the parallel version reduce the communication amount as well as the round number, since the same q is commonly used by all t round messages.

5   Conclusion

We have proposed a new proof system, the minimum knowledge interactive bi-proof system, and constructed an undeniable signature scheme using a formulation of the new system.

We have also defined a pair of languages, the common witness problem, based on the random self-reducible problem, and shown that any common witness problem has the minimum knowledge interactive bi-proof system.

A practical undeniable signature scheme was proposed based on such a proof system, in which confirmation and disavowal can be done with the same protocol (or at the same time).

Acknowledgement

The authors wish to thank Toshiya Itoh, Kenji Koyama, Kouichi Sakurai, Hiroki Shizuya, Kazue Tanaka, Yasuyuki Tsukada, and Yuliang Zheng for their valuable comments.

References

[BCC] G. Brassard, D. Chaum, and C. Crépeau, "Minimum Disclosure Proofs of Knowledge", *Journal of Computer and System Sciences*, Vol.37, No.2, pp.156–189 (Oct., 1988).

[BMO] M. Bellare, S. Micali, and R. Ostrovsky, "Perfect Zero-Knowledge in Constant Rounds", Proceedings of 22nd annual ACM Symposium on Theory of Computing, pp.482–493 (May, 1990).

[Ch] D. Chaum, "Zero-Knowledge Undeniable Signatures", in *Advances in Cryptology — EUROCRYPT '90*, Lecture Notes in Computer Science 473, Springer–Verlag, Berlin, pp.458–464 (1991).

[CA] D. Chaum and H. van Antwerpen, "Undeniable Signatures", in *Advances in Cryptology — CRYPTO '89*, Lecture Notes in Computer Science 435, Springer–Verlag, Berlin, pp.212–216 (1990).

[DH] W. Diffie and M. E. Hellman, "New Directions in Cryptography", IEEE Transactions on Information Theory, Vol.IT-22, No.6, pp.644–654 (Nov., 1976).

[FFS] U. Feige, A. Fiat, and A. Shamir, "Zero Knowledge Proofs of Identity", Proceedings of 19th annual ACM Symposium on Theory of Computing, pp.210–217 (May, 1987).

[GHY] Z. Galil, S. Haber, and C. Yung, "Minimum-Knowledge Interactive Proofs for Decision Problems", *SIAM Journal on Computing*, Vol.18, No.4, pp.711–739 (Aug., 1989).

[GL] O. Goldreich and L. Levin, "A Hard-Core Predicate for all On-Way Functions", Proceedings of 21st annual ACM Symposium on Theory of Computing, pp.25–32 (May, 1989).

[GMR] S. Goldwasser, S. Micali, and C. Rackoff, "The Knowledge Complexity of Interactive Proof-Systems", Proceedings of 17th annual ACM Symposium on Theory of Computing, pp.291–304 (May, 1985).

[ILL] R. Impagliazzo, L. Levin, and M. Luby, "Pseudo-Random Number Generation from One-Way Functions", Proceedings of 21st annual ACM Symposium on Theory of Computing, pp.12–24 (May, 1989).

[Na] M.Naor, "Bit Commitment Using Pseudo-Randomness", in *Advances in Cryptology — CRYPTO '89*, Lecture Notes in Computer Science 435, Springer–Verlag, Berlin, pp.128–136 (1990).

[TW] M. Tompa and H. Woll, "Random Self-Reducibility and Zero Knowledge Interactive Proofs of Possession of Information", 28th Annual Symposium on Foundations of Computer Science, IEEE, pp.472–482 (Oct., 1987).

Group Signatures

David Chaum

Eugène van Heyst

CWI Centre for Mathematics and Computer Science,
Kruislaan 413, 1098 SJ Amsterdam, The Netherlands.

Abstract. In this paper we present a new type of signature for a group of persons, called a group signature, which has the following properties:

 (i) only members of the group can sign messages;

 (ii) the receiver can verify that it is a valid group signature, but cannot discover which group member made it;

 (iii) if necessary, the signature can be "opened", so that the person who signed the message is revealed.

These group signatures are a "generalization" of the credential/ membership authentication schemes, in which one person proves that he belongs to a certain group.

We present four schemes that satisfy the properties above. Not all these schemes are based on the same cryptographic assumption. In some of the schemes a trusted centre is only needed during the setup; and in other schemes, each person can create the group he belongs to.

1. Introduction

In this paper we present a new type of signature, which will be illustrated with the following example:

A company has several computers, each connected to the local network. Each department of that company has its own printer (also connected to the network) and only persons of that department are allowed to use their department's printer. Before printing, therefore, the printer must be convinced that the user is working in that department. At the same time, the company wants privacy: the user's name may not be revealed. If, however, someone discovers at the end of the day that a printer has been used too often, the director must be able to discover who misused that printer, to send him a bill.

More formally: a group of persons wants to create a signature scheme, which we will call a *group signature scheme*, that has the following three properties:

 (i) only members of the group can sign messages;

 (ii) the receiver of the signature can verify that it is a valid signature of that group, but cannot discover which member of the group made it;

 (iii) in case of dispute later on, the signature can be "opened" (with or without the help of the group members) to reveal the identity of the signer.

Group signatures are a "generalization" of *credential mechanisms* ([Ch85]) and of *membership (authentication) schemes* (cf. [OOK90], [SKI90]), in which a group member can convince a verifier that he belongs to a certain group, without revealing his identity. In [OOK90] and [SKI90], several of these schemes are proposed in which the same secret key is given to each group member. We define the following assumptions.

Assumption 1. *For each person it is unfeasible to compute RSA roots (hence it is unfeasible to split numbers that are the product of some large primes; and it is unfeasible to compute discrete logarithms modulo a large composite number).*

Assumption 2. *For each person it is unfeasible to compute the discrete logarithm modulo a large prime number.*

In this paper, only one group of persons will be considered (the hierarchical situation will not be treated here); and four different group signature schemes are presented. These schemes are compared.

Cryptographic assumption. In the first scheme every public key system can be used; the other schemes are based on Assumption 1 or 2. In all schemes (except in some modifications of the first scheme), the privacy of the signer is protected computationally. Not even a person from the group can determine who made a certain signature (except of course for the person who made that signature). Care must of course be taken in the selection of the exponents used in order to protect the anonymity of the signer. See Section 6.

Trusted authority. Let Z be a trusted authority, which sets the group signature scheme (it may be possible to distribute the power of Z). Except for the first scheme, Z is no longer needed after the setup. In the last scheme, a group signature scheme can be created from a "normal" setup, without a trusted authority.

Creation of the group. In the first two schemes the group of persons is fixed in advance. In the last two schemes, it is assumed that there is already a setup, based on RSA or discrete logarithm. If in these schemes someone wants to sign a message without revealing his name, then *at that moment* he creates some group of persons (for instance by picking them from a Trusted Public Directory of public keys) and proves that he belongs to that group. In case of dispute later on, the other "group members" are able to deny that signature.

Type of signature. In the last three schemes, the signatures made by the group members are undeniable signatures, but it is possible to make digital signatures. This can be realized as in [FS86], by doing the k iterations of the confirmation protocol in parallel and let the recipient choose the challenge vector not randomly, but as the outcome of a one-way-function on the received numbers. Because this protocol is no longer zero-knowledge, the signature and the confirmation protocol together will be a digital signature. Still to be proven is that this parallel protocol gives "no useful knowledge" to the recipient.

Costs. In all schemes the length of the public key (i.e., the number of bits of the group's public key) is linear in the number of group members. The numbers of bits and of computations are only compared in the case of the confirmation protocol, because in one disavowal protocol, these numbers are independent of the number of group members. We have not taken into account the looking-up of some public keys in a Trusted Public Directory.

Scheme number	Based on assumption	Z needed to open a signature	Group fixed in advance	Type of signature	Length of the group's public key	Number of computations during conf. pr.	Number of bits transmitted during conf. pr.
1	Any	Yes	Yes	Any type	Linear	Independent	Independent
2	1	No	Yes	Undeniable	Linear	Linear	Independent
3	1	No	No	Undeniable	Linear	Linear	Independent
4	2	No	No	Undeniable	Linear	Linear	Linear

Fig. 1. Comparison of the four group signature schemes presented in this paper. "Independent, linear" means that the number is independent respectively linear in the number of group members.

2. First group signature scheme

Z chooses a public key system, gives each person a list of secret keys (these lists are all disjunct) and publishes the complete list of corresponding public keys (in random order) in a Trusted Public Directory.

Each person can sign a message with a secret key from his list, and the recipient can verify this signature with the corresponding public key from the public list. Each key will be used only once, otherwise signatures created with that key are linked. Z knows all the lists of secret keys, so that in case of dispute, he knows who made the disputed signature. Hence Z is needed for the setup and for "opening" a signature.

If each person gets the same number of secret keys, then the length of the public key of this group signature scheme (i.e. the length of the Trusted Public Directory) is linear in the number of persons; but the number of messages a person can sign is fixed.

A problem with this scheme is that Z knows all the secret keys of the group members and can therefore also create signatures. This can be prevented by using *blinded public keys*. Let the public key system used be based on Assumption 2: for instance the ElGamal scheme [ElG85] or the undeniable signature scheme [CvA89]. Let g be a generator of the multiplicative group $\mathbb{Z}_p^*$, where p is a prime. Group member i creates his own secret key s_i and gives $g^{s_i} \pmod{p}$ to Z. Thus Z has a list of all these public keys together with the group member's name. Each week Z gives each group member i a randomly chosen number $r_i \in \{1,...,p-1\}$ and publishes the list of all the blinded public keys $(g^{s_i})^{r_i}$. During this week group member i will use $s_i r_i \pmod{p-1}$ as secret key.

The advantages of this modification are that Z cannot fake signatures, and that each group member only has to have one "really secret key" (for instance in a smart card), which can be blinded in order to make other secret keys. Only the one week's signatures can be linked, so that each group member can have only a few secret keys in his smart card to prevent this linking. If an r_i is accidentally revealed, still no more information about the secret key s_i is revealed.

In another modification, no trusted authority is needed: each user untraceably sends one (or more) public keys to a public list, which will be the public key of the group. But only group members must be able to send public keys to that list.

3. Second group signature scheme

Z chooses two different large primes p,q together with a one-way-function f of which the outcome may be assumed to be coprime with $N=pq$. Z gives person i of the group a secret key s_i, which is a large prime randomly chosen from the set $\Phi = \{\lceil\sqrt{N}\rceil, \ldots, \lfloor 2\sqrt{N}\rfloor - 1\}$, computes $v = \prod s_i$, and publishes N, v and f. If group member i wants to sign message n, his signature will be

$$(f(n))^{s_i} \bmod N,$$

and he has to prove to the recipient that $s_i|v$ and that $s_i \in \Phi$, without revealing anything more about s_i (see Section 3.1). In case of dispute later on, the recipient can perform a confirmation/disavowal protocol with each group member, without the help of $\mathcal{Z}$ (see Section 3.2). To prove the security of these schemes we need Assumption 1.

3.1. Confirmation protocol

We first consider the following instance, which is solved by [BCDvdG87] by using Protocol 1, which uses computationally secure blobs $\mathcal{B}$.

$\mathcal{P}$'s secret	: c.
public	: $N, x, y, \Omega;$ $x, y \in \mathbb{Z}_N^*, \Omega = \{\alpha, \ldots, \alpha + \beta\} \subset \mathbb{IN}$.
prove to $\mathcal{V}$	: $x^c \equiv y \pmod{N} \land c \in \Omega$.

Instance 1.

If this protocol is iterated k times, $\mathcal{V}$ will be convinced (with probability $1 - 2^{-k}$) that $c \in \tilde{\Omega} = \{\alpha - \beta, \ldots, \alpha + 2\beta\}$, but $\mathcal{V}$ will receive no knowledge other than the fact that $c \in \Omega = \{\alpha, \ldots, \alpha + \beta\}$[†].

Protocol 1. (for Instance 1)

(1) $\mathcal{P}$ chooses $r \in \{0, \ldots, \beta\}$. He computes blobs on $z_1 \equiv x^r \pmod{N}$ and $z_2 \equiv x^{r-\beta} \pmod{N}$, and sends the unordered pair $\{\mathcal{B}(z_1), \mathcal{B}(z_2)\}$ to $\mathcal{V}$.

(2) $\mathcal{V}$ chooses randomly $b \in \{0,1\}$ and sends it to $\mathcal{P}$.

(3) $\mathcal{P}$ sends $\mathcal{V}$ in case

   $b=0$: r and opens both blobs.

   $b=1$: $\tilde{r}$ which is $(c+r)$ or $(c+r-\beta)$, whichever is in the set Ω, and opens respectively the blob on z_1 or z_2 (which is called $\tilde{z}$).

(4) $\mathcal{V}$ verifies in case

   $b=0$: that $r \in \{0, \ldots, \beta\}$ and that the blobs contain x^r and $x^{r-\beta}$ in some order.

   $b=1$: that $\tilde{r} \in \Omega$, that one of the blobs contains $\tilde{z}$ and that $\tilde{z}$ satisfies $x^{\tilde{r}} \equiv \tilde{z}y$.

If $c \in \Omega$, then the distribution of $\tilde{r}$ is uniform over Ω and is thus independent of c. With this protocol we will create a confirmation protocol, so let $\mathcal{P}$ be a fixed group member who wants to convince the recipient (verifier $\mathcal{V}$) that he gave him a valid signature S. So the following instance (in which we write m in stead of $f(n)$) has to be solved:

[†] Hence, by using $\Omega = \{1, \ldots, N\}$, one can prove that he knows a discrete logarithm modulo N, without knowing $\varphi(N)$.

$\mathcal{P}$'s secret	: s.
public	: N,v,m,S,Φ; $m,S \in \mathbb{Z}_N^*$.
prove to $\mathcal{V}$	: $S \equiv m^s \pmod N \wedge s \in \Phi \wedge s|v$.

Instance 2.

Protocol 2. (for Instance 2)

Step 1. *Prove the knowledge of s such that $S \equiv m^s \pmod N$ and that $s \in \Phi$ with Protocol 1, iterated k times (take $\Omega = \Phi$, $x = m$, $y = S$ and $c = s$).*

Step 2. *Prove that $s|v$ as follows*

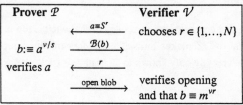

Note that for all x the probability distributions of $x^r \pmod N$ where $r \in \{1,...,\varphi(N)\}$ or $r \in \{1,...,N\}$ are polynomially indistinguishable [CEvdG87]. Step 1 of this protocol was already proven to be sound, complete, and zero-knowledge. Step 2 is trivially complete and zero-knowledge (the blobs $\mathcal{B}$ are computationally secure zero-knowledge). Because in Step 1 it is proved that $S \equiv m^s$, one can easily see that it is feasible to compute $b \equiv (m^r)^v$ from $\{s, v, a \equiv (m^r)^s\}$ if and only if $s|v$ (under the assumption that it is unfeasible to compute RSA roots, so here we use that N is not a prime). Hence Step 2 is also sound. $\square$

3.2. Disavowal protocol

If $\mathcal{P}$ wants to prove to $\mathcal{V}$ that S is not his signature on m, the following instance has to be solved:

$\mathcal{P}$'s secret	: s.
public	: N,v,m,S,Φ; $m,S \in \mathbb{Z}_N^*$.
prove to $\mathcal{V}$	: $S \not\equiv m^s \pmod N \wedge s \in \Phi \wedge s|v$.

Instance 3.

There are no zero-knowledge disavowal protocols to prove that $\alpha^x \not\equiv \beta^x \pmod N$, for given $\{N, \alpha, \beta, \alpha^x\}$, where $\varphi(N)$ is unknown. Therefore we use the following modification of [Ch90] to solve Instance 3. $\mathcal{Z}$ publishes $<\tilde{g}, \tilde{h}>$, which generates the whole group $\mathbb{Z}_N^*$ (see the next section how to construct $\tilde{g}$ and $\tilde{h}$), together with a Trusted Public Directory containing $\{$name group member, $\tilde{g}^s, \tilde{h}^s\}$. Let l be a very small constant such that exhaustive search over $\{0,...,l\}$ is feasible. Note that if $S \equiv m^s$, then $\mathcal{P}$ can not compute a from $(\frac{m^s}{S})^a$, because $(\frac{m^s}{S})^a \equiv 1$. So he has to guess a.

Prover $\mathcal{P}$		Verifier $\mathcal{V}$
	$\xleftarrow{\quad m^a \tilde{g}^{r_1} \tilde{h}^{r_2}, S^a (\tilde{g}^s)^{r_1} (\tilde{h}^s)^{r_2} \quad}$	chooses $r_1, r_2 \in \{1,\ldots,N\}$ and $a \in \{0,\ldots,l\}$
computes a from $(\frac{m^r}{S})^a$ by exhaustive search verifies numbers	$\xrightarrow{\quad \mathcal{B}(a) \quad}$	
	$\xleftarrow{\quad r_1 \cdot r_2 \quad}$	
	$\xrightarrow{\quad \text{open blob} \quad}$	verifies opening

Protocol 3. (for Instance 3)

3.3. Some remarks on this group signature scheme

If all group members except one conspire, the secret key of that one person is revealed. This threat can be easily eliminated if the authority Z makes himself a member of the group, i.e., if Z computes v as $v = s_Z \cdot \prod s_i$, where s_Z is a secret key only known to Z. With this trick, the group can also consist of two members.

The number of bits of the public key v is linear in the number of persons, so raising a number to the power v will take a time linear in the number of group members.

The set Φ can also be chosen in other ways, but it must satisfy the following conditions. If $\Phi = \{\varphi_1, \ldots, \varphi_1 + \varphi_2\} \subset \mathbb{N}$, then $1, N, \varphi_1^2 \notin \tilde{\Phi} = \{\varphi_1 - \varphi_2, \ldots, \varphi_1 + 2\varphi_2\}$. The first condition is necessary to avoid the use of $s=1$. According to the last condition the following conspiracy attack is avoided: if two group members, say i and j, conspire, they can create signatures $S \equiv m^{s_i s_j}$, which they can both disavow later. But $s_i s_j \notin \tilde{\Phi}$, so this signature will not be accepted in Step 1 of Protocol 2. Hence also the choice of v/s or v as exponent in the signature is avoided.

The blob $\mathcal{B}$ can be implemented in the following way: Z chooses generators g_p and h_q of $\mathbb{Z}_p^*$ and $\mathbb{Z}_q^*$ respectively, and constructs with the use of the Chinese Remainder Theorem $g \equiv \begin{cases} g_p \mod p \\ 1 \mod q \end{cases}$ and $h \equiv \begin{cases} 1 \mod p \\ h_q \mod q \end{cases}$. So $<g,h>$ generates $\mathbb{Z}_N^*$ uniformly, but it reveals the factorization of N. Therefore he chooses integers a_1, a_2, b_1, b_2 satisfying $\gcd(a_1, b_1, p-1) = \gcd(a_2, b_2, q-1) = \gcd(a_1 b_2 - a_2 b_1, \frac{\varphi(N)}{\lambda(N)}) = 1$ and publishes $\tilde{g} \equiv g^{a_1} h^{a_2}$ and $\tilde{h} \equiv g^{b_1} h^{b_2}$. It is not difficult to see also that $< \tilde{g}, \tilde{h} >$ generates the whole group $\mathbb{Z}_N^*$ uniformly, if the exponents are chosen from $\{1, \ldots, \varphi(N)\}$. Hence, in order for $\mathcal{P}$ to make $\mathcal{B}(y)$, he chooses $r_1, r_2 \in \{1, \ldots, N\}$ and creates $\mathcal{B}(y)$ as $y g^{r_1} h^{r_2} \pmod N$.

Another method of implementation is the following: $\mathcal{P}$ chooses randomly k numbers $g_1, \ldots, g_k$ from $\{1, \ldots, N\}$. Then with high probability $<g_1, \ldots, g_k>$ generates $\mathbb{Z}_N^*$ nearly uniformly, for k sufficiently large. In this case no trusted centre is needed [Ch87].

4. Third group signature scheme

For the security of this scheme we need Assumption 1, and we assume that there is a Trusted Public Directory in which each person's RSA modulus is listed (the public RSA exponent is not needed in this group signature scheme).

The secret key of group member i will be the factorization of his own RSA modulus $N_i = p_i q_i$.

During the setup, $\mathcal{Z}$ chooses an RSA-modulus N, which is independent of all the N_i's. Let M be a public integer such that $p_i \in \Phi = \{\lceil \sqrt{M} \rceil, \ldots, \lfloor 2\sqrt{M} \rfloor - 1\}$ and $q_i > 4\sqrt{M}$ (for all i). If person i wants to sign message n, he chooses randomly some set Γ of persons (including himself); his signature will be

$$\Gamma, \quad (f(n))^{p_i} \bmod N,$$

and he has to give a zero knowledge proof that the used exponent $p_i \in \Phi$ and that p_i is a divisor of the product of the RSA moduli of the persons of Γ. This can be done with Protocol 2 (with $\Omega = \Phi$), because $N_i > q_i > 4\sqrt{M}$ and thus all moduli, every product of two prime divisors of different moduli and each q_i are no elements of $\tilde{\Phi} = \{\lceil \sqrt{M} \rceil, \ldots, \lfloor 3\sqrt{M} \rfloor\}$. Hence the exponent used in the signature must be p_i. If a group member wants to deny a signature, he can use Protocol 3.

5. Fourth group signature scheme

The fourth group signature scheme is based on Assumption 2. Let p be a large public prime and let g, h be public generators of $\mathbb{Z}_p^*$. Person i has a secret key s_i and a public key $k_i \equiv g^{s_i} \pmod p$. If person i wants to sign message $m = f(n)$, he randomly chooses some set Γ of persons (including himself); and his signature will be

$$\Gamma, m^{s_i} \pmod p,$$

and he has to give a zero-knowledge proof that the secret exponent used in that signature is also used in the public key of somebody of the group Γ, i.e. the protocol has to solve the following instance:

$\mathcal{P}$'s secret	:	s_i.
public	:	p, g, h, S, Γ.
to prove to $\mathcal{V}$	:	$S \equiv m^{s_i} \pmod p \wedge g^{s_i} \in \{k_j \mid j \in \Gamma\}$.

Instance 4.

To prove this, $\mathcal{P}$ uses the following protocol, which gives no additional information about i and s_i. We have compressed the proofs that S is of the correct form, that the exponents used in S and in some public key are the same, and that the public key is used by somebody in Γ into one protocol.

Protocol 4. (for Instance 4)

(1) $\mathcal{P}$ chooses numbers $r_1, \ldots, r_{|\Gamma|}, t_1, t_2, t_3 \in \{1, \ldots, p-1\}$ and a permutation τ of Γ. He sends $\mathcal{V}$ the numbers: $x \equiv \left(\frac{g}{m}\right)^{t_1} h^{t_2} \pmod p$, $y \equiv m^{t_3} \pmod p$ and $z_{\tau(j)} \equiv k_j h^{r_j} \pmod p$ (for all $j \in \Gamma$).

(2) $\mathcal{V}$ chooses $b \in \{0, 1\}$ and sends b to $\mathcal{P}$.

(3) $\mathcal{P}$ sends $\mathcal{V}$ in case

$b=0$: $r_1, \ldots, r_{|\Gamma|}, t_1, t_2, t_3$ and τ.

$b=1$: $t_1 + s_i, t_2 + r_i, t_3 + s_i$ and index $\tau(i)$.

(4) $\mathcal{V}$ verifies in case

$b=0$: that the numbers $x, y, z_1, \ldots, z_{|\Gamma|}$ are formed correctly.

$b=1$: that $yS \equiv m^{t_3 + s_i} \pmod p$ and that $xz_{\tau(i)} \equiv Sh^{t_2 + r_i} (g/m)^{t_1 + s_i} \pmod p$.

If $\mathcal{P}$ can answer both questions, then he knows s_i; it is easy to see that this s_i satisfies $S \equiv m^{s_i}$ and $k_i \equiv g^{s_i}$. Hence if this protocol is iterated k times, then $\mathcal{V}$ will be convinced with confidence $1-2^{-k}$. This protocol is also zero-knowledge because it can be simulated (with the same probability distributions) by:

(1) *Choose a permutation τ of Γ, numbers $r_1,\ldots,r_{|\Gamma|},t_1,t_2,t_3 \in \{1,\ldots,p-1\}$ and $e \in \{0,1\}$.*

   Compute and send the numbers: $z_{\tau(j)} \equiv k_j h^{r_j} \pmod{p}$ $(j \in \Gamma)$, $y \equiv m^{t_3} / S^e \pmod{p}$ *a n d*

   $x \equiv \left(\frac{g}{m}\right)^{t_1} h^{t_2} (S / z_{\tau(i)})^e \pmod{p}$.

(2) *Receive $b \in \{0,1\}$.*

(3) *Send in case*

   $e=b=0$: $r_1,\ldots,r_{|\Gamma|},t_1,t_2,t_3$ *and* τ.

   $e=b=1$: *index $\tau(i)$ and t_1, t_2, t_3.*

   $e \neq b$: *restart this algorithm.*

If a person wants to deny a group signature, he can for instance use the disavowal protocol of [Ch90].

6. Some open problems

We have presented several group signature schemes, in which to open a signature the recipient asks $\mathcal{Z}$ or he performs a disavowal protocol with each group member. Is it possible to create other situations, such as: a majority of the group members can open a signature?

Is it possible to make digital group signatures other than by using [FS86] on undeniable signatures?

Can the results of [SS90] and [Per85] be applied to show that specific choices of the exponents in the schemes of Sections 2-4 and 5, respectively, protect anonymity in ways equivalent to known computational problems?

Is it possible to modify the fourth group signature system in such a way that the number of transmitted bits during the confirmation protocol is independent of the number of group members?

Acknowledgements

We would like to thank Jurjen Bos very much for his patience in listening to all the earlier schemes we proposed, and for his enthusiasm in breaking those; we also thank Gilles Brassard, Adam Cornford, Matthijs Coster, Jan-Hendrik Evertse, Maarten van der Ham, and Thijs Veugen for their help.

References

[BCDvdG87] Ernest Brickell, David Chaum, Ivan Damgård and Jeroen van de Graaf, Gradual and verifiable release of a secret, *Advances in Cryptology -CRYPTO 87*, C. Pomerance ed., Lecture Notes in Computer Science 293, Springer-Verlag, pp. 156-166.

[Ch85]   David Chaum, Showing credentials without identification, *Advances in Cryptology - EUROCRYPT 85*, F. Pichler ed., Lecture Notes in Computer Science 219, Springer-Verlag, pp. 241-244.

[Ch87]   David Chaum, Blinding for unanticipated signatures, *Advances in Cryptology -*

EUROCRYPT 87, D. Chaum, W. Price eds., Lecture Notes in Computer Science 304, Springer-Verlag, pp. 227-233.

[Ch90]   David Chaum, Zero-knowledge undeniable signatures, *Advances in Cryptology - EUROCRYPT 90*, I. Damgård ed., Lecture Notes in Computer Science 473, Springer-Verlag, pp. 458-464.

[CvA89]   David Chaum and Hans van Antwerpen, Undeniable signatures, *Advances in Cryptology - CRYPTO 89*, G. Brassard ed., Lecture Notes in Computer Science 435, Springer-Verlag, pp. 212-216.

[CEvdG87]   David Chaum, Jan-Hendrik Evertse and Jeroen van de Graaf, An improved protocol for demonstrating possession of discrete logarithms and some generalizations, *Advances in Cryptology -EUROCRYPT 87*, D. Chaum, W. Price eds., Lecture Notes in Computer Science 304, Springer-Verlag, pp. 127-141.

[ElG85]   Taher ElGamal, A public key cryptosystem and a signature scheme based on discrete logarithm, *IEEE IT* **31** (1985), pp. 469-472.

[FS86]   Amos Fiat and Adi Shamir, How to prove yourself: practical solution to identification and signature problems, *Advances in Cryptology -CRYPTO 86*, A.M. Odlyzko ed., Lecture Notes in Computer Science 263, Springer-Verlag, pp. 186-194.

[OOK90]   Kazuo Ohta, Tatsuaki Okamoto and Kenji Koyama, Membership authentication for hierarchical multigroup using the extended Fiat-Shamir scheme, *Advances in Cryptology -EUROCRYPT 90*, I. Damgård ed., Lecture Notes in Computer Science 473, Springer-Verlag, pp. 446-457.

[Per85]   René Peralta, Simultaneous security of bits in the discrete log, *Advances in Cryptology - EUROCRYPT 85*, F. Pichler ed., Lecture Notes in Computer Science 219, Springer-Verlag, pp. 62-72.

[SKI90]   Hiroki Shizuya, Kenji Koyama and Toshiya Itoh, Demonstrating possession without revealing factors and its applications, *Advances in Cryptology AUSCRYPT 90*, J. Seberry and J. Pieprzyk eds., Lecture Notes in Computer Science 453, Springer-Verlag, pp. 273-293.

[SS90]   Schrift and Shamir, The discrete log is very discreet, *Proc. 22nd STOC 1990*, pp. 405-415.

Enhancing Secrecy by Data Compression : Theoretical and Practical Aspects

Colin Boyd
Communications Research Group
Electrical Engineering Laboratories
University of Manchester
Manchester M13 9PL, UK
(Email: BOYD@uk.ac.man.ee.v1)

Abstract

It was recognised by Shannon that data compression increases the strength of secrecy systems when applied prior to encryption. Compression techniques have advanced considerably in recent years. This paper considers the extent to which these techniques can increase security. Estimates are obtained for how far practical compression schemes can increase unicity distance of symmetric ciphers. It is noted that there are other good reasons for using data compression prior to encryption. Comparison is made with homophonic coding and it is suggested that data compression is more worthwhile for practical sources such as natural language.

1   Introduction

Shannon's theory of secrecy systems [11] uses key equivocation as an index to measure the security of a cryptosystem. The key equivocation is the conditional entropy of the key given the ciphertext, and can be expressed as a function of the number of plaintext characters encrypted. Shannon showed that the rate at which this equivocation falls is approximately linear with slope equal to the redundancy of the source language.

The unicity distance U can be defined as the least number of symbols such that the key equivocation, after U symbols are encrypted, is expected to be zero. Shannon also showed that U is approximately inversely proportional to the source redundancy in bits per symbol, D, for all reasonable cryptosystems

[11]. If $H(K)$ is the initial key entropy then U is approximated by

$$U = \frac{H(K)}{D}$$

An alternative definition of U is the average number of plaintext symbols required so that the redundancy (in bits) exceeds the key length. If the length of the encrypted message is less than the unicity distance then it is not possible to decide the key or plaintext uniquely from knowledge of the ciphertext alone. It is quite possible for ciphers to have an infinite U, and Shannon called such ciphers *ideal*.

In Shannons other landmark paper [12] he showed that it is possible to reduce the redundancy of sources by suitable coding. He realised that this source coding, or *data compression*, if implemented prior to encryption, would strengthen secrecy systems by reducing the rate at which the key equivocation function decreases or, equivalently, increasing U. If all source redundancy can be removed before encryption then any reasonable cipher will be ideal. The use of data compression has become widespread in recent years due to the availability of easily programmed algorithms. The benefits of data compression are obvious in terms of savings in storage and communications costs.

This principle of using compression prior to encryption is now widely known and has been repeated often, for example in modern texts such as [14]. However, the literature has not been helpful in providing quantitative measures for how far security can be extended when using practical techniques. In this paper the practical, as well as the theoretical, aspects of applying compression prior to encryption are considered, with particular reference to recent advances in data compression techniques. As a result a quantitative measure for how far the best compression schemes can be expected to increase unicity distance is obtained.

The paper is divided into three main sections, the first two of which are concerned solely with the question of how far unicity distance can be extended by practical compression. Firstly modern coding techniques are examined to see how close they can get to achieving zero redundancy. In order to do this, new bounds on the overhead of arithmetic coding are obtained which show that unicity distance can be made very large if the only overheads are due to coding inaccuracies. The next section considers the complementary problem of modelling real sources and how this affects practical compression. This allows quantitative statements to be made on how far modern compression techniques can be expected to extend unicity distance. We conclude that in the practice, for English text, only a modest increase of unicity distance is possible, by a factor of between 3 and 6. The final main section considers other aspects of using compression prior to encryption, in particular the effects on known and chosen plaintext attacks, and the possible effects on processing speed.

When considering the effect of compression on unicity distance, comparison is made with the alternative source coding technique of homophonic coding [6]. Although homophonic coding appears best in a purely theoretical approach, we suggest that it is probably not worthwhile for practical encryption of complex sources such as natural language, in comparison with compression methods.

1.1   Huffman, Ziv-Lempel and arithmetic coding

In a theoretical sense the compression coding problem was solved in 1952 when Huffman published his coding algorithm [5]. He showed that it could not be improved upon in the sense that there is no prefix free code with a shorter average word length. Despite this, the most successful modern methods of practical compression do not use Huffman coding. The reason is partly that modern methods do not encode in a symbolwise manner as Huffman coding does, but instead deal with source symbols many at a time. In addition, and perhaps more importantly, Huffman coding is not well suited to exploit the adaptive models used in the most successful methods.

The most common modern methods are arithmetic coding and dictionary coding [1]. The set of dictionary coding methods, which are variations on the method of Ziv and Lempel [18], have proved very popular recently largely due to their speed and ease of implementation, as well as their very good compression. Arithmetic coding, although less widely used, is a very simple and effective idea. It has the property that it separates the coding and modelling functions very clearly which not only makes it suitable for virtually any modelling technique, but also makes it amenable to analysis. With sophisticated modelling techniques arithmetic coding is frequently the most effective choice in terms of achievable compression.

1.2   Coding and Modelling

One of the most important recent influences on data compression has been the realisation that the whole compression process can be divided into two essentially distinct parts [10]; the modelling process, which provides a probability distribution for the source alphabet, and the coding process which uses the stream of source symbols to be compressed, together with the probability distributions from the model, to produce an encoding. In an information theoretic model of communication various kinds of source model are usually considered. For example, symbols may be assumed to be independently emitted, or more generally a Markov model may be assumed. A practical approach to compression, and to cryptography, needs to take into account that a real source may not conform to any tractable model, or if it does then the exact probability distribution may be unknown.

The next two sections reflect the coding and modelling viewpoint. First we ignore the modelling problem by making an assumption that an exact model for the source is known. Following that we turn to the practical situation by including the modelling problem. For dictionary methods the division between modelling and coding is rather difficult to define. For Huffman and arithmetic coding the division is very clean, so we concentrate on these.

2 Coding

By Shannon's Noiseless Coding Theorem [12] it is known that for a given source it is possible to compress the output arbitrarily close to its entropy, but no further without loss of information. We are only concerned here with compression that can be completely reversed since this is necessary in practice for text.

For any message m, which is a sequence of l source symbols, we may define its information content by $I(m) = -\log p_m$ if m occurs with probability p_m. The overhead for a particular message m is then:

$$coding\ overhead = \frac{encoded\ length - I(m)}{l}$$

We assume that all encodings are binary so that the coding overhead is measured in bits per symbol (*bps*). A conventional way of measuring the effectiveness of a source code is to find the *expected* coding overhead. It will suit our purposes to look simply at bounds on the coding overhead for any message. This makes calculations simpler and also conforms to the convention in cryptography of assuming worst case conditions.

2.1 Limitations of Huffman Coding

The basic algorithm for Huffman coding [5] assumes that the model of the source is fixed and that symbols are emitted independently. Schemes for adaptive Huffman coding have also been developed but they are not as flexible as arithmetic coding in accepting different models. The limitation of Huffman coding is that an exact number of bits must be used for the encoding of each symbol. To illustrate worst case conditions note that when a binary source of just two symbols is encoded, each symbol must occupy one bit. If one symbol is far more likely than the other then the information content of that bit will be very small. As a result, the best general bound for the coding overhead is one bit per symbol. It is well known that there is zero coding overhead if all symbols have probabilities equal to an integral power of 1/2.

For a source with 'random' symbol probabilities we might expect an average overhead of 1/2 bit per symbol.

A common way of reducing the overhead is to extend the source alphabet by using blocks of two or more symbols. In this way the overhead is spread over the block, so that for an alphabet of two-symbol blocks the maximum overhead is 1/2 bit per symbol. This idea can be exploited as far as is desired in theory by taking larger and larger blocks, but the practical drawback is that the storage required increases exponentially in the block size. For ASCII text a block length of 3 or 4 is about as far as is reasonable, leading to a maximum overhead of 0.25 bits per symbol.

2.2 Limitations of arithmetic coding

Arithmetic coding encodes a source string as a number in the unit interval $[0, 1)$. Unlike Huffman Coding, there is no fixed codeword for each symbol, but how each symbol is encoded depends on the rest of the string. A complete description can be found in [7] or [17]. The idea is that each symbol in the message is assigned a distinct subinterval of the unit interval of length equal to its probability. This is the *coding interval* for that symbol. As encoding proceeds a nesting of subintervals is defined. Each successive subinterval is defined by reducing the previous subinterval in proportion of the current symbol's probability. The final interval, when all symbols have been encoded, has length equal to the product of all the symbol probabilities and can be transmitted by sending any member of it. It can be easily shown that in any interval of length L there is a number that can be represented in a number of bits that is the least integer greater than $-\log L$. This is equal to the entropy of the message encoded so in theory virtually perfect compression is achieved.

The limitations of arithmetic coding are a little harder to evaluate than those of Huffman coding, since they depend on parameters defined by the implementation. In order to make reasonable estimates we use the parameters reported for a published implementation [17]. Alternative concrete implementations are considered in [2] and [7]. The overhead can be divided into three parts.

- Overhead due to finite arithmetic. Because only finite arithmetic is used to calculate the current interval at each stage, a truncation must be made, resulting in a smaller interval than would be obtained with infinite precision arithmetic. Using arithmetic to 32 bits of precision, this has a very small effect on the compression obtained, since the interval has to be increased to twice its correct size before one extra bit is used.

In [17] the overhead due to finite arithmetic is stated to be around 10^{-4}

bits per symbol, from empirical calculations. A concrete bound may also be obtained which indicates that this is, if anything, an overestimate of the effect.

- Overhead due to end effects. In practice it is not necessary to encode all symbols of a message before obtaining some output bits. However, after the final symbol is encoded it is necessary to send some additional bits to disambiguate the final symbol. This results in an overhead of not more than 2 bits per message (see [17, p. 535]).

- Overhead due to halting problem. The decoder needs to have some means of knowing when to stop decoding since the transmitted string represents any interval it is contained in. A naive way of achieving this is to send the message length prior to the message, and this clearly results in an overhead of $\log l$ bits for a message of length l. In practice this method may not be very satisfactory and so in [17] an end-of-message symbol (eom) is included in the model, which is appended to each message as the last symbol. The effect of this is that extra bits are used to send this symbol, and also that the coding interval of every other symbol is slightly shortened to accommodate the coding interval for eom. The exact overhead depends on the way that the end-of-message symbol is modelled. In [17] both a fixed and an adaptive model are implemented.

For the the fixed model each source character is given a weight, the sum of all weights being 8000. In addition the eom symbol also has weight 1 and so has probability $1/8001$, and each other symbol has its probability reduced by the factor $8000/8001$. The resulting overhead for one message is

$$-\log(8000/8001)bps + \log 8001 = 0.00018bps + 13.$$

For the adaptive model the eom symbol is given a fixed weight of 1 while all other characters start off with weight 1 but can increase, subject to a maximum total weight of 2^{14}. Thus if the eom symbol originally has probability $1/257$ then it has probability $1/(257 + l)$ at the end of a message of length l. Thus the overhead for a message of length l is $\log(257 + l)$ for coding the eom symbol itself plus

$$-\log(256/257)(257/258)...(256 + l)/(257 + l) = \log 257 + l - 8.$$

In other words the total overhead due to eom is $2\log(257 + l) - 8$.

Because of the maximum allowed total weight, the weights are all halved periodically and so the above formula is no longer valid. Instead, for long messages the eom symbol has a frequency in the adaptive model of between 1 in 2^{13} and 1 in 2^{14}. This results in a minimum probability of eom of 2^{-14}, while the reduction to other symbols is not more than $1 - 2^{-13}$. For long messages then, the eom results in an overhead of not more than $14 + 0.00018bps$.

In conclusion, adding the three factors together we arrive at a fair estimate for the overhead in an implementable arithmetic coding scheme of

$$0.00028 \; bits \, per \, symbol + 16 \; bits \, per \, message$$

The bounds derived above were verified by performing some simple experiments using the implementation of arithmetic coding in 'C' given in [17]. Using simple fixed models it was found that the overhead was almost exactly as predicted by the estimates.

2.3 Homophonic coding

Although arithmetic coding has very small redundancy it is possible to do better. Homophonic coding actually achieves zero redundancy even though it may result in data expansion. A useful way of viewing this surprising effect is to consider that homophonic coding works by 'adding randomness' to the source. Since an ideal cipher requires only zero redundancy, and not compression, this method is just as useful from a cryptographic viewpoint. The recent methods of Günther [4], and of Jendal, Kuhn and Massey [6] are guaranteed to have small data expansion. The links between homophonic coding and data compression are strong - using the model of [6] homophonic coding can be viewed as a homophonic mapping followed by perfect compression. Homophonic coding allocates a number of homophones (infinite in general) to each source symbol. The coding space of each symbol is divided up in such a way that each of its homophones has a part and so that the homophones can be perfectly compressed.

In comparison with compression methods, homophonic coding has two disadvantages. Firstly the implementation is more expensive - a random source of bits is required to choose the homophones and more resources are required to store or calculate the codewords. Secondly there is considerable loss in data compression. It was shown [6] that the expected coding overhead for homophonic coding is not more than 2 bits per symbol, and that this can be further reduced for memoryless sources by blocking as explained for Huffman coding. However, even in this simple case the overhead will be considerably worse than for arithmetic coding.

2.4 The Effects of Compression Coding on Unicity Distance

For Huffman coding the coding overhead will depend on the extent to which the source alphabet may be extended. If we assume an overhead of 0.125

bits per symbol, which may be typical for a source with alphabet extended to sets of four symbols, then the unicity distance for a cryptosystem will become eight times the key length in bits. For example a cryptosystem with 56 bit key length should achieve around a 450 character unicity distance.

Consider next the situation for arithmetic coding. If we assume again a cipher with a key length of 56 bits then the unicity distance U is defined by

$$16 + 0.00028U = 56$$

so that U is over 142 000 characters. This is quite a large size of message (about four times the size of this paper) and represents a vast increase compared with using ASCII, and around 300 times better than with Huffman coding.

Finally for homophonic coding we have zero redundancy and so an infinite unicity distance is achieved. Thus in a theoretical sense homophonic coding allows achievement of ideal ciphers.

3   Practical Compression Schemes

We are only concerned here with 'one-pass' compression schemes - those that use models that are either chosen beforehand and fixed, or which adapt according to the statistics of previous symbols encoded. The alternatives are two pass schemes which examine the statistics of the message first and then transmit a model along with the compressed message. There are a number of reasons that this restriction is made. From the viewpoint of increasing unicity distance, transferring a model ensures that there is a considerable amount of redundancy present. From the point of view of achieving good compression it has been shown [1] that two pass schemes are in practice no better then one-pass. Finally, one-pass schemes are far more convenient in a communications environment.

Practical compression schemes often use adaptive models which change the statistics of the source model according to those symbols encoded so far. Arithmetic coding is particularly suited to adaptive modelling since a new probability distribution can be used after every symbol is encoded. As long as the procedure for updating the model is well defined both encoder and decoder maintain the same model at each stage. A comprehensive survey of such modelling techniques is presented by Bell, Cleary and Witten [1].

3.1   The effects of the best compression methods on unicity distance

It is very difficult to make a definitive statement on what is the best data compression method currently known. For one thing techniques are constantly improving and there is much active research. But in any case we need to define what is meant by 'best'. Perhaps the first concern in the present context is how much compression is achieved, but even this matter will normally depend on the type of data being compressed. Just as important in a communications environment is the question of the cost of compression, particularly in terms of time but also in memory required. As might be expected, there is in general a trade-off between compression achieved and resources required. We will try to give a brief summary of the current situation concentrating on how well "ordinary" English text can be compressed, since this is the case for which the data exists to compare the effect on unicity distance.

A comparison of ten different compression schemes is presented in by Bell, Cleary and Witten [1]. This comparison ranges over a variety of samples including technical and non-technical English prose encoded in ASCII, binary object code, programming source code in ASCII and graphics images. Over the English text the best compression achieved (using the PPMC method with arithmetic coding) was 2.25 bits per character for technical prose, and 2.48 bit per character for fiction prose. The unicity distance achieved on encrypting such compressed text will depend crucially on the true figure of the information content per English character for the source used. There have been various methods devised for estimating the entropy of ordinary English, many using human experiments. (See [15] for a survey, and [3] for a recent method of computer analysis.) The figures obtained typically vary between 1 and 1.3 bits per symbol and depend on authors and styles of writing. However there are no studies which suggest that the entropy of English is above 1.3 bits per symbol for messages of any reasonable length and we may safely take this value as an upper bound. Thus even for best compression schemes the redundancy per symbol is at least 1 bit per character. This compares with 3.7 bits per character of redundancy for the basic 26 letter alphabet, or 6 bits per character for English text encoded as 7-bit ASCII.

Coding	Bits per char	Redundancy per char
26 letter alphabet	4.7	3.4
7 bit ASCII	7	5.7
Best compression schemes	2.3	1

Table 1: Redundancies for English Text

Thus, since unicity distance is inversely proportional to redundancy, the effect of the best compression schemes on unicity distance is to increase it between 3 and 6 times, depending on the coding used and on the true value of the information content. The best methods use arithmetic coding for which the coding overhead is a small fraction of one bit per symbol and thus contributes a small part of the total redundancy. The only way to significantly improve unicity distance for natural languages beyond these levels is to use better modelling techniques. These are the subject of much current research.

Estimates for the redundancy of real sources other than natural languages do not seem to be so readily available. Clearly many examples, such as programming source code, can be expected to have a less rich structure than natural language, and it may well be that redundancy per character can be made much lower than 1 bit per character for these sources. In [1] Lisp and Pascal source code is reported to be compressed to 1.9 and 1.84 bits per character respectively. It is possible to conceive of sources for which extremely accurate models are available and where practically infinite unicity distance may be obtained. At present this does not appear to be achievable for natural languages.

Although unicity distance may be improved by a factor of 3 to 6 it will still be far too small in general to allow keys to be changed before the unicity distance is achieved, which would guarantee some unconditional security. For example, the 56 bit key length of DES would result in a unicity distance of no more than 56 characters of plaintext. Even so, the removal of so much structure of the plaintext gives good confidence that breaking the cryptosystem using a ciphertext-only attack will be made considerably harder than without compression. It is well understood that a small unicity distance does not mean that a cryptosystem is weak - thus with ASCII encoded English, DES has a unicity distance of about 8 characters, but nobody knows a better way to break DES than with a brute force key search.

Shannon defined the *work factor* associated with a cryptosystem [11, p. 702] to be the amount of work required to break it from a given amount of ciphertext. The idea is that with more plaintext redundancy being used, the effort needed to break the cipher would be reduced. Shannon suggests that there is a strong relationship between work factor and unicity distance. If the work factor were directly proportional to the unicity distance then using compression would increase this also by a factor of 3 to 6. In practice, however, the work factor may be asymptotic to some value, and since there is frequently practically limitless ciphertext available, this should perhaps not be taken as very comforting.

3.2 Is homophonic coding worthwhile?

It was shown in section 2 that practical coding methods can compress with a coding overhead of around 0.0003 bits per symbol for long messages. However, as we have just seen, the best compression methods (including those which achieve this sort of coding efficiency) can only compress natural language with remaining redundancy at least 1 bit per character. In other words nearly all the redundancy remaining is due to approximations in the modelling and not to problems of coding. Even with Huffman coding the majority of the overhead is due to modelling.

The reason for the modelling overhead is that the incorrect probabilities are used for each message. Thus a particular message m of length l may have an actual probability p_m of ocurring, but the model assumes that it has a probability of p'_m. Thus if we write

$$Modelling\ Overhead = \frac{\log(p_m/p'_m)}{l}$$

then the total overhead for compression is

$$\frac{Encoded\ length - I(m)}{l} = Coding\ Overhead + Modelling\ Overhead$$

For homophonic coding the coding overhead is zero but the modelling problem, and thus the modelling overhead, is the same as for compression coding. Thus, for natural language, using homophonic coding would achieve little advantage in loss of redundancy while resulting in considerably higher implementational costs and loss of much compression. Thus from the viewpoint of reducing redundancy there seems little point in using homophonic coding. The reason that homophonic coding does not achieve optimal compression, even though it does achieve optimal coding, is that randomness is introduced. We cannot say that this addition of randomness will not make cryptanalysis harder, but equally other methods of adding randomness may be just as effective.

4   Other Factors

Up till now we have been considering the benefits of compression only in terms of increasing the unicity distance of a cipher - in other words we have been aiming at an approximation to an ideal cipher of Shannon. In this section other factors are considered, including the benefits of compression against other forms of attack, and the implications for speed of processing.

4.1   Using adaptive modelling to increase security

Consider a known plaintext attack against a cryptosystem to which compression is applied beforehand. On the surface it may seem that compression provides no extra defence against such an attack. For an attacker who obtains known ciphertext and the corresponding plaintext which was compressed before encryption, may compress the plaintext himself to obtain plaintext/ciphertext pairs for the basic cryptosystem. It is here that the use of adaptive modelling can provide additional security.

The use of adaptive modelling for cryptographic purposes has previously been considered by Witten and Cleary [16]. They proposed the use of arithmetic coding with adaptive modelling as a cryptosystem itself, using the initial state of the source model as the key. They argue that the model will become so complex and dependent on the whole of the plaintext that analysis for a cryptanalyst is impractical. However they do not provide any concrete evidence that the idea is secure.

By using instead the compressed output as the input to a cryptosystem in which confidence has been established, we can be fairly sure of having made cryptanalysis considerably harder. However, the benefits of the above idea can also be claimed. Instead of using a key to initialise an adaptive model, a random initialiser can be used as a prefix for each message. This will indeed make the model unpredictable and have a complicated affect on its future states (note that such models usually expand in size over time). In addition such a randomizer would make a known or chosen plaintext attack more difficult to mount if the initialiser were not itself known or chosen, much in the manner that initialisation values for block ciphers can. This initialiser need not be sent in advance as long as its length is agreed beforehand.

It is perhaps worth extending this analogy with block ciphers. A common mode of operation of block ciphers is to chain the ciphertext blocks together so that the ciphertext of each block depends on all the preceding blocks. This property is also true when adaptive modelling is used but now on a character by character basis. This property ensures that recurring pieces of plaintext are encrypted differently. It is also useful in maintaining the integrity of the message, in that parts of the encrypted text cannot be deleted or transposed without completely altering the subsequent decrypted text.

4.2 Speed

When considering the practical implication of using data compression prior to encryption it is important to examine the speed of compression. In a communications environment it may not be tolerable for a large delay to be introduced. Not surprisingly there is again a trade-off here, this time between speed of compression and compression achieved. Nevertheless even the best compression techniques are not likely to have too problematic an effect. In [1] the speed of the PPMC method mentioned above is reported as 2000 characters per second on a Vax. Schemes which achieve less compression go faster - a version of Ziv-Lempel coding is reported in [1] to run at 6000 characters per second for encoding and nearly twice as fast decoding.

The effects of speed when applying compression prior to encryption will depend also on the speed of the underlying encryption. There will of course be less material to encrypt if compression is used. If we assume also that pipelining of algorithms is possible then we are looking for compression algorithms which run at similar speeds to the encryption algorithm in order that there is similar performance. Implementations of DES in software run typically between 20 and 100 kbit/s [13]. (More recent products claim speeds of around 200 kbit/s.) If 8-bit ASCII is used for encrypting English this translates to between 2500 and 12 000 characters per second. Clearly it is difficult to draw precise conclusions from these figures on different machines, but it appears that compression may result in a small slow down in running speed, perhaps around a half in some cases.

Hardware encryption with, say, DES, can go much faster than this, up to 45 Mbit/s [13]. Compression in software cannot match these speeds. Hardware designs exist [9] which promise adaptive data compression at 100 Mbit/s. If this can be achieved then the use of data compression prior to encryption will be able to increase the speed of encrypting a message, in addition to its other benefits. For slower encryption algorithms, such as RSA, compression prior to encryption may also result in an increase of speed.

4.3   Error propagation

The one clear disadvantage in using data compression is the effect it has upon error propagation. Whilst Huffman coding with a fixed model has quite good re-synchronisation properties [8], coding with adaptive models appears not to have any such properties. Once a single bit is lost or changed the whole model thereafter is out of synchronisation and will have catastrophic effects. Whether this is a major problem will depend on the channel being used and if essentially error free transmission can be achieved. A silver lining to this cloud is the benefit of such a property in terms of authentication of the message as discussed in 4.1.

5   Conclusion

In this paper we have made the following points.

1. Modern coding techniques can reduce the coding overhead to less than 0.0003 bits per symbol plus 16 bits per message in practice.

2. The major overhead is due to limitations in modelling. This results in a current best achievement of around 2.3 bits per symbol for ordinary English text.

3. Practical compression of English text results in increase of unicity distance of between 3 and 6 times.

4. Homophonic coding suffers from the same modelling limitations and thus has little benefit over compression coding in reducing redundancy.

5. Using compression coding helps reduce resources used, and may sometimes even improve the speed of encryption.

6. Using a random initialiser with an adaptive model appears to make practical cryptanalysis very hard.

In summary we have seen that ideal cryptosystems cannot be achieved either by using compression or homophonic coding. However modern compression, such as arithmetic coding, used prior to encryption, results in both theoretical and practical strengthening of the cryptosystem with little or no loss of performance while also saving on storage and/or transmission costs. The only negative consideration is whether errors are likely. Further research on practical implementations of combined compression and encryption would be useful.

6   Acknowledgement

I am very grateful to Ian Witten for his interest in this paper and for making suggestions for important improvements.

References

[1] T.Bell, I.H.Witten and J.G.Cleary, *Modeling for Text Compression*, ACM Computing Surveys, 21,4, December 1989.

[2] G.V.Cormack and R.N.S.Horspool, *Data Compression using Dynamic Markov Modelling*, The Computer Journal, 30, 6, 1987.

[3] P.Grassberger, *Estimating the Information Content of Symbol Sequences and Efficient Codes*, IEEE Transactions on Information Theory, IT-35, 3, pp 669-675, 1989.

[4] C.G.Günther, *A Universal Algorithm for Homophonic Coding*, Proceedings of Eurocrypt 88, Springer-Verlag, 1988.

[5] D.A.Huffman, *A method for the Construction of Minimum-Redundancy Codes*, Proceedings of the IERE, 40,9,1952.

[6] H.N.Jendal, Y.J.B.Kuhn and J.L.Massey, *An Information-Theoretic Treatment of Homophonic Substitution*, Proceedings of Eurocrypt 89, Springer-Verlag, 1990.

[7] G.G.Langdon, *An Introduction to Arithmetic Coding*, IBM Journal of Research and Development, 28,2, 1984.

[8] D.A.Lelewer and D.S.Hirschberg, *Data Compression*, ACM Computing Surveys, 13,3,1987.

[9] R.Phillips and S.Jones, *A 100 MBit/s Adaptive Compressor Chip*, Abstracts of Second Bangor Symposium on Communications, May 1990.

[10] J.Rissanen and G.G.Langdon, *Universal Modelling and Coding*, IEEE Transactions on Information Theory, IT-27, 1, pp 12-23, 1981.

[11] C.E.Shannon, *Communication Theory of Secrecy Systems*, Bell Systems Technical Journal, 656-715, 1949.

[12] C.E.Shannon and W.Weaver, *The Mathematical Theory of Communication*, University of Illinois Press, 1949.

[13] M.Smid and D.Branstad, *The Data Encryption Standard: Past and Future*, Proceedings of the IEEE, 76,5,1988.

[14] H.C.A.van Tilborg, *An Introduction to Cryptology*, Kluwer Academic Publishers, 1988.

[15] D.Welsh, *Codes and Cryptography*, Clarendon Press, Oxford, 1988.

[16] I.H.Witten and J.G.Cleary, *On the Privacy Afforded by Adaptive Text Compression*, Computers and Security, 7, 1988, pp397-408.

[17] I.H.Witten, R.Neal and J.G.Cleary, *Arithmetic Coding for Data Compression*, Communications of the ACM, 30,6,1987.

[18] J.Ziv and A.Lempel, *A universal algorithm for sequential data compression*, IEEE Transactions on Information Theory, IT-23,3,pp 337-343, 1977.

Factoring Integers and Computing Discrete Logarithms via Diophantine Approximation

C. P. Schnorr
Universität Frankfurt
Fachbereich Mathematik/Informatik
6000 Frankfurt am Main
Germany

email: schnorr@informatik.uni-frankfurt.de

Abstract

Let N be an integer with at least two distinct prime factors. We reduce the problem of factoring N to the task of finding random integer solutions $(e_1, \ldots, e_t) \in \mathbb{Z}^t$ of the inequalities

$$\left| \sum_{i=1}^{t} e_i \log p_i - \log N \right| \leq N^{-c} \quad \text{and}$$

$$\sum_{i=1}^{t} |e_i \log p_i| \leq (2c - 1) \log N + o(\log p_t),$$

where $c > 1$ is fixed and $p_1, \ldots, p_t$ are the first t primes. We show, under the assumption that the smooth integers distribute "uniformly", that there are $N^{\epsilon + o(1)}$ many solutions $(e_1, \ldots, e_t)$ if $c > 1$ and if $\epsilon := c - 1 - (2c - 1) \log \log N / \log p_t > 0$. We associate with the primes $p_1, \ldots, p_t$ a lattice $L \subset \mathbb{R}^{t+1}$ of dimension t and we associate with N a point $\mathbf{N} \in \mathbb{R}^{t+1}$. We reduce the problem of factoring N to the task of finding random lattice vectors $\mathbf{z}$ that are sufficiently close to $\mathbf{N}$ in both the ∞−norm and the 1−norm. The dimension t of the lattice L is polynomial in $\log N$. For $N \approx 2^{512}$ it is about 6300. We also reduce the problem of computing, for a prime N, discrete logarithms of the units in $\mathbb{Z}/N\mathbb{Z}$ to a similar diophantine approximation problem.

1 Summary

The task of factoring large composite integers N has a long history and is still a challenging problem. In this paper we reduce this task to the following problem of diophantine approximation. Find about $t+2$ integer vectors $(e_1, \ldots, e_t) \in \mathbb{Z}^t$ so that $|\sum_{i=1}^{t} e_i \log p_i - \log N| \leq N^{-c}$ and $\sum_{i=1}^{t} |e_i \log p_i| \leq (2c-1) \log N + o(\log p_t)$ hold for some $c > 1$ where $p_1, \ldots, p_t$ are the first t prime numbers.

Given these $t+2$ diophantine approximations of $\log N$ we can factorize N as follows. The integer $u := \prod_{e_j > 0} p_j^{e_j}$ must be a close approximation to $v N$ where $v = \prod_{e_j < 0} p_j^{|e_j|}$. In fact we show in Lemma 2 that $|u - vN| = p_t^{o(1)}$. Hence the residue $u(\bmod N)$ factorizes completely over the primes $p_1, \ldots, p_t$ and we obtain a non trivial congruence $\prod_{e_j > 0} p_j^{e_j} = \pm \prod_{j=1}^{t} p_j^{b_j} (\bmod N)$. Using about $t+2$ of these congruences we can factorize N according to the method in section 2.

The above diophantine approximation problem can be formulated as a closest lattice vector problem. In section 3 we associate with N a point $\mathbf{N} \in \mathbb{R}^{t+1}$ and with the primes $p_1, \ldots, p_t$ a lattice L so that the desired approximations $\sum_{i=1}^{t} e_i \log p_i$ of $\log N$ can be generated from the lattice vectors $\mathbf{z}$ such that $\|\mathbf{z} - \mathbf{N}\|_1$ and $\|\mathbf{z} - \mathbf{N}\|_\infty$ are sufficiently small. We show in Lemma 2 that every lattice vector that is sufficiently close to $\mathbf{N}$ yields a desired approximation of $\log N$. Under a reasonable hypothesis we show in Theorem 7 that, for some fixed $\varepsilon > 0$, there are at least $N^{\varepsilon + o(1)}$ sufficiently close lattice vectors provided that the number t of primes is larger than $(\log N)^2$. These results reduce the problem of factoring N to the task of finding lattice vectors in L that are close to $\mathbf{N}$ in both the 1–norm and the ∞–norm.

The lattice basis reduction algorithm of Lenstra, Lenstra, Lovász (1982) apparently let some experts think on the possibility to factorize N by finding good approximations to N by a linear combination of $\log$'s of small primes. Since this approach seemed to be impractical it has never been analysed. We introduce negative coefficients into the approximation problem and we set up this problem as a nearest lattice vector problem. We also obtain explicit numbers on the size of the lattice and error bounds needed to make the method work.

We have solved the diophantine approximation problem using a prime basis of $t = 125$ primes. We reduce the lattice basis by blockwise Korkine Zolotarev reduction, a concept that has been introduced by Schnorr (1987). Schnorr and Euchner (1991) give improved practical algorithms for lattice basis reduction. For a basis of 125 primes the diophantine approximation problem can be solved within a few hours on a SPARC 1+ computer. In general it may be hard to find a lattice vector that is very close in both the 1-norm and the ∞-norm. Our experience with the particular problem indicates that it is sufficient to reduce by a strong reduction algorithm for the Euclidean norm, the lattice basis $b_1, \ldots, b_t, N$ described in section 3. In order to factor integers N that are 500 bits long the basis should have about 6300 primes. It is difficult to estimate the required computer time.

The paper is organized as follows. In section 2 we show how to factor N if we are given about $t + 2$ pairs of integers (u_i, v_i) such that u_i is of the form $\prod_{j=1}^{t} p_j^{a_j}$ and $|u_i - v_i N| \le p_t$. In section 3 we show that these pairs (u_i, v_i) can be generated from the lattice vectors in the lattice L that is associated with the primes $p_1, \ldots, p_t$ that are sufficiently close to the point N We show in section 4 that there are $N^{\epsilon+o(1)}$ lattice vectors that are sufficiently close to N. In section 5 we reduce the problem of computing discrete logarithms to the task of solving a closest lattice vector problem in an associated lattice.

2   Factoring integers via smooth numbers

Notation   Let $\mathbb{N}, \mathbb{Q}, \mathbb{R}$ be the sets of natural, integer, real numbers. Let $\log x$ denote the natural logarithm of $x \in \mathbb{R}, x > 0$.

The factoring method

Input. N   (a composite integer with at least two distinct prime factors and $\alpha, c \in \mathbb{Q}$ with $\alpha, c > 1$. The choice for α, c is discussed in section 3)

1. Form the list $p_1, \ldots, p_t$ of all primes smaller than $(\log N)^{\alpha}$.

2. Generate from lattice vectors, as explained in section 3, a list of $m \ge t+2$ pairs $(u_i, v_i) \in \mathbb{N}^2$ with the property that

$$u_i = \prod_{j=1}^{t} p_j^{a_{i,j}} \quad \text{with } a_{i,j} \in \mathbb{N} \tag{1}$$

$$|u_i - v_i N| \le p_t \tag{2}$$

3. Factorize $u_i - v_i N$ for $i = 1, \ldots, m$ over the primes $p_1, \ldots, p_t$ and $p_0 = -1$. Let $u_i - v_i N = \prod_{j=0}^{t} p_j^{b_{i,j}}$, $b_i = (b_{i,0}, \ldots, b_{i,t})$ and $a_i = (a_{i,0}, \ldots, a_{i,t})$ with $a_{i,0} = 0$.

4. Find a nonzero $0, 1$-solution $(c_1, \ldots, c_m)$ of the equation

$$\sum_{i=1}^{m} c_i(a_i - b_i) = 0 \ (\mathrm{mod}\, 2)$$

5.
$$x := \prod_{j=0}^{t} p_j^{\sum_{i=1}^{m} c_i(a_{i,j}+b_{i,j})/2} \ (\mathrm{mod}\, N) \ ,$$

$$y := \prod_{j=0}^{t} p_j^{\sum_{i=1}^{m} c_i b_{i,j}} = \prod_{j=1}^{m} u_i^{c_i} (\mathrm{mod}\, N) \ .$$

(The construction implies that $x^2 = y^2 (\mathrm{mod}\, N)$.)

6. If $x \neq \pm y (\mathrm{mod}\, N)$ then *output* $gcd(x + y, N)$ and stop. Otherwise go to 4 and generate a different solution $(c_1, \ldots, c_m)$.

Remarks. 1. If x, y in step 5 behave like a random solution of $x^2 = y^2 (\mathrm{mod}\ N)$ then the success rate of step 6 is at least $1/2$. Therefore the time that the algorithm takes to factorize N is essentially the time to generate the list of $m \geq t + 2$ pairs (u_i, v_i) required in step 2.
2. Steps $4 - 6$ of the algorithm only require that u_i and $u_i (\mathrm{mod}\, N)$ factorize completely over the prime basis $p_1, \ldots, p_t$. In case of the weaker inequality $|u_i - v_i N| = p_t^{O(1)}$ we expect that $u_i - v_i N$ factorizes completely over the prime basis for at least some fixed positive fraction of the pairs (u_i, v_i).
3. In the next section we introduce a lattice $L_{\alpha, c}$ and we show that essentially every vector in $L_{\alpha, c}$ that is sufficiently close to the point $\mathbf{N}$ yields some pair $(u_i, v_i) \in \mathbb{N}^2$ such that (1), (2) hold. Moreover assuming an unproved but reasonable hypothesis we show that if $\alpha > (2c-1)/(c-1)$ then the lattice vectors that are close to $\mathbf{N}$ yield sufficiently many suitable pairs (u_i, v_i) satisfying (1) and (2).
4. By the prime number theorem the number t of primes $\leq (\log N)^\alpha$ is

$$t = (\log N)^\alpha / \alpha \log\log N \ (1 + o(1)) \ .$$

3 How to generate u_i, v_i from lattice vectors that are close to N

Let $L = L_{\alpha, c} \subset \mathbb{R}^{t+1}$ be the lattice that is generated by the column vectors $b_1, \ldots, b_t$ of the following $(t+1) \times t$ matrix B and let $\mathbf{N} \in \mathbb{R}^{t+1}$ be represented by the following column vector:

$$
B = \begin{bmatrix}
\log 2 & 0 & \cdots & 0 \\
0 & \log 3 & & 0 \\
\vdots & \vdots & & \vdots \\
0 & 0 & \cdots & \log p_t \\
N^c \log 2, & N^c \log 3 & \cdots & N^c \log p_t,
\end{bmatrix}
\qquad
N = \begin{bmatrix}
0 \\
0 \\
\vdots \\
0 \\
N^c \log N
\end{bmatrix}
$$

We let the rational numbers $\alpha, c > 1$ vary only slightly with the size of N. The real entries of the matrix B must be approximated by rational numbers. We show below that it is sufficient to approximate them with an error less than $1/2$, i.e. we can approximate them by the nearest integer.

Notation. We associate with a lattice vector $z = (z_1, \ldots, z_{t+1}) = \sum_{i=1}^{t} e_i b_i$, $e_1, \ldots, e_t \in \mathbb{Z}$, the pair of integers $g(z) := (u, v) \in \mathbb{N}^2$ with

$$
u := \prod_{e_j > 0} p_j^{e_j}, \qquad v := \prod_{e_j < 0} p_j^{|e_j|}.
$$

The *maximum norm* of a vector $z = (z_1, \ldots, z_{t+1}) \in \mathbb{R}^{t+1}$ is by definition $\|z\|_\infty = \max_i |z_i|$; the *1-norm* is $\|z\|_1 = \sum_{i=1}^{t+1} |z_i|$. We call an integer $\pm \prod_{i=1}^{t} p_i^{e_i}$ γ-smooth if $p_i^{e_i} \leq \gamma$ for $i = 1, \ldots, t$. A pair (u, v) of integers is γ-smooth if both u and v are γ-smooth.

Lemma 1. *If* $z \in L$ *and* $\|z - N\|_\infty \leq \log p_t$ *then* $(u, v) = g(z)$ *is* p_t-*smooth.*

Proof. Let $z = \sum_{i=1}^{t} e_i b_i$. We have $|e_i \log p_i| = \log p_i^{|e_i|} \leq \log p_t$ for $i = 1, \cdots, t$. **QED**

For any lattice vector $z = (z_1, \ldots, z_{t+1}) = \sum_{i=1}^{t} e_i b_i$ with $(u, v) = g(z)$ we have

$$
\|z - N\|_1 = \log u + \log v + N^c |\log(u/vN)|. \tag{3}
$$

$$
z_{t+1} = N^c \log(u/v) \tag{4}
$$

Lemma 2. *If* $z \in L$ *satisfies the inequalities*

$$
\|z - N\|_\infty \leq \log p_t \tag{5}
$$

$$
\|z - N\|_1 \leq (2c - 1) \log N + o(\log p_t) \tag{6}
$$

then we have for $(u, v) := g(z)$ *that* $|u - vN| = p_t^{o(1)}$. *The asymptotic is for* $N \to \infty$.

We see from Fact 1 and Lemma 2 that if $z \in L$ satisfies (5) and (6) for sufficiently large N then the pair $(u, v) = g(z)$ satisfies the conditions (1), (2) in step 2 of the factoring algorithm.

Proof. We let β denote $z_{t+1} - N^c \log N$, i.e. $\beta = (z - N)_{t+1}$. From the inequality (5) we only use that $|\beta| \leq \log p_t$. We see from (4) and (5) that

$$\left| \log \left(1 + \frac{u - vN}{vN} \right) \right| = |\log(u/vN)| \overset{(4)}{=} N^{-c}\beta$$

$$\overset{(5)}{\leq} N^{-c} \log p_t = o(1).$$

Using that $\log(1 + x) = x + o(1)$ for small x this yields

$$|u - vN| \leq vN^{1-c} \log p_t (1 + o(1))$$

Since $\log p_t = p_t^{o(1)}$ it remains to show that $v \leq N^{c-1}p_t^{o(1)}$. We have

$$\log v \overset{(3)}{=} \|z - N\|_1 - \log u - |\beta|$$

$$\overset{(4)}{=} \|z - N\|_1 - \log vN - \beta N^{-c} - |\beta|$$

$$\leq \|z - N\|_1 - \log vN.$$

By (6) this implies $2 \log v \leq 2(c - 1) \log N + o(\log p_t)$, and thus $v \leq N^{c-1}p_t^{o(1)}$.

QED

If we replace in Lemma 2 the inequality (6) by the weaker bound

$$\|z - N\|_1 \leq (2c - 1) \log N + O(\log p_t)$$

it follows that $|u - vN| = p_t^{O(1)}$. This latter inequality is still sufficient for our factoring method.

Lemma 3. *In the proof of Lemma 2 we have used from the inequalities (5), (6) only that*

$$\left| \sum_{i=1}^{t} e_i \log p_i - \log N \right| \leq N^{-c} \log p_t \tag{7}$$

$$\sum_{i=1}^{t} |e_i \log p_i| \leq (2c - 1) \log N + o(\log p_t) \tag{8}$$

Therefore in order to find an integer pair (u, v) for our factoring method it is sufficient to solve the inequalities (7), (8) with $e_1, \ldots, e_t \in \mathbb{Z}$. The factor $\log p_t$ in (7) is negligible. It can be eliminated by replacing c by $c' = c - \log\log p_t / \log N$. This substitution does not affect the inequality (8) since $\log\log p_t = o(\log p_t)$.

Rational approximation of the basis matrix. In practice we must approximate the real entries of the basis matrix $B = [\mathbf{b}_1, \ldots, \mathbf{b}_t]$ by rational vectors $\overline{\mathbf{b}}_1, \ldots, \overline{\mathbf{b}}_t$. The approximation must be sufficiently close so that the error in $|z_{t+1}| N^{-c}$ for $\mathbf{z} = \sum_{i=1}^{t} e_i \, \mathbf{b}_i$ is negligible whenever $|e_i \log p_i| \le \log p_t$ for $i = 1, \ldots, t$. For this it is sufficient to approximate $N^c \log p_i$, $N^c \log N$, $\log p_i$ by the nearest integer. Then the bit length of $N^c \log p_i$, $N^c \log N$ is $c \log_2 N$ and the bit length of $\log p_i$ is $\log_2 p_t$. If we choose for N^c a power of 2 (10, resp.) then $N^c \log p_i$, $N^c \log N$ is the initial segment of the binary (digital, resp.) representation of $\log p_i$, $\log N$ shifted to the right of the point.

4   There are sufficiently many lattice vectors that are close to N

We show under a reasonable hypothesis that at least $N^{\varepsilon + o(1)}$ lattice vectors $\mathbf{z} \in L$ satisfy the inequalities (5), (6) of Lemma 2 for $\varepsilon = c - 1 - (2c - 1)\log\log N / \log p_t$. Therefore we can factorize N efficiently if $\varepsilon > 0$ and if we can efficiently generate random lattice vectors $\mathbf{z} \in L$ satisfying (5) and (6).

Our argument showing the existence of suitable lattice vectors $\mathbf{z} \in L$ is not constructive. We derive these lattice vectors from smooth integers u, v satisfying $|u - vN| = O(1)$. The existence of these smooth integers follows from the assumption that the smooth integers distribute "uniformly".

Let $\mathbb{N}_t$ denote the set of integers that factorize completely over the primes $p_1, \ldots, p_t$. For $u = \Pi_i p_i^{e_i}$, $v = \Pi_i p_i^{e_i'} \in \mathbb{N}_t$ let $f(u, v) = \sum_{i=1}^{t} (e_i - e_i') \mathbf{b}_i$. The mapping $f : \mathbb{N}_t \times \mathbb{N}_t \to L$ is inverse to g, i.e. $fgf = f$. f is not one–one since we have $f(u, v) = f(uw, vw)$ for all $w \in \mathbb{N}_t$. At most one preimage (u, v) of each $\mathbf{z} \in f(\mathbb{N}_t^2)$ can be used in step 2 of the factoring algorithm. We can always use the minimal preimage $(u, v) = g(\mathbf{z})$.

Lemma 4. *If $u, v \in \mathbb{N}_t$, $|u - vN| = o(\log p_t)$ and $v = \Theta(N^{c-1})$ then $\mathbf{z} = f(u, v)$ satisfies $\|\mathbf{z} - \mathbf{N}\|_1 \le (2c - 1)\log N + o(\log p_t)$ and $|(\mathbf{z} - \mathbf{N})_{t+1}| = o(\log p_t)$.*

Proof. Let $z = (z_1, \ldots, z_{t+1}) = \sum_{i=1}^{t} e_i b_i$. We put $\beta := (z - N)_{t+1} = z_{t+1} - N^c \log N$. We have by (4) $|\beta| N^c| \log(u/vN)| = N^c |\log(1 + \frac{u-vN}{vN})| \le N^c \frac{|u-vN|}{vN} + O(N^c((\log p_t)/vN)^2)$.

It follows from $N^{c-1} = O(v)$, $|u - vN| = o(\log p_t)$ that $|\beta| = o(\log p_t)$. From this and $v = \Theta(N^{c-1})$ we see that

$$\|z - N\|_1 \overset{(3)}{=} \log u + \log v + |\beta| \overset{(4)}{\le} \log v^2 N + |\beta|(1 + N^{-c})$$

$$\le (2c - 1) \log N + o(\log p_t).$$

$$|(z - N)_{t+1}| = |\beta| = o(\log p_t).$$

QED

We put $p_t = (\log N)^\alpha$, $\log p_t = \alpha \log \log N$. In order to estimate the number of pairs $(u, v) \in \mathbb{N}_t^2$ with $|u - vN| \le \alpha \log \log N$ we will assume the following

Hypothesis. *The fraction of pairs (u, v) in $\{(u, v) \in \mathbb{N}^2 \mid N^{c-1}/2 < v < N^{c-1}, |u - vN| \le \alpha \log \log N\}$ for which u and v are $(\log N)^\alpha$-smooth is at least $1/(\log N)^{O(1)}$-times as large as the probability that a random pair in $\{(u, v) \in \mathbb{N}^2 \mid u \le N^c, v \le N^{c-1}\}$ is $(\log N)^\alpha$-smooth in u and v.*

Theorem 5. (Norton 1971 and Canfield, Erdös, Pomerance, 1983)
Let $\varepsilon > 0$ be fixed, let r satisfy $N^{1/r} \ge (\log N)^{1+\epsilon}$. Then $\#\{x \le N \mid x$ is free of primes $> N^{1/r}\}/N = r^{-r+o(r)}$ where $\lim_{N \to \infty} o(r)/r = 0$.

Remark The proof of Theorem 5 also shows that
$\#\{x \le N \mid x$ is free of prime powers $p^e > N^{1/r}\}/N = r^{-r+o(r)}$
where $\lim_{N \to \infty} o(r)/r = 0$ provided that $N^{1/r} \ge (\log N)^{1+\epsilon}$, with $\varepsilon > 0$ fixed.

Let

$$M_{\alpha,c,N} = \left\{ (u, v) \in \mathbb{N}^2 \ \middle| \ \begin{array}{l} |u - vN| \le \alpha \log \log N \\ N^{c-1}/2 < v < N^{c-1}, \ u, v \ (\log N)^\alpha - \text{smooth} \end{array} \right\}$$

Proposition 6. *If the hypothesis holds, $c > 1$ and $\alpha > (2c-1)/(c-1)$ are fixed then we have $\#M_{\alpha,c,N} \ge N^{\varepsilon+o(1)}$ with $\varepsilon = (c-1) - (2c-1)/\alpha$ where $\lim_{N \to \infty} o(1) = 0$.*

Proof. Let $r = \log N / \alpha \log\log N$, and thus $(\log N)^\alpha = N^{1/r}$. By the hypothesis, Theorem 5 and the remark we have for sufficiently large N and $\alpha > 1$ that

$$\# M_{\alpha,c,N} \geq N^{c-1} \left[r(c-1) \right]^{-r(c-1)} cr^{-cr+o(r)} / (\log N)^{O(1)}.$$

Hence

$\log \# M_{\alpha,c,N}$

$$\geq \quad (c-1)\log N - \frac{\log N}{\alpha \log\log N} \left((c-1)\log[r(c-1)] + c\log cr \right)$$
$$+ o(r \log cr)$$

$$\overset{cr \leq \log N}{\geq} \quad [(c-1) - (2c-1)\alpha^{-1}] \log N + o(\log N)$$

$$\geq \quad (\varepsilon + o(1)) \log N \quad \text{with} \quad \varepsilon = (c-1) - (2c-1)\alpha^{-1}.$$

Hence $\# M_{\alpha,c,N} \geq N^{\varepsilon + o(1)}$. **QED**

Theorem 7. *If the hypothesis holds there are $N^{\varepsilon + o(1)}$ many vectors $z \in L$ that satisfy the inequalities (5) and (6), where $\varepsilon = (c-1) - (2c-1)/\alpha$.*

Proof. By Lemma 4 the number of vectors $z \in L$ that satisfy (5), (6) is at least $\# f(M_{\alpha,c,N})$. It will be sufficient to show for all $z \in L$ the inequality

$$\# f^{-1}(z) \cap M_{\alpha,c,N} \leq \alpha \log\log N = N^{o(1)}$$

This inequality and Proposition 6 implies the claim:

$$\# f(M_{\alpha,c,N}) \geq \# M_{\alpha,c,N} / N^{o(1)} = N^{\varepsilon + o(1)}.$$

For any $z \in f(M_{\alpha,c,N})$ there exists $(u,v) \in M_{\alpha,c,N}$ with $f(u,v) = z$ and $\gcd(u,v) = 1$. We get (u,v) from any preimage $(\overline{u},\overline{v}) \in f^{-1}(z)$ by dividing both u and v by $\gcd(u,v)$. The pair (u,v) is the "minimal" preimage of z and any preimage $(\overline{u},\overline{v}) \in f^{-1}(z)$ is of the form $(\overline{u},\overline{v}) = (uw, vw)$ with $w \in \mathbb{N}_t$. We have $w \mid (\overline{u} - \overline{v}N)$. Since $|\overline{u} - \overline{v}N| \leq \alpha \log\log N$ holds for all $(\overline{u},\overline{v}) \in M_{\alpha,c,N}$ we see that $w \leq \alpha \log\log N$. The desired upper bound on $\# f^{-1}(z) \cap M_{\alpha,c,N}$ follows from $w \leq \alpha \log\log N$. **QED**

Conclusion. We have reduced, by the algorithm in section 2, Lemma 2 and Theorem 7, the problem of factoring N to the problem of finding a random solution $(e_1, \ldots, e_t)$ of the inequalities (7), (8) (to the problem of finding random lattice vectors z satisfying (5), (6), resp.). Our reduction is polynomial time. Its correctness uses two heuristic arguments. First, we assume that $x \neq \pm y \pmod{N}$ holds with positive probability for the solution of the congruence $x^2 = y^2 \pmod{N}$ that generated by the algorithm. Second, we assume in the hypothesis that the set of smooth integers is somewhat "uniformly" distributed.

The condition $\alpha > (2c-1)/(c-1)$ in Proposition 6 can be relaxed for small N. We give some examples of parameters α, c so that $\#M_{\alpha,c,N}$ is larger than t.

A scenario for factoring $N \approx 2^{512}$

Let $c = 3$, $\alpha = 1.9$. Hence $(\log N)^\alpha = 70013$, $t \approx (\log N)^\alpha / \alpha \log\log N \approx 6276$ and $r = \log N / \alpha \log\log N \approx 31.8$.
We have

$$\log \#M_{\alpha,c,N} \approx (c-1)\log N - r(c-1)\log r(c-1) - rc\log rc$$

$$\geq 710 - 264.3 - 435.2$$

$$\geq 10.5 > \log t \approx 8.75$$

At present this seems to be a formidable task. So far we have no experience with lattice basis reduction for lattices with dimension 6300. Moreover the bit length of the input vectors is at least 1500 and a substantial part of the arithmetic has to be done with 1500 precision bits. On the other hand congruences can be constructed within only a few hours computation time in case of dimension 125.

Example solutions of the inequalities (7), (8) using a basis of 125 primes.

Using $t = 125$ primes with the largest prime $p_t = 691$ we have solved the inequalities (7), (8) ((1), (2), resp.) using variants of the LLL–algorithm. Simple LLL–reduction did not generate any solution of the inequalities (7), (8) for this N. We have reduced the lattice basis B of section 3 with 4 precision bits to the right of the point using blockwise Korkine Zolotarev reduction with block size 32. The general concept of blockwise Korkine Zolotarev reduction has been developed in SCHNORR (1987). SCHNIORR and EUCHNER (1991) give practical algorithms and evaluate their performance in solving subset sum problems. For $N = 2131438662079$, $N^c = 10^{25}$, $c \approx 2.03$ we have found the following solutions:

1. $u = 2^4 \cdot 11 \cdot 29 \cdot 37^2 \cdot 43 \cdot 61^2 \cdot 71 \cdot 79 \cdot 97 \cdot 107 \cdot 139 \cdot 167 \cdot 211$
   $v = 5^3 \cdot 7 \cdot 41^2 \cdot 53^2 \cdot 683$, $u - vN = 69$.
   The vector $z = f(u,v)$ satisfies $\|z - N\|_1 \approx 95.88 \approx (2c-1)\log N + 9.19$.

2. $u = 2^4 \cdot 11 \cdot 31^2 \cdot 37 \cdot 61 \cdot 73 \cdot 97 \cdot 107 \cdot 113 \cdot 127 \cdot 149 \cdot 163 \cdot 241 \cdot 257$
   $v = 5^2 \cdot 7^2 \cdot 43 \cdot 47 \cdot 59 \cdot 67 \cdot 83 \cdot 173 \cdot 271$, $u - vN = 29 \cdot 137$.
   The vector $z = f(u,v)$ satisfies $\|z - N\|_1 \approx 102.5 \approx (2c-1)\log N + 15.81$.

3. $u = 3^4 \cdot 5^3 \cdot 11^2 \cdot 17 \cdot 19 \cdot 61 \cdot 67 \cdot 73 \cdot 109 \cdot 193 \cdot 211 \cdot 263$
   $v = 2 \cdot 59 \cdot 101 \cdot 127 \cdot 163 \cdot 173 \cdot 353,\ u - vN = 7.$
   The vector $z = f(u, v)$ satisfies $\|z - N\|_1 \approx 91.$

4. $u = 3 \cdot 19 \cdot 47 \cdot 67 \cdot 71 \cdot 97 \cdot 113 \cdot 151 \cdot 157 \cdot 199 \cdot 239 \cdot 269 \cdot 359$
   $v = 17 \cdot 31 \cdot 107 \cdot 137 \cdot 211 \cdot 223 \cdot 373,\ u - vN = 166.$
   The vector $z = f(u, v)$ satisfies $\|z - N\|_1 \approx 99$

5. $u = 3^3 \cdot 13 \cdot 23 \cdot 31 \cdot 43 \cdot 47 \cdot 101 \cdot 103 \cdot 107 \cdot 173 \cdot 239 \cdot 251 \cdot 283 \cdot 401$
   $v = 2 \cdot 7 \cdot 17 \cdot 29 \cdot 59 \cdot 61 \cdot 89 \cdot 223 \cdot 631,\ u - vN = 139.$
   The vector z satisfies $\|z - N\|_1 \approx 97.$

Note that in our example solutions we have $\|z - N\|_1 \approx (2c-1)\log N + 2\log|u - vN|$.

5 Computing discrete logarithms

We reduce the problem of computing discrete logarithms in $\mathbb{Z}_N^*$ to the closest vector problem in an associated lattice L. The dimension of L is polynomial in $\log N$.

Let N be a prime and let $z \in \mathbb{Z}_N = \mathbb{Z}/N\mathbb{Z}$ be a primitive root of the subgroup of units $\mathbb{Z}_N^* \subset \mathbb{Z}_N$. The logarithm of $y \in \mathbb{Z}_N^*$ to base z, denoted as $\log_z(y)$, is the number $x \in \mathbb{Z}_{N-1}$ satisfying $y = z^x (\bmod N)$.

Let $p_1, \ldots, p_t$ be the t smallest prime numbers and let $p_0 = -1$. We can compute $\log_z(y)$ and $\log_z(p_i)$ for $i = 0, \ldots, t$ if we are given $m > t + 2$ general congruences of the form

$$\prod_{j=1}^{t} p_j^{a_{i,j}}\, z^{a_{i,t+1}}\, y^{a_{i,t+2}} = \prod_{j=0}^{t} p_j^{b_{i,j}} (\bmod N) \text{ for } i = 1 \ldots m \tag{9}$$

with $a_{i,j}, b_{i,j} \in \mathbb{N}$. These congruences can be written as

$$\sum_{j=0}^{t} (a_{i,j} - b_{i,j}) \log_z(p_j) + a_{i,t+1} + a_{i,t+2} \log_z(y) = 0 (\bmod N - 1)$$

This is a system of m linear equations in the $t + 2$ unknowns $\log_z(p_j)$ $j = 0, \ldots, t$, $\log_z(y)$. If we have $t + 2$ linearly independent equations then we can determine these unknowns by solving these equations modulo $N - 1$.

The congruences (9) can be obtained from vectors in the following lattice $L = L_{\alpha,c,z,y} \subset \mathbb{R}^{t+3}$ that are $\| \ \|_1$–close to the vector $\mathbf{N}$. The lattice L is generated by the column vectors $\mathbf{b}_1, \ldots, \mathbf{b}_{t+2}$ of the following $(t+3) \times (t+2)$ matrix and $\mathbf{N} \in \mathbb{R}^{t+3}$ is the following column vector.

$$
\begin{bmatrix}
\log 2 & 0 & \cdots & & 0 \\
0 & \log 3 & & & \\
& & \ddots & & \vdots \\
\vdots & \vdots & \log p_t & & \vdots \\
& & \log y & & \\
0 & 0 & & \log z & \\
N^c \log 2 & N^c \log 3 & \cdots \quad \cdots \quad \cdots & N^c \log z
\end{bmatrix}
\qquad
\mathbf{N} =
\begin{bmatrix}
0 \\
\vdots \\
\vdots \\
0 \\
N^c \log N
\end{bmatrix}
$$

We associate with a lattice vector $\mathbf{z} = (z_1, \ldots, z_{t+3}) = \sum_{i=1}^{t+2} e_i \, \mathbf{b}_i$ the integer $u = \prod p_j^{e_j}$ where j ranges over the set of indices $j \leq t+2$ with $e_j > 0$ and where $p_{t+1} = y$, $p_{t+2} = z$. If the residue $u(\bmod N)$ factorizes completely over the basis $p_0 = -1, p_1, \ldots, p_t$ this yields a congruence

$$
\prod_{e_j > 0} p_j^{e_j} = \prod_{j=0}^{t} p_j^{b_j} \ (\bmod N)
$$

as in (9).

Conclusion. Computing the discrete logarithm in $\mathbb{Z}_N^*$ via closest lattice vectors takes about the same time as factoring, via closest lattice vectors, integers having the same length as N.

References

E.R. CANFIELD, P. ERDÖS, C. POMERANCE: *On a problem of Oppenheim concerning "Factorisatio Numerorum"*. J. Number Theory 17, (1983), pp. 1 – 28.

M.J. COSTER, B.A. LMACCHIA, A.M. ODLYZKO and C.P. SCHNORR: *An Improved low–density subset sum algorithm*. Proceedings EUROCRYPT'91. Springer LNCS.

R. KANNAN: *Minkowski's convex body theorem and integer programming*. Math. Oper. Res. 12 (1987), pp. 415 – 440.

J.C. LAGARIAS, H.W. LENSTRA, JR. and C.P. SCHNORR: *Korkin–Zolotarev bases and successive minima of a lattice and its reciprocal lattice.* To appear in Combinatorica.

A.K. LENSTRA, H.W. LENSTRA, JR. AND L. LOVÁSZ: *Factoring polynomials with rational coefficients.* Math. Annalen 261, (1982), pp. 515–534.

K.K. NORTON: *Numbers with small prime factors, and the least kth power non–residue.* Memoirs of the AMS, 106 (1971) 106 pages.

C.P. SCHNORR: *A hierarchy of polynomial time lattice basis reduction algorithms.* Theoret. Comp. Sci. 53, (1987), pp. 201 – 224.

C.P. SCHNORR: *A more efficient algorithm for lattice basis reduction.* Journal of Algorithms 9, (1988), pp. 47 – 62.

C.P. SCHNORR and M. EUCHNER: *Lattice basis reduction: improved practical algorithms and solving subset sum problems.* Proceedings of FCT–symposium 1991, Altenhof near Berlin, Germany, September – To appear in Springer LNCS.

Some Considerations concerning the Selection of RSA Moduli

Klaus Huber

Deutsche Bundespost TELEKOM

Research Institute

Am Kavalleriesand 3

P.O. Box 10 00 03

6100 Darmstadt

Germany

Abstract

In this contribution two conditions are stated which safe RSA moduli $n = p \cdot q$ must fulfill. Otherwise the factors of n can be found. First we consider the cycle-lengths of the recursion $c \leftarrow c^{\varphi(n)-1} + 1 \bmod n$ which leads to a condition in terms of Fibonacci numbers. The second condition involves a property of Euler's function. We introduce a number-theoretic distance measure – the power-of-two distance (ptd) – which may be useful for evaluating the security of RSA moduli against 'number-theoretic integration'. The ptd of an RSA prime p must not be too small.

1   Introduction

The factorization of large numbers is a very old mathematical problem, which has found increasing interest since the advent of the RSA public-key cryptosystem (see [1]), whose security essentially relies on the difficulty of factoring. Nowadays – for security reasons – every user gets a different RSA modulus $n = p \cdot q$. As result thereof, a great amount of "secure" RSA moduli have to be generated. Hence there will not be enough (CPU-) time and resources to try all known factorization algorithms for a sufficiently long time on each RSA modulus n. For this reason it is of interest to have criteria telling whether a particular modulus n may be insecure (e.g. it is well known that $p - 1$ and $q - 1$ must contain at least one large prime factor). In this contribution we state two conditions which secure RSA moduli must fulfill.

2 The first Condition

We start by giving a 'small' example. The "RSA number"

$$n = 5251695219926276145833441195951527749$$

can be factored easily by assigning c the initial value 1 and then using the iteration

$$c \leftarrow c^{-1} + 1 \bmod n \qquad (1)$$

until the greatest common divisor of c and n is greater than 1. c^{-1} denotes the inverse of c modulo n. A program implementing (1) on a powerful computer rapidly (much less than a second) finds the factor $p = 8242065050061761$. Hence the second factor is $q = 637181966690123467909$.

Now neither $p - 1$ nor $q - 1$ do have only 'small' prime divisors:

$$p - 1 \;=\; 2^6 \cdot 5 \cdot 53 \cdot 107 \cdot 109 \cdot 41667737$$
$$q - 1 \;=\; 2^2 \cdot 3 \cdot 13 \cdot 67 \cdot 6096268340042429 \;,$$

and the primes dividing $p + 1$ and $q + 1$ are not all 'small' either:

$$p + 1 \;=\; 2 \cdot 3^3 \cdot 17 \cdot 577 \cdot 15560284867$$
$$q + 1 \;=\; 2 \cdot 5 \cdot 11 \cdot 59 \cdot 431 \cdot 449 \cdot 9677 \cdot 5242693 \;.$$

The reason why the program handles this number so well is that the index u_p of the smallest Fibonacci number F_{u_p} which contains p as a factor is quite small, we have $u_p = 107$ (for Fibonacci numbers see the appendix), and, clearly, for initial value 1 the recursion (1) computes the convergents F_{j+1}/F_j. Before we study the cycle-lengths of (1) for arbitrary initial value a, we state the first condition:

Condition 1 *A prime p selected as factor of an RSA modulus n must have a large index u_p, where F_{u_p} is the smallest Fibonacci number which contains p as a divisor.*

To find the cycle-lengths of (1) we use continued fractions and set

$$
\begin{aligned}
a \;&=\; 1 + \cfrac{1}{1 + \ldots \frac{1}{1+\frac{1}{a}}} \\
&=\; [1, 1, 1, \ldots, 1, a] = [b_0, b_1, b_2, \ldots, b_l, a] \;,
\end{aligned}
$$

where computations are done modulo n. Note that if we set $c^{-1} \equiv c^{\varphi(n)-1} \mod n$ the recursion (1) does make sense even if $\gcd(n, c) > 1$.

Let us first consider the recursion modulo a prime p. We set c equal to an initial value a and start the recursion

$$c \leftarrow c^{p-2} + 1 \mod p .\tag{2}$$

The question we ask is how many calls of (2) do we need until we come back to the initial value a.

The answer to this question can be obtained by considering the jth convergents $f_j = A_j/B_j$ of the continued fraction $[1, 1, \ldots, a]$. We get

$$
\begin{aligned}
A_j &= A_{j-1} + A_{j-2} , & 1 \le j \le l; & \quad \text{where } A_{-1} = A_0 = 1 \\
B_j &= B_{j-1} + B_{j-2} , & 1 \le j \le l; & \quad \text{where } B_{-1} = 0, B_0 = 1 \\
&\Rightarrow A_j = F_{j+2}, \quad B_j = F_{j+1} .
\end{aligned}
$$

$$\text{Hence} \quad a = f_{l+1} = \frac{aF_{l+2} + F_{l+1}}{aF_{l+1} + F_l} .$$

If $a \neq -F_j/F_{j+1}$ we get $(a^2 - a - 1)F_{l+1} \equiv 0 \mod p$ and the cycle-length is u_p or 1, otherwise the cycle-length equals $u_p - 1$. To summarize, the possible cycle-lengths of (2) are

$$
\begin{array}{ll}
1 & \text{for } a = \frac{1 \pm \sqrt{5}}{2} \\
u_p - 1 & \text{for } a = -\frac{F_j}{F_{j+1}} \\
u_p & \text{else}
\end{array}
\tag{3}
$$

The cycle-length 1 occurs if 5 is a quadratic residue of p, i.e. if the last digit of p is 1 or 9. From the properties of the Fibonacci numbers we find that there is only one cycle of length $u_p - 1$. The remaining $\frac{p - (5/p) - u_p}{u_p}$ cycles all have length u_p.

Example: $p = 101$, $u_{101} = 50$

a	cycle-length
1	49
4	50
23	1
79	1

Having this result for primes we infer that for RSA-moduli n the possible cycle-lengths of (1) are given by the least common multiples of the cycle-lengths of its prime-factors. Let us consider two examples:

First: $n = 77 = 7 \cdot 11$, $u_7 = 8$, $u_{11} = 10$

a	cycle-length
1	$63 = \text{lcm}(7, 9) = \text{lcm}(u_7 - 1, u_{11} - 1)$
4	$7 = \text{lcm}(7, 1) = \text{lcm}(u_7 - 1, 1)$
8	$7 = \text{lcm}(7, 1) = \text{lcm}(u_7 - 1, 1)$

Second: $n = 611 = 13 \cdot 47$, $u_{13} = 7$, $u_{47} = 16$

a	cycle-length
1	$30 = \text{lcm}(6, 15) = \text{lcm}(u_{13} - 1, u_{47} - 1)$
3	$105 = \text{lcm}(7, 15) = \text{lcm}(u_{13}, u_{47} - 1)$
4	$112 = \text{lcm}(7, 16) = \text{lcm}(u_{13}, u_{47})$
6	$48 = \text{lcm}(6, 16) = \text{lcm}(u_{13} - 1, u_{47})$
$\vdots$	$\vdots$

We now give a simple combined test for primality of p and large u_p. We use the well-known matrix description of Fibonacci numbers which follows immediately from the definition in eqn. (12):

$$\begin{pmatrix} F_{j+1} & F_j \\ F_j & F_{j-1} \end{pmatrix} = \begin{pmatrix} 1 & 1 \\ 1 & 0 \end{pmatrix}^j. \tag{4}$$

By 'square and multiply' any $F_j \bmod n$ can be computed with $O(\log n)$ operations. For a prime p we get (see appendix)

$$\begin{pmatrix} 1 & 1 \\ 1 & 0 \end{pmatrix}^{p - \left(\frac{5}{p}\right)} \equiv \begin{pmatrix} \left(\frac{5}{p}\right) & 0 \\ 0 & \left(\frac{5}{p}\right) \end{pmatrix} \bmod p. \tag{5}$$

Equation (5) can be used as primality test (for a composite number $\left(\frac{5}{n}\right)$ denotes Jacobi's symbol). There are 7 odd composite numbers smaller than 50000 which fulfill equation (5), namely $\{4181, 5777, 6721, 10877, 13201, 15251, 34561\}$. Even if a composite odd number fulfills eqn. (5) its compositeness can sometimes be established within the test, e.g. for $n = 6721$ we have $n - (5/n) = 2^6 \cdot 105$ and

$$\begin{pmatrix} 1 & 1 \\ 1 & 0 \end{pmatrix}^{2^4 \cdot 105} \equiv \begin{pmatrix} 6579 & 0 \\ 0 & 6579 \end{pmatrix} \bmod n$$

$$\Rightarrow 6579^2 \equiv (-1)^{2^4 \cdot 105} \equiv 1 \bmod n \Rightarrow \gcd(n, 6579 \pm 1) = \begin{cases} 47 \\ 143 \end{cases}.$$

As $F_p \equiv 5^{\frac{p-1}{2}} \bmod p$ we can extend eqn. (5) to give the following *primality test*:

$$\begin{pmatrix} 1 & 1 \\ 1 & 0 \end{pmatrix}^{n-(\frac{5}{n})} \stackrel{?}{\equiv} \begin{pmatrix} (\frac{5}{n}) & 0 \\ 0 & (\frac{5}{n}) \end{pmatrix} \stackrel{?}{\equiv} \begin{pmatrix} 5^{\frac{n-1}{2}} & 0 \\ 0 & 5^{\frac{n-1}{2}} \end{pmatrix} \bmod n . \qquad (6)$$

None of the seven odd composite numbers given above passes this test.

Eventually the number u_p can be found among the divisors of $p - (5/p)$. This follows from eqn. (5), for further details see e.g. ([4] or [5]).

To increase confidence in the primality of a number, we may still run e.g. Miller's test for one or two bases. Essentially, however, the combined test for primality and large u_p given above does not increase the cost of selecting an RSA-prime, if the primes are generated from the bottom up (as in [1] p.124), i.e. if the factors of $p - (5/p)$ are known.

To summarize, for an RSA number $n = p \cdot q$ we must demand that u_p and u_q are both large. Otherwise either the recursion (1) with initial value $a = 1$ or – faster –

$$\gcd(n, F_i \bmod n) \qquad i = 1, 2, 3, \ldots \qquad (7)$$

will factor n with $\min\{u_p, u_q\}$ steps. (The only case that $\gcd(n, F_{u_p})$ does not factor n is if $u_p = u_n$. Note that (7) may also be useful to extract small factors from large composite numbers.)

To get very long cycles of (1), we may demand – according to the cycle-lengths which do occur – that $\gcd(u_p, u_q)$, $\gcd(u_p - 1, u_q)$, $\gcd(u_p, u_q - 1)$, $\gcd(u_p - 1, u_q - 1)$ are small. $\gcd(u_p, u_q)$ is small if $\gcd(p - (5/p), q - (5/q))$ is small, this can be checked even if the factors of $p - (5/p)$ and $q - (5/q)$ are not known. To be sure against other ideas exploiting Fibonacci numbers (e.g. the Iteration Theorem in [5]), it is reasonable to demand that u_p and u_q contain a large prime. Finally note that safe primes of the form $p = 2p' + 1$, where p' is also prime, do ensure a very large u_p if $(5/p) = 1$, but not if $(5/p) = -1$.

3 The second Condition

In this section a number-theoretic distance function – the power-of-two distance (ptd) – is introduced. The ptd of RSA moduli should not be too small in order to give security against cryptanalytic attacks.

Euler's function $\varphi(n)$, given in equation (8), plays a central role in the RSA cryptosystem and for factoring as well.

$$\varphi(n) = |\{i \mid gcd(i, n) = 1, 1 \le i \le n\}| \qquad (8)$$

$$\varphi(n) \;=\; n \cdot \prod_{p|n} \frac{p-1}{p} \qquad \text{where } p \text{ means prime.} \tag{9}$$

Now let us define the iterated function $\varphi^{\{j\}}(n)$:

$$\varphi^{\{j\}}(n) = \varphi(\varphi^{\{j-1\}}(n)) \qquad j = 1, 2, \ldots \tag{10}$$

where $\varphi^{\{0\}}(n) = n$. By applying Euler's function φ repeatedly, we will in most cases arrive quite rapidly at a power of two. This follows immediately from eqn. (9), as in each step every prime factor is reduced by one and thus contributes at least one factor of two. For illustration consider the following example:

$$
\begin{aligned}
n &= 98765432109876543210 \\
n = \varphi^{\{0\}}(n) &= 2 \cdot 3^2 \cdot 5 \cdot 17^2 \cdot 101 \cdot 3541 \cdot 27961 \cdot 379721 \\
\varphi^{\{1\}}(n) &= 2^{17} \cdot 3^3 \cdot 5^5 \cdot 11 \cdot 17 \cdot 59 \cdot 233 \cdot 863 \\
\varphi^{\{2\}}(n) &= 2^{29} \cdot 3^2 \cdot 5^5 \cdot 29^2 \cdot 431 \\
\varphi^{\{3\}}(n) &= 2^{34} \cdot 3 \cdot 5^5 \cdot 7 \cdot 29 \cdot 43 \\
\varphi^{\{4\}}(n) &= 2^{40} \cdot 3^2 \cdot 5^4 \cdot 7^2 \\
\varphi^{\{5\}}(n) &= 2^{43} \cdot 3^2 \cdot 5^3 \cdot 7 \\
\varphi^{\{6\}}(n) &= 2^{46} \cdot 3^2 \cdot 5^2 \\
\varphi^{\{7\}}(n) &= 2^{48} \cdot 3 \cdot 5 \\
\varphi^{\{8\}}(n) &= 2^{50} = 1125899906842624
\end{aligned}
$$

In a way Euler's function behaves like a 'number-theoretic derivative' – it makes big primes small. Therefore the function $\varphi^{\{j\}}(n)$ is refered to as j–th (number-theoretic) derivative. For most numbers repeated application of Euler's function leads quite rapidly to a power of two. This simple observation leads to the following definition of the power-of-two distance:

Definition 1 *The power-of-two-distance (ptd) of a number $n > 1$ is defined by*

$$ptd(n) := \min\{j \mid \varphi^{\{j\}}(n) = 2^i, i = 1, 2, \ldots\} \;.$$

For example $ptd(2^{16}) = 0$, $ptd(2^{16} + 1) = 1$, $ptd(3977) = 2$. From the fact that almost all numbers around n have about $\ln\ln n$ prime divisors (see [3]), we obtain the following crude approximation for the average value of ptd for a randomly chosen number n:

$$E\{ptd(n)\} \approx \frac{\log_2 n}{\ln\ln n} \;.$$

Our second condition is now:

Condition 2 *A prime p selected as factor of an RSA modulus n must have a sufficiently big value of ptd(p).*

Clearly, we have

$$\max\{\mathrm{ptd}(a), \mathrm{ptd}(b)\} \leq \mathrm{ptd}(a \cdot b) \leq \mathrm{ptd}(a) + \mathrm{ptd}(b) \ .$$

The left half of the above inequality may be useful to bound the ptd if a number can be factored only partially.

In analogy to 'number-theoretic differentiation' we can refer to 'number-theoretic integration' of a number r as finding a number which belongs to the set Ψ_r, which is defined by

$$\Psi_r := \{i \mid \varphi(i) = r\} \ . \tag{11}$$

We refer to finding the whole set Ψ_r as complete integration of r. For example integrating $r = 100$ completely gives $\Psi_{100} = \{101, 125, 202, 250\}$.

If the factors of r are known, integration of r is an easy task. It can be done in a systematic way from the representations $r = \prod \varphi(p_i) \cdot p_i^{f_{p_i}}$. For integration note, that all odd numbers ≥ 3 are non-integrable, and if an odd number t belongs to Ψ_r then $2t$ is also in Ψ_r. Also the density of non-integrable even numbers increases the larger the numbers get. If the ptd(p) is too 'small', the factors of $n = p \cdot q$ can be found by repeated integration, starting from a power of 2 close to $\sqrt{n}$.

Since the set $\Psi_{\varphi(q)}$ of a safe prime q contains only one even number – thus reducing its effective ptd – we should measure the ptd of primes which lead to long chains of safe primes by the ptd of the smallest prime in the chain (e.g. 2879, 1439, 719, 359, 179, 89 is a chain of length 5, hence it is ptd$(89) = 3$ which measures the security of $p = 2879$).

4 Appendix: Fibonacci numbers

To make this paper self-contained we recall the most important properties of Fibonacci numbers (see e.g. [2] pp.78-86, or [3] p.150). Fibonacci numbers are defined by the recursion

$$F_{j+2} = F_{j+1} + F_j \qquad j = 2, 3, \ldots \tag{12}$$

with initial values $F_0 = 0$ and $F_1 = 1$. From the roots of the characteristic equation $x^2 - x - 1 = 0$ we get the n-th Fibonacci number as $F_n = ((\frac{1+\sqrt{5}}{2})^n - (\frac{1-\sqrt{5}}{2})^n)/\sqrt{5}$.

This leads to $2^{n-1} F_n = n + \binom{n}{3} 5 + \binom{n}{5} 5^2 + \ldots + \begin{cases} 5^{\frac{n-1}{2}} & n \text{ odd} \\ n 5^{\frac{n}{2}-1} & n \text{ even} \end{cases}$. $\tag{13}$

Thus for a prime p from the above equation and Euler's criterion we get

$$F_p \equiv 5^{\frac{p-1}{2}} \equiv (5/p) \bmod p \, , \tag{14}$$

where $(5/p)$ denotes Legendre's symbol. Using Gauß's law of quadratic reciprocity we find

$$\left(\frac{5}{p}\right) = \left(\frac{p}{5}\right) = \begin{cases} 1 & \text{for } p \equiv 1 \text{ or } 4 \bmod 5 \\ -1 & \text{for } p \equiv 2 \text{ or } 3 \bmod 5 \end{cases} \, .$$

It is easily seen (e.g. from the determinant of the matrices of eqn. (4)) that $F_{n+1}F_{n-1} - F_n^2 = (-1)^n$ holds. Hence $F_{p+1}F_{p-1} \equiv 0 \bmod p$. It can be shown that either F_{p-1} or F_{p+1} contains p as divisor. More precisely, using (13) we find

$$F_{p-1} \equiv 0 \bmod p \quad \text{for } p \equiv 1, 4 \bmod 5$$
$$F_{p+1} \equiv 0 \bmod p \quad \text{for } p \equiv 2, 3 \bmod 5 \, .$$

By induction one can show that $F_{n+m} = F_m F_{n+1} + F_{m-1} F_n$, and an important divisibility property of Fibonacci numbers follows, namely F_a divides $F_{a \cdot b}$ where a, b are integers. Thus $F_{u_p} \equiv 0 \bmod p \Rightarrow F_{k \cdot u_p + 2} \equiv F_{k \cdot u_p + 1} \bmod p$.

References

[1] R.L.Rivest, A.Shamir, L.Adleman: "A Method for Obtaining Digital Signatures and Public Key Cryptosystems", Communications of the ACM, Vol.21 Nr.2, pp.120-126, Feb.1978.

[2] D.E.Knuth: "The Art of Computer Programming" Vol.1, Fundamental Algorithms, Reading, MA:Addison-Wesley, 1968.

[3] G.H.Hardy, E.M.Wright: "An Introduction to the Theory of Numbers", Oxford University Press: Oxford, Fifth edition 1979.

[4] K.Barner: "Zur Fibonacci-Folge modulo p", Monatshefte für Mathematik. Bd.69/2, pp.97-104, 1965.

[5] J.D.Fulton, W.L.Morris: "On Arithmetical functions related to the Fibonacci numbers", Acta Arithmetica, XVI, pp.105-110, 1969.

On the Use of Interconnection Networks in Cryptography

Michael Portz
RWTH Aachen
Lehrstuhl für angewandte Mathematik insb. Informatik
Ahornstr. 55
D-5100 Aachen
michaelp@terpsichore.informatik.rwth-aachen.de

Cryptosystems can be viewed as sets of permutations from which one permutation is chosen as cryptofunction by specifying a key. Interconnection networks have been widely studied in the field of parallel processing. They have one property that makes them very interesting for cryptology, i.e. they give the opportunity to access and perform permutations at the same time. This paper presents two examples of how cryptology can benefit from the use of interconnection networks. One is a new construction of a pseudo-random permutation (generator) from one single pseudo-random function (generator). The search for such constructions has been of major interest since Luby and Rackoff gave the first construction in 1986. The second example presents a cryptosystem based on interconnection networks and a certain class of boolean functions. Some arguments for its security are given. Although there is a relation between the two examples they complement each other in using different properties of interconnection networks. This can be regarded as an argument that exploiting the full potential of interconnection networks can establish completely new techniques in cryptology.

1 Introduction

Interconnection netwo ks have been widely studied in the field of parallel processing. They have one property that makes them very interesting for cryptology, i.e. they give the opportunity to specify and perform permutations at the same time. This paper introduces a new class of cryptosystems which is constructed using boolean functions and interconnection networks. The construction is secure in the sense that it can be used to construct pseudo-random permutation generators from pseudo-random Boolean function generators ([$LuRa$86], [GGM86], [$Schn$88], [$Piep$90], [$Piep$91]). It is proposed, to use simpler functions instead of pseudo-random functions to construct cryptosystems, e.g. theoretical pseudo-random number generators (as proposed by $[Yao81],[BBS]$,etc), practical pseudo-random number generators (linear shift register etc.) or oneway functions $[Yao81]$. The security of a specific cryptosystem based on boolean functions fulfilling the strict avalanche criterion $[Lloy89]$ is investigated.

Chapter 2 gives a short introduction to the theory of interconnection networks. In chapter 3 a new construction of pseudo-random permutation generators from pseudo-random function generators is described. In chapter 4 a new one-key cryptosystem based on interconnection networks and boolean functions fulfilling the strict avalanche criterion $[Lloy89]$ is presented. Some arguments for its security are given. An outlook on further research is given in chapter 5. The rest of this introduction is used to give a short review of known results. 1.1 contains the results concerning pseudo-randomness and 1.2 the results concerning boolean functions as mentioned above.

1.1 Pseudo-randomness and Permutation Generators

During the last years a lot of work has been spend on the construction of permutation generators. One reason for this is, that most cryptosystems (e.g. RSA, DES) are nothing more than generators of permutations. Specifying a certain key in such a cryptosystem means specifying (or **generating**) a certain permutation on a very large ordered set. On the other hand there has been a cryptographical interest in pseudo-randomness for a long time, too, dealing mostly with the (pseudo)randomness of numbers or bitstrings. In $[GGM86]$ the notion of pseudo-randomness is extended to functions and a construction of pseudo-random functions from pseudo-random bitstrings is described. Luby and Rackoff were the first to look at the special case of pseudo-random **bijective** functions $[LuRa86][LuRa88]$. They proved, that such pseudo-random permutations (which bijective functions can be identified with) can be constructed from pseudo-random functions.

The construction given by Luby and Rackoff has the same iterative structure as the DES (Fig. 1). Three (instead of 16) of these iterations are performed and in each iteration a different pseudo-random function is used (Fig. 2). Naturally the question arises, whether the number of functions used can be reduced $[Schn88]$. Zheng, Matsumoto and Imai $[ZMI89]$ give a positive answer to that question and proved that two functions are the minimum if three iterations are performed (Fig. 3). Pieprzyk $[Piep90]$ was able to perform a construction based on one pseudo-random function and four iterations (Fig. 4).

In this paper only a short review of some of the basic definitions is given. Let throughout the definitions n and k represent any positive integers. With $I = \{0, 1\}$ let F_n and $\mathcal{F}$ be defined as:

$$F_n = \{f \mid f : I^n \to I^n\} \qquad \mathcal{F} = \bigcup_{n>0} F_n$$

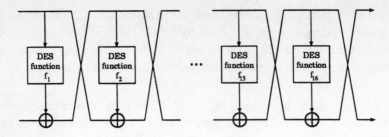

Fig. 1: Iterationstructure of DES

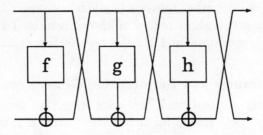

Fig. 2: Lubys and Rackoffs Construction

Definition: A **function generator** with key length function $klf(n)$ (klf a polynomial) is a collection $\mathcal{H} = \bigcup_{n>0} H_n$, $H_n = \{h_{n,k} \mid \log k \leq klf(n)\}$, where each $h_{n,k}$ is a function from F_n. It is required that, given a key k of length $klf(n)$, and an input α of length n, $h_{n,k}(\alpha)$ can be computed in time polynomial in n.

The following definition defines function generators mapping to I instead of mapping to I^n. B_n and $\mathcal{B}$ be defined as:

$$B_n = \{f \mid f : I^n \to I^n\} \qquad \mathcal{B} = \bigcup_{n>0} B_n$$

Definition: A **Boolean function generator** with key length function $klf(n)$ (klf a polynomial) is a collection $\mathcal{H} = \bigcup_{n>0} H_n$, $H_n = \{h_{n,k} \mid \log k \leq klf(n)\}$, where each $h_{n,k}$ is a function from B_n. It is required that, given a key k of length $klf(n)$, and an input α of length n, $h_{n,k}(\alpha)$ can be computed in time polynomial in n.

Definition: A **permutation generator** $\mathcal{H}$ is a function generator such that each function $h_{n,k}$ is bijective. Let $\overline{\mathcal{H}} = \bigcup_{n>0} \overline{H_n}$ where $\overline{H_n} = \{h_{n,k}^{-1}\}$. We say $\mathcal{H}$ is invertible if $\overline{\mathcal{H}}$ is also a permutation generator. In this case, $\overline{\mathcal{H}}$ is the inverse permutation generator for $\mathcal{H}$.

Luby and Rackoff give a formal definition of pseudo-randomness which is based on a definition of "undistinguishability". Informally a function generator is called

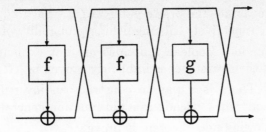

Fig. 3: Ohnishis Construction

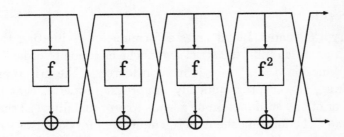

Fig. 4: Pieprzyks Construction

pseudo-random if for large n no function $h_{n,k}$ can for randomly generated k be distinguished from a really random function.

Definition: A (Boolean) function generator $\mathcal{H}$ is **pseudo-random** if there is no distinguishing circuit family for $\mathcal{H}$. A distinguishing circuit family for $\mathcal{H}$ is an oracle circuit family $\{C_{n_1}, C_{n_2}, \ldots\}$ where $n_1 < n_2 < \ldots$, such that for some polynomial Q_1 and for each n for which there is a circuit C_n the $\{H_n, F_n\}$ (or $\{H_n, B_n\}$ respectively) distinguishing probability of C_n is at least $\frac{1}{Q_1(n)}$.

An oracle circuit family is an infinite family of circuits $\{C_{n_1}, C_{n_2}, \ldots\}$ such that for some polynomial Q_2 and for each n for which there is a circuit C_n:

1. C_n is a circuit which contains the usual boolean gates together with oracle gates, where each oracle gate has n inputs and n outputs. C_n has one boolean output, where the value of the output depends on the way the oracle gates are evaluated. Such a circuit is called an oracle circuit.

2. The size of C_n is less than or equal to $Q_2(n)$ (size defined as number of inter-gate connections)

The $\{H_n, F_n\}$ ($\{H_n, B_n\}$ respectively) distinguishing probability of C_n is defined as follows. Let x_n be the output value of C_n. Let $r_n = P[x_n = 1]$ when a function is randomly chosen from F_n and this function is used to evaluate the oracle gates in C_n. Let $p_n = P[x_n = 1]$ when a key k of length $klf(n)$ is randomly chosen and $h_{n,k}$ is used to evaluate the oracle gates in C_n. Then $d_n = |p_n - r_n|$ is the $\{H_n, F_n\}$ ($\{H_n, B_n\}$ respectively) distinguishing probability of C_n.

Note, that pseudo-random Boolean functions are not explicitly defined in the previous papers, but their existence is implicitly proven in [GGM86].

Theorem:[LuRa88] There is a way to construct an invertible pseudo-random permutation generator from a pseudo-random function generator.

In this paper the following new theorem is proven:

New Theorem: There is a way to construct an invertible pseudo-random permutation generator from a pseudo-random Boolean function generator.

1.2 Lloyds result

In her Eurocrypt'89 paper Lloyd gives a formula for estimating the number of boolean functions which fulfil the strict avalanche criterion of order $(m - 2)$. Here only boolean function $f : I^m \rightarrow I$ are considered. The criterion guarantees, roughly speaking, the cryptographically important property, that changing one input-bit of f or of any subfunction of f leads to a probability $1/2$ that the output bit changes, too. The formula she uses to count the functions can as well be used to choose one of these functions randomly. The formula for an n-bit function f (given here for $0 - 1$-values, Lloyd gives it for the function $\hat{f}(x) := (-1)^{f(x)}$) is as follows:

(Let h be the Hamming weight function (number of 1's in the bitstring representation of its argument), e_i be the i-th unity vector, e_0 be the zero vector and $x \in I^m$.)

$$f(x) = \frac{h(x)(h(x) - 1)}{2} + f(e_0)(h(x) + 1) + \sum_{e_i \oplus x > 0; i \in [1:m]} f(e_i)$$

Obviously the function f is completely defined by its values on $\{e_0, \ldots, e_m\}$ and so it is very easy definable and accessible. On the other hand f can be completely reconstructed from knowing only $m + 1$ of its function values. This can be done by solving a system of linear equations, taking the values $\{f(e_0), f(e_1), \ldots, f(e_m)\}$ as variables.

2 Interconnection Networks

Interconnection networks are commonly dealt with in the context of concurrent processing. They are used to connect a set of input elements (usually processors or memory locations) with a set of output elements (usually processors or memory locations, too). Research on interconnection networks deals in most cases with finding routing algorithms (i.e. how can a given set of connections be realized by a given interconnection network) or finding new topologies which are both efficient and capable of realizing given sets of connections. In our context a different property of interconnection networks is used: they are a very easy way to specify and perform permutations at the same time. The following terminology is according to [Feng81].

2.1 Control strategy

An interconnection network is build up from **switching elements** (sometimes called β-elements). A switching element takes two inputs and produces two outputs. Whether the inputs should be exchanged in the specific switching element or not is determined by a control-setting function h. This function maps the unique index of any switching element of the interconnection network onto the set $I = \{0,1\}$ ($0 \hat{=}$ don't exchange,$1 \hat{=}$ exchange).

2.2 Topology

The topology of an interconnection network specifies how the switching elements are connected to each other. Any topology describes a set of permutations. Choosing the control-setting function h means choosing a specific permutation from this set. This is an interesting property which interconnection networks and cryptosystems have in common. Even more interesting in this context are to-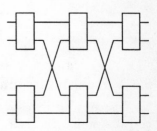
pologies which are capable of generating all permutations on the input-set. Such networks were introduced by Benes [Bene65]. Waksman gives a topology which uses asymptotically the minimal number of switching elements [Waks68]. Here the Benes-topology is used, because of its slightly simpler design. At the right-hand side a Benes-network for 4 input-elements is shown. Figure 5 shows one for 8 elements. The recursive structure of these networks can easily be seen, so its not stated formally: a Benes-network N_n with 2^n input-elements is build from two Benes-networks N_{n-1} and 2^n additional switching elements.

This subsection is completed by an example. Let $h : I^m \to I$ be a boolean function. Note that in the case of an Benes-network N_n m must at least have the value $\lceil \log(2^{n-1}(2n - 1)) \rceil$. In the following example $n = 3$ and $m = 5$. Then $N(h)$ denotes the permutation which results from using h as the control-setting function in a Benes-network of appropriate size. Let further $N(\mathcal{H})$ denote the resulting set of permutations, if $\mathcal{H}$ is a set of boolean functions. Figure 5 shows an example of an interconnection network with Benes-topology and control-setting function $h : I^5 \to I$ and resulting permutation $N(h)$.

x	0	1	2	3	4	5	6	7	8	9	10	11	12	13	14	15	16	17	18	19	20	...	31
h(x)	1	0	0	0	1	1	0	0	0	1	1	1	0	0	1	0	1	0	0	1	x	...	x

$$N(h) = (0, 5, 3, 6, 4, 2, 1, 7)$$

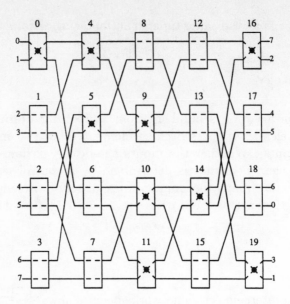

Fig.5: Activated Benes-Network with 8 Inputs

2.3 Virtual Interconnection Networks

To be ready to investigate the use of interconnection networks in the design of cryptosystems one has to overcome one last difficulty: If one chooses the input size of an interconnection network according to the security constraints normally put on cryptosystems, one cannot establish the interconnection network physically any more. Cryptosystems like DES and RSA usually describe sets of permutations on 2^{64} elements or $\sim 2^{512}$ elements respectively. A solution to this is dealing with a virtual interconnection network, which could be derived from the topology.

A virtual interconnection network only realizes those parts of an interconnection network, which are absolutely necessary to compute a certain output. This is done by additionally defining the next-index-function ni. This function computes the index of the next switching element out of the index of the present switching element and its relative output position.

3 The New Construction

The new construction can be described very short: Let $\mathcal{H}$ be a pseudo-random Boolean function generator. Then $N(\mathcal{H})$ should be the constructed permutation generator.

Theorem: If $\mathcal{H}$ is a generator for pseudo-random Boolean functions, then $N(\mathcal{H})$ is an invertible pseudo-random permutation generator.

This theorem is proven as corollary to the following lemma, where $\mathcal{S} = \bigcup_{n>0} S_{2^n}$, S_k denoting the set of all permutations of k elements.

Lemma 1: There is no distinguishing circuit family for $N(\mathcal{B})$ and $\mathcal{S}$.

The proof of the theorem shows that if lemma 1 holds and if there were a distinguishing circuit family for $N(\mathcal{H})$ and $\mathcal{S}$ there would be a distinguishing circuit family for $\mathcal{H}$ and $\mathcal{B}$ as well, contradicting the assumption that there is none.

3.1 Proof of the Lemma 1

The idea of the proof is to prove that the output-distribution of any polynomial-sized sample of $N(f)$ is approximately the same as the output-distribution of any polynomial-sized sample of $\pi \in S_{2^n}$, namely the Laplace-distribution. The following remarks give an impression of the proof technique.

Remark 1: Each single input-value to a Benes-network is uniformly distributed onto the outputs by $N(f)$, if f is a uniformly distributed random variable mapping to B_n for some n.

Remark 2: The decision, whether an input-value is mapped to the upper half or to the lower half of the output-set $[0 : 2^n - 1]$ is made in the middle (the n-th) column (Fig. 6). A similiar statement holds for all further "halfs": the decision, whether an input-value is mapped to the upper half or the lower half of the half which has been chosen in column n is made in column $n+1$. The decision, whether an input-value is mapped to the upper half or the lower half of the quarter (half of half) which was specified in columns n and $n + 1$ is made in column $n + 2$, and so on. From this remark it follows immediately, that if two values decide for different output-intervals, they cannot collide anywhere behind the column, where they made their decision.

One special case, which is of interest for the rest of the proof, is the situation in column $\frac{n}{2} + n - 1$: in this column the decision is made, into which intervall of size $2^{\frac{n}{2}}$ each output is mapped.

Remark 3: No matter what $k \leq 2^{\frac{n}{2}}$ sample points one chooses, the probability that not two of them will enter the same internal box in column $2^{\frac{n}{2}}$ is bigger than $\frac{(2^{\frac{n}{2}})^k}{(2^{\frac{n}{2}})^k}$. (An **internal box** is any of the sub-Benes-networks $N_{k<n}$ of a Benes-network N_n(see section 2.2))

From these three remarks it follows, that for large n (virtually with probability 1):
  - each input-value chooses a different internal box of a certain size (remark 3).
  - thus the input-values are mapped uniformly distributed onto the outputs of these internal boxes (remark 1).
  - they are mapped uniformly distributed onto the output-intervals of size $2^{\frac{n}{2}}$ (remark 2).
  - there will be no collision in the columns starting from $\frac{n}{2}$ up to $2n - 1$, which is the last one (remark 3 and remark 2).

These remarks and their conclusions roughly describe the proof. They show that it is simply not possible to choose input-values, so that one can learn anything on

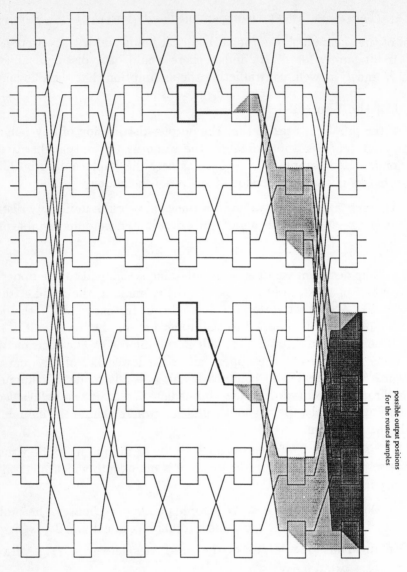

possible output positions
for the routed samples

In ▯ the decision is made wether the value is mapped to the upper or to the lower half

Fig. 6: Illustration of remark 2, N_4

the resulting outputs of the permutation. The reason for that is, that as long as one is restricted to polynomially many (in n) input-values, the input-values are routed independently through the main part of the network.

Preliminaries: Let throughout the rest of this section denote $B_m = \{f : I^m \to I\}$ and $\mathcal{B} = \bigcup_m B_m$. To emphasize the fact, that m depends on n as described in subsection 2.3, m is replaced by $l(n)$ as follows: For real numbers r let from now on I^r denote the set $[0 : \lfloor 2^r \rfloor - 1]$. If $r \in N$ nothing changes; if $r = \log x \notin N$ although one cannot deal anymore with bitstrings, one has at least a set which contains the right number of elements. Now we are able to replace m by $l(n) = \log(2^{n-1}(2n-1))$.

First of all one has to define an appropriate probability space. Here the space must describe the following event. For a certain n
- with probability $\frac{1}{2}$ one set out of $\{B_{l(n)}, S_{2^n}\}$ is chosen.
- from the chosen set one element is drawn uniformly distributed.

To describe this experiment it turns out to be best to choose

$$\Omega_{n,1} = B_{l(n)}$$
$$\Omega_{n,2} = S_{2^n}$$
$$P_{n,i} = \mathcal{L}(\Omega_{n,i}) \quad , i \in \{1,2\}$$
$$\Omega_n = \Omega_{n,1} \cup \Omega_{n,2}$$
$$P_n(A) = \frac{P_{n,1}(A \cap \Omega_{n,1}) + P_{n,2}(A \cap \Omega_{n,2})}{2} \quad , A \subset \Omega_n$$

with $\mathcal{L}$ being the Laplace-distribution. Further some notations have to be given, to be able to describe certain events in this probability space.

Notations: The probability, that a random function mapping to a set of 2^l different elements does not map any two of k randomly picked arguments onto the same value, is described by:

$$G_{l,k} = \frac{(2^l)^{\underline{k}}}{(2^l)^k}$$

where $(x)^{\underline{k}}$ denotes the Pochhammer-symbol which is defined as:

$$(x)^{\underline{k}} = x \cdot (x-1) \cdot \ldots \cdot (x-k+1)$$

The notation π_ω describes the permutation which results from ω. Formally:

$$\pi_\omega = \begin{cases} N(\omega) & \omega \in \Omega_{n,1}(= B_{l(n)}) \\ \omega & \omega \in \Omega_{n,2}(= S_{2^n}) \end{cases}$$

Additionally, if ω is a control-setting function (i.e. drawn from $\Omega_{n,1}$), π_{ω_l} denotes the permutation one gets, if one cuts the Benes-network vertically at the inputs of the $\frac{n}{2} + 1$-th column. Thus ω_l is the subfunction of the control-setting function ω which suffices to compute the settings of the switching elements in the first $\frac{n}{2}$ columns.

Definition: The (partial) output $\begin{bmatrix} o_1 \\ \vdots \\ o_k \end{bmatrix}$ of a permutation is said to fulfil the **least distance condition** (LDC), if not two of the $\{o_1, \ldots, o_k\}$ are in the same output interval of size $2^{\frac{n}{2}}$.

The following random variables and subsets of Ω_n are defined:

$$X_n^{\begin{bmatrix} i_1 \\ \vdots \\ i_k \end{bmatrix}}(\omega) = \begin{bmatrix} o_1 \\ \vdots \\ o_k \end{bmatrix} \quad \text{with:} \quad o_j = \pi_\omega(i_j), 0 \le i_1 < i_2 < \ldots < i_k < 2^n$$

$$L1_n^{\begin{bmatrix} i_1 \\ \vdots \\ i_k \end{bmatrix}} = \{\omega \mid \pi_{\omega_l}(\begin{bmatrix} i_1 \\ \vdots \\ i_k \end{bmatrix}) \quad \text{fulfils the LDC}\}$$

$$L2_n^{\begin{bmatrix} i_1 \\ \vdots \\ i_k \end{bmatrix}} = \{\omega \mid \pi_\omega(\begin{bmatrix} i_1 \\ \vdots \\ i_k \end{bmatrix}) \quad \text{fulfils the LDC}\}$$

The set $L1_n^{\begin{bmatrix} i_1 \\ \vdots \\ i_k \end{bmatrix}}$ describes those control-setting functions, which map each input $i_j, j \in [1:k]$ into a different internal box of size $2^{\frac{n}{2}} (= \text{sub-Benes-Network } N_{2^{\frac{n}{2}}})$,
whereas $L2_n^{\begin{bmatrix} i_1 \\ \vdots \\ i_k \end{bmatrix}}$ contains those ω, which spread the inputs good enough regarding the output intervals of size $2^{\frac{n}{2}}$. With these notations and definitions it is now possible to formulate the necessary lemmata.

Lemma 2: Let Q and q be any polynomials. There is no probabilistic algorithm which is restricted to at most $k < q(n)$ queries to an oracle realizing a permutation π_ω, ω chosen according to P_n from Ω_n, which can choose inputs $\begin{bmatrix} i_1 \\ \vdots \\ i_k \end{bmatrix}$ so that for more than finite many n:

1
$$P(\omega \notin L2_n^{\begin{bmatrix} i_1 \\ \vdots \\ i_k \end{bmatrix}} \mid \omega \in \Omega_{n,2}) \ge \frac{1}{Q(n)} \quad \text{and further:}$$

2
$$P(\omega \notin L2_n^{\begin{bmatrix} i_1 \\ \vdots \\ i_k \end{bmatrix}} \cap L1_n^{\begin{bmatrix} i_1 \\ \vdots \\ i_k \end{bmatrix}} \mid \omega \in \Omega_{n,1}) \ge \frac{1}{Q(n)}$$

Lemma 3: For all $\begin{bmatrix} i_1 \\ \vdots \\ i_k \end{bmatrix}$ and $\begin{bmatrix} o_1 \\ \vdots \\ o_k \end{bmatrix}$ the following holds:

$$P(X_n^{\begin{bmatrix} i_1 \\ \vdots \\ i_k \end{bmatrix}} = \begin{bmatrix} o_1 \\ \vdots \\ o_k \end{bmatrix} \mid L2_n^{\begin{bmatrix} i_1 \\ \vdots \\ i_k \end{bmatrix}}, L1_n^{\begin{bmatrix} i_1 \\ \vdots \\ i_k \end{bmatrix}}, \Omega_{n,1}) = P(X_n^{\begin{bmatrix} i_1 \\ \vdots \\ i_k \end{bmatrix}} = \begin{bmatrix} o_1 \\ \vdots \\ o_k \end{bmatrix} \mid L2_n^{\begin{bmatrix} i_1 \\ \vdots \\ i_k \end{bmatrix}}, \Omega_{n,2})$$

The proofs of lemma 2, lemma 3 and lemma 1 (the latter one being a corollary to the former two) can be found in [$Port91$].

3.2 Proof of the Theorem

The proof of the theorem now can make use of lemma 1. Let again be $\mathcal{H}$ be a pseudo-random Boolean function generator, $\mathcal{B}$ be the set of all Boolean functions and S be the set of all permutations. It shows, that if there is no distinguishing circuit for S and $N(\mathcal{B})$ (i.e. lemma 1 holds) and if there were a distinguishing circuit family for S and $N(\mathcal{H})$ there were a distinguishing circuit family for $\mathcal{H}$ and $\mathcal{B}$ as well. Note that the invertibility is trivially achieved using this construction. The full version of this proof like all the other proofs can be found in [Port91].

4 Other Control-setting Functions

In this context naturally one question arises: how simple can the functions be which are used as control-setting functions without making the resulting cryptosystem crytpographically insecure. One proposal which is made here is to use "simple" boolean functions mapping I^m to I which fulfil the strict avalanche criterion of order $m-2$. This properties guarantees a "statistical perfectness", in that changing one input bit means that the output bit changes exactly with probability $\frac{1}{2}$. S.Lloyd gives an enumeration, which shows, that there are 2^{m+1} such functions [Lloy89]. Each of these functions can be expressed as

$$f(x) = \frac{h(x)(h(x)-1)}{2} + f(e_0)(h(x)+1) + \sum_{e_i \oplus x > 0; i \in [1:m]} f(e_i)$$

for an appropriate choice of $f(e_j), j \in [0:m]$, e_0 being the zero-vector and $e_j, j > 0$ being the j-th unity vector in I^m. h denotes the Hamming-weight function, which computes the number of 1's in the binary representation of its argument.

These functions are easy in that each function is easily accessible and each function value is computable fast. Only $m+1$ bits (namely $f(e_j), j \in [0:m]$) are needed to define such a function. All operations which are involved in computing any function value are done modulo 2. The most complex computation is the one of $h(x)$, which is nevertheless fast.

One has to be careful, if one wants to use such simple functions. Only $m+1$ function values $x_0, \ldots, x_m$ are needed to reconstruct the whole function. This can be done by solving the following set of linear equations ($j \in \{0, \ldots, m\}$):

$$f(e_0)(h(x_j)+1) + \sum_{e_i \oplus x_j > 0; i \in [1:m]} f(e_i) = f(x_j) - \frac{h(x_j)(h(x_j)-1)}{2}$$

The main argument for the security of such a system is, that interconnection networks prevent the cryptanalyst from completely determining any value $f(x_j)$ of the control-setting function. So he will never be absolutely sure, which set of linear equations he has to solve.

Up to now it is not known, whether there is a less expensive way of choosing the correct set of equations than doing an exhaustive search, assuming a chosen plaintext attack. The system is breakable, if one assumes a combined chosen plaintext/chosen ciphertext attack, but this kind of attack does not seem to be very realistic. Even this attack can be prevented, if one uses additional design criteria on the network [*BHP*91].

5 Future Research

In section 1 it has already been pointed out, that cryptosystems and interconnection networks are related in that both are able to generate permutations. The main question for future research is, what classes of "cryptograpically interesting" boolean functions define secure cryptosystems, if one uses them as control-setting functions for a Benes-network.

A related question is, whether it is possible to construct pseudo-random permutation generators immediately from pseudo-random number generators or even from oneway-functions? A positive answer to this question would allow more efficient cryptosystems to be built which are "provable secure". The author conjectures that both constructions are possible if one uses interconnection networks.

Finally it must be pointed out, that Benes-networks are only one possible network topology, and that there are numerous other topologies with different properties, which possibly are useful for the construction of cryptosystems, too [*BHP*91].

6 Conclusion

The notion of interconnection networks has been viewed from the cryptographic point of view. It has been shown, how to construct a set of permutations out of a set of Boolean functions. The appropriateness of two classes of Boolean functions as control-setting functions has been investigated: Pseudo-random Boolean functions as control-setting functions result in pseudo-random permutations and Boolean functions fulfilling the strict avalanche criterion of higher order result in fast computable permutation generators, which possibly turns out to be a good cryptosystem. Finally it has been proposed to use different network topologies and different Boolean functions to define cryptosytems.

7 Acknowledgements

Many thanks to René Peralta, who encouraged me to do this work.

8 Literature

[*BBS*] L.Blum, M.Blum, M.Shub: "A simple unpredictable pseudo-random number generator", SIAM Journal on Computing, Vol. 15, 1986, pp. 364-383

[*Bene*65] V.E.Benes: "Mathematical theory of connecting networks and telephone traffic", Academic Press, New York, 1965

[*BHP*91] T.Beth, P.Horster, M.Portz: "Verbindungsnetzwerke in der Kryptologie"; to appear as report of the European Institute for System Security (E.I.S.S.)

[*Feng*81] Tse-yun Feng: "A survey of interconnection networks"; Computer: IE^3; Dec 1981, pp. 12-27

[*GGM*86] O.Goldreich, S.Goldwasser, S.Micali: "How to construct random functions"; Journal of the ACM, Vol. 33, No. 4, Oct. 1986, pp. 792-807

[*Lloy*90] S.Lloyd: "Counting Functions satisfying a higher order strict avalanche criterion"; Advances in Cryptology - EUROCRYPT '89, Lecture Notes in Computer Science 434, Springer Verlag, 1990

[*LuRa*86] M.Luby, C.Rackoff: "Pseudo-random permutation generators and cryptographic composition"; Proceedings of the 18th ACM Symposium on the Theory of Computing, ACM, 1986, pp. 356-363

[*LuRa*88] M.Luby, C.Rackoff: "How to construct pseudo-random permutations from pseudorandom functions"; SIAM Journal of Computing, Vol. 17 (2), 1988, pp. 373-386

[*OpTs*71] D.C.Opferman, N.T.Tsao-Wu: "On a class of rearrangeable switching networks" "Part I: Control Algorithm"; The Bell System Technical Journal, Vol. 50, No. 5, May-June 1971, pp. 1579-1600; "Part II: Enumeration Studies and Fault Diagnosis"; The Bell System Technical Journal, Vol. 50, No. 5, May-June 1971, pp. 1601-1618

[*Ohni*88] Y. Ohnishi: "A study on data security"; Master Thesis (in Japanese); Tohoku University, Japan, 1988

[*Piep*90] J.Pieprzyk: "How to construct pseudorandom permutations from single pseudorandom functions"; Advances in Cryptology - EUROCRYPT '90, Lecture Notes in Computer Science 473, Springer Verlag, 1991

[*Port*91] M. Portz: "A new class of cryptosystems based on interconnection networks"; Aachener Informatik-Berichte, Nr. 91-4, RWTH Aachen, Fachgruppe Informatik; ISSN 0935-3232, 1991

[*Schn*88] C.P.Schnorr: "On the construction of random number generators and random function generators"; Advances in Cryptology - EUROCRYPT '88, Lecture Notes in Computer Science 330, Springer Verlag, 1989

[*Waks*68] A.Waksman: "A permutation network"; Journal of the ACM, Vol. 15, No. 1, Jan. 1968, pp. 159-163

[*ZMI*89] Y. Zheng, T. Matsumoto, H. Imai: "On the construction of block ciphers provably secure and not relying on any unproved hypothesis"; Advances in Cryptology-CRYPTO 89; Lecture Notes in Computer Science 435; Springer; 1990

[*Yao*91] A.C.Yao: "Theory and application of trapdoor functions"; Proceedings of the 23rd IEEE Symposium on Foundation of Computer Science, New York, 1982

Non Supersingular Elliptic Curves for Public Key Cryptosystems

T. Beth

F. Schaefer

Institut für Algorithmen und Kognitive Systeme

Universität Karlsruhe

Fasanengarten 5

D-7500 Karlruhe 1

Abstract

For public key cryptosystems multiplication on elliptic curves can be used instead of exponentiation in finite fields. One attack to such a system is: embedding the elliptic curve group into the multiplicative group of a finite field via weilpairing; calculating the discrete logarithm on the curve by solving the discrete logarithm in the finite field. This attack can be avoided by constructing curves so that every embedding in a multiplicative group of a finite field requires a field of very large size.

1   Introduction

In 1985 [10] Miller has suggested to use the chord tangent group law over elliptic curves for public key cryptosystems. These elliptic curve groups are used in a way similar to multiplicative groups of finite fields à la Diffie/Hellman (see [5][6]).

In this paper we discuss different possibilities to choose elliptic curves over finite fields with respect to application for such cryptosystems. The supersingular curves E with $\#E(GF(q)) = q + 1$ elements on the curve earlier proposed by Koblitz ([7]) are not well suited for that purpose. Cryptosystems based on such a type of curves can be attacked by a new discrete logarithm algorithm recently presented by A. Menezes, T. Okamoto and S. Vanstone([9]).

This algorithm uses the Weil pairing for embedding the group of the curve into the multiplicative group of a finite field. By that the discrete logarithm problem on the curve is reduced to the discrete logarithm problem in the finite field. Menezes, Okamoto and Vanstone propose to use some other supersingular elliptic curves instead, because this class of elliptic curves provides some advantages with respect to implementation. However, these curves can still be embedded in finite fields of a somewhat larger size.

In this paper we show, that the crucial embedding can be hardened by using curves over $GF(p^n)$ with p prime and $p \gg 2$ or by using non supersingular curves over $GF(2^n)$. Then the breaking algorithm sketched above cannot feasibly be applied even if some progress in solving discrete logarithms is obtained. Due to the advantages provided by the use of fields with characteristic 2, especially for purposes of VLSI design, we concentrate in this paper on the arithmetic on non supersingular curves over these fields.

2 Mathematical Preliminaries

An elliptic curve $E(k)$ over a field k is defined to consist of all points $(x, y) \in k \times k$, which are solutions of a socalled Weierstrass equation:

$$E : y^2 + a_1 xy + a_3 y = x^3 + a_2 x^2 + a_4 x + a_6,$$

where $a_1, ..., a_6 \in k$ are constants such that E has no singularities,

together with an additional point 0, the "point at infinity".

We have to regard these curves in projective instead of affine coordinates. Then one has to consider the homogeneous equation:

$$(*) \quad E_h : Y^2 Z + a_1 XYZ + a_3 YZ^2 = X^3 + a_2 X^2 + a_4 X + a_6.$$

Points on this curve are described as equivalence classes of tripels (X, Y, Z) fulfilling the equation $(*)$, where the equivalence relation $(**)$ is defined:

$$(**) \quad (X, Y, Z) \cong (Xo, Yo, Zo) \text{ iff } \exists\, c \in k \text{ with } X = cXo, Y = cYo \text{ and } Z = cZo.$$

Then the point at infinity 0 can be represented by $(0, 1, 0)$, because this represents the only solution of the homogenous equation $(*)$ for $Z = 0$.

On elliptic curves an additive group operation can be defined in such a way, that the point at infinity becomes the zero element of this group. Using the affine coordinate representation of above, the group operation can be calculated as follows:

Let $P := (x_1, y_1)$ and $Q := (x_2, y_2)$ be two points on the curve $E(k)$ and $P + Q =: (x_3, y_3)$ be the sum. Then:

For $x_1 \neq x_2$ define:

$$\lambda := \frac{y_2 - y_1}{x_2 - x_1}, \quad \nu := \frac{y_1 x_2 - y_2 x_1}{x_2 - x_1}.$$

For $x_1 = x_2$, but $y_1 + y_2 + a_1 x_2 + a_3 \neq 0$ define:

$$\lambda := \frac{3x_1^2 + 2a_2 x_1 + a_4 - a_1 y_1}{2y_1 + a_1 x_1 + a_3},$$

$$\nu := \frac{-x_1^3 + a_4 x_1 + 2a_6 - a_3 y_1}{2y_1 + a_1 x_1 + a_3}.$$

Using this definition of λ and ν the line $y = \lambda x + \nu$ passes through P and Q, or is a tangent to E if $P = Q$.

Now $P + Q =: (x_3, y_3)$ is given by:

$$x_3 := \lambda^2 + a_1 \lambda - a_2 - x_1 - x_2 \,,$$
$$y_3 := -(\lambda + a_1)x_3 - \nu - a_3 \,.$$

Thus the sum $P + Q$ is the third intersection point of the line $y = \lambda x + \nu$ with $E(k)$ reflected at the symmetry line of the curve E.

If $x_1 = x_2$ and $y_1 + y_2 + a_1 x_2 + a_3 = 0$, then:

$$P + Q = 0$$

From this addition on the curve a multiplication with a scalar $m \in \mathbf{N}$ can be defined:

$$m \in \mathbf{N}, \; m \cdot P := P + \ldots + P.$$

With elliptic curves one usually asserts certain quantities. The fact, that E should not have any singularities can be expressed in terms of the discriminant. Let c_4, c_6 be:

$$c_4 := (a_1^2 + 4a_2)^2 - 24(2a_4 + a_1 a_3)$$
$$c_6 := (a_1^2 + 4a_2)^3 + 36(a_1^2 + 4a_2)(2a_4 + a_1 a_3) - 216(a_3^2 + 4a_6).$$

Then for the discriminant Δ holds:

$$1728\,\Delta = c_4^3 - c_6^2 \ .$$

For elliptic curves $\Delta \neq 0$ is supposed. This ensures that there are no singularities on the curve.

Closely related to the dicriminant is the j–invariant. It is defined by:

$$j := \frac{c_4^3}{\Delta}\ ,$$

and characterizes curves over algebraic closed fields up to isomorphism.

Another important tool for analysing elliptic curves is the endomorphism ring over the curve, where the curve is considered over the algebraic closure of the underlying field:

$$End(E) := End(E(\overline{k})).$$

The multiplication defined above gives a natural embedding of the ring of integers Z into $End(E)$. A curve is said to have *complex multiplication*, if $End(E)$ is stricly larger than Z. For curves over finite fields this is always the case.

An elliptic curve is called *supersingular*, iff the endomorphism ring $End(E)$ is non–commutative. The commutativity of $End(E)$ is only dependent on the structure of the curve over algebraic closures. Therefore it can be related to the j–invariant. For curves over fields with characteristic 2 the supersingular curves are exactly those with j–invariant $= 0$ (see [12] for proofs and further details).

3 Elliptic Curve Cryptosystem

A general concept to find one way functions is to construct a large finite cyclic group $(G, \circ)$ together with a generator $g \in G$, such that it is "easy" to calculate $m \cdot g := g \circ \ldots \circ g$ for all $m \in$ N but "difficult" to retrieve the m for some arbitrary element $h \in G$, such that $m \cdot g = h$ holds. Here "easy" to calculate means solvable in polynomial time, where the polynom has a degree in the size of $\log |G|$, and "difficult" to calculate means has more than polynomial time complexity, at least for the best known algorithms.

One realization using this construction is given by the exponentiation in large finite fields proposed by Diffie and Hellman. This principle is also used here to construct a public key cryptosystem based on elliptic curves using the above defined group operation:

Choose an elliptic curve $E(GF(q))$ over a finite field $GF(q)$ together with a base point $P \in E(GF(q))$. This base point should be of high order. Then it is comparatively easy to calculate a scalar multiplication mP ($:= P + \ldots + P$ m-times), but difficult to calculate m given P and mP.

The later problem is called the discrete logarithm problem for elliptic curves. The best algorithm for descrete logarithms working for every type of elliptic curves is the GiantStepBabyStep algorithm. It has a complexity of $O(\sqrt{l_p})$, where l_p is the largest primefactor of the order of the base point P. This algorithm can be used to calculate discrete logarithms in any finite cyclic groups.

4 The Weil Pairing and the Discrete Logarithm

To motivate our further reasoning on how the curves should be choosen, a short review of the reduction algorithm due to A. Menezes, T. Okamoto and S. Vanstone is given([9]). The main idea is to reduce the calculation of a discrete logarithm in the elliptic curve group $E(k)$ to a discrete logarithm problem in a finite field GF by embedding the elliptic curve group $E(k)$ into the multiplicative group of a finite field GF. This embedding is delivered by the Weil pairing:

$$e_N : E[N] \times E[N] \to \mu_N,$$

which maps the n-torsion group over the algebraic closure of the field

$$E[N] := \{P \in E(\overline{k}) \mid N \cdot P = 0\}$$

into the set of N-th roots of unity (for details see [12]). Using the bilinearity and the non–degeneracy of the Weil pairing, such an embedding of an elliptic curve group into a finite field can be constructed.

By choosing the second component of the map in such a way, that the image of P under e_N is a primitive root, one gets a multiplication preserving function. Thus calculating a discrete logatithm in an elliptic curve group can be reduced to calculating a discrete logarithm in a finite field containing the N-th roots of unity.

Discrete logarithms in finite fields $GF(2^n)$ can be calculated by Coppersmith's algorithm([3]) with a complexity of

$$O(\exp(cn^{\frac{1}{3}}(\ln n)^{\frac{2}{3}})).$$

Thus the calculation of a discrete logarithm in an elliptic curve group is fastened up by this embedding as long as we can find the N-th roots of unity in a finite field of low extension degree over the basic field.

For the special case of the curve

$$E : y^2 * y = x^3$$

over fields with characteristic 2 the Weil pairing gives an embedding:

$$E(GF(2^n)) \hookrightarrow GF(2^{2n})^*$$

(see [9]). That means that in this case the embedding leads to much faster algorithm for the calculation of discrete logarithms.

In general this is only true, if the roots of unity are in an extension field with low degree over the field $GF(q)$. To avoid this kind of attack in [9] the following curves are proposed:

$$E_1 : y^2 * y = x^3 + x \; ,$$
$$E_2 : y^2 * y = x^3 + x + 1 \; .$$

For these two curves the Weil pairing deliveres an embedding of $E(GF(q))$ into $GF(q^4)^*$, i.e. a field with a representation of four times the bitlength. Then the time for computing discrete logarithms with the reduction algorithm rises properly.

	GiantStepBabyStep		Discr. Log in $GF(q^4)$
$E(GF(2^{100}))$	$\approx 10^{16}$	$GF(2^{4*100})$	$\approx 10^{23}$
$E(GF(2^{200}))$	$\approx 10^{31}$	$GF(2^{4*200})$	$\approx 10^{31}$
$E(GF(2^{300}))$	$\approx 10^{46}$	$GF(2^{4*300})$	$\approx 10^{37}$

Table 1: The complexity of discrete logarithm algorithms in $E(GF(q))$ by GiantStep-BabyStep method compared to the complexity of discrete logarithms in $GF(q^4)$ calculated by Coppersmith's method.

The figures in Table 1 shows, that the exponent of 4 is not satisfying for implementations with higher level of security and with respect to further progress in algorithm technique and machine speed. Already for curves over fields of size larger than 2^{200} it is easier to attack the cryptosystem by embedding and solving discrete logarithm than by using the GiantStepBabyStep method.

5 The Number of Points on Elliptic Curves

To avoid the attack described in the previous paragraph, we consider different types of curves. The following theorem gives the possible number of points on elliptic curves depending on the supersingularity. It is formulated in this way in Waterhouse' thesis, but its content is going back to Deurings work on elliptic function fields in the 1940os ([4]).

Theorem 1 *Let E be an elliptic curve over the finite field $GF(q)$ with $q = p^n$ a power of the prime p. Let the number of points on E be:*

$$\sharp E(GF(q)) = q + 1 - \beta.$$

In the case of supersingular curves one of the following condition holds:

(i) n even: $\beta = \pm 2\sqrt{q}$,

(ii) n even and $p \not\equiv 1 \pmod 3$: $\beta = \pm\sqrt{q}$,

(iii) n odd and $p = 2$ or 3: $\beta = \pm\sqrt{pq}$,

(iv) either n odd or n even and $p \not\equiv 1 \pmod 4$: $\beta = 0$.

In the case of non supersingular curves, β fulfills the following properties:

- *$|\beta| \leq 2\sqrt{q}$ (Hasse-bound) and*

- *$gcd(\beta, p) = 1$.*

The inverse statement is also valid in the sense that all the cases above occur.

(For proofs see [14] and [4]). For illustration of the theorem we give an example, which will be used later on:

Example 2 Over the finite field $GF(16)$ the possible sizes of elliptic curves are

$$\sharp E(GF(16)) = 16 + 1 - \beta \in \{9, 13, 17, 21, 25\}$$

for supersingular curves, and

$$\sharp E(GF(16)) = 16 + 1 - \beta \in \{10, 12, 14, 16, 18, 20, 22, 24\}$$

for non supersingular curves.

Note that in general, there are at most 5 supersingular elliptic curves over a finite field $GF(2^n)$ and $2 \times 2^{\lfloor \frac{n}{2} \rfloor}$ non–supersingular ones. As shown in [9] all elliptic curves over $GF(2^n)$ with $j(E) = 0$, i.e. supersingular curves, allow an embedding in a finite field of at most four times the bitlength. For the reasons explained above we look for curves which can not be embedded in extension fields of such small degree.

One possibility is to change the characteristic of the underlying field. For example in fields with characteristic 3 the supersingular curves with $q + 1 \pm \sqrt{q}$ points require fields with six times the bitlength for such embeddings. But due to faster and smaller implementations of arithmetic in fields of characteristic 2 these are of more interest. The non–supersingular curves give suitable candidates.

6 Construction of Suitable Non Supersingular Elliptic Curves

Over finite fields with characteristic 2 the non supersingular curves can be represented as:

$$E : \quad y^2 + xy = x^3 + a_2 x^2 + a_6,$$

where the j–invariant $j(E) = \frac{1}{a_6}$. As shown in the previous paragraph we find curves with $\sharp E(GF(2^n)) = 2^n + 1 - \beta$ for any given β with β odd and $|\beta| \le 2\sqrt{q}$ by choosing the coefficients a_2 and a_6 in $GF(2^n)$ and $a_6 \ne 0$.

An important point for the security of such a crypto system is to guarantee that there is a very large prime factor $p_{E(GF(2^n))}$ in the number of points calculated. Otherwise the GiantStepBabyStep algorithm can be applied succesfully to the subgroups. Thus the cyclic subgroup of order $p_{E(GF(2^n))}$ is the cryptographic essential part of the elliptic curve group.

To embed this cyclic subgroup into the multiplicative group of some extension field of $GF(2^n)$, let say $GF((2^n)^i)$, the following condition is necessary:

$$p_{E(GF(2^n))} | 2^{ni} - 1.$$

We are interested in curves where this *divisibility property* does not hold at least up to some extension degree k. This can be checked by calculating the following *gcdos*:

$$\gcd(p_{E(GF(2^n))}, 2^{ni} - 1) \quad (i = 1, \dots, k).$$

or respectively:

$$\gcd(\sharp E(GF(2^n)), 2^{ni} - 1) \quad (i = 1, \ldots, k).$$

How can we construct examples of curves fulfilling the divisibility property for k large enough and at the same time having a large prime factor in the group order. The algorithms to count the number of points on curves have rather high complexity. Therefore it is difficult to find curves for a given β in very large fields in general. If the number of points of a fixed curve over a finite field is known, then the number of points over any extension of this field can be calculated easily.

One proceeds as follows: We start with some small extension field of $GF(2)$, say $GF(q)$. Here it is easy to determine curves for all the possible number of points:

$$\sharp E(GF(q)) = q + 1 - \beta_0 \quad \beta_0 \text{ odd and } |\beta| \leq 2\sqrt{q}.$$

Using the weil conjecture (see [12]) we find the number of points of this curves for any extension field of $GF(q)$:

$$\sharp E(GF(q^k)) = q^k + 1 - \beta_k,$$

where $\beta_k = a^k + b^k$ and a, b are the complex solutions of $1 - \beta_0 T + qT^2 = (1 - aT)(1 - bT)$.

Obviously $E(GF(q))$ is a subgroup of $E(GF(q^k))$. Therefore $\sharp E(GF(q^k))$ has a small factor, namely $\sharp E(GF(q))$. It can be checked, whether the remaining factor

$$\frac{\sharp E(GF(q^k))}{\sharp E(GF(q))}$$

is prime. For $l \in \mathbf{N}$ with $l \nmid k$, $E(GF(q^l)) \subseteq E(GF(q^k))$ is a subgroup. Thus it is sufficient to consider only extensions of prime degree over $GF(q)$.

By this method it is possible to find curves over $GF(2^n)$ fulfilling the divisibility property for relatively large k with a large prime factor in the group order.

For illustration a special example suited for public key cryptosystems is constructed. In Example 2 we considered the number of elements on curves over $GF(16)$. The smallest non–supersingular elliptic curve group over this field has order 10. Computer search gives all curves with 10 elements over $GF(16)$. Representing the field as $GF(2)[x]/(x^4 + x + 1)$ and the curve as $y^2 + xy = x^3 + a_2 x^2 + a_6$, the coefficient a_2 can be choosen as a polynomial of degree 3 and a_6 as one of the polynomials $x^2 + x$ or $x^2 + x + 1$.

Enlarging $GF(16)$ by a finite field extension of degree 47 we get a group of order

$$2 * 5 * 392318858461667547739736838942997715128064667934031507 29,$$

where the last factor is a probable prime with 56 digits. These curves fulfills the divisibility property for $k = 2 \ldots 100$. The factor 10 is due to the subgroup $E(GF(16))$.

7 Implementation

In this chapter some ideas are given how to implement the group operation on non–supersingular curves over fields of characteristic 2. In comparison to supersingular curves the addition here is slightly harder to compute, because doubling of a point is more complicated to calculate.

The complexity of the basic arithmetic operations in finite fields differs considerably. The additions are negligable in comparison to multiplications. The inversions are by fare the most time consuming operations. Therefore the curve is represented in projective coordinates. Then the inversions can be eliminated. Only at the end of each calculation two inversions are needed to get a unique representation (see [2],[8],[11]).

The homogeneous equation for non–supersingular curves over fields with characteristic 2 is:

$$Y^2 Z + XYZ = X^3 + a_2 X^2 Z + a_6 Z^3$$

with points $P = (X, Y, Z)$.

From a base point $P = (x, y, 1)$, we calculate $m * P$ with a double and add algorithm. Starting with the highest bit of m, we need only doublings of a point and additions of two different points of the form $(x, y, 1) + (x_i, y_i, z_i)$, i.e. we can assume that one of the points in the sums is given in affine coordinates. Then the following addition formulas are obtained:

Given $P_1 = (x_1, y_1, 1)$ and $P_2 = (x_2, y_2, z_2) \cong \left(\frac{x_2}{z_2}, \frac{y_2}{z_2}, 1\right)$,

and let $A := (z_2 x_1 + x_2)$ and $B := (z_2 y_1 + y_2)$, then

$$z_2 A^2 x_3 \;=\; z_2 B^2 + z_2 AB + A^2(x_1 z_2 + x_2 + a_2 z_2)$$
$$z_2 A^3 y_3 \;=\; z_2 A^2(y_1 x_2 + x_1 y_2) + (A + B)(z_2 A^2 x_3),$$

thus :

$$P_1 + P_2 \;=\; (z_2 A^3 x_3, \; z_2 A^3 y_3, \; z_2 A^3) \cong (x_3, y_3, 1).$$

For the doubling of a point $P = (x, y, z)$, defining $A = (yz + x^2)$, we have:

$$x^2 z^2 x_d \;=\; A^2 + xzA + a_2 x^2 z^2$$
$$x^3 z^3 y_d \;=\; x^5 z + (A + xz)(x^2 z^2 x_3)$$

thus $2P \;=\; ((x^3 z^3) x_d, \; (x^3 z^3) y_d, \; (x^3 z^3)) \cong (x_d, y_d, 1).$

The addition of above can be calculated with 12 multiplications and 1 squaring and the doubling of a point with 7 multiplications and 2 squarings.

Implementing the elliptic curve group operation in a VLSI design, the squarings can be calculated parallel with the multiplications, if the polynomial bases multiplier unit, invented by D. Gollman ([1]), is used. By using three multiplier units, these multiplications can be executed parallel. Thus the computing time is reduced to 3 repectively 4 multiplication steps for doubling and addition. Assuming that the factor m has a bit representation with half zeros and half ones, this means, that the average computation time would be 5 multiplication steps per bit. Additionaly there are around $4 \cdot \log n$ final multiplications for two inversions.

8   Conclusion

For public key cryptosystems based on problems like discrete logarithms, large groups are needed. The security depends on the structure of these groups.

Elliptic curves give the possibility to choose between a lot of different groups with different orders, especially if non supersingular curves are considered. This variety is the main advantage in comparison to the use of multiplicative groups of finite fields, where we have only one candidate for every field.

For algorithms, as the different index calculus methods, a large data base is calculated once for every candidate of group and out of this database single logarithms can be derived quickly. Also in this respect elliptic curves are a powerfull tool because of the richness of the many occuring cases.

References

[1] T. Beth, D. Gollmann; *Algorithm Engineering for Public Key Algorithms*; IEEE Journal on Selected Areas in Comm., Vol. 7, No. 4, 1989, pp. 458-466.

[2] T. Beth, W. Geiselmann, F. Schaefer; *Arithmetics on Elliptic Curves*; Algebraic and Combinatorical Coding Theory, 2nd int.workshop, Leningrad, 1990, pp. 28-33.

[3] D. Coppersmith; *Fast evaluation of logarithms in fields of characteristic two*; IEEE Trans. Inform. Theory, IT 30, 1984, pp. 587-594.

[4] M. Deuring; *Die Typen der Multiplikatorenringe elliptischer Funktionenkoerper*; Abh. Math. Sem. Hamburg, Bd. 14, 1941, pp. 197-272.

[5] W. Diffie, M. Hellman; *New directions in cryptography*; IEEE Trans. Inform. Theory, IT 22, 1976, pp. 644-654.

[6] T. ElGamal; *A public key cryptosystem and a signature scheme based on discrete logarithms*; IEEE Trans. Inform. Theory, IT 31, 1985, pp. 469-472.

[7] N. Koblitz; *Elliptic Curve Cryptosystems*; Mathematics of Computation, Vol. 48, No177, 1987, pp. 203-209.

[8] A. Menezes, S. A. Vanstone; *The Implementation fo Elliptic Curve Cryptosystems*; Advances in Cryptology-Auscrypt 90, Springer LNCS 453,1990, pp. 2-13.

[9] A. Menezes, T. Okamoto, S. A. Vanstone; *Reducing Elliptic Curve Logarithms to Logarithms in a Finite Field*; University of Waterloo, preliminary version, sep. 1990.

[10] V. S. Miller; *Use of Elliptic Curves in Cryptography*; Advances in Cryptology: Proceedings of Crypto 85, Springer LNCS 218, 1986, pp. 417-426.

[11] P. Montgomery; *Speeding the Pollard and elliptic curve methods of factorization*; Math. Comp., Vol. 48, 1977, pp 243-264.

[12] J. H. Silverman; *The Arithmetic of Elliptic Curves*; Springer, New York, 1986.

[13] J. T. Tate; *The Arithmetic of Elliptic Curves*; Inventiones math. 23, Springer, 1974, pp. 179-206.

[14] W. C. Waterhouse, *Abelian Varieties over finite fields*; Ann. scient. Ec. Norm. Sup., 4th serie, 1969, pp. 521-560.

BUILDING CYCLIC ELLIPTIC CURVES
MODULO LARGE PRIMES

François Morain [*]

INRIA, B. P. 105

78153 LE CHESNAY CEDEX (France)

morain@inria.inria.fr

Abstract

Elliptic curves play an important rôle in many areas of modern cryptology such as integer factorization and primality proving. Moreover, they can be used in cryptosystems based on discrete logarithms for building one-way permutations. For the latter purpose, it is required to have cyclic elliptic curves over finite fields. The aim of this note is to explain how to construct such curves over a finite field of large prime cardinality, using the ECPP primality proving test of Atkin and Morain.

1 Introduction

Elliptic curves prove to be a powerful tool in modern cryptology. Following the original work of H. W. Lenstra, Jr. [18] concerning integer factorization, many researchers have used this new idea to work out primality proving algorithms [8, 14, 2, 4, 22] as well as cryptosystems [21, 16] generalizing those of [12, 1, 9]. Recent work on these topics can be found in [20, 19].

More recently, Kaliski [15] has used elliptic curves in the design of one-way permutations. For this, the author needs elliptic curves which are cyclic and the easiest solution is to build elliptic curves with squarefree order. The aim of this paper is to show how ;o construct such elliptic curves using some byproducts of the Elliptic Curve Primality Proving (ECPP) algorithm of Atkin and Morain [4].

The problem of building elliptic curves of given order in finite fields of small characteristic is dealt with in [5] and our work can be seen as solving the same problem in large characteristic.

---

[*]On leave from the French Department of Defense, Délégation Générale pour l'Armement.

The paper is organized as follows. Section 2 contains a brief summary of the properties of elliptic curves modulo some prime p. Section 3 gives the heart of ECPP. Section 4 describes a theoretical means of building curves of given order and it is shown that the running time of this procedure would be exponential in $\log p$. Section 5 explains how ECPP can be used to find cyclic curves in a faster way, the running time of the process being that of ECPP that is conjectured to be polynomial with complexity $O((\log p)^{5+\epsilon})$.

2 Elliptic curves modulo p

2.1 Group law

We briefly describe some properties of elliptic curves. For more information, see [25].

An elliptic curve E over a field $\mathbf{Z}/p\mathbf{Z}$ with p a prime greater than 3 can be described as a pair (a, b) of elements of $\mathbf{Z}/p\mathbf{Z}$ such that $\Delta(E) = -16(4a^3 + 27b^2)$ is invertible in $\mathbf{Z}/p\mathbf{Z}$. This quantity is called the *discriminant* of E. The set of points of E, noted $E(\mathbf{Z}/p\mathbf{Z})$ is the set of triples $(x : y : z)$ of elements of $\mathbf{Z}/p\mathbf{Z}$ that are solution of

$$y^2 z \equiv x^3 + axz^2 + bz^3.$$

These triples can be interpreted as the coordinates of points in the projective plane of $\mathbf{Z}/p\mathbf{Z}$. There is a well known law on $E(\mathbf{Z}/p\mathbf{Z})$. This is called the *tangent-and-chord* method and the law is noted additively. The neutral element is just the point at infinity: $O_E = (0 : 1 : 0)$.

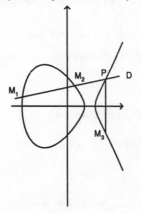

Figure 1: An elliptic curve over $\mathbf{R}$.

In order to add two points $M_1 = (x_1 : y_1 : 1)$ and $M_2 = (x_2 : y_2 : 1)$ on E, resulting in $M_3 = (x_3 : y_3 : z_3)$, the equations are

$$\begin{cases} x_3 &= \lambda^2 - x_1 - x_2, \\ y_3 &= \lambda(x_1 - x_3) - y_1, \end{cases}$$

where

$$
\lambda = \begin{cases} (y_2 - y_1)(x_2 - x_1)^{-1} & \text{if } x_2 \neq x_1, \\[2ex] (3x_1^2 + a)(2y_1)^{-1} & \text{otherwise.} \end{cases}
$$

We define also the *invariant* of the curve E, noted $j(E)$:

$$
j(E) = -\frac{12^3 a^3}{\Delta(E)}.
$$

We then have the following easy result.

Proposition 1 *All elements of $\mathbf{Z}/p\mathbf{Z}$ are invariant of an elliptic curve.*

Proof: Let j_0 be an element of $\mathbf{Z}/p\mathbf{Z}$. We look for an elliptic curve $E = (a, b)$ such that $j(E) = j_0$. If $j_0 = 0$, take $a = 0$, and any nonzero b. If $j_0 = 1728$, take any nonzero a and $b = 0$. In the general case, let $k = j_0/(1728 - j_0)$ and choose $a = 3k, b = 2k$.

Among the interesting and deep properties of these objects, we note the following. (We use the notation $\#\mathcal{A}$ to designate the cardinality of a set $\mathcal{A}$.)

Theorem 1 (Hasse) *Let m be the cardinality of an elliptic curve $E(\mathbf{Z}/p\mathbf{Z})$, then*

$$
(\sqrt{p} - 1)^2 \leq m \leq (\sqrt{p} + 1)^2. \tag{1}
$$

We use the notations of [18] for what follows and we refer the reader to it for more information.

Theorem 2 (Deuring [11]) *Let t be any integer such that $|t| \leq 2\sqrt{p}$. Letting $K(d)$ denote the Kronecker class number of d, there exists $K(t^2 - 4p)$ elliptic curves over $\mathbf{Z}/p\mathbf{Z}$ with number of points $m = p + 1 - t$, up to isomorphisms.*

Concerning the group structure of $E(\mathbf{Z}/p\mathbf{Z})$, we have:

Theorem 3 (Cassels [7]) *The group $E(\mathbf{Z}/p\mathbf{Z})$ is either cyclic or the product of two cyclic groups or order m_1 and m_2 that satisfy*

$$
m_1|m_2, \quad m_1|\gcd(m, p - 1), \tag{2}
$$

where $m = \#E(\mathbf{Z}/p\mathbf{Z})$.

Note that if m is squarefree, then surely $E(\mathbf{Z}/p\mathbf{Z})$ is cyclic.

2.2 Twists

We define the *twisted* curve E' of E as the curve

$$E' : y^2 z = x^3 + ac^2 xz^2 + bc^3 z^3,$$

where c is any non-quadratic residue modulo p. The main point in this is that if the cardinality of E is $m = p + 1 - t$, then $\#E'(\mathbf{Z}/p\mathbf{Z}) = p + 1 + t$. Note that E and its twist have the same invariant j_0.

2.3 Computing $\#E(\mathbf{Z}/p\mathbf{Z})$

From a theoretical point of view, there exists an algorithm of Schoof's that solves the problem in time polynomial in $\log p$, see [23]. However, it appears difficult to implement, even after some improvements of Atkin [3] and Elkies [13]. In practice, it is not feasible as soon as p has more than 65 decimal digits.

3 Overview of ECPP

The following results are at the heart of the Elliptic Curve Primality Proving algorithm in [4]. The first one can be found as [10, Prop. (5.29)] and the second one is a summary of the theory involved in [4].

Theorem 4 *Let p be a prime number and D any positive integer. Then $4p = x^2 + Dy^2$ has a solution in integers (x, y) if and only if $-D$ is a quadratic residue modulo p and the polynomial $H_D(X)$ has a root modulo p, where $H_D(X)$ is a monic polynomial with integer coefficients depending on D only.*

Theorem 5 *Let p be a prime that can be written as $4p = x^2 + Dy^2$ for a given D. Then there exists an elliptic curve E defined over $\mathbf{Z}/p\mathbf{Z}$ such that $4\#(E(\mathbf{Z}/p\mathbf{Z})) = (x - 2)^2 + Dy^2$. Moreover, this curve can be computed explicitly using any root of the polynomial $H_D(X)$ modulo p.*

The algorithm then proceeds as in the classical DOWNRUN process of the well known primality proving algorithms based on the converse of Fermat's Theorem [6, 22].

4 Building curves of given order

Let p be a given prime number greater than 3. Suppose we want to build an elliptic curve of order m, where m satisfies (1). We will use the theory of ECPP to achieve this. The algorithm runs as follows:

procedure BuildCurveGivenM(p)

1. compute $t = p + 1 - m$ and $D = 4p - t^2$;

2. compute $H_D(X)$, the minimal polynomial of $j(\sqrt{D})$ where

$$j(z) = \frac{\left(1 + 240 \sum_{k \geq 1} \frac{k^3 q^k}{1 - q^k}\right)^3}{q \prod_{k \geq 1} (1 - q^k)^{24}}$$

with $q = \exp(2i\pi z)$ (see [4]);

3. find a root j_0 of $H_D(X) \equiv 0 \bmod p$;

4. build the curve E of invariant j_0 and cardinality m.

5. **end.**

The validity of this method is easily seen once we remark that $4p = t^2 + D$ and that the Theorems 4 and 5 of the preceding section apply.

Note also that there are a lot of technical details involved in such computations and the interested reader should consult [4, 22].

Example. Suppose that $p = 101$. By Hasse's theorem, a good m satisfies: $82 \leq m \leq 122$. Let us try to build a curve of cardinality $m = 85$. We get $t = 17$ and $D = 5 \times 23$. Using the algorithms described in [4], we compute

$$H_{115}(X) = X^2 + 427864611225600X + 130231327260672000.$$

This polynomial has two roots modulo 101, namely $\{67, 96\}$. We choose $j_0 = 67$ and get

$$k = 98, a = 3k = 92, b = 2k = 95.$$

Next, we select the point $(1 : 17 : 1)$ on the curve

$$E : y^2 z = x^3 + axz^2 + bz^3 \bmod p.$$

But we find that

$$85P = (24 : 88 : 1)$$

and thus the cardinality of $E(\mathbf{Z}/101\mathbf{Z})$ is not m. We then consider the twisted curve E' obtained by replacing a (resp. b) by ac^2 (resp. bc^3) with $c = 2$. On

$$E' : y^2 z = x^3 + 65xz^2 + 53z^3$$

we take $P' = (7 : 12 : 1)$ and find that

$$85P' = O_{E'}.$$

It is now easy to verify that P' is a point of maximal order on E'.

A rough analysis. We can now state the following result.

Proposition 4.1 *The running time of* `BuildCurveGivenM` *is exponential in* $\log p$.

Proof: By Siegel's Theorem [24], we know that $h(-D)$ is $O(D^{1/2+\epsilon})$. Hence, we may want to find D small. If we brutally apply the preceding algorithm, we require that m be as close of $(\sqrt{p} \pm 1)^2$ as possible. This implies that D is $O(\sqrt{p})$, yielding $h(-D) = O(p^{1/4+\epsilon})$.

5 Finding cyclic curves

Let p be as usual a given (large) prime. Suppose now that we do not insist on having a curve with given number of points, but simply that the curve be cyclic. This is the case in [15]. The easiest way to do this is to find a curve with squarefree order. It then follows from Theorem 3 that the resulting curve is cyclic. Note that we can relax this condition by imposing that any prime factor dividing m with a multiplicity greater than 1 does not divide $p - 1$:

$$q^2 \mid m \Rightarrow q \nmid p - 1.$$

5.1 Brute force

Let us first consider the following brute force algorithm.

procedure `BruteForce`(p)

repeat

  choose E (i.e. a and b) at random and compute $m = \#E(\mathbf{Z}/p\mathbf{Z})$ using Schoof's algorithm

until m is squarefree.

From a theoretical point of view, this is quite nice, since the proportion of squarefree numbers is $6/\pi^2 \approx 0.608$ and that Schoof's algorithm runs in polynomial time. However, this is not a practical algorithm.

Let us turn to a more subtle way. We simply use ECPP and just modify it in such a way that we select a squarefree number of points in the process. The idea is that we will find a good squarefree m by looking at a list of D with small class numbers for which $4p = x^2 + Dy^2$. Once we find a good m, we can build the curve by using a process similar to that of `BuildCurveGivenM`, but this time, the degree of H_D is small. The algorithm is then

procedure ModifiedECPP(p)

1. **repeat**

    1. find D such that $4p = x^2 + Dy^2$; compute $m = ((x-2)^2 + Dy^2)/4$

    until m is squarefree and m is completely factored, maybe with a large prime cofactor.

2. Build E as in BuildCurveGivenM. It is cyclic.

3. **end.**

To examplify this idea, take the smallest 100-digit prime number, namely

$$p = 10^{99} + 289.$$

Using ECPP, we find that

$$4p = A^2 + 1435B^2$$

with

$$A = 2122739902357851560845466093533544718303747803 6989,$$

$$B = 15727198595366658251567998967349766422560087 20081.$$

We get

$$m = p + 1 - A = 7 \times 73 \times p_1$$

where p_1 is a probable prime. In order to prove the primality of p, we have to find a curve E of cardinality m. The degree of $H_{1435}(X)$ is equal to 4 and it is easy to compute this polynomial. We find that the right curve is $E : y^2z = x^3 + axz^2 + bz^3$ with

$a = 89332580780315577971243129589054863098634217387660751864455044211315789505524515985449257586521766,$

$b = 18613904516032152217956335334173823605916083569265109985354760506956584258703397376281607375649 8461$

and E is cyclic with generator $P = (x : y : 1)$ where

$x = 90873632635092532442296404364966023081742894541464194966484332541963500928363746628169821126842 2360,$

$y = 80986435510174523280537324569786186770629268711002368057061282745039814087286072570490165561028 0810.$

We end this by the following results.

Conjecture 5.1 *Procedure* ModifiedECPP *has running time* $O((\log p)^{5+\epsilon})$.

Proof: It is easy to see that the complexity of ModifiedECPP is at most that of ECPP, which can be heuristically estimated to $O((\log p)^{5+\epsilon})$ (see [17]).

Acknowledgments. The author wants to thank A. Miyaji for some valuable remarks on the preliminary version of this paper.

References

[1] L. M. ADLEMAN, R. L. RIVEST, AND A. SHAMIR. A method for obtaining digital signatures and public-key cryptosystems. *Comm. ACM 21*, 2 (1978), 120–126.

[2] A. O. L. ATKIN. Manuscript. Lecture Notes of a conference, Boulder (Colorado), August 1986.

[3] A. O. L. ATKIN. The number of points on an elliptic curve modulo a prime. Preprint, january 1988.

[4] A. O. L. ATKIN AND F. MORAIN. Elliptic curves and primality proving. Research Report 1256, INRIA, Juin 1990. To appear in *Math. Comp.*

[5] T. BETH AND F. SCHAEFER. Non supersingular elliptic curves for public key cryptosystems. In *Advances in Cryptology - EUROCRYPT '91* (1992), D. Davies, Ed., Springer–Verlag. Proceedings of the Workshop on the Theory and Application of Cryptographic Techniques, Brighton, United Kingdom, April 8–11, 1991.

[6] J. BRILLHART, D. H. LEHMER, J. L. SELFRIDGE, B. TUCKERMAN, AND S. S. WAGSTAFF, JR. *Factorizations of* $b^n \pm 1$, $b = 2, 3, 5, 6, 7, 10, 11, 12$ *up to high powers*, 2 ed. No. 22 in Contemporary Mathematics. AMS, 1988.

[7] J. W. S. CASSELS. Diophantine equations with special reference to elliptic curves. *J. London Math. Soc. 41* (1966), 193–291.

[8] D. V. CHUDNOVSKY AND G. V. CHUDNOVSKY. Sequences of numbers generated by addition in formal groups and new primality and factorization tests. Research report RC 11262, IBM, Yorktown Heights, 1985.

[9] D. COPPERSMITH, A. M. ODLYZKO, AND R. SCHROEPPEL. Discrete logarithms in $GF(p)$. *Algorithmica 1* (1986), 1–15.

[10] D. A. COX. *Primes of the form* $x^2 + ny^2$. John Wiley & Sons, 1989.

[11] M. DEURING. Die Typen der Multiplikatorenringe elliptischer Funktionenkörper. *Abh. Math. Sem. Hamburg 14* (1941), 197–272.

[12] W. DIFFIE AND M. E. HELLMAN. New directions in cryptography. *IEEE Trans. on Information Theory IT-22-6* (nov 1976).

[13] N. ELKIES. Computing the number of points on an elliptic curve modulo p. Email to Morain, 1990.

[14] S. GOLDWASSER AND J. KILIAN. Almost all primes can be quickly certified. In *Proc. 18th STOC* (Berkeley, May 28–30 1986), pp. 316–329.

[15] B. S. KALISKI, JR. One-way permutations on elliptic curves. To appear in Journal of Cryptology, 1991.

[16] N. KOBLITZ. Elliptic curve cryptosystems. *Math. Comp. 48*, 177 (January 1987), 203–209.

[17] A. K. LENSTRA AND H. W. LENSTRA, JR. Algorithms in number theory. In *Handbook of Theoretical Computer Science*, J. van Leeuwen, Ed., vol. A: Algorithms and Complexity. North Holland, 1990, ch. 12, pp. 674–715.

[18] H. W. LENSTRA, JR. Factoring integers with elliptic curves. *Annals of Math. 126* (1987), 649–673.

[19] A. MENEZES, T. OKAMOTO, AND S. A. VANSTONE. Reducing elliptic curves logarithms to logarithms in a finite field. Tech. rep., University of Waterloo, 1990. Preliminary version.

[20] A. MENEZES AND S. A. VANSTONE. The implementation of elliptic curve cryptosystems. In *Advances in Cryptology* (1990), J. Seberry and J. Pieprzyk, Eds., no. 453 in Lect. Notes in Computer Science, Springer–Verlag, pp. 2–13. Proceedings Auscrypt '90, Sysdney (Australia), January 1990.

[21] V. MILLER. Use of elliptic curves in cryptography. In *Advances in Cryptology* (1987), A. M. Odlyzko, Ed., vol. 263 of *Lect. Notes in Computer Science*, Springer-Verlag, pp. 417–426. Proceedings Crypto '86, Santa Barbara (USA), August11–15, 1986.

[22] F. MORAIN. *Courbes elliptiques et tests de primalité.* PhD thesis, Université Claude Bernard–Lyon I, Septembre 1990.

[23] R. SCHOOF. Elliptic curves over finite fields and the computation of square roots mod p. *Math. Comp. 44* (1985), 483–494.

[24] C. L. SIEGEL. Über die Classenzahl quadratischer Zahlkörper. *Acta Arithmetica 1* (1935), 83–86.

[25] J. H. SILVERMAN. *The arithmetic of elliptic curves*, vol. 106 of *Graduate Texts in Mathematics.* Springer, 1986.

On the Complexity of Hyperelliptic Discrete Logarithm Problem

Hiroki Shizuya

Department of Electrical Communications,
Faculty of Engineering, Tohoku University
Aramaki-Aza-Aoba, Aoba-ku, Sendai, 980 Japan
shizuya@jpntohok.bitnet

Département d'I.R.O., Université de Montréal
C.P.6128, Succ.A, Montréal, Québec, CANADA, H3C 3J7
shizuya@iro.umontreal.ca

Toshiya Itoh

Department of Information Processing,
The Graduate School at Nagatsuta,
Tokyo Institute of Technology,
4259 Nagatsuta, Midori-ku,
Yokohama 227, Japan
titoh@cc.titech.ac.jp

Kouichi Sakurai

Computer & Information Systems Laboratory,
Mitsubishi Electric Corporation,
5-1-1 Ofuna, Kamakura 247, Japan
sakurai@isl.melco.co.jp

Abstract

We give a characterization for the intractability of hyperelliptic discrete logarithm problem from a viewpoint of computational complexity theory. It is shown that the language of which complexity is equivalent to that of the hyperelliptic discrete logarithm problem is in $\mathcal{NP} \cap$ co-$\mathcal{AM}$, and that especially for elliptic curves, the corresponding language is in $\mathcal{NP} \cap$ co-$\mathcal{NP}$. It should be noted here that the language of which complexity is equivalent to that of the discrete logarithm problem defined over the multiplicative group of a finite field is also characterized as in $\mathcal{NP} \cap$ co-$\mathcal{NP}$.

1   Introduction

In the early times when Diffie and Hellman [DH] proposed a public key-distribution system based on the discrete logarithm problem over the multiplicative group of a finite field, the intractability of the problem was not exactly characterized. However, Brassard [Br] soon pointed out that the language of which complexity is equivalent to that of the discrete logarithm problem is in $\mathcal{NP} \cap$co-$\mathcal{NP}$. Since then, the discrete logarithm problem associated with a finite group has been well studied, but the problem is not known to be solved in polynomial time.

In 1985, Miller [Mi1] showed that there is an alternative for the finite group over which the discrete logarithm problem can be defined, the abelian group of points on an elliptic curve over a finite field. The same idea was also proposed by Koblitz [Ko1] independently of Miller's work, and the notion of the elliptic curve discrete logarithm problem was clarified by Koblitz and Kaliski [Ka1, Ka2, Ko2]. Informally, the elliptic curve discrete logarithm problem is, given two points X and B on an elliptic curve E over a finite field, to find an integer m such that $X = mB$. In 1989, Koblitz [Ko3] extended the elliptic curve discrete logarithm problem to cover hyperelliptic curves, which is the hyperelliptic discrete logarithm problem we discuss in this paper.

Among those works of forerunners, Miller, Kaliski, and Koblitz, what we should recognize is that they have a common observation on the intractability of the hyperelliptic discrete logarithm problem (including the elliptic curve discrete logarithm problem), i.e., the hyperelliptic discrete logarithm problem seems to be more difficult than the discrete logarithm problem defined over the multiplicative group of a finite field. It is remarkable that Menezes, Okamoto, and Vanstone [MOV] announced that if the elliptic curve is supersingular, the elliptic curve discrete logarithm problem is probabilistic polynomial time reducible to the discrete logarithm problem defined over the multiplicative group of the finite field. Although the reduction is restricted to specific curves, this is the first result concerning the relationship between two distinct kind of discrete logarithm problems. However, in general, the intractability of the hyperelliptic discrete logarithm problem is not yet exactly characterized. So we challenge to this work just as Brassard did for the discrete logarithm problem.

In this paper, it is shown that the language of which complexity is equivalent to that of the hyperelliptic discrete logarithm problem is in $\mathcal{NP} \cap$co-$\mathcal{AM}$, and that especially for elliptic curves, the corresponding language is in $\mathcal{NP} \cap$ co-$\mathcal{NP}$, where $\mathcal{AM}$ denotes the set of languages that have constant round Arthur-Merlin games [Ba]. This is the first characterization for the intractability of hyperelliptic discrete logarithm problem from a viewpoint of structural complexity theory. Note that $\mathcal{NP}$ is contained in $\mathcal{AM}$, but the converse inclusion is not known to hold. It should also be noted here that the language of which complexity is equivalent to that of the discrete logarithm problem defined over the multiplicative group of a finite field is characterized as in $\mathcal{NP} \cap$ co-$\mathcal{NP}$.

To our best knowledge, unlike other languages known to be in $\mathcal{NP} \cap$ co-$\mathcal{AM}$ (such as graph isomorphism [GMW2, Sc2]), the hyperelliptic discrete logarithm problem is the first candidate of *number-theoretic* problems that are characterized as in $\mathcal{NP} \cap$ co-$\mathcal{AM}$ but not known to be in $\mathcal{NP} \cap$ co-$\mathcal{NP}$.

2 Preliminaries

2.1 The Mathematical Background

We start with the definitions of notions and notations related to hyperelliptic curves [Ca, Ko3].

Let K be an arbitrary field, and $\overline{K}$ denote its algebraic closure. A hyperelliptic curve C of genus g over K is the set of solutions $(u, v) \in K^2$ to an equation of the form $v^2 + h(u)v = f(u)$, where $h(u)$ is a polynomial of degree at most g and $f(u)$ is a monic polynomial of degree $2g + 1$. We require that the curve has no singular points.

Let L be a field containing K. By an L-point $P \in C$, we mean either the symbol ∞ or else a finite point, that is a solution $u = x \in L$, $v = y \in L$ of the equation $v^2 + h(u)v = f(u)$. Given a finite point $P = P_{x,y} \in C$, we define its opposite $\tilde{P}$ to be $\tilde{P} = (x, -y - h(x))$.

To introduce the jacobian of the curve C, we define in advance a divisor on C. A divisor is a finite formal sum of $\overline{K}$-points $D = \sum m_i P_i$. The degree of D is defined to be the integer $\sum m_i$, and denoted by $\deg D$. The divisors form an additive group $\mathbf{D}$, and the divisors of degree 0 form a subgroup $\mathbf{D}^0 \subseteq \mathbf{D}$. Given $D \in \mathbf{D}$, we set $D^0 = D - (\deg D)\infty$ so that $D^0 \in \mathbf{D}^0$. Given two divisors $D_1 = \sum m_i P_i$ and $D_2 = \sum n_i P_i$ in $\mathbf{D}^0$, we define g.c.d.$(D_1, D_2) \in \mathbf{D}^0$ to be $\sum \min(m_i, n_i)P_i - (\sum \min(m_i, n_i))\infty$.

For a polynomial $q(u, v)$ with coefficients in $\overline{K}$, the discrete valuation for $q(u, v)$ at a point $P \in C$ can be defined, which is called the order and denoted by $\mathrm{ord}_P\, q$. The divisor $\sum (\mathrm{ord}_P\, q)P$ is denoted by (q), where the summation is taken over all points P on the curve (including ∞). It can be shown that $(p) \in \mathbf{D}^0$. For polynomials p and q, a divisor of the form $(p) - (q)$ is called principal, and such divisors form a subgroup $\mathbf{P}$ of $\mathbf{D}^0$. The jacobian $\mathbf{J}$ of the curve C is the quotient group $\mathbf{D}^0/\mathbf{P}$. If $D_1, D_2 \in \mathbf{D}^0$, we write $D_1 \sim D_2$ if $D_1 - D_2 \in \mathbf{P}$, i.e., if D_1 and D_2 are equal when considered as elements of $\mathbf{J}$. We let $\mathbf{J}(C; L)$ denote the set of L-points of $\mathbf{J}$ associated with the curve C.

A divisor $D = \sum m_i P_{x_i, y_i} - (\sum m_i)\infty$ can be uniquely respresented as the g.c.d. of two principal divisors of polynomials of the form $a(u)$ and $b(u) - v$, that is, g.c.d.$((a(u)), (b(u) - v))$. We write $D = \text{div}(a, b)$ in short to denote such D.

Let $K = \mathbf{F}_q$, a finite field of q elements, and let $\mathbf{F}_{q^n}$ be its extension. We regard them as fixed. Given a divisor D, the unique representation $\text{div}(a, b)$ can be obtained in $O(n^2)$ bits operations. Furthermore, given $D \in \mathbf{J}(C; \mathbf{F}_{q^n})$, the multiples of the divisor, denoted by mD, can be computed efficiently by the repeated doubling method, which takes $O(n^3)$ bits operation. Informally, the hyperelliptic discrete logarithm problem is, given two divisors X and B in $\mathbf{J}$ associated with a hyperelliptic curve C over a finite field, to find an integer m such that $X \sim mB$.

2.2 HEDL and the Related Languages

Throughout this paper, all strings will be over the finite alphabet $\Sigma = \{0, 1\}$. We use $|x|$ to represent the length of string x. We let Σ^* designate the set of all possible strings including zero-length string λ. A language is a set of strings. A class is a set of languages. For a language L, we use $\overline{L}$ to denote $\Sigma^* \setminus L$. For a class $\mathcal{C}$, we use co-$\mathcal{C}$ to denote its class of complements, i.e. the set of any L such that $\overline{L}$ is in $\mathcal{C}$. For any finite set A, we let $\sharp A$ designate its cardinality.

We now define HEDL, the hyperelliptic discrete logarithm problem on $\mathbf{J}(C; \mathbf{F}_{q^n})$.

Definition 1 (HEDL) :
HEDL(q, n, C, X, B) is a computing problem, where q is prime power, n is a positive integer, C is a hyperelliptic curve (with no singular points) defined over $\mathbf{F}_q$, and X and B are divisors in $\mathbf{J}(C; \mathbf{F}_{q^n})$. If there exists an integer m such that $X \sim mB$ and $0 \le m < \sharp\mathbf{J}(C; \mathbf{F}_{q^n})$, then the answer is the smallest m, and if such m does not exist, the answer is a special string "$\perp$".

Given q, n, and C, we can check in probabilistic polynomial time that the curve C has a singular point. Note that, by the definition, HEDL is the elliptic curve discrete logarithm problem when the genus of the curve is 1.

Two languages L_s and L_ℓ are also introduced to explore the intractability of this problem. The language L_s is the set of instances of *solvable* hyperelliptic discrete logarithm problem, of which membership problem is to answer *yes* if the input causes HEDL to return a non-negative integer and *no* otherwise. The language L_ℓ is the set of instances of *location* problem associated with hyperelliptic discrete logarithms, of which membership problem is to answer *yes* if the input causes HEDL to return an integer $\geq k$ and *no* otherwise.

Definition 2 (L_s):
$L_s = \{< q, n, C, X, B > | (\exists m \geq 0)[\text{HEDL}(q, n, C, X, B) = m]\}$.

Definition 3 (L_ℓ) :
$L_\ell = \{< q, n, C, X, B, k > | (k \in \mathbf{Z}_{\geq 0}) \wedge (\text{HEDL}(q, n, C, X, B) \geq k)\}$.

Obviously, L_s is deterministic polynomial time Turing reducible to L_ℓ. Furthermore, it is easy to see that the complexity of the language L_ℓ is equivalent to the complexity of the problem HEDL.

2.3   The Order of Jacobian

It is important to note that $\mathbf{J}(C; \mathbf{F}_{q^n})$ is not necessarily a cyclic group but a (finite) abelian group. We also define the problem OrdJ and the language L_{NJ} to investigate the complexity of computing the exact order of $\mathbf{J}(C; \mathbf{F}_{q^n})$.

Definition 4 (OrdJ) :
OrdJ(q, n, C) is a counting problem, where q is prime power, n is a positive integer, C is a hyperelliptic curve (with no singular points) defined over $\mathbf{F}_q$. If the input is valid, the answer is the exact order of $\mathbf{J}(C; \mathbf{F}_{q^n})$, and if invalid, the answer is "$\perp$".

Definition 5 (L_{NJ}) :
$L_{NJ} = \{< N, q, n, C > | (N$ is a positive integer$)$
$$\wedge (N = \text{OrdJ}(q, n, C)) \}.$$

Clearly, the language L_{NJ} is in P if there exists a deterministic polynomial time algorithm fo computing OrdJ. Pila [20] showed the following theorem as an extension of Schoof's result [Sch].

Theorem A (Pila [Pi]): Let A be an abelian variety over a finite field $\mathbf{F}_q$. Then one can compute the characteristic polynomial of the Frobenius endomorphism of A in time $O((\log q)^\Delta)$ where Δ and the implied constant depend only on the form of the equations defining A.

Theorem A implies that we can compute the order of $\mathbf{J}(C; \mathbf{F}_{q^n})$ in polynomial time. Thus, we have the following theorem, which will later become important.

Theorem B: The language L_{NJ} is in $\mathcal{P}$.

3 Main Results

Recall that the complexity of the language L_ℓ, the set of instances of *location* problem associated with HEDL, is equivalent to that of HEDL. This implies that L_ℓ completely characterizes the complexity of HEDL. We show in this section the following results.

Theorem 1 : L_ℓ is in $\mathcal{NP} \cap$ co-$\mathcal{AM}$.

Theorem 2 : For any elliptic curve E, let L_ℓ be denoted by L_ℓ^E. Then, L_ℓ^E is in $\mathcal{NP} \cap$ co-$\mathcal{NP}$.

Whereas other complexity-theoretic properties of HEDL and L_s are investigated in the appendix, where we show the followings as well as some immediate corollaries.

Theorem A1: The problem HEDL is random self-reducible in the sense of the definition in [TW].

Theorem A2: There exists a perfect zero-knowledge interactive proof system for the language L_s.

Theorem A3: There exists a perfect zero-knowledge interactive proof system for the language $\overline{L}_s$.

We now restrict ourselves to the discussion on the complexity of L_ℓ. In 1988, Goldreich and Kushilevitz [GK] showed a perfect zero-knowledge interactive proof for the language of which complexity is equivalent to that of the discrete logarithm problem over a multiplicative group of a finite field, and they mentioned that their protocol would be extended to cover the general discrete logarithm problem defined over a finite abelian group. However, they assume in [GK] that the structure of finite abelian group is known, whereas we do not. To investigate the complexity of HEDL without such assumption, we take into account the complexity of determining the structure of finite abelian group. Thus, the context in this paper is crucially different from that in [GK].

Proof of Theorem 1 :

L_ℓ **is in** $\mathcal{NP}$:   It is easily seen that L_ℓ is in $\mathcal{NP}$ if $N =\text{OrdJ}(q, n, C)$ is given. In fact, a nondeterministic polynomial time Turing machine can guess $m = \text{HEDL}(q, n, C, X, B)$ among positive integers less than N, and then check in a straightforward manner that $m \geq k$. Here, by Theorem B, L_{NJ} is in $\mathcal{P}$. Thus, L_ℓ is in $\mathcal{NP}$.

L_ℓ **is in co-**$\mathcal{AM}$:   We show that $\overline{L}_\ell$ is in $\mathcal{AM}$. $\overline{L}_\ell$ is expressed as follows:

$\overline{L}_\ell = \{x|\ x$ does not satisfy at least one of the specifications for $q, n, C, X, B,$ and $k\}$

$\cup \{< q, n, C, X, B, k > |\ (\exists m \geq 0)[\text{HEDL}(q, n, C, X, B) = m < k]\} \cup L_{us},$

where

$$L_{us} = \{ < q, n, C, X, B > \mid \text{HEDL}(q, n, C, X, B) = \text{``} \perp \text{''} \},$$

that is, the set of instances of *unsolvable* hyperelliptic discrete logarithm problem.

For $\overline{L}_\ell$, the first two sets are both in $\mathcal{NP}$. Thus, it suffices to show that there exists a constant round interactive proof system for the language L_{us}, because Goldwasser and Sipser showed in [GS] that any language having a constant round interactive proof system can be simulated by a constant round Arthur-Merlin game.

The interactive protocol over P and V on input $< q, n, C, X, B >$ consists of three parts, where we use P and V to designate the all-powerful prover and the probabilistic polynomial time bounded verifier, respectively. Informally saying, in Part 1, P and V share a set of points on $\mathbf{J}(C; \mathbf{F}_{q^n})$ that are seemingly the generators of $\mathbf{J}(C; \mathbf{F}_{q^n})$. Note that $\mathbf{J}(C; \mathbf{F}_{q^n})$ is generated by at most $2g$ cyclic groups, where g is the genus of curve C (the proof for the case $g = 1$ will be found in [Sil]). In Part 2, P shows V that the set is actually the set of generators of $\mathbf{J}(C; \mathbf{F}_{q^n})$. This part is inspired by the constant round interactive protocol for graph non-isomorphism [GMW1]. In Part 3, P shows V that there exists no m such that $X \sim mB$.

The protocol works as follows:

Input to (P,V) : $< q, n, C, X, B >$

Part 1:

V: does nothing.

P: chooses $G = (\xi_1, \ldots, \xi_\ell)$, the tuple of generators of abelian decomposition of $\mathbf{J}(C; \mathbf{F}_{q^n})$. That is, each $\xi_i \in G$ $(1 \le i \le \ell)$ has the order of prime power, namely $\text{ord}(\xi_i) = p_i^{n_i}$, and G generates $\mathbf{J}(C; \mathbf{F}_{q^n})$ itself: $\mathbf{J}(C; \mathbf{F}_{q^n}) \cong \langle \xi_1 \rangle \oplus \cdots \oplus \langle \xi_\ell \rangle$, where $\oplus$ denotes the direct sum, and $N = \Pi_{i=1}^\ell p_i^{n_i} = \text{OrdJ}(q, n, C)$.

P→V: G, $\{p_i\}$, $\{n_i\}$, and $\mathcal{NP}$-proofs [Pr] for the fact that p_i is prime $(1 \le i \le \ell)$.

V: continues if $\text{ord}(\xi_i) = p_i^{n_i}$ and $N = \Pi_{i=1}^k p_i^{n_i}$ with p_i prime $(1 \le i \le \ell)$ else rejects and halts.

Part 2:

V: randomly picks $\sigma \in S_\ell$ and $r_i \in \mathbf{Z}_{\text{ord}(\xi_{\sigma(i)})} \setminus \{0\}$, and computes $T_i \sim r_i \xi_{\sigma(i)}$ $(1 \le i \le \ell)$, where S_ℓ denotes the symmetric group of degree ℓ.

V→P: $T_1, \ldots, T_\ell$

P: computes $\tau \in S_\ell$ such that $T_i \sim \tilde{r}_i \xi_{\tau(i)}$ $(1 \le i \le \ell)$.

P→V: τ

V: continues if $\tau = \sigma$ else rejects and halts.

Part 3:

P: computes $(x_1, \ldots, x_\ell)$ and $(b_1, \ldots, b_\ell)$ such that
$$X = [\xi_1^{x_1}, \ldots, \xi_\ell^{x_\ell}] \text{ and } B = [\xi_1^{b_1}, \ldots, \xi_\ell^{b_\ell}].$$

P→V: $(x_1, \ldots, x_\ell)$ and $(b_1, \ldots, b_\ell)$.

V: accepts if
$$X = [\xi_1^{x_1}, \ldots, \xi_\ell^{x_\ell}], B = [\xi_1^{b_1}, \ldots, \xi_\ell^{b_\ell}],$$

and there exists no m satisfying the linear equations
$$(\forall j)[x_j \equiv b_j m \bmod \operatorname{ord}(\xi_j)],$$

else rejects and halts. (End of Protocol)

Note that in the last step, V checks that $\neg(\exists m)[X \sim mB]$. Because

$$\neg(\exists m)[X \sim mB] \Leftrightarrow \neg(\exists m)[(\forall j)[\xi_j^{x_j} = (\xi_j^{b_j})^m]]$$
$$\Leftrightarrow \neg(\exists m)[(\forall j)[x_j \equiv b_j m \bmod \operatorname{ord}(\xi_j)]].$$

This protocol constitutes a constant round interactive proof system for L_{us}. Thus, it is immediate from the result in [GS] that L_{us} is in $\mathcal{AM}$. $\square$

It is clearly seen that determining the structure of $\mathbf{J}(C; \mathbf{F}_{q^n})$ is in $\mathcal{AM}$, hence L_{us} is in $\mathcal{AM}$. In other words, if the structure is determined in nondeterministic polynomial time, then L_{us} is in $\mathcal{NP}$, and consequently L_ℓ is in $\mathcal{NP} \cap \text{co-}\mathcal{NP}$. To prove Theorem 5, we show that for an elliptic curve E, the structure of $\mathbf{J}(E; \mathbf{F}_{q^n})$ is determined in nondeterministic polynomial time. The idea is based on Miller's algorithm [Mi2] to compute the value of Weil e_m-pairing, which also plays an important role in [MOV] to prove the reduction from the (supersingular) elliptic curve discrete logarithm problem to the discrete logarithm problem defined over the multiplicative group over the finite filed.

Proof of Theorem 2:

It suffices to show that for any elliptic curve E, L_{us}^E is in $\mathcal{NP}$, where L_{us}^E is a subset of L_{us} for the case of genus $g = 1$. We use the notion of Weil e_m-pairing defined as follows (see also [Sil, p.95]).

> **Weil e_m-pairing [Mi2]:** Given an elliptic curve E and a non-negative integer m, there is a unique function e_m such that
> $$e_m : E[m] \times E[m] \to \overline{\mathbf{F}}_{q^n},$$
> where
> $$E[m] = \{S \in \mathbf{J}(E; \overline{\mathbf{F}}_{q^n}) \mid m \neq 0, mS = O\}.$$

Here, we use O to denote the identity element in $\mathbf{J}(E; \mathbf{F}_{q^n})$.

Weil e_m-pairing has the following properties:

1. $e_m(S, T)$ is an m-th root of unity for all $S, T \in E[m]$.
2. Identity: $e_m(S, S) = 1$ for all $S \in E[m]$.
3. Skew-symmetry: $e_m(S, T) = e_m(T, S)^{-1}$ for all $S, T \in E[m]$.
4. Linearity: $e_m(S + U, T) = e_m(S, T)e_m(U, T)$ for all $S, T, U \in E[m]$.
5. Non-degeneracy: If $e_m(S, T) = 1$ for all $S \in E[m]$, then $T = O$.

To determine the structure of $\mathbf{J}(E; \mathbf{F}_{q^n})$, the following facts are essential:

1. $\mathbf{J}(E; \mathbf{F}_{q^n})$ is always either cyclic, or the direct sum of two cyclic groups of orders α and β where $\alpha | \beta$.

2. Let ξ_1 and ξ_2 be points on $\mathbf{J}(E; \mathbf{F}_{q^n})$ of orders α and β respectively. If $\alpha | \beta$, $\alpha\beta = N = \mathrm{OrdJ}(q, n, E)$, and $e_\beta(\xi_1, \xi_2) \neq 1$, then $\mathbf{J}(E; \mathbf{F}_{q^n})$ is the direct sum of two cyclic groups $\langle \xi_1 \rangle$ and $\langle \xi_2 \rangle$. In fact, by the properties 1 and 4 of Weil pairing, if $\xi_1 = t\xi_2$ for some $t \in \mathbf{Z}_N$, $e_\beta(\xi_1, \xi_2) = e_\beta(t\xi_2, \xi_2) = e_\beta(\xi_2, \xi_2)^t = 1^t = 1$.

3. Miller [Mi2] showed an algorithm that on input an elliptic curve E over $\mathbf{F}_{q^n}$, a natural number m, and two points $P, Q \in E[m]$, outputs the value $e_m(P, Q)$, which runs in expected polynomial (in $\log q$) time. (This is now converted into a deterministic polynomial time algorithm by V. S. Miller.) To compute $e_m(P, Q)$, the algorithm first picks additional points $T, U \in \mathbf{J}(E; \mathbf{F}_{q^n})$ at random repeatedly until T and U satisfy the specific conditions [Ka2, Mi2]. The conditions for the choice depends only on inputs m, P, Q, and they can be checked in deterministic polynomial time. Note that such points T, U always exist for any m, P, Q. Once T and U are appropriately fixed, the subsequent steps are executed in deterministic polynomial time. The reason why the running time is *expected* polynomial is explained by the random choice of the additional points T, U.

By the above facts, we show that L_{us}^E is in $\mathcal{NP}$.

We guess $\xi \in \mathbf{J}(E; \mathbf{F}_{q^n})$ and the factorization of $N = \mathrm{OrdJ}(q, n, E)$, and check in deterministic polynomial time that $\mathrm{ord}(\xi) = N$. If the check is passed, we determine that $\mathbf{J}(E; \mathbf{F}_{q^n}) = \langle \xi \rangle$. Otherwise, we guess $\xi_1, \xi_2 \in \mathbf{J}(E; \mathbf{F}_{q^n})$ and the additional points $T, U \in \mathbf{J}(E; \mathbf{F}_{q^n})$ to be used in Miller's algorithm. Then, we check in deterministic polynomial time that $\mathrm{ord}(\xi_1) \cdot \mathrm{ord}(\xi_2) = \alpha\beta = N$, $\alpha | \beta$, and $e_\beta(\xi_1, \xi_2) \neq 1$. If the checks are passed, we determine that $\mathbf{J}(E; \mathbf{F}_{q^n}) \cong \langle \xi_1 \rangle \oplus \langle \xi_2 \rangle$. At this time, the structure of $\mathbf{J}(E; \mathbf{F}_{q^n})$ has been determined in nondeterministic polynomial time. Next, we check that $\neg(\exists m)[X \sim mB]$, which is an $\mathcal{NP}$-statement as shown in Part 3 in the interactive protocol for L_{us}. Thus, L_{us}^E is in $\mathcal{NP}$, and consequently L_ℓ^E is in $\mathcal{NP} \cap$ co-$\mathcal{NP}$. $\square$

4 Concluding Remarks

We showed that for curves with genus $g \geq 2$, the complexity of hyperelliptic discrete logarithm problems is characterized as in $\mathcal{NP} \cap$ co-$\mathcal{AM}$. Whereas, for curves with $g = 1$, the complexity is characterized as in $\mathcal{NP} \cap$ co-$\mathcal{NP}$. The latter is the same characterization for the discrete logarithm problem defined over the multiplicative group of a finite field.

To characterize the complexity of hyperelliptic discrete logarithm problem as in $\mathcal{NP} \cap$ co-$\mathcal{NP}$ for any g, it suffices to positively solve the question: Is L_{us}, the set of instances of *unsolvable* hyperelliptic discrete logarithm problem, in $\mathcal{NP}$ for any $g \geq 2$? However, we have not yet solved it. If Miller's algorithm can be used to determine the structure of jacobian $\mathbf{J}(C; \mathbf{F}_{q^n})$ for C with any g, L_{us} is in $\mathcal{NP}$. But this requires an extension and redefinition of Weil pairing to cover curves with $g \geq 2$. It is worth noting that the attempt to define such extended Weil pairing and to positively solve this open question has already been started by Okamoto and Sakurai [OS].

Acknowledgements

We wish to thank Neal Koblitz of Washington University, Tatsuaki Okamoto of NTT, and Jonathan S. Pila of Columbia University for their invaluable suggestions on our work. Eyal Kushilevitz of Technion gave us helpful comments on [GK]. Victor S. Miller of IBM kindly informed us of the existence of deterministic polynomial time version of his algorithm for computing Weil pairing. We are also grateful to Mitsuru Matsui of Mitsubishi Electric Corporation for his helpful advice on algebraic geometry and number theory.

References

[AH] W. Aiello and J. Håstad, "Statistical zero-knowledge languages can be recognized in two rounds," Proc. 28th FOCS, pp.439-448 (1987).

[Ba] László Babai, "Trading group theory to randomness," Proc. 17th STOC, pp.421-429 (1985).

[Br] Gilles Brassard, "A note on the complexity of cryptography," IEEE Trans. Inf. Theory, vol.IT-25, no.2, pp.232-233 (1979).

[Ca] David G. Cantor, "Computing in the Jacobian of a hyperelliptic curve," Math. Comp., vol.48, no.177, pp.95-101 (1987).

[DH] W. Diffie and M. Hellman, "New directions in cryptography," IEEE Trans. Inf. Theory, vol.IT-22, no.6, pp.644-654 (1976).

[Fo] Lance J. Fortnow, "The complexity of perfect zero-knowledge," Proc. 19th STOC, pp.204-209 (1987).

[GK] O. Goldreich and E. Kushilevitz, "A perfect zero-knowledge interactive proof for a problem equivalent to discrete logarithm," Proc. CRYPTO'88 (1988).

[GMR] S. Goldwasser, S. Micali, and C. Rackoff, "The zero-knowledge complexity of interactive proof-systems," Proc. 17th STOC, pp.291-304 (1985).

[GMW1] O. Goldreich, S. Micali, and A. Wigderson, "Proofs that yield nothing but their validity and a methodology of cryptographic protocol design," Proc. 27th FOCS, pp.174-187 (1986).

[GMW2] O. Goldreich, S. Micali, and A. Wigderson, "Proofs that yield nothing but their validity or All languages in $\mathcal{NP}$ have zero-knowledge proofs," Technical Report 554, Technion (1989).

[GS] S. Goldwasser and M. Sipser, "Private coins versus public coins in interactive proof systems," Proc. 18th STOC, pp.59-68 (1986).

[Ka1] Burton S. Kaliski, Jr., "A pseudo-random bit generator based on elliptic logarithms," Proc. CRYPTO'86, pp.84-103 (1986).

[Ka2] Burton S. Kaliski, Jr., "Elliptic curves and cryptography: a pseudorandom bit generator and other tools," MIT/LCS/ TR-411, MIT (1988).

[Ko1] Neal Koblitz, "Elliptic curve cryptosystems," Math. Comp., vol.48, no.177, pp.203-209 (1987).

[Ko2] Neal Koblitz, "A Course in Number Theory and Cryptography," GTM114, Springer-Verlag, New York (1987).

[Ko3] Neal Koblitz, " Hyperelliptic cryptosystems," J. Cryptology, vol.1, no.3, pp. 139-150 (1989).

[Mi1] Victor S. Miller, "Use of elliptic curves in cryptography," Proc. CRYPTO'85, pp.417-426 (1985).

[Mi2] Victor S. Miller, "Short programs for functions on curves," manuscript (1986).

[MOV] A. Menezes, T. Okamoto, and S. Vanstone, "Reducing elliptic curve logarithms to logarithms in a finite field," announced at CRYPTO'90 rump session (1990) (to appear in Proc. STOC'91).

[OS] T. Okamoto and K. Sakurai, "On the complexity of problems associated with hyperelliptic curves," Proc. SCIS91, 9C (1991).

[Pi] Jonathan S. Pila, "Frobenius maps of abelian varieties and finding roots of unity in finite fields," Ph.D Thesis, Stanford University (to appear in Math. Comp.) (1988).

[Pr] Pratt,V., "Every Prime has a succinct certificate," SIAM J. COMPUT. vol.4, pp.214-220 (1975).

[Sc1] Uwe Schöning, "A low and high hierarchy within $\mathcal{NP}$," J. Comp. Syst. Sci., vol.27, pp.14-28 (1983).

[Sc2] Uwe Schöning, "Graph isomorphism is in the low hierarchy," J. Comp. Syst. Sci., vol.37, pp.312-323 (1988).

[Sch] René Schoof, "Elliptic curves over finite field and the computation of square roots mod p," Math. Comp., vol.44, pp.483-494 (1985).

[Shi] Hiroki Shizuya, "Zero-knowledge interactive proofs for hyper- and elliptic-discrete logarithm problems," Proc. WCIS'89, pp.143-152 (1989).

[SI] H. Shizuya, and T. Itoh, "A group-theoretic interface to random self-reducibility," Trans. IEICE, vol.E-73, no.7, pp.1087-1091 (1990).

[Sil] Joseph H. Silverman, "The Arithmetic of Elliptic Curves," GTM 106, Springer-Verlag, New York (1986).

[TW] M. Tompa and H. Woll, "Random self-reducibility and zero knowledge interactive proofs for possession of information," Proc. 28th FOCS, pp.472-482 (1987).

Appendix

A.1 Random Self-Reducibility of HEDL

HEDL reduces to the elliptic curve discrete logarithm problem when $g = 1$, and we know that the elliptic curve discrete logarithm is random self-reducible [Shi] in the sense of definition in [TW]. We show here that HEDL is also random self-reducible.

Theorem A1 : HEDL is random self-reducible.

A lemma is required for the proof. For a finite group G under a binary operation, we mean by the accessibility of G that any element in G can be picked randomly and uniformly in time polynomial in $|\sharp G|$, and that the binary operation for any pair of elements is computed in time polynomial in $|\sharp G|$.

Lemma A1 ([SI]) :

Let G_1 and G_2 be accessible finite groups, respectively, and φ be a homomorphism from G_1 onto G_2. For any $\xi \in G_1$, let $\xi^{-1} \in G_1$ and $\varphi(\xi)$ be computed in time polynomial in $|\sharp G_1|$. Then, given $x \in G_2$, the problem to compute some $y \in G_1$ such that $x = \varphi(y)$ is random self-reducible.

Proof of Theorem A1 :

Let φ be the homomorphism from the finite abelian group $\mathbf{Z}_N$ onto $\langle B \rangle$ such that $\varphi(\xi) = \xi B$, where $N = \mathrm{OrdJ}(q, n, C)$, and $\langle B \rangle$ is the group of divisors that consists of any multiple of B. By Pila's theorem, N is computed in polynomial time. This implies that we can determine the range of elements in $\mathbf{Z}_N$ to pick, thus $\mathbf{Z}_N$ is accessible. In addition, given any element in $\mathbf{Z}_N$, its inverse is computed in a straightforward manner. Since φ is computed in polynomial time by using the repeated doubling algorithm, any element in $\langle B \rangle$ can be picked randomly by computing $\varphi(r)$ with r chosen randomly from $\mathbf{Z}_N$. This implies that $\langle B \rangle$ is also accessible. Thus, by Lemma A1, HEDL is random self-reducible.

□

A.2 Perfect Zero-Knowledge Interactive Proof for L_s

Theorem A2 : There exists a perfect zero-knowledge interactive proof system for L_s.

Proof : The computing model is based on that in [TW], i.e., we consider the interaction between the prover (P) of unbounded power and the verifier (V) of probabilistic polynomial time bounded power. The construction of protocol is almost the same as shown in [TW] for the language membership. A perfect zero-knowledge protocol for L_s on input (q, n, C, X, B) works as follows:

P: picks $r \in [0, N)$ randomly and computes R such that $R \sim rB$, where $N = \mathrm{OrdJ}$ (q, n, C).

P→V: R

V→P: $e \in \{0, 1\}$ chosen at random.

P→V: σ such that $R \sim \sigma B - eX$.

By [TW], the above protocol forms a perfect zero-knowledge interactive proof system for the language membership in L_s. □

A.3 Perfect Zero-Knowledge Interactive Proof for $\overline{L}_s$

We mean by $\overline{L}_s$ the complement of L_s. More precisely,

$$\overline{L}_s = \{x \mid x \text{ does not satisfy at least one of the specifications for } q, n, C, X, \text{ and } B\}$$
$$\cup \{< q, n, C, X, B > \mid X \in \mathbf{J}(C; \mathbf{F}_{q^n}) \setminus \langle B \rangle\}.$$

The latter set is equivalent to L_{us} which we discussed in Section 3.

Theorem A3 : There exists a perfect zero-knowledge interactive proof system for $\overline{L}_s$.

Proof : The protocol is essentially the same as the statistical zero-knowledge interactive proof for the language membership in $\{< p, a, b > \mid b \in \mathbf{Z}_p^* \setminus \langle a \rangle_p\}$ shown in [TW]. However, the following construction of the protocol is converted into perfect zero-knowledge, based on the idea of perfect zero-knowledge interactive proof for graph non-isomorphism [GMW2]. Note that in the protocol, steps to check the validity of input are omitted since V of probabilistic polynomial time power can check it without interaction.

$$\text{Input to (P,V)} : < q, n, C, X, B >$$

V: chooses $r \in \mathbf{Z}_N \setminus \{0\}$ and $\alpha \in \{0, 1\}$ randomly and uniformly, and computes $Z \sim rB + \alpha X$, where $N = \mathrm{OrdJ}$ (q, n, C). V also generates $T_i = (T_{i0}, T_{i1})$ $(1 \le i \le t = 2|N|)$ such that $T_{i0} \sim Z + s_{i0}B - \beta_i X$ and $T_{i1} \sim Z + s_{i1}B - (1 - \beta_i)X$, where $s_{ij} \in \mathbf{Z}_N \setminus \{0\}$ $(j = 0, 1)$ and $\beta_i \in \{0, 1\}$ are chosen randomly, uniformly and independently.

V→P: Z, $T_i (1 \leq i \leq t)$

    P: chooses at random, a subset $I \subseteq \{1, 2, \ldots, t\}$.

P→V: I

    V: rejects and halts if $I \not\subseteq \{1, 2, \ldots, t\}$. Otherwise, V generates $w_i (1 \leq i \leq t)$ such that if $i \in I$, $w_i = (\beta_i, s_{i0}, s_{i1})$; if $i \notin I$, $w_i = (\gamma_i, u_i)$ where $\gamma_i \equiv \alpha + \beta_i \pmod{2}$ and $u_i \equiv r + s_{i\gamma_i} \pmod{N}$.

V→P: $w_i (1 \leq i \leq t)$

    P: checks that for $w_i (1 \leq i \leq t)$, $((i \in I) \wedge (T_{i0} \sim Z + s_{i0}B - \beta_i X) \wedge (T_{i1} \sim Z + s_{i1}B - (1 - \beta_i)X)) \vee ((i \notin I) \wedge (T_{i\gamma_i} \sim u_i B))$. If either condition is violated, P stops. Otherwise, P computes δ such that $\delta = 0$ if $Z \in \langle B \rangle$; $\delta = 1$ if $Z \notin \langle B \rangle$.

P→V: δ

    V: accepts if $\alpha = \delta$. Otherwise, V rejects and halts.

Completeness, soundness, and perfect zero-knowledgeness of the protocol are proven in a way like [GMW2]. In the proof of perfect zero-knowledgeness, it is essential that $t = 2|N|$, because $2^{-t} \cdot 2N < 1$. □

A.4 Immediate Corollaries

Combining Theorem A2 and the results of Fortnow [Fo] and Aiello-Håstad [AH], we can show that L_s is in $\mathcal{AM} \cap$ co-$\mathcal{AM}$. However, L_s is polynomial time Turing reducible to L_ℓ, and our main results show that L_ℓ is in $\mathcal{NP} \cap$ co-$\mathcal{AM}$, and that for elliptic curves L_ℓ^E is in $\mathcal{NP} \cap$ co-$\mathcal{NP}$. Thus,

Corollary A1: L_s is in $\mathcal{NP} \cap$ co-$\mathcal{AM}$, and L_s^E is in $\mathcal{NP} \cap$ co-$\mathcal{NP}$, where L_s^E designates L_s for the case of genus $g = 1$.

It immediately follows from [Fo] that neither L_s nor L_s^E will be $\mathcal{NP}$-complete unless the polynomial time hierarchy collapses to the second level. Furthermore, by Schöning's results on his low and high hierarchies within $\mathcal{NP}$ [Sc1, Sc2], we can show

Corollary A2: Neither L_s nor L_ℓ will be $\mathcal{NP}$-complete unless the polynomial time hierarchy collapses to the second level.

Corollary A3: Neither L_s^E nor L_ℓ^E will be $\mathcal{NP}$-complete unless the polynomial time hierarchy collapses to the first level.

An Expanded Set of S-box Design Criteria Based on Information Theory and its Relation to Differential-Like Attacks

M. H. Dawson and S. E. Tavares

Department of Electrical Engineering
Queens University at Kingston
Kingston, Ontario, Canada, K7L 3N6
Phone (613) 545–2925
Fax (613) 545–6615

Abstract

The security of DES-like cryptosystems depends heavily on the strength of the Substitution boxes (S-boxes) used. The design of new S-boxes is therefore an important concern in the creation of new and more secure cryptosystems. The full set of design criteria for the S-boxes of DES has never been released and a complete set has yet to be proposed in the open literature. This paper introduces a unified S-box design framework based on information theory and illustrates how it provides immunity to the differential attack.

Introduction

In private-key cryptosystems which are based on substitution-permutation (S-P) networks (i.e., DES-like systems), the strength of the cryptosystem depends directly on the quality of the substitution boxes (S-boxes) used by the algorithm. Biham and Shamir, in their recent paper on Differential Cryptanalysis [1] showed that DES could be broken if poor S-boxes were used. The design of good S-boxes is therefore an important part of designing a DES-like cryptosystem.

In this work we present an expanded set of design criteria for creating good S-boxes based on information theoretic concepts and show that an S-Box that meets these criteria is immune to differential cryptanalysis[1]. We also discuss the analysis of the DES S-boxes and the creation of new S-boxes of various sizes using the new design framework. The new criteria give us new insights into the design of good S-boxes which is of considerable interest as any new private-key cryptosystem that replaces DES will require new S-boxes for copyright and security reasons.

Background

Cryptographic substitutions, first introduced by Shannon in [2], were further refined and explained in [3][4]. It has been shown in [5][6] and more recently in [1] that poor S-boxes can lead to weak cryptosystems. The S-boxes of DES [7] have been subject to much analysis (see [8][9][10][11] and others).

Work on defining desirable properties of S-boxes has been presented in [12][13][14] [15][16][17]. More recently, some properties based on information theory were presented by Forré in [11]. Despite the previous investigations of desirable properties of S-boxes, a comprehensive set of design criteria for S-boxes has yet to be presented.

We will extend the set of desirable properties of S-boxes using information theory and use these properties to propose a set of design criteria for S-boxes.

Static and Dynamic Views of an S-box

S-Boxes can be viewed in two distinct ways. The first is the static view of the S-box which describes the S-box when the inputs are not changing. The second is the dynamic view of the S-box which describes the S-box when the inputs are changing.

Much of the previous work on S-boxes has focussed on the static properties of S-boxes. The **static** view of an S-box, with inputs $X = [x_1, ..., x_m]$ and outputs $Y = [y_1, ..., y_n]$, can be envisioned as shown in Figure 1.

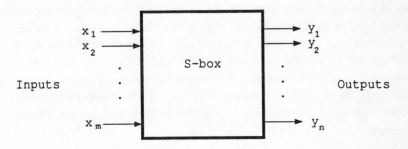

Figure 1 Static View of an m×n S-box

The importance of certain **dynamic** properties of an S-box were introduced by Feistel in [3] and refined in [14]. More recently Biham and Shamir's work on differential cryptanalysis[1] stimulated us to discover that a broader range of dynamic properties of S-boxes are important in DES-like cryptosystems. When considering the dynamic properties of an S-box, it is useful to refer to the delta S-box shown in Figure 2.

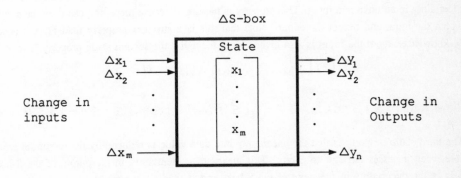

Figure 2 Dynamic View of an m×n S-box

In Figure 2 the values of the vector $X = [x_1, ..., x_m]$ are the current inputs to the S-box and can be viewed as the state of the delta S-Box. The $\triangle x_i$ and the $\triangle y_i$ are the changes in the inputs and outputs respectively. The current state X is usually unknown and it is assumed that any relation found between the $\triangle x_i$ and the $\triangle y_i$ is over all possible states.

Properties of Ideal S-boxes Based on Information Theory

For a random variable $\mathbf{z}$ with possible values $z_1, ..., z_n$, the uncertainty in $\mathbf{z}$ is $H(\mathbf{z}) = \sum_{i=1}^{n} P(z_i) log_2 \left(\frac{1}{P(z_i)} \right)$. The mutual information between two random variables $\mathbf{X}$ and $\mathbf{Y}$ is $I(\mathbf{X}; \mathbf{Y}) = H(\mathbf{X}) - H(\mathbf{X} \mid \mathbf{Y})$. The information theoretic basis for our criteria is to minimize the information which can be gained about unknown inputs and outputs of an S-box from known inputs and outputs. If the random variable $\mathbf{U}$ describes the known values and the random variable $\mathbf{V}$ represents the unknown values we want $I(\mathbf{V}; \mathbf{U}) = H(\mathbf{V}) - H(\mathbf{V} \mid \mathbf{U}) = 0$. An "Ideal" S-box should have $I(\mathbf{V}; \mathbf{U}) = 0$ for $\mathbf{U}$ representing any combination of the inputs and outputs. However, due to the deterministic nature of an S-box the input-output relation is known. The best an Ideal S-box can do then is to have $I(\mathbf{V}; \mathbf{U}) = 0$ when $\mathbf{U}$ represents any combination of a subset of the inputs and a subset of the outputs. By minimizing the information which leaks through the S-box the amount of information available to a cryptanalyst is reduced and thus the cryptosystem is strengthened. In [11] Forré developed two properties of an Ideal m×n bit S-box based on these ideas. The first property was that the uncertainty in the output bits is not reduced by the knowledge of any subset of the input bits. The second property was that the uncertainty in any unknown output bits is not reduced by the knowledge of the other output bits.

We have defined a set of six properties that an Ideal S-box is required to meet. This set of properties has a broader scope than those of Forré and any S-box that meets these properties will also meet Forré's. The properties are grouped into a set of static properties and a set of dynamic properties.

Static Properties

The first static property is that the partial information about the inputs and outputs does not reduce the uncertainty in an unknown output. Note that this is a stronger property than Forré's because partial knowledge about the output is also given. More formally, the first static property is that:

$$H(y_i \mid x_{j_1}, ..., x_{j_k}, y_{l_1}, ..., y_{l_s}) = H(y_i)$$

for all $i, k, l, s, p \mid 1 \leq i \leq n, 1 \leq k \leq m - 1, 1 \leq j_1, ..., j_k \leq m, 1 \leq s \leq n - 1, 1 \leq (l_1, ..., l_s, p) \leq n, l_p \neq i$.

The second static property is that the partial information about the inputs and outputs does not reduce the uncertainty in an unknown input. This property is required because the S-box can often be attacked from both the input and output directions. Note that this is a stronger property than Forré's because partial knowledge about the input is also given. More formally, the second static property is that:

$$H(x_i \mid x_{j_1}, ..., x_{j_k}, y_{l_1}, ..., y_{l_s}) = H(x_i)$$

for all $i, k, l, s, p \mid 1 \leq i \leq m, 1 \leq k \leq m - 1, 1 \leq (j_1, ..., j_k, p) \leq m, 1 \leq s \leq n - 1, 1 \leq l_1, ..., l_s \leq n, j_p \neq i$.

The third static property is that the uncertainty in a data value is reduced by the minimum amount possible when it passes through an S-box. This means that uncertainty in the output of the S-box is as great as the uncertainty in the input of the S-box, and if this is not possible, because m > n, that the uncertainty in the output is the maximum for the number of output bits. This property is desirable so that one cannot guess the output of the S-box more easily that the input. More formally, let $\mathbf{X} = [x_1, ..., x_m]$, $\mathbf{Y} = [y_1, ..., y_n]$ where $m \geq n$, then the third static properties is that:

$$H(\mathbf{Y}) = \left\{ \begin{array}{ll} H(\mathbf{X}), & if \ H(\mathbf{X}) \leq n \\ n, & if \ H(\mathbf{X}) > n \end{array} \right\}$$

Dynamic Properties

The dynamic properties are similar to the static properties except that they deal with the changes in the inputs and outputs. These definitions refer to the delta S-box. The first dynamic property is that partial information about the changes in the inputs and outputs does not reduce the uncertainty in changes of the unknown outputs. More formally, the first dynamic property is that:

$$H(\triangle y_i \mid \triangle x_{j_1}, ..., \triangle x_{j_k}, \triangle y_{l_1}, ..., \triangle y_{l_s}) = H(\triangle y_i)$$

for all $i, k, l, s, p \mid 1 \leq i \leq n, 1 \leq j_1, ..., j_k, k \leq m, 1 \leq s \leq n - 1, 1 \leq (l_1, ..., l_s, p) \leq n, l_p \neq i$.

The second dynamic property is that partial information about the changes in the inputs and outputs does not reduce the uncertainty in changes of the unknown inputs. Again, this property is required because an S-box may be attacked from both the input and output directions. More formally, the second dynamic property is that:

$$H(\triangle x_i \mid \triangle x_{j_1}, ..., \triangle x_{j_k}, \triangle y_{l_1}, ..., \triangle y_{l_s}) = H(\triangle x_i)$$

for all $i, k, l, s, p \mid 1 \leq i \leq m, 1 \leq k \leq m - 1, 1 \leq (j_1, ..., j_k, p) \leq m, 1 \leq l_1, ..., l_s, s \leq n, j_p \neq i$.

The third dynamic property is that the uncertainty in the changes in a data value is reduced by the minimum amount possible when it passes through an S-box. This means that uncertainty in the output changes of the S-box is as great as the uncertainty in the input changes of the S-box, and if this is not possible, because m > n, that the uncertainty in the output changes is the maximum for the number of output bits. This property is desirable so that one cannot guess the output changes of the S-box more easily that the input changes. More formally, let $\triangle X = [\triangle x_1, ..., \triangle x_m]$, $\triangle Y = [\triangle y_1, ..., \triangle y_n]$ where $m \geq n$, then the third dynamic property is that:

$$H(\triangle Y) = \begin{Bmatrix} H(\triangle X), & if\ H(\triangle X) \leq n \\ n, & if\ H(\triangle X) > n \end{Bmatrix}$$

Again, this property is important to ensure that repeated use of S-boxes does not reduce the uncertainty in the changes of the outputs of the S-boxes and therefore reduce the work required for cryptanalysis.

Static Design Criteria

This section defines the static design criteria for m×n S-boxes which are based on the static properties of an Ideal S-box. Note that invertibility only applies to n×n S-boxes. The definitions are for an m×n bit S-box with inputs X and outputs Y. In the definition of the design criteria we use the requirement that $P(u_j \mid V) = P(u_j)$ to enforce that $I(U; V) = 0$. This is the same as requiring that $H(U) - H(U \mid V) = 0$. We chose this description because it makes the implications of the criteria clearer.

Input-output Independence

The Input-output Independence criterion of order r is used to select S-boxes for which knowledge of r input values does not reduce the uncertainty in the output values. Formally, an S-box meets the Input-output Independence criterion of order r, r < m, iff:

$$Prob(y_j \mid a_1 x_1, ..., a_m x_m) = Prob(y_j)$$

for all $x_i, y_j, a_k \mid 1 \leq j \leq n, 1 \leq i, k \leq m, (a_k, x_i, y_j) \in \{0,1\}, A = [a_1, ..., a_m], W(A) = r$, where $a_k = 1$ denotes that x_k is given and $a_k = 0$ denotes that x_k is not given. Note that the highest order of Input-output Independence that can be met is m-1. To meet Input-output Independence of order m the input-output relation would have to be unknown and this is never true due to the deterministic nature of S-boxes.

Output-input Independence

The Output-input Independence criterion is used to select S-boxes for which knowledge of some of the outputs does not reduce the uncertainty in the inputs. This criterion is defined in exactly the same way as Input-output Independence except that the inputs and outputs are reversed.

Output-output Independence

The Output-output Independence criterion is used to select S-boxes for which partial information about the outputs bits does not reduce the uncertainty in the unknown output bits. Formally, an S-box meets the Output-output Independence criterion of order r, r < n, iff:

$$Prob(y_j \mid a_1 y_1, ..., a_n y_n) = Prob(y_j)$$

for all $y_j, a_k \mid 1 \leq j, k \leq n, (a_k, y_j) \in \{0,1\}, a_j = 0, A = [a_1, ..., a_n], W(A) = r$, where $a_k = 1$ denotes that x_k is given and $a_k = 0$ denotes that x_k is not given. This criterion is important in order to prevent attacks which use correlation between the outputs of the S-boxes from succeeding.

An important result which we discovered is that this criterion is met, for all orders of n-1 or less, by all invertible n×n bit S-boxes. The proof is quite simple and is as follows. The possible outputs of an invertible n×n bit S-box include all the values from 0 to $2^n - 1$. For this reason if the output value $y_1, y_2, ..., y_{l-1}, 1, y_{l+1}, ..., y_n$ exists, the value $y_1, y_2, ..., y_{l-1}, 0, y_{l+1}, ..., y_n$ must also exist and therefore the values of y_i , $i \neq l$ cannot be used to predict the value of y_l. It follows that the output bits of an invertible S-box are independent. This proof can be extended to show that any m×n bit S-box made up of invertible n×n bit S-boxes meets the Output-output Independence criterion for all orders up to n-1 because, assuming all input values occur, each possible output value will occur 2^{m-n} times and thus the same argument holds except that the output values $y_1, y_2, ..., y_{l-1}, 1, y_{l+1}, ..., y_n$ and $y_1, y_2, ..., y_{l-1}, 0, y_{l+1}, ..., y_n$ each occur 2^{m-n} times.

Nonlinearity

Nonlinearity is a crucial property of an Ideal S-box. It is the nonlinearity of an S-box that prevents it from being expressed as a set of linear equations, which could then be used to break any cryptosystem using that S-box. It is therefore important to use S-boxes with the highest possible nonlinearity. Nonlinearity has been proposed as a design criterion previously and is defined in [12].

Information Completeness

The criterion of Completeness was proposed by Kam and Davida in [13]. They define Completeness as:

for every possible input value every output bit depends on all input bits and not just a proper subset of the input bits.

As noted by Forré in [11] this is a weak concept. We extend this definition, to define *Information Completeness*, by requiring that each output bit depend on all the information in each input bit as opposed to depending on only part of the information in each bit. This means that no function of the inputs, whose output set has less information content than the original set of inputs, can produce the same set of outputs for the S-box. In Figure 3 this means that if the set $\mathbf{X}' = \left\{ x_1', ..., x_m' \right\}$ produced by the mapping $F(\mathbf{X}) = \mathbf{X}'$, produces the same outputs, from the S-box, as the set $\mathbf{X} = \{x_1, ..., x_m\}$ and has less information content than $\mathbf{X}$, the S-box is not Information Complete.

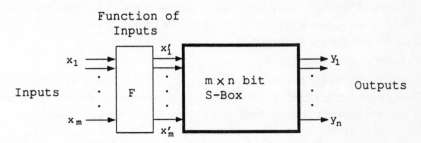

Figure 3 Illustration of Information Completeness for an m×n bit S-box

More formally, an m×n S-box, S, will be Information Complete iff there exists no function F such that: $F(\mathbf{X}) = \mathbf{X}'$ and

$$H\left(\mathbf{X}'\right) < H(\mathbf{X})$$

and $S\left(\mathbf{X}'\right) = S(\mathbf{X})$ for all values of $\mathbf{X}$.

It is clear that Information Completeness includes the notion of Completeness because if any output bit of the S-box does not depend on input bit k, the function:

$$F_{inc}(x_1, ..., x_m) = (x_1, ..., x_{k-1}, x_k, x_{k+1}, ..., x_m), \; x_k = 0$$

exists and $H(F_{inc}(\mathbf{X})) < H(\mathbf{X})$ and $S(F_{inc}(\mathbf{X})) = S(\mathbf{X})$ for all values of $\mathbf{X}$, and therefore the S-box will fail the test of Information Completeness.

This criterion is proposed because all Ideal S-boxes are Information Complete. In the case where an output only depends on a subset of the inputs, partial information (the inputs that the output depends on) can be used to reduce the uncertainty in the output value. This is also the case if the output depends on all the inputs but only on part of the information in the inputs. As an example, consider a 4×4 bit S-box that is not Information Complete and that the Function $F(x_1, x_2, x_3, x_4) = F(x_1, x_2, x_3 + x_4, x_4)$ exists whose outputs produce the same values for output1 of the S-box as $x_1, ..., x_4$ (+ is the standard inclusive or function). In this case the uncertainty in output1 of the S-box is reduced by the partial information of the values of x_1, x_2, x_4. This is because the value of $x_3 + x_4$ can be guessed with probability greater than 1/2. Any S-box that meets the third static property of an Ideal S-box must be Information Complete.

This criterion is important because if an S-box is not Information Complete the outputs may be reduced to a function of fewer inputs (it can be produced by a smaller S-box), and this will reduce the strength of the system as smaller S-boxes have poorer properties than larger ones.

Invertibility

This criterion is generally known to be a desirable property of n×n S-boxes. An S-box is invertible iff it is a one to one mapping. More formally, an n bit S-box, S, is invertible iff:

$$S(\mathbf{X_1}) = S(\mathbf{X_2}) \; iff \; \mathbf{X_1} = \mathbf{X_2}$$

for all inputs X_1 *and* X_2. This criterion fits into our information theoretic framework because an Ideal n×n S-box must meet this criterion. If an S-box is not invertible there are fewer output values than there are input values. If there are fewer output values than input values then there is less uncertainty in the output than in the input, and therefore the third static property of an Ideal S-box will not be met.

Dynamic Design Criteria

The following section defines the dynamic design criteria for m×n S-boxes. The definitions are for an m×n bit S-box with inputs X and outputs Y and use the concept of the delta S-box with changes to the inputs Δx and changes to the outputs Δy.

Dynamic Input-output Independence

The Dynamic Input-output Independence criterion, of order r, is used to select S-boxes for which knowledge of the changes in r inputs bits, does not reduce the uncertainty in the changes of the outputs. Formally, an S-box meets the Dynamic Input-output Independence criterion of order r, $r \leq m$ iff:

$$Prob(\Delta y_j \mid a_1 \Delta x_1, ..., a_m \Delta x_m) = Prob(\Delta y_j)$$

for all $\Delta x_i, \Delta y_j, a_k \mid 1 \leq j \leq n, 1 \leq i, k \leq m, (a_k, \Delta x_i, \Delta y_j) \in \{0,1\}, A = [a_1, ..., a_m], W(A) = r$, where $a_k = 1$ denotes that Δx_k is given and $a_k = 0$ denotes that Δx_k is not given. This criterion is related to previous work in that the Strict Avalanche Criterion introduced and defined by [14, 18] and its extensions are a subset of Dynamic Input-output Independence of order m. The Strict Avalanche Criterion is met if:

$$Prob(\Delta y_j \mid \Delta x_1, ..., \Delta x_m) = Prob(\Delta y_j)$$

for all $\Delta x_i, \Delta y_j \mid 0 \leq j \leq n, 1 \leq i, k \leq m, (\Delta x_i, \Delta y_j) \in \{0,1\}, \Delta X = [\Delta x_1, ..., \Delta x_m], W(\Delta X) = 1$, and the extension to order r, $r \leq m$, is met if:

$$Prob(\Delta y_j \mid \Delta x_1, ..., \Delta x_m) = Prob(\Delta y_j)$$

for all $\Delta x_i, \Delta y_j \mid 0 \leq j \leq n, 1 \leq i, k \leq m, (\Delta x_i, \Delta y_j) \in \{0,1\}, \Delta X = [\Delta x_1, ..., \Delta x_m], W(\Delta X) = r$.

The requirements of SAC are clearly a subset of the requirements of Dynamic Input-output Independence of order m. The extension of SAC given above is also a subset of Dynamic Input-output Independence of order m as it simply enlarges the set of the values of $(\Delta x_1, ..., \Delta x_m)$ for which the condition must hold. In the extreme case, SAC of order m = Dynamic Input-output Independence of order m. We want it to be clear that Dynamic Input-output Independence is not a direct extension of SAC because it originated from a completely different viewpoint, but that SAC happens to be a subset of the highest order of it.

Dynamic Output-input Independence

The Dynamic Output-input Independence criterion is used to select S-boxes for which knowledge of some of the output changes does not reduce the uncertainty in the input changes. This criterion is defined in exactly the same way as Dynamic Input-output Independence except that the input changes and output changes are reversed.

Dynamic Output-output Independence

The Dynamic Output-output Independence criterion, of order r, is used to specify S-boxes for which the knowledge of r of the output changes and a particular pattern of input changes, does not reduce the uncertainty in the unknown output bits. Formally, an S-box meets the Dynamic Output-output Independence criterion of order r, r < n, iff:

$$Prob(\Delta y_j \mid a_1\Delta y_1, ..., a_n\Delta y_n, \Delta x_1, ..., \Delta x_m) = Prob(\Delta y_j \mid \Delta x_1, ..., \Delta x_m)$$

for all $\Delta x_i, \Delta y_j, a_k \mid 1 \leq j \leq n, 1 \leq i, k \leq m, (a_k, \Delta x_i, \Delta y_j) \in \{0,1\}, a_j = 0, A = [a_1, ..., a_m], W(A) = r$, where $a_k = 1$ denotes that Δx_k is given and $a_k = 0$ denotes that Δx_k is not given.

Resistance to Differential Cryptanalysis.

Biham and Shamir introduced differential cryptanalysis in [1]. The attack is based on using the imbalances in the "pairs XOR distribution table", for an S-box, to predict the output XOR from the input XOR. Consider an m×n S-box that meets the Dynamic Input-output Independence criterion of order m and the Dynamic Output-output Independence criterion of order n–1. Since no information about the output changes can be gained from the knowledge of the input changes, each output XOR must occur with equal probability for each input XOR. The "pairs XOR distribution table", for an m×n S-box meeting the Dynamic Input-output Independence criterion of order m would be as shown in Figure 4.

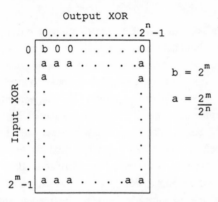

Figure 4 XOR Distribution Table for an S-box which Meets the
Dynamic Input-output and Output-output Independence Criteria.

It is clear that the freedom from imbalances in the "pairs XOR distribution table" shown in Figure 4 makes the S-box immune from the differential attack. Any m×n S-box that meets the Dynamic Input-output Independence criterion of order m and the Output-output Independence criterion of order n–1 is therefore immune to the differential attack.

Avalanche Criteria

Many of the previously proposed design criteria for S-boxes are used to ensure that the cryptosystem in which they are used possess certain kinds of avalanche. We do not view the properties which these criteria require as fundamental properties of S-boxes, however they may be necessary when S-boxes are used in certain types of cryptosystems. The avalanche properties can be divided into three classes: Probabilistic Avalanche, Directed Avalanche, and Minimal Avalanche. *Probabilistic Avalanche* criteria require that each output of an S-box change with probability 1/2 whenever the input is changed. The changes in the outputs must also be independent. All S-boxes which meet the dynamic information theoretic criteria will posses Probabilistic Avalanche and this is regarded as the only type of avalanche which is a fundamental property of a good S-box. *Directed Avalanche* criteria require that each output of an S-box change with probability 1/2 whenever certain patterns of change are made in the input. Again, the changes in the output bits must be independent. Examples of Directed Avalanche criteria are the Strict Avalanche Criterion (SAC) and all of its extensions. *Minimal Avalanche* criteria require that a minimum number of output bits changes when certain patterns of change are made in the input. The DES design criteria that requires that at least two output bits change when one input is changed is a good example of a Minimal Avalanche criterion. Neither Minimal nor Directed avalanche properties are fundamental to good S-boxes, however they may be useful whenever smaller S-boxes are used to create the larger substitutions required in SP network based cryptosystems. When smaller S-boxes are used in SP network based cryptosystems, the permutations used ensure that the outputs of individual S-boxes are distributed to the inputs of distinct S-boxes in the next round. This distribution has the effect of forcing certain patterns of changes in the input (those where 1 or 2 bits change) to be the most likely to occur in the early rounds. Due to this effect it is justified to used Minimal or Directed avalanche criteria to ensure that adequate avalanche will occur for those patterns of change. In other cryptosystems where all of the patterns of change in the inputs are equally likely it does not make sense to require Minimal or Directed Avalanche.

Application of the Criteria

The evaluation of S-boxes using the set of information theoretic design criteria would be simple if all of the criteria could be met simultaneously. In this case either the S-box would meet all the criteria and be acceptable or it would not. Unfortunately, all the criteria cannot be met simultaneously. We must therefore formulate a measure of how close an S-box comes to meeting each of the design criteria. This approach is somewhat new as most of the previous criteria were proposed on a pass/fail type of evaluation. Dropping the requirement that S-boxes meet a particular criterion perfectly complicates the evaluation and design of S-boxes. There are many possible ways to measure the criteria and the formulation of the method used to evaluate an S-box based on all the criteria simultaneously requires some difficult decisions. Since we based our criteria on information theoretic ideas, the natural basis for the required measures is information theory. For the criteria which require a form of independence, such as Input-output Independence, the measure used will be the average amount of information revealed about the unknown bits by the knowledge of partial information about the other bits. This is simply a measure of the average mutual information between the known input or output bits of the S-box and the unknown input or output bits. We will refer to this measure as the *Information Leakage measure* to emphasize that an increase in mutual information is undesirable and that for an Ideal S-box all the measures would be zero. To illustrate how this measure is used to judge how close an S-box comes to meeting the criteria, consider the Input-output Independence criterion. The Information Leakage measure for the Input-output Independence criterion of order 1 is the average amount of information revealed about an output bit by the knowledge of one input bit. Similarly, the Information Leakage measure for the Input-output Independence criterion of order 2 is the average amount of information revealed about an output bit by the knowledge of two input bits. The measures for the higher orders of the criterion are defined in the same manner. The design criteria which will be evaluated using the Information Leakage measure are :

1. Input-output Independence
2. Output-input Independence
3. Output-output Independence
4. Dynamic Input-output Independence

5. Dynamic Output-input Independence

6. Dynamic Output-output Independence

Each of the three remaining criteria will be evaluated using different methods.

Nonlinearity will be measured in the normal way as defined by Pieprzyk and Finkelstein [12]. The nonlinearity of each individual vector will be measured as its Hamming distance from the closest linear vector. In previous analyses of the nonlinearity of DES [12], it seems that the measure used to judge the nonlinearity of the 6×4 bit DES S-boxes was formed by adding the nonlinearities of the four 4×4 bit sub S-box vectors for each output of a 6×4 bit DES S-box. We feel that a better measure for the nonlinearity of the 6×4 bit S-box vectors is to compute the hamming distance of the complete output vector from the closest linear vector of the same length. This method produces the true nonlinearity of the 6×4 bit S-box vectors (which can be greater than 16) and is therefore a better measure of nonlinearity for these vectors.

The Information Completeness criterion will be evaluated using a set of measures. Each measure will be calculated to be the average information in k input bits on which the output of the vector does not depend. This measure will be referred to as the *Information Degeneracy measure* to emphasize that the measures for an Ideal S-box would all be zero. As an example, the Information Degeneracy measure of order 1 is the average amount of information in an individual input bit on which the output bit does not depend. Similarly, the Information Degeneracy measure of order 2 is the average amount of information in a pair of input bits on which the output bit does not depend and so on for the other orders. The Information Degeneracy measure is only meaningful up to order m-1 for an m×n bit S-box.

There will be no measure for the criterion of Invertibility because an S-box is either invertible or it is not.

Analysis of DES S-boxes Using The Design Criteria

We first applied the new design framework to analyze the DES S-boxes. We investigated both the properties of the DES 6×4 bit S-boxes and the DES 4×4 S-boxes. The investigations revealed that we could not find S-boxes with substantially better information theoretic properties than the S-boxes of DES and which also meet the acknowledged DES design criteria. This indicates that the S-boxes of DES may be some of the best possible based on a combination of our information theoretic properties and the acknowledged DES design criteria. It is important to note that there were many S-boxes found which met the acknowledged DES design criteria but had poor information theoretic properties.

It was also revealed that the properties of the inverses of the DES 4×4 S-boxes were as good as those of the S-boxes themselves. In addition, we discovered that the inverses of the DES 4×4 S-boxes meet the acknowledged DES design criterion which requires that at least two bits change in the output whenever one input bit is changed. These two discoveries indicate that the designers of DES placed an equal emphasis on the properties of the S-boxes and their inverses.

In every case we found that the properties of the complete 6×4 S-boxes were better than any individual 4×4 sub-box. We concluded that using multiple sub-boxes to form a larger S-box is an important method which can be used to create S-boxes that have better properties than are possible in a single sub-box. This gives a possible explanation for why multiple sub-boxes were used to create the S-boxes of DES. Some of the unexplained DES design criteria may have been included to ensure that the properties of the S-boxes created from the 4×4 S-boxes were acceptable.

One important fact noted in this investigation is that no n×n S-box can meet the Dynamic criteria perfectly because, due to the nature of the XOR function, output XOR values always occur in pairs (since $a \oplus b = b \oplus a$).

Further details of the investigations into the properties of the S-boxes of DES are contained in [19]

Creation of New DES-like S-boxes

The second application for our the new design framework was to design new S-boxes. In order to further evaluate the DES S-boxes we first chose to create S-boxes which met the acknowledged DES design criteria and met our criteria as well as the S-boxes of DES. These S-boxes will be called *DES-like*. We created over 12000 new 4×4 DES-like S-boxes and 257 new 6×4 DES-like S-boxes. During the process of creating these new S-boxes we discovered several important results. First, the inverse of an S-box with good information theoretic properties does not necessarily have good properties. Second, that there are many S-boxes which met the acknowledged DES design criteria which have poor information theoretic properties. Last, we found no S-boxes, of similar size, which had significantly better information theoretic properties than the S-boxes of DES. These results indicate that our set of criteria impose different requirements than the acknowledged DES design criteria and that it is not likely that the good information theoretic properties exhibited by the S-boxes of DES and their inverses is accidental.

Creation of other new S-boxes

Since we do not believe that the Minimal Avalanche requirements of DES are fundamental to all good S-boxes we wanted to check if S-boxes with better information theoretic properties could be created if the requirements of the acknowledged DES design criteria were removed. We created many new 4×4 and 6×4 S-boxes which did not meet the acknowledged DES design criteria but that possessed better information theoretic properties. This result suggests that care should be taken when choosing the required avalanche criteria so that one does not reduce the attainable information theoretic properties.

There is considerable interest in the creation of larger S-boxes. In order to demonstrate that our design framework could be used to create larger S-boxes we produced more than fifty 5×5 bit S-boxes using two methods which are applicable to the construction of larger S-boxes. Further details about these methods is available in [19, 20]

Comparision of Information Theoretic Properties

As a final demonstration that our new criteria impose requirements on the design of S-boxes which differ from those proposed in previous work we will present the values of the Information theoretic values for four 4×4 S-boxes. The first was generated at random, the second was listed in [14] by Webster, the third is a sub-box of the first DES S-box, and the last is a new S-box we created. The measures of the information theoretic properties of these S-boxes appear in Figures 5 to 8. From the measures given for each S-box it should be clear that using our design framework results in S-boxes with better information theoretic properties.

```
S-BOX vectors
-------------
0001010110100111   Nonlin:4      Inverse Nonlin:4
1100000010011111   Nonlin:4      Inverse Nonlin:2
1001101000110110   Nonlin:4      Inverse Nonlin:2
0011110000011101   Nonlin:2      Inverse Nonlin:4
```

Figure 5 Properties of Random S-box   (Continued ...)

```
COMPLETENESS METRICS
--------------------
              S-BOX                    Order        INVERSE S-BOX
      1         2         3         4           1         2         3         4
--------------------------------------------------------------------------------
0.000000 0.000000 1.219361 3.000000 --- 0.000000 0.000000 1.156861 3.000000
0.000000 0.250000 1.183572 3.000000 --- 0.000000 0.250000 1.234680 3.000000
0.000000 0.000000 1.125000 3.000000 --- 0.000000 0.250000 1.266541 3.000000
0.000000 0.250000 1.266541 3.000000 --- 0.000000 0.250000 1.183572 3.000000


INPUT - OUTPUT METRICS
----------------------
          IO INDEPENDENCE             Order        OI INDEPENDENCE
      1         2         3         4           1         2         3         4
--------------------------------------------------------------------------------
0.045566 0.177694 0.500000 1.000000 --- 0.034174 0.177694 0.500000 1.000000
0.058572 0.203634 0.500000 1.000000 --- 0.034174 0.094361 0.250000 1.000000
0.022783 0.078634 0.375000 1.000000 --- 0.022783 0.078634 0.375000 1.000000
0.022783 0.161967 0.500000 1.000000 --- 0.058572 0.203634 0.500000 1.000000


DYNAMIC INPUT - OUTPUT METRICS
------------------------------
         DYN IO INDEPENDENCE          Order      DYN OI INDEPENDENCE
      1         2         3         4           1         2         3         4
--------------------------------------------------------------------------------
0.002820 0.020966 0.059213 0.133271 --- 0.002115 0.020966 0.059213 0.133271
0.012096 0.033804 0.068362 0.133271 --- 0.002115 0.005650 0.011391 0.290132
0.001410 0.004709 0.034578 0.133271 --- 0.001410 0.004709 0.072456 0.290132
0.001410 0.044809 0.133521 0.290132 --- 0.012096 0.033804 0.068362 0.133271


DYNAMIC OUTPUT - OUTPUT METRICS
-------------------------------
      S-BOX DYN OO INDEP   Order   INVS S-BOX DYN OO INDEP
      1         2         3         1         2         3
-----------------------------------------------------------------
0.318081 0.624428 0.827975 --- 0.334970 0.647912 0.794066
```

Figure 5 Properties of Random S-box

```
S-BOX vectors
-------------
1111000010011001   Nonlin:4    Inverse Nonlin:4
1011111000010100   Nonlin:4    Inverse Nonlin:4
0010011100011011   Nonlin:4    Inverse Nonlin:4
0101001100110101   Nonlin:4    Inverse Nonlin:4

COMPLETENESS METRICS
-------------------- -
              S-BOX                    Order        INVERSE S-BOX
      1         2         3         4           1         2         3         4
--------------------------------------------------------------------------------
0.000000 0.416667 1.125000 3.000000 --- 0.000000 0.333333 1.297180 3.000000
0.000000 0.416667 1.125000 3.000000 --- 0.000000 0.250000 1.250000 3.000000
0.000000 0.166667 1.250000 3.000000 --- 0.250000 0.666667 1.500000 3.000000
0.000000 0.166667 1.250000 3.000000 --- 0.000000 0.416667 1.125000 3.000000
```

Figure 6 Properties of Webster S-box   (Continued ...)

```
INPUT - OUTPUT METRICS
-----------------------
          IO INDEPENDENCE           Order        OI INDEPENDENCE
     1        2        3        4              1        2        3        4
--------------------------------------------------------------------------------
0.047180 0.177694 0.500000 1.000000 --- 0.047180 0.146241 0.375000 1.000000
0.047180 0.177694 0.500000 1.000000 --- 0.094361 0.240602 0.500000 1.000000
0.094361 0.209148 0.500000 1.000000 --- 0.094361 0.312907 0.625000 1.000000
0.094361 0.209148 0.500000 1.000000 --- 0.047180 0.177694 0.500000 1.000000

DYNAMIC INPUT - OUTPUT METRICS
------------------------------
        DYN IO INDEPENDENCE         Order      DYN OI INDEPENDENCE
     1        2        3        4              1        2        3        4
--------------------------------------------------------------------------------
0.011391 0.038510 0.094361 0.250000 --- 0.011391 0.030915 0.070771 0.250000
0.011391 0.038510 0.094361 0.250000 --- 0.022783 0.053698 0.094361 0.250000
0.022783 0.046104 0.094361 0.250000 --- 0.022783 0.062369 0.133271 0.250000
0.022783 0.046104 0.094361 0.250000 --- 0.011391 0.038510 0.094361 0.250000

DYNAMIC OUTPUT - OUTPUT METRICS
-------------------------------
      S-BOX DYN OO INDEP   Order   INVS S-BOX DYN OO INDEP
     1        2        3          1        2        3
--------------------------------------------------------------
0.333333 0.550000 0.850000 --- 0.333333 0.400000 1.000000
```

Figure 6 Properties of Webster S-box

```
S-BOX vectors
-------------
1010011101010100   Nonlin:4    Inverse Nonlin:2
1110010000111001   Nonlin:4    Inverse Nonlin:2
1000111011100001   Nonlin:4    Inverse Nonlin:4
0011011010001101   Nonlin:4    Inverse Nonlin:2

COMPLETENESS METRICS
--------------------
              S-BOX              Order          INVERSE S-BOX
     1        2        3        4              1        2        3        4
--------------------------------------------------------------------------------
0.000000 0.083333 1.172180 3.000000 --- 0.000000 0.250000 1.266541 3.000000
0.000000 0.166667 1.117951 3.000000 --- 0.000000 0.250000 1.402933 3.000000
0.000000 0.166667 1.141541 3.000000 --- 0.000000 0.083333 1.172180 3.000000
0.000000 0.166667 1.117951 3.000000 --- 0.000000 0.250000 1.402933 3.000000

  INPUT - OUTPUT METRICS
  ----------------------
          IO INDEPENDENCE           Order        OI INDEPENDENCE
     1        2        3        4              1        2        3        4
--------------------------------------------------------------------------------
0.022783 0.120301 0.437500 1.000000 --- 0.022783 0.078634 0.375000 1.000000
0.011391 0.078634 0.375000 1.000000 --- 0.011391 0.047180 0.312500 1.000000
0.022783 0.110088 0.375000 1.000000 --- 0.022783 0.120301 0.437500 1.000000
0.011391 0.078634 0.375000 1.000000 --- 0.011391 0.047180 0.187500 1.000000
```

Figure 7 Properties of DES S-box   (Continued ...)

```
DYNAMIC INPUT - OUTPUT METRICS
--------------------------------
          DYN IO INDEPENDENCE          Order      DYN OI INDEPENDENCE
   1         2        3        4        1        2        3        4
--------------------------------------------------------------------------
0.001410 0.012367 0.047620 0.133271 --- 0.001410 0.004709 0.072456 0.290132
0.000705 0.010419 0.043727 0.133271 --- 0.000705 0.002825 0.069608 0.290132
0.001410 0.012303 0.034578 0.133271 --- 0.001410 0.012367 0.047620 0.133271
0.000705 0.010419 0.043727 0.133271 --- 0.000705 0.002825 0.008544 0.290132

DYNAMIC OUTPUT - OUTPUT METRICS
--------------------------------
       S-BOX DYN OO INDEP   Order   INVS S-BOX DYN OO INDEP
   1        2        3           1        2        3
--------------------------------------------------------------
0.271739 0.604401 0.829044 --- 0.336366 0.600914 0.783518
```

Figure 7 Properties of DES S-box

```
S-BOX vectors
-------------
0001100111101001    Nonlin:4    Inverse Nonlin:4
1101000110100110    Nonlin:4    Inverse Nonlin:4
1010100100111100    Nonlin:4    Inverse Nonlin:4
1001001101011010    Nonlin:4    Inverse Nonlin:4

COMPLETENESS METRICS
--------------------
                 S-BOX                 Order             INVERSE S-BOX
   1        2        3        4        1        2        3        4
--------------------------------------------------------------------------
0.000000 0.166667 1.117951 3.000000 --- 0.000000 0.166667 1.117951 3.000000
0.000000 0.166667 1.117951 3.000000 --- 0.000000 0.166667 1.117951 3.000000
0.000000 0.166667 1.117951 3.000000 --- 0.000000 0.166667 1.117951 3.000000
0.000000 0.166667 1.117951 3.000000 --- 0.000000 0.166667 1.117951 3.000000

INPUT - OUTPUT METRICS
----------------------
          IO INDEPENDENCE            Order        OI INDEPENDENCE
   1        2        3        4        1        2        3        4
--------------------------------------------------------------------------
0.011391 0.078634 0.375000 1.000000 --- 0.011391 0.078634 0.375000 1.000000
0.011391 0.078634 0.375000 1.000000 --- 0.011391 0.078634 0.375000 1.000000
0.011391 0.078634 0.375000 1.000000 --- 0.011391 0.078634 0.375000 1.000000
0.011391 0.078634 0.375000 1.000000 --- 0.011391 0.078634 0.375000 1.000000

DYNAMIC INPUT - OUTPUT METRICS
--------------------------------
          DYN IO INDEPENDENCE          Order      DYN OI INDEPENDENCE
   1        2        3        4        1        2        3        4
--------------------------------------------------------------------------
0.000705 0.010419 0.043727 0.133271 --- 0.000705 0.010419 0.043727 0.133271
0.000705 0.010419 0.043727 0.133271 --- 0.000705 0.010419 0.043727 0.133271
0.000705 0.010419 0.043727 0.133271 --- 0.000705 0.010419 0.043727 0.133271
0.000705 0.010419 0.043727 0.133271 --- 0.000705 0.010419 0.043727 0.133271
```

Figure 8 Properties of New S-box   (Continued . . .)

```
DYNAMIC OUTPUT - OUTPUT METRICS
-------------------------------
    S-BOX DYN OO INDEP   Order   INVS S-BOX DYN OO INDEP
     1       2       3            1       2       3
-------------------------------------------------------------
0.198651 0.500727 0.735700 --- 0.198651 0.500727 0.735700
```

Figure 8 Properties of New S-box

Conclusions

In this paper we introduced the static and dynamic views of an S-box and used these abstractions to define the properties of an Ideal S-box based on information theoretic ideas. We then presented a new set of design criteria for S-boxes based on the properties of an Ideal S-box. We then demonstrated the usefulness of the new design framework by using it to analyze the S-boxes of DES and to create new S-boxes of various sizes. The new set of design criteria should be a valuable tool that can be used to create S-boxes for cryptosystems of the future.

Bibliography

[1] E. Biham and A. Shamir, "Differential cryptanalysis of DES-like cryptosystems," in *CRYPTO 90 Abstracts*, pp. 1–19, August, 1990.

[2] C. E. Shannon, "Communication theory of secrecy systems," *Bell Systems Technical Journal*, vol. 28, pp. 656–715, 1949.

[3] H. Feistel, "Cryptography and computer privacy," *Scientific American*, vol. 228, no. 5, pp. 15–23, 1973.

[4] H. Feistel, W. Notz, and J. L. Smith, "Some crytptographic techniques for machine-to-machine data communications," in *Proceedins of the IEEE*, vol. 63, pp. 1545–1554, 1975.

[5] B. den Boer, "Crptanalysis of F. E. A. L.," in *Advances in Cryptology: Proc. of EUROCRYPT 88*, pp. 167–173, Springer-Verlag, 1989.

[6] W. Fumy, "On the F-function of FEAL," in *Advances in Cryptology:Proc. of CRYPTO 87*, pp. 434–437, Springer-Verlag, 1988.

[7] National Bureau of Standards (U.S.), "Data Encryption Standard (DES)," Tech. Rep. Publication 46, Federal Information Processing Standards, 1977.

[8] M. E. Hellman and et. al., "Results of an initial attempt to cryptanalyze the NBS Data Encryption Standard," tech. rep., Information Systems Laboratory, Stanford University, November, 1976.

[9] A. Shamir, "On the security of DES," in *Advances in Cryptology. Proc. of CRYPTO 85*, pp. 280–281, Springer-Verlag, 1986.

[10] E. F. Brickell, J. H. Moore, and M. R. Purtill, "Structure in the S-boxes of the DES(extended abstract)," in *Advances in Cryptology: Proc. of CRYPTO 86*, pp. 3–8, Springer-Verlag, 1986.

[11] R. Forré, "Methods and instruments for designing S-boxes," *Journal of Crytology*, vol. 2, no. 3, pp. 115–130, 1990.

[12] J. Pieprzyk and G. Finkelstein, "Towards effective nonlinear cyptosystem design," in *IEE proceedings, Part E: Computers and Digital Techniques*, vol. 135, pp. 325–335, 1988.

[13] J. B. Kam and G. I. Davida, "Structured design of substituion-permutation encryption networks," *IEEE Transactions on Computers*, vol. C-28, pp. 747–753, 1979.

[14] A. F. Webster, "Plaintext/ciphertext bit dependencies in cryptographic systems," Master's thesis, Queen's University, 1985.

[15] B. Preneel, W. VanLeewijck, L. VanLinden, R. Govaerts, and J. Vandewalle, "Propagation characteristics of boolean functions," in *EUROCRYPT 90 — Abstracts*, pp. 155–165, 1990.

[16] S. Lloyd, "Properties of binary functions," in *EUROCRYPT 90 — Abstracts*, pp. 126–135, 1990.

[17] C. M. Adams and S. E. Tavares, "The structured design of cryptographically good S-boxes," *Journal of Cryptology*, vol. 3, pp. 27–41, 1990.

[18] A. F. Webster and S. E. Tavares, "On the design of S-boxes," in *Advances in Cryptology:Proc. of CRYPTO 85*, (New York), pp. 523–534, Springer-Verlag, 1986.

[19] M. H. Dawson, "A unified framework for Substitution box design based on information theory," Master's thesis, Department of Electrical Engineering, Queens University, April 1991.

[20] M. H. Dawson, "An implementation of the algorithms required to measure the information theoretic properties of an S-box and the algorithms to use these measures to create new S-boxes," tech. rep., Department of Electrical Engineering, Queen's University, Feb. 1991.

Enumerating Nondegenerate Permutations

Luke O'Connor
Department of Computer Science
University of Waterloo, Ontario, Canada, N2L 3G1
email: ljpoconn@watmath.uwaterloo.ca

Abstract

Every cryptosystem with an n-bit block length may be modeled as a system of n-bit boolean equations. The cipher is said to be nondegenerate if the equation f_i that describes the output c_i is nondegenerate, for $1 \leq i \leq n$. Let $\mathcal{N}^{n,n}$ be the set of nondegenerate permutations. We will derive an exact expression for $|\mathcal{N}^{n,n}|$, and show that

$$\frac{|\mathcal{N}^{n,n}|}{2^n!} = 1 + o\left(\frac{\sqrt{2^n}}{2^{2^{n-1}+n}}\right).$$

1 Introduction

One of the basic design criteria for a block encryption function is to ensure that each ciphertext bit depends nonlinearly on each message bit, for each fixed key. For example, this property is essential if the encryption function is to be used as the basis for an authentication algorithm [7], or if we are to avoid meet-in-the-middle attacks based on bit independence [3]. More generally, total nonlinear dependence between the message and ciphertext is a necessary condition for small changes in the message to produce large unpredictable changes in the ciphertext. This phenomenon, known as the avalanche effect [6], reduces the information that a cryptanalyst can gain by considering the encryption of similar messages. For a discussion of other design criteria for block ciphers see [1] [6] [14] [18].

A boolean equation f is nondegenerate if its output depends on all the input bits to the equation. As each ciphertext bit can be described by a boolean equation in the message and the key, we are then interested in encryption functions for which the output, or the ciphertext, is described by a system of nondegenerate equations. Ciphers with this property will be called *nondegenerate ciphers*.

Kam and Davida [11] were the first to show that large nondegenerate product ciphers, the so-called SP-networks, can be constructed from small nondegenerate substitutions, or S-boxes. The Kam and Davida algorithm selects special transpositions at each round of the product cipher, which cause the influence of a variable to propagate throughout the intermediate ciphertext in a regular and controlled manner, such that the final round the propagation is complete (for a reason possibly similar to this, Kam and Davida called such functions *complete* rather than nondegenerate). Subsequently, Ayoub has shown that a similarly constructed product cipher, employing only *random* transpositions, would almost certainly guarantee the nondegeneracy property of the product cipher [2]. Ayoub derives a combinatorial expression for the probability that a product cipher is nondegenerate, and then demonstrates empirically that a randomly constructed product cipher attains the nondegeneracy property after a small number of rounds.

From the work of Ayoub we may hypothesize that *most product ciphers are nondegenerate*. We further observe that product ciphers give rise to a very general class encryption functions, and in fact it has been shown that for a given block size n, these ciphers can generate the alternating group of the set $\{0, 1, \cdots 2^n - 1\}$ [4][5][12]. Thus we may further hypothesize that for a given n, most *n-bit permutations* are nondegenerate.

Our main result is to show that almost all systems of boolean equations which describe a permutation will be nondegenerate. Consider the problem of determining the number of n-bit to m-bit boolean functions that are nondegenerate. The case where $m = 1$ has been solved by Harrison [9], and also by Hu [10]. If we let $\mathcal{N}^n$ denote the set of n-bit nondegenerate functions, then the number of n-bit to m-bit degenerate functions is simply $(|\mathcal{N}^n|)^m$. However, as noted by Mitchell [14], the difficulty of this problem seems to increase if we further require that the functions be nonsingular ($n = m$ and the functions are invertible).

Let $\mathcal{N}^{n,n}$ denote the set of nondegenerate n-bit nonsingular functions, or nondegenerate n-bit permutations. In this paper we will prove that

$$\frac{|\mathcal{N}^{n,n}|}{2^n!} = 1 + O\left(\frac{n^2}{2^{2^{n-1}}}\right),\tag{1}$$

and it clearly follows that $|\mathcal{N}^{n,n}| \sim 2^n!$. The immediate implication is that as n increases, the probability of randomly selecting a nondegenerate n-bit permutation tends to unity.

This paper is organized as follows. Section 2 contains the definitions and notations that will be used throughout the paper. In §3 we consider asymptotic estimates for the number of degenerate n-bit functions. In §4 we prove our main theorem by deriving an expression for $|\mathcal{N}^{n,n}|$ using the inclusion-exclusion principle.

2 Definitions and Notations

The following definitions will be used throughout the paper when describing boolean functions and permutations.

Definition 2.1 Let f be an n-bit function where $f : \{0,1\}^n \to \{0,1\}$. For $0 \le i \le 2^n - 1$, let $b(i)$ denote that element of $\{0,1\}^n$ whose decimal representation is i. The *vector representation* V_f of a function f is defined as $V_f = v_0, v_1, \cdots v_{2^n-1} \in \{0,1\}^{2^n}$ where $v_i = f(b(i))$, $0 \le i \le 2^n - 1$. The *distance between two n-bit functions* f and g is defined as $d(f,g) = w(V_f \oplus V_g)$ where $w(\cdot)$ is the hamming weight function. □

Let the symmetric group on 2^n elements be denoted as S_{2^n}.

Definition 2.2 For $P \in S_{2^n}$, define $V_P^i = v_0, v_1, \cdots v_{2^n-1} \in \{0,1\}^{2^n}$ as $v_j = y_i$, where $P(j) = Y = y_1, y_2, \cdots y_m \in \{0,1\}^m$, $0 \le j \le 2^n - 1$, $1 \le i \le m$. The n-tuple of boolean functions $F = [f_1, f_2, \cdots f_m]$ is said to *realize the permutation* P if $w(V_P^i \oplus V_{f_i}) = 0$, $1 \le i \le m$. □

Definition 2.3 Let $F = [f_1, f_2 \cdots f_k]$ be a k-tuple of n-bit functions. Let $\mathcal{E}(F)$ be defined as the set

$$\mathcal{E}(F) = \{ F' \mid F' = [f_1, \cdots f_k, f'_{k+1}, \cdots f'_n] \in S_{2^n} \}. \tag{2}$$

Then $\mathcal{E}(F)$ will be called the *extension set of F*. If $|\mathcal{E}(F)| > 0$ then we will say that F is *extendible*. □

The following theorem was used implicitly by Gordon and Retkin [8].

Theorem 2.1 For k, $0 \le k \le n - 1$, and an arbitrary k-tuple F of n-bit functions, if F is extendible then $|\mathcal{E}(F)| = (2^{n-k}!)^{2^k}$.

proof. Proof by induction on k [16]. □

3 Nondegenerate Functions

An n-bit function f is *vacuous* in variable x_i if for all of $x_1, x_2, \cdots x_n \in \{0,1\}^n$,

$$f(x_1, \cdots x_i, \cdots, x_n) = f(x_1, \cdots, \overline{x_i}, \cdots x_n). \tag{3}$$

If f is vacuous in any variable then f is *degenerate*, otherwise f is *nondegenerate*. Let $\mathcal{N}_k^n$ be the set of n-bit nondegenerate functions of weight k, and let $\mathcal{N}^n = \bigcup \mathcal{N}_k^n$. For degenerate functions, we may similarly define the sets $\mathcal{D}^n$ and $\mathcal{D}_k^n$. It follows that $|\mathcal{D}_k^n| = \binom{2^n}{k} - |\mathcal{N}_k^n|$.

The number of nondegenerate functions has been determined by Harrison using inversion formulae [9, p169], and it follows that $|\mathcal{N}^n| \sim 2^{2^n}$. Thus most n-bit functions are nondegenerate.

Theorem 3.1 (Harrison) The number of degenerate n-bit functions of weight k is

$$|\mathcal{D}_k^n| = \sum_{1 \le j \le \nu_2(k)} (-1)^{j-1} \binom{n}{j} \binom{2^{n-j}}{k \cdot 2^{-j}}. \tag{4}$$

$\square$

For $1 \le j \le n-1$, let $A_k^n(j) = \binom{2^{n-j}}{k2^{-j}}$, which are the coefficients of the sum in eq. (??). In general, $A_k^n(1)$ dominates the sum, and we will prove this for the case where $k = 2^{n-1}$, as we will require an asymptotic estimate of $|\mathcal{D}_{2^{n-1}}^n|$ in a later section.

Theorem 3.2

$$|\mathcal{D}_{2^{n-1}}^n| = A_{2^{n-1}}^n(1)\left(1 + o\left(\frac{1}{2^{2^{n-2}}}\right)\right). \tag{5}$$

proof. Using bounds for the factorial function [15, p183], we have that for $2 \le j \le n-1$,

$$\frac{A^n(j)}{A_{2^{n-1}}^n(1)} = \frac{(2^{n-2}!)^2 \cdot 2^{n-j}!}{2^{n-1}! \cdot (2^{n-j-1}!)^2}, \tag{6}$$

$$< \frac{2^{2^{n-j}}}{2^{2^{n-1}}} \cdot \sqrt{\pi \cdot 2^{j-1}} \cdot \frac{exp\left[\frac{2}{12 \cdot 2^{n-2}} + \frac{1}{12 \cdot 2^{n-j}}\right]}{exp\left[\frac{2}{12 \cdot 2^{n-j-1}+1/4} + \frac{1}{12 \cdot 2^{n-1}+1/4}\right]}, \tag{7}$$

$$= o\left(\frac{1}{2^{2^{n-2}}}\right). \tag{8}$$

The theorem follows from

$$|\mathcal{D}_{2^{n-1}}^n| = \sum_{j=1}^{n-1} (-1)^{j-1} \binom{n}{j} A_{2^{n-1}}^n(j), \tag{9}$$

$$= A_{2^{n-1}}^n(1) \cdot \left[\sum_{j=1}^{n-1} (-1)^{j-1} \binom{n}{j} \frac{A_{2^{n-1}}^n(j)}{A_{2^{n-1}}^n(1)}\right], \tag{10}$$

$$= A_{2^{n-1}}^n(1) \cdot \left[1 + o\left(\frac{1}{2^{2^{n-2}}}\right) \cdot \sum_{j=2}^{n-1} (-1)^i \binom{n}{j}\right], \tag{11}$$

$$= A_{2^{n-1}}^n(1) \cdot \left[1 + o\left(\frac{1}{2^{2^{n-2}}}\right)\right]. \tag{12}$$

$\square$

4 Nondegenerate Permutations

In this section we will determine the number of n-bit permutations that are nondegenerate.

Definition 4.1 Let $\mathcal{N}^{n,n}$ be the set of permutations $P \in S_{2^n}$, such that if P is realized by $F = [f_1, f_2, \cdots f_n]$ then $f_i \in \mathcal{N}^n_{2^{n-1}}$, $1 \le i \le n$. $\qquad\square$

Our technique is to enumerate all sets $F = [f_1, f_2, \cdots f_k]$ where $f_i \in \mathcal{D}^n_{2^{n-1}}$, and then compute the extension set of F. This method allows us to compute the necessary coefficients in the inclusion-exclusion expansion for $|\mathcal{N}^{n,n}|$.

Definition 4.2 For k, $1 \le k \le n$, let $C^n(k)$ denote the number of tuples $F = [f_1, f_2, \cdots f_k]$ such that

1. $\mathcal{E}(F) \ne \emptyset$;

2. $f_i \in \mathcal{D}^n_{2^{n-1}}$, $1 \le i \le k$. $\qquad\square$

Definition 4.3 For k, $1 \le k \le n$, let C^n_k be the set of all n-bit permutations P such that if P is realized by $F = [f_1, f_2, \cdots f_n]$ then $f_i \in \mathcal{D}^n_{2^{n-1}}$, $1 \le i \le k$. $\qquad\square$

Thus $C^n(k)$ is the number of degenerate k-tuples that realize the first k bits of some permutation, and C^n_k is the set of all k-tuples of degenerate functions that can be extended to permutations. The next theorem shows that the $|C^n_i|$ can be expressed in terms of the $C^n(i)$, which leads to an expression for $|\mathcal{N}^{n,n}|$.

Theorem 4.1 For $n > 1$,

$$|\mathcal{N}^{n,n}| = 2^n! + \sum_{i=1}^{n} (-1)^i \binom{n}{i} C^n(i) \cdot (2^{n-i}!)^{2^i}. \tag{13}$$

proof. We have that

$$|\mathcal{N}^{n,n}| = 2^n! - \left| \bigcup_{1 \le i \le n} C^n_i \right|. \tag{14}$$

Let $C^n_{i_1, i_2, \cdots i_k} = \bigcap_{i \in \{i_1, i_2, \cdots i_k\}} C^n_i$ where $i_1, i_2, \cdots i_k \in \{1, 2, \cdots, n\}$. By symmetry we have that $|C^n_{1,2,\cdots,k}| = |C^n_{i_1,i_2,\cdots,i_k}|$. Then from Theorem 2.1 we have that

$$|C^n_{1,2,\cdots,k}| = C^n(k) \cdot (2^{n-k}!)^{2^k}. \tag{15}$$

The theorem now follows using the inclusion-exclusion principle. $\qquad\square$

It remains to calculate the coefficients $C^n(i)$. These coefficients can be calculated exactly [16], but the resulting expression is cumbersome. As we will show, the first term dominates the sum in eq. (14), and we will concentrate on estimating this term.

Theorem 4.2 For $n > 1$, $1 \leq k \leq n$,

$$C^n(k) \leq |\mathcal{D}_{2^{n-1}}^n| \cdot \prod_{i=1}^{k-1} \left(|\mathcal{D}_{2^{n-i-1}}^{n-i}|^{2^i} + \sum_{j=1}^{i} (-1)^{j-1} \binom{i}{j} \binom{2^{i-j}}{2^{i-j-1}}^{2^{i-j}} \right). \quad (16)$$

proof. By induction on k.

Basis. Let $k = 1$. Then $C^n(1)$ is the number of balanced n-bit degenerate functions which is exactly $|\mathcal{D}_{2^{n-1}}^n|$, and thus the theorem is true when $k = 1$.

Induction Hypothesis. Assume that the theorem is true for k, $1 < k < n$.

Inductive Step. Let $F_k = [f_1, f_2, \cdots f_k]$ such that $f_i \in \mathcal{D}_{2^{n-1}}^n$, and F is extendible. We wish to determine the number of number of n-bit degenerate functions f such that $F_{k+1} = [f_1, f_2, \cdots f_k, f]$ is extendible.

Let f depend on the variables $x_1, x_2, \cdots x_n$, and partition V_f into 2^k blocks of size 2^{n-k}. Denote these blocks as $V_{g_1}, V_{g_2}, \cdots V_{g_{2^{n-k}}}$, and let $G = \{g_1, g_2, \cdots g_{2^k}\}$.

We may consider each function g_i as depending on a subset of the variables $x_1, x_2, \cdots x_n$, and w.l.o.g., let these variables be $x_1, x_2, \cdots x_{n-k}$. Now f is degenerate in the variable $x_j \in \{x_1, x_2, \cdots x_{n-k}\}$ if and only if g_i is degenerate in x_j, $\forall g_i \in G$. Then it follows that the number of functions f that are degenerate in some variable from the set $\{x_1, x_2, \cdots x_{n-k}\}$ is less than $|\mathcal{D}_{2^{n-k-1}}^{n-k}|^{2^k}$.

The function f will be degenerate in a variable from the set $\{x_{n-k+1}, x_{n-k+2}, \cdots x_n\}$ if $g_{i \oplus 2^j} = g_i$, for some j, $1 \leq j \leq k$. The number of 2^k-tuples G for which $g_{i \oplus 2^j} = g_i$ is given by

$$\sum_{j=1}^{k} (-1)^{j-1} \binom{k}{j} \binom{2^{n-k}}{2^{n-k-1}}^{2^{k-j}}, \quad (17)$$

where we have used the inclusion-exclusion principle.

It follows $C^n(k+1)/C^n(k)$ gives the number of ways a degenerate function can be added to F such that the resulting $(k+1)$-tuple is still extendible. Then using the induction hypothesis, we have that

$$C^n(k+1)/C^n(k) < |\mathcal{D}_{2^{n-k-1}}^{n-k}|^{2^k} + \sum_{j=1}^{k} (-1)^{j-1} \binom{k}{j} \binom{2^{n-k}}{2^{n-k-1}}^{2^{k-j}}, \quad (18)$$

$$C^n(k+1) < |\mathcal{D}_{2^{n-1}}^n| \cdot \prod_{i=1}^{k} \left(|\mathcal{D}_{2^{n-i-1}}^{n-i}|^{2^i} + \sum_{j=1}^{i} (-1)^{j-1} \binom{i}{j} \binom{2^{n-k}}{2^{n-k-1}}^{2^{i-j}} \right). \quad (19)$$

Thus the induction hypothesis is true for $k + 1$. $\qquad \square$

Corollary 4.1 For k, $1 < k \leq n$,

$$C^n(k) < n^{2^k-2} \cdot (2^{n-1}!) \cdot \binom{2^{n-1}}{2^{n-2}} \cdot (2^{n-k}!)^{2^k-1}. \quad (20)$$

proof. Using the estimates of $|\mathcal{D}_k^n|$ from Theorem 3.2, and the fact that the sum in eq. (17) is dominated by its first term, it follows that

$$C^n(k) \; < \; n\binom{2^{n-1}}{2^{n-2}} \cdot \prod_{i=1}^{k-1} (n-i)^{2^i} \cdot \binom{2^{n-i-1}}{2^{n-i-2}}^{2^i} + i \cdot \binom{2^{n-i}}{2^{n-i-1}}^{2^{i-1}} \tag{21}$$

Using Stirling's approximation it can be shown that $\binom{2^{n-i}}{2^{n-i-1}} > \binom{2^{n-i-1}}{2^{n-i-2}}^2$, and with the observation that $(n-i)^{2^i} + i < n^{2^i}$ for $n \ge 2, i \ge 1$, the estimate of $C^n(k)$ in eq. (21) can be simplified to

$$C^n(k) \; < \; n\binom{2^{n-1}}{2^{n-2}} \cdot \prod_{i=1}^{k-1} n^{2^i} \cdot \binom{2^{n-i}}{2^{n-i-1}}^{2^{i-1}}, \tag{22}$$

$$< \; n^{2^k-2} \cdot \binom{2^{n-1}}{2^{n-2}} \cdot (2^{n-1}!) \cdot \frac{2^{n-1}!}{(2^{n-k}!)^{2^{k-1}}}, \tag{23}$$

since

$$\prod_{i=1}^{k-1} n^{2^i} \cdot \binom{2^{n-i}}{2^{n-i-1}}^{2^{i-1}} = n^{2^k-2} \cdot \frac{2^{n-1}!}{(2^{n-k}!)^{2^{k-1}}}. \tag{24}$$

$\square$

Using theses estimates of the $C^n(k)$ we can in turn estimate $|C_{1,\cdots k}|$, and thus give a lower bound on $|\mathcal{N}^{n,n}|$.

Theorem 4.3

$$|\mathcal{N}^{n,n}| \; = \; 2^n! - |C_1^n| \cdot (1 + o(1)). \tag{25}$$

proof. Using bounds for the factorial function [15], we have that for $2 \le k \le n$,

$$\frac{|C_{1,\cdots,k}^n|}{|C_1^n|} \; < \; \frac{n^{2^k-1} \cdot \binom{2^{n-1}}{2^{n-2}} (2^{n-k}!)^{2^{k-1}}}{(2^{n-1}!) \cdot (1 + o(1)) \cdot n \cdot \binom{2^{n-1}}{2^{n-2}}}, \tag{26}$$

$$= \; \frac{n^{2^k-2} \cdot (2^{n-k}!)^{2^{k-1}}}{(2^{n-1}!) \cdot (1 + o(1))}, \tag{27}$$

$$< \; \frac{(2^{\log n+n-k})^{2^k}}{\sqrt{2^n \pi} \cdot (2^{k-1})^{2^{n-1}}}, \tag{28}$$

$$< \; \frac{(2^{\log n-n+2})^{2^{n-1}}}{(1 + o(1))}, \tag{29}$$

$$= \; o\left((2^{\log n-n+2})^{2^{n-1}}\right). \tag{30}$$

Then from Theorem 4.1 we have that

$$|\mathcal{N}^{n,n}| = 2^n! + \sum_{i=1}^{n}(-1)^i \binom{n}{i} \cdot |C_{1,2,\cdots i}^n|, \tag{31}$$

$$= 2^n! - |C_1^n| \cdot \left[\sum_{i=1}^{n}(-1)^i \binom{n}{i} \cdot \frac{C_{1,2,\cdots i}^n}{|C_1^n|} \right], \tag{32}$$

$$= 2^n! - |C_1^n|(1 + o(1)). \tag{33}$$

$\square$

Corollary 4.2

$$\frac{|\mathcal{N}|}{2^n!} = 1 + o\left(\frac{\sqrt{2^n}}{2^{2^{n-1}+n-1}} \right). \tag{34}$$

proof. Using estimates of the factorial function we have that

$$\frac{|\mathcal{N}^{n,n}|}{2^n!} = 1 + \frac{|C_1^n|(1 + o(1))}{2^n!}, \tag{35}$$

$$= 1 + \frac{\binom{2^{n-1}}{2^{n-2}}(1 + o(1))}{2^n!}, \tag{36}$$

$$= 1 + o\left(\frac{\sqrt{2^n}}{2^{2^{n-1}+n-1}} \right). \tag{37}$$

$\square$

5 Conclusion

Our main theorem states that nonlinearity and nondegeneracy are naturally occurring properties for permutations. The the denseness of nonlinear permutations is not unexpected given that the the set of nondegenerate permutations are dense (there are only two linear functions that are nondegenerate, viz. $f = x_1 \oplus x_2 \cdots x_n$, $\overline{f} = x_1 \oplus x_2 \cdots x_n \oplus 1$). These result provide strong evidence that DES is both nondegenerate and nonlinear, which has been justified previously through theoretical arguments [13], and empirical results [17]. The inclusion-exclusion principle provides a convenient form for asymptotic estimates. In the case of degenerate functions, the coefficients of the expansion are exponentially decreasing in magnitude, and the first coefficient of the expansion provides an asymptotic estimates of the sum itself. We may be able to apply similar techniques to decide whether or not most permutations are correlation immune, or satisfy the strict avalanche criterion.

Acknowledgements

The author would like to thank Prabhakar Ragde for his helpful comments in the preparation of this manuscript.

References

[1] A. Adams and S. Tavares. The structured design of cryptographically good S-boxes. *Journal of Cryptology*, 3(1):27–41, 1990.

[2] F. Ayoub. Probabilistic completeness of substitution-permutation encryption networks. *IEE proceedings*, 129, part E(5):196–199, 1982.

[3] D. Chaum and J. H. Everste. Cryptanalysis of DES with a reduced number of rounds. *Advances in Cryptology, CRYPTO 85, H. C. Williams ed., Lecture Notes in Computer Science, vol. 218, Springer-Verlag*, pages 192–211, 1986.

[4] D. Coppersmith and E. Grossman. Generators for certain alternating groups with applications to cryptography. *SIAM Journal of Applied Mathematics*, 29(4):624–627, 1974.

[5] S. Even and O. Goldreich. DES-like functions can generate the alternating group. *IEEE Transactions on Information Theory*, IT-29(6):863–865, 1983.

[6] H. Feistel. Cryptography and computer privacy. *Scientific American*, 228(5):15–23, 1973.

[7] H. Feistel, W. A. Notz, and J. Lynn Smith. Some cryptographic techniques for machine-to-machine data communications. *proceedings of the IEEE*, 63(11):1545–1554, 1975.

[8] J. Gordon and H. Retkin. Are big S-boxes best? In T. Beth, editor, *Cryptography, proceedings, Burg Feuerstein*, pages 257–262, 1982.

[9] M. A. Harrison. *Introduction to Switching and Automata Theory*. McGraw-Hill, Inc., 1965.

[10] S. T. Hu. *Mathematical Theory of Swithcing Circuits and Automata*. Berkeley, University of California Press, 1968.

[11] J. B. Kam and G. I. Davida. A structured design of substitution-permutation encryption networks. *IEEE Transactions on Computers*, 28(10):747–753, 1979.

[12] A. Konheim. *Cryptography: a primer*. Wiley, 1981.

[13] C. Meyer. Ciphertext/plaintext and ciphertext/key dependence vs. number of rounds for the data encryption standard. In *AFIPS Conference proceedings, 47*, pages 1119–1126, 1978.

[14] C. Mitchell. Enumerating boolean functions of cryptographic significance. *Journal of Cryptology*, 2(3):155–170, 1990.

[15] D. S. Mitrinovic. *Analytic Inequalities*. Springer–Verlag, 1970.

[16] L O'Connor. Enumerating nondegenerate permutations. Technical Report 2527, University of Waterloo, Waterloo, Ontario, Canada, 1991.

[17] W. L. Price and D. W. Davies. *Security for computer networks*. Wiley, 1984.

[18] R. A. Rueppel. *Design and Analysis of Stream Ciphers*. Springer–Verlag, 1986.

Perfect nonlinear S-boxes

Kaisa Nyberg

Finnish Defense Forces and University of Helsinki

Abstract. A perfect nonlinear S-box is a substitution transformation with evenly distributed directional derivatives. Since the method of differential cryptanalysis presented by E. Biham and A. Shamir makes use of nonbalanced directional derivatives, the perfect nonlinear S-boxes are immune to this attack. The main result is that for a perfect nonlinear S-box the number of input variables is at least twice the number of output variables. Also two different construction methods are given. The first one is based on the Maiorana-McFarland construction of bent functions and is easy and efficient to implement. The second method generalizes Dillon's construction of difference sets.

1. Introduction

The study of the properties of the substitution transformations of DES has resulted in a wealth of nonlinearity criteria for Boolean functions, whose applications are not restricted to DES-like block ciphers but are useful in the analysis of any cryptographic algorithm where nonlinear transformations are used. An overview of nonlinearity criteria with extensive bibliography is given in [16].

The two most successful publicly presented attacks on DES make use of the so called linear structures of S-boxes. Chaum and Evertse [3] were able to find six-bit blocks such that when they are xored to the input of an S-box the output is always changed by a same (zero or nonzero) block. By chaining these linear structures they are able to successfully attack DES up till six rounds.

Biham and Shamir develop in [2] this idea further and are able to attack more rounds. They only require that with certain changes in the input of an S-box the change in the output is known with a high probability. Therefore they look for input changes with most unevenly distributed output changes.

In this paper we study substitution transformations with evenly distributed output changes. Their importance is also noticed in [4] We shall show that such perfect nonlinear transformations exist and can be efficiently implemented but only when the input block is twice as long as the output block.

In [12] Meier and Staffelbach discuss perfect nonlinear Boolean functions, which are defined to be at maximum distance from linear structures. These functions are the same as the previously known bent functions [15]. To construct perfect nonlinear S-boxes it is necessary that each output bit is a perfect nonlinear function of the input. But it is not sufficient, indeed, also every linear combination of the output variables have to be perfect nonlinear. We present two different constructions to achieve this property.

In §2 we recall the basic facts of q-ary bent functions as their definition and construction by the Maiorana-McFarland method. We also present a second construction which makes use of the field structure of $GF(p^n)$ and generalizes Dillon's construction of difference set in $GF(2^n)$ given in [6]. The property of perfect nonlinearity for functions from $\mathbf{Z}_p^n$ to $\mathbf{Z}_p^m$, p prime, is studied in §3. The main result is that perfect nonlinear functions, such that all linear combinations of output variables are regular bent functions of the input, exist only if $n \geq 2m$. Using a linear feedback shift register to generate a suitable set of permutations an efficient construction of perfect nonlinear functions is given in §4. Since perfect nonlinear functions are quite rare it might be a good idea to begin a construction of a cryptographic function from a perfect nonlinear function and then modify it to satisfy other requirements. In §4 we present an example how balancedness can be achieved without completely destroying the original good property. In §5 a different construction is presented which also gives a wealth of perfect nonlinear functions.

2. Bent functions

Let q be a positive integer and denote the set of integers modulo q by $\mathbf{Z}_q$. Let

$$u = e^{i\frac{2\pi}{q}}$$

be the qth root of unity in $\mathbf{C}$, where $i = \sqrt{-1}$. Let f be a function from the set $\mathbf{Z}_q^n$ of n-tuples of integers modulo q to $\mathbf{Z}_q$. Then the *Fourier transform* of u^f is defined as follows

$$F(\mathbf{w}) = \frac{1}{\sqrt{q^n}} \sum_{\mathbf{x} \in \mathbf{Z}_q^n} u^{f(\mathbf{x}) - \mathbf{w} \cdot \mathbf{x}}, \quad \mathbf{w} \in \mathbf{Z}_q^n.$$

The following definition is given in [7].

DEFINITION 2.1. *A function* $f : \mathbf{Z}_q^n \to \mathbf{Z}_q$ *is bent if* $|F(\mathbf{w})| = 1$, *for all* $\mathbf{w} \in \mathbf{Z}_q^n$.

Let f and g be two functions from $\mathbf{Z}_q^n$ to $\mathbf{Z}_q$. Then their *shifted cross-correlation*

$$c(f, g)(\mathbf{w}) = \frac{1}{q^n} \sum_{\mathbf{x} \in \mathbf{Z}_q^n} u^{f(\mathbf{x} + \mathbf{w}) - g(\mathbf{x})}.$$

From these definitions the following characterization is immediate.

THEOREM 2.1. *A function* $f : \mathbf{Z}_q^n \to \mathbf{Z}_q$ *is bent if and only if*

$$|c(f, L)(\mathbf{w})| = \frac{1}{\sqrt{q^n}}$$

for all linear (or affine) functions $L : \mathbf{Z}_q^n \to \mathbf{Z}_q$ *and* $\mathbf{w} \in \mathbf{Z}_q^n$.

Analogously to the binary case it then follows that the q-ary bent functions have the minimum correlation to the set of all affine functions (see Theorem 3.5 in [12]).

In [7] also the following result can be found.

THEOREM 2.2. *A function* $f : \mathbf{Z}_q^n \to \mathbf{Z}_q$ *is bent if and only if*

$$c(f, f)(\mathbf{w}) = 0, \text{ for all } \mathbf{w} \neq \mathbf{0}.$$

This is in the binary case exactly the property of perfect nonlinearity used by Meier and Staffelbach [12] to define bent functions. In [13] the following generalization is made.

DEFINITION 2.2. *A function $f : Z_q^n \to Z_q$ is perfect nonlinear if for every fixed $\mathbf{w} \in Z_q^n$, $\mathbf{w} \neq 0$, the difference*

$$f(\mathbf{x} + \mathbf{w}) - f(\mathbf{x})$$

obtains each value $k \in Z_q$ for exactly q^{n-1} values of $\mathbf{x} \in Z_q^n$.

THEOREM 2.3. *A perfect nonlinear function from Z_q^n to Z_q is bent. The converse is true if q is a prime.*

The following theorem is due to Kumar, Scholtz and Welch [7]. For $q = 2$ it was proved by Maiorana (unpublished, see [6]) generalizing the construction method of Rothaus [15]. An equivalent method is given by McFarland in [11].

THEOREM 2.4. *Let $g : Z_q^m \to Z_q$ be any function and $\pi : Z_q^m \to Z_q^m$ any permutation. Then the function*

$$f : Z_q^{2m} = Z_q^m \times Z_q^m \to Z_q, \; f(\mathbf{x}_1, \mathbf{x}_2) = \pi(\mathbf{x}_1) \cdot \mathbf{x}_2 + g(\mathbf{x}_1)$$

is a regular bent function.

A third equivalent way of looking at this construction in the binary case is to make use of Hadamard matrices as described in [8]. This method is also discussed in [14]. The constructions given in [1] and [17] are special cases of the Maiorana-MacFarland construction.

A completely different construction of bent functions in $GF(2^n)$ with an even n is due to Dillon. Indeed, the main result of [5] is that this method gives bent functions which are not affinely equivalent to any Maiorana function. We have the following generalization of Dillon's construction.

THEOREM 2.5. *Let p be a prime and $n = 2m$. Denote by $G = GF(p^m)$ the subfield of $F = GF(p^n)$ and let α be a primitive element in F. Then the cosets of G^**

$$H_i = \alpha^i G^*, \; i = 0, 1, \ldots, p^m,$$

are all distinct and their union is the set of non-zero elements of F. Assume that the set of indices $1, 2, \ldots, p^m$ is divided into p disjoint subsets $A_0, A_1, \ldots, A_{p-1}$ of cardinality p^{m-1} each. Then the function $f : GF(p^n) \to GF(p)$,

$$f(0) = 0$$
$$f(\mathbf{x}) = 0, \text{ for } x \in H_0,$$
$$f(\mathbf{x}) = k, \text{ for } x \in H_i, \; i \in A_k, \; k = 0, 1, \ldots, p-1,$$

is a bent function in F.

The proof of this theorem is a straightforward but lengthy checking of the condition on perfect nonlinearity. The main argument is that for every nonzero $\mathbf{w}$ the elements $\mathbf{x} + \mathbf{w}$ belong to distinct cosets of G for distinct elements $\mathbf{x}$ in a fixed coset.

3. Perfect nonlinear transformation

We give the following further generalization of perfect nonlinearity.

DEFINITION 3.1. *A function* $\mathbf{f} : \mathbf{Z}_q^n \to \mathbf{Z}_q^m$ *is perfect nonlinear if for every fixed* $\mathbf{w} \in \mathbf{Z}_q^n$ *the difference*

$$\mathbf{f}(\mathbf{x} + \mathbf{w}) - \mathbf{f}(\mathbf{x})$$

obtains each value $\mathbf{y} \in \mathbf{Z}_q^m$ *for* q^{n-m} *values of* $\mathbf{x}$.

We call the function

$$D_\mathbf{w}\mathbf{f} : \mathbf{Z}_q^n \to \mathbf{Z}_q^m, \ \mathbf{x} \mapsto \mathbf{f}(\mathbf{x} + \mathbf{w}) - \mathbf{f}(\mathbf{x}),$$

the derivative of $\mathbf{f}$ to the direction $\mathbf{w}$. Then we can say that $\mathbf{f}$ is perfect nonlinear if and only if its derivatives to all nonzero directions are balanced functions. By definition, a function $\mathbf{g} : \mathbf{Z}_q^n \to \mathbf{Z}_q^m$ is balanced if and only if for every $\mathbf{c} \in \mathbf{Z}_q^m$, $\mathbf{c} \neq \mathbf{0}$ the function $\mathbf{x} \mapsto \mathbf{c} \cdot \mathbf{g}(\mathbf{x})$ is balanced. Since moreover,

$$D_\mathbf{w}(\mathbf{c} \cdot \mathbf{f}) = \mathbf{c} \cdot D_\mathbf{w}\mathbf{f},$$

we have the following characterization.

THEOREM 3.1. *A function* $\mathbf{f} : \mathbf{Z}_q^n \to \mathbf{Z}_q^m$ *is perfect nonlinear if and only if for every nonzero* $\mathbf{c} \in \mathbf{Z}_q^m$ *the function*

$$\mathbf{x} \mapsto \mathbf{c} \cdot \mathbf{f}(\mathbf{x})$$

is perfect nonlinear in the sense of Definition 2.2.

In other words, a blockfunction is perfect nonlinear if and only if every linear combination of its output coordinates is perfect nonlinear.

Assume now that p is a prime. Then perfect nonlinearity and bentness of a $\mathbf{Z}_p$-valued function in $\mathbf{Z}_p^n$ are equivalent concepts, see Theorem 2.3. The value distributions of p-ary bent functions are derived in [13]. Let us now consider the value distributions of perfect nonlinear blockfunctions. Recall that a function $f : \mathbf{Z}_p^n \to \mathbf{Z}_p$ is called a regular bent function if there is a function $g : \mathbf{Z}_p^n \to \mathbf{Z}_p$ such that $F(\mathbf{w}) = u^{g(\mathbf{w})}$, for all $\mathbf{w} \in \mathbf{Z}_p^n$ ([7], [13]). If $p = 2$ then all bent functions are regular.

THEOREM 3.2.. *Let* n *be even and* $\mathbf{f} : \mathbf{Z}_p^n \to \mathbf{Z}_p^m$ *a perfect nonlinear function such that the functions*

$$\mathbf{x} \mapsto \mathbf{c} \cdot \mathbf{f}(\mathbf{x}), \ \mathbf{c} \in \mathbf{Z}_p^m, \mathbf{c} \neq \mathbf{0},$$

are regular bent functions. Let

$$a_\mathbf{y} = \#\{\mathbf{x} \in \mathbf{Z}_p^n \mid \mathbf{f}(\mathbf{x}) = \mathbf{y}\}, \ \mathbf{y} \in \mathbf{Z}_p^m.$$

Then

$$a_\mathbf{y} = p^{\frac{n}{2}-m}b_\mathbf{y}, \ \text{for every } \mathbf{y},$$

where $b_\mathbf{y}$ *is a positive integer not divisible by* p. *Also,*

$$p^{n-m} + p^{\frac{n}{2}-m} - p^{\frac{n}{2}} \le a_\mathbf{y} \le p^{n-m} - p^{\frac{n}{2}-m} + p^{\frac{n}{2}}.$$

PROOF: Let $c \in Z_p^m$, $c \neq 0$ and denote the Fourier transform of the function $x \mapsto c \cdot f(x)$ by $F_c(0)$. Then

$$p^{\frac{n}{2}} F_c(0) = \sum_{x \in Z_p^n} u^{c \cdot f(x)} = \sum_{y \in Z_p^m} a_y u^{c \cdot y}.$$

Taking the sum over $c \neq 0$ we obtain

$$\sum_y a_y \sum_{c \neq 0} u^{c \cdot y} = p^{\frac{n}{2}} \sum_{c \neq 0} F_c(0).$$

Let $S = \sum_{c \neq 0} F_c(0)$. Then we have

$$\sum_{y \neq 0} a_y(-1) + a_0(p^m - 1) = p^{\frac{n}{2}} S$$

from which

$$S = p^{n - \frac{n}{2}} + a_0 p^{m - \frac{n}{2}}.$$

To prove the claim it suffices to show that S is an integer not divisible by p. Since n is even, S is a rational number. Let

$$r_k = \#\{c \in Z_p^m \setminus \{0\} \mid F_c(0) = u^k\}, \quad k = 0, 1, \ldots, p - 1.$$

Then, due to the regularity assumption,

$$\sum_{k=0}^{p-1} r_k = p^m - 1 \quad \text{and} \quad S = \sum_{k=0}^{p-1} r_k u^k$$

and hence

$$r_0 - S = r_1 = r_2 = \cdots = r_{p-1},$$

from which it follows that S is an integer and p devides $\sum r_k - S = p^m - 1 - S$, which proves the claim.

The estimates for a_y follow from the estimates

$$-p^m + 1 \leq S \leq p^m - 1.$$

Indeed, in the context of this theorem, we always have $n \geq 2m$. Since a_y is an integer and binary bent functions are regular and exist only if the input space is of even dimension, we have the following

COROLLARY. *For a perfect nonlinear binary S-box the dimension of the input space is at least twice the dimension of the output space.*

4. A construction based on Maiorana-McFarland method

Let n be an even positive integer, $\mathbf{f} : \mathbf{Z}_p^n \to \mathbf{Z}_p^m$ a function and denote the m output coordinate functions of $\mathbf{f}$ by $f_1, f_2, \ldots, f_m$. Assume that every f_i, $i = 1, 2, \ldots, m$, is a Maiorana function, i.e., has the form

$$f_i(\mathbf{x}) = f_i(\mathbf{x}_1, \mathbf{x}_2) = \pi_i(\mathbf{x}_1) \cdot \mathbf{x}_2 + g_i(\mathbf{x}_1),$$

where π_i is a permutation of the space $\mathbf{Z}_p^{\frac{n}{2}}$ and g_i is a function from $\mathbf{Z}_p^{\frac{n}{2}}$ to $\mathbf{Z}_p$. Then $\mathbf{f} = (f_1, f_2, \ldots, f_m)$ is perfect nonlinear if every nonzero linear combination of the permutations π_i, $i = 1, 2, \ldots, m$ is again a permutation of $\mathbf{Z}_p^{\frac{n}{2}}$. Since Maiorana functions are regular bent we have by the remark at the end of §3 that $n \geq 2m$.

One way of constructing a family of permutations with the required property, is to use a linear feedback shift register of length $\frac{n}{2}$ and with a primitive feedback polynomial. Let A be the state transition function of such a shift register. Then A is a permutation of the space $\mathbf{Z}_p^{\frac{n}{2}}$ as well as the powers A^i of A,

$$A^i = \overbrace{A \circ \cdots \circ A}^{i \text{ times}}, \ i = 1, 2, \ldots.$$

Moreover, it is a wellknown property of linear feedback shift registers that generate maximal length sequences that every non-trivial linear combination of the permutations

$$I, A, A^2, \ldots, A^{\frac{n}{2}-1}$$

is a power of A and hence a permutation.

Now an elementary implementation of a perfect nonlinear S-box with n input variables and m output variables, $n \geq 2m$, is obtained in the following way. Take a $\frac{n}{2}$-shift register with a primitive feedback polynomial. Devide the input block of length n into two halves $\mathbf{x}_1$ and $\mathbf{x}_2$. The first digit of the output block of length m is obtained by calculating the dot product $\mathbf{x}_1 \cdot \mathbf{x}_2$. To obtain the second digit the shift register is shifted once and the dot product of its new contents with $\mathbf{x}_2$ is calculated. In this manner every shift of the register produces a new output digit. This basic arrangement is very efficient and suitable for on-line applications. If the functions g_i are used their complexity may cause reduction of the speed.

Let us still consider the properties of the basic arrangement,

$$\mathbf{f} = (f_1, f_2, \ldots, f_m), \ f_i(\mathbf{x}_1, \mathbf{x}_2) = A^{i-1}(\mathbf{x}_1) \cdot \mathbf{x}_2.$$

This perfect nonlinear function $f : \mathbf{Z}_p^n \to \mathbf{Z}_p^m$ is not balanced. The all-zero output block is obtained for

$$p^{n-m} - p^{\frac{n}{2}-m} + p^{\frac{n}{2}}$$

different inputs and the other possible outputs are obtained for equally many, i.e., for

$$p^{n-m} - p^{\frac{n}{2}-m}$$

different inputs. In some applications it might be possible that the first half x_1 of the input that goes to the shift register is never the all zero block. With this restriction the function f is balanced. Let us see what is the effect of this restriction to the directional derivatives.

Let the nonzero increment w have two halves w_1 and w_2 corresponding to the division of the input. Then

$$f_i(x + w) - f_i(x) = A^{i-1}(x_1) \cdot w_2 + A^{i-1}(w_1) \cdot x_2 + A^{i-1}(w_1) \cdot w_2,$$

for every $i = 1, 2, \ldots, m,$. Now we have two cases.

$1°$ $w_1 = 0$. In this case the directional derivative

$$D_w f(x) = f(x + w)) - f(x)$$

is a linear function of x_1 and obtains each nonzero value for p^{n-m} different inputs and the zero value for $p^{n-m} - p^{\frac{n}{2}}$ different inputs.

$2°$ $w_1 \neq 0$. Then the directional derivative is balanced.

As a conclusion we can say that the restriction to the inputs with nonzero first halves gives a balanced and almost perfect nonlinear function.

Other possible families of permutations $\{\pi_1, \pi_2, \ldots, \pi_m\}$ to be used in the Maiorana-McFarland based construction are, for example

$$\pi_i(x) = a_i x,$$

where $\{a_1, a_2, \ldots, a_m\}$ are linearly independent elements of the Galois field $GF(p^{\frac{n}{2}})$, or as a special case,

$$\pi_i(x) = \alpha^i x,$$

where α is a primitive element of $GF(p^{\frac{n}{2}})$.

The problem of finding suitable permutations is related to the problem of complete mappings and orthogonal Latin squares (see [9],§9.4 and [10]). The following theorem illustrates this relationship. For more evolved constructions of orthogonal Latin squares we refer to [5], Ch. 7.

THEOREM 4.1.. *Let π and σ be permutations of $\mathbf{Z}_p^n$ and let $a_0, a_1, \ldots, a_{p^n-1}$ be the elements of $\mathbf{Z}_p^n$. Then the $p^n \times p^n$ matrices*

$$(\pi(a_i) + a_j)_{ij} \text{ and } (\sigma(a_i) + a_j)_{ij}$$

are orthogonal Latin squares if and only if $\pi - \sigma$ is a permutation.

It is not difficult to check that if the sum of two permutations of $\mathbf{Z}_2^3$ is a permutation then these permutations are affinely equivalent mappings. For $n \geq 4$ nonlinear permutations can have a permutation sum even if they are not affinely equivalent.

Example. The following nonlinear permutations π and σ of $\mathbf{Z}_2^4$ have a sum which is a permutation.

x	=	1	2	3	4	5	6	7	8	9	A	6	B	C	D	E	F
$\pi(x)$	=	0	2	D	1	3	8	A	9	C	F	B	E	7	5	4	6
$\sigma(x)$	=	0	3	4	2	1	D	E	F	6	7	C	5	8	B	9	A
$(\pi + \sigma)(x)$	=	0	1	9	3	2	5	4	6	A	8	7	B	F	E	D	C

Also π and σ are not affinely equivalent, i.e., $\pi^{-1}\sigma$ is nonlinear.

5. A second construction

Let f_i, $i = 1, 2, \ldots, m$ be bent functions from $GF(p^n)$ to $GF(p)$ constructed by the method given in Theorem 2.5. Assume that the assignments of the values $0, 1, \ldots, p-1$ to the different cosets of G for different f_i satisfy the following compatibility condition. For every nonzero $\mathbf{c} = (c_1, c_2, \ldots, c_m) \in GF(p^m)$ the function $c_1 f_1 + c_2 f_2 + \cdots + c_3 f_3$ obtains each of the values $1, 2, \ldots, p-1$ on $p^{\frac{n}{2}-1}$ cosets from $H_1, H_2, \ldots, H_{p^{\frac{n}{2}}}$. Then the function $\mathbf{f} = (f_1, f_2, \ldots, f_m)$ is perfect nonlinear. In fact, the given compatibility condition is also necessary for $\mathbf{f}$ to be perfect nonlinear.

The assignment of values for f_i can be done by using a function $h_i : \mathbf{Z}_{p^{\frac{n}{2}}} \to \mathbf{Z}_p$ defined in the following way. For $k \in \mathbf{Z}_p$ and $i = 1, 2, \ldots, m$ we set

$$h_i(a) = k, \text{ if } f_i(\mathbf{x}) = k \text{ for } \mathbf{x} \in H_{a+1}.$$

THEOREM 5.1. *Let f_i, $i = 1, 2, \ldots, m$ be bent functions in $GF(p^n)$ constructed by the generalization of Dillon's method. Let h_i be the value assignment function for f_i, $i = 1, 2, \ldots, m$. Then the function*

$$\mathbf{f} : GF(p^n) \to GF(p^m), \ \mathbf{f}(\mathbf{x}) = (f_1(\mathbf{x}), f_2(\mathbf{x}), \ldots, f_m(\mathbf{x})),$$

is perfect nonlinear if and only if for every nonzero $\mathbf{c} = (c_1, c_2, \ldots, c_m) \in GF(p^m)$ the function $c_1 h_1 + c_2 h_2 + \cdots + c_m h_m$ is balanced.

In the terminology of [9], Ch. 7, the statement of the theorem says that $\mathbf{f}$ is perfect nonlinear if and only if the functions h_i, $i = 1, 2, \ldots, m$, form an orthogonal system of permutation polynomials. Hence especially, for $m = \frac{n}{2}$, every permutation of the space $\mathbf{Z}_p^{\frac{n}{2}}$ gives, via this construction, a perfect nonlinear function from $\mathbf{Z}_p^n$ to $\mathbf{Z}_p^{\frac{n}{2}}$ and different permutations give different functions. Since the fixed coset H_0 can be chosen in $(p^{\frac{n}{2}} + 1)$ ways the number of perfect nonlinear functions with maximal output given by this construction is $(p^{\frac{n}{2}} + 1)!$.

Acknowledgement

I wish to thank Ossi Ojala for useful computer programs.

REFERENCES

1. C. M. Adams and S. E. Tavares, *The use of bent sequences to achieve higher-order strict avalanche criterion in S-box design*, IEE Proceedings (to appear).
2. E. Biham and A. Shamir, *Differential cryptanalysis of DES-like cryptosystems*, Proceedings of Crypto '90 (to appear).
3. D. Chaum and J. H. Evertse, *Cryptanalysis of DES with a reduced number of rounds*, Advances in Cryptology, Proceedings of Crypto '85, Springer-Verlag 1986, 192–211.
4. M. H. Dawson and S. E. Tavares, *An expanded set of s-box design criteria based on information theory and its relation to differential-like attacks*, These Proceedings.
5. J. Denes and A. D. Keedwell, "Latin squares and their applications," The English Universities Press Ltd, London, 1974.
6. J. F. Dillon, *Elementary Hadamard difference sets*, Proceedings of the Sixth Southeastern Conference on Combinatorics, Graph Theory and Computing, Boca Raton, Florida (1975), 237–249; Congressus Numerantium No. XIV, Utilitas Math., Winnipeg, Manitoba (1975).
7. P. V. Kumar, R. A. Scholtz and L. R. Welch, *Generalized bent functions and their properties*, J. Combinatorial Theory, Ser. A 40 (1985), 90–107.

8. A. Lempel and M. Cohn, *Maximal families of bent sequences*, IEEE Trans. Inform. Theory **IT-28** (1982), 865–868.

9. R. Lidl and H. Niederreiter, "Finite fields. Encyclopedia of Mathematics and its applications, Vol. 20," Addison-Wesley, Reading, Massachusetts, 1983.

10. H. B. Mann, *The construction of orthogonal Latin squares*, Ann. Math. Statist. **13** (1942), 418–423.

11. R. L. McFarland, *A family of difference sets in non-cyclic groups*, J. Combinatorial Theory, Ser. A **15** (1973), 1–10.

12. W. Meier and O. Staffelbach, *Nonlinearity criteria for cryptographic functions*, Proceedings of Eurocrypt '89, Springer 1990, 549–562.

13. K. Nyberg, *Constructions of bent functions and difference sets*, Proceedings of Eurocrypt '90, Springer-Verlag 1991, 151–160.

14. B. Preneel et al.,, *Propagation characteristics of Boolean bent functions*, Proceedings of Eurocrypt '90, Springer-Verlag 1991, 161–173.

15. O. S. Rothaus, *On "bent" functions*, J. Combinatorial Theory, Ser. A **20** (1976), 300–305.

16. R. A. Rueppel, *Stream Ciphers*, in "Contemporary Cryptology: The Science of Information Integrity," edited by Gustavus Simmons, IEEE Press (to appear).

17. R. Yarlagadda and J. E. Hershey, *Analysis and synthesis of bent sequences*, IEE Proceedings **136** (1989), 112–123.

A Formal Approach to Security Architectures[1]

Rainer A. Rueppel

R^3 Security Engineering, 8623 Wetzikon

Eidgenössische Technische Hochschule, Zürich

Switzerland

Abstract

We define a formal language whose symbols are security goals and mechanisms. This allows us to express every security architecture as a string. Designing a security architecture becomes the task of generating a word in the language. Analysing a security architecture becomes the task of parsing a string and determining if it belongs to the language. Since not every complete security architecture achieves its goals equally efficient, we associate a complexity parameter to every goal and mechanism. This allows us to identify complexity- reducing and complexity-increasing mechanisms.

1 Introduction

In computer systems development, formal methods are applied to tasks such as requirements analysis, system design, system verification, system validation, and system analysis and evaluation. In computer security, formal methods are applied in particular to the problem of access control [14]. For example, in the Bell-LaPadula model [1] a computer system is modelled as a finite-state machine where user actions cause state transitions; the main interest is in determining if the system can ever reach an insecure state.

In cryptology, formal methods have been applied to the analysis of protocols [11, 2, 6]. Here the main interest is in verifying the assumptions on which the security of the protocol depends, and in verifying that the protocol achieves the desired goals while not releasing any compromising information. Typically, these formal methods are too restricted to be applicable to the general task of analysing and designing a security architecture.

In the standards arena, as exemplified by the treatment of security in the OSI-model [7], there is a great uncertainty about how the various security services, security mechanisms, and the corresponding security management are to be interconnected or to be embedded into the system architecture[13, 8, 9, 10, 5].

Another aspect, although important in practice, has only received little attention in theory. This is the problem of assessing the management complexity that results from specific choices of security services and mechanisms [18].

Now suppose you are the designer of a secure system. You would like to know

1. what design choices are available at a specific layer of the security architecture,

---

[1]This work was supported in part by the Hasler-Foundation, Switzerland

2. what the consequences of these choices are, in particular, if the management complexity can be reduced using appropriate security techniques and mechanisms,

3. when the security architecture is complete.

The methodology presented in this paper helps to answer all of these questions. We identify security goals and mechanisms with symbols in a formal language. The various ways in which security mechanisms can be combined or can be used to achieve certain security goals are governed by a set of productions (rewriting rules). In a given stage of the design, the subset of applicable productions are exactly the available design choices. A security architecture is complete, when all security goals have been satisfied. Moreover, to each security goal and mechanism we associate a parameter, its inherent complexity (measured by the number of secure channels). This allows us to identify complexity- reducing and complexity-increasing mechanisms. It also allows us to detect over- and under-achievement of security goals. Summarizing, the presented approach has applications as a formal design tool or as an analysis and evaluation tool, revealing unstated assumptions, inconsistencies, and unintentional incompleteness. In section 1.3 we give examples for both uses.

In this paper we limit ourselves to channels and trusted authorities as architectural components in a homogeneous environment (one in which all participants have the same capabilities). But it is obvious that our approach can be extended in various ways, for instance, to include the problem of key generation. It is beyond the scope of this paper to provide an exhaustive list of productions for all security goals and mechanisms. Instead, the purpose is to show that even complex concepts such as certificate or identity- based systems are amenable to analysis in our language.

1.1 Confidentiality and Authenticity

In practice there exists a confusing multiplicity of security services. Take for instance the security architecture of the OSI model [7]. There are such services as data origin authentication, peer-entity authentication, data integrity, confidentiality, non-repudiation. Moreover, most services distinguish between connectionless and connection-oriented mode, and between selective-field message, and traffic flow security. But fundamentally, there are only two basic security goals

Confidentiality: the sender is certain that, whoever might receive his message, only the legitimate receiver can read it. Imagine a channel, to which everybody can write, but from which only the legitimate receiver can read.

Authenticity: the receiver is certain that, when he can read the message, it must have been created by the legitimate sender. Imagine a channel to which only the legitimate sender can write, but from which everybody can read.

We will use **security** to denote the combined goal of both confidentiality and authenticity.

1.2 The Underlying Logic

There is a strict logic supporting our constructions. Suppose we use a symmetric cryptosystem to encrypt the basic data channels. Then we write

$$Secu(N^2) \rightarrow sym(secu, N^2), Secu(N^2)$$

where $Secu(N^2)$ on the left of the production denotes the goal of securing N^2 (data) channels, $sym(secu, N^2)$ denotes the symmetric cryptosystem used for security, and $Secu(N^2)$ on the right of the production denotes the goal of securing N^2 (key) channels. Clearly, security on the data links can only be achieved if the keys for the symmetric cryptosystem are securely transmitted. Hence, security of the data link implies security of the key link. Similarly, for all other productions, **achievement of the security goal on the left-hand side of the rewriting rule implies achievement of the security goal(s) on the right-hand side of the rewriting rule.** And since, while building a security architecture, we replace lower layer security goals by higher layer security goals, we achieve the original goal only if we resolve all goals by some suitable means during the construction process.

1.3 Examples

We want to illustrate our approach with some simple and self-explanatory examples.

1.3.1 Designing a Security Architecture

Suppose your task is to design a system with N participants which achieves **homogeneous individual authentication** (what we mean is, that every participant upon reception of a message can convince himself about the authenticity of the message). Your idea might be to use a symmetric cryptosystem for the data channel, which leaves you with the task of finding means to distribute the keys securely. What are your options here? Should you use another symmetric or an asymmetric cryptosystem, or a specialized key distribution protocol like Diffie-Hellman, or a tamper-proof device? Applying the construction rules given by our language and making the corresponding decision you might arrive at the following security architecture:

$$Auth(N) \rightarrow sym(secu, N^2), Secu(N^2)$$
$$Secu(N^2) \rightarrow asym(secu, N), Auth(N)$$
$$Auth(N) \rightarrow phys(auth, N), ta(auth, N), asym(auth, 1), Auth(1)$$
$$Auth(1) \rightarrow phys(auth, 1)$$

First line: You have decided to achieve the original security goal $auth(N)$ using a symmetric system. This implies that you use (roughly) N^2 secret keys, one for each pair of participants. If more than two participants were to share the same key, the receiver could no longer authenticate the sender. Thus, the new security goal is $secu(N^2)$, that is, the secure distribution of N^2 keys. The first line also indicates that your choice has increased the complexity of the problem from N to N^2.

Second line: Now you decide to use a public-key system to solve the key distribution problem, which leaves you with the problem of authentically distributing the public keys, indicated by the new goal $auth(N)$. This choice reduces the complexity of the management problem from N^2 to N. Actually, it seems as if you have not gained anything. Since you are back at your original goal. This is not true since public keys do not change as often as the data in the basic link.

Third line: Now you decide to employ a trusted center (ta) which certifies the public keys. The participants use physically secure channels to the ta (for instance, they go there with their public keys), the center signs the public keys using its asymmetric system and distributes them back to the participants. For the certificates to be verifiable, the participants need to receive an authentic copy of the center's public key, indicated by the new goal $Auth(1)$. Note that, by employing a center, you have reduced the management complexity from N to 1. Note also that you do not have to entrust your secrets to the center.

Fourth line: In order to distribute the center's public key you decide to use an authentic physical technique. For instance, you publish it every morning in the Newspaper. There is no more security goal to be achieved. So you know that your architecture is complete.

1.3.2 Analyzing a Security Architecture

A certain vendor has a product where the data links are encrypted using a symmetric cryptosystem. For the key distribution he uses the following protocol:

1. A and B initialize a session; independently they choose secret keys k_1 and k_2.

2. Both A and B encrypt their secret keys using the public key P_{KMC} of the center and send them to the center:

$$A \rightarrow KMC: \quad P_{KMC}(k_1)$$
$$B \rightarrow KMC: \quad P_{KMC}(k_2)$$

3. The KMC decrypts k_1 and k_2 using its secret key S_{KMC}; then the KMC selects a session key k_s for A and B and sends k_s back to them on the symmetric channels established by k_1 and k_2:

$$KMC \rightarrow A: \quad E_{k_1}(k_s)$$
$$KMC \rightarrow B: \quad E_{k_2}(k_s)$$

4. A and B decrypt k_s with their independent keys k_1 and k_2 and are now ready to have a private session using the symmetric cryptosystem.

The center broadcasts its public key P_{KMC} continuously to all N participants.

Translating this information into our language we arrive at the following security architecture:

$$Secu(N^2) \rightarrow sym(secu, N^2), Secu(N^2)$$
$$Secu(N^2) \rightarrow sym(secu, N), ta(secu), Secu(N)$$
$$Secu(N) \rightarrow asym(conf, 1), Auth(1)$$
$$Auth(1) \rightarrow cont(1)$$

Parsing this architecture, we get an error message at layer 3: "impossible to achieve $Secu(N)$ with $asym(conf, 1)$". The flaw is that any participant (in fact anybody in possession of the center's public key P_{KMC}) could impersonate any other participant in the system. Thus, the above architecture neither achieves confidentiality (the sender cannot be certain about the receiver of his message) nor authenticity (the receiver cannot be certain about the sender of a received message) and, as a consequence, security breaks down.

2 A Formal Language for Security Architectures

We define a language for security architectures by specifying a grammar where

1. the terminals are security mechanisms.

2. the nonterminals are security goals.

3. the productions give the available constructions, that is, the different ways in which security goals may be replaced (achieved) by security mechanisms and, possibly, other security goals.

As is customary, we designate the nonterminals by symbols which start with upper- case letters, and the terminals by symbols which start with lower- case letters.

2.1 Security Goals

For the moment we wish to deal only with homogeneous security goals, that is, with goals where each participant in the network is given the same capabilities, except possibly for a distinguished participant such as a trusted center. We will distinguish between distributed and centralized security goals, which both appear frequently in a network of N participants. They will form the nonterminals in our formal language.

2.1.1 Distributed Security Goals

$Conf(N)$ denotes homogeneous individual confidentiality. Every participant has associated a (unidirectional) channel from which he can read, but to which everybody else can only write.

$Auth(N)$ denotes homogeneous individual authenticity. Every participant has associated a (unidirectional) channel to which he can write, but from which everybody else can only read.

$Secu(N^2)$ denotes homogeneous individual security. Every pair of participants share a private channel.

Note that

$$Secu(N^2) \rightarrow Auth(N), Conf(N)$$

that is, achieving homogeneous individual confidentiality and authenticity is equivalent to achieving homogeneous individual security.

2.1.2 Security Goals Involving a Center

$Conf(ta, 1)$ denotes distinguished (or centralized) confidentiality. The center has associated a channel to which everybody can write, but from which only the center can read.

$Auth(ta, 1)$ denotes distinguished (or centralized) authenticity. The center has associated a channel from which everybody can read, but to which only the center can write.

$Secu(ta, N)$ denotes distinguished (or centralized) security. The center shares with every participant a private channel.

Because $Conf(ta,1)$ and $Auth(ta,1)$ do not amount to $Secu(ta,N)$ we must introduce two more security goals:

$Auth(ta,N)$ denotes individual authenticity towards the center. Every participant has associated a channel to which only he can write and, from which only the center can read.

$Conf(ta,N)$ denotes individual confidentiality from the center. Every participant has associated a channel from which only he can read and, to which only the center can write.

Note that

$$Secu(ta,N) \rightarrow Auth(ta,N), Conf(ta,N)$$

2.2 Elementary Components and Constructions

In order to achieve our security goals we must employ protection mechanisms and, possibly, trusted authorities. We will distinguish the following elementary channels:

1. Physical channel: the message is protected by some physical means.

2. Symmetric channel: the message is protected by a symmetric cryptographic technique.

3. Asymmetric channel: the message is protected by a public-key technique.

2.2.1 The physical channel

A physical channel is typically used to achieve security, that is, for confidentiality and authentication jointly. Supposedly secure physical channels are couriers, fibre optics, tamper-proof devices etc. We shall write

$phys(secu, N^2)$ to denote a homogeneous system with a secure physical channel between each pair of participants. The corresponding production is

$$Secu(N^2) \rightarrow phys(secu, N^2)$$

But it is also possible to use a physical channel for authentication only. Supposedly authentic physical channels are hardcopy, newspapers, books and $WORMs$ (write-once-read-many-times devices) such as compact disks. Write access to the channel is determined by the ability to print. We shall write

$phys(auth, N)$ to denote a homogeneous system with an authentic physical channel associated to each participants. The corresponding production is

$$Auth(N) \rightarrow phys(auth, N)$$

The distinguishing feature of a physical system is that is does not require any further (secure) distribution of information in order to achieve its security goals.

2.2.2 The symmetric channel

When a symmetric channel is used for confidentiality then the sender encrypts the message M under control of a secret key K, and the data written on the channel is $E_K(M)$. When a symmetric channel is used for authentication then the sender computes a message authentication code under control of a secret key K which is then appended to the message, and the data written on the channel is $M, A_K(M)$ where A is the authentication algorithm. When a symmetric channel is used for security then the properties confidentiality and authenticity must both be enforced. One often reads the statement that authentication is implicitly provided by encryption. In general this is not true as illustrated by the one-time pad. Therefore it is advisable to use two algorithms, one for confidentiality, the other one for authentication, both with independent keys, in order to achieve security in a symmetric channel. Who can access a symmetric channel is determined by the corresponding keys. We write

$sym(secu, N^2)$ to denote a homogeneous symmetric system that allows for a secure logical channel between each pair of participants. In such a system, N^2 secret keys are needed, one for each channel.

$sym(secu, N)$ to denote a centralized system that allows for a secure symmetric channel between every participant and the center. In such a system N keys are needed, one for each channel.

We have only used the mode $secu$ in the above system descriptions, since with a symmetric cryptosystem possession of the key implies the ability to read and write from the associated channel, and hence, no distinction is necessary between authenticity, confidentiality, and security (as far as security management is concerned). If a symmetric cryptosystem is used to achieve a security goal, we are then faced with the problem of distributing the corresponding keys in a secure fashion. This amounts to a new security goal. The most obvious production is

$$Secu(N^2) \rightarrow sym(secu, N^2), Secu(N^2)$$

where we establish a secure channel between every pair of participants using a symmetric cryptosystem and, as a consequence, must establish another secure channel between every pair of participants to distribute the keys. When the goal is only confidentiality or authenticity then the use of a symmetric cryptosystem will result in an overachievement (in the sense that the mechanism used does more than is required by the goal). The following two productions illustrate the situation.

$$Conf(N) \rightarrow sym(secu, N^2), Secu(N^2)$$
$$Auth(N) \rightarrow sym(secu, N^2), Secu(N^2)$$

Moreover, they are complexity-increasing since, by using N^2 symmetric channels, we must then distribute N^2 keys securely.

2.2.3 The asymmetric channel

When an asymmetric channel [4, 16] is used for confidentiality then the sender encrypts the message M with the public key E_α of the recipient α, and the data written on the channel is $E_\alpha(M)$. Only the recipient α has full access to the asymmetric channel defined by E_α since only he can decrypt the ciphertexts with his secret key D_α. But everybody with access to E_α can write messages on the channel. When an asymmetric channel is used for authentication then the sender A signs the message M with his private signature key S_A, and the data written on the channel is $S_A(M)$. Everybody with access to the public verification key V_A can check the signature (read messages form the channel) but only A has the capability to also write messages on the asymmetric channel. We shall write

$asym(mode, N)$ to denote a homogeneous asymmetric system that associates with every partici-
pant his own asymmetric channel. Assuming that the participants create their asymmetric channels themselves, the remaining problem is to distribute the N public keys in an authentic fashion among the participants. According to the use of the asymmetric system we set $mode = auth, conf$, or $secu$.

The corresponding productions are

$$Conf(N) \rightarrow asym(conf, N), Auth(N)$$
$$Auth(N) \rightarrow asym(auth, N), Auth(N)$$

where the new goal $Auth(N)$ denotes the problem of distributing the public keys authentically among the participants. A secure channel between two communicants may be built by composing two asymmetric channels, one for authentication and one for confidentiality. First the sender A signs the message M under his private signature key S_A and then he encrypts $S_A(M)$ under the recipients B public encryption key E_β to produce $E_\beta(S_A(M))$. The corresponding production is

$$Secu(N^2) \rightarrow asym(secu, N), Auth(N)$$

where, in fact, we have allowed $asym(secu, N)$ to stand for two different asymmetric channels (one for confidentiality and one for authenticity) for every participant. The new goal $Auth(N)$ is to distribute the public keys authentically among the participants. Note that this is a complexity-reducing production since we replace the management of N^2 secure channels by the management of N authentic channels.

2.2.4 The trusted authority

A participant may instead of directly establishing a secure channel with another participant send his message to a trusted authority, and let the authority forward his message to the intended recipient in the desired secure mode. Introducing a trusted authority means switching from a distributed to a centralized concept in the corresponding layer of the security architecture. We shall write

$ta(secu, N)$ to denote an authority which is trusted with handling the secrets of the participants.

$ta(auth, N)$ to denote an authority which is trusted with handling the participants' data in an authentic fashion.

$ta(conf, N)$ to denote an authority which is trusted with handling the participants' data in a confidential fashion.

The classical centralized security concept where the trusted authority shares a secure channel with each participant and acts as a central agent relaying information forth and back is described by the following production:

$$Secu(N^2) \rightarrow ta(secu, N), Secu(ta, N)$$

When the goal is only authenticity or confidentiality, then the following productions apply:

$$Auth(N) \rightarrow Auth(ta, N), ta(auth, N), Auth(ta, 1)$$
$$Conf(N) \rightarrow Conf(ta, 1), ta(conf, N), Conf(ta, N)$$

An asymmetric channel can be used, if the goal is confidentiality towards the center, or authenticity from the center:

$$Auth(ta, 1) \rightarrow asym(auth, 1), Auth(ta, 1)$$
$$Conf(1, ta) \rightarrow asym(conf, 1), Auth(ta, 1)$$

where $Auth(ta, 1)$ stands for the authentic distribution of the ta's public key to all the participants. For more constructions which involve a trusted authority, please compare the sections on certificate systems and identity- based systems.

2.3 Compound Constructions

2.3.1 Diffie-Hellman Key Agreement

The Diffie-Hellman key agreement [3] (also called exponential key exchange) is a protocol which allows two participants, without prior exchange of secret information, to establish a common secret key using public messages only. The resulting secret key is used for encryption with their symmetric cryptosystems. The main problem is to guarantee authenticity of the transmitted public messages. The corresponding production is

$$sym(secu, N^2), Secu(N^2) \rightarrow sym(secu, N^2), expka(N), Auth(N)$$

where $expka(N)$ denotes the exponential key agreement. The complexity is N since we need N authentic channels, one for each participant. Note that the above production is context- sensitive; the exponential key agreement can only be applied in combination with a symmetric cryptosystem. Note also, that the exponential key exchange is complexity- reducing. Since in this paper we are not interested in the internal functioning of the protocol, the term $expka(N)$ may stand for any protocol exhibiting the same characteristics as the Diffie- Hellman protocol (compare [17]).

2.3.2 The Certificate System

The certificate system [12] is an asymmetric system used by the trusted authority for authentication of a participant's individual data. It is utilized as follows:

1. The participants register their data with the trusted authority.

2. The trusted authority signs the participant's data with its secret key S_{ta} to produce a certificate for the data.

3. The certified data is made available to all participants.

The major application of the certificate channel is the authentic distribution of the participant's public keys. The certificate channel is modelled by the following production:

$$Auth(N) \rightarrow phys(auth, N), ta(auth, N), asym(auth, 1), Auth(ta, 1)$$

A system with N authentic public keys may be implemented using N authentic physical transmissions from each participant to a trusted authority ta, which distributes the public keys via an asymmetric channel used for authenticity (in other words, it signs the public keys). But authenticity of the public keys of the participants is only achieved if the ta's public key is distributed authentically and if the trust placed in the ta is justified. Note that we do not entrust any secret information to the ta. Note also that we have reduced the management complexity from N to 1 at the expense of a trusted authority.

2.3.3 The Identity-based Asymmetric System

The basic idea due to Shamir [19] is that the identity of each participant may directly serve as the public key giving partial access to the participant's asymmetric channel. But, if participant A was able to compute his private key from his ID_A (his public key) then so would be any other participant. Therefore we need a trusted authority ta which under control of its own secret key can do this computation. The concept of an identity-based asymmetric channel is as follows:

1. The participants identify themselves and register with the ta. This requires physical appearance at the ta.

2. The ta computes the secret key S_A from ID_A with the help of its own secret key K_{ta} and hands it back to A in a tamper-proof device. This creates a secure physical channel form the ta to the participant A.

3. A is now in the position to sign messages with S_A and everybody with access to ID_A is able to verify A's signatures. Equivalently, if the ta computes a secret decryption key D_A for A, then A is able to decrypt whereas everybody with access to ID_A is only able to encrypt messages for A.

We conclude that an identity-based system is modelled by the production

$$Auth(N) \rightarrow phys(auth, N), ta(secu, N), phys(secu, N), (Auth(N))$$

The goal of establishing asymmetric channels for each participant may be implemented by N authentic physical channels, a trusted authority which computes (and hence knows) the participants' secrets, and N secure physical channels to distribute the secret keys. Note that the apparent advantage of an identity-based system largely stems from the assumption that the ID's have been globally distributed in an authentic fashion. If this assumption is in doubt, then we are left with the security goal of authentically distributing N ID's to all the participants.

3 Conclusions

We have defined a formal language whose symbols are security goals and mechanisms. As a consequence, the design choices are made explicit as productions of the language, and completeness is achieved when all the goals are satisfied. Moreover, since one of the most important aspects of a security architecture is the resulting security management complexity, we have associated a complexity parameter to every goal and mechanism. This allows to assess which mechanisms are most effective to achieve a given goal. The presented methodology has applications as a formal design tool or as an evaluation tool. Moreover, it can be extended in various ways, for instance, to cover aspects such as key generation.

Acknowledgements

I wish to thank James L. Massey, Christian Waldvogel, Xuejia Lai, and Peter Landrock for stimulating discussions.

References

[1] D.E. Bell, L.J. LaPadula, "Secure computer system: unified exposition and Multics interpretation", Tech. Report MTR-2997, Mitre Corp., Bedford, Mass., Mar. 1976.

[2] M. Burrows, M. Abadi, R. Needham, "A logic of authentication", Tech. Report 39, DEC Systems Research Center, 1989.

[3] W. Diffie and M.E. Hellman, "Multiuser cryptographic techniques," in S. Winkler, Ed., AFIPS Conference Proceedings Vol. 45: National Computer Conference, New York, NY, June 7-10, 1976, pp. 109-112. Montvale, NJ: AFIPS Press, 1976.

[4] W. Diffie and M.E. Hellman, "New directions in cryptography," IEEE Transactions on Infomation Theory, Vol. IT-22, No. 6, November 1976, pp. 644-654. key management scheme for implementing the Data Encryption Standard", IBM Systems Journal, Vol. 17, No. 2, 1978, pp. 106-125.

[5] W. Fumy, M. Leclerc "Integrating key management protocols into the OSI architecture", Proc. of Symposium on Computer Security 90, Rome, Italy, Nov. 22-23, 1990.

[6] K. Gaarder, E. Snekkenes, "Applying a formal analysis technique to the CCITT X.509 strong two-way protocol", to appear in JCrypt. Special Issue on Applications of Cryptology.

[7] ISO 7498-2, "Information processing systems - Open Systems Interconnect - Basic reference model - Part 2: Security Architecture", First Ed. 1989.

[8] IEC/ISO JTC1/SC27 Working Draft: "Key management part 1: overview", 1990.

[9] IEC/ISO JTC1/SC27 Working Draft: "Key management part 2: key management using symmetric cryptographic techniques", 1990.

[10] IEC/ISO JTC1/SC27 Working Draft: "Key management part 3: key management using public key techniques", 1990.

[11] R. Kemmerer, "Analyzing encryption protocols using formal verification techniques", Advances in Cryptology - Proc. of Crypto'87, Springer - Verlag, 1988.

[12] L.M. Kohnfelder, "A method for certification," MIT Laboratory for Computer Science, Cambridge, MA May 1978.

[13] P. Landrock, W. Fumy, "User identification and key management using public key techniques", Proc. of Symposium on Computer Security 90, Rome, Italy, Nov. 22-23, 1990.

[14] J. McLean, "The specification and modeling of computer security", IEEE Computer, Jan. 1990.

[15] R.M. Needham and M.D. Schroeder, "Using encryption for authentication in large networks of computers, "Communications of the ACM, Vol. 21, No. 12, December 1978, pp. 993-999.

[16] R.L. Rivest, A. Shamir and L. Adleman, "A method for obtaining digital signatures and public-key cryptosystems", Communications of the ACM, Vol. 21, No. 2, February 1978, pp. 120-127.

[17] R.A. Rueppel, "Key agreements based on function composition", Advances in Cryptology: Proceedings Eurocrypt'88, Springer - Verlag, 1988.

[18] R.A. Rueppel, "Security management", Proc. of Symposium on Computer Security 90, Rome. Italy, Nov. 22-23, 1990.

[19] A. Shamir, "Identity - based cryptosystems and signature schemes", Advances in Cryptology: Proceedings Crypto'84, Springer - Verlag, 1985.

Discrete Logarithm Based Protocols

Patrick Horster
Hans-Joachim Knobloch

University of Karlsruhe
European Institute for System Security
Am Fasanengarten 5
D-7500 Karlsruhe 1
FR Germany

Abstract

The Exponential Security System (TESS) developed at the European Institute for System Security is the result of an attempt to increase the security in heterogenous computer networks.

In this paper we present the cryptographic protocols in the kernel of TESS. We show how they can be used to implement access control, authentication, confidentiality protection, key exchange, digital signatures and distributed network security management.

We also look at the compatibility of TESS with existing standards, like the X.509 Directory Authentication Framework, and compare it to established systems like Kerberos. A comparison of TESS with the non-electronic "paper"-world of authentication and data exchange shows strong parallels.

Finally we give a short overview of the current state of development and availability of different TESS components.

1 Introduction

During the last years a workinggroup at the European Institute for System Security developed the network security system SELANE (SEcure Local Area Network Environment) [Baus90]. The main part of the system is a family of cryptographic protocols based on the discrete logarithm problem. After the possible scope of applications of these protocols had been extended far beyond the originally anticipated area of LAN security, a larger system called TESS (The Exponential Security System) was formed. SELANE is the part of TESS dealing with network security. Another part is an electronic signature system named EES (Exponential Electronic Signature).

2 Protocols

2.1 The Discrete Logarithm Problem

One of the most important one way functions in cryptography is based on the discrete logarithm problem in the finite field $\mathrm{GF}(p)$.

Given a large prime p and a primitive element $\alpha \in \mathrm{GF}(p)$ it is feasible to compute the value of $y := \alpha^x$ (using $O(\log x)$ modular multiplications via the square-and-multiply algorithm). It is, however, (except for trivial cases) infeasible to compute the value of x, given y, α and p [PoHe78]. For the solution of this discrete logarithm problem $O(\exp(const \cdot \sqrt{\log p \log \log p}))$ long integer multiplications are needed [Odly84]. Similar discrete logarithm problems can be found in finite fields $\mathrm{GF}(p^k)$ of prime characteristic p or in the group of points on an elliptic curve [Kobl87].

It should be noted that these are true one way functions, where no intrinsic trap door has to be kept secret, in contrast to the RSA trap door one way function [RiSA78].

For the rest of this paper we will assume that the parameters p and α are known to all participants of the schemes mentioned.

2.2 The Diffie-Hellman Public Key Distribution Scheme

The Diffie-Hellman scheme [DiHe76] uses this one way property to allow two principals, let us call them A and B, to exchange a secret key using a public channel. Each principal i chooses a secret random number x_i and publishes the value $y_i := \alpha^{x_i}$. Then both can compute a common key $K = y_A^{x_B} = y_B^{x_A}$.

A well-known attack on this scheme uses the fact that the authenticity of the y_i is not assured. Suppose an attacker C can control the communication channel between A and B. Upon receiving y_A from A he will send $y_C := \alpha^{x_C}$ to B instead. Similarly he sends y_C to A instead of y_B. Using this attack he will share one key $K' = \alpha^{x_A x_C}$ with A and another key $K'' = \alpha^{x_B x_C}$ with B and may thus decrypt, read, modify and re-encrypt messages between A and B. A method to detect this attack has been developed in [RiSh84].

2.3 The ElGamal Signature Scheme

For an ElGamal signature [Elga85] the signer chooses a random number $x \in \mathbf{Z}_{p-1}$ and computes $y := \alpha^x$. He publishes y as public key and keeps x secret. These values are constant for all messages to be signed. Any message to be signed must be encoded as a number $m \in \mathbf{Z}_{p-1}$, e.g. by concatenating ASCII representations of letters. To sign m the signer chooses a random $k \in \mathbf{Z}_{p-1}^*$. k may never be reused to sign another message. The signer computes $r := \alpha^k$ and solves the congruence $m \equiv xr + ks \pmod{p-1}$. The triple (m, r, s) is the signed message. It may be verified by checking the equation $\alpha^m = y^r r^s$.

Note that the signed message has the triple size of the message alone. Furthermore verification of the signature depends on the knowledge of the system parameters p and α and the signer's public key y, which has to be authentic.

2.4 The modified ElGamal Signature Scheme

A modification of the ElGamal signature was presented by Agnew, Mullin and Vanstone [AgMV90]. Instead of $m \equiv xr + ks \pmod{p-1}$ the signer may solve the congruence $m \equiv xs + kr \pmod{p-1}$. (In this case x must have been chosen from $\mathbf{Z}_{p-1}^*$.) The signature (m, r, s) is verified by checking the equation $\alpha^m = y^s r^r$.

The advantage of this scheme over the standard ElGamal signature is, that, in order to compute the signature by solving the congruence for s, the signer only needs to compute y^{-1} in $\mathbf{Z}_{p-1}^*$ once, instead of computing k^{-1} for every signature.

2.5 The Testimonial Scheme

There is a variation of a signature we call a "testimonial". Whereas a signature involves a signer and a verifier, a testimonial involves three parties, called claimer, notary and verifier. For a testimonial the notary chooses x and y, like the signer does in the signature schemes. The claimer, who wants to have the message m testified, chooses $h \in \mathbf{Z}_{p-1}^*$ random, computes $a := \alpha^h$ and passes a on to the notary. Now, the notary chooses a random $k \in \mathbf{Z}_{p-1}^*$ and computes $r := a^k$. Again h and k may never be reused for another message. The notary solves the congruence $m \equiv xr + kb \pmod{p-1}$ and passes the triple (m, r, b) to the claimer. The claimer then acknowledges the receipt of the triple, e.g. by a handwritten or electronic signature. Afterwards he computes $s = bh^{-1}$ in $\mathbf{Z}_{p-1}$. The triple (m, r, s) is the testified message. It may be verified by checking the equation $\alpha^m = y^r r^s$.

Note that it is possible for the notary to issue a signature (m, r', s') that may be verified instead of the testimonial (m, r, s). But it seems infeasible for him to compute a signature using the particular r (being acknowledged by the claimer) and s or to obtain s if it is not published by the claimer. And obviously nobody else (besides the claimer of course) will have a better chance to fool the claimer than the notary. The claimer may prove the knowledge of his secret s using a zero-knowledge protocol or use it as his secret key in a public key system.

If $s \in \mathbf{Z}_{p-1}^*$ (i.e. $\gcd(s, p-1) = 1$) reconstructing s by the notary is equivalent to computing the discrete logarithm h of $a = \alpha^h$, since

$$h = bs^{-1} \bmod p - 1.$$

Thus, any algorithm which allows the notary to efficiently compute s from (a, m, r, k, b) leads to a probabilistic algorithm for computing the discrete logarithm h of a by simply trying different values m' and/or k', until the result will be $s' \in \mathbf{Z}_{p-1}^*$. The efficiency of this algorithm depends on the chance to find a proper s'. Under the assumption that the values s' are equidistributed over $\mathbf{Z}_{p-1}$ for appropriately chosen m' and k' this chance is $\phi(p-1)/(p-1)$, where ϕ is the Euler totient function.

On the other hand the claimer gets no more information about the notary's secrets if the testimonial scheme is used instead of a standard ElGamal signature issued by the notary. This can be proven using similar arguments as for proving the zero-knowledge property of an interactive protocol. In the testimonial scheme the notary sends the claimer a triple (m, r, b) which satisfies the modular equation

$$\alpha^m = y^r (r^{h^{-1}})^b,$$

where $h \in \mathbf{Z}_{p-1}^*$ is chosen by the claimer. As a standard ElGamal signature the notary sends the claimer a triple (m, r, s) which satisfies the equation

$$\alpha^m = y^r r^s.$$

The claimer may then compute the corresponding value b for an arbitrary $h \in \mathbf{Z}_{p-1}^*$ by simply multiplying s with h, resulting in the equation

$$\alpha^m = y^r (r^{h^{-1}})^{hs}.$$

If the factorization of $p - 1$ is known, the notary can easily check whether the particular h was indeed chosen from $\mathbf{Z}_{p-1}^*$ by testing if $a = \alpha^h$ is a primitive element. The claimer might also use a zero-knowledge proof of membership to convince the notary about the proper choice of h.

2.6   The Beth Zero Knowledge Identification Scheme

Soon after the invention of zero knowledge proofs Chaum, Evertse and van de Graaf published a zero knowledge scheme to prove the possession of discrete logarithms [ChEG87].

Beth later presented a zero knowledge identification scheme based on the discrete logarithm problem [Beth88]. This scheme, like most other protocols that involve authentication or identification, rests on a trusted authority. Here this trusted authority is called Secure Key Issuing Authority (SKIA). A principal A is characterized by an attribute list m_A, containing his name and other relevant data in encoded form.

The SKIA chooses l independent random numbers $x_1, \ldots, x_l \in \mathbf{Z}_{p-1}$ and computes $y_j := \alpha_j^x$ for $j = 1, \ldots, l$. It publishes the y_j as public keys and keeps x_j secret. These values are constant for all principals in the system. Additionally the SKIA chooses and publishes a one way hashing function $f : \mathbf{Z}_{p-1} \times \mathbf{Z} \to \mathbf{Z}_{p-1}$.

When principal A is registered, the SKIA computes $m'_{A,j} := f(m_A, j)$ for $j = 1, \ldots, l$ and signs these $m'_{A,j}$ with an ElGamal signature, using the key pairs (x_j, y_j) but only one pair $(k, r) = (k_A, r_A)$ for all l signatures. The identification data, afterwards given to A, is the $(l + 2)$-tuple $(m_A, r_A, s_{A,1}, \ldots, s_{A,l})$.

When A wants to identify himself towards another principal B, he sends the values m_A and r_A to B wich can then compute the $m'_{A,j}$.

A then chooses a random $t \in \mathbf{Z}_{p-1}$, computes $z := r_a^{-t}$ and sends t to B. B chooses l random values $b_1, \ldots, b_l$ from a suitably chosen subset of $\mathbf{Z}_{p-1}$, and sends them to A. A computes $u := t + \sum_{j=1}^{l} b_j s_j \bmod p - 1$ and sends u to B. B accepts the identification, if $r_A^u z \prod_{j=1}^{l} y_j^{r_A b_j} = \alpha^{\sum_{j=1}^{l} b_j m'_{A,j}}$. This step of the protocol may be repeated to increase security.

Schnorr published a similar identification scheme [Schn89], which is optimized with respect to the time/computation constraints of smartcards.

2.7   Four KATHY Protocols

Several protocols have been developed to overcome the weakness of the Diffie-Hellman scheme that the exchanged keys are not necessarily authentic [BaKn89, Günt89]. We call these protocols KATHY protocols, K-ATH-Y standing for KeY exchange with embedded AuTHentication.

All KATHY protocols rely on a trusted authority, which is needed to assure the principals about each others identity (not necessarily during the authentic key exchange itself). Like in section 2.6 we call this trusted authority SKIA and characterize a principal i by an attribute list m_i.

For the basic form of KATHY the SKIA signs each principal's attribute list using the ElGamal scheme, publishes y and hands the signature (m_i, r_i, s_i) out to the principal i. If principal A wants to exchange an authentic key with principal B, A passes the values m_A and r_A to B. B chooses $t \in \mathbf{Z}_{p-1}$ random, computes $v := r_A^t$ and passes v to A. A can now compute the key $K_A := v^{s_A}$. B can compute the same key $K_A = (\alpha^{m_A} y^{-r_A})^t$. As A's attribute list m_A is directly used to compute K_A, B can be sure that the only principal sharing the key is A (besides eventually the SKIA).

In a first variation of KATHY the SKIA uses the modified ElGamal scheme to sign m_i. The authentic key exchange is the same as for the basic KATHY, except that B computes $v := y^t$ and $K_A = (\alpha^{m_A} r_A^{-r_A})^t$. This modification enables B to precompute v without even knowing A beforehand.

In the second variation of KATHY the SKIA also uses the modified ElGamal scheme to sign m_i. After two principals A and B exchanged (m_A, r_A) and (m_B, r_B), they compute a common key $K_{AB} = (\alpha^{m_A} r_A^{-r_A})^{s_B} = (\alpha^{m_B} r_B^{-r_B})^{s_A}$. This key is authentic for both, however it is fixed for each pair of principals and all communication between them.

In the third variation of KATHY the SKIA uses the testimonial scheme to testify m_i, where principal i is the claimer. After i has computed s_i, the authentic key exchange works exactly the same way as in the basic KATHY protocol. Now the SKIA can not recompute the key K_A using only the information that passes the public channel, even if it memorizes all the data about i during the testimonial.

2.8   EES

The electronic signature package comprises the original and modified ElGamal signature schemes. Additionally, extending the possible applications, the KATHY setup may be used to generate electronic signatures.

If principal A wants to sign a message M he chooses $k \in \mathbf{Z}_{p-1}^*$ random and computes $t := r_A^k$. Then he solves the congruence $M \equiv s_A t + ku \pmod{p-1}$.

(M, m_A, r_A, t, u) is the authentically signed message. It may be verified by checking the equation $r_A^M = (\alpha^{m_A} y^{-r_A})^t t^u$.

For the KATHY variation using the modified ElGamal scheme t must be computed as $t := y^k$ and the congruence to solve is $M \equiv s_A u + kt \pmod{p-1}$. This leads to the verification equation $y^M = (\alpha^{m_A} r_A^{-r_A})^u t^t$.

Note that the verifier of such a signature only needs to be confident in the public SKIA parameters, not in the parameters of each signing principal.

2.9 SELANE

Only in the second KATHY variation both principals can be sure about the authenticity of the exchanged key. For network security applications, however, a different key is desired for each communication session.

The solution is to use one of the three other KATHY protocols twice (or two variations once), once for each direction of the communication. This may be done in parallel for both directions to reduce the overall running time.

This solution yields two keys K_A and K_B, each authentic for one of the principals. A simple interlock protocol ensures the mutual key authenticity. Principal A chooses a random value z_A, encrypts it using key K_A and sends ist to B. B does the same with a random value z_B and key K_B. Upon reception, both principals decrypt the random value, re-encrypt it with the other of the two keys and return it. After successful decryption and comparison with the original value, A can be sure that the authentic B, who knows key K_B, is also the one with whom he shares key K_A and vice versa.

In the case of a cleartext communication over an insecure network, a third party might impersonate one of the communicating principals after the authentication. Therefore it is necessary to use a message authenticator algorithm or to encrypt the whole communication to keep up the authenticity of the session.

At present SELANE uses a stream cipher algorithm to encipher the communication with authentic keys. However, any other symmetric cipher, like DES, could be used instead.

3 Established Systems

3.1 X.509

The CCITT recommendation X.509 [CCIT88] describes a certificate-based system, where a certification authority (CA) authenticates registered users' public keys. To this purpose the CA issues certificates, which are essentially digital signatures of the users' names and public keys. Different CAs may mutually certify their public keys, resulting in a connected graph of CAs. The initial point of trust for a particular user is the CA which registered him. For reasons of simplicity this graph is often looked upon as a tree (with optional additional connections).

In contrast to that the KATHY protocols are in the terminology of Girault [Gira91] not certificate-based but self-certified public key systems. (Note that different versions of the KATHY protocols obtain either trust level 1 or trust level 2 as defined by Girault).

It is possible to group SKIAs hierarchically, in a way that higher level SKIAs' signatures authorize lower level SKIAs to act as such. These lower level SKIAs use the KATHY protocol with the signature scheme described in section 2.8 instead of the standard El-Gamal signature. In this case knowledge of the top level SKIA's public parameters is sufficient to authenticate all principals registered at lower level SKIAs. Thus, the initial point of trust for all users is the top level SKIA.

This hierarchy tree may be mapped to the X.509 directory tree and makes it possible, if desired, to start all authentication paths at the root of the directory tree.

3.2 Kerberos

The Kerberos authentication scheme [MNSS87] uses a modified form of the Needham-Schroeder key distribution protocol [NeSc78]. Here we will only describe the basic ideas of the scheme. Our description may differ in some details from the actual implementation of Kerberos. These differences are, however, irrelevant for the review of Kerberos in the context of this paper. For a more complete description of the Kerberos scheme the reader is refered to the original publications.

The basis of the scheme is that every principal u has a secret key K_u in common with the trusted authority, which is here called *Kerberos authentication server*. K_u is exchanged upon registration of the user and known only to u and the authentication server.

When principal c wants to communicate with principal s, he contacts the authentication server, denoting his name and the name of s. The authentication server creates a session key $K_{c,s}$. It encrypts $K_{c,s}$ using the secret key K_s. This encryption is called *seal* and denoted by $\{K_{c,s}\}K_s$. Then the authentication server seals $K_{c,s}$ and $\{K_{c,s}\}K_s$ using K_c. $\{K_{c,s}\}K_s$ is called a *ticket*. In addition to the session key a ticket contains both principal's names, addresses, a time stamp, the ticket life time and other data, mainly used to prevent replay attacks or to make the handling of the authentication system easier for the user.

The authentication server passes $\{K_{c,s}, \{K_{c,s}\}K_s\}K_c$ to c, who unwraps the seal with K_c. Then it passes the ticket on to s, which can decrypt $K_{c,s}$ using its own secret key. Thereafter $K_{s,c}$ is the common secret between c, s and the authentication server.

In the standard Kerberos scheme the session key is used only to encrypt a test message, here called *authenticator*, from c to s. The authenticator consists of the name and address of c and a time stamp. Additionally the session key may be used for mutual authentication or to encrypt a session or compute a message authentication code.

Areas administered by different authorities are called *realms*. Every realm has its own authentication server. Authentication between principals of different realms is possible by registering the authentication server of one realm as a principal at the authentication server of the other realm.

The major drawback of Kerberos is the existence of the authentication server. It must be physically secure, however it must have network access as it is needed online for every authentic connection within its realm. Discreditation of the authentication server would be fatal to the whole authentication system.

It is possible to replicate the authentication server to provide fault tolerance, but this replication introduces the need for a protocol to keep the database containing the users' secret keys consistent among all instances of the authentication server. Additionally, replication increases the necessary efforts to protect the authentication server from unauthorized access.

Finally it is possible for the administrator of the authentication server to pretend any desired identity and to decipher any network communication even if the session key is used to encrypt a complete session. To obtain privacy even with respect to the Kerberos administrator, it is necessary to put an independent key distribution and authentication system on top of Kerberos.

One obvious advantage of SELANE over Kerberos is, that it does not need a trusted online authentication server and thus does not depend on the security and fault tolerance of such a server to establish authentic communication.

Another important advantage occurs if the KATHY variation with testimonials is used. The SKIA can not decrypt authentic communication, whereas the Kerberos server always can do this, as it itself generates the session keys.

3.3 Conventional passports

In many points the presented protocols are directly equivalent to what can be found in the "paper"-world of authentication and data exchange.

The SKIA's role is that of a passport office. To recognize an authentic passport (signature/testimonial on an attribute list) one only has to know how the imprint of an authentic seal of the passport office (public key y of the SKIA, the seal itself corresponds to the private key x) looks like, not to ask the passport office itself (like one has to do in Kerberos).

The KATHY variation using testimonials is equivalent to the case of a passport, which is not valid until its bearer has signed it. It is possible to use different variations of the KATHY protocols for the two directions of the authentication similar to two persons presenting different types of passports for mutual inspection.

4 Implementation

The basis of the current implementation of TESS is a toolbox comprising arithmetic functions in $GF(p)$ and $\mathbf{Z}^*_{p-1}$, including tests for primality and primitivity, and some symmetric cipher systems, including DES. This toolbox is coded in C with optimized assembler parts for several popular processors. An optional hardware accelerator box for arithmetics and en-/deciphering has been developed. This box can be connected to various standard interfaces.

Support for smart cards as storage devices for secret data is available for a wide range of PCs and workstations. Additional hardware is supported that uses inductively coupled personalized tags, which may be attached e.g. to a watch, to indicate the presence of a certain user in front of his terminal/workstation.

The TESS toolbox has been used to implement the most interesting of the protocols presented in section 2.

Combining these results, a prototype of SELANE has been realized for a UNIX server with client applications on UNIX and several PC types. The possible footholds for the authentication service in UNIX are the same as for Kerberos. For easy handling the users' authentication data are stored in PIN protected smart cards. Optionally the PIN is taken from an inductively coupled tag.

Future development will address the computation of the session key within a smart card. We expect that this will be feasible with the next smart card generation which is announced to be available within 1991 from several manufacturers.

References

[AgMV90] G. B. Agnew, R. C. Mullin, S. A. Vanstone, *Improved digital signature scheme based on discrete exponentiation*, Electronics Letters 26, 1990, pp. 1024-1025.

[BaKn89] F. Bauspieß, H.-J. Knobloch, *How to Keep Authenticity Alive in a Computer Network*, Adv. in Cryptology - EUROCRYPT '89, Springer, Berlin 1990, pp. 38-46.

[Baus90] F. Bauspieß, *SELANE - An Approach to Secure Networks*, Abstracts of SE-CURICOM '90, Paris 1990.

[Beth88] Th. Beth, *Zero-Knowledge Identification Scheme for Smart Cards*, Adv. in Cryptology - EUROCRYPT '88, Springer, Berlin 1988, pp. 77-84.

[CCIT88] CCITT, Recommendation X.509: *The Directory - Authentication Framework*, Blue Book - Melbourne 1988, Fascicle VIII.8: Data communication networks: directory, International Telecommunication Union, Geneva 1989, pp. 48-81.

[ChEG87] D. Chaum, J. H. Evertse, J. van de Graaf, *An Improved Protocol for Demonstrating Possession of Discrete Logarithms and some Generalizations*, Adv. in Cryptology - EUROCRYPT '87, Springer, Berlin 1988, pp. 127-141.

[DiHe76] W. Diffie, M. E. Hellman, *New Directions in Cryptography*, IEEE Trans. on Information Theory 22, 1976, pp. 644-654.

[Elga85] T. ElGamal, *A Public Key Cryptosystem and a Signature Scheme Based on Discrete Logarithms*, IEEE Trans. on Information Theory 31, 1985, pp. 469-472.

[Gira91] M. Girault, *Self-Certified Public Keys*, Adv. in Cryptology - EUROCRYPT '91, this volume.

[Günt89] C. G. Günther, *Diffie-Hellman and El-Gamal Protocols with One Single Authentication Key*, Adv. in Cryptology - EUROCRYPT '89, Springer, Berlin 1990, pp. 29-37.

[HoKn91] P. Horster, H.-J. Knobloch, *Protocols for Secure Networks*, Abstracts of SE-CURICOM '91, Paris 1991.

[Kobl87] N. Koblitz, *Elliptic Curve Cryptosystems*, Math. of Computation 48, 1987, pp. 203-209.

[MNSS87] S. P. Miller, B. C. Neuman, J. I. Schiller, J. H. Saltzer, *Section E.2.1: Kerberos Authentication and Authorization System*, MIT Project Athena, Cambridge, Ma., 1987.

[NeSc78] R. M. Needham, M. D. Schroeder, *Using Encryption for Authentication in Large Networks of Computers*, Comm. of the ACM 21, 1978, pp. 993-999.

[Odly84]   A. M. Odlyzko, *Discrete Logarithms in Finite Fields and their Cryptographic Significance*, Adv. in Cryptology - EUROCRYPT '84, Springer, Berlin 1985, pp. 224-314.

[PoHe78]   S. C. Pohlig, M. E. Hellman, *Am Improved Algorithm for Computing Logarithms Over GF(p) and its Cryptographic Significance*, IEEE Trans. on Information Theory 24, 1978, pp. 106-110.

[RiSA78]   R. L. Rivest, A. Shamir, L. Adleman, *A Method for Obtaining Digital Signatures and Public-Key Cryptosystems*, Comm. of the ACM 21, 1978, pp. 120-126.

[RiSh84]   R. L. Rivest, A. Shamir, *How to Expose an Eavesdropper*, Comm. of the ACM 27, 1984, pp. 393-395.

[Schn89]   C. P. Schnorr, *Efficient Identification and Signatures for Smart Cards*, Adv. in Cryptology - CRYPTO '89, Springer, Berlin 1990, pp. 239-251.

Human Identification Through Insecure Channel

Tsutomu MATSUMOTO

Hideki IMAI

Division of Electrical and Computer Engineering
YOKOHAMA NATIONAL UNIVERSITY
156 Tokiwadai, Hodogaya, Yokohama 240, Japan
Fax: +81-45-338-1157, Tel: +81-45-335-1451
Internet: tsutomu@mlab.dnj.ynu.ac.jp

Abstract This paper examines a relatively new problem of how to securely identify a human through an insecure channel. It proposes a simple but powerful cryptographic scheme that fits human ability of memorizing and processing. Typical applications of the scheme are the identification verification of an user at an on-line terminal of a central computer or holder verification done by an IC card which can communicate its holder only through an equipment like an automatic vendor machine.

Keywords   Identification Verification, Human Identification, User Identification, Authentication, Cryptography, Access Control, Password, IC Card, Smart Card, Insecure Channel, Human Interface

1 Introduction

Human identification, or user identification, is one of the most important items for information security. Based on biometrics (eg., fingerprints), something memorized (eg., passwords), belongings (eg., tokens), and their combinations, a variety of human identification schemes have been developed and utilized actually. A compact and excellent survey appears in [1]. This paper proposes a scheme to securely identify a human through an insecure channel.

A popular human identification scheme is that a verifier V firstly requires a human prover P to simply exhibit a password and then accepts P if and only if the received password coincides with its registered counterpart. This scheme is very convenient and often used. However, for an attacker who can watch the interaction between a verifier and an accepted prover, it is an easy task to obtain the password between them and to masquerade as the prover as long as the same password is being used. Consider the following cases to make clear the crucial points.

Case 1: Suppose there is a terminal connected to a central computer V through a communication network.   Let's call the path to V from a human P via the terminal

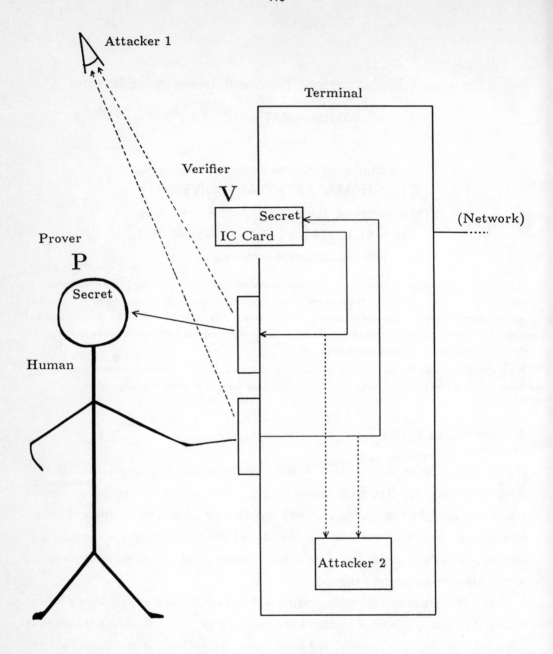

Figure 1. Insecure Channel

as the channel C. When human P requests an access to computer V, how should V verify the identity of P or how should P prove its identity to V by an interaction through channel C ? The line between the terminal and V can be protected by encipherment. However, it is hard to expect that channel C is always secure since how P operates the terminal may be watched by somebody standing behind P or some subliminal equipment set inside the terminal or everywhere in the network. As well as watching, the equipment might also behave as a true verifier to actively steal the secret of P.

Case 2: Imagine a human P keeping her/his own IC card (smart card) V with no direct human interfaces (i.e., no built-in keyboard and display). IC card V may be used for identification by belongings based on highly secure cryptographic techniques, which include brand-new zero-knowledge identification schemes. Suppose a system in which if P wants to use IC card V then P should connect V to a device C with IC card interface and direct human interfaces and P should give appropriate commands to C. Some automatic vendor machines and some automatic teller machines are existing examples of such C. Assume that IC card V is made to correctly work only when it has succeeded in verifying operator P as the true holder through device C. Thus C is the unique channel for communication between P and V. But it is hard to expect that channel C is always secure for P and V. The reason is that all the data transferred through C can be watched by somebody standing behind P or a subliminal equipment set inside C which may also masquerade as true V to actively steal the secret of P. How should P and V conduct secure identification through such C ? (See Figure 1.)

This paper considers the problem of how a prover and a verifier securely conduct an identification procedure through an insecure communication channel. Here, the term 'secure' is used in the following two meanings:

- The event that a prover not knowing true secret is accepted by a verifier occurs only with negligible probability. The value of the probability can be set appropriately owing to the strategy in which the verifier discontinues the identification for a prover who has consecutively failed over predetermined times.

- It is computationally infeasible to infer the secret from the observations of interactions between a true prover and a true or fake verifier. Though "computationally" can be replaced by "unconditionally" if so-called one-time password schemes are adopted, but they require huge amount of memory and are impractical for direct human identification to be considered in this paper.

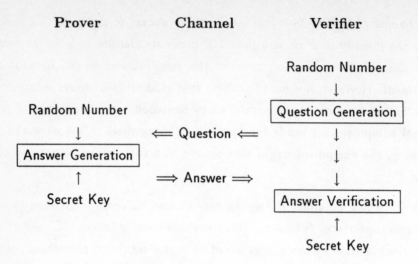

Figure 2. Outline of Interaction

This paper examines a solution to this problem under the following conditions.

- Any attacker cannot directly observe the secret activity concerning the identification inside human brains.

- Any human can easily separate each character of a given sequence into the character she/he remembers and others.

- Any human can memorize a sequence of characters of certain length.

- Any human can select a character randomly from a predetermined small alphabet.

- Unlike conventional so-called dynamic password schemes, no auxiliary devices like pocket calculators are required to assist human provers.

The basic scheme to be proposed is a two-move protocol as illustrated in Figure 2. It is based on common-key cryptography. The verifier asks a random question to the prover. In reply to the question, the human prover generates and sends a random answer based on the common secret key of the prover and the verifier. Finally, the verifier uses the secret key to decide whether the transferred answer matches the question or not. Typical requirement for a human prover is to memorize 10 to 25 characters and to read and input dozens of characters.

The rest of this paper is organized as follows. Section 2. proposes a concrete scheme. Section 3. shows that the scheme is effective. And finally Section 4. concludes this paper.

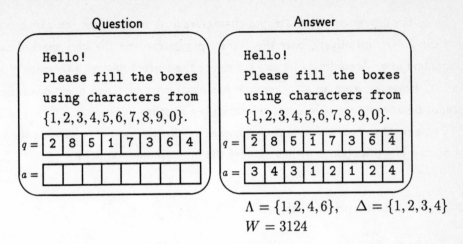

Figure 3. Example of Question and Answer

2 An Identification Scheme

This section proposes a concrete scheme for human identification.

2.1 Demonstration

Figure 3. illustrates a quite simple example of the human identification scheme. In this example, the verifier challenges the prover a question q, a sequence of characters randomly selected from a predetermined alphabet, and requires him to exhibit a sequence a on the alphabet $\{1,2,3,4,5,6,7,8,9,0\}(= \Omega)$ as an answer to q. Ω is called the whole alphabet.

The correct prover remembers a secret key consisting of a window alphabet $\Lambda = \{1,2,4,6\}$, a secret word $W = 3124$, and an answer alphabet $\Delta = \{1,2,3,4\}(\subset \Omega)$.

The correct answer a matching the question q is defined as follows. A hidden window f is embedded in q. The window is a sequence of positions where the characters belonging to Λ are located. At the positions in the answer a corresponding to those in the window f, the characters in the secret word W are located in order. That is, the first character of W (i.e., 3) is assigned to the first position of f (where 2 lies in q), the second character of W (i.e., 1) is assigned to the second position of f (where 1 lies in q), and so on. And at the other positions in a, characters randomly chosen from the answer alphabet Δ are assigned.

Since the prover can separate the characters in Λ from others, he can extract the window f. Or, intuitively, only the correct prover can see the bars marked over the characters in q. Accordingly he can construct the correct answer a by using f and W and Δ. However, even an attacker who has observed a matched question–answer pair cannot be advantageous in correctly answering another question.

Consequently, such a simple trick provides an effective way of enhancing the security of human identification schemes against the insecure environment.

2.2 Notation and Definition

To rigorously describe the identification protocol, the above notions like 'questions', 'answers', and 'windows' should be redefined in terms of functions.

Notation

- The number of elements of a finite set S is denoted by $\#S$.

- The set of all positive integers less than or equal to n is denoted by $\langle n \rangle$.

- The set of all functions (surjections, bijections, resp.) from a set S into a set T is denoted by $\mathrm{Ft}(S,T)$ ($\mathrm{St}(S,T)$, $\mathrm{Bt}(S,T)$, resp.).

- The composite function of functions f and g is denoted by $g \circ f$.

Definition 1. For a totally ordered finite set $(S, \leq)$, let define a function $\mathrm{sort}(S)$ as the bijection $b \in \mathrm{Bt}(\langle \#S \rangle, S)$ such that

$$b(1) \leq b(2) \leq \cdots \leq b(\#S).$$

2.3 Protocol Description

Preparation

A prover P and a verifier V agree on integers ω, γ, λ, δ, β, α, and sets Ω, Γ, Λ, Δ, and a function W, defined in Table 1. See also Figure 4. Among these, Λ, Δ, W constitute a secret key between P and V, while ω, γ, λ, δ, β, α, Ω, Γ are not required to be kept secret.

Table 1. Objects

symbol	name	definition	unit
ω	the whole alphabet size		characters
γ	the question alphabet size	integers satisfying	characters
λ	the window size	$2 \leq \delta \leq \lambda < \gamma \leq \omega$	characters
δ	the answer alphabet size		characters
β	the number of blocks	integers satisfying	
α	the threshold	$1 \leq \alpha \leq \beta$	
Ω	the whole alphabet	a finite set of characters	
Γ	the question alphabet	a subset of Ω with $\#\Gamma = \gamma$	
Λ	a window alphabet	a subset of Γ with $\#\Lambda = \lambda$	
Δ	an answer alphabet	a subset of Ω with $\#\Delta = \delta$	
W	a secret word	a surjection from $\langle \lambda \rangle$ onto Δ	
q_j	a question block	a bijection from $\langle \gamma \rangle$ onto Γ	
Q	a question	$Q = [q_1, \ldots, q_\beta]$	
f_j	a window	an injection from $\langle \lambda \rangle$ into $\langle \gamma \rangle$ such that $f_j = \mathbf{sort}\{i \in \langle \gamma \rangle | q_j(i) \in \Lambda\}$	
F	a window tuple	$F = [f_i, \ldots, f_\beta]$	
J	a sieve	a subset of $\langle \beta \rangle$ with $\#J = \alpha$	
a_j	an answer block	a surjection from $\langle \gamma \rangle$ onto Δ such that $a_j \circ f_j = W$ iff $j \in J$	
A	an answer	$A = [a_1, \ldots, a_\beta]$	
D	a decision	a predicate such that $D = \mathbf{accept}$ if $\#\{j \in \langle \beta \rangle | a_j \circ f_j = W\} \geq \alpha$; $D = \mathbf{reject}$ otherwise	
ν	the question size (the answer size)	$\nu = \beta \cdot \gamma$	characters
μ	an upperbound of required human memory	$\mu = 2\lambda$	characters

416

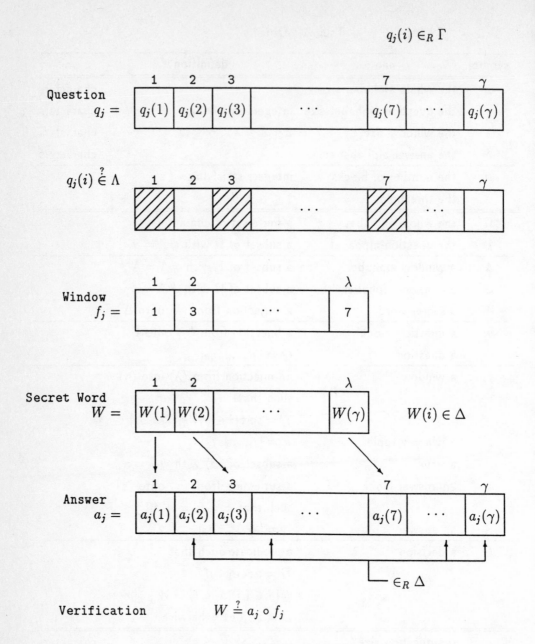

$$q_j(i) \in_R \Gamma$$

Question
$q_j =$ | 1 | 2 | 3 | 7 | γ |

$q_j(i) \stackrel{?}{\in} \Lambda$

Window
$f_j =$

Secret Word
$W =$ $W(i) \in \Delta$

Answer
$a_j =$

$\in_R \Delta$

Verification $W \stackrel{?}{=} a_j \circ f_j$

Figure 4. Illustration of Protocol

Interaction   (see Figure 4 and Table 1.)

1. **Question Generation:** V selects β question blocks q_1, ..., q_β randomly and uniformly from $\mathsf{Bt}(\langle\gamma\rangle, \Gamma)$.

2. **Question Transfer:** V transfers the question $Q = [q_1, \ldots, q_\beta]$ to P.

3. **Answer Generation:** P generates β answer blocks a_1, ..., $a_\beta \in \mathsf{St}(\langle\gamma\rangle, \Delta)$ as follows:

   3-1. **Sieve Selection:** P selects α distinct elements randomly and uniformly from $\langle\beta\rangle$ to form a sieve $J \subseteq \langle\beta\rangle$.

   3-2. **Correct Answer Block Generation:** P generates answer block a_j for each $j \in J$ as follows:

   3-2-1. **Question Block Check:** If $q_j \in \mathsf{Bt}(\langle\gamma\rangle, \Gamma)$ then P proceeds. Otherwise P quits.

   3-2-2. **Window Detection:** P computes the window
   $$f_j = \mathsf{sort}(\{i \in \langle\gamma\rangle | q_j(i) \in \Lambda\}) \in \mathsf{Ft}(\langle\lambda\rangle, \langle\gamma\rangle).$$

   3-2-3. **Secret Word Embedding:** For each
   $i \in f_j(\langle\lambda\rangle) = \{i \in \langle\gamma\rangle | \exists h \in \langle\lambda\rangle, i = f_j(h)\}$, P determines $a_j(i)$ as
   $a_j(i) = W(h)$.

   3-2-4. **Random Padding:** For each $i \in \langle\gamma\rangle - f_j(\langle\lambda\rangle)$, P selects an element randomly and uniformly from Δ and allocates it to $a_j(i)$.

   3-3. **Random Answer Block Generation:** For each $j \in \langle\beta\rangle - J$, P selects a surjection randomly and uniformly from $\mathsf{St}(\langle\gamma\rangle, \Delta)$ and allocates it to a_j.

4. **Answer Transfer:** P transfers the answer $A = [a_1, \ldots, a_\beta]$ to V.

5. **Answer Verification:** V evaluates the decision D as follows:

   5-1. **Window Detection:** For each $j \in \langle\beta\rangle$, V computes the window
   $f_j = \mathsf{sort}(\{i \in \langle\gamma\rangle | q_j(i) \in \Lambda\}) \in \mathsf{Ft}(\langle\lambda\rangle, \langle\gamma\rangle)$ to form $F = [f_1, \ldots, f_\beta]$.

   5-2. **Embedded Secret Word Check:** If $\#\{j \in \langle\beta\rangle | a_j \circ f_j = W\} \geq \alpha$ then V puts $D = $ accept and accepts P. Otherwise V puts $D = $ reject and rejects P.

Remark: V can do **5-1.** at any time after **1.** and before **5-2.**

3 Evaluation

This section shows the effectiveness of the proposed identification scheme.

3.1 Logical Completeness

Proposition 1. In the proposed scheme, any prover knowing correct Λ, Δ, W and obeying the protocol is certainly accepted by the verifier.

3.2 Tolerance against Random Attacks

The followings are some typical attacks done without secret keys.

Definition 2.

A **known-Δ random attack** means the following attack conducted by an attacker who knows the protocol itself and knows the concrete values of ω, γ, λ, δ, Ω, Γ, and Δ, but doesn't know concrete values of Λ and W. In reply to any question Q the attacker transfers an answer $A = [a_1, \ldots, a_\beta]$, each block a_j of which is selected randomly and uniformly from $\mathrm{St}(\langle \gamma \rangle, \Delta)$.

The **success probability of a known-Δ random attack** is the probability p_Δ that a question Q and an answer A by a known-Δ random attack satisfy $D =$ accept.

A **Δ-guessing random attack** means the following attack conducted by an attacker who knows the protocol itself and knows the concrete values of ω, γ, λ, δ, Ω, and Γ, but doesn't know concrete values of Λ, Δ, and W. In reply to any question Q, the attacker firstly guesses Δ as a subset of Ω with δ elements, then transfers an answer $A = [a_1, \ldots, a_\beta]$, each block a_j of which is selected randomly and uniformly from $\mathrm{St}(\langle \gamma \rangle, \Delta)$.

The **success probability of a Δ-guessing random attack** is the probability p_δ that a question Q and an answer A by a Δ-guessing random attack satisfy $D =$ accept.

By straightforward calculation the success probability of each attacks can be estimated as follows.

Proposition 2. The success probability of a known-Δ attack is given by

$$p_\Delta = \sum_{j=\alpha}^{\beta} \binom{\beta}{j} p^j (1-p)^{\beta-j} \le \binom{\beta}{\max\{\alpha, \lfloor \beta/2 \rfloor\}} p^\alpha,$$

where

$$p = \frac{1}{\delta^\lambda (1 - \sum_{i=1}^{\delta-1} \binom{\delta}{i} (\frac{i}{\delta})^\gamma)}.$$

And the success probability of a Δ-guessing random attack is given by

$$p_\delta = \frac{p_\Delta}{\binom{\omega}{\delta}}.$$

In summary, an attacker E not knowing Δ but knowing δ only can do a Δ-guessing random attack which succeeds with probability p_δ. But, if E can observe a question Q and an answer A transferred between a verifier V and a prover P who is accepted by V, then E can obtain Δ and can do a known-Δ random attack with success probability $p_\Delta = \binom{\omega}{\delta} \cdot p_\delta$. An interesting problem arising here is to look for more powerful attacks which can be done by such an attacker E observing interactions of P and V.

3.3 Complexity of Inferring Secret

Let's analize the case $\alpha = \beta = 1$. Similar results hold for the general case.

Definition 3. For any $\Lambda \subset \Gamma$ and any bijection $q : \langle \gamma \rangle \longrightarrow \Gamma$, let define an injection

$$f_{\Lambda,q} = \text{sort}(\{i \in \langle \gamma \rangle | q(i) \in \Lambda\}),$$

and call it the window determined by a window alphabet Λ and a question (block) q.

Definition 4. For any $\Lambda \subset \Gamma$ and any surjection $W : \langle \lambda \rangle \longrightarrow \Delta$, let define a set $C_{\Lambda,W}$ by

$$C_{\Lambda,W} = \{(q,a) | q : \langle \gamma \rangle \longrightarrow \Gamma, a : \langle \gamma \rangle \longrightarrow \Delta, a \circ f_{\Lambda,q} = W\}.$$

Also define a set C by

$$C = \{C_{\Lambda,W} | \Lambda \subset \Gamma, W : \langle \lambda \rangle \longrightarrow \Delta\}.$$

An attacker can obtain a set O such that $O \subseteq C_{\Lambda,W} \in C$ for unknown Λ and W, by observing correct interactions between a prover and a verifier, or even by masquerading as a verifier to collect answers from a prover. Such a set O is called an observation.

Definition 5. Let B denote the set of all observations, *i.e.*,

$$B = \{O | \exists C_{\Lambda,W} \in C \quad \text{such that} \quad O \subseteq C_{\Lambda,W}\}.$$

A target of an attacker given an observation $O \in B$ is to determine $\Lambda \subset \Gamma$ and $W : \langle \lambda \rangle \longrightarrow \Delta$ such that $O \subseteq C_{\Lambda,W}$.

It is easy to see the following proposition holds.

Proposition 3. For any observation $O \in B$, there exists a window alphabet $\Lambda(\subset \Gamma)$ such that

$$a \circ f_{\Lambda,q} = a' \circ f_{\Lambda,q'}$$

for any $(q,a), (q',a') \in O$.

Accordingly, the following strategy of attack can be derived.

Strategy. Since an attacker given O can check for each $\Lambda(\subset \Gamma)$ with $\#\Lambda = \lambda$ whether the condition in Proposition 3 holds or not, the attacker can find out correct Λ in at most $\begin{pmatrix} \gamma \\ \lambda \end{pmatrix}$ trials. From this correct Λ, the attacker can obtain the secret word W as $W = a \circ f_{\Lambda,q}$.

3.4 Viability

Let's consider the following examples.

Example 1. If $\omega = \gamma = 36$, $\lambda = 18$, $\delta = 2$, and $\beta = \alpha = 1$, then

$$p_\delta \simeq 6.06 \times 10^{-9},$$
$$p_\Delta \simeq 3.81 \times 10^{-6},$$
$$\begin{pmatrix} \gamma \\ \lambda \end{pmatrix} \simeq 9.08 \times 10^9 > 2^{33},$$

and $\nu = 36$ and the required human memory is at most 18 characters + 5 hexadecimal digits.

Example 2. If $\omega = \gamma = 50$, $\lambda = 10$, $\delta = 3$, and $\beta = \alpha = 1$, then

$$p_\delta \simeq 8.64 \times 10^{-10},$$
$$p_\Delta \simeq 1.69 \times 10^{-6},$$
$$\binom{\gamma}{\lambda} \simeq 1.03 \times 10^{10},$$

and $\nu = 50$ and the required human memory is at most 10 characters + 5 nonary digits.

From these examples, with memory, computational and communication complexity acceptable for a human prover and even for a human verifier, the proposed scheme can keep enough security over human identification through insecure channel.

4   Conclusion

This paper has described the importance of the problem of human identification through insecure channels, and proposed a concrete scheme which is matching to human ability of memorizing and processing. The following items are listed for further research :

- Applying the proposed scheme into practice.

- Developing much simpler (lower complexity) versions.

- Studying simple schemes for a human to read a message from an entity through an insecure channel and to reply a confirmation of receiving it through the channel.

- Studying the case where not the both but one of the channel from which a human receives messages and the channel to which a human sends messages is insecure.

Acknowledgment

It is a pleasure to thank Steve Babbage, Donald Davies, Hiroyuki Masumoto, James Massey, Hiroshi Miyano, Satoshi Ozaki, Yuichi Saitoh, Minoru Sasaki, Taroh Sasaki, Kazue Tanaka, Yacov Yacobi, Hiroharu Yoshikawa for their interest and comments.

Reference

[1] D. W. Davies and W. L. Price, *Security for Computer Networks*, Chapter 7, John Wiley & Sons, 1984.

The Automated Cryptanalysis of Analog Speech Scramblers

B Goldburg**, E Dawson*,   S Sridharan**

*School of Mathematics
and
Information Security Research Centre
Queensland University of Technology
GPO Box 2434
Brisbane Qld 4001
Australia

**School of Electrical and Electronic Systems Engineering
Queensland University of Technology
GPO Box 2434
Brisbane Qld 4001
Australia

Abstract

An automated method of attacking commonly used speech scramblers is presented.   The cryptanalysis relies on the availability of the scrambled speech only and makes use of the characteristics of speech. It is shown that some of the currently available time and frequency domain scramblers, based on a fixed permutation, can be cryptanalysed. For systems where the permutation is changed with time, methods for partial recovery of the encrypted speech for several existing systems are given. In the case of the frequency domain scramblers a novel method of attack using a codebook is presented.

1.   Introduction

Most commercially available analog speech scrambling systems are based on permutation of components in either the time domain or the frequency domain. This paper describes a systematic computer attack on several analog speech scramblers. The scramblers attacked consist of the hopping window scrambler as described in [1], bandsplitter as described in [1] and Discrete Fourier Transform (DFT) scrambler as described in [10]. A description will be given of the method used to attack each cipher.

In Carroll [2], [3] and [4] there are descriptions of methods for systematic computer cryptanalysis of simple ciphers, using permutation and substitution, for encryption of written text. These attacks referenced a large amount of data concerning the nature of the language. For example letter frequency in terms of single characters, digraphs and trigraphs were used. Speech has more redundancy than written text. However it is inherently difficult to use this redundancy when conducting a computer cryptanalysis of scrambled speech since much of the redundancy depends on the perception of the listener.

In assessing the security of an encryption algorithm it is assumed that an attacker has complete knowledge of the encryption system. Under this assumption the entire security of the cipher resides in the key. This assumption will be made in all the attacks discussed in this paper. For many analog scrambling systems this is a reasonable assumption to make since some designers present details of the system as part of the marketing exercise. It may also be possible for an attacker to purchase the scrambler to determine what type of system is used. In this paper ciphertext only attacks will be described. This attack assumes that a cryptanalyst has access to only an encrypted version of a conversation. A cipher which can be compromised under such an attack is very insecure. To the understanding of the authors this is the first time that the results of such attacks have been reported in the literature.

2. Cryptanalysis of Hopping Window Scrambler

A hopping window type time domain speech scrambler achieves security by first dividing a continuous speech signal into equal length frames, typically half a second in duration. These frames are further subdivided into a fixed number of time segments of equal length. The scrambling algorithm reorders the time segments within a given frame according to the current permutation. This scrambled frame is then sent in place of the original frame. Figure 1 indicates the process used for a six segment scrambler.

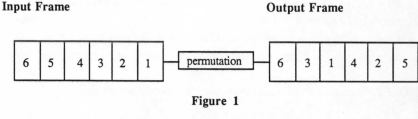

Figure 1

Hopping Window Scrambler

Suppose that a hopping window scrambler is used with a fixed permutation. Knowledge of the speech characteristics can be applied to give the cryptanalyst information about the permutation being used. The frequency content of the speech signal either side of a segment boundary will not change significantly. It should be therefore possible to match the end of one segment with the beginning of its succeeding segment as suggested in [1]. A spectral distance measure is calculated between the end of each segment and the start of all other segments in the frame. Two segments having minimum distance constitute a match. Each segment is used in turn as a starting segment. The second segment is found using the technique described above. The second segment can in turn be used to locate the third and so on until the end of the frame is reached.

There are several different spectral distances that one can apply to match segments. The spectral distances which were used were the Log Spectral Distance (LSD) as described in [6], the Frequency Weighted Log Spectral Distance (FWLSD) as described in [9], the Frequency Variant Spectral Distance (FVSD) as described in [9] and the Segmental Spectral Signal to Noise Ratio (SSNR) as described in [8].

In practice there will be a finite probability of error when choosing a successor to any segment. To reduce this error the most probable matches can be stored. When investigating the correct segment sequence it becomes necessary to employ dynamic programming techniques in the form of a path search algorithm. After choosing a starting segment, a path is traced until it violates the conditions for an allowable path. Paths which encounter the same segment twice represent a violation. If an illegal segment is found the routine is required to backtrack and try an alternative route until the sequence is completed successfully. The path which yields the minimum total distance between segments is selected as the best approximation to the permutation for the current frame. In general this algorithm is unable to determine the correct permutation using a single frame. It is necessary therefore to collect evidence until a definite decision can be made. Information concerning the succeeding segment, for each segment in a frame, is stored together with the most common succeeding segments from previous frames in a matrix. A permutation approximation is constructed from this information using the path search algorithm described above.

The attack process is outlined in the following using m time segments over N speech frames.

Step 1:   Input ciphertext frame $i = 1, 2, ..., N$.

Step 2:   For each frame i calculate the spectral distance measure for the end of each segment and the start of all other segments.

Step 3:   For $j = 1, ..., m$ using a path search algorithm, calculate the most likely permutation with segment j as a starter.

Step 4:   For the m permutations choose the path with the minimum total distance between segments.

Step 5:   Update the table containing the most common succeeding segments for each segment in the frame.

Step 6:   After N frames use above matrix to generate the most likely permutation.

Attacks were conducted, using the algorithm described above, on hopping window scramblers using eight, and sixteen segments. In each case the correct permutation was recovered using less than twenty seconds of encrypted speech. The frame size was kept constant at 0.512 seconds, which is equivalent to 4096 samples at an 8 KHz sampling rate. The average number of half second frames required to make a successful attack as the segment size is varied is shown in Table 1. These values are given for each of the four spectral distance measures namely LSD, FWLSD, FVSD and SNR. The eight and sixteen segment scramblers on average required 3 and 12 $\frac{\text{sec}}{\text{frame}}$ respectively to make an attack. These results indicate that the FWLSD measure offers a reliable and efficient method to use in attacking the hopping window scrambler. These results demonstrate the poor security offered by the fixed permutation hopping window type scrambler. There is an increase in the average number of frames required for a successful attack as the number of segments is increased. This result is demonstrated by the increase in key entrophy when more segments are added. It should be noted that the number of frames required to attack is very sensitive to the position of the segment boundaries.

Eight Segment Hopping Window Scrambler	
Average Number Measure	**Distance of Frames Required**
LSD	5
FWLSD	4
FVSD	4
SSNR	6

Sixteen Segment Hopping Window Scrambler	
Average Number Measure	**Distance of Frames Required**
LSD	9
FWLSD	7
FVSD	11
SSNR	18

Table 1
Results of Fixed Permutation
Attack on Hopping Window Scrambler

Now consider a hopping window device which chooses a different permutation with which to encrypt each frame. The attack proposed for the fixed permutation system described previously is directly applicable to the varying permutation case. It is not possible, however, to use information extracted from previous frames to aid the recovery of permutations. The permutation must be determined from a single frame. The results above from Table 1 indicate that a single frame is not sufficient to recover the correct permutation. Experimentation proved this to be true. Very little intelligibility could be recovered from the ciphertext.

3. Cryptanalysis of Bandsplitter

The bandsplitter scrambles speech by partitioning the original speech spectrum into a fixed number of frequency bands, usually 16 or less. The current permutation then defines how these bands will be rearranged within the frequency space. Figure 2 illustrates the technique for five bands. This scrambling algorithm need not be frame based and can be done on a continuous basis. The receiver must be made aware of the point at which the permutation is changed however.

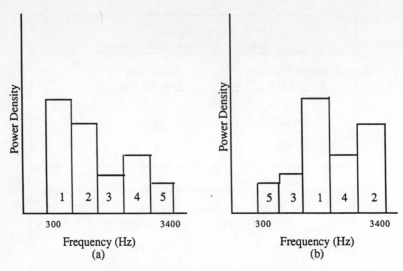

Figure 2

Bandsplitter (a) Original   (b) Scrambled

A ciphertext only attack on the bandsplitter is possible, in which a pattern matching technique is used to return the scrambled spectral envelope to its original state. The attack requires a spectral template representative of the speech waveform. This template is used for comparison when trying to recover the original spectral envelope from the scrambled spectrum. For each frequency subband in the template the attack aims to locate the subband in the scrambled speech (ciphertext) which gives the best match. A mean square error (MSE) criterion is used to make this choice. The ciphertext subbands can thus be rearranged so that the scrambled spectrum conforms to the shape of the spectral template.

Recent work in speech coding has shown that the speech waveform can be represented by a finite number of speech parameter vectors or a codebook [5]. Consider a codebook in which the vectors contain spectral components obtained from a large set of training data. A codebook vector can be used as the required template for the above mentioned attack. A ciphertext only attack is proposed in which each of these codebook vectors is used to decrypt the scrambled spectrum under attack. The resulting decrypted spectrum giving the best match with its corresponding codebook vector following the attack is assumed to be the recovered speech spectrum. It is beneficial to use information from previous frames in order to recover the true permutation for a fixed permutation system. Following an attack on a given frame the position of each band is used to update a table. The table contains the frequency with which each band was assigned to a certain position. The correct permutation should be able to be constructed by selecting the bands with maximum frequency. The Hungarian assignment algorithm [6] was used to obtain an optimum solution from the table.

The attack process is outlined in the following using n frequency bands over N speech frames where k codebook vectors are used.

Step 1:   Transform ciphertext frame i to frequency domain.

Step 2:   Partition into n bands.

Step 3:   For codebook vector j = 1, ..., k do a pattern match and calculate mean square error.

Step 4:   Record the permutation used to match the ciphertext vector to the codebook vector giving the minimum mean square error.

Step 5:   Update possible permutation matrix.

Step 6:   Use matrix to derive most probable permutation.

With a codebook size as small as 180 vectors it is possible to completely cryptanalyse eight and sixteen band frequency scramblers using the above ciphertext alone attack. The average number of half second frames required to make a successful attack were 16 and 26 for the eight and sixteen bands frequency scramblers respectively. The average time to attack in sec/frame was 4.6 and 10.6 seconds for the eight and sixteen band frequency scrambler respectively. These results demonstrate the poor security offered by the fixed permutation bandsplitter.

A bandsplitter encryption scheme, using a continuously varying permutation, was attacked in the same manner as the fixed permutation system. Using the codebook template matching technique, the best match was used as the decrypted spectrum for each frame in turn. Previous frames can no longer be used to provide information about the current permutation since the permutation is different for each frame. It is well known that if the most significant bands in each frame can be located correctly the resulting speech will be intelligible. The decrypted speech resulting from an attack on the eight and sixteen band systems was clearly recognisable. Table 2 shows the probability with which a given band was located correctly. The table shows that the first band in each case was positioned correctly with the highest probability. This band contains a large proportion of the voice speech energy and hence a high proportion of the speech information. It is clear from the table that as the number of bands was increased it became more difficult to correctly position the vital low frequency bands. The results of these attacks demonstrate the poor security offered by the bandsplitter even in the case where a different permutation is used for each frame.

Number of Bands : k = 8		Number of bands : k = 16	
Band	Probability	Band	Probability
1	1.00	1	0.83
2	0.53	2	0.67
3	0.46	3	0.48
4	0.29	4	0.32
5	0.49	5	0.29
6	0.43	6	0.29
7	0.44	7	0.28
8	0.67	8	0.21
		9	0.33
		10	0.32
		11	0.32
		12	0.27
		13	0.33
		14	0.32
		15	0.24
		16	0.46

Table 2
Results of Varying Permutation Attack on Bandsplitter

4. Cryptanalysis of DFT Scrambler

A DFT scrambler typically operates on speech frames containing 256 speech samples, giving a frame length of 32ms. Application of the DFT to these speech samples produces 256 spectral components. The spectral components with in the band of the channel undergo a permutation before the inverse DFT is used to return the frame to the time domain. In the scrambler simulated for the attacks described in this section 88 spectral components were permuted. The scrambling process is indicated in block diagram fashion in Figure 3. Permutation of spectral components results in the destruction of formant and pitch structures, leaving little information with which an attack can be performed. The scrambling process is frame based since the discrete transform operation is performed on a fixed number of time samples, N.

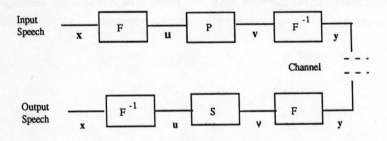

Figure 3

DFT Scrambler

The attack described for use with bandsplitter encryption devices is also applicable to the DFT scrambler. The only modification required is in the method for obtaining the plaintext/ciphertext mapping. In the case of the bandsplitter a frequency subband in the plaintext frame is mapped to a subband in the ciphertext frame. For the DFT scrambler however, it is necessary to map a single transform component in the plaintext frame to a single component in the ciphertext frame. This is achieved by locating the largest component in the plaintext frame and assigning it to the largest component in the ciphertext frame. This mapping is recorded and the next largest in the corresponding frames are assigned. This process continues until all components have been mapped. Again a MSE criterion is used to choose the codebook vector giving the best spectral match. The mapping used for this vector becomes the permutation estimate for the frame under attack.

The attack process is outlined in the following where 88 DFT coefficients are permutated, each codebook vector has dimension 88 and N speech frames are used.

Step 1:   Obtain the 88 transform coefficients from time frame i. i = 1, ..., N.
Step 2:   For codebook vector j = 1, ..., k pattern match the scrambled frame i to the codebook vector j and calculate M.S.E.
Step 3:   Record the permutation giving the minimum M.S.E.
Step 4:   Update possible permutation matrix.
Step 5:   Use matrix to derive most probable permutation.

A DFT scrambler permuting 88 coefficients, with a frame size N = 256, was cryptanalysed using the procedure described above. The attack was performed on a system using a fixed permutation, as well as one using a constantly varying permutation. The attack was able to correctly position only a small number of coefficients, however in each case this was sufficient to recover intelligible speech. As expected, the fixed permutation attack gave more intelligible speech. The improvement in the intelligibility of the recovered speech in each case with respect to the original is shown in Table 3 which gives the % of components which are placed within two positions of their correct location. In the case of a fixed permutation the large number of components (23%) which are "close" to the correct position demonstrates the improvement in the intelligibility of the recovered speech.

Speech Segments Compared	% of Components
Original and Scrambled	3.7%
Original and Recovered (Using Varying Permutation)	8.9%
Original and Recovered (Using Fixed Permutation)	23%

Table 3
Results of DFT Scrambler Cryptanalysis

5. Conclusion

It has been shown that it is possible to conduct a computer cryptanalysis of several analog scramblers based on ciphertext alone. These attacks have demonstrated the poor security offered by many of the commonly used analog speech scramblers. The results from this paper can be used as a guideline for attacking speech ciphers as well as improving the security of existing scramblers. It should be noted that the actual attack on a cipher is dependent on the quality of the intercepted signal and the voice characteristics of the individual speaker.

References

1. H. Beker, and F. Piper, **Secure Speech Communications**, Academic Press, 1985.
2. J.M. Carroll, and S. Martin, "The Automated Cryptanalysis of Substitution Ciphers", **Cryptologia**, Vol. 10, 1986, pp 193 - 209.
3. J.M. Carroll, and L.E. Robbins, "The Automated Cryptanalysis of Polyalphabetic Ciphers", **Cryptologia**, Vol. 11, 1987, pp 193 - 205.
4. J.M. Carroll, and L.E. Robbins, **Computer Cryptanalysis**, Technical Report No. 223, Dept. of Computer Science, The University of Western Ontario, Dec. 1988.
5. R.M. Gray, "Vector quantization", **IEEE ASSP Mag.**, April 1984, pp 4 - 29.
6. N. Kitawaki, H. Nagabuch and Itok, "Objective quality evaluation for low bit rate speech coding systems", **IEEE Journal on Selected Areas in Communication**, Vol. 6, No. 2, February 1988, pp 282 - 248.
7. R.W. Llewellyn, **Linear Programming**, Hold, Rinehart and Windston, 1964.
8. A. Matsunaga, K. Koga, and M. Ohkawa, "An analog speech scrambling system using the FFT technique with high level security" **IEEE Journal in Selected Areas in Communications**, Vol. 7, May 1989, pp. 540 - 547.
9. S.R. Quackenbush, T.P. Barnwell, and M.A. Clements, **Objective Measures of Speech Quality**, Prentice Hall, 1988.
10. S. Sridharan, E. Dawson, B. Goldburg, "A Fast Fourier Transform Based Speech Encryption System", to appear in **IEE Proceedings Part I Communications**, Speech and Vision.

ACKNOWLEDGEMENT

This work was supported by a QUT Research and Development grant.

A Construction for
One Way Hash Functions
and
Pseudorandom Bit Generators

Babak Sadeghiyan
and
Josef Pieprzyk[1]

Department of Computer Science,
University College,
University of New South Wales,
Australian Defence Force Academy,
Canberra, A.C.T. 2600,
Australia.

Abstract

We prove that if f is a n-bit one-way permutation, i.e., it has some hard bits, a one-way permutation with $n - k$ provably simultaneous hard bits can be constructed with it. We apply this construction to improve the efficiency of Blum-Micali pseudo-random bit generator. Then, we apply the construction to propose a new approach for building universal one-way hash functions. This approach merges Damgard's design principle (or Merkle's meta-method) and the method proposed by Zheng, Matsumoto and Imai for the construction of hash functions for long messages.

1   Introduction

Consider a situation when a communicant A, sends a message to a receiver B. In order to protect the message against forgery, A should sign the message. If the length of the message is long, the efficient method is *transforming all the message to a short string with a public hash function h, then signing the hash value.*

The hash function simply maps messages of arbitrary length to some small fixed length, and should satisfy four properties:

1. h should have the property that for any given message x and hash value $h(x)$, finding another message y such that $h(y) = h(x)$, $x \neq y$, is computationally hard. In other words, a hash function has to be collision free.

---

[1]Support for this project was provided in part by Telecom Australia under the contract number 7027 and by the Australian Research Council under the reference number A48830241.

2. h should be one-way so that messages are not disclosed by their signatures.(Properties 1 and 2 are related to each other.)

3. h should have the property to be computed over the entire message (with different lengths).

4. h should destroy the homomorphic structure of the underlying public key cryptosystem used for the signature scheme (for a detailed discussion see [9],[14],[15],[21]).

Several approaches for constructing hash functions based on DES have been proposed (see [1]). Unfortunately, DES suffers from small key space and also has some undesired properties such as complementation property, i.e., $e_{\overline{k}}(\overline{m}) = \overline{e_k(m)}$. In [20], it is shown that some of these hash functions are not collision free. Several other proposals based on DES appear in [19],[23],[18], [28],[29], which try to overcome these drawbacks. Some other hash functions based on RSA and squaring modulo n appear in [16],[10]. Attacks to some of these constructions appear in [6],[10]. Later, Damgard [7] constructed hash functions based on the existence of a claw free pair of permutations, which was the first for which collision freeness could be proven.

The current trend in cryptography is to provide the construction of basic primitives with general cryptographic assumptions that are also as weak as possible (it is theoretically important to base cryptographic primitives and basic tools on reduced complexity assumptions). It is also practically important to give efficient implementation of such constructions [24].

Two formal complexity-theoretic definitions have been suggested for cryptographic hash function families. The first family of hash functions, defined by Damgard, is the Collision Free Hash Functions (CFHF) or Collision Intractable Hash Functions (CIH). In this family, the function is given but finding a pair which map to the same output is difficult (see [8] for the precise definition). The second family, defined by Naor and Yung [22], is the Universal One Way Hash Functions (UOWHF). This family is weaker and if given an input and any function from the family, it is difficult to find another input which collides with it.

Naor and Yung [22] showed that a secure signature scheme reduces to the existence of UOWHF. They constructed a family of UOWHF from any one-way permutation and a family of strongly universal$_2$ hash functions, which was introduced in [5],[27], with collision accessibility property. In their construction, the one-way permutation provides the one-wayness of the UOWHF, and the strongly universal$_2$ family of hash functions performs the mapping to the small length output. When a member is chosen randomly and uniformly from the family, the output is distributed randomly and uniformly over the output space.

Santias and Yung [25] constructed the family of UOWHF from any 1 to 1 one-way function. They also proposed another construction from any one-way function with almost known pre-image size. Zheng, Matsumoto and Imai [32] built a family of UOWHF from any quasi-injection one-way function with the application of a pair-wise independent uniformiser and a family of strongly universal$_2$ hash functions. Rompel [24] gave a construction for one-way hash functions from any one-way function and proved that existence of one-way functions is a necessary and sufficient condition for constructing hash functions. However, although his work is theoretically optimal, it is less than practical.

In this area, each successive paper has assumed weaker conditions for the one-way function and has made hashing and additional procedures more complicated, such that Rompel's scheme can be constructed from any one-way function but needs too many additional procedures. In contrast, in this paper we construct a one-way permutation with some stronger properties but apply a simple hashing procedure, simply chopping or selecting arbitrarily some bits of the output.

On the other hand, for the construction of pseudo-random bit generators (PBG), Blum and Micali [3] discovered hard-core predicates b of functions f. Such $b(x)$ cannot be efficiently obtained, given $f(x)$. They applied this notion to construct a PBG based on the intractability of the discrete logarithm problem. Yao [30] generalises this by showing that a PBG can be constructed from any one-way permutation. He transforms any one-way permutation into a more complicated one which has a hard-core predicate. Similarly, later works in this area have tried to make generalisations and assume weaker conditions (for example see [12], [13]).

In this paper, we present a method such that given an n-bit one-way permutation, i.e., it has some hard bits, a one-way permutation with n hard bits can be constructed, which we call a strong permutation. We apply this strong permutation to present a construction for pseudo-random bit generators with maximum efficiency, based on the Blum-Micali pseudo-random bit generator. We also present a method to build a universal one-way hash function from the strong permutation. Hence, given a one-way permutation, we can construct both an efficient pseudo-random generator and a universal one-way hash function. Zheng, Matsumoto and Imai [31] revealed a duality between pseudo-random bit generators and UOWHF. Applying the revealed duality, they presented a construction for UOWHF which is a dual of the construction of Blum-Micali PBG. We show that by the application of the strong permutation, Zheng et al.'s scheme and Damgard's design principle for construction of hash functions merge with each other, and would yield the same result. As the result, our proposal yields an algorithm that can be used both for generating pseudorandom bits, and hashing long messages. This has a practical significance, since it would not be necessary to use two different algorithms for implementing these two cryptographic tools.

2 Notations

The notation we use here is similar to [31]. The set of all integers is denoted by N. Let $\Sigma = \{0,1\}$ be the alphabet we consider. For $n \in N$, Σ^n is the set of all binary strings of length n. The concatenation of two binary strings x, y is denoted by $x \parallel y$. The length of a string x is denoted by $\mid x \mid$.

Let l be a monotone increasing function from N to N and f a function from D to R, where $D = \bigcup_n D_n$, $D_n \subseteq \Sigma^n$ and $R = \bigcup_n R_n$, $R_n \subseteq \Sigma^{l(n)}$. D is called the domain and R the range of f. Denote by f_n the restriction of f on Σ^n. f is a permutation if each f_n is a 1 to 1 and onto function. f is polynomial time computable if there is a polynomial time algorithm computing $f(x)$ for all $x \in D$. The composition of two functions f and g is defined as $f \circ g(x) = f(g(x))$. The i-fold composition of f is denoted by $f^{(i)}$.

A (probability) ensemble E, with length $l(n)$, is a family of probability distributions $\{E_n \mid E_n : \Sigma^{l(n)} \to [0,1], n \in N\}$. The uniform ensemble U with length $l(n)$ is the family of uniform probability distributions U_n, where each U_n is defined as $U_n(x) = \frac{1}{2^{l(n)}}$, for all $x \in \Sigma^{l(n)}$. By $x \in_E \Sigma^{l(n)}$ we mean that x is randomly selected from $\Sigma^{l(n)}$ according to E_n, and in particular by $x \in_r S$ we mean that x is chosen from the set S uniformly at random. E is samplable if there is an algorithm M that on input n, outputs an $x \in_E \Sigma^{l(n)}$, and polynomially samplable if the running time of M is also polynomially bounded.

3 Preliminaries

Definition 1 *A <u>statistical test</u> is a probabilistic algorithm T that on an input x, where x is an n-bit string, halts in $O(n^t)$ and outputs a bit $0/1$, where t is some fixed positive integer.*

Definition 2 *Let l be a polynomial, and E^1 and E^2 be ensembles both with length $l(n)$. E^1 and E^2 are called* <u>*indistinguishable*</u> *from each other, if for each statistical test T, for each polynomial Q, for all sufficiently large n,*

$$| Prob\{T(x_1) = 1\} - Prob\{T(x_2) = 1\} | < \frac{1}{Q(n)}$$

where $x_1 \in_{E^1} \Sigma^{l(n)}$, $x_2 \in_{E^2} \Sigma^{l(n)}$.

Definition 3 *A polynomially samplable ensemble E is* <u>*pseudorandom*</u> *if it is indistinguishable from the uniform ensemble U with the same length.*

Definition 4 *Let $f : D \to R$, where $D = \bigcup_n \Sigma^n$ and $R = \bigcup_n \Sigma^{l(n)}$, be a polynomial time computable function. We say that f is* <u>*one-way*</u> *if for each probabilistic polynomial time algorithm M, for each polynomial Q and for all sufficiently large n,*

$$Prob\{f_n(M(f_n(x))) = f_n(x)\} < \frac{1}{Q(n)}$$

where $x \in_U D_n$.

Note that the one-way property of a function is relative to a specific model of computation with a specific amount of computing resources.

Definition 5 *We say we have a* <u>*computing resource for k bits*</u> *if given the output of a one-way function and $n - k$ bits of the input string, one can define the remaining k bits of the input string by exhaustive search.*

For the remaining of this paper we assume that we have a computing resource for at most k bits.

4 Hard Bits

If a function f is one-way then given $f(x)$ the argument x must be unpredictable. If every bit of the argument x were easily computable from $f(x)$, then f would not be a one-way function. Therefore, some specific bits of the argument are unpredictable, and we cannot guess them better than by flipping a coin. We call these bits hard bits of f.

Definition 6 *Let $f : D \to R$ be a one-way function, where $R = \bigcup_n \Sigma^n$ and $D = \bigcup_n \Sigma^{l(n)}$. Let $i(n)$ be a function from N to N with $1 \le i(n) \le n$. If for each probabilistic polynomial time algorithm M, for each Q and for all sufficiently large n,*

$$Prob\{M(f_n(x)) = x'_{i(n)}\} < \frac{1}{2} + \frac{1}{Q(n)}$$

where $x \in_r \Sigma^n$ and $x'_{i(n)}$ is the $i(n)$-th bit of an $x' \in \Sigma^n$ satisfying $f(x) = f(x')$, then $i(n)$-th bit is a <u>*hard bit*</u> *of f [31].*

Note that the definition of hard bits implies that a hard bit depends on all bits of $f(x)$ under f^{-1}, where f^{-1} is a hard problem.

Lemma 1 *The number of hard bits defines the difficulty of inverting a one-way function.*

Proof : Assume that only a small number of bits of a function are hard bits and, when the output is given, we can obtain every remaining bit with a probability better than $\frac{1}{2} + \frac{1}{Q(n)}$ in polynomial time. A probabilistic algorithm M that first predicts the easy bits and then does an exhaustive search for finding hard bits can inverse the function f in polynomial time with a probability at least better than $\frac{1}{Q(n)}$. For example, consider that a function has been proven to have only $\log_2(n)$ hard bits and $n = 512$ then only 9 bits are hard. If we have a computing resource for more than 9 bits, which we usually have, then given the output, the input can be obtained in polynomial time with a probability better than $\frac{1}{Q(n)}$. $\qquad \square$

Hence, a one-way function should have at least $k + 1$ hard bits.

Lemma 2 *All the hard bits are independent of one another.*

Proof : (By contradiction) assume that the i_1, i_2-th bits are hard bits that are dependent on each other and there is a probabilistic algorithm M that can calculate i_1-th bit given both $f(x)$ and i_2-th bit with a probability better than $\frac{1}{Q(n)}$. Then, we can construct a probabilistic algorithm M' for guessing i_1-th bit.
  Algorithm M':

1. Guess i_2-th bit with flipping a coin (guess with probability 0.5).

2. Given i_2-th bit and $f(x)$, run M and find i_1-th bit.

then $Prob\{M'(f(x)) = x_{i_1}\} > \frac{1}{2} + \frac{1}{Q(n)}$; which is a contradiction. $\qquad \square$

From the above Lemma we draw the following corollary.

Corollary 1 *Let $f : D \to R$ be a one-way function, where $D = \bigcup_n \Sigma^n$ and $R = \bigcup_n \Sigma^{l(n)}$. Assume f has t hard bits, $t < n - k$, and $j < k$ of them and $f(x)$ are given, we cannot predict any of the remaining $t - j$ hard bits with a probability better than $\frac{1}{2} + \frac{1}{Q(n)}$.*

Definition 7 *Let l be a polynomial, and E be an ensemble with length $l(n)$. We say that E passes the <u>next bit test</u> if for each statistical test T, for each polynomial Q, for all sufficiently large n, the probability that on input the first i bits of a sequence x randomly selected according to E and $i < l(n)$, T outputs the $(i+1)$th bit of x is:*

$$Prob\{T(x_1, \ldots, x_i) = 1\} < \frac{1}{2} + \frac{1}{Q(n)}$$

where $x \in_E \Sigma^{l(n)}$.

The following theorem is derived from [Yao 82] and has been stated in [2], [3], [11] in different terms.

Theorem 1 *Let E be an polynomially samplable ensemble, the following statements are equivalent:*
  (i) E passes the next bit test.
  (ii) E is indistinguishable from the uniform ensemble U.

In other words, the indistinguishability test is equivalent to the unpredictability test.

Corollary 2 *Assume that $f : D \to R$ is a one-way function, where $D = \bigcup_n \Sigma^n$ and $R = \bigcup_n \Sigma^{l(n)}$. Also assume that $i_1, i_2, \ldots, i_t$ are functions from N to N, with $1 \le i_j(n) \le n$ for each $1 \le j \le t$, $t < k$ and each i_j denotes a hard bit of f. Denote by E_n^1 and E_n^2 the probability distributions defined by the random variables $x_{i_t(n)} \ldots x_{i_2(n)} \, x_{i_1(n)} \parallel f(x)$ and $r_t \ldots r_2 \, r_1 \parallel f(x)$ respectively, where $x \in_r \Sigma^n$, $x_{i_j(n)}$ is the $i_j(n)$-th bit of x and $r_j \in_r \Sigma$. Let $E^1 = \{E_n^1 \mid n \in N\}$ and $E^2 = \{E_n^2 \mid n \in N\}$, then E^1 and E^2 are indistinguishable from each other.*

Proof : From Corollary 1, it can be concluded that every string of $t < k$ hard bits passes the next bit test. This is equivalent to saying that given $f(x)$, any string of $t < k$ hard bits is indistinguishable from a string chosen uniformly at random from Σ^t, according to Theorem 1. □

In other words, given $f(x)$, any string of $t < k$ hard bits is indistinguishable from random strings. Such hard bits are called <u>simultaneous hard bits</u> of f. Note that the maximum number of simultaneous hard bits of any one way function can not be more than $n - k$.

Blum and Micali discovered the notion of hard core predicates of functions and applied it to construct pseudorandom bit generators (PBG).

Definition 8 *Let l be a polynomial with $l(n) > n$. A <u>pseudorandom bit generator</u> is a deterministic polynomial time function g that upon receiving a random n-bit input, extends it into a sequence of $l(n)$-bit pseudorandom bits $b_1, b_2, \ldots, b_{l(n)}$ as the output.*

In other words:

1. Each bit b_k is easy to compute.

2. The output bits are unpredictable, in other words the output string passes the next bit test, i.e., given the generator g and the first s output bits $b_1, \ldots, b_s$, but not the input string, it is computationally infeasible to predict the $(s + 1)$th bit in the sequence [3].

The following theorem describes Blum-Micali PBG [3].

Theorem 2 *Let l be a polynomial with $l(n) > n$, and let f be a one-way permutation on $D = \bigcup_n \Sigma^n$ and $i(n)$-th bit is proven to be a hard bit of f. Let g_n be a function defined as follows:*

1. *Generate the sequence $f_n^{(1)}(x), f_n^{(2)}(x), \ldots, f_n^{(l(n))}(x)$, where $x \in \Sigma^n$.*

2. *From right to left (!), extract i-th bit from each element in the above sequence and output that bit.*

so, $g_n(x) = b_{l(n)}(x) \ldots b_2(x) \, b_1(x)$ where $x \in \Sigma^n$ and $b_j(x) = $ (the i-th bit of $f_n^{(j)}(x)$). The $g = \{g_n \mid n \in N\}$ is a pseudorandom bit generator extending n-bit into $l(n)$-bit output strings.

If $i_1(n), \ldots, i_t(n)$-th bits are simultaneous hard bits of f, then the efficiency of g can be improved by defining the $b_j(x)$ to be a function which extracts all known simultaneous hard bits of $f^{(j)}(x)$.

In [2], it has been proven that the $\log_2(n)$ least significant bits of RSA and Rabin encryption functions are simultaneously hard. Hence, if we use RSA or Rabin functions instead of the one-way permutation, with each iteration of the function we can extract $\log_2(n)$ bits. For example, if n is equal to 512 and we would like to produce a 512 bit pseudorandom string, we should iterate the one-way function for $\lceil \frac{l(n)}{\log_2(n)} \rceil = \lceil \frac{512}{\log_2(512)} \rceil = 57$ times. If a one-way permutation has more known hard bits, we can use it instead of RSA or Rabin function and obtain a better efficiency.

5 A Strong One Way Permutation

In this section we construct a one-way permutation with maximum number of hard bits, which can be used for the construction of both the Blum-Micali pseudorandom bit generator and one-way hash functions. Before describing the construction some preliminary definitions are given.

Definition 9 *A transformation is called* complete *if each output bit depends on all input bits. In other words, the simplest Boolean expression for each output bit contains all the input bits.*

Definition 10 *If the inverse of a complete transformation is also complete, it is described as being* two way complete. *In other words, each output bit depends on all the input bits and vice-versa.*

Lemma 3 *If a permutation is complete, then it is also two way complete.*

Definition 11 *If the correlation between two binary variables is zero, they are called* independent variables.

(See [26], for the definition of correlation.)

Definition 12 *Let v be a complete permutation and all the output bits be pairwise independent. We call v a* perfect permutation.

Kam and Davida [17] presented a method where an entire substitution-permutation network could be guaranteed to be complete if all the substitution boxes used in the procedure were complete. DES is an example of a complete cryptographic transformation. Since DES is reversible and the reverse function (decryption) has the same structure as encryption, DES is a two way complete transformation. Webster and Tavares [26] showed that there is very little correlation between output variables of DES. So, we can conclude that DES is an example of a perfect permutation, in our definitions. Brown [4] has used the known design criteria of DES to build an extended 128-bit DES and has shown that his scheme has similar cryptographic properties to DES. Extending the DES structure for more bits, for example 512 bits, has the disadvantage that the running time would be relatively high and would be comparable to public key cryptosystem. For the following theorems, we use a two way complete permutation such that only $k+1$ output bits are independent of other bits and we call it a $k + 1$-bit perfect permutation, which has much looser requirements than a perfect permutation. If we consider $k = 63$, a $k + 1$-bit perfect permutation can easily be constructed with the Kam and Davida method, plus a single DES block.

Lemma 4 *Let f be an n-bit one-way permutation and V be the set of all n-bit permutations, then $m = f \circ v \circ f$ is also a one-way permutation with a probability better than $1 - \frac{1}{Q(n)}$, when $v \in_r V$.*

Proof : Both f and v are permutations and f is a one-way permutation, so the result of their composition would be a permutation. The probability that m would not be a one way permutation is equal to the probability of finding f^{-1} (or any linear function of f^{-1}) from V by chance and is equal to $\frac{1}{Q(n)}$. □

If we put some conditions on v and f, m can be made to be a permutation with the desired properties.

Theorem 3 *Let $m : D \to D$ be a one-way permutation where $D = \bigcup_n \Sigma^n$ and $m = f \circ v \circ f$, where f is a one-way permutation, i.e., it has at least $k + 1$ hard bits, and v is a $k + 1$-bit perfect permutation where the positions of independent output bits comply with the position of hard bits of f. For each probabilistic polynomial time algorithm M, for each Q and for all sufficiently large n,*

$$Prob\{M(m(x)) = x_i\} < \frac{1}{2} + \frac{1}{Q(n)}$$

where $x \in_r \Sigma^n$ and x_i is the i-th bit of the x, and $1 \leq i \leq n$. In other words, each bit of x is a hard bit of m.

Proof : (By contradiction) we show that if an algorithm could find x_i, it would be able to invert f. For simplicity of notation, we indicate the first one-way function with f_1 and the second one with f_2, so $m = f_2 \circ v \circ f_1$. Assume that M is an algorithm that given $m(x)$, can predict x_i with a probability bigger than $\frac{1}{2} + \frac{1}{Q(n)}$ (x_i is not a hard bit of m). Two situations may arise;

(a) when x_i is not a hard bit of f_1:

Since the i-th bit is not a hard bit of f_1, then given $f_1(x)$, there exists an algorithm M' that can find the i-th bit with a probability bigger than $\frac{1}{2} + \frac{1}{Q(n)}$.

Without loss of generality, consider v to be an invertible permutation. Due to the two way completeness property of v, all bits of $v \circ f_1(x)$ depend on all bits of $f_1(x)$ and vice-versa. So, to obtain $f_1(x)$, we need to know all bits of $v \circ f_1(x)$. Since v is an invertible function in polynomial time, then given $v \circ f_1(x)$, it is possible to find the i-th bit of x,

$$Prob\{M'(v \circ f_1(x)) = x_i\} > \frac{1}{2} + \frac{1}{Q'(n)}$$

the probability equation simply says that we can predict x_i by tossing a coin with probability $1/2$ or estimating it given $v \circ f_1(x)$ with a probability better than $1/Q'(n)$. In other words,

$$Prob\{\text{estimating } x_i \mid v \circ f_1(x)\} > \frac{1}{Q'(n)}$$

Without loss of generality, we assume that f_2 is a one way permutation such that given a $f_2(y)$, we can guess $n - k - 1$ bits of y efficiently. Moreover, the $k + 1$ independent bits of v comply with hard bits of f_2, and knowing some other bits of $v \circ f_1(x)$ (i.e., other than independent output bits of v) and v, we cannot calculate all bits of $v \circ f_1(x)$. In accordance with the assumption that the i-th bit is not a hard bit of m, the following is also held:

$$\frac{1}{Q(n)} < Prob\{\text{estimating } x_i \mid f_2 \circ v \circ f_1(x)\}$$
$$= Prob\{\text{estimating } x_i \mid v \circ f_1(x)\}.Prob\{\text{obtaining } v \circ f_1(x) \mid f_2 \circ v \circ f_1(x)\}$$

Since the multiplication of two polynomial expressions is another polynomial expression, then for some polynomial Q'', the following holds:

$$Prob\{\text{obtaining } v \circ f_1(x) \mid f_2 \circ v \circ f_1(x)\} > \frac{1}{Q''(n)}$$

This is equivalent to inverting f_2 and contradicts our assumption that f_2 is a one-way permutation.

(b) when the x_i is a hard bit of f_1:

by performing a procedure similar to the case (a), it is obvious that the i-th bit should also be a hard bit of m. □

Lemma 5 *Let $m = f_2 \circ v \circ f_1$ be a one way permutation defined in Theorem 3. In addition, consider f_1 to be a one way permutation such that given a $t < n - k$ bits of x, no $\ell > k$ bits of $f(x)$ can be guessed with a probability better than $\frac{1}{2^k}$, then given $m(x)$ and the $t < n - k$ bits of x, $m(x)$ can not still be reversed.*

Proof : Since $t < n - k$ bits of x is known, the value of $f_1(x)$ can be guessed with a probability equal to $\frac{1}{2^{n-t}}$, where $n - t > k$. Hence, with v being a two way complete permutation, any bit of $v \circ f_1(x)$ can not be estimated with a probability better than $\frac{1}{2^{n-t}} < \frac{1}{2^k}$. On the other hand we assumed that given $f_2 \circ v \circ f_1(x)$, $n - k - 1$ bits of $v \circ f_1(x)$ could be guessed efficiently. Since the position of hard bits of f_2 comply with the positions of independent bits of v, given $n - k - 1$ bits of $v \circ f_1(x)$, we can not still estimate the $k + 1$ independent output bits of v with a probability better than $\frac{1}{2^{k+1}}$. Then the only possibility for reversing m is that the hard bits of f_2 and the $t < n - k$ bits of x be related to each other with some function such that revealing the t bits of x makes estimating the hard bits of f_2 probable. Such possibility has been excluded by assuming that f_1 is a one way permutation such that given a $t < n - k$ bits of x, no $\ell > k$ bits of $f(x)$ can be guessed with a probability better than $\frac{1}{2^k}$. Because, even if $v \circ f_1(x)$ and $f_1(x)$ are related to each other with a system of linear equations, knowing $n - k - 1$ bits of $v \circ f_1(x)$ and $\ell < k$ bits of the $f_1(x)$, the system of equations can not still be solved. $\square$

Note that, the conditions of Lemma 5 for f_1 only excludes one way permutations that split into two or more parts, for example $f(x_1 \parallel x_2) = x_1 \parallel g(x_2)$.

Lemma 6 *Let $m = f_2 \circ v \circ f_1$ be the one way permutation defined in Theorem 3. In addition, consider f_1 to be a one way permutation such that given any string of $t < n - k$ bits of x, any $\ell < k$ bits of $f_1(x)$ can not be evaluated with a probability better than $\frac{1}{2^k}$, then given $m(x)$ and any string of $t < n - k$ bits of x, m can not be reversed.*

Lemma 6 simply suggested a construction for a one-way permutation m such that each bit of x is a hard bit of m and given any $t < n - k$ bits of x and $m(x)$, m can not be reversed. We call such a permutation m a *strong one-way permutation* or simply a *strong permutation*. The following corollary can be drawn from Lemma 6.

Corollary 3 *Assume that $m : D \to D$ is a strong one-way permutation, where $D = \bigcup_n \Sigma^n$. Also assume that $i_1, i_2, \ldots, i_t$ are functions from N to N, with $1 \le i_j(n) \le n$ for each $1 \le j \le t$, $t < n - k$. Denote by E_n^1 and E_n^2 the probability distributions defined by the random variables $x_{i_t(n)} \cdots x_{i_2(n)} x_{i_1(n)} \parallel m(x)$ and $r_t \ldots r_2 r_1 \parallel m(x)$ respectively, where $x \in_r \Sigma^n$, $x_{i_j(n)}$ is the $i_j(n)$-th bit of x and $r_j \in_r \Sigma$. Let $E^1 = \{ E_n^1 \mid n \in N \}$ and $E^2 = \{ E_n^2 \mid n \in N \}$, then E^1 and E^2 are indistinguishable from each other.*

In other words, any string of $t < n - k$ bits of x is indistinguishable from random strings.

We can now construct an efficient Blum-Micali pseudo-random bit generator with the strong one-way permutation suggested in Theorem 3.

Theorem 4 *Let l be a polynomial with $l(n) > n$ and m be a strong one-way permutation. Let g be a function defined as follows:*

1. *Generate the sequence $m_n^{(1)}(x), m_n^{(2)}(x), \ldots, m_n^{(l(n))}(x)$, where $x \in \Sigma^n$.*

2. *From right to left, extract $n - k - 1$ bits from each element in the above sequence and output them.*

Then g is a pseudorandom bit generator extending n-bit into $(n - k - 1)l(n)$ bit output strings.

Since we have a computing resource for k bits then the above scheme yields the maximum possible efficiency. If $k = 128$ (!) and n is 512, then with 2 iterations of m, or 4 iterations of f, we can extract 766 pseudorandom bits. This yields nearly 192 pseudo-random bits per iteration of f, which is 21 times more efficient than using RSA or Rabin function with the scheme described in Theorem 2.

Note that since the output string is pseudorandom, we can also draw the following corollary.

Corollary 4 *The $n - k - 1$ extracted bits of each iteration is distributed uniformly and randomly in Σ^{n-k-1}.*

6 UOWHF Construction and PBG

Damgard in [8] suggested the use of pseudorandom bit generators for hash functions and extraction of a small portion of the output string, due to their one-way property, provided that the collision freeness of the concrete instance is analysed. Moreover, Zheng et al. [31] revealed a duality between the construction of pseudorandom bit generators and one-way hash functions. We show that the construction presented in Theorem 5 for PBG, can also be used for the construction of UOWHF. Before entering this discussion we give the background and some preliminary definitions.

There are two kinds of one-way hash functions, i.e., universal one way hash functions, or weak one-way hash functions, and collision free hash functions, or strong one-way hash functions. The main property of the former is that given a random initial string x, it is computationally infeasible to find a different string y that collides with x, i.e., $h(x) = h(y)$. The main property of the latter is that it is computationally difficult to find a pair (x, y) of strings, $x \neq y$, that collide with each other.

In universal one-way hash functions, there is no guarantee that it is computationally infeasible to find pairs of input that map onto the same output and for some inputs $z \neq z'$ might $h(z) = h(z')$. However, there should not be too many z, z' pairs. So, choosing x randomly should make it unlikely that anyone can find an x' such that $h(x) = h(x')$ [19]. However, if we assume that h is random, i.e., hashing is accomplished by looking up the correct value in a large table of random numbers, then it is possible to choose x in a non-random way since any method of choosing x that does not depend on h is random with respect to h.

Another problem with universal one-way hash functions is that repeated use weakens them. To deal with this problem, we can simply define a family of one-way hash functions with the property that each member h_i of the family is different from all other members, so any information about how to break h_i will provide no help in breaking h_j for $i \neq j$ (see [19]). If the system is designed so that every use of a weak one-way hash function is parameterized by a different parameter, then the overall system security can be kept high. Naor and Yung [22] constructed such a family of functions with a one-way permutation and a strongly universal$_2$ family of hash functions. The precise definition of UOWHF is given in Definition 13 below.

6.1 Preliminaries

Let l be a polynomial with $l(n) > n$, H is a family of hash functions defined by $H = \bigcup_n H_n$, where H_n is a set of functions from $\Sigma^{l(n)}$ to Σ^n. For two strings $x, y \in \Sigma^{l(n)}$ with $x \neq y$, we say that x

and y collide under $h \in H_n$ or (x, y) is a collision pair for h, if $h(x) = h(y)$. H is polynomial time computable if there is a polynomial time algorithm computing all $h \in H$, and accessible if there is a probabilistic polynomial time algorithm that on input $n \in N$ outputs uniformly at random a description of $h \in H_n$. Let F be a collision finder. F is a probabilistic polynomial time algorithm such that on input $x \in \Sigma^{l(n)}$ and $h \in H_n$ outputs either ? (cannot find) or a string $y \in \Sigma^{l(n)}$ such that $x \neq y$ and $h(x) = h(y)$.

Definition 13 *Let H be a computable and accessible hash function compressing $l(n)$-bit input into n-bit output strings and F a collision string finder. H is a universal one-way hash function if for each F, for each Q and for all sufficiently large n,*

$$Prob\{F(x, h) \neq ?\} < \frac{1}{Q(n)}$$

where $x \in \Sigma^{l(n)}$ and $h \in_r H_n$. The probability is computed over all $h \in_r H_n$, $x \in \Sigma^{l(n)}$ and the random choice of F.

6.2 UOWHF Based on the Strong One-Way Permutation

Theorem 5 *Assume that $m : D \to D$ is a strong one-way permutation, where $D = \bigcup_n \Sigma^n$, and $chop_1 : \Sigma^n \to \Sigma^{n-1}$ simply chops the last bit, then $h = chop_1 \circ m$ is a universal one-way hash function.*

Proof : (By contradiction), assume that there is a probabilistic algorithm F that can find a collision, then we show that we can make an algorithm that can invert m. Consider that we first choose an x at random, then run m on x to get $m(x)$, then we obtain $h(x) = chop_1(m(x))$. There is only one element that can collide with $m(x)$ under $chop_1$. This element differs with $m(x)$ in one bit. Let us notate this element $m(y)$. If a collision finder can find an y such that collides with x under h with probability bigger than $\frac{1}{Q(n)}$, it can obtain y from $m(y)$ with the same probability. This contradicts our assumption that m is a one-way permutation. □

Lemma 7 *If we define $1chop : \Sigma^n \to \Sigma^{n-1}$ simply to chop one bit and the position of chopped bit is defined in the description of the function and can be any bit, then $h = 1chop(m(x))$ is also a universal one-way hash function.*

Proof Sketch: The problem of finding a collision for h, defined in Lemma 7, can be reformulated to finding x, y and $x \neq y$, such that $m(x)$ and $m(y)$ match at all bits except at the one defined in the definition of $1chop$ function. By repeating a procedure similar to the procedure for the proof of Theorem 5 the claim of Lemma can be shown to be true. □

Since according to Corollary 3 and Corollary 4 the output of m is distributed uniformly and randomly in Σ^n, then for finding y with exhaustive search, we need to perform 2^{n-1} operations on the average. If this much computation is bigger than 2^k, then it is infeasible to find the collision.

If we chop t bits of $m(x)$, then there are $(2^t - 1)$ elements which collide with x under h. If these elements are distributed randomly in 2^n elements; then, we need to do 2^{n-t} search operations to find a collision for x. Since our computational resource can do at most 2^k search operations then t should be less than $n - k$.

Corollary 5 *Let* $\text{chop}_t : \Sigma^n \to \Sigma^{n-t}$ *simply to chop t last bits and* $t < n - k$, *then* $h = \text{chop}_t \circ m$ *is a universal one-way hash function.*

Note that the scheme described in the above corollary increases the efficiency of the hash function scheme, so for hashing long messages, we need to do less iterations. We can also generalise the above scheme by introducing *tchop* to be a function which chops t bits of the output. In this case, we need $(n - k - 1) \log_2 n$ bits to specify the positions of the chopped bits.

6.3 Parameterization

Since the hash function presented in Corollary 5 is a universal one-way hash function, we should parameterize it to make it secure in a practical scenario. The parameterization can be done in two different ways:

1. we can parameterize h by selecting v from a family of $k + 1$-bit perfect permutations. Then $H = \{h = \text{chop}_t \circ f \circ v \circ f \mid v \in V_n\}$ where V_n is the $k + 1$-bit perfect permutation family and chop_t simply chops the t last bits.

2. we can parameterize h by selecting the function for the compressing procedure from a family of hash functions. We may consider this family to be a family of *chop* functions. In this case, the number of bits required to specify a member of the family is at most equal to $(n - k - 1) \log_2 n$. However, we may also consider this family to be a family of t to 1 strongly universal hash function as proposed in [22].

6.4 Compressing Arbitrary Length Messages

One of the main properties of hash functions is that they should be applied to any argument of any size. Damgard suggested a design principle in [8] based on fixed size collision free hash functions. Another method has been appeared in [31] and is the dual of Blum-Micali pseudorandom bit generator (let us call it ZMI method). We show that using the perfect one-way permutation proposed in Theorem 4, these two methods actually yield one scheme for hashing long messages.

Damgard's design principle: Let $l(n)$ be a polynomial with $l(n) > n$, let f be a collision free one-way hash function $f : \Sigma^{n+t} \to \Sigma^n$, $\alpha \in_r \Sigma^n$, split $l(n)$-bit message x into t bit blocks, let the blocks be denoted by $x_1, x_2, \ldots, x_{\frac{l(n)}{t}}$. Let

$$y_0 = \alpha$$
$$\vdots$$
$$y_{i+1} = f(y_i \parallel x_{i+1})$$

then $h(x) = y_{\frac{l(n)}{t}}$ would be the hash value of the long message x.

ZMI method: Let f be a one-way permutation $f : \Sigma^{n+t} \to \Sigma^{n+t}$, let $I(n) = (i_1, i_2, \ldots, i_t)$ denote the known simultaneously hard bits of f, let $x = x_t \ldots x_2 x_1 \in \Sigma^t$, $b \in \Sigma^n$, define:

$$\text{ins}_{I(n)}(b, x) = \ldots b_i x_1 b_{i-1} \ldots b_2 b_1$$

Let $z \in \Sigma^{n+t}$, denote by $\text{drop}_{I(n)}(z)$ a function dropping the i_1-th, $\ldots$, i_t-th bits of z. Let l be a polynomial with $l(n) > n$, $\alpha \in \Sigma^n$, split $l(n)$-bit message x into t bit blocks be denoted by

$x_1, x_2, \ldots, x_{\frac{l(n)}{t}}$, where $x_i \in \Sigma^t$ for each $1 \leq i \leq \frac{l(n)}{t}$. Let h be the function from $\Sigma^{l(n)}$ to Σ^n defined by:

$$y_0 = \alpha$$
$$y_1 = \text{drop}_{I(n)}(f(\text{ins}_{I(n)}(y_0, x_{\frac{l(n)}{t}})))$$
$$\vdots$$
$$y_i = \text{drop}_{I(n)}(f(\text{ins}_{I(n)}(y_{i-1}, x_{\frac{l(n)}{t}-i+1})))$$

then $h(x) = y_{\frac{l(n)}{t}} = \text{drop}_{I(n)}(f(\text{ins}_{I(n)}(y_{\frac{l(n)}{t}-1}, x_1)))$. (In the original ZMI scheme $h(x) = f(\text{ins}_{I(n)}(y_{\frac{l(n)}{t}-1}, x_1))$). If we use the strong one-way permutation m in ZMI scheme for f, since the t least significant bits are simultaneously hard bits, then $\text{drop}_{I(n)}$ function performs identically to the chop_t function defined in Corollary 5. So, $\text{drop}_{I(n)}(f(x))$ in ZMI method would be identical to $\text{chop}_t(m(x))$ of Corollary 5, which is a universal one-way hash function from Σ^{n+t} to Σ^n. On the other hand, when t last bits of a function are simultaneously hard bits, then $\text{ins}_{I(n)}(y_0, x_{\frac{l(n)}{t}})$ would yield the same result as $(y_0 \parallel x_{\frac{l(n)}{t}})$. So, practicing the strong one-way permutation with ZMI scheme, would yield the same result as either practicing the one-way hash function proposed in Corollary 5 with Damgard's design principle, when the message blocks are fed in a similar order.

7 A Single construction for PBG and UOWHF

Each iteration of the pseudorandom bit generator presented in Theorem 5 is identical to the hash function presented in Corollary 5. Assume that we have a computational resource for at most $k=63$ bits. For the construction of the PBG of Theorem 5, an algorithm should extract at most $n - k - 1$ bits, and throw away at least $k + 1$ bits on each iteration. On the other hand, for the construction of the one-way hash function according to Corollary 5, we may chop at most $n - k - 1$ bits, and leave $k + 1$ bits as the hash value. If we choose $k < t < n - k$, for example for $n = 512$ we choose $64 \leq t \leq 448$, then the algorithm can be used both for pseudorandom bit generation and universal one-way hashing.

8 Conclusions and Extensions

1. We constructed a strong permutation with a $k+1$-bit perfect permutation, namely a complete permutation whose $k + 1$ output bits are independent. A $k + 1$-bit perfect permutation can be constructed easily as follows:

$$v(x) = c(x) \oplus PBG_{k+1}(x_l, \ldots, x_1)$$

where $x \in \Sigma^n$, and $c(x)$ is a complete permutation, and $PBG_{k+1}(x_l, \ldots, x_1)$ denotes $k + 1$ output bits of a pseudorandom bit generator where the seed is $l > k$ bits of the x. Then, we constructed a UOWHF and also an efficient pseudorandom bit generator with the strong permutation. This confirms Naor and Yung's conjecture [22] that if pseudorandom bit generators exist then UOWHF exist.

2. For the construction of the strong permutation we assumed that the position of $k + 1$ hard bits of the one-way function f complies with $k + 1$ independent bits of v. The following generalisation can easily be shown to be true.

If v is a perfect permutation then $m = f \circ v \circ f$ is a strong one-way permutation, where f is a one way permutation.

In other words, there is no need to know the exact positions of hard bits of f. As we mentioned earlier, the running time of a perfect permutation based on DES structure for large enough n, e.g., $n=512$, is rather big.

A reasonable question is whether we can apply some simpler mathematical functions or a compositions of such functions for v, for example $y = (a_i x)^3 \bmod m$, and/or $y = (ax + b) \bmod m$.

ACKNOWLEDGMENT

We would like to thank the members of the CCSR for their support and assistance during the preparation of this work.

References

[1] Selim G. Akl. On the security of compressed encoding. In *Advances in Cryptology - CRYPTO '83*, pages 209–230. Plenum Publishing Corporation, 1983.

[2] W. Alexi, B. Chor, O. Goldreich, and C. P. Schnorr. RSA and Rabin functions: Certain parts are as hard as the whole. *SIAM Journal on Computing*, 17(2):194–209, 1988.

[3] M. Blum and S. Micali. How to generate cryptographically strong sequences of pseudo-random bits. *SIAM Journal on Computing*, 13(4):850–864, 1984.

[4] L. Brown. A proposed design for an extended DES. In *Computer Security in the Age of Information*. North-Holland, 1989. Proceedings of the Fifth IFIP International Conference on computer Security, IFIP/Sec '88.

[5] J. L. Carter and M. N. Wegman. Universal classes of hash functions. *Journal of Computer and System Sciences*, 18:143–154, 1979.

[6] D. Coppersmith. Analysis of ISO/CCITT Document X.509 Annex D, 1989.

[7] I. B. Damgard. Collision free hash functions and public key signature schemes. In *Advances in Cryptology - EUROCRYPT '87*, volume 304 of *Lecture Notes in Computer Science*, pages 203–216. Springer-Verlag, 1987.

[8] I. B. Damgard. A design principle for hash functions. In *Advances in Cryptology - CRYPTO '89*, volume 435 of *Lecture Notes in Computer Science*, pages 416–427. Springer-Verlag, 1989.

[9] D. E. Denning. Digital signatures with RSA and other public-key cryptosystems. *Communications of the ACM*, 27(4):388–392, 1984.

[10] M. Girault. Hash-functions using modulo-n operations. In *Advances in Cryptology - EUROCRYPT '87*, volume 304 of *Lecture Notes in Computer Science*, pages 218–226. Springer-Verlag, 1987.

[11] O. Goldreich, S. Goldwasser, and S. Micali. How to construct random functions. *Journal of the ACM*, 33(4):792–807, 1986.

[12] O. Goldreich and L. A. Levin. A hard-core predicate for all one-way functions. In *the 21st ACM Symposium on Theory of Computing*, pages 25–32, 1989.

[13] R. Impagliazzo, L. A. Levin, and M. Luby. Pseudo-random generation from one-way functions. In *the 21st ACM Symposium on Theory of Computing*, pages 12–24, 1989.

[14] W. De Jonge and D. Chaum. Attacks on some RSA signatures. In *Advances in Cryptology - CRYPTO '85*, volume 218 of *Lecture Notes in Computer Science*, pages 18–27. Springer-Verlag, 1985.

[15] W. De Jonge and D. Chaum. Some variations on RSA signatures and their security. In *Advances in Cryptology - CRYPTO '86*, volume 263 of *Lecture Notes in Computer Science*, pages 49–59. Springer-Verlag, 1986.

[16] R. R. Jueneman. Electronic document authentication. *IEEE Network Magazine*, 1(2):17–23, 1987.

[17] J. B. Kam and G. I. Davida. Structured design of substitution-permutation encryption networks. *IEEE Transactions on Computers*, 28(10):747–753, 1979.

[18] S. M. Matyas, C. H. Meyer, and J. Oseas. Generating strong one-way functions with cryptographic algorithm. *IBM Technical Disclosure Bulletin*, 27(10A):5658–5659, 1985.

[19] R. C. Merkle. One way hash functions and DES. In *Advances in Cryptology - CRYPTO '89*, volume 435 of *Lecture Notes in Computer Science*, pages 428–446. Springer-Verlag, 1989.

[20] S. Miyaguchi, K. Ohta, and M. Iwata. Confirmation that some hash functions are not collision free. In *Abstracts of EUROCRYPT '90*, pages 293–308, 1990.

[21] J. H. Moore. Protocol failures in cryptosystems. *Proceedings of the IEEE*, 76(5):594–601, 1988.

[22] Moni Naor and Moti Yung. Universal one-way hash functions and their cryptographic applications. In *the 21st ACM Symposium on Theory of Computing*, pages 33–43, 1989.

[23] J. Quisquater and M. Girault. 2n-bit hash functions using n-bit symmetric block cipher algorithms. In *Abstracts of EUROCRYPT '89*, 1989.

[24] J. Rompel. One-way functions are necessary and sufficient for secure signatures. In *the 22nd ACM Symposium on Theory of Computing*, pages 387–394, 1990.

[25] A. De Santis and M. Yung. On the design of provably-secure cryptographic hash functions. In *Abstracts of EUROCRYPT '90*, pages 377–397, 1990.

[26] A. F. Webster and S. E. Tavares. On the design of S-boxes. In *Advances in Cryptology - CRYPTO '85*, Lecture Notes in Computer Science, pages 523–534. Springer-Verlag, 1985.

[27] M. N. Wegman and J. L. Carter. New hash functions and their use in authentication and set equality. *Journal of Computer and System Sciences*, 22:265–279, 1981.

[28] R. S. Winternitz. Producing a one-way hash function from DES. In *Advances in Cryptology - CRYPTO '83*, pages 203–207. Plenum Publishing Corporation, 1983.

[29] R. S. Winternitz. A secure one-way hash function built from DES. In *the 1984 IEEE Symposium on Security and Privacy*, 1984.

[30] A. C. Yao. Theory and applications of trapdoor functions. In *the 23rd IEEE Symposium on the Foundations of Computer Science*, pages 80–91, 1982.

[31] Y. Zheng, T. Matsumoto, and H. Imai. Duality between Two Cryptographic Primitives. In *the 8-th International Conference on Applied Algebra, Algebraic Algorithms and Error Correcting Codes*, page 15, 1990.

[32] Y. Zheng, T. Matsumoto, and H. Imai. Structural properties of one-way hash-functions. In *CRYPTO '90*, pages 263–280, 1990.

ESIGN: An Efficient Digital Signature Implementation for Smart Cards

Atsushi Fujioka   Tatsuaki Okamoto   Shoji Miyaguchi

NTT Laboratories
Nippon Telegraph and Telephone Corporation
1-2356, Take, Yokosuka-shi, Kanagawa-ken, 238-03 Japan

Abstract

ESIGN is an efficient digital signature algorithm [OkS, Ok], whose computation speed is more than twenty times faster than that of the RSA scheme, while its key length and signature length are comparable to those of the RSA scheme. This paper presents a software implementation of ESIGN on an 8bit micro-processor smart card. This realizes a computation time for signature generation of about 0.2 seconds. To achieve this remarkable speed for signature generation, appropriate implementation techniques such as pre-computation and table look-up techniques are effectively used. Moreover, this software implementation is compact enough for smart cards; the program size and the data size including the work area are at most 3Kbytes each. Practical identification schemes based on ESIGN are also presented.

1   Introduction

Recently, smart cards are the basis of many services such as prepaid cards, banking cards, and credit cards. In these applications, the integrity and authenticity of digital messages and documents are often required to be ensured by digital information in place of manual signatures written on paper documents. These functions can usually be achieved through the use of *digital signatures*, and they should be implemented through software.

Many digital signature schemes have been developed since Diffie and Hellman's seminal paper on public key cryptosystems [DH] was presented in 1976. Among these schemes, the RSA scheme [RSA] and the Fiat-Shamir signature scheme [FS] are the most respected schemes from the practical viewpoint. However, the RSA scheme has the disadvantage of very low processing speed. Usually a specific hardware chip is needed to perform the RSA function [Br]. If the RSA scheme is implemented in software on an 8bit microprocessor smart card, one complete cycle takes at least several minutes. On the other hand, although the Fiat-Shamir signature scheme is more efficient than the RSA scheme, signature generation still takes more than several seconds with a software implementation on an 8bit microprocessor smart card, even if the fast implementation technique introduced by [OnS] is used*. Moreover, the Fiat-Shamir scheme involves a trade-off between signature size and key size, and their product is relatively large. For example, when the key size equals that of the RSA scheme, then the signature size is at least seventy times as long as that of the RSA scheme[†]. Although a modified scheme which overcomes this trade-off problem has been proposed [GQ, OhO], it is somewhat slower than the original scheme.

In 1985, Okamoto *et al.* proposed a fast signature scheme based on polynomial operations [OkS]. The new scheme had significantly better efficiency. It is much (e.g., more than twenty times even with unsophisticated implementation) faster than the RSA scheme, and its key and signature lengths are comparable to those of the RSA scheme. Many versions of this signature scheme were suggested in [Ok], and, hereafter, we will simply call the most typical of them ESIGN (**Section 2**).

In this paper, we report the remarkable performance of our software implementation of ESIGN on an 8bit microprocessor smart card. In our implementation, a pre-computation technique plays an essential role in increasing the speed of signature generation. In addition, residue and division operations by the table look-up method utilizing the EEPROM area is also a key technique in our implementation. By utilizing both techniques, the computation time for signature generation is just about 0.2 seconds (effectively instantaneous for humans)[‡]. Thus we can ignore the time taken for signature generation in almost all smart card applications.

As for identification schemes, the Fiat-Shamir identification [FS] scheme is currently

---

*It seems to take more than 20 seconds in the implementation of [Kno], because roughly the Fiat-Shamir *signature* scheme is more than three times slower than the Fiat-Shamir *identification* scheme, which is reported to take about 6 seconds.

†Note that the trade-off level of the Fiat-Shamir *identification* scheme is often less than that of the signature scheme, because identification is done under real-time circumstances.

‡Note that in this estimation we select parameters offering a security level equivalent to that of the RSA scheme with a 64byte (512bit) composite modulus.

the most promising. In this paper, we also introduce practical identification schemes based on ESIGN, which are at least as efficient as the Fiat-Shamir identification scheme.

2 ESIGN

2.1 Notations

Z_n denotes the set of numbers between 0 and $n-1$, and Z_n^* denotes the set of numbers between 0 and $n-1$ which are relatively prime to n. $\lceil M \rceil$ denotes the least integer which is larger than or equal to M. $\lfloor M \rfloor$ denotes the greatest integer which is less than or equal to M. $x \equiv y \pmod{n}$ denotes that n divides $x - y$. $f(x) \bmod n$ denotes an integer such that n divides $f(x) - (f(x) \bmod n)$ and $f(x) \bmod n \in Z_n$. $x/y \bmod n$ denotes an integer such that n divides $x - y(x/y \bmod n)$ and $x/y \bmod n \in Z_n$. $|X|_b$ denotes $\lceil \log_b X \rceil$. In other words, $|X|_2$ denotes the bit size of X, and $|X|_{64}$ denotes the byte size of X. $a\|b$ denotes the concatenation of a and b.

2.2 Procedures

- *Keys, message and signature:*

    o *Secret key:*   large prime numbers P, Q $(P > Q)$.

    o *Public key:*   positive integers $N = P^2 Q$.

    o *Message:*   a positive integer M.

    o *Signature:*   an integer $S \in Z_N^*$.

- *Key generation:*

    o When originator A joins the system, he generates the secret and public keys and publishes the public key. The secret key is known only to A.

- *Signature generation:*

    o A signature S of a message M is computed by originator A as follows:

    * Pick a random number $X \in Z_{PQ}^*$.
    * Compute S such that

    $$W = \left\lceil \frac{H(M) - (X^K \bmod N)}{PQ} \right\rceil,$$

    $$Y = W/(KX^{K-1}) \bmod P,$$

$$S = X + YPQ,$$

where H is a one-way hash function ($H(M) \in Z_N$ for any positive integer M), K is an integer ($K \geq 4$). Function H and parameter K can be fixed in the system.

- *Signature sending:*

  o After generating the signature S, originator A sends message M along with S to receiver B, who verifies it.

- *Signature verification:*

  o The signature message (S, M) is considered valid if the following verification inequality holds.

$$H(M) \leq S^K \bmod N < H(M) + 2^{2 \cdot |N|_2 / 3}.$$

2.3 Security of ESIGN

The quadratic version (parameter K is 2) was broken by Brickell and DeLaurentis in 1985 ([Ok], page 49), several months after this signature scheme was presented [OkS]. However, no attack on the higher degree versions (K is more than 3) has been reported in the last 5 years, although many excellent researchers such as Brickell, Girault, Shamir, and Vallée attempted this ([Ok], pp.49-50). We conjecture that to break our higher degree version (ESIGN) is as hard as factoring N ([Ok] p.52).

3 Implementation on Smart Cards

3.1 Preparation

To implement ESIGN on a smart card, we must determine the parameters carefully because a smart card doesn't have high processing speed or much memory.

In our implementation, K is chosen as a power of 2, i.e., 4, 8, 16, and so on. Our implementation target consists of the following steps:

- $X \in Z_{PQ}^*$,

- $F = X^K \bmod N$,

- $W = \left\lceil \dfrac{H(M) - F}{PQ} \right\rceil$,

- $G = KX^{K-1} \bmod P,$

- $Y = W/G \bmod P,$

- $S = X + YPQ.$

We choose 16, 24, 32, and 40bytes as the lengths of prime P in order to appraise the performance of ESIGN on a smart card.

Our software implementation works on a smart card with 8bit microprocessor that has clock cycle of 5MHz. The memory area consists of 384bytes RAM, 10Kbytes ROM and 8Kbytes EEPROM.

Our implementation is not straightforward. The residue and division operations take more time than addition or multiplication. Therefore, we developed an iterated table look-up method to reduce the processing time of the residue and division operations. In addition, the signature generation procedure of ESIGN has the good property that it contains some computations that do not depend on the message to be signed. Hence, when a smart card is idling, it can do pre-computation and store the computation value, to generate a signature later. This is based on the same idea as "on-line/off-line digital signatures" [EGM].

In the following subsections, we will discuss the table look-up method and pre-computation. Finally proposed implementation is appraised.

3.2 Hash Functions

We can use any secure hash function H for implementing ESIGN [Da]. In our implementation, we adopt the hash function named N-Hash [MOI] because of the compactness of its program and high execution speed. That is, the program size is about 300bytes (to be stored in ROM), and the execution speed is about 150Kbps (bits per second) in our smart card implementation, which implies that $H(M)$ can be computed within 0.06 seconds when the size of M is about 1Kbytes.

3.3 Iterated Table Look-up Method

Residue and division operations take much more processing time than addition or multiplication. To increase the computation speed of residue and division operations, several table look-up methods have been presented [KH]. However, these methods need a large amount of memory for storing the table, therefore, they are not suitable for typical smart card implementations. This subsection introduces a new table look-up method for these operations, in which all primitive operations are performed on

8bit words. It is suitable for smart card implementation, because our method needs only 9 values in the table and is based on 8bit word primitive operations for 8bit microprocessors of smart cards.

In ESIGN, residue and division operation are performed in the following steps:

- $F = X^K \bmod N$,

- $W = \left\lceil \dfrac{H(M) - F}{PQ} \right\rceil$,

- $G = KX^{K-1} \bmod P$,

- $T = 1/G \bmod P$.

In these steps, modulus P and N are fixed numbers for the smart card, and the divider PQ is also a fixed number. The residue table is stored in EEPROM.

Our residue table regarding modulus N consists of 9 one-bit-shifted numbers of a modulus, $N_1, \ldots, N_9$, such that $N_i = N \cdot 2^{z(N)+9-i}$, $|N_i|_2 = |N|_2 + 8$, $(i = 1, \ldots, 9)$, where $z(N)$ means the number of zeros succeeding the most significant bit of N.

For example, if the modulus number N is 11011010 00001001 (DA09 in hexadecimal), then the residue table consists of

N_1	11011010 00001001 00000000	DA0900
N_2	01101101 00000100 10000000	6D0480
N_3	00110110 10000010 01000000	368240
N_4	00011011 01000001 00100000	1B4120
N_5	00001101 10100000 10010000	0DA090
N_6	00000110 11010000 01001000	06D048
N_7	00000011 01101000 00100100	036824
N_8	00000001 10110100 00010010	01B412
N_9	00000000 11011010 00001001	00DA09 $\quad (= N)$.

This residue table can be constructed when the smart card is issued, because the values of P, Q and N are fixed when the card is issued.

The residue algorithm using the residue table is as follows;

Algorithm MOD :

Input B and N

Output $A = B \bmod N$

Step 1 Compare the length of B and N.

  Step 1-1 if $|B|_2 < |N|_2$ then output B as A.

  Step 1-2 if $|B|_2 = |N|_2$ then go to **Step 2**.

Step 1-3 Search i such that the first byte of N_i is greater than the first byte of B.

Step 1-4 Compute $B := B - N_i 2^{|B|_2 - |N_i|_2}$.

Step 1-5 Return **Step 1**.

Step 2 Compare B and N.

Step 2-1 if $B < N$ then output B as A.

Step 2-2 Compute $B := B - N$.

Step 2-3 Return **Step 2**.

3.4 Pre-computation

In this subsection, we will show the other technique for speeding up signature generation.

The signature generation procedure of ESIGN contains some computations independent of the message to be signed. Hence, these steps can be carried out before receiving a message to be signed. This technique dramatically reduces the processing time for signature generation.

The below steps are computed in the *pre-computation phase*.

- $X \in_R Z_{PQ}^*$,

- $F = X^K \bmod N$,

- $G = K X^{K-1} \bmod P$,

- $T = 1/G \bmod P$.

The steps which depend on M are as follows (in other words, these steps are computed in the *signature generation phase*):

- $W = \left\lceil \dfrac{H(M) - F}{PQ} \right\rceil$,

- $Y = WT \bmod P$,

- $S = X + YPQ$.

After the pre-computation, triplet (X, F, T) is stored in EEPROM. When message M is input, only three steps (computing W, Y, S) are needed to generate signature S. Note that each triplet (X, F, T) is used for each signature S.

Clearly, the pre-computation phase including the power and inversion operations is much more computationally demanding than the signature generation phase, which consists of only addition, multiplication and division operations.

3.5 Performance

This subsection introduces the experimental data of our implementation of ESIGN.

Table. 1 shows the memory size of the program and data area. This table was estimated assuming $|P|_{64} = 32$ (P's size is 32bytes), or $|N|_{64} = 96$. This sizes of P and N guarantee that the degree of security of our digital signature scheme is comparable to that of the RSA scheme with 64byte (512bit) modulus, assuming that the security of our scheme and the RSA scheme only depend on factoring each modulus (or N in our scheme). This table shows that our implementation satisfies the memory restriction of a typical smart card.

Table 1: Required memory size for ESIGN

Memory Area	Required Memory Size
RAM (bytes)	352
ROM (bytes)	2,882
EEPROM	
P (bytes)	32
Residue Table of P (bytes)	297
PQ (bytes)	64
Residue Table of PQ (bytes)	585
N (bytes)	96
Residue Table of N (bytes)	873
X, F, T (bytes)	192
Total (bytes)	2,139

Table. 2 lists the processing speeds, when $K = 4^{\S}$. When the size of P is 32bytes, the running time of pre-computation is just under 4 seconds. Therefore, a smart card can do pre-computation easily in any idling time such as a time waiting for a message to be input. Then, the digital signature can be generated within 0.2 seconds.

Note that signature verification is also fast (about 2 seconds); fast enough for most applications, although verification is usually executed in centers and terminals, not in smart cards.

---

§The recommended values of K are 4, 8, 16, 32, 64, and 128. When parameter K is one of these recommended values, the computation times for signature generation and pre-computation are at most twice as much as those of $K = 4$.

Our implementation uses a straightforward algorithm (or standard extended Euclidean algorithm) for computing the modular division (computing T from G and P). If we use a more efficient algorithm (e.g., [Knu], algorithm L and B, pp.321-339), then the speed of pre-computation will increase a few times, although the program size may increase.

Table 2: Performance of ESIGN

$|P|_{64}$	16	24	32	40
Card Issuing (sec)	0.02	0.04	0.07	0.10
Pre-Computation (sec)	0.67	1.86	3.88	7.28
Generating Signature (sec)	0.04	0.09	0.18	0.24
Verifying Signature (sec)	0.45	0.98	2.05	2.50

4 Identification Schemes

This section introduces two practical identification schemes based on ESIGN, which are at least as efficient as the Fiat-Shamir identification scheme [FS]. The two schemes are the three round version and the two round version. We omit the description of the identity-based versions [Sh] of these identification schemes, because we can easily modify these public-key file versions into the identity-based versions by using Kohnfelder's idea [De].

(1) Identification Scheme 1 (*three* round version)

Protocol:

Step 1 (Key generation and registration) Prover P generates ESIGN's secret key, p_P, q_P, and public key, n_P, and publishes the public key with his name.

Step 2 Prover P generates random numbers r, u, and calculates $x = f(r\|u)$, where f is a one-way function. P sends x to verifier V.

Step 3 V generates random number y and sends y to P.

Step 4 P calculates $m = r \oplus y$. P generates ESIGN's signature s of m using P's secret key, and sends (s, r, u) to V.

Step 5 V checks whether $x = f(r\|u)$ holds and whether s is a valid signature of m using P's public key.

(2) Identification Scheme 2 (*two* round version)

Protocol:

Step 1 (Key generation and registration) Same as **Step 1** of Scheme 1.

Step 2 V generates random number r and sends y to P.

Step 3 P generates random number u and calculates $m = f(r\|u)$. P generates ESIGN's signature s of m using P's secret key, and sends (s, u) to V.

Step 4 V checks whether $m = f(r\|u)$ holds and whether s is a valid signature of m using P's public key.

5   Conclusion

We have presented a practical digital signature implementation scheme for smart cards. We have shown that the signature generation time is just about 0.2 seconds. This is achieved using pre-computation and table look-up techniques. The required memory size is small enough for smart card implementation. The program size and the data size including the work area are at most 3Kbytes each.

Thus, we can conclude that our smart card digital signature scheme can be put to practical use, from the viewpoints of processing time and the required memory size.

Acknowledgment

The authors wish to thank Masahiko Iwata for his basic idea of the table look-up method.

References

[Br] E. F. Brickell, "A Survey of Hardware Implementation of RSA", in *Advances in Cryptology — CRYPTO '89*, Lecture Notes in Computer Science 435, Springer–Verlag, Berlin, pp.368–370 (1990).

[Da] D. W. Davies, "Applying the RSA Digital Signature to Electronic Mail", *Computer*, Vol.16, No.2, pp.55–62 (Feb., 1983).

[De] D. E. Denning, *Cryptography and Data Security*, Addison-Wesley, pp.170 (1982).

[DH] W. Diffie and M. E. Hellman, "New Directions in Cryptography", *IEEE Transactions on Information Theory*, Vol.IT-22, No.6, pp.644–654 (Nov., 1976).

[EGM] S. Even, O. Goldreich, and S. Micali, "On-line/Off-line Digital Signatures", in *Advances in Cryptology — CRYPTO '89*, Lecture Notes in Computer Science 435, Springer–Verlag, Berlin, pp.263–275 (1990).

[FS] A. Fiat and A. Shamir, "How to Prove Yourself: Practical Solutions to Identification and Signature Problems", in *Advances in Cryptology — CRYPTO '86*, Lecture Notes in Computer Science 263, Springer–Verlag, Berlin, pp.186–194 (1987).

[GQ] L. C. Guillou and J. J. Quisquater, "A Practical Zero-Knowledge Protocol Fitted to Security Microprocessors Minimizing both Transmission and Memory", in *Advances in Cryptology — EUROCRYPT '88*, Lecture Notes in Computer Science 330, Springer–Verlag, Berlin, pp.123–128 (1988).

[KH] S. Kawamura and K. Hirano, "A Fast Modular Arithmetic Algorithm Using a Residue Table", in *Advances in Cryptology — EUROCRYPT '88*, Lecture Notes in Computer Science 330, Springer–Verlag, Berlin, pp.246–250 (1988).

[Kno] H. Knobloch, "A Smart Card Implementation of the Fiat-Shamir Identification Scheme", in *Advances in Cryptology — EUROCRYPT '88*, Lecture Notes in Computer Science 330, Springer–Verlag, Berlin, pp.87–95 (1988).

[Knu] D. E. Knuth, *The Art of Computer Programming* 2nd Edition, Vol.2, *Semi-Numerical Algorithms*. Reading, Massachusetts: Addison-Wesley (1981).

[MOI] S. Miyaguchi, K. Ohta, and M. Iwata, "A 128-bit Hash Function (N-Hash)", *Proceedings of SECURICOM'90*, pp.123–137 (Mar., 1990).

[OhO] K. Ohta and T. Okamoto, "A Modification of the Fiat-Shamir Scheme", in *Advances in Cryptology — CRYPTO '88*, Lecture Notes in Computer Science 403, Springer–Verlag, Berlin, pp.232–243 (1990).

[Ok] T. Okamoto, "A Fast Signature Scheme Based on Congruential Polynomial Operations", *IEEE Transactions on Information Theory*, Vol.IT-36, No.1, pp.47–53 (Jan., 1990).

[OkS] T. Okamoto and A. Shiraishi, "A Digital Signature Scheme Based on Quadratic Inequalities", *Proceeding of Symposium on Security and Privacy*, IEEE, pp.123–132 (Apr., 1985).

[OnS] H. Ong and C. P. Schnorr, "A Fast Signature Generation with the Fiat-Shamir Scheme", in *Advances in Cryptology — EUROCRYPT '90*, Lecture Notes in Computer Science 473, Springer–Verlag, Berlin, pp.432–440 (1991).

[RSA] R. Rivest, A. Shamir, and L. Adleman, "A Method for Obtaining Digital Signatures and Public-Key Cryptosystems", *Communications of the ACM*, Vol.21, No.2, pp.120–126 (Feb., 1978).

[Sh] A. Shamir, "Identity-based Cryptosystems and Signature Schemes", *Advances in Cryptology — CRYPTO '84*, Lecture Notes in Computer Science 196, Springer–Verlag, Berlin, pp.47–53 (1985).

New Approaches to the Design
of Self-Synchronizing Stream Ciphers[1]

Ueli M. Maurer

Department of Computer Science
Princeton University
Princeton, NJ 08544

Abstract. Self-synchronizing stream ciphers (SSSC) are a commonly used encryption technique for channels with low bit error rate but for which bit synchronization can present a problem. Most presently used such ciphers are based on a block cipher (e.g. DES) in 1-bit cipher feedback mode. In this paper, several alternative design approaches for SSSCs are proposed that are superior to the design based on a block cipher with respect to encryption speed and potentially also with respect to security. A method for combining several SSSCs is presented that allows to prove that the combined SSSC is at least as secure as any of the component ciphers. The problem of designing SSSCs is contrasted with the problem of designing conventional synchronous additive stream ciphers and it is shown that different security criteria must be applied.

Furthermore, an efficient algorithm is presented for finding a function of low degree that approximates a given Boolean function, if such an approximation exists. Its significance for the cryptographic security of SSSCs and its applications in coding theory are discussed.

1. Introduction

Cryptographic protocols and techniques are often designed under the assumption that the communication channels are error-free. Such protocols can therefore be extremely vulnerable to unexpected errors on the channel. Many existing communication channels introduce some errors because their complete removal by the use of error-correcting codes would be too costly in terms of transmission rate reduction or encoder/decoder complexity. When encryption has

---

[1]This work was supported by Omnisec AG, CH-8105 Regensdorf, Switzerland.

to be built into an existing application on such a channel then no reduction of the data rate can be tolerated and thus no synchronization bits nor redundancy can be introduced for the purpose of error-correction. Therefore the encryption algorithm itself must be designed to be as error-resistant as possible to ensure that errors on the channel result in as little distortion of the deciphered plaintext as possible. For instance, when the channel introduces single bit errors, the optimal solution is to use a (conventional) synchronous additive stream cipher because every bit error in the ciphertext results in only a single bit error in the corresponding deciphered plaintext. This is in contrast to a block cipher in electronic codebook mode where a single bit error destroys the entire corresponding plaintext block. If the channel introduces bit slips (deletion or insertion of bits), however, both synchronous stream ciphers and block ciphers behave catastrophically since loss of synchronization results in a completely erroneous decryption of the entire following ciphertext.

A well-known cryptographic technique (e.g., see [5]) that is resistant against bit slips on the transmission channel (without introducing additional synchronization bits and without using an interactive higher-level protocol for recovering lost synchronization) is the use of a self-synchronizing stream cipher (SSSC for short). Properties and advantages of SSSCs are discussed in Section 2, and in Section 3 a theoretical treatment of SSSCs is given and several new design strategies for SSSCs are presented. The cryptographic security of SSSCs is discussed in Section 4. In Section 5, an efficient algorithm is presented for finding a function of low degree that approximates a given Boolean function, if such an approximation exists, and its significance in cryptography and coding theory is discussed.

2. Self-Synchronizing Stream Ciphers (SSSC)

The basic idea behind an SSSC (see Figure 1 for a canonical representation of an SSSC) is to encipher every plaintext digit using an encryption transformation that depends only on a fixed number M of previous ciphertext digits and on the secret key, but that does not depend on past plaintext digits other than through its dependence on past ciphertext digits. Therefore every ciphertext digit can be deciphered correctly when the previous M ciphertext digits have been received correctly. This self-synchronizing mechanism not only allows to resynchronize after bit slips on the channel, but it also enables the receiver to switch at any time into an ongoing enciphered transmission without knowing the current bit position within the message.

SSSCs are resistant against bit slips but on the other hand are less resistant than synchronous stream ciphers against single bit errors because every bit error in the ciphertext results in an error burst of length M in the deciphered plaintext. Hence SSSCs are suitable only when the bit error rate on the channel is sufficiently small. The trade-off between security and error-propagation is discussed in Section 4.

An alternative synchronization technique for stream ciphers is described in [7]. The running key generator of an ordinary additive stream cipher is reset whenever a given (secret or public) synchronization pattern (of length for example 16 bits) occurs in the ciphertext. The reset state of the generator is different each time since it depends not only on the secret key but also on a certain number of ciphertext bits following the synchronization pattern. For every bit error probability and bit slip probability on the channel, this technique, even when modified so that a set of synchronization patterns rather than a single one triggers resynchronization, can be shown to have no advantages over SSSCs with respect to error-tolerance. Note that an SSSC can be viewed as a special case of this synchronization technique where the length of the synchronization pattern is zero, i.e., the generator is synchronized after every bit.

In addition to the resynchronization feature, SSSCs also offer two advantages over synchronous additive stream and block ciphers from a security point of view. First, the fact that single bit errors in the ciphertext result in error bursts in the plaintext prevents active eavesdroppers from undetectable tampering with the plaintext, thus assuring message authenticity. Note that when a synchronous additive stream cipher is used, plaintext bits can selectively be flipped by flipping the corresponding ciphertext bits. This would for instance allow an enemy to selectively modify the account number of an encrypted financial transaction. The second advantage is that unlike in additive stream ciphers or block ciphers, every plaintext bit influences the entire following ciphertext. Compared to block ciphers which are insecure when the plaintext is strongly redundant, i.e., when some plaintext blocks are likely to occur repeatedly, SSSCs are more resistant against attacks based on plaintext redundancy.

Most presently used SSSCs are based on a block cipher (e.g. DES) in 1-bit cipher feedback mode [13]. This mode is quite inefficient in terms of encryption speed since one block cipher operation is required for enciphering a single plaintext bit. Moreover, the published design criteria, security analysis and cryptanalytic attacks [4] for most block ciphers is restricted to the electronic codebook mode. While some design and security criteria are known for synchronous stream ciphers and block ciphers, only little is known about the design of SSSCs. The major goals of this paper are to narrow this gap and to contrast the problem of designing SSSCs with that of designing conventional synchronous additive stream ciphers.

3. Theoretical Foudations and Design Strategies

Without essential loss of generality, only binary SSSCs are considered in this paper. Let $B = \{0,1\}$. Let $\underline{X} = X_1, X_2, \ldots$, $\underline{Y} = Y_1, Y_2, \ldots$ and $\underline{W} = W_1, W_2, \ldots$ denote the binary plaintext, ciphertext and keystream sequences, respectively, and let Z denote the secret key that is chosen randomly (and uniformly) from the set $\mathcal{Z}$ of possible keys. The encryption transformation can be described by

$$Y_i = X_i \oplus W_i \tag{1}$$

for $i = 1, 2, \ldots$, where every keystream digit W_i depends on the previous M ciphertext digits $Y_{i-M}, \ldots, Y_{i-1}$ and the secret key Z, and where $Y_{-M+1}, \ldots, Y_0$ are predefined constants. Figure 1 shows a canonical representation of an SSSC.

The feedback part of an SSSC is a finite automaton with input the ciphertext sequence $\underline{Y} = Y_1, Y_2, \ldots$, with output the keystream sequence $\underline{W} = W_1, W_2, \ldots$ and with state sequence $\sigma_0, \sigma_1, \sigma_2, \ldots$. It has the special property that the input memory is finite and equal to M, i.e., the state depends only on the previous M input digits and the secret key, but is independent of all other input digits. This automaton is characterized by the state space Σ and the (possibly) key-dependent state-transition and output functions captured in the following definition.

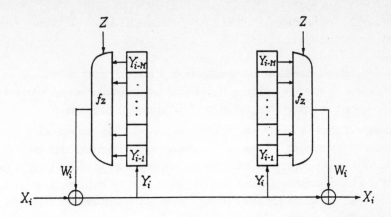

Figure 1: Canonical representation of a self-synchronizing stream cipher as a length M shift-register with a memoryless feedback function.

Definition: A *keyed state-transition function* for state space Σ, with memory M and key space $\mathcal{Z}$ is a family $G_{\mathcal{Z}} = \{g_z : z \in \mathcal{Z}\}$ of functions $g_z : \Sigma \times B \to \Sigma$ such that for all $z \in \mathcal{Z}$, when z is given, $g_z(\sigma, y)$ is easy to compute for all $\sigma \in \Sigma$ and $y \in B$, and such that the corresponding automaton has input memory M. A *keyed output function* for state space Σ and with key space $\mathcal{Z}$ is a family $H_{\mathcal{Z}} = \{h_z : z \in \mathcal{Z}\}$ of functions $h_z : \Sigma \to B$ such that for all $z \in \mathcal{Z}$, when z is given, $h_z(\sigma)$ is easy to compute for all $\sigma \in \Sigma$.

The encryption transformation of an SSSC with state-transition function $G_{\mathcal{Z}} = \{g_z : z \in \mathcal{Z}\}$ and output function $H_{\mathcal{Z}} = \{h_z : z \in \mathcal{Z}\}$, secret key Z and initial state σ_0 is specified by equation (1) and the two equations

$$W_i = h_Z(\sigma_{i-1}) \qquad (2)$$
$$\text{and} \quad \sigma_i = g_Z(\sigma_{i-1}, Y_i) \quad \text{for } i = 1, 2, \ldots. \qquad (3)$$

Every finite automaton with finite input memory M can be represented in a *canonical form* that consists of an input shift-register of length M with an attached memoryless function whose input is the shift-register state. In other words, the encryption transformation specified by equations (1)-(3) can equivalently be described by (1) and

$$W_i = f_Z(Y_{i-1}, \ldots, Y_{i-M}),$$

for $i = 1, 2, \ldots$, where the feedback function f_Z is completely specified by the secret key Z (capital letters denote random variables whereas small letter denote particular values that a random variable can take on), the state-transition function g_Z and the output function h_Z and where $Y_{-M+1}, \ldots, Y_0$ are specified by the secret key and the (for the key Z reachable) initial state σ_0 (see Figure 1). The concept of a memoryless key-dependent function is captured in the following definition.

Definition: A *keyed Boolean function (KBF)* of size M and with key space $\mathcal{Z}$ is a family

$F_{\mathcal{Z}} = \{f_z : z \in \mathcal{Z}\}$ of functions $f_z : B^M \to B$ such that for all $z \in \mathcal{Z}$, when z is given, $f_z(x)$ is easy to compute for all $x \in B^M$.

The above defined canonical representation of a finite-memory automaton assigns a keyed Boolean function $F_{\mathcal{Z}}$ to every pair $(G_{\mathcal{Z}}, H_{\mathcal{Z}})$ of state-transition and output function. The security of an SSSC is determined by the properties of the corresponding KBF $F_{\mathcal{Z}}$.

The design of most presently used SSSCs was motivated by the canonical representation of a finite-memory automaton. These SSSCs consist of a ciphertext shift-register of length M and a memoryless key-dependent function with input the state of the register (see Figure 1). Most often, a block cipher algorithm (e.g. DES) is used for implementing the key-dependent memoryless function, where the block cipher's input is the shift-register state and where all but one of the block cipher output bits are discarded. This mode of using a block cipher is usually referred to as 1-bit cipher feedback mode [13].

Note that in the canonical form, the state-transition function is extremely simple and independent of the secret key. Therefore the security of ciphers based on a block cipher in 1-bit cipher feedback mode relies entirely on the security of the output function. In this paper we suggest to design SSSCs that are based on a cryptographically secure state-transition function as well as on a cryptographically secure output function such that the SSSC is secure unless both functions are simultaneously insecure. In particular, we suggest to choose a state space with cardinality much greater than 2^M where clearly for a given key, at most 2^M states can be reached. The idea is that unlike for the conventional 1-bit cipher feedback mode, it should be infeasible for an enemy knowing the input sequence to even determine the state of the automaton. In addition, it should also be infeasible for an enemy to determine the output of the automaton, even if an oracle provided the (actually hidden) state sequence for free.

A general finite automaton has infinite input memory. In the following we present a method for designing state-transition functions that are guaranteed to correspond to an automaton with finite input memory M. Without essential loss of generality we assume in the following that the state can be represented by $T \geq M$ binary digits, i.e. $\sigma_i = (\sigma_i[1], \ldots, \sigma_i[T])$. Hence $\Sigma = B^T$. For $1 \leq k \leq T$, $\sigma_i[k]$ is a (memoryless) generally key-dependent function of the ciphertext digit Y_i, some of the variables $\sigma_{i-1}[1], \ldots, \sigma_{i-1}[T]$ and the secret key Z, but it is independent of the time i. One can show that there always exists a relabeling of the memory cells such that for $1 \leq k \leq T$, $\sigma_i[k]$ only depends on $\sigma_{i-1}[1], \ldots, \sigma_{i-1}[k-1]$, Y_i and Z and is independent of $\sigma_{i-1}[k], \ldots, \sigma_{i-1}[T]$. The dependence structure of such an automaton A is characterized by a loop-free directed graph G_A with vertex set $V = \{I, \sigma[1], \sigma[2], \ldots, \sigma[T], O\}$ and edge set E, where I and O denote the input and output, respectively. A directed edge from $\sigma[j]$ to $\sigma[k]$ indicates that $\sigma_i[k]$ functionally depends on $\sigma_{i-1}[j]$. Similarly, an edge from I to $\sigma[k]$ indicates that $\sigma_i[k]$ functionally depends on Y_i, and an edge from $\sigma[k]$ to O indicates that W_i depends on $\sigma_{i-1}[k]$. I has no incoming edges and O has no outgoing edges, and there exists no edge from I to O. The memory of A is given by the length of the longest path from I to O and can be determined as $\mu(O)$ where the function μ maps the vertices of G_A to the integers and is defined by $\mu(I) = 0$ and

$$\mu(k) = 1 + \max_{j:(j,k)\in E} \mu(j).$$

For a given dependence structure (i.e., a given matrix G_A), M can efficiently be determined by

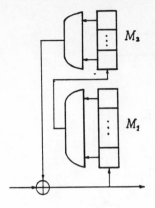 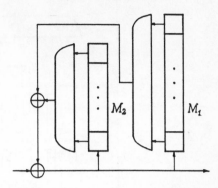

Figure 2: Serial composition (left) and parallel composition (right) of two SSSCs in the canonical form with memories M_1 and M_2, respectively. The serial and parallel compositions are equivalent to SSSCs with memory $M = M_1 + M_2$ and $M = \max(M_1, M_2)$, respectively.

a dynamic program.

An important concept in cryptography is that of composition. In the following we consider two different ways of combining two or more finite automata: parallel and serial composition. By the parallel composition of several automata we mean the automaton that is realized by connecting its input to every of the component automata's inputs and taking as its output the modulo-2 sum of the components' outputs. The memory of the parallel composition is the maximum memory of the component automata. By the serial composition of two automata A_1 and A_2 we mean the automaton whose input is the input of A_1, whose output is the output of A_2 and where the output of A_1 is connected to the input of A_2. The memory of the serial composition of two or more automata is equal to the sum of the component memories. Parallel composition allows to increase the number T of memory cells, i.e., the size of the state space, without increasing the memory. A theorem about the security provided by parallel feedback is stated in the next section. Figure 2 shows the serial and the parallel composition of two SSSCs in the canonical form.

By iterative application of parallel and serial composition, many component SSSCs that are relatively simple in terms of implementation complexity and memory length can be combined to form an SSSC realizing a very complicated keyed Boolean function with desired memory size. One possible architecture for realizing the state-transition function of an SSSC with memory $M = 8L$ and state space of size 2^{2M} using 16 SSSCs of memory length L is shown in Figure 3. The component SSSCs can all be different and can either be realized by a shift-register with a memoryless key-dependent output function or they can themselves be designed as the combination of several smaller component SSSCs. The design of Figure 3 consists of the serial composition of four component SSSCs, each component SSSC consisting of the parallel composi-

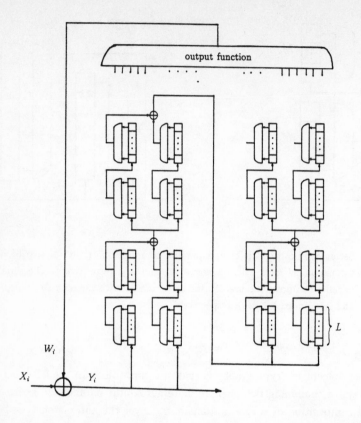

Figure 3: A possible design for the state-transition function of an SSSC by iterative application of serial and parallel composition of component SSSCs.

tion of two further component SSSCs, each of which is the serial composition of two elementary SSSCs with memory L. For instance, L could be 16 such that the resulting SSSC has memory $M = 128$, or L could be as small as 3 such that the resulting SSSC would have a memory of $M = 24$. Such an SSSC would not be secure by itself, but could be used as one component SSSC in the design of Figure 3 such that the finally resulting SSSC has memory $M = 192$. Clearly, the design of Figure 3 is only one example of a vast number of ways several component SSSCs can be combined. It should also be pointed out that only the state transition function is specified by the suggested design and that the output function would have to be some cryptographically secure function of all or part of the state.

The goal of a design strategy similar to the one described above, is to realize a cryptographically secure key-dependent state-transition function having the property that it should be infeasible to determine the state corresponding to a given input sequence. In addition to the potential improvement in cryptographic security compared the conventional design method of using a block cipher in 1-bit cipher feedback mode, another major advantage of the suggested architecture is the very high achievable encryption speed. When such a cipher is implemented in hardware, all the component functions can be evaluated in parallel. The time required for enciphering one plaintext bit is the maximum of the execution times of all the memoryless component functions, including state transition and output functions. These memoryless functions can be realized by tables which could for instance be compiled by a key-dependent precomputation. The most time-consuming component function will usually be the overall output function that is applied to all or at least a substantial part of the state, which can for instance be realized by combining the results of several table lookups.

4. Cryptographic Security of SSSCs

A necessary condition for an SSSC to be secure is that M is sufficiently large such that the probability is negligible that a length M ciphertext pattern is repeated before the secret key is changed. When an enemy can observe two occurrences of the same length M ciphertext pattern he is able to compute the modulo-2 sum of the corresponding two plaintext bits.

For the purpose of determining the minimum memory M required to achieve a certain level of security, assume that the ciphertext can be modeled as a random sequence and moreover, that consecutive (overlapping) ciphertext patterns are independent. The probability $q(N, M)$ that in a sequence of N random binary length M patterns all patterns are distinct is given by

$$q(N, M) = \prod_{i=0}^{N-1} (1 - i2^{-M}).$$

Using the fact that $\ln(1 - x) \approx -x$ for small x we obtain

$$\ln q(N, M) = \sum_{i=0}^{N-1} \ln(1 - i2^{-M}) \approx -2^{-M} \sum_{i=0}^{N-1} i = -N(N - 1)2^{-M-1}.$$

Thus when a probability p of a ciphertext pattern repeating can be tolerated and the expected plaintext length for a given secret key is N, M must be chosen such that $p < 1 - q(N, M) \approx \ln q(N, M)$, hence

$$M > \log_2 \left(\frac{N^2}{p} \right).$$

For example, for $p = 10^{-9}$ and $N = 10^{12}$, one should choose $M \geq 110$. Because bit errors on the channel propagate over the following M deciphered plaintext bits, M should on the other hand be as small as possible. To choose M between 80 and 128 seems to be a reasonable compromise for the tradeoff between security and error performance.

An important observation for SSSCs is that essentially no security can be gained by letting the initial state σ_0 of the finite automaton depend on the secret key because the states $\sigma_M, \sigma_{M+1}, \ldots$ are independent of the initial state and therefore an enemy can simply discard the first M ciphertext bits and attack the cipher based on the remaining ciphertext.

Although no presently-used cipher can rigorously be proved computationally secure, some necessary security criteria are known for synchronous stream ciphers [1, 15]. A synchronous stream cipher is insecure unless the period and the linear complexity of the keystream sequence are sufficiently large. These criteria cannot be applied to SSSCs because there exists no sequence in the encipherment process that is independent of the plaintext and has the property that the SSSC is insecure unless the sequence's period and the linear complexity are large. However, it is shown in Section 4 that a necessary condition for an SSSC to be secure is that the corresponding KBF is (for all but a negligible fraction of the keys) not approximable by a Boolean function of low degree. Considering the limitations of the cryptographic significance of linear complexity for synchronous stream ciphers, this result is somewhat surprising for two reasons. First, the concept of linear complexity looses its original significance when generalized to quadratic or higher order complexity while such a generalization is possible in our case. Second, there exists no known efficient method for cryptanalyzing a synchronous stream cipher whose keystream sequence can only be *approximated* by a sequence with low linear complexity. For SSSCs, only the approximability by a low degree function is required for breaking the cipher. On the other hand, it should be pointed out that while lower bounds on the linear complexity of practical keystream generators can be proved, it seems to be extremely difficult to design SSSCs whose KBF can be proved to have no low degree approximation.

For the purpose of analyzing the security of a cipher it is generally assumed that the enemy cryptanalyst knows the cipher system precisely, but that he has no *a priori* information about the secret key. Moreover, one generally assumes that the enemy is capable of intercepting the ciphertext completely. Regardless of the particular implementation of an SSSC, an enemy can always consider its canonical form, i.e., he can analyze the corresponding KBF. Cryptanalytic attacks against a cipher are usually classified according to the type and amount of information about the plaintext the enemy cryptanalyst is assumed to have available. Commonly considered attacks are ciphertext-only, known-plaintext, chosen-plaintext and chosen-ciphertext attacks. Unlike for block ciphers where a chosen-plaintext attack is in general much more powerful than a known-plaintext attack (see [4]), these two attacks seem for SSSCs to be both equivalent to the enemy seeing certain randomly selected input/output pairs of the SSSCs keyed Boolean function.

The by far most powerful type of attack against an SSSC is the *chosen-ciphertext attack*. It allows an enemy to choose arguments of the KBF as he wishes, except that he is assumed to be unable to choose arguments occurring in the actual ciphertext. The task of cryptanalyzing an SSSC with KBF F_Z and key space Z in a chosen-ciphertext attack is equivalent to the problem of predicting $f_Z(\xi_1), f_Z(\xi_2), \ldots$, where $\xi_1, \xi_2, \ldots \in B^M$ are given and where Z is a randomly and uniformly (from Z) selected secret key, when one can obtain for free the values of $f_Z(\tilde{\xi}_1), f_Z(\tilde{\xi}_2), \ldots$ for arbitrarily chosen $\tilde{\xi}_1, \tilde{\xi}_2, \ldots \in B^M$ such that the two sets $\{\xi_1, \xi_2, \ldots\}$ and $\{\tilde{\xi}_1, \tilde{\xi}_2, \ldots\}$ are disjoint.

The design goal for a cryptographic system is usually to make it secure against the most powerful conceivable attack for the strongest possible definition of security. Not only should it be infeasible for the enemy to determine any useful information about the plaintext or the secret key, but it should even be infeasible to determine any information whatsoever about the system that cannot be computed in an obvious way. It should for instance be infeasible to obtain any information about not obviously accessible intermediate results of the encryption process, even if this seems to be of no help in deriving information about the plaintext. In particular, it should be infeasible to distinguish the ciphertext from a truly random sequence for an appropriate definition of distinguishing.

For SSSCs, one of the strongest conceivable definitions of security is that the corresponding KBF be indistinguishable from a random function. We define a cryptographically secure KBF as follows. Let H_M be the set of 2^{2^M} Boolean functions with M inputs. Consider the following random experiment. Let S be a binary random variable that takes on the values 0 and 1 equally likely. S is assumed to be secret. Let g be a Boolean function with M inputs that is selected randomly from the set H_M when $S = 0$ and that is selected randomly from the set F_Z when $S = 1$.

Definition: A keyed Boolean function F_Z of size M and with key space Z is *cryptographically secure* if it is computationally infeasible to distinguish F_Z from H_M, i.e., to predict S defined above with probability of being correct significantly greater than $1/2$, when an oracle for the function g is available.

This paper is focussed mainly on the practical aspects of designing SSSCs and therefore the definitions are by intention only stated informally for the sake of simplicity. The above definition (as well as other definitions in this paper) could however be further formalized similar to the definition of a pseudorandom function generator (PRFG) introduced by Goldreich, Goldwasser and Micali [6] and Luby and Rackoff [9]. For instance, one could consider a family $\mathcal{F} = \{F_{B^{t(k)}}^k :$ $k = 1, 2, \ldots\}$ of KBFs where for every $k \geq 1, 2, \ldots, F_{B^{t(k)}}^k$ is a KBF of size k with key space $B^{t(k)}$, and where $t(k)$ is an integer-valued key-length function. Such a family $\mathcal{F}$ of KBFs could be defined to be cryptographically secure if there exists no polynomial Q and polynomial-time (in k) algorithm T such that for all sufficiently large k, when given k as an input and when given access to an oracle for g corresponding to the KBF $F_{B^{t(k)}}^k$ as defined above, T can guess S with success probability at least $1/Q(k)$. A KBF could then be shown to be equivalent to a PRFG: A KBF can trivially be obtained from a PRFG by discarding all but one of the output bits and a KBF can be transformed into a PRFG by letting the function argument be the initial state of a feedback shift-register whose feedback function is the KBF, and defining the state of the shift-register after $k - 1$ shifts as the output of the pseudo-random function generator.

The following proposition demonstrates that a cryptocraphically secure SSSC can be transformed into a cryptographically secure synchronous additive stream cipher. This demonstrates that the design strategies presented in this paper have also applications to the design of conventional stream ciphers.

Proposition: *The autonomous finite automaton resulting by feeding the output of a finite automaton realizing a cryptographically secure KBF back to its input, is a pseudo-random number generator.*

The following theorem about the cryptographic security of the parallel composition of SSSCs or, equivalently, the sum of KBFs, can be proved using a similar argument as the one used in [11] for proving that the cascade of several conventional synchronous stream ciphers is at least as secure as the most secure component cipher. The theorem holds for virtually every reasonable definition of distinguishing and under virtually every assumption about the enemy's computational resources and knowledge.

Theorem: *The modulo-2 sum of several keyed Boolean functions with statistically independent keys is at least as difficult to distinguish from a random function as any of the component*

KBFs. Hence the parallel composition of several SSSCs with independent keys is at least as cryptographically secure as any of the component SSSCs.

This theorem suggests to design an SSSC as the parallel combination of two or more SSSCs with independent keys. Each component SSSC can be based on an entirely different design principle. As long as at least one of the component SSSCs is secure, the combined SSSC is provably at least as secure, but intuitively even much more secure. The risk that all design strategies fail simultaneously is much smaller than the risk that each design strategy fails individually.

The goal of designing an SSSC must be to make the corresponding KBF cryptographically secure, i.e., indistinguishable from a random function. The design approaches discussed in this paper try to achieve this goal by designing the state-transition and the output function of the finite automaton *both* to be cryptographically secure.

A state-transition function can be defined to be cryptographically secure if it is infeasible to determine the state for a given length M input sequence, even when an oracle would provide the state for free for any other length M input sequence. Note that for the state-transition function of Figure 3 to be secure against such a hypothetical attack it would have to be improved by introducing additional dependencies between the component SSSCs. The reason is that for every memoryless function with only few inputs, a table realizing the function could be determined by exhaustive search using the above mentioned oracle.

5. Low Degree Approximations for Boolean Functions

Assume that the algebraic normal form of the feedback function $f_z(x_1, \ldots, x_M)$ in an SSSC is of the special form that almost all coefficients are known to be zero, and only few coefficients can possibly be non-zero. Then an enemy who is able to perform a chosen-ciphertext attack can break the cipher since he can determine the coefficients of f by solving a system of linear equations of size the number of potential non-zero coefficients.

Assume now it is only known that there exists a simple function $g(x_1, \ldots, x_M)$ that ϵ-approximates f, i.e., that agrees with f for at least a fraction $1 - \epsilon$ of the 2^M arguments. Knowing g would allow the enemy to determine the plaintext bits with error rate ϵ. When the plaintext is sufficiently redundant, even an error rate of $25 - 30\%$ would allow to determine the plaintext precisely. However, the problem of finding g corresponds to the problem of *approximately* solving a system of linear equations over $GF(2)$, i.e., of finding the solution that satisfies the most equations. This problem is equivalent to the problem of decoding a linear code to the nearest codeword, which is for general linear codes believed to be a very difficult problem. In fact, this problem is NP-complete [2].

However, for certain special types of codes there do exist efficient decoding algorithms. Moreover, a significant step towards decoding general linear codes has recently been announced [8]. Because the codewords in our application have length 2^M and are thus too long to be even only read in feasible time, general decoding algorithms are of no use however. In this section we present a *local decoding algorithm* for certain classes of codes that not only provides necessary security criteria for SSSCs but also has applications in coding theory.

Consider as a first example the problem of determining the best affine approximation

$$g(x_1, \ldots, x_M) \;=\; a_0 + a_1 x_1 + a_2 x_2 + \cdots + a_M x_M$$

to a given function $f(x_1, \ldots, x_M)$. Every coefficient a_i for $1 \leq i \leq M$ can be expressed in many different ways as the sum of two function values. More precisely, a_1 can for every choice of $x_2, \ldots, x_M$ be expressed as $a_1 = g(0, x_2, \ldots, x_M) + g(1, x_2, \ldots, x_M)$ and therefore 2^{M-1} independent estimates of a_1 of the form $f(0, x_2, \ldots, x_M) + f(1, x_2, \ldots, x_M)$ can be obtained. When f agrees with some affine function g for more than $3/4$ of the arguments, a majority decision for the above 2^{M-1} values yields the coefficient a_1. The coefficients $a_2, \ldots, a_M$ can be determined analogously, and a_0 can be determined by a majority decision over all 2^M bits $f(x_1, \ldots, x_M) - a_1 x_1 - \cdots - a_M x_M$.

When only linear rather than affine functions are considered (i.e., $a_0 = 0$), the described procedure can be interpreted as a decoding algorithm for the dual code of a $(2^M - 1, 2^M - M - 1)$ Hamming code [12]. The minimum distance of this code is 2^{M-1} so that only 25% errors are guaranteed to be corrected, but when errors occur randomly and independently, close to 50% errors can be corrected with high probability using the above procedure. Observe that for large M, even when a majority decision is made only from a small subset of the 2^{M-1} terms, this procedure still allows to correct close to 50% errors with high probability. In other words, this code can be decoded with a local decoding procedure that examines only a small fraction of the word to be decoded.

Consider now the more difficult problem of finding the best approximation $g(x_1, \ldots, x_M)$ of degree at most r to a given Boolean function $f(x_1, \ldots, x_M)$. g can be expressed in the algebraic normal form as

$$g(x_1, \ldots, x_M) \;=\; \sum_{S \subseteq \{1, \ldots, M\}: |S| \leq r} a_S \prod_{i \in S} x_i.$$

The sum is over all index sets $S \subseteq \{1, \ldots, M\}$ of cardinality at most r.

One can show that any two Boolean functions of degree at most r differ for at least a fraction 2^{-r} of the arguments. This is equivalent to saying that the minimum distance of an r-th order Reed-Muller code of length 2^M is 2^{M-r} [3]. Hence it is theoretically possible to uniquely determine the best r-th degree approximation g to a given function f provided that it differs in less than a fraction 2^{-r-1} of the function values. For instance, an error rate of up to $1/8$ can be tolerated for finding the best second order approximation.

However, it is completely infeasible to examine all 2^M values of f, and therefore it seems to be infeasible to find an r-th degree approximation when the error rate is not considerably less than 2^{-r-1}. Surprisingly, a solution to this problem exists that is based on a novel local decoding procedure for Reed-Muller codes. Instead of finding several orthogonal expressions for every coefficient individually, we find systems of linear expressions for small subsets of the coefficients that can be solved by the (complete) decoding algorithm for much shorter Reed-Muller codes. We choose sets of $L > r$ variables $\{x_{i_1}, x_{i_2}, \ldots, x_{i_L}\}$ and consider the 2^L values of f for those arguments where the remaining variables take on the value 0. These function values depend solely on the $\sum_{i=0}^{r} \binom{L}{i}$ coefficients of the form $a_{S'}$ for $S' \subseteq \{i_1, \ldots, i_L\}$ and thus a system of 2^L linear expressions for $\sum_{i=0}^{r} \binom{L}{i} < 2^L$ unknowns is obtained or, equivalently, the codeword of an r-th order Reed-Muller code of length 2^L evaluated for the information bits equal to the coefficients with indices in the set $\{i_1, , \ldots, i_L\}$, i.e., the coefficients $a_0, a_{i_1}, \ldots, a_{i_L}, a_{i_1 i_2}, \ldots, a_{i_{L-1} i_L}, a_{i_1 i_2 i_3}, \ldots, a_{i_1, i_2, \ldots, i_L}$. The decoding procedure for Reed-Muller codes that is fast for short codes can thus be used to determine these coefficients correctly when no more than $2^{L-r-1} - 1$ errors are among the 2^L function values.

There exist two somewhat different strategies for repeatedly using this local decoding procedure to determine all coefficients of the approximating function g. A first strategy is to choose sufficiently many sets of L variables such that all coefficients of g appear in at least one of the systems. The problem of choosing the subsets of variables of size L is related to the graph-theoretic problem of covering the edges of a complete hypergraph on M vertices with complete subgraphs on L vertices. The second strategy, in which L must be chosen smaller than in the first strategy in order for the algorithm to be feasible, is to consider all $\binom{M}{L}$ size L sets of variables and to make a majority decision over all obtained solutions for every coefficient. For a coefficient of order s $(0 \leq s \leq r)$ the number of solutions is $\binom{M-s}{L-s}$.

The second strategy suggests a new class of linear error-correcting codes with $\sum_{i=0}^{r} \binom{M}{r}$ information bits and codeword length $\sum_{i=0}^{L} \binom{M}{L}$ for some choices $r < L < M$. The encoding procedure is simply to evaluate the r-degree function of size M defined by the information bits taken as coefficients at all arguments of Hamming weight at most L. The information rate of these codes is much higher than that of the corresponding Reed-Muller codes while their error-resistance is nevertheless comparable to that of Reed-Muller codes. This is true although the minimum distance of the new codes is only

$$d_{\min} = \sum_{i=0}^{L-r} \binom{M-r}{i}$$

compared to 2^{M-L} for the corresponding Reed-Muller code. In other words we propose a decoding procedure for strongly truncated Reed-Mullers codes that is efficient even when decoding (and even encoding) the full length 2^M code is completely infeasible.

6. Conclusions

New approaches to designing self-synchronizing stream ciphers have been presented whose security is based both on a cryptographically-secure state-transition function of the corresponding finite automaton as well as on a cryptographically-secure output function and is argued to be potentially much higher than for the conventional design based or a block cipher in 1-bit cipher feedback mode. Another advantage of the presented design strategy is its suitability for high-speed applications. A necessary condition for an SSSC to be secure is that there exists no function of sufficiently small degree r (e.g. $r \leq 10$) that agrees with the feedback function in at least a fraction $1 - 2^{-r-1}$ of the function values.

Acknowledgements

I am grateful to Dr. P. Schmid and Martin Benninger of Omnisec AG for many helpful discussions and for their generous support, and to Laszlo Lovász and Jim Massey for their comments.

References

[1] H. Beker and F. Piper, *Cipher systems: the protection of communications*, New York, NY: Van Nostrand, 1982.

[2] E.R. Berlekamp, R.J. McEliece and H.C.A. van Tilborg, On the inherent intractability of certain coding problems, *IEEE Transactions on Information Theory*, vol. 24, pp. 384-386, 1978.

[3] R.E. Blahut, *Theory and practice of error control codes*, Reading, MA: Addison-Wesley, 1984.

[4] E. Biham and A. Shamir, Differential analysis of DES-like cryptosystems, presented at CRYPTO'90 (to appear in the proceedings).

[5] D.E.R. Denning, *Cryptography and data security*, Reading, MA: Addison-Wesley, 1982.

[6] O. Goldreich, S. Goldwasser and S. Micali, How to construct random functions, *Journal of the ACM*, vol. 33, no. 4, pp. 792-807, Oct. 1986.

[7] H.-J. Klemenz and W.R. Widmer, Swiss Patent Nr. CH 658 759 A5.

[8] V.I. Korzhik and A.I. Turkin, Cryptanalysis of McEliece's public-key cryptosystem, these proceedings.

[9] M. Luby and C. Rackoff, How to construct pseudorandom permutations from pseudorandom functions, *SIAM Journal on Computing*, vol. 17, no. 2, pp. 373-386, 1988.

[10] J.L. Massey, Shift-register synthesis and BCH decoding, *IEEE Transactions on Information Theory*, vol IT-15, no. 1, pp. 122-127, Jan. 1969.

[11] U.M. Maurer and J.L. Massey, Cascade ciphers: the importance of being first, presented at the 1990 IEEE Int. Symp. on Information Theory, San Diego, CA, Jan. 14-19, 1990 (also submitted to J. of Cryptology).

[12] F.J. MacWilliams and N.J. Sloane, *The theory of error-correcting codes*, Amsterdam: North-Holland, sixth printing, 1988.

[13] National Bureau of Standards, DES modes of operation, Fed. Inform. Proc. Standards Publication 81, Nat. Inform. Service, Springfield, VA, Dec. 1980.

[14] N. Proctor, A self-synchronizing cascaded cipher system with dynamic control of error propagation, *Advances in Cryptology - CRYPTO '84*, Lecture Notes in Computer Science, vol. 196, Berlin: Springer Verlag, pp. 174-190, 1985.

[15] R.A. Rueppel, *Analysis and design of stream ciphers*, Berlin: Springer Verlag, 1986.

Randomized Authentication Systems

Josef Pieprzyk
Reihaneh Safavi-Naini*

Department of Computer Science
University College
University of New South Wales
Australian Defence Force Academy
Canberra, ACT 2600, AUSTRALIA

Department of Mathematic, Statistic and Computing
University of New England
Armidale, NSW 2351, AUSTRALIA

Abstract

In this work, the application of Luby-Rackoff randomizers for authentication purposes is examined. First randomized authentication codes are introduced. In these codes, the assignment of a cryptogram to a given message is done in two stages. In the first, the redundancy is introduced and in the second, the concatenation of several Luby-Rackoff randomizers is used. Next, perfect A-codes are defined. The quality of the authentication codes (A-codes) is measured using the concept of distinguishing circuits. Three A-codes with different redundancy stages are examined and proven that they are perfect if the suitable number of Luby-Rackoff randomizers is used in the second stage of the A-code.

1   Introduction

We are going to consider authentication systems whose quality can be rigorously proven. It is known [8] that randomizers can be applied to construct provably secure cryptosystems. The main quality measurements of such cryptosystems is their indistinguishability from truly random generators ([2], [7]).

We construct a class of authentication systems (codes) that consists of two stages. The first stage introduces redundancy to the message by applying some encoding rule ([3],[4],[5], [6]) while the second stage spreads this redundancy over the whole cryptogram.

To be more precise, we assume that messages are n-bit long and we add the redundancy by concatenating $(m - n)$-bit strings to the message $(m > n)$. The resulting message of length

---

*Support for this project was provided in part by TELECOM Australia under the contract number 7027 and by the Australian Research Council under the reference number A48830241.

m (later we consider the case when $m = 2n$) is submitted to the second stage which is a randomizer. The resulting cryptogram of length m is transmitted to the receiver over a publicly exposed channel ([5]).

The receiver first recovers the redundant message and next compares the $(m - n)$-bit redundant string to the original one. They accept the messages as authentic only if the two redundant strings are the same.

2 Preliminaries

Let $I_n = \{0, 1\}^n$ be the set of all 2^n binary strings of length n and let the set $F_{n,m}$ of all functions from I_n to I_m be defined as

$$F_{n,m} = \{f \mid f : I_n \to I_m\}.$$

$F_{n,m}$ consists of 2^{m2^n} elements (we will use F_n for the case $m = n$). In general, $f \in F_{n,m}$ might not have an inverse. In fact if $n > m$ then such an inverse function doesn't exist.

The definition of a generalized function generator can be given similar to that of a function generator (see [1], [2]).

Definition 2.1 *Let $l(n)$ and $m(n)$ be polynomials in n. A generalized function generator with index k of length $l(n)$ is a collection $\mathbf{f} = \{f^{n,m}\}$ where the index k specifies a function $f_k^{n,m} \in f^{n,m}$. For given index $k \in I_{l(n)}$ and $x \in I_n$, the function $f_k^{n,m}(x)$ is computable in polynomial time.*

Also the concept of distinguishing circuit family can be extended to this case:

Definition 2.2 *A distinguishing circuit $C_{n,m}$ for $f^{n,m}$ is an acyclic circuit which consists of Boolean gates (AND, OR, NOT), constant gates ("0" and "1") and r oracle gates ($r < 2^n$). The circuit has one bit output only. Oracle gates accept binary inputs of length n and generate binary outputs of the length m. Each oracle gate is evaluated using some function from the space $F_{n,m}$.*

Definition 2.3 *A family of distinguishing circuits for $\{f^{n,m}\}$ is an infinite sequence of circuits $C_{n_1,m_1}, C_{n_2,m_2}, \cdots (n_1 < n_2 < \cdots)$ such that for two constants c_1 and c_2 and for each pair of parameters n, m, there exists a circuit $C_{n,m}$ which has the following properties:*

- *The size of $C_{n,m}$ is smaller than n^{c_1} (the size is defined as the number of all connections between gates).*

- *Let $Pr[C_{n,m}(F_{n,m})]$ be the probability that the output bit of $C_{n,m}$ is one when a function is randomly and uniformly selected from $F_{n,m}$ and used to evaluate the oracle gates. Let $Pr[C_{n,m}(f^{n,m})]$ be the probability that the output bit of $C_{n,m}$ is one when the oracle gates are evaluated using a function randomly and uniformly selected from $f^{n,m}$ (by random selection of the index k). The probability of distinguishing the truly random function from the one generated by $f^{n,m}$, is*

$$\mid Pr[C_{n,m}(F_{n,m})] - Pr[C_{n,m}(f^{n,m})] \mid \geq \frac{1}{n^{c_2}}$$

We say that a function generator $\{f^{n,m}\}$ does not have a family of distinguishers if for almost all parameters n

$$\mid Pr[C_{n,m}(F_{n,m})] - Pr[C_{n,m}(f^{n,m})] \mid \leq \frac{1}{n^{c_2}} = \frac{p(r)}{2^n}$$

where r is the number of oracle gates in the distinguisher and $p(r)$ is a polynomial in r. A generalized pseudorandom function generator is a generalized function generator that does not have a family of distinguishing circuits.

The construction of a pseudorandom function generator from a cryptographically secure pseudorandom bit generator (CSB) is given in [1] where it is noted that the construction is extendable to generalized pseudorandom function generators.

For a function $f \in F_n$, we can determine a DES-type permutation $D_f \in F_{2n}$ as

$$D_f(L, R) = (R, L \oplus f(R))$$

where L and R are n-bit input strings ($L, R \in I_n$). Having a sequence of functions $f_1, f_2, \cdots, f_i \in F_n$, we can determine the concatenation of their DES-type permutations ψ and

$$\psi(f_1, f_2, \cdots, f_i) = D_{f_i} \circ D_{f_{i-1}} \circ \cdots \circ D_{f_1}$$

Of course, $\psi(f_1, f_2, \cdots, f_i) \in F_{2n}$.

Note that a generator $\psi(f_1, \ldots, f_i)$ (where $f_j \in F_n$ for all $j = 1, 2, \ldots, i$) should be seen as a class of permutations for different parameters $n = 1, 2, 3, \ldots$.

Obviously, the quality of permutation generators $\psi(f_1, \cdots, f_i)$ depends upon the selection of their functions f_j ($1 \leq j \leq i$). Luby and Rackoff [2] showed that $\psi(f, g, h)$ does not have a distinguisher and

$$| Pr[C_{n,n}(F_{2n})] - Pr[C_{n,n}(\psi(f, g, h))] | \leq \frac{r^2}{2^n}$$

where $r \leq 2^n$ is the number of oracle gates in a distinguishing circuit and the functions f, g, h are randomly and uniformly selected from the space F_n i.e. $f, g, h \in_R F_n$. It means that for all possible distinguishing circuits C_{2n} which contain r oracle gates (all statistical tests with the access to r observations of input/output pairs), the probabilities $Pr[C_{2n}(F_{2n})]$, $Pr[C_{2n}(\psi(f, g, h))]$ are very close to each other and their difference can be made as small as required by selecting a large enough parameter n.

The Luby-Rackoff module $\psi(f, g, h)$ can be used in two different ways, as a pseudorandom permutation generator when the three functions f, g, h are pseudorandom (it will be called L-R module), and as a randomizer when f, g, h are randomly and uniformly selected from F_n (it will be called L-R randomizer).

Note that a L-R randomizer no longer constitutes a pseudorandom function generator as the three random functions f, g, h create an index whose length is not polynomial in n. Therefore for a given index and input $x \in I_n$, the output is not computable in polynomial time.

3 Perfect Authentication Codes

3.1 A-Codes

Authentication codes (A-codes) were introduced by Simmons [6] in the study of authentication systems. An A-code $A^{n,m} = \{A_k^{n,m}\}$ is a set of invertible one-to-one functions from I_n to I_m, where each function is indexed by a key k. It is required that if k is known, $A_k^{n,m}(x)$ ($x \in I_n$) can be computed in polynomial time. An A-code can provide security only if $n < m$, i.e., there is redundancy in the system.

There is an attack on authentication systems that is called a spoofing of order T. In this attack, an enemy has intercepted T cryptograms and attempts an impersonation or substitution attack on the system. We say that an A-code provides security of order T (T a polynomial in n) if for infinitely many n, the best strategy of an enemy in the spoofing of order T attack on

$\{A^{n,m}\}$ is random selection with uniform distribution from the set I_m when the T intercepted cryptograms are excluded.

So for security against the spoofing of order T, it is required that the enemy cannot use their knowledge of the T intercepted cryptograms in designing a better strategy. Using a distinguishing circuit family for assessing A-code generators is in fact equivalent to an attack stronger than spoofing, i.e., the attack in which pairs of message/cryptogram are accessible to the enemy. Moreover the distinguishing circuit (the attacker) can choose messages and collect cryptograms from the oracle gates. We assume that the distinguishing circuit computing resources (the attacker's resources) are not polynomially bounded but the number of accessible pairs of message/cryptogram (the number of oracle gates) is limited.

3.2   Randomized A-Codes

We give the construction of randomized A-codes (also called randomized authentication systems). The construction has two stages (see [4]). The first stage introduces redundancy while the second stage serves to diffuse the redundant information over the whole block of cryptogram using the concatenation of several L-R randomizers.

Definition 3.1 *A randomized A-code $\mathcal{A}_n = \{A^{n,2n}\}$ is a family of functions $A^{n,2n} = \{A_k^{n,2n}\} \subset F_{n,2n}$. The assignment of the cryptogram (the output) for a given message (the input) $M \in I_n$, is done in the following two stages:*

- *in the first stage redundancy is introduced into the message $M \in I_n$ by creating the redundant message $M' = (M, \vartheta) \in I_{2n}$ where ϑ is a string of redundant bits added to M;*

- *in the second stage, the message M' is transformed using the concatenation of i ($i = 1, 2, \ldots$) L-R randomizers $\psi(f, g, h)$ ($f, g, h \in_R F_n$). The resulting randomizer is $\Psi_i = \underbrace{\psi \circ \psi \circ \cdots \circ \psi}_{i}$. The random functions f, g, h are a part of the system cryptographic keys and are kept secret (known to the sender and receiver only).*

Clearly, randomized A-codes are not pseudorandom function generators as they are based upon L-R randomizers for which neither the indexing nor the polynomial time evaluation are satisfied. However, the quality of randomized A-codes can be assessed by using distinguishing circuits $\{C_{n,m}\}$ as given in Definition 2.3 ($m = 2n$).

In the following, we define a class of perfect randomized A-codes.

Definition 3.2 *A randomized A-code $\mathcal{A}_n = \{A^{n,2n}\}$ is perfect if for any distinguisher $C_{n,2n}$, all outputs of the oracle gates (evaluated by the A-code) are independent from input random variables.*

Let us consider a randomized A-code $\mathcal{A}_n = \{A^{n,2n}\}$ for which in the first stage for each message $M \in I_n$, ϑ is selected independently and with the uniform probability from the space I_n (the selected ϑ is kept secret). In the second stage, there is a single L-R randomizer. The quality of the A-code is given by the following theorem.

Theorem 3.1 *A single L-R randomizer $\psi_1(f, g^*, h)$ is enough ($\Psi_1 = \psi_1(f, g^*, h)$, $f, h \in_R F_n$ and $g^* \in_R F_n$ is a random permutation) for the second stage of $\mathcal{A}_n = \{A^{n,2n}\}$ to obtain a perfect randomized A-code provided that in the first stage for each message $M_i \in I_n$, there is an independent and uniformly distributed random variable ϑ_i (the distinguisher has $r \leq 2^n$ oracle gates).*

Proof. If we have r ($r \leq 2^n$) oracle gates, then all oracle gates should produce r independent random variables. This happens only if for any pair of oracle gates (O_i, O_j) ($0 \leq i < j \leq r$), their outputs are independent from their inputs. Let us consider a single pair of oracle gates (O_i, O_j). They are fed by two different messages M_i, M_j (they are random variables which can take on different values) and the A-code generate two independent random variables ϑ_i, ϑ_j for them (note that ϑ_i and ϑ_j are not accessible to the distinguisher). If random variables ϑ_i and ϑ_j are independent and uniform, then the outputs y_{i_1} and y_{j_1} are independent as well (see Figure 1). Now consider random variables y_{i_2} and y_{j_2}. We have the two following cases.

(a) If random variables ϑ_i and ϑ_j take on different values. It results that the function f assigns two independent random variables. So y_{i_2} and y_{j_2} are independent (ϑ_i and ϑ_j are not accessible to the distinguisher) from the input random variables x_{i_1}, x_{j_1}.

(b) If ϑ_i and ϑ_j have happened to have the same value $\vartheta = \vartheta_i = \vartheta_j$. Then $\alpha_i = M_i \oplus f(\vartheta)$ and $\alpha_j = M_j \oplus f(\vartheta)$. As random variables α_i, α_j can take on different values only, the outputs $y_{i_1} = g^*(\alpha_i) \oplus \vartheta$, $y_{j_1} = g^*(\alpha_j) \oplus \vartheta$ have different values and the random function h generates two independent random variables so y_{i_2}, y_{j_2} are independent from the input as well.

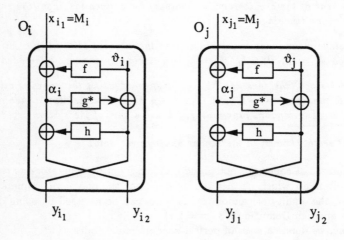

Figure 1: Two oracle gates evaluated using an A-code with $\psi(f, g^*, h)$

As this happens for all pairs of oracle gates, it means that all oracle gates generate independent random variables (from all inputs of oracle gates) when the oracle gates are evaluated by the randomized A-code $\mathcal{A}_n$.

□

Theorem 3.1 basically states that perfect security for messages of length n can be achieved if each message is padded by a randomly chosen string of length at least n and a single L-R randomizer $\psi(f, g^*, h)$ is used for diffusing the random information over the whole block. The random permutation g^* can be substituted by identity permutation ($g = 1$) as ϑ_i and ϑ_j are already independent.

It is interesting to note that if the redundant strings ϑ_i ($1 \leq i \leq r$, r is the number of oracle gates) are kept constant for all messages (source states), the system will still be perfect if a second L-R randomizer is added.

Let the random string ϑ be fixed (and publicly known - accessible to the distinguisher) for the whole transmission session i.e., $\vartheta_i = \vartheta$ for all $i = 1, \ldots, r$. It means that the randomizer $\Psi_2 = \psi_1(f, g, h) \circ \psi_2(h, g^*, f)$ is fed by the pair of random variables: the current message M_i and ϑ.

Theorem 3.2 *Given A-code $\mathcal{A}_n = \{A^{n,2n}\}$. Assume that in the first stage, each message is assigned a common random variable $\vartheta \in I_n$ (the distinguisher knows it but it cannot change its value), then $\mathcal{A}_n$ is perfect provided the following two conditions are satisfied:*

- *the redundant string ϑ is placed to the left hand input of L-R randomizer (Figure 2) i.e., $x_{i_1} = \vartheta$ and $x_{i_2} = M_i$ where $i = 1, \ldots, r$ (r is the number of oracle gates in the distinguishing circuit; $r \leq 2^n$),*

- *the randomizer used in the second stage consists of concatenation of two L-R elementary randomizers i.e., $\Psi = \Psi_2 = \psi_1(f, g, h) \circ \psi_2(h, g^*, f)$ (where $f, g, h \in_R F_n$, and a permutation $g^* \in_R F_n$).*

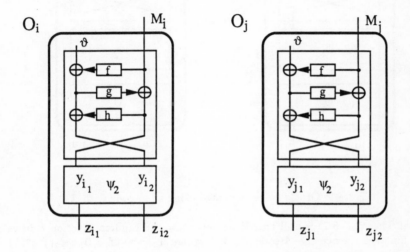

Figure 2: Oracle gates evaluated using an A-code with Ψ_2

Proof: As in the previous theorem, we consider a pair of oracle gates (O_i, O_j) where $0 \leq i < j \leq r$ and we prove that their outputs are independent from the inputs. Figure 2 shows the two oracle gates (O_i, O_j). As the random variables M_i, M_j have always different values, the random variables y_{i_2} and y_{j_2} are independent from the input (the random function f generates independent random variables for different arguments). Now consider the second pair of the outputs y_{i_1} and y_{j_1}. They are also independent as long as the random function g generates two independent random variables (this happens only if the values of $\vartheta \oplus f(M_i)$ and $\vartheta \oplus f(M_j)$ are different). Otherwise, y_{i_1} and y_{j_1} are related and then

$$g(\vartheta \oplus f(M_i)) = g(\vartheta \oplus f(M_j)) = Y$$

This may happen if the random function f collides i.e. $f(M_i) = f(M_j)$ (in [2] this case was called X *is bad*). So we have

$$y_{i_1} = M_i \oplus Y \quad \text{and} \quad y_{j_1} = M_j \oplus Y$$

Note that although related, the random variables y_{i_1}, y_{j_1} take on different values. Now if we put (y_{i_1}, y_{i_2}) and (y_{j_1}, y_{j_2}) to ψ_2 of O_i and O_j, respectively, we face the same situation as in the previous theorem and the final result follows.

□

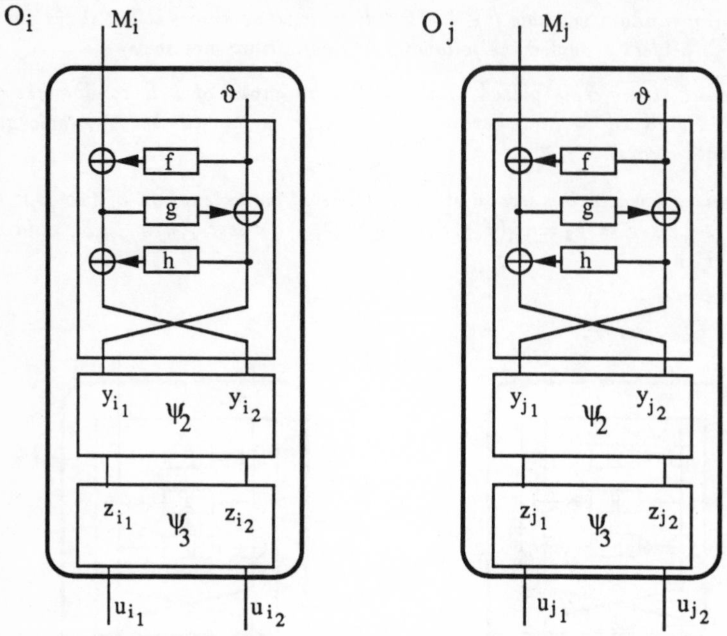

Figure 3: Oracle gates evaluated using an A-code with Ψ_3

Note that Theorem (3.2) is still true if we substitute the random function h in ψ_1 by the constant $\mathbf{0}$ function. Hence the A-code $\mathcal{A}_n(\Psi_2)$, where $\Psi_2 = \psi_1(f, g, \mathbf{0}) \circ \psi_2(f, g^*, h)$, is also perfect.

It is easy to check that, $\mathcal{A}_n(\Psi_2)$ is not perfect if the redundant string ϑ and the message M_i are swopped i.e.,

$$x_{i_1} = M_i$$
$$x_{i_2} = \vartheta$$

However, it will be perfect if we add another L-R randomizer so the resulting A-code applies the randomizer $\Psi_3 = \psi_1(f, g, h) \circ \psi_2(h, g^*, f) \circ \psi_3(h, g^*, f)$. Let us consider the resulting A-code. The random variable ϑ is fixed for all oracle gates so the function f assigns the same random variable $f(\vartheta)$ for all gates. The random variables $M_i \oplus f(\vartheta)$ $(i = 1, \ldots, r)$ always take on different values for all oracle gates. So the random function g assigns r independent random variables and all outputs y_{i_1} are independent from the inputs. Let us consider a single pair of oracle gates (O_i, O_j) (Figure 3). We have already concluded that $y_{i_1} = g(M_i \oplus f(\vartheta)) \oplus \vartheta$ and $y_{j_1} = g(M_j \oplus f(\vartheta)) \oplus \vartheta$ are independent from M_i and M_j. The second pair y_{i_2}, y_{j_2} is also independent from the input if $g(M_i \oplus f(\vartheta)) \neq g(M_j \oplus f(\vartheta))$. However if they collide, i.e. $Y = g(M_i \oplus f(\vartheta)) = g(M_j \oplus f(\vartheta))$, the random variables $y_{i_2} = M_i \oplus f(\vartheta) \oplus h(Y)$ and $y_{j_2} = M_j \oplus f(\vartheta) \oplus h(Y)$ are related although they take on different values.

Therefore if outputs y_{i_2}, y_{j_2} are related to the input, they always have different values (and $y_{i_1} = y_{j_1}$). Note that y_{i_1}, y_{j_1} are independent. The second randomizer ψ_2 does not change the situation - z_{i_2}, z_{j_2} are independent from the input but z_{i_1}, z_{j_1} may be related to the input (with some probability). According to Theorem (3.1), ψ_3 cuts the statistical relation with the input.

Note that if $x_{i_1} = \vartheta$ and $x_{i_2} = M_i$ (for $i = 1, \ldots, r$), then the outputs (z_{i_1}, z_{i_2}) are already independent from the input (see Theorem (3.2)) and ψ_3 preserves the independency.

Thus, we have shown that the following theorem is true.

Theorem 3.3 *Given A-code $\mathcal{A}_n = \{A^{n,2n}\}$. Assume that in the first stage, each message is assigned a common random string $\vartheta \in I_n$ (the distinguisher knows it but it cannot change its value), then $\mathcal{A}_n$ is perfect provided the following two conditions are satisfied:*

- *the redundant string ϑ is placed to the same half of input of L-R randomizer (Figure 3) i.e., $(x_{i_1} = M_i$ and $x_{i_2} = \vartheta)$ or $(x_{i_1} = \vartheta$ and $x_{i_2} = M_i)$, where $i = 1, \ldots, r$ (r is the number of oracle gates in the distinguishing circuit; $r \leq 2^n$),*

- *the randomizer used in the second stage consists of concatenation of three L-R elementary randomizers i.e., $\Psi = \Psi_3 = \psi_1(f, g, h) \circ \psi_2(h, g^*, f) \circ \psi_3(h, g^*, f)$ (where $f, g, h \in_R F_n$)*

Note that the A-code considered in Theorem 3.3 is perfect even if the redundant string ϑ is made public (although public it cannot be changed by the distinguisher).

The above results can be summarised as follows:

A-codes $\mathcal{A}_2(\Psi)$ are perfect if:

- $\Psi = \psi_1(f, g^*, h)$ and the inputs to the randomizer are $x_{i_1} = M_i$ and $x_{i_2} = \vartheta_i$, where ϑ_i is independently selected for each message M_i with the uniform probability distribution.

- $\Psi = \psi_1(f, g, h) \circ \psi_2(h, g^*, f)$ and the inputs to the randomizer are $x_{i_1} = \vartheta$ and $x_{i_2} = M_i$, where the random variable ϑ is fixed for the whole session (for all messages),

- $\Psi = \psi_1(f, g, h) \circ \psi_2(h, g^*, f) \circ \psi_3(h, g^*, f)$ and the inputs to the randomizer are either $(x_{i_1} = M_i$ and $x_{i_2} = \vartheta)$ or $(x_{i_1} = \vartheta$ and $x_{i_2} = M_i)$, where the random variable ϑ and its position in the input are fixed for the whole session (for all messages).

We have discussed the case of A-codes $\mathcal{A}_n(\Psi)$ when the length of redundant strings is the same as the length of messages. The same comments can be made for the case of A-codes when redundant strings are longer than messages.

Randomized A-codes are perfect if all outputs of the oracle gates (evaluated using the A-code) are independent from the input random variables. It also means that perfect A-codes resist the spoofing attack of order $T = r$ (where r specifies the number of oracle gates in distinguishing circuits). Hence the knowledge of r message/cryptogram pairs does not reveal any information to the attacker in forming a substitution message and their best strategy is random selection with uniform distribution from the rest of cryptograms ([3],[5]). Therefore if an enemy wished to make the receiver accept a false cryptogram, they would have to select such a cryptogram randomly from the rest of $2^m - r$ elements. The probability of an enemy's success is equal to:

$$\frac{2^n - r}{2^m - r}$$

where 2^n is the size of the message space and 2^m is the size of the cryptogram space.

There is a problem with an implementation of randomized A-codes, as their random functions f, g, h are not polynomially computable and to store them in a computer, requires exponential size of memory. To make the A-code implementable, the random functions $f, g, h \in_R F_n$ in L-R randomizers have to be substituted by pseudorandom ones ($f, g, h \in_{PS} F_n$). It is easy to check that the resulting A-code is pseudorandom and its quality depends upon the quality of pseudorandom functions used.

4   Conclusions

It is well known [6] that secrecy and authenticity are related. If the message source has redundancy, then any cryptosystem applied for secrecy also gives authentication of messages. If the message source has no redundancy, then any cryptogram injected by an enemy is accepted by the receiver as a genuine one. In general, to provide authenticity, it is necessary to introduce redundancy, which divides redundant messages into two classes. The first one consists of all meaningful messages whose cryptograms can appear in the communication channel. All meaningless redundant messages create the second class. Their cryptograms never occur in the channel (see [4]).

We defined randomized A-codes and gave some constructions for them. Our considerations are limited to the case when n-bit long messages are transformed into $2n$-bit cryptograms. In these codes, the assignment of the cryptogram to a given message is done in two stages. The first introduces redundancy and the second applies the concatenation of i Luby-Rackoff randomizers ($i = 1, 2, 3$).

The number of required stages in an L-R randomizer is directly affected by the way the redundancy is introduced. If a known constant padding is used for all messages (this padding sequence can be made public) but its position in the randomizer input (although fixed for the session) is not known, concatenation of three L-R randomizers guarantees that the resulting A-code is perfect. Perfection implies that the authentication code is indistinguishable from a truly random function generator $F^{n,m}$ which assigns independently and uniformly distributed random cryptograms for each message (the number of oracle gates $r \leq 2^n$).

If two communicating parties agree beforehand that they will always place the redundant string at the left hand input of the randomizer, then it is possible to obtain a perfect A-code for a simpler randomizer $\Psi = \Psi_2$ that applies the concatenation of two L-R randomizers. Note that the positions of redundant string and message are important - the message should always be input to the right hand input of the randomizer (to the input of the random function f).

To be perfect, a randomized A-code with a single L-R randomizer needs to assign an independent and uniformly distributed random variable ϑ_i for each message M_i.

Perfect randomized A-codes have the advantage that they are resistant to a spoofing of order T attack, as an enemy has to select a cryptogram from the remaining equally probable elements and their probability of success is strictly related to the redundancy.

Perfect randomized A-codes can be readily converted to pseudorandom A-codes whose quality depends on the quality of underlying pseudorandom functions used in L-R modules.

According to the definition, perfect A-codes do not leak information about the input to the output as all outputs are independent random variables. However, some information about the A-code structure can be extracted from the output.

ACKNOWLEDGMENT

We would like to thank Jacques Patarin, Babak Sadeghiyan and Yuliang Zheng for their critical comments and help. We thank Professor Jennifer Seberry for her continuous support and encouragement. Also we thank Cathy Newberry, Thomas Hardjono and other members of the CCSR for their assistance.

References

[1] O. Goldreich, S. Goldwasser, and S. Micali. How to construct random functions. *Journal of the ACM*, 33(4):792–807, October 1986.

[2] M. Luby and Ch. Rackoff. How to construct pseudorandom permutations from pseudorandom functions. *SIAM Journal on Computing*, 17(2):373–386, April 1988.

[3] J.L. Massey. Cryptography - a selective survey. In *Digital Communication*. Elsevier Science Publishers, 1986.

[4] R. Safavi-Naini and J. Seberry. Error correcting codes for authentication and subliminal channels. to appear in IEEE Transactions on Information Theory.

[5] R. Safavi-Naini and J. Seberry. On construction of practically perfect authentication codes. Technical report, Department of Computer Scienee, The University of New South Wales, ADFA, 1990.

[6] G.V. Simmons. A survey of information authentication. *Proceedings of IEEE*, 76:603–620, 1988.

[7] Andrew C. Yao. Theory and application of trapdoor functions. In *Proceedings of the 23rd IEEE Symposium on Fundation of Computer Science*, pages 80–91, New York, 1982. IEEE.

[8] Y. Zheng, T. Matsumoto, and H. Imai. On the construction of block ciphers provably secure and not relying on any unproved hypotheses. Abstracts of CRYPTO'89, Santa Barbara, CA, July 1989.

Ideals over a Non-Commutative Ring
and their Application in Cryptology

E. M. Gabidulin, A. V. Paramonov and O. V. Tretjakov
Moscow Institute of Physics and Technology
141700 Dolgoprudnii
Moscow Region, USSR

Abstract: A new modification of the McEliece public-key cryptosystem is proposed that employs the so-called maximum-rank-distance (MRD) codes in place of Goppa codes and that hides the generator matrix of the MRD code by addition of a randomly-chosen matrix. A short review of the mathematical background required for the construction of MRD codes is given. The cryptanalytic work function for the modified McEliece system is shown to be much greater than that of the original system. Extensions of the rank metric are also considered.

1. INTRODUCTION

The purpose of this paper is to show that error-correcting codes for the rank metric, as introduced recently in [1], can advantageously be used to replace codes for the usual Hamming metric in McEliece's public-key cryptosystem [2]. The next section develops the necessary mathematical background for describing codes over the rank metric. The codes themselves are derived in Section 3. Section 4 describes how these codes are used in the McEliece system and quantifies the increase in security compared to the system based on codes for the Hamming metric.

2. MATHEMATICAL PRELIMINARIES

A *linearized polynomial* with coefficients in the finite field $GF(q^N)$ is a polynomial of the form

$$F(z) = \sum_{i=0}^{n} f_i \, z^{[i]}$$

where here and hereafter "[i]" in an exponent is shorthand for "q^i". The largest i such that $f_i \neq 0$ will be called the *norm* of the polynomial. By way of convention, the norm of the linearized polynomial 0 is taken to be $-\infty$. We write $R_N[z]$ to denote the set of all linearized polynomials with coefficients in $GF(q^N)$. Addition and multiplication in $R_N[z]$ are defined by

$$F(z) + G(z) = \sum_{i=0}^{n} (f_i + g_i) \, z^{[i]}$$

and by

$$F(z) * G(z) = \sum_{i=0}^{n} (\sum_{k+s=i} f_s \, g_k^{[s]}) \, z^{[i]},$$

respectively, It is important to note that multiplication in $R_N[z]$ is *not* commutative. The set $R_N[z]$ under these two operations is a non-commutative ring whose multiplicative identity is the polynomial z.

The polynomial $z^{[N]}$ - z commutes under multiplication with every polynomial $F(z)$ in $R_N[z]$. Moreover, if $G(z)$ and $H(z)$ are polynomials in $R_N[z]$ with leading coefficients 1 and such that $G(z) * H(z) = z^{[N]}$ - z, then $G(z)$ and $H(z)$ also commute under multiplication, i.e., $G(z) * H(z) = H(z) * G(z)$. Thus, one can speak unambiguously of the divisors of $z^{[N]}$ - z. We will write $L_N[z]$ to denote the *quotient ring* $R_N[z]/(z^{[N]} - z)$, i. e., the ring whose operations are addition and multiplication modulo the polynomial $z^{[N]}$ - z. The ring $L_N[z]$ is a non-commutive ring with q^m elements where $m = N^2$. Every left (or right) ideal in this ring is a principal ideal generated by a polynomial $G(z)$ that divides $z^{[N]}$ - z. The elements of this left ideal are all the polynomials in $R_N[z]$ of the form $F(z) * G(z)$ with $F(z)$ in the ring $L_N[z]$.

3. IDEALS ON $L_N[z]$ AS ERROR-CORRECTING CODES

We will consider left ideals of $L_N[z]$ as *codes* over the "large" field $GF(q^N)$. Instead of the Hamming metric that is most frequently used to study the error-correcting properties of codes, we will instead use a family of metrics induced by the so-called *rank metric*. This metric was introduced in [1], where a complete theory of codes with maximal rank distance (MRD) was given, including encoding and decoding techniques.

We will write F^N to denote the N-dimensional vector space of N-tuples over the "large" field $GF(q^N)$. Let $x = (x_0, x_1, ... x_{N-1})$ be a vector in F^N. Then the *rank norm* of x, denoted $r(x)$, is defined to be the maximum number of components of x that are linearly independent when $GF(q^N)$ itself is considered as an N-dimensional vector space over the "small" field $GF(q)$. The *rank distance* between x and y, denoted $d(x, y)$, is then defined as $r(x - y)$. It is easy to show that the minimum rank distance d of an (N, k) linear code over $GF(q^N)$ satisfies $d \leq N - k + 1$, a code for which $d = N - k + 1$ is called a *maximum-rank-distance* (MRD) code.

The vector $\tilde{x} = (x_{N-1}^{[s]}, x_0^{[s]}, \ldots x_{N-2}^{[s]})$ will be called the *[s]-cyclic shift* of **x**. Note that $\tilde{x}$ is obtained from **x** first by a right cyclic shift of its components followed by raising these components to the q^s power. A code $\mathcal{M}$ will be call an *[s]-cyclic code* if the [s]-cyclic shift of a code word is always itself a code word. Note that **x** and $\tilde{x}$ have the same rank norm. The main construction of [1]-cyclic codes is given by the following theorem.

Theorem 1 [1]: Let γ be an element of $GF(q^N)$ such that $\gamma = \gamma^{[0]}, \gamma^{[1]}, \ldots, \gamma^{[N-1]}$ are linearly independent over the "small" field $GF(q)$ [or, equivalently, such that these elements form a so-called *normal basis* for $GF(q^N)$], then the linear code $\mathcal{M}$ over $GF(q^N)$ with parity-check matrix

$$H = \begin{bmatrix} \gamma^{[0]} & \gamma^{[1]} & \ldots & \gamma^{[N-1]} \\ \gamma^{[1]} & \gamma^{[2]} & \ldots & \gamma^{[0]} \\ \vdots & \vdots & \vdots & \vdots \\ \gamma^{[d-2]} & \gamma^{[d-1]} & \ldots & \gamma^{[d-3]} \end{bmatrix}$$

is a [1]-cyclic MRD code of length N over $GF(q^N)$ with minimum rank distance d and dimension $k = N - d + 1$.

We now wish to treat code words and other N-tuples over the "large" field $F = GF(q^N)$ as $N \times N$ matrices over the "small" field $GF(q)$ so as to pave the way for consideration of "errors" in the digits lying in the "small" field. To do this, we suppose that a normal basis $\gamma^{[0]}, \gamma^{[1]}, \ldots, \gamma^{[N-1]}$ for F has been fixed, and we associate the vector **x** with the matrix

$$X = \begin{bmatrix} x_{00} & x_{01} & \cdots & x_{0:N-1} \\ x_{10} & x_{11} & \cdots & x_{1:N-1} \\ \vdots & \vdots & \vdots & \vdots \\ x_{N-1:0} & x_{N-1:1} & \cdots & x_{N-1:N-1} \end{bmatrix}$$

whose entries are elements of $GF(q)$ determined from the components of **x** according to the representation of these components in the normal basis, i.e.,

$$x_i = \sum_{i=0}^{N-1} x_{ji}\, \gamma^{[i]}.$$

In this manner, single errors **e** in the rank metric correspond to matrices **E** with rank 1 and have the form

$$E = CJD,$$

where C, J and D are $N \times N$ matrices over $GF(q)$ such that J has N identical non-zero columns, C is nonsingular, and D is a non-zero diagonal matrix.

4. APPLICATION TO THE McELIECE PUBLIC-KEY CRYPTOSYSTEM

In [2], McEliece introduced a public-key cryptosystem based on algebraic codes that can be described as follows. The cryptographer chooses a $k \times n$ generator matrix G for a t-error-correcting binary Goppa code, for which a fast decoding algorithm is known, and chooses also a $k \times k$ nonsingular "scrambling" matrix S and an $n \times n$ permutation matrix P. He then computes the matrix $K = S G P$, which is also the generator matrix of an (n, k) linear t-error-correcting code, but one for which no fast decoding algorithm is known [3] if S, G, and P are not individually known. He then publishes K as his public encryption key. When someone wishes to send him a message, that person fetches K from the public directory, then encrypts his k-bit message m as

$$c = m K + e$$

where e is a randomly chosen pattern of t or fewer errors. The legitimate receiver, i. e., the cryptographer, upon receipt of c first computes $c P^{-1} = (m S) G + e P^{-1}$. He then applies his fast decoding algorithm to this vector to obtain $m S$, and finally recovers the message m as $(m S) S^{-1}$.

The cryptanalyst's *work function* for breaking this scheme by the attack considered by McEliece [2] is

$$W \approx \beta k^3 \binom{n}{k} / \binom{n-t}{k},$$

where βk^3 is the number of computations required to invert a non-singular $k \times k$ matrix; $\beta = 1$ will be used in all examples hereafter. For the parameters suggested by McEliece (n = 1024, k = 524, t = 50), this gives $W \approx 2^{80.7}$. Adams and Meijer [4] determined that the value of t that maximizes W for n = 1024 was t = 37, which gives k = 654 and $W \approx 2^{84.1}$.
Lee and Brickell [5] improved the attack; against their attack the best choice is t = 38 which gives $W \approx 2^{73.4}$.

The main disadvantages of McEliece's public-key cryptosystem are its large public key (about 2^{19} bits for McEliece's original parameters), its expansion of the plaintext by a factor n/k (about 2), and the existence of a systematic attack for the cryptanalyst. We will see that these disadvantages can be overcome at least partially by the use of codes for the rank metric and its induced metrics.

To adapt McEliece's scheme to MRD codes requires some modification. First, because there are no distinguished coordinates in an MRD code, there is no point to using the permutation matrix P when G is the generator matrix of a MRD code. However, the matrix $S G$ is still the generator matrix of another MRD code so this structure must be hidden in another way to make the decoding problem "hard". We suggest hiding this structure by adding a matrix $\alpha^T e_g$ to $S G$ where α is a non-zero k-tuple and e_g is a non-zero n-tuple over $GF(q^n)$ such that $r(e_g) \leq t_g < t$, where t_g is a design parameter and t is the rank-error-correcting capability of the code.

The modified McEliece cryptosystem works as follows. The cryptographer chooses a k × n generator matric G for a t-rank-error-correcting code, and chooses also a k × k nonsingular "scrambling" matrix S together with a matrix $\alpha^T e_g$ as described above. He then computes the matrix $K = S G + \alpha^T e_g$. He then publishes K as his public encryption key. When someone wishes to send him a message, that person fetches K from the public directory, then encrypts his k-bit message m as

$$c = m K + e_e$$

where e_e is a randomly chosen pattern of $t_e = t - t_g$ or fewer rank errors. The legitimate receiver applies his fast decoding algorithm to this c to remove the error pattern $m \alpha^T e_g + e_e$ (which has rank weight at most t) to obtain $m S$, and finally recovers the message m as $(m S) S^{-1}$.

There are two possible attacks on this modified scheme. The first is similar to that in [4] and [5] for the original scheme. The difference is that, with high probability, there will be no subset of k code coordinates that is error-free, which means that the cryptanalyst must search through all error patterns of rank t_e or less in some selected set of k coordinates. The number of k-tuples e over $GF(q^n)$ with $r(e) \leq t_e$ is much greater than the number of such e with Hamming weight at most t_e when $t_e < n/2$. Thus, the complexity of this attacking algorithm for the rank metric is much greater than for the Hamming metric. The work function for the rank metric is

$$W \approx k^3 L(k, t_e)$$

where $L(k, t_e)$ is the number of k-tuples e over $GF(q^n)$ with $r(e) = t_e$. This number is given by

$$L(k, i) = \begin{bmatrix} k \\ i \end{bmatrix} (q^n - 1)(q^n - q) \ldots (q^n - q^{i-1}),$$

where

$$\begin{bmatrix} k \\ i \end{bmatrix} = \frac{(q^k - 1)(q^k - q) \ldots (q^k - q^{i-1})}{(q^i - 1)(q^i - q) \ldots (q^i - q^{i-1})}$$

is the number of i-dimensional subspaces of a k-dimensional vector space over $GF(q^n)$.

The second attack is for the cryptanalyst to try to determine from the public key K a generator matrix for the code for which he can find a decoding algorithm. The complexity of the best attack of this kind that we have been able to formulate is

$$W \approx L(k, t_g) (q^n - 1)^k n^3.$$

The complexity of this second attack is much greater than that of the first, but it must be remembered that the second attack needs to be carried out only once to solve any number of cryptograms whereas the first attack must be carried out for each cryptogram to be solved.

As a numerical example, consider the case where $n = 20, k = 12$ and $t_e = 3$. The code rate is then $k/n = 3/5$, i. e., the plaintext is expanded by a factor of $5/3$. The size of the public key is $n^2 k = 4800 \approx 2^{12}$ bits. The work functions for the first and second attack are about 2^{100} and 2^{290}, respectively. [Note that the operations counted are in $GF(2^n)$ rather than in $GF(2)$.] All parameters are substantially better than for the original McEliece system that uses codes based on the Hamming metric.

5. EXTENSIONS OF THE RANK METRIC

The rank metric matches [s]-cyclic shifting for any s in the sense that a vector x and its [s]-cyclic shift have the same rank norm. But it is also possible to introduce a new set of metrics that apply for specific values of s, as we shall now do.

Consider now the mapping φ_s (where $0 \leq s < N$) defined by

$$\varphi_s(x) = (x_0^{[0]}, x_1^{[s]}, x_2^{[2s]}, \dots, x_{N-1}^{[(N-1)s]}).$$

This mapping is a bijection on F^N but is nonlinear for $s \neq 0$. We will call the metric D_s defined by

$$D_s(x, y) = r(\varphi_s^{-1}(x - y))$$

the *metric on F^N induced by* φ_s. Single errors in the induced metric D_s have the same structure $C J D$ as for the rank metric except that the matrix J now may have any non-zero first column. One now considers this first column as representing an element of $GF(q^N)$, say $x_0^{[0]}$, and forms subsequent elements $x_0^{[s]}, x_0^{[2s]}, \dots, x_0^{[(N-1)s]}$, then returns to the matrix representation. If one uses a normal-basis representation, then each subsequent column of the maxtrix is simply the cyclic shift by s positions of the components of the previous column.

If a code $\mathcal{M}$ is optimal for the rank metric, then the *image code* $\varphi_s(\mathcal{M})$ is optimal for the induced metric D_s. Moreover, encoding and decoding schemes for the original code in the rank metric are easily adapted to the image code in the induced metric.

It was shown in [1] that any left ideal l of $L_N[z]$ is a [1]-cyclic MRD code. The following theorem is an immediate consequence.

Theorem 2: Let l be a left ideal of $L_N[z]$ and let $\mathit{l}_s = \varphi_s(\mathit{l})$. Then l_s is an [s+1]-cyclic codes with maximal minimum distance for the induced metric D_s.

The choice $s = N - 1$ in Theorem 2 gives nonlinear codes over $GF(q)$ that are cyclic in the usual sense and that have maximal minimum distance in the induced metric D_s.

The public encryption key when the metric D_s is used in McEliece's cryptosystem is the matrix

$$K_s = S\,\phi_s(G) + \alpha^T\,\phi_s(e_g)$$

where, as above, G is the $k \times n$ generator matrix for a t-rank-error-correcting code, e_g is a vector of rank norm t_g, and $\phi_s(G)$ is the matrix obtained by applying the mapping ϕ_s to each row of G. The k-bit message m is encrypted as

$$c = m\,K_s + \phi_s(e)$$

where e is a randomly chosen vector of rank norm at most $t - t_g$.

The use of these induced norms in the McEliece system allows one to increase the number of possible public encryption keys compared to the case where only the rank metric is used. For a fixed $s \neq 0$, the system based on the D_s metric is equivalent to that based on the rank metric. We are currently investigating whether it would be possible to increase the security of the system by somehow making s part of the private key only.

REMARK

We point out that MRD codes can also be useful in implementing perfect local randomizers. Maurer and Massey's bound [6] on the degree δ of perfect local randomizers obtained with maximum-distance-separable (MDS) codes for the Hamming metric also applies to MRD codes, since MRD codes are also MDS. However, this bound can sometimes be improved for MRD codes.

REFERENCES

[1] E. M. Gabidulin, "Theory of Codes with Maximum Rank Distance", *Problems of InformationTransmission* , vol. 21, no. 1, pp. 1-12, July, 1985 (Russian Original, January-March, 1985).

[2] R. J. McEliece, "A Public-Key Cryptosystem Based on Algebraic Coding Theory", pp. 114-116 in *DSN Progress Report 42-44*, Jet Propulsion Lab., Pasadena, CA, January-February, 1978.

[3] E. R. Berlekamp, R. J. McEliece and H. C. A. van Tilborg, "On the Inherent Intractability of Certain Coding Problems", *IEEE Trans. Inf. Th.*, vol. IT-24, pp. 384-386, May 1978.

[4] C. M. Adams and H. Meijer, "Security-Related Comments Regarding McEliece's Public-Key Cryptosystem", pp. 224-228 in *Advances in Cryptology--CRYPTO '87* (Ed. C. Pomerance), Lecture Notes in Computer Sci. No. 293. Heidelberg and New York: Springer-Verlag, 1988.

[5] P. J. Lee and E. F. Brickell, "An Observation on the Security of the McEliece Public-Key Cryptosystem", pp. 275-280 in *Advances in Cryptology--EUROCRYPT '88* (Ed. C. Günther), Lecture Notes in Computer Sci. No. 330. Heidelberg and New York: Springer-Verlag, 1988.

[6] U. M. Maurer and J. L. Massey, "Perfect Local Randomness in Pseudo-Random Sequences, pp. 100-112 in *Advances in Cryptology--CRYPTO '89* (Ed. G. Brassard), Lecture Notes in Computer Sci. No. 435. Heidelberg and New York: Springer-Verlag, 1990.

Self-certified public keys

Marc Girault

Service d'Etudes communes de la Poste et de France Télécom (SEPT)
Groupement PEM
42 rue des Coutures, B.P. 6243
14066 CAEN-CEDEX, France

Abstract   *We introduce the notion, and give two examples, of self-certified public keys, i.e. public keys which need not be accompanied with a separate certificate to be authenticated by other users. The trick is that the public key is computed by both the authority and the user, so that the certificate is "embedded" in the public key itself, and therefore does not take the form of a separate value.*

Self-certified public keys contribute to reduce the amount of storage and computations in public key schemes, while secret keys are still chosen by the user himself and remain unknown to the authority. This makes the difference with identity-based schemes, in which there are no more certificates at all, but at the cost that secret keys are computed (and therefore known to) the authority.

1. Introduction

A lot of public-key schemes have been designed since their discovery in 1976 [DH]. In such schemes, every user has a key-pair (s,P). The first one, s, is a secret key, only known to this user. The second one, P, is a public key, which anybody may know. The two keys, secret and public, are mathematically strongly connected, but knowing only the second one is insufficient to retrieve the first one in reasonable time.

By definition, public keys need not be protected for confidentiality ; on the contrary, they have to be made as public as possible. But this "publicity" makes them particularly vulnerable to active attacks, such as the substitution of a "false" public key to a "true" one in a directory. This is why, in addition to the key-pair (s,P) and his identification string (or identity) I, the attributes of a user must also contain a "guarantee" that P is really the public key of user I, and not the one of an impostor I'.

Depending on the form of this guarantee, we may distinguish several types of schemes. Their common point is to require the existence of an authority, in which every user "trusts" (in a sense to define ...). It seems difficult to get rid of such a requirement, except that there may be several authorities, each user trusting at least one of them.

In certificate-based schemes, the guarantee G takes the form of a digital signature of the pair (I,P), often called certificate, computed and delivered by the authority. In such a case, the four attributes $(I, s, P$ and $G)$ are distinct ; three ones are public $(I, P$ and $G)$ and should be available in a directory. When somebody needs, for example, to authenticate user I, he gets his public triplet (I,P,G), checks G with the help of the authority's public key, that everybody is supposed to know, and afterwards makes use of P to authenticate this user. This is CCITT X509 approach [CCI].

In identity-based schemes, introduced by Shamir [Sh] in 1984 (see e.g. [FS] or [GQ]), the public key is nothing but the identity I (i.e. $P=I$). And the guarantee is nothing but the secret key itself (i.e. $G=s$), so that only two attributes exist $(I$ and $s)$ instead of four. This approach is very attractive, since there is no certificate to store and to check, but has its drawbacks. In particular, the authority can impersonate any user at any moment since secret keys are calculated by it.

In this paper, we propose a new type of scheme, intermediary between certificate-based and identity-based ones. In such schemes, the guarantee is equal to the public key (i.e. $G=P$), which therefore may be said *self-certified*, and each user has three attributes $(I, s$ and $P)$.

Schemes using self-certified public keys are neither certificate-based, since there is no separate certificate, nor identity-based, since the public key is not restricted to the identity. As a consequence, they contribute to reduce the amount of storage and computations (in particular, they do not require hash-functions at authority level) while secret keys are still chosen by the user himself and remain unknown to the authority.

Our paper is organized as follows : after the present introduction (section 1), we give some general features on public-key schemes using self-certified public keys (section 2), then provide two examples of such schemes (sections 3 and 4). The first one is based on factorization and discrete logarithm problems. The second one is only based on discrete logarithm problem.

2. General

The authority mentioned in the introduction is the link between all the users connected to a same network. Thanks to it, two people who have never "met" before and who share nothing (except universal parameters related to the authority) may set up an authenticated or confidential channel. Of course, this works if and only if users trust this authority. But what does "trust" mean here ?

With secret-key schemes, such authorities know all the secret keys held by the users and these users must have every confidence in it. With public-key schemes, this drastic condition can be greatly relaxed, but a careful analysis shows that several levels of trust can be defined. In this paper, we essentially distinguish three levels (1, 2 and 3).

At level 1, the authority knows (or can easily compute) users' secret keys and, therefore, can impersonate any user at any time without being detected. At level 2, the authority does not know (or cannot easily compute) users' secret keys. Nevertheless, the authority can still impersonate a user by generating false guarantees (e.g. false certificates). This is why we also require, to reach level 3, the frauds of the authority to be detectable. More precisely, a public-key scheme will be said of level 3 if the authority cannot compute users' secret keys, and if it can be proven that it generates false guarantees of users if it does so.

Clearly, the level 3 is the most desirable one, and is achieved by certificate-based schemes. Indeed only the authority is able to produce certificates. As a consequence, the existence of two (or more) different certificates for the same user is in itself a proof that the authority has cheated.

Now, as the storage and the verification of certificates lead to additional parameters to store, exchange and more computations to perform, it would be pleasant to design schemes which are not certificate-based, while they still achieve level 3. Identity-based schemes fail to do that since they only achieve level 1, which may be highly insufficient in some applications. The two schemes that we are going to present now use self-certified public keys and reach level 3.

Before describing these schemes, we wish to point out that, as in certificate-based schemes and contrary to identity-based ones, the channel used by a user and the authority needs not be a confidential one.

3. A scheme using RSA/Rabin digital signature scheme

3.1 Set-up

At SECURICOM'89 conference, Paillès and the author have presented a scheme

[PG] using self-certified public keys (but without employing this name). A similar scheme has also been proposed by Tanaka and Okamoto at SECURICOM'90 [TO]. A new version of PG scheme has been presented at ESORICS'90 conference [GP] (or [Gi]). All these proposals use RSA digital signature scheme but only reach level 2. The reason why is the possibility for each user to create other valid public keys linked to his identity I, after he has been given one by the authority. As a consequence, a judge cannot distinguish between a cheating authority and a cheating user (we will now call Alice).

In our scheme, the authority generates a RSA key-pair [RSA], that is a large integer n, product of two prime factors p and q, an integer e coprime to p-1 and q-1, and the converse d of e modulo $(p-1)(q-1)$. Then it computes an integer g of maximal order in the multiplicative group $(Z/nZ)^*$, with usual notations. The parameters n, e, and g are published by the authority whilst p, q and d are kept secret.

Actually, this RSA key could be replaced by a Rabin's one [Ra] (i.e. with $e = 2$), in order to reduce the number of multiplications to carry out, but only RSA case is described here.

Now, Alice randomly chooses a (say) 150-bit secret key s, computes the integer $v = g^{-s}$ *(mod n)* and gives v to the authority. Then she proves to the authority that she knows s without revealing it, by using the protocol described below (paragraph 3.2). Afterwards the authority computes Alice's public key P as a RSA signature of the modular difference of g^{-s} and I :

$$P = (g^{-s} - I)^d \bmod n$$

So the following equation, called (E), holds :

$$P^e + I = g^{-s} \quad (mod\ n)$$

Now, this set-up will enable Alice to prove her identity with the help of a minimum-knowledge identification protocol, or exchange secret keys with other users in an authenticated manner.

3.2 Identification protocol

Alice proves to Bob she is Alice, by convincing him that she knows a discrete logarithm modulo n (the one of $v = (P^e + I)$), while ignoring the factorization of n. This can be done with the following protocol, related to Beth's [Be] or Schnorr's one [Sc], and also to a protocol from Okamoto and Ohta [OO] :

1) Alice sends I and P to Bob, who computes $v = (P^e + I) \bmod n$.

2) Alice selects a (say) 220-bit random integer x, computes $t = g^x \ (mod \ n)$, and sends t to Bob.

3) Bob selects a (say) 30-bit random integer c and sends it to Alice.

4) Alice computes $y = x + sc$ and sends it to Bob.

5) Bob checks that $g^y \ v^c = t \ (mod \ n)$.

It can be proven that :
- Alice will be accepted by Bob with probability almost 1 (completeness)
- an impostor, who does not know s, will be detected with probability $1\text{-}2^{-30}$ (soundness)
- the protocol hardly reveals anything about s (minimum-knowledgeness).

The same protocol (steps 2 to 5) is used by Alice and the authority at the set-up of the scheme (see paragraph 3.1).

Note that there is no certificate to check : public-keys are "self-certified". Note also that another user cannot infer Alice's secret key from her public key, provided discrete logarithm problem is hard. Moreover, though it holds the factors of n, the authority is also unable to compute s (from $g^{-s} \ (mod \ n)$) if these factors are large enough (say 350 bit).

Of course, the authority can still compute "false" public keys linked to Alice, by choosing a number s' and computing P' as described in paragraph 3.1. But, since only the authority is able to produce valid keys (i.e. satisfying equation (E)), the existence of two (or more) different valid public keys for the same user is in itself a proof that the authority has cheated. This shows that the scheme reaches level 3, as promised.

3.3 Key exchange protocol

Let (I,s,P) be the attributes of Alice, (I',s',P') those of Bob. They can simply exchange an authenticated key by choosing :

$$K = (P^e + I)^{s'} = (P'^e + I')^s = g^{-ss'} \ (mod \ n)$$

This protocol is clearly related to Diffie-Hellman's one, but, contrary to it, makes Alice sure that she shares K with Bob and conversely.

4. A scheme using El-Gamal digital signature scheme

Contrary to the preceding one, this scheme is only based on the difficulty to compute discrete logarithms modulo a prime number. It results from a combination of Beth's scheme and Horster-Knobloch "testimonial scheme" [HK].

Beth's scheme is an identity-based identification scheme, in that Alice's secret key is computed by the authority as an El-Gamal [El] signature of her identity I. Actually, only one part of this signature is the secret key, and the other part has to be transmitted to those who wish to authenticate Alice. In our paradigm, this second part can be viewed as a self-certified public key. But only level 1 is achieved.

In order to reach level 3, we can combine Beth's scheme with the so-called testimonial digital signature scheme. This gives the following :

The authority generates a large prime p such that $p-1$ has also a large prime factor (e.g. $(p-1)/2$) and a primitive element g of $(Z/pZ)^*$. Then it selects an integer a in $[0,p-2]$ and computes $b = g^a \pmod{p}$. The parameters p, g, and b are published by the authority whilst a is kept secret.

Now, Alice chooses a random integer h, computes $u = g^h \pmod{p}$ and gives u to the authority. The authority chooses a random integer k, computes $P = u^k \pmod{p}$ and solves in x the equation :

$$aP + kx = I \mod (p-1)$$

Then the authority returns (P,I,x) to Alice, who calculates : $s = xh^{-1} \pmod{p}$ so that :

$$b^P P^s = g^I \pmod{p}$$

Alice's secret key is s and her self-certified public key is P. Note that the pair (s,P) is an El-Gamal authority's signature of I, but that the authority ignores s ! (A sort of paradox ...). That makes the difference with original Beth's scheme and explains why level 3 is reached by this one.

Now, Alice can be authenticated by Bob, using Beth's protocol, as described in [Be].

Acknowledgements

I would like to thank E. Okamoto for his careful analysis of section 3, and H.J. Knobloch for having informed me of the testimonial scheme.

References

[Be] T. Beth, "A Fiat-Shamir-like authentication protocol for the ElGamal scheme", Advances in Cryptology, Proc. of EUROCRYPT'88, LNCS 330, Springer-Verlag, 1988, pp.77-86.

[CCI] "The Directory-Authentication Framework", CCITT Recommendation X509.

[DH] W. Diffie and M. Hellman, "New directions in cryptography", IEEE Transactions on Information Theory, Vol.IT-22, Nov.1976, pp.644-654.

[El] T. El Gamal, "A public key cryptosystem and a signature scheme based on discrete logarithms", Advances in Cryptology, Proc. of CRYPTO'84, LNCS 196, Springer-Verlag, 1985, pp.10-18.

[FS] A. Fiat and A. Shamir, "How to prove yourself : Practical solutions to identification and signature problems", Advances in Cryptology, Proc. of CRYPTO'86, LNCS 263, Springer-Verlag, 1987, pp.186-194.

[Gi] M. Girault, "An identity-based identification scheme based on discrete logarithms modulo a composite number", Proc. of EUROCRYPT'90, LNCS 473, Springer-Verlag, 1991, pp.481-486.

[GP] M. Girault and JC. Paillès, "An identity-based identification scheme providing zero-knowledge authentication and authenticated key exchange", Proc. of ESORICS'90, pp.173-184.

[GQ] L.C. Guillou and J.J. Quisquater, "A practical zero-knowledge protocol fitted to security microprocessors minimizing both transmission and memory", Advances in Cryptology, Proc. of EUROCRYPT'88, LNCS 330, Springer-Verlag, 1988, pp.123-128.

[HK] P. Horster and H.J. Knobloch, "Discrete logarithm based protocols", these Proceedings.

[OO] T. Okamoto and K. Ohta, "How to utilize the randomness of zero-knowledge proofs", Proc. of CRYPTO'90, to appear.

[PG] J.C. Paillès and M. Girault, "CRIPT : A public-key based solution for secure data communications", Proc. of SECURICOM'89, pp.171-185.

[Ra] M.O Rabin, "Digitalized signatures and public-key functions as intractable as factorization", MIT, Lab. for Computer Science, MIT/LCS/TR-212, Jan.1979.

[RSA] R.L. Rivest, A. Shamir and L. Adleman, "A method for obtaining digital signatures and public-key cryptosystems", CACM, Vol.21, n°2, Feb.1978, pp.120-126.

[Sc] C.P. Schnorr, "Efficient identification and signatures for smart cards", Advances in Cryptology, Proc. of CRYPTO'89, LNCS 435, Springer-Verlag, pp.239-252.

[Sh] A. Shamir, "Identity-based cryptosystems and signature schemes", Advances in Cryptology, Proc. of CRYPTO'84, LNCS 196, Springer-Verlag, 1985, pp.47-53.

[TO] K. Tanaka and E. Okamoto, "Key distribution system using ID-related information directory suitable for mail systems", Proc. of SECURICOM'90, pp.115-122.

Non-interactive Public-Key Cryptography[1]

Ueli M. Maurer [2]

Dept. of Computer Science
Princeton University
Princeton, NJ 08544
umm@cs.princeton.edu

Yacov Yacobi

Bellcore
445 South St.
Morristown, NJ 07962
yacov@bellcore.com

Abstract. An identity-based non-interactive public key distribution system is presented that is based on a novel trapdoor one-way function allowing a trusted authority to compute the discrete logarithm of a given number modulo a publicly known composite number m while this is infeasible for an adversary not knowing the factorization of m. Without interaction with a key distribution center or with the recipient of a given message a user can generate a mutual secure cipher key based solely on the recipient's identity and his own secret key and send the message, encrypted with the generated cipher key using a conventional cipher, over an insecure channel to the recipient. Unlike in previously proposed identity-based systems, no public keys, certificates for public keys or other information need to be exchanged and thus the system is suitable for many applications such as electronic mail that do not allow for interaction.

1. Introduction

Public-key distribution systems and public-key cryptosystems suffer from the following well-known authentication problem. In order to prevent an adversary from fraudulently impersonating another user, it must be possible to verify that a received public key belongs to the user it is claimed to belong to. A commonly used solution to this authentication problem is the certification of public keys by a trusted authority which, after checking a user's identity, signs the concatenation of his name and public key using a digital signature scheme. Systems based on either the RSA [23] or the ElGamal [3] signature schemes have been proposed [5, 6].

---

[1]A more detailed version of this paper has been submitted to the IEEE Transactions on Information Theory.
[2]Work performed while consulting for Omnisec AG, Switzerland, prior to joining Princeton University.

Shamir [25] suggested as a simple but ingenious method for solving the authentication problem in public-key cryptography to let each user's public key be his (publicly-known) identification information. Because it must be infeasible for users to compute the secret key corresponding to a given identity (including their own), the secret keys must be computed by a trusted authority who knows some secret trapdoor information. The security of such an identity-based system depends on the trusted authority in a more crucial way than the security of a public-key certification system because in the former the trusted authority knows all secret keys.

Because a user's identity can be assumed to be publicly known (the identity can be defined as that part of the identification information that *is* publicly known), the public keys of an identity-based public-key cryptosystem need not be transmitted. Therefore an identity-based system can be used in a completely non-interactive manner.

A simple way to set up an identity-based public-key cryptosystem would seem to be to use the RSA-system with a universal modulus where each user's public encryption exponent is his (odd, and relatively prime to $\varphi(m)$) identity and in which a trusted authority knowing the factorization of the modulus computes the secret decryption exponents for users. However, this system is insecure because knowledge of a matching (secret/public) key pair allows to easily factor the modulus.

While Shamir presented an identity-based signature scheme, he left and proposed as an open problem to find an identity-based public-key cryptosystem or public-key distribution system [25]. In the context of signature schemes, however, an identity-based system is less advantageous than it would be in the context of public-key cryptosystems (which can be made non-interactive) because in a signature scheme, public keys can be certified by a trusted authority and a user's certified public key can be disclosed together with the signature, thus requiring no additional protocol steps for the transmission of the public keys.

Many previously proposed systems [5, 7, 19, 20, 27] have been called identity-based public-key distribution systems because they make use of Shamir's idea for self-authentication of public keys. However, none of these (with the exception of the quite impractical and also insecure version of a scheme discussed in [27]) is an identity-based system in Shamir's sense because the public key is a function not only of the identity but also of some random number selected either by the user or by the trusted authority. As a consequence, these systems are bound to be interactive. A major achievement of this paper is that it presents the first truly identity-based public-key distribution system. It should be mentioned that the key predistribution system of Matsumoto and Imai [13], which is based on a completely different approach, also achieves non-interactive key distribution.

The original Diffie-Hellman public key distribution system [2] with a prime modulus p cannot be used as an identity-based system in Shamir's sense because if the scheme is secure, that is when discrete logarithms modulo p are infeasible to compute, it is infeasible even for a trusted authority to compute the secret key corresponding to a given public key, i.e., a given identity. This comment applies to any public-key distribution system based on a one-way function without trapdoor. One of the major achievement of this paper is that a method for building a *trapdoor into the modular exponentiation one-way function* is proposed which allows a trusted authority to feasibly compute discrete logarithms whereas this is nevertheless completely infeasible for an adversary using present technology and algorithmic knowledge. This allows a trusted authority to set up a non-interactive public-key distribution system. Non-interactiveness is crucial in some applications (e.g. electronic mail, some military applications) and in some other applications allows at least to simplify the protocols. The computational effort that the trusted authority must spend is considerable but the key distribution protocol is efficient.

In Section 2, the preferred version of our system is presented. A security and feasibility analysis is given in Section 3 and some alternative implementation approaches are discussed in Section 4. The final section summarizes some conclusions.

2. A Non-interactive Public Key Distribution System

From a protocol viewpoint, the difference between a public-key distribution system and a public-key cryptosystem is that in the former, both parties must receive the other party's public key whereas in the latter, only the sending party must receive the public key of the receiving party. Therefore, a public-key distribution system, when combined with a conventional symmetric cryptosystem used for encryption, cannot be used as a public-key cryptosystem. In contrast, a non-interactive public-key distribution system *can* be used as a public-key cryptosystem by sending as one message the sender's identity and the enciphered plaintext, where the cipher key is computed from the receiver's identity and the sender's secret key and where some agreed conventional cipher is used for encryption of the message.

Our non-interactive public key distribution system is based on a variant of the Diffie-Hellman system with composite modulus m. By choosing the prime factors of m appropriately such that discrete logarithms modulo each prime factor can feasibly be computed but such that computing discrete logarithms modulo m is nevertheless infeasible, a trusted authority can set up a public key distribution system based on exponentiation modulo m.

Two different ways of generating such a modulus m are presented below and in Section 4, respectively. To use a composite modulus $m = pq$ with p and q prime in the Diffie-Hellman scheme has previously been proposed by Shmuely [26] and McCurley [15] in order to exhibit a system which to break requires the ability both to factor m and to compute discrete logarithms modulo p and q.

Our approach to identity-based public key distribution differs in a crucial way from previous approaches [5, 6, 7, 19, 20, 27] in that the public key consists entirely of public identity information (e.g. name, address, physical description), but does not depend on an additional random number selected either by the user or the trusted authority. This is the reason why our system can be used in a truly non-interactive manner. Clearly, the type and amount of information about a user that can be assumed to be publicly known depends on the application, but note that in most applications, at least part of the identification information is indeed publicly known. For instance, the receiver's address, which must be known in every communication system in order to send a message, can serve as his public key.

One problem that arises in the proposed system is that the multiplicative group Z_m^* is cyclic if and only if m is either 2, 4, a power of an odd prime or twice the power of an odd prime. When m is the product of distinct odd primes there hence exists no element that generates the entire group Z_m^*. Thus not every identity number that corresponds to some valid identification information is guaranteed to have a discrete logarithm with respect to some universal base α. This problem could be solved by adding the smallest offset to every identity number that makes the new number have a discrete logarithm. However, the resulting system would have to be interactive since the offsets must be exchanged between the users. Two different solutions to this problem are presented below and in Section 4, respectively. Both are computationally more efficient (for the trusted authority) than the offset method and at the same time allow to preserve the advantage of non-interactiveness of our scheme.

Let $m = p_1 \cdot p_2 \cdots p_r$ where the primes $p_1, \ldots, p_r$ are in the following assumed to be odd and distinct. The maximal order of an element of the multiplicative group Z_m^* is given by $\lambda(m) = \mathrm{lcm}(p_1 - 1, \ldots, p_r - 1)$, which is at most 2^{-r+1} times the group order $\varphi(m)$. $\lambda(m)$ is strictly less than $\varphi(m)/2^{r-1}$ unless the numbers $(p_1 - 1)/2, \ldots, (p_r - 1)/2$ are pairwise relatively prime. Let α be an element of Z_m^* that is primitive in each of the prime fields $GF(p_1), \ldots, GF(p_r)$, i.e., such that for $1 \leq i \leq r$, $p_i - 1$ is the smallest exponent t_i for which $\alpha^{t_i} \equiv 1 \pmod{p_i}$. Then α has maximal order $\lambda(m)$ in Z_m^*. The discrete logarithm of a number y modulo m to the base α is defined as the smallest non-negative integer x such that $\alpha^x \equiv y \pmod{m}$ (if such an x exists) and can, when the complete factorization of m is given, be obtained by computing for $i = 1, \ldots, r$ the discrete logarithm x_i of y to the base α modulo p_i, i.e., by computing x_i satisfying $\alpha^{x_i} \equiv y \pmod{p_i}$, and solving the system

$$x \equiv x_1 \pmod{p_1 - 1},$$

$$\cdot$$

$$\cdot$$

$$x \equiv x_r \pmod{p_r - 1}$$

of r congruences for x by the Chinese remainder technique. As mentioned above, this system need not have a solution because the numbers $p_1 - 1, \ldots, p_r - 1$ are not pairwise relatively prime. In particular, the system has no solution unless either all x_i are odd or all x_i are even.

The following Lemma is a special case of a more general result proved in the journal version of this paper. It suggests an easy to compute publicly-known function that transforms, without use of the secret trapdoor, any identity number into a modified identity number that is guaranteed to have a discrete logarithm.

Lemma. *Let m and α be as defined above where the numbers $(p_i - 1)/2, \ldots, (p_r - 1)/2$ are pairwise relatively prime. Then every square modulo m has a discrete logarithm modulo m to the base α.*

A complete description of the preferred version of the proposed non-interactive public key distribution system follows. The following three paragraphs describe the system set up by a trusted authority, the user registration phase and the user communication phase, respectively.

To set up the system we suggest that a trusted authority choose the primes p_i such that the numbers $(p_i - 1)/2$ are odd and pairwise relatively prime [14]. Preferably, $(p_i - 1)/2$ are chosen to be primes themselves. The primes p_i are chosen small enough such that computing discrete logarithms modulo each prime is feasible (though not trivial) using for instance the algorithm of [1] but such that factoring the product, even with the best known method for finding relatively small prime factors [10] of a number, is completely infeasible. The trusted authority then computes the product

$$m = p_1 \cdot p_2 \cdots p_r$$

of the selected primes, determines an element α of Z_m^* that is primitive in every of the prime fields $GF(p_i)$ and publishes m and α as system parameters. We refer to Section 3 for an analysis of the security versus the feasibility for different sizes of parameters. To choose 3 to 4 primes of between 60 and 70 decimal digits seems at present to be appropriate, but these figures can vary according to future progress in computer technology and number-theoretic algorithms. An alternative approach to making the discrete logarithm problem feasible other than by choosing the prime factors of m sufficiently small is described in Section 4.

When a user A wants to join the system she visits the trusted authority, presents her identification information ID_A together with an appropriate proof of her identity (e.g. a passport) and receives the secret key s_A corresponding to ID_A. The secret key s_A is computed by the trusted authority as the discrete logarithm of $ID_A{}^2$ modulo m to the base α:

$$s_A \equiv \log_\alpha(ID_A{}^2) \pmod{m}.$$

Due to the squaring of ID_A, s_A is guaranteed to exist as a consequence of the above lemma.

In order to send a message M securely to a user B without interaction, user A establishes the mutual secure cipher key K_{AB} shared with user B by computing

$$K_{AB} \equiv (ID_B)^{2s_A} \pmod{m}.$$

Note that $K_{AB} \equiv \alpha^{s_A s_B} \pmod{m}$. She then uses a conventional symmetric cryptosystem (e.g. DES) to encipher the message M using the cipher key K_{AB}, which results in the ciphertext C. User A then sends C together with her identity number ID_A to user B. In order to decipher the received ciphertext C, user B proceeds symmetrically and computes

$$K_{BA} \equiv (ID_A)^{2s_B} \equiv \alpha^{s_B s_A} \equiv K_{AB} \pmod{m}.$$

He then deciphers C using the conventional cryptosystem with the secret key K_{AB}, which results in the plaintext message M.

Note that the trusted authority is only required for the initial system set up and for user registration, but not in the user communication phase described above. In fact, the trusted authority could close itself down if no additional users need to be registered, thereby irreversibly erasing the factorization of m.

In the described system the secret key shared by two users is the same when the protocol is repeated several times. This in many applications undesirable property can easily be removed without losing non-interactiveness by having user A choose a random number R and use $f(K_{AB}, R)$ as the mutual cipher key, where f is a cryptographically secure hash function. R is sent to B together with the ciphertext C. In order to prevent an adversary knowing a previously cipher key from impersonating at a later time, a time stamp can be used as an additional argument of the hash function. It is possible to build a dynamic key distribution system using no hash function, that is provably as hard (on the average) to break against a disruptive adversary as factoring the modulus [28].

Although in the proposed trapdoor one-way function the trapdoor is the factorization of the modulus as in the RSA trapdoor one-way function [23], the two functions are nevertheless entirely different. In the RSA function, the argument is the base and the exponent e is a constant whereas in our exponentiation trapdoor one-way function the argument is the exponent and the base α is a constant. Accordingly, the inverse operations are the extraction of the e-th root and the discrete logarithm to the base α, respectively, and are infeasible to compute without knowledge of the trapdoor.

3. Security and Feasibility Analysis

The following fact has previously been observed but is not widely known nor published. A proof is given in the journal version of this paper.

Proposition. *Let m be the product of distinct odd primes $p_1, \ldots, p_r$ and let α be primitive in each of the prime fields $GF(p_i)$ for $1 \leq i \leq r$. Then computing discrete logarithms modulo m to the base α is at least as difficult as factoring m completely.*

The function

$$L_x(a, b) = e^{b(\log x)^a (\log \log x)^{1-a}}$$

is commonly used to express the conjectured asymptotic running time of number-theoretic algorithms. The fastest known algorithm for computing discrete logarithms in $GF(p)$ [1] has asymptotic running time $L_p(1/2, 1)$. The largest primes for which this algorithm is at present feasible with massively parallel computation have between 90 and 100 decimal digits. For primes of up to 65-70 decimal digits the algorithm is feasible on a small to medium size computer. An important feature of this algorithm is that most of the running time is spent in a precomputation phase that is independent of actual elements for which the logarithm is to be computed. After the precomputation, individual logarithms can be computed much faster in asymptotic running time $L_p(1/2, 1/2)$. The algorithm is well suited for a parallel implementation.

The largest general integers that can at present feasibly be factored using massively parallel computation have on the order of 110 decimal digits [9]. The factoring algorithm with the best conjectured asymptotic running time $L_m(1/3, c)$ for some constant $c < 2$ is the number field sieve [11], but for the size of general integers m that can be factored within reasonable time a variant of the quadratic sieve with asymptotic running time $L_m(1/2, 1)$ is more efficient [9]. The running time of both these algorithms is independent of the size of the factor that is found. The best known algorithm for finding factors of moderate size is the elliptic curve algorithm [10] which is with massively parallel computation successful for factors with up to 40 decimal digits [8, 18]. Its asymptotic running time is $L_p(1/2, \sqrt{2})$ where p is the factor to be found. It is the ratio $L_p(1/2, \sqrt{2})/L_p(1/2, 1) = L_p(1/2, \sqrt{2} - 1)$ of the running times of the elliptic curve factoring algorithm and the discrete logarithm algorithm [1] that provides a range for the size of the primes for which our public-key distribution system is both practical and secure.

It seems at present to be appropriate to choose 3 to 4 prime factors of between 60 and

70 decimal digits. To factor such a modulus is for all presently known factoring algorithms completely infeasible. The largest factor that has been found by the elliptic curve algorithm has 38 decimal digits [8]. Odlyzko [18] estimated that with the same computational effort that was spent on the factorization of the 106-digit number of [12], one could compute discrete logarithms for 92-digit prime moduli. To find a 70 digit factor with the elliptic curve factoring algorithm takes about $L_{10^{70}}(1/2, \sqrt{2})/L_{10^{38}}(1/2, \sqrt{2}) \approx 270.000$ times more time than to find a 38 digit factor. On the other hand, computing discrete logarithms for a 70-digit prime modulus is about $L_{10^{92}}(1/2, 1)/L_{10^{70}}(1/2, 1) \approx 157$ times faster than for a 92-digit prime modulus. An asymptotic analysis of the work factor of our system is given in the journal version of the paper.

4. Alternative Implementations

There exists a discrete logarithm algorithm for $GF(p)$ due to Pohlig and Hellman [21] whose running time is proportional to the square root of the largest prime factor of $p - 1$, if the factorization of $p - 1$ is known. Hence the primes p_i can be chosen such that $(p_i - 1)/2$ is the product of some primes of a certain relatively small size. Unfortunately, there also exists a special purpose factoring algorithm due to Pollard [22] that is particularly efficient for finding prime factors p for which $p - 1$ has only relatively small prime factors. However, the running time of Pollard's algorithm is proportional to the largest prime factor of $p - 1$ rather than its square root. Therefore there may exist a range for the size of the largest prime factors of $p_i - 1$ for which a system based on this idea is both practical and secure. A possible choice could be to let m be the product of 2 primes p_1 and p_2 of about 100 decimal digits each, where $(p_1 - 1)/2$ and $(p_2 - 1)/2$ both are the product of several 13- to 15-digit primes.

When the computational effort spent by the trusted authority is increased by a factor k, this forces an adversary to increase his computational effort by a factor k^2. Thus when k-fold faster computer hardware becomes available this system's security can also be increased by a factor of k. This system is asymptotically superior to the system of Section 2 for which the work factor could be increased only by a factor $k^{\sqrt{2}-1} = k^{.414}$.

The lemma in the previous section suggests a way to derive an identity number from a user's identity such that the discrete logarithm of this number modulo m to the base α is guaranteed to exists. In the case where m is the product of only two prime factors there exists an alternative though less practical approach which is mentioned here for the sake of completeness. Let $m = p_1 p_2$ and let $\gcd(p_1 - 1, p_2 - 1) = 2$. The (without knowledge of the factorization of m) easily computable Jacobi symbol $(x|m)$ is equal to 1 if and only if x is a quadratic residue either for both $GF(p_1)$ and $GF(p_2)$ or for none of them. Equivalently, $(x|m) = 1$ if and only if the discrete logarithms in $GF(p_1)$ and $GF(p_2)$ are congruent modulo 2, i.e., if and only if x possesses a discrete logarithm modulo m. Hence a user's identity number can be defined as the smallest integer x greater or equal to the number representing his name and such that $(x|m) = 1$. No interaction is required for transmitting the offset since it can easily be determined without knowing the factorization of m.

5. Conclusions

A remarkable property of the presented systems is that not only the cryptanalyst, but also the trusted authority must spend time super-polynomial in the input size. However, because the system is used for an appropriate fixed size of parameters, the trusted authority's computation is nevertheless feasible. Progress in computer technology can be exploited to increase the security of the system.

There may exist other approaches than those presented to making the discrete logarithm problem feasible only when given the factorization of the modulus. Any progress in the discrete logarithm problem not leading to a comparable progress in the factorization problem, especially when applicable to primes of a certain special form, has the potential of leading to an improvement of the presented system. An interesting open question is whether it is possible to construct primes p of a special form containing a trapdoor such that computing discrete logarithms modulo p is feasible if and only if the trapdoor is known.

Acknowledgements

We are grateful to Marc Girault, Stuart Haber, Neal Koblitz, Arjen Lenstra, Kevin McCurley, Andrew Odlyzko, Ron Rivest and Rich Graveman for their helpful comments. We would also like to thank Tom Berson and Jim Massey for highly appreciated discussions, and Dr. K. Ohta for drawing our attention to the paper [17] written in Japanese, which contains a scheme possibly similar to those presented in this paper. The first author would like to thank Dr. P. Schmid and Martin Benninger of Omnisec AG for their comments and generous support of this work.

References

[1] D. Coppersmith, A.M. Odlyzko and R. Schroeppel, Discrete Logarithms in $GF(p)$, *Algorithmica*, vol. 1, pp. 1-15, 1986.

[2] W. Diffie and M.E. Hellman, New directions in cryptography, *IEEE Transactions on Information Theory*, vol. IT-22, pp. 664-654, Nov. 1976.

[3] T. ElGamal, A public key cryptosystem and a signature scheme based on discrete logarithms, *IEEE Transactions on Information Theory*, vol. IT-31, pp. 469-472, July 1985.

[4] M. Girault, Self-certified public keys, these proceedings.

[5] C.G. Günther, An identity-based key-exchange protocol, *Advances in Cryptology - EUROCRYPT '89*, Lecture Notes in Computer Science, vol. 434, Berlin: Springer Verlag, pp. 29-37, 1990.

[6] L. Kohnfelder, Towards a practical public-key cryptosystem, B.S. Thesis, MIT, 1979.

[7] K. Koyama and K. Ohta, Identity-based conference key distribution systems, *Advances in Cryptology - CRYPTO '87*, Lecture Notes in Computer Science, vol. 293, Berlin: Springer Verlag, pp. 175-184, 1988.

[8] A.K. Lenstra, personal communication, 1991.

[9] A.K. Lenstra and M.S. Manasse, Factoring with two large primes, *Advances in Cryptology - EU-ROCRYPT '90*, Lecture Notes in Computer Science, vol. 473, Berlin: Springer Verlag, pp. 69-80, 1991.

[10] H.W. Lenstra, Factoring integers with elliptic curves, *Annals of Mathematics*, vol. 126, pp. 649-673, 1987.

[11] A.K. Lenstra, H.W. Lenstra, M.S. Manasse and J.M. Pollard, The number field sieve, to appear.

[12] A.K. Lenstra and M.S. Manasse, Factoring with electronic mail, *Advances in Cryptology - EURO-CRYPT '89*, Lecture Notes in Computer Science, vol. 434, Berlin: Springer Verlag, pp. 355-371, 1990.

[13] T. Matsumoto and H. Imai, On the key predistribution system: a practical solution to the key distribution problem, *Advances in Cryptology - CRYPTO '87*, Lecture Notes in Computer Science, vol. 293, Berlin: Springer Verlag, pp. 185-193, 1988.

[14] U.M. Maurer, Fast generation of secure RSA-moduli with almost maximal diversity, *Advances in Cryptology - EUROCRYPT '89*, Lecture Notes in Computer Science, vol. 434, Berlin: Springer Verlag, pp. 636-647, 1990.

[15] K.S. McCurley, A key distribution system equivalent to factoring, *Journal of Cryptology*, vol. 1, no. 2, pp. 95-106, 1988.

[16] G.L. Miller, *Riemann's hypothesis and tests for primality*, Journal of Computer and System Sciences, vol. 13, pp. 300-317, 1976.

[17] Y. Murakami and M. Kasahara, An ID-based key distribution system, Proc. of ISEC90, pp. 33-40, 1990 (in Japanese).

[18] A.M. Odlyzko, personal communications, 1990-91.

[19] T. Okamoto and K. Ohta, How to utilize the randomness of zero-knowledge proofs, presented at CRYPTO'90 (to appear in the proceedings), Santa Barbara, CA, Aug. 11-15, 1990.

[20] E. Okamoto and K. Tanaka, Key distribution based on identification information, *IEEE Journal on Selected Areas in Communications*, vol. 7, no. 4, pp. 481-485, May 1989.

[21] S.C. Pohlig and M.E. Hellman, An improved algorithm for computing logarithms over $GF(p)$ and its cryptographic significance, *IEEE Transactions on Information Theory*, vol IT-24, pp. 106-110, Jan. 1978.

[22] J.M. Pollard, Theorems on factorization and primality testing, *Proc. Cambridge Philos. Society*, vol. 76, pp. 521-528, 1974.

[23] R.L. Rivest, A. Shamir and L. Adleman, A method for obtaining digital signatures and public-key cryptosystems, *Communications of the ACM*, vol. 21, pp. 120-126, 1978.

[24] R.J. Schoof, Elliptic curves over finite fields and the computation of square roots mod p, *Mathematics of Computation*, vol. 44, pp. 483-494, 1985.

[25] A. Shamir, Identity-based cryptosystems and signature schemes, *Advances in Cryptology - CRYPTO '84*, Lecture Notes in Computer Science, vol. 196, Berlin: Springer Verlag, pp. 47-53, 1985.

[26] Z. Shmuely, Composite Diffie-Hellman public-key generating systems are hard to break, TR 356, CS Dept., Technion, Feb. 1985.

[27] S. Tsujii and T. Itoh, An ID-based cryptosystem based on the discrete logarithm problem, *IEEE Journal on Selected Areas in Communications*, vol. 7, no. 4, pp. 467-473, May 1989.

[28] Y. Yacobi, A key distribution "paradox", presented at CRYPTO'90 (to appear in the proceedings), Santa Barbara, CA, Aug. 11-15, 1990.

Hash Functions And Graphs With Large Girths

G. Zémor

E.N.S.T.
Dept. Réseaux
46 rue Barrault
75634 Paris Cedex 13
FRANCE

ABSTRACT

We propose and analyse an easily computable cryptographic hash function, for the purpose of signing long variable length texts, which is related to the construction of graphs with large girths.

EXTENDED ABSTRACT

We focus on the problem of devising an easily computable hash function, for integrity purposes. Such a function should be defined on the set of finite words over an alphabet, say $\{0, 1\}^*$, and should take values on a small finite set ; its purpose is to provide long variable length texts (in practice of length several megabytes), with a "signature" (of a few hundred bits), without using a secret key. Computation should be fast, and finding a text with a given signature, or two texts with the same signature, (i.e. devising a forgery), difficult.

Several schemes have been proposed and analysed, one of which (see [God]), makes use of error-correcting codes, and has the attractive feature that modification of less than d bits of text will necesserily yield a modification of the hashed value, where d is the minimal distance of an appropriately chosen code. Unfortunately, such schemes are based on linear computations which are well known for their cryptographic weakness. We have tried to devise a hash function based on nonlinear computations which retains something of in the modular group $\Gamma = SL_2(Z)/\{1, -1\}$, we have $T^2 = 1$ and $(TS)^3 = 1$, furthermore it is well known that Γ is isomorphic to the free product of a cyclic group generated by an x of order 2, and a cyclic group generated by a y of order 3, where x corresponds to T and y corresponds to TS. From this it can easily be deduced that an equality of the form :

$$X_1 X_2 \ldots X_k X_h'^{-1} \ldots X_2'^{-1} X_1'^{-1} = 1 \tag{2}$$

with $X_i = A$ or B, and $X_j' = A$ or B, cannot hold in Γ, unless $x_1 \ldots x_k$ and $x_1' \ldots x_h'$ are identical strings.

Hence, if $x_1 \ldots x_k$ and $x_1' \ldots x_h'$ are not identical :

$$\|X_1 X_2 \ldots X_k - X_1' X_2' \ldots X_h'\| \geq p \tag{3}$$

where $\|M\| = \sup_{\xi \neq 0} \|M\xi\|/\|\xi\|$ and the norm of $\xi = \begin{pmatrix} \xi_1 \\ \xi_2 \end{pmatrix}$ is $\|\xi\| = \sqrt{\xi_1^2 + \xi_2^2}$.

By elementary linear algebra, $\|A\| = \sqrt{\|{}^t A A\|} = \sqrt{\lambda}$ where λ is the largest eigenvalue of ${}^t A A$. Hence $\|A\| = \|B\| = \phi = \frac{1+\sqrt{5}}{2} \approx 1.62$.

(3) implies

$$\max(\|X_1 X_2 \ldots X_k\|, \|X_1' X_2' \ldots X_h'\|) \geq p/2$$

and by the submultiplicativity of the norm of matrices

$$\max(k, h) \geq \log_\phi \frac{p}{2}.$$

We have proved :

Proposition 1 *If k consecutive bits of text are replaced (nontrivially) by h consecutive bits with $\max(k, h) < \log_\phi \frac{p}{2}$, then the signature is modified.*

Compare this with an analogous result (obtained in very much the same way) stated in the language of graphs :

Proposition 2 *The directed Cayley graph $C(SL_2(F_p), A, B)$ has a girth (smallest circuitsize) $g \geq 2 \log_\phi \frac{p}{2} - 1$.*

The idea of using $SL_2(F_p)$ for constructing Cayley graphs with large girths originates in [Mar].

Hashed values range over $SL_2(F_p)$: A and B are easily seen to generate $SL_2(F_p)$, but do texts of length a polynomial in $\log p$, yield arbitrary elements of $SL_2(F_p)$ as a hashed value ? (Clearly a necessary feature of an attractive hash function). This is indeed the case, i.e. we can prove :

the features of the coding-based schemes ; for that purpose, we substituted the original tool, i.e. the minimum distance of a code, by the girth of a Cayley graph. This will be made clear shortly.

The scheme we propose is the following : to an arbitrary string of $\{0,1\}^*$ (the text) associate the string of $\{A,B\}^*$ obtained by substituting 0 for A and 1 for B, then assign to A and B values of adequately chosen matrices of $SL_2(Z)$, those could be, for example :

$$A = \begin{pmatrix} 1 & 1 \\ 0 & 1 \end{pmatrix} \qquad B = \begin{pmatrix} 1 & 0 \\ 1 & 1 \end{pmatrix}$$

then evaluate the product associated with the string of A's and B's in the group $SL_2(F_p)$ where F_p is the field on p elements, p being a chosen large prime number (e.g. of 150 bits). The hashed value S is the computed product (its size is $3 \log p$ bits).

A multiplication by A or B in $SL_2(F_p)$ requires essentially 4 additions, so hashing an n bit text requires $4n$ additions of $\log p$ bits, which is reasonably fast. Signatures based on associating an alphabet with basic matrices and multiplying them in $GL_2(F_p)$ have been proposed before, but with basic matrices of arbitrary size, so that a large p could not be chosen without damaging the speed of computation, and forging could be achieved with probabilistic methods of factoring, see [Cam], which do not seem to be appliable here.

The problem of devising a forgery involves factoring elements of $SL_2(F_p)$ into a product of A's and B's. Trivial factorisations of an arbitrary matrix of $SL_2(F_p)$ can be exhibited but they have a length in $O(p)$, so are useless as a forgery (no text has 2^{150} bits !). What is needed is a short factorisation of elements of $SL_2(F_p)$ which seems to be quite difficult, see [Bab] ; besides, recall that the general problem of finding the shortest factorisation of an arbitrary element of a group over a given set of generators is P-space complete, (see [Jer]).

"Local" modifications of the text change the signature : Suppose that a subset of k consecutive bits $x_1 x_2 \ldots x_k$ of a text is changed into h consecutive bits $x_1' x_2' \ldots x_h'$, with $x_1 \neq x_1'$ and $x_k \neq x_h'$. If the signature is unchanged, then the corresponding products of A's and B's are equal in $SL_2(F_p)$:

$$X_1 X_2 \ldots X_k = X_1' X_2' \ldots X_h' \qquad \mod p \qquad (1)$$

Evaluate those two products in $SL_2(Z)$; they are necessarily different : to see this, recall that $SL_2(Z)$ is classically generated by the matrices

$$S = A \text{and } T = \begin{pmatrix} 0 & 1 \\ -1 & 0 \end{pmatrix} = -S^{-1}BS^{-1} = (S^{-1}BS^{-1})^3$$

Proposition 3 *The diameter of the directed Cayley graph $C(SL_2(F_p), A, B)$ is in $O(\log p)$.*

The proof involves powerful (and nonconstructive) arithmetic : it can be shown (see [Bab] and the references therein) that there is a constant c (independant of p) such that for any set X of vertices of the nondirected Cayley graph $C(G = PSL_2(F_p), A, B, A^{-1}, B^{-1})$, such that $|X| \leq \frac{1}{2}|G|$

$$|\partial X| \geq c|X| \qquad (4)$$

where ∂X denotes the set of neighbours of S, not in X. Following [AlM] it can be deduced that the diameter of $C(PSL_2(F_p), A, B, A^{-1}, B^{-1})$ is in $O(\log p)$.

We can adapt those combinatorial techniques to obtain (4) in the directed graph case and hence proposition 3.

Generalisations to strings over larger alphabets can be envisaged, using matrices that generate graphs with a large girth and a small diameter.

References

[AlM.85] N. Alon, and V.D. Milman, "λ_1, isoperimetric inequalities for graphs, and superconcentrators", *J. Comb. Theory. Ser. B*, 38 (1985), 73-88.

[Bab.89] L. Babai, W.M. Kantor, and A. Lubotsky, "Small-diameter Cayley Graphs for Finite Simple Groups," *Europ. J. Combinatorics*, 1989, 10, 507-522.

[Cam.87] P. Camion, "Can a Fast Signature Scheme Without Secret Key be Secure ?", in *AAECC, Lecture Notes in Computer Science*, n 228, Springer-Verlag.

[Jer.85] M.R. Jerrum, "The Complexity of Finding Minimum Length Generator Sequences ", *Theoretical Computer Science*, April 1985.

[God.88] P. Godlewski and P. Camion, "Manipulations and Errors, Detection and Localization", *Advances in Cryptology, EUROCRYPT-88*, Springer-Verlag, pp.96-106.

[Mar.82] G.A. Margulis, "Explicit Constructions of Graphs Without Short Cycles and Low Density Codes," *COMBINATORICA* 2 (1), 1982, 71-78.

Dickson Pseudoprimes and Primality Testing*)

Winfried B. Müller
Institut für Mathematik
Universität Klagenfurt
A-9022 Klagenfurt
Austria

Alan Oswald
School of Computing and Mathematics
Teesside Polytechnic
Middlesbrough, Cleveland TS1 3BA
Great Britain

Abstract: The paper gives a general definition for the concept of strong Dickson pseudoprimes which contains as special cases the Carmichael numbers and the strong Fibonacci pseudoprimes. Furthermore, we give necessary and sufficient conditions for two important classes of strong Dickson pseudoprimes and deduce some properties for their elements. A suggestion of how to improve a primality test by Baillie&Wagstaff concludes the paper.

1. Carmichael Numbers

Fermat's Little Theorem plays an important role in many primality tests and in motivating the concept of pseudoprimes. An equivalent formulation of this theorem states that for any prime n and an arbitrary integer b one has

$$b^n \equiv b \bmod n. \tag{1}$$

An odd composite number n for which $b^n \equiv b \bmod n$ for a certain integer b is called a *pseudoprime to the base b* (abbreviated $psp(b)$). If n is not a prime then it is still possible, but not very likely, that (1) holds for a randomly chosen integer b, and even less likely, that (1) holds for all integers b. An odd composite integer n such that $b^n \equiv b \bmod n$ for every $b \in \mathbb{Z}$ is called a *Carmichael number*. An odd composite integer n is a Carmichael number if and only if n is square-free and $(p-1) \mid (n-1)$ for every prime p dividing n (cf. KOBLITZ [7]). The smallest Carmichael number is $n = 561 = 3 \cdot 11 \cdot 17$. CHERNICK [1] gave a method for obtaining Carmichael numbers with three prime factors. For a positive integer t the number $n = (6t + 1)(12t + 1)(18t + 1)$ is a Carmichael number if all three factors of n are prime. A fast method for finding (also very large) Carmichael numbers of this form is due to DUBNER [2]. A table with all Carmichael numbers $\leq 10^{12}$ was calculated by JAESCHKE [6]. However, it is not known if there are infinitely many Carmichael numbers.

---

*) This work peformed in part at the University of Klagenfurt was supported by the Forschungskommission of the University of Klagenfurt and by the Österreichischer Fonds zur Förderung der wissenschaftlichen Forschung under project no. P6174.

2. Generalizations of Fermat's Little Theorem

Let b, c be nonzero integers and α, β be the roots of the polynomial $x^2 - bx + c$. Assume that $d = b^2 - 4c \neq 0$. Then the sequences

$$U_n(b, c) = \frac{\alpha^n - \beta^n}{\alpha - \beta} \quad \text{and} \quad V_n(b, c) := \alpha^n + \beta^n, \quad n \geq 0$$

are called the *Lucas sequences associated to the pair* (b, c) (cf. RIBENBOIM [14]). If n is an odd prime and $\gcd(n, d) = 1$, then

$$U_{n-(d/n)} \equiv 0 \bmod n, \tag{2}$$

where (d/n) is the Jacobi symbol. An odd composite integer n such that (2) holds is called a *Lucas pseudoprime with parameters* (b, c) (abbreviated $lpsp(b, c)$).

Comparing probable prime tests based on Fermat's Theorem (1) and on the Lucas test (2) one obtains e.g. 22 $psp(2)$s and only 9 $lpsp(1, c)$s less than 10^4, where $c = \frac{1}{4}(1 - d)$ and d is the first element of the sequence $5, -7, 9, -11, 13, \cdots$ for which $(d/4) = -1$. As by test (1) with different bases b at least the Carmicheal numbers cannot be exposed as composite, BAILLIE AND WAGSTTAFF [3] suggested a primality test combining Fermat's Theorem with Lucas pseudoprimes. They proved that all of the 21853 $psp(2)$s under $25 \cdot 10^9$ fail the Lucas test (2), where b and c are chosen as above.

At EUROCRYPT'88 DI PORTO AND FILIPPONI [4] proposed another method for finding large probable primes based on the fact that for any prime number n and an arbitrary integer b there holds

$$V_n(b, -1) \equiv b \bmod n. \tag{3}$$

Composite odd integers n with $V_n(1, -1) \equiv 1 \bmod n$ are called *Fibonacci pseudoprimes* (abbreviated $fpsp(1, -1)$) and have been studied already by SINGMASTER [15]. FILIPPONI [5] verified experimentally that there exist only 7 $fpsp(1, -1)$ under 10^4 and 852 $fpsp(1, -1)$ less than 10^8. Numerical tests on odd composite integers n up to 10^{100} suggest that very few such numbers satisfy a combination of congruences $V_n(b, -1) \equiv b \bmod n$ for several b.

According to LIDL, MÜLLER AND OSWALD [10] an odd composite number n is called a *strong Fibonacci pseudoprime* if n satisfies the congruence (3) for every $b \in \mathbb{Z}$. In contrast to Fermat's Theorem there are no strong Fibonacci pseudoprimes $n \leq 10^{13}$ (cf. [10]). In particular, there is no odd composite integer $n \leq 10^8$ which satisfies (2) for all $b \in \mathbb{Z}$ with $1 \leq b \leq 8$ (cf. [5]). However, the question of existence of strong Fibonacci pseudoprimes n has not yet been answered.

3. Strong Dickson Pseudoprimes

By using *Waring's formula* it can be verified that

$$V_n(b,c) = \alpha^n + \beta^n = \sum_{i=0}^{[n/2]} \frac{n}{n-i} \binom{n-i}{i} (-c)^i \, b^{n-2i} =: g_n(b,c), \tag{4}$$

where $[n/2]$ denotes the greatest integer $i \leq \frac{n}{2}$. The polynomial $g_n(x,c)$ is called the
Dickson polynomial of parameter c and degree n. It is not difficult to show that the
coefficients of $g_n(x,c)$ are integers for any positive integer n and any $c \in \mathbb{Z}$.
Properties of Dickson polynomials and their application in cryptography have been studied
in great detail (cf. LIDL AND MÜLLER [8], MÜLLER [11], MÜLLER AND NÖBAUER R.
[12]). From (4) it can be seen immediately that for any prime n and an arbitrary $b \in \mathbb{Z}$
there holds

$$V_n(b,c) = g_n(b,c) \equiv b \bmod n. \tag{5}$$

Generalizing the definition of strong Fibonacci pseudoprimes, we call an odd composite
integer n a *strong Dickson pseudoprime of the kind c* (in short: a *strong c-Dickson pseudoprime*) if $g_n(b,c) \equiv b \bmod n$ for all $b \in \mathbb{Z}$.
Obviously, the strong 0-Dickson pseudoprimes are exactly the Carmichael numbers and
the strong (-1)-Dickson pseudoprimes the strong Fibonacci pseudoprimes.

The following theorem gives a reformulation of Theorem 1 in [10].

Theorem 1: *An odd integer n is a strong (-1)-Dickson pseudoprime if and only if*
(i)   *n is Carmichael number,*
(ii)   *$2(p_i + 1) \mid (n - 1)$ or $2(p_i + 1) \mid (n - p_i)$ for every prime p_i dividing n.*

Improving the results on the minimal number of prime factors of strong (-1)-Dickson
pseudoprimes given in [10] we state

Corollary 1: *Any strong (-1)-Dickson pseudoprime $n \equiv 1 \bmod 4$ must be the product
of at least four distinct primes.*
*Any strong (-1)-Dickson pseudoprime $n \equiv 3 \bmod 4$ must be the product of at least five
distinct primes.*

Proof: For the first statement, let $n = p_1 p_2 p_3$, whereby p_1, p_2, p_3 are primes with
$p_1 < p_2 < p_3$. If n is a strong (-1)-Dickson pseudoprime with $(p_3 - 1) \mid (n - 1)$ and
$2(p_3+1) \mid (n-1)$ then $(p_3^2-1) \mid (n-1)$, i.e. $(p_3^2-1) \mid (p_1p_2p_3-1)$. Hence $(p_3^2-1) \mid (p_1p_2-p_3)$,
which yields a contradiction.
If n is a strong (-1)-Dickson pseudoprime with $(p_3 - 1) \mid (n - 1)$ and $2(p_3 + 1) \mid (n - p_3)$

then $(p_3 - 1) \mid (p_1 p_2 - 1)$ and $2(p_3 + 1) \mid (p_1 p_2 - 1)$. Hence $(p_3^2 - 1) \mid (p_1 p_2 - 1)$, which yields a contradiction too.

The second statement was proved already as Corollary 4 in [10]. $\square$

The following necessary und sufficient conditions for strong $(+1)$-Dickson pseudoprimes can be derived similarly as for (-1)-Dickson pseudoprimes in [10], using a formula for the number of fixed points of the permutation $x \to g_n(x,1)$ on $\mathbb{Z}/(n)$ given in [13].

Theorem 2. *An odd integer n is a strong $(+1)$-Dickson pseudoprime if and only if*

(i) n *is square-free,*

(ii) $((p_i - 1) \mid (n - 1)$ *or* $(p_i - 1) \mid (n - p_i))$ *for every prime p_i dividing n,*

(iii) $((p_i + 1) \mid (n - 1)$ *or* $(p_i + 1) \mid (n - p_i))$ *for every prime p_i dividing n.*

Corollary 3. *Any strong (-1)-Dickson pseudoprime is also a strong $(+1)$-Dickson pseudoprime.*

Lemma 1. *A Carmichael number of the form*

$$n = (6t + 1)(12t + 1) \prod_{i=1}^{r-2} (9 \cdot 2^i t + 1) \text{ with } t, r \in \mathbb{Z}, \ t \geq 1, \ r \geq 3$$

(cf. [14]) is not a strong (-1)-Dickson pseudoprime.

Proof. If n is a strong (-1)-Dickson pseudoprime then $(p+1) \mid (n-1)$ for each prime p dividing n (Theorem 1(ii)). Now $(12t + 1) + 1 = 2(6t + 1)$ and so $(6t + 1) \mid (n - 1)$. But $(6t + 1) \mid n$ and this is a contradiction. $\square$

4. Conclusions and Remarks

It is an open problem if there exist strong c-Dickson pseudoprimes for $c \neq 0$. The numerical evidence collected so far indicates that there are very few odd composite integers n satisfying a combination of congruences $V_n(b, +1) \equiv b \bmod n$ for several arbitrarily chosen b. In accordance with Corollary 3, even fewer integers n satisfy the congruences $V_n(b, -1) \equiv b \bmod n$ for several b (cf. LIDL AND MÜLLER [9]). The scarcity of odd composite integers passing only a small number of tests by congruence (5) with different parameters c suggests a fast probabilistic primality test combining such tests. In general, one needs less tests to disclose an odd composite integer n as not prime using congruence (5) with negative parameters c rather than positive ones. E.g., there are only 24 composed odd numbers under 10^6 passing test (5) with $(b, c) = (3, -3)$ and up to 3.7×10^6 only the composed odd number $1\,909\,001$ with the factor 461 passes the tests (5) for $(b, c) =$

$(1,-1)$ and $(b,c) = (3,-3)$. But this number is disclosed by the test with $(b,c) = (2,-1)$ too. Hence, a combination of several tests by congruence (5) with a few different negative parameters c seems to be more efficient than the proposed primality test by Baillie&Wagstaff combining tests by congruence (1) and (2). Numerical evidence for this statement for the numbers up to 10^9 is in progress.

References

[1] CHERNICK J.: On Fermat's simple theorem. Bull.Amer.Math.Soc. **45**, 269–274 (1939).

[2] DUBNER H.: A New Method for Producing Large Carmichael Numbers. Math.Comp. **53**, No. 187, 411–414 (1989).

[3] BAILLIE, R., WAGSTAFF JR., S.S.: Lucas pseudoprimes. Math.Comp. **35**, 1391–1417 (1980).

[4] DI PORTO, A., FILIPPONI, P.: A Probabilistic Primality Test Based on the Properties of Certain Generalized Lucas Numbers. In: Advances in Cryptology – Eurocrypt'88, Lecture Notes in Computer Science **330**, Springer–Verlag, New York–Berlin–Heidelberg, pp. 211–223, 1988.

[5] FILIPPONI, P.: Table of Fibonacci Pseudoprimes to 10^8. Note Recensioni Notizie **37**, No. 1–2, 33–38 (1988).

[6] JAESCHKE, G.: Math.Comp. **55**, No. 191, 383–389 (1990).

[7] KOBLITZ, N.: A Course in Number Theory and Cryptography. Springer–Verlag, New York–Berlin–Heidelberg, 1987.

[8] LIDL, R., MÜLLER, W.B.: Permutation polynomials in RSA-cryptosystems. Advances in Cryptology - Crypto '83 (ed. D.Chaum), New York, Plenum Press, pp. 293–301, 1984.

[9] LIDL, R., MÜLLER, W.B.: Generalizations of the Fibonacci Pseudoprimes Test. To appear in Discrete Mathem. **92** (1991).

[10] LIDL, R., MÜLLER, W.B., OSWALD A.: Some Remarks on Strong Fibonacci Pseudoprimes. Applicable Algebra in Engineering, Communication and Computing (AAECC) **1**, 59–65 (1990).

[11] MÜLLER, W.B.: Polynomial Functions in Modern Cryptology. In: Contributions to General Algebra **3**, Teubner–Verlag, Stuttgart, pp. 7–32, 1985.

[12] MÜLLER, W.B., NÖBAUER R.: Cryptanalysis of the Dickson-scheme. In: Advances in Cryptology – Eurocrypt'85, Lecture Notes in Computer Science **219**, Springer–Verlag, New York–Berlin–Heidelberg, pp. 50–61, 1986.

[13] NÖBAUER, W.: Über die Fixpunkte der Dickson–Permutationen. Sb.d.Österr.Akad.-d.Wiss., math.-nat.Kl., Abt.II, Bd. **193**, 115–133 (1984).

[14] RIBENBOIM, P.: The Book of Prime Number Records. Springer–Verlag, New York–Berlin–Heidelberg, 1988.

[15] SINGMASTER, D.: Some Lucas pseudoprimes. Abstracts Amer.Math.Soc. **4**, No.83T-10-146, p.197 (1983).

Equivalent Goppa Codes and Trapdoors to McEliece's Public Key Cryptosystem

J. K. Gibson

Department of Computer Science, Birkbeck College,
Malet Street, London WC1E 7HX, England

Abstract
We show that contrary to a published statement, any instance of McEliece's Public Key Cryptosystem always has many trapdoors. Our proof leads to a natural equivalence relation on monic polynomials over a finite field F such that any two irreducible Goppa codes over F whose Goppa polynomials are equivalent under this relation are equivalent as codes.

1. Introduction

McEliece [7] introduced the idea of using an error correcting code as the basis of a Public Key Cryptosystem, which we abbreviate to PKC. Let C be a linear code which corrects t errors and for which a fast decoder is known, and let G be a generator matrix for C such that it is hard to find any fast decoder for C from knowledge of G. To encipher a message M, introduce t random errors and encode the result with G. In the McEliece PKC, C is an irreducible binary Goppa code. Since for an arbitrary linear code finding the nearest codeword to a given received word is an NP-complete problem, it can be expected that only the holder of the decoder for C will be able to decrypt messages. Thus the decoder acts as a trapdoor to the decipherment function and is the secret key of the system, while G is the public key. Experience with the knapsack PKC has shown however that the NP-completeness of a problem used to construct a PKC in this way is no guarrantee of security, since only special cases of the problem are used [2]. Part of the difficulty lies in the fact that there may be many trapdoors to a given decipherment function. Adams and Meijer [1] state that for the McEliece system there is usually only one. We show that their statement is incorrect, although there are probably sufficiently few that finding one by brute force is out of the question. A more serious cloud has been cast on the security of the McEliece PKC by the announcement by Korzhik and Turkin [5] of an algorithm for decoding a linear code that succeeds for received words whose distance from the nearest codeword is strictly less than half the minimum distance of the code, and which is polynomial in the length of the code. They do not find a trapdoor for the McEliece PKC, and indeed they estimate a time of 60 hours on a personal computer to decipher one block of ciphertext. Their algorithm assumes the usual Hamming metric, so Gabidulin [3] has suggested using codes that employ a non-Hamming metric instead.

There are two main thrusts to this paper. The first is an examination of just what is involved in finding a fast decoder for an irreducible binary Goppa code when its generator matrix G is given. We show there are many fast decoders, each corresponding to a permutation of the columns of G. Each such permutation may be regarded as a trapdoor to the instance of the McEliece PKC with public key G. The second thrust is the introduction of an equivalence relation $\sim$ on the set P of monic polynomials of degree t over $F = GF(2^m)$. We define $g \sim h$ if some affine transformation over F composed with some automorphism of F maps roots of g to roots of h, and show that any two irreducible Goppa codes over F with equivalent Goppa polynomials are equivalent as codes. Although the converse is not true, this does suggest that it would be worthwhile to count and classify the equivalence classes of P, which has not to our knowledge been previously attempted. Some results in this direction have been obtained, and will appear in a forthcoming paper. Certainly it can be hoped that this kind of detailed study of the structure of Goppa codes will lead eventually to a determination of whether or not the problem of finding a trapdoor to an instance of the McEliece PKC is NP-complete.

There is not a large body of literature on the McEliece PKC. Several authors [1] [6] [9] show how to reduce the work needed to decipher messages without finding a trapdoor. Heiman [4] is the only previous author to address the problem of finding a trapdoor. Goppa codes are a special case of the class of Alternant codes [8], and Heiman shows how to find a fast decoder for any Alternant code from its generator matrix. Fortunately the irreducible binary Goppa codes used in the McEliece PKC have fast decoders that will correct more errors, twice as many in fact, as Heiman's decoders will, and they are the only Alternant codes known with this property! The papers [3] [5] already referred to complete the current picture.

2. Finding a fast decoder from the generator matrix

Let $F = GF(n)$, $n = 2^m$, and let $\alpha = (\alpha_0, \alpha_1 \ldots \alpha_{n-1})$ be any vector of all the n members of F. Let g be an irreducible monic polynomial of degree t over F. The irreducible binary Goppa code of degree t with field vector α and Goppa polynomial g is the code $\Gamma(\alpha, g)$ whose codewords are the binary vectors $c = (c_0, c_1 \ldots c_{n-1})$ with $\sum_{i=0}^{n-1} c_i/(x-\alpha_i) = 0 \mod g(x)$. $\Gamma(\alpha, g)$ is determined up to equivalence by g, and knowledge of α and g provides a fast decoder correcting up to t errors. More details can be found in [8].

To create an instance of the McEliece PKC from a k × n generator matrix G for Γ, a designer chooses at random a non-singular k × k binary matrix S, and an n × n permutation matrix P, and uses K = SGP as the public key. Let C denote the code whose generator matrix is K. We examine in this section the task that a cryptanalyst faces in finding a fast decoder for C that corrects t errors, and show in the next that there are many such decoders.

An important point, first noted by Heiman [4], is that the matrix S has no cryptographic significance, though it may be useful in hiding any obvious structure of G. The reason is simply that S does not change the set of codewords of C, and messages can be recovered from codewords using K without knowing what S is. We now show that in a sense, P has no cryptographic significance either. We show that if α permuted with P can be found then a fast decoder for C correcting t errors can be obtained easily. In other words, a trapdoor is just a suitable field vector.

The cryptanalyst first chooses a representation of F, and any vector $\rho = (\rho_0, \rho_1 \ldots \rho_{n-1})$ of all the n members of F. He then seeks a permutation of the coordinates of ρ that transforms ρ into $\omega = (\omega_0, \omega_1 \ldots \omega_{n-1})$ for which $C = \Gamma(\omega, h)$ for some h. (An entirely equivalent procedure is to keep ρ fixed and look for a suitable permutation of the columns of K). g and α permuted with P are known to be possible values for h and ω, but there are many others. Once ω is found, h, and consequently a fast decoder for C, can be found quickly by a method described in [8] p341 in a different context. The rows of K are codewords of C. Let $c = (c_0, c_1 \cdots c_{n-1})$ be any codeword of C, and let $p(x) = \prod_{i=0}^{n-1} c_i(x-\omega_i)$. Then the formal derivative p' of p is a multiple of h^2. Thus the cryptanalyst has only to find ω for which the polynomials p' obtained using each row of K have non-trivial greatest common divisor.

We will show that there are at least $mn(n-1)$ permutations that work, and each may be regarded as a trapdoor to the instance of the McEliece PKC with public key K. McEliece suggested $m = 10$, giving the cryptanalyst over 10 million permutations to choose from, though since they have to be selected from all 1024! permutations of the coordinates of ρ he will not find one by brute force.

3. The equivalence of codes and polynomials

Let $F = GF(n)$, $n = 2^m$. Let $\alpha = (\alpha_0, \alpha_1 \cdots \alpha_{n-1})$ be any vector of all the n members of F. Let g be an irreducible monic polynomial of degree t over F. Let $a, b \in F$, $a \neq 0$. We use the same symbol b to denote the n-vector $(b, b \cdots b)$. Let j be an integer, $0 \leq j < m$. Let h be the be the monic polynomial of degree t over F for which $a^t[g(x)]^{2^j} = h(ax^{2^j}+b)$, and let $\rho = (\rho_0, \rho_1 \cdots \rho_{n-1}) = a\alpha^{2^j}+b$, powers of a vector being taken coordinatewise. It is not difficult to show that if $c = (c_0, c_1 \cdots c_{n-1})$ is any binary n-vector then $\sum_{i=0}^{n-1} c_i/(x-\alpha_i) = 0$ mod $g(x)$ if and only if $\sum_{i=0}^{n-1} c_i/(x-\rho_i) = 0$ mod $h(x)$, ie. $\lceil(\alpha,g) = \lceil(\rho,h)$. This prompts what follows.

Let P be the set of monic polynomials of degree t over F. Define the equivalence relation $\sim$ on P by $g \sim h$ if for some $a, b \in F$, $a \neq 0$, and some integer j, $0 \leq j < m$, $a^t[g(x)]^{2^j} = h(ax^{2^j}+b)$. Equivalently $g \sim h$ if, in the splitting field of g, some affine transformation over F composed with some automorphism of F maps roots of g to roots of h. In terms of coefficients, $\sum_{i=0}^{t} g_i x^i \sim \sum_{i=0}^{t} a^{t-i} g_i^{2^j} (x+b)^i$.

It is clear that any two irreducible Goppa codes over F with equivalent Goppa polynomials are equivalent as codes. Indeed this is true for any two codes of the same length and degree, whether irreducible or not. The converse is not true. The irreducible Goppa codes over GF(32) with Goppa polynomials $x^6 + x + 1$ and $x^6 + x^5 + 1$ are equivalent codes with inequivalent polynomials.

Let L denote the group generated under composition by affine transformations over F and automorphisms of F. Then the order of L is mn(n-1), and each member of L applied to the coordinates of a vector α of all the n members of F maps α to a different vector, justifying the assertion made in the last section that there are at least mn(n-1) successful permutations available to a cryptanalyst of an instance of the McEliece PKC of degree t over F with given public key K. There may be far more. If eg. two columns of K are equal, any successful permutation composed with the appropriate interchange will be successful, though it will not in general be a permutation induced by any member of L. This happens when m = 3 and t = 2.

Summarising, let α,ρ be vectors of all the n members of F, and let g,h be irreducible monic polynomials of the same degree over F. If a member of L maps α to ρ and roots of g to roots of h then $\lceil(α,g) = \lceil(ρ,h)$. There will always be more than one polynomial describing $\lceil(α,g)$ up to equivalence, but there may be fewer than mn(n-1). The exact number will be discussed in a forthcoming paper.

References

[1] ADAMS C.M. and MEIJER H. 'Security Related Comments Regarding McEliece's Public-Key Cryptosystem'. Lecture Notes in Computer Science vol 293, Eurocrypt 87. Springer-Verlag 1987.

[2] BRICKELL E.F. 'Breaking Iterated Knapsacks'. Lecture Notes in Computer Science vol 196, Crypto 84. Springer-Verlag 1984.

[3] GABIDULIN E.M. 'Ideals over a Non-Commutative Ring and their Applications in Cryptography'. These Proceedings.

[4] HEIMAN R. 'On the Security of Cryptosystems Based on Linear Error Correcting Codes'. MSc. Thesis, Feinberg Graduate School of the Weizmann Institute of Science. August 1987.

[5] KORZHIK V.I. and TURKIN A.I. 'Cryptanalysis of McEliece's Public Key Cryptosystem'. These Proceedings.

[6] LEE P.J. and BRICKELL E.F. 'An Observation on the Security of McEliece's Public Key Cryptosystem'. Lecture Notes in Computer Science vol 330, Eurocrypt 88. Springer-Verlag 1988.

[7] McELIECE R.J. 'A Public Key Cryptosystem Based on Algebraic Coding Theory'. DSN Progress Report (Jan,Feb), Jet Propulsion Lab., Calif. Inst. Tech. 1978.

[8] McWILLIAMS F.J.and SLOANE N.J. 'The Theory of Error Correcting Codes'. North Holland Publishing Co. 1977.

[9] Van TILBURG J. 'On the McEliece Public Key Cryptosystem.' Lect. Notes in Comp. Sc. vol 403, Crypto 88. Springer-Verlag 1988.

A Threshold Cryptosystem
without a Trusted Party

(Extended abstract)

Torben Pryds Pedersen
Aarhus University, Computer Science Department

Abstract

In a threshold cryptosystem n members share the secret key of an organization such that k members ($1 \leq k \leq n$) must cooperate in order to decipher a given ciphertext. In this note it is shown how to implement such a scheme without having a trusted party, which selects the secret key and distributes it to the members. In stead, the members choose the secret key and distribute it verifiably among themselves. Subsequently, this key can be used for authentication as well as secret communication.

1 Introduction

The concept of group oriented cryptography was introduced in [Des88] as a means of sending messages to a group of people, such that only certain subsets of the members are able to read the message (decipher the ciphertext).

The members of a group are said to be *known* if the sender has to know them (a public key for each member), and a group is called *anonymous* if there is a single public key for the group independently of the members. In general, an anonymous group has a much shorter public key than groups with known members, but it is difficult to handle the situation where a member leaves the group, as this usually requires a new secret key to be selected. Desmedt presents crypto-systems for both types of groups in the case where deciphering requires the cooperation of all members.

Group-oriented cryptography has been further studied in [Fra90], [DF90] and [Hwa91]. Frankel used in [Fra90] the organization of individuals in groups to reduce the problem of distributing and managing public keys. His solution required clerks at the sending as well as the receiving organization.

In [DF90], Desmedt and Frankel modified the El Gamal public key cryptosystem [EG85] so that any k members of the organization can decipher the received ciphertext (for anonymous groups), and in [Hwa91] this property was obtained for organizations with known members.

In this paper only anonymous groups are considered. The main purpose is to improve the threshold cryptosystem proposed by Desmedt and Frankel in two ways. First, it is shown how to avoid the trusted party, who selects and distributes the secret key. Secondly, it is shown how to share the secret key (chosen by the members) such that each member of the group can verify, that the share is correct. This property is important as the shares are no longer computed by a trusted party, and therefore it is not reasonable to expect that they are computed correctly.

In the next section some notation is introduced. Then the protocols for selecting and distributing the key are presented, and in Section 4 possible applications of the these keys are presented. Finally a conclusion and an open problem are given.

2   Notation

In this note p and q denote large primes such that q divides $p-1$, G_q is the unique subgroup of $\mathbb{Z}_p^*$ of order q, and g is a generator of G_q. For all elements a and $b \neq 1$ in G_q, the discrete logarithm of a with respect to b is defined and it is denoted $\log_b(a)$. It is easy to test if an element $a \in \mathbb{Z}_p^*$ is in G_q since

$$a \in G_q \quad \Longleftrightarrow \quad a^q = 1.$$

3   Selection of the Keys

In this section we show how n members of a group $(P_1, \ldots, P_n)$ can select a public of the form (p, q, g, h), where $g, h \in G_q$ and the corresponding secret key is $x = \log_g h$, such that for a fixed parameter k $(1 \leq k \leq n)$, k members must cooperate in order to use the secret key. It will be assumed that $n \geq 2k - 1$. As (k, n)-threshold schemes allow at most $k - 1$ cheating participants, this means that a majority of the participants is assumed to be honest. It is not hard to generalize the protocols such that l members select the secret key and distribute it to the n members of the group (where $n \geq l \geq 2k - 1$).

It will be assumed that the members of the group have previously agreed on the primes p and q and the generator g of G_q.

3.1   Selecting and Distributing the Keys

Let $C(m, r)$ denote a commitment to $m \in \{0, 1\}^*$ using the random string r. Then the keys are selected as follows:

1. P_i chooses $x_i \in \mathbb{Z}_q$ at random (uniform distribution) and computes $h_i = g^{x_i}$. Then a random string r_i is chosen and $C_i = C(h_i, r_i)$ is broadcast to all members.

2. When all n members have broadcast a commitment, each P_i opens C_i.

3. The public key, h, is computed as $h = \prod_{i=1}^{n} h_i$.

Now all members know the public key, but they cannot find the secret key $x = \sum_{i=1}^{n} x_i$ unless they all work together (or some of them can find discrete logarithms).

If P_i chooses x_i at random then the distribution of the secret key is polynomially indistinguishable from the uniform distribution.

Next it is shown how x can be distributed such that any k members can find it if necessary (if $k = 1$ or $k = n$ this is trivial). The proposed method extends the ideas presented in [IS91] to verifiable secret sharing. P_i distributes x_i as follows ($h_1, \ldots, h_n$ are publicly known):

1. P_i chooses at random a polynomial $f_i(z) \in \mathbb{Z}_q(z)$ of degree at most $k - 1$ such that $f_i(0) = x_i$. Let

$$f_i(z) = f_{i0} + f_{i1}z + \ldots + f_{i,k-1}z^{k-1}$$

where $f_{i0} = x_i$.

2. P_i computes $F_{ij} = g^{f_{ij}}$ for $j = 0, \ldots, k - 1$ and broadcasts $(F_{ij})_{j=1,\ldots,k-1}$ ($F_{i0} = h_i$ is known beforehand).

3. When everybody have sent these $k - 1$ values, P_i sends $s_{ij} = f_i(j)$ secretly and a signature on s_{ij} to P_j for $j = 1, \ldots, n$ (in particular P_i keeps s_{ii}).

4. P_i verifies that the share received from, P_j (s_{ji}) is consistent with the previously published values by verifying that

$$g^{s_{ji}} = \prod_{l=0}^{k-1} F_{jl}^{i^l}.$$

If this fails, P_i broadcasts that an error has been found, publishes s_{ij} and the signature and then stops.

5. P_i computes his share of x as the sum of all shares received in step 3 $s_i = \sum_{j=1}^{n} s_{ji}$. Finally P_i signs h.

When all members have signed h, a key authentication center verifies the signatures, and if they are correct, it makes a certificate showing that h is the public key of the group.

Let f be the following polynomial over $\mathbb{Z}_q$: $f(z) = f_1(z) + \ldots + f_n(z)$. By construction $s_i = f(i)$ for every $i = 1, \ldots, n$, and thus s_i is a share of $f(0) = x$ (see [Sha79]). For each share s_i of x let σ_i denote g^{s_i}. If P_i has received correct shares, then each P_j ($j \neq i$) can compute σ_i as

$$\sigma_i = \prod_{j=1}^{n} g^{s_{ji}} = \prod_{j=1}^{n} (h_j \prod_{l=1}^{k-1} F_{jl}^{i^l}).$$

3.2 Properties of the Key Selection Scheme

The following theorem shows that any group of k people have sufficient information to find x if they have followed the key distribution protocol.

Theorem 3.1
Let $(P_i)_{i \in H}$ be a group of k members who have followed the key distribution protocol and accepted their shares. Let $f'(z) = \varphi_0 + \varphi_1 z + \ldots + \varphi_{k-1} z^{k-1}$ be the (unique) polynomial of degree at most $k - 1$ such that $f'(i) = s_i$ for $i \in H$. Then $g^{\varphi_i} = \prod_{j=1}^{n} F_{ji}$ for $i = 0, \ldots, k - 1$.

This theorem implies that $\varphi_0 = x$ as

$$\prod_{j=1}^{n} F_{j0} = \prod_{j=1}^{n} h_j = h.$$

During the key distribution protocol P_i publishes much information about x_i. The following lemma shows that this information is of no use to a collusion of l members $(1 \le l < k)$

Lemma 3.2
Given a group of $l < k$ members $(P_j)_{j \in D}$. For any h_i and any set of shares $(s_{ij})_{j \in D}$, it is possible to generate in polynomial time (in $|q|$) a random set $(F_{it})_{t=1,\ldots,k-1}$ satisfying

$$g^{s_{ij}} = \prod_{t=0}^{k-1} F_{it}^{j^t} \qquad \text{for } j \in D,$$

where $F_{i0} = h_i$.

4 Applications

The keys selected as described in Section 3 can be used for secret communication as well as authentication. Someone knowing the public key can encipher the plaintext $m \in G_q$ as (see [EG85])

$$(c_1, c_2) = (g^y, h^y m) \qquad \text{where } y \in \mathbb{Z}_q^* \text{ is chosen at random.}$$

Any k members can decipher the ciphertext (c_1, c_2) using the deciphering protocol described in [DF90]. Using Lemma 3.2 it can be shown that

Theorem 4.1
The group-oriented crypto-system is as secure as the ElGamal public-key crypto-system against all kinds of attack.

In the full version of the paper it is shown that any k members can represent the organization in an identification scheme and that any k members can construct digital signatures on behalf of the organization. Furthermore, these authentication schemes are proven secure.

5 Conclusion

In this note we have improved the threshold cryptosystem suggested in [DF90] on two points:

1. A trusted party for selecting and distributing the secret is no longer needed.

2. Each member of the group can verify that his share of the secret key corresponds to the public key.

Even though a trusted party is still needed when deciphering (see [DF90]), this paper shows that no trusted party needs to know the secret key of any member.

This paper still leaves open the problem of constructing an efficient anonymous threshold cryptosystem secure against chosen ciphertext attack without any a trusted party at all.

References

[Des88]   Y. Desmedt. Society and group oriented cryptography: A new concept. In *Advances in Cryptology - proceedings of CRYPTO 87*, Lecture Notes in Computer Science, pages 120 – 127, 1988.

[DF90]   Y. Desmedt and Y. Frankel. Threshold cryptosystems. In *Advances in Cryptology - proceedings of CRYPTO 89*, Lecture Notes in Computer Science, pages 307 – 315, 1990.

[EG85]   T. El Gamal. A public key cryptosystem and a signature scheme based on discrete logarithms. In *Advances in Cryptology - proceedings of CRYPTO 84*, Lecture Notes in Computer Science. Springer-Verlag, 1985.

[Fra90]   Y. Frankel. A practical protocol for large group oriented networks. In *Advances in Cryptology - proceedings of EUROCRYPT 89*, Lecture Notes in Computer Science, pages 56 – 61. Springer-Verlag, 1990.

[Hwa91]   T. Hwang. Cryptosystem for group oriented cryptography. In *Advances in Cryptology - proceedings of EUROCRYPT 90*, Lecture Notes in Computer Science, pages 352 – 360. Springer-Verlag, 1991.

[IS91]   I. Ingemarsson and G. J. Simmons. A protocol to set up shared secret schemes without the assistance of a mutually trusted party. In *Advances in Cryptology - proceedings of EUROCRYPT 90*, Lecture Notes in Computer Science, pages 266 – 282. Springer-Verlag, 1991.

[Sha79]   A. Shamir. How to share a secret. *CACM*, 22:612–613, 1979.

A COMPARISON OF CRYPTANALYTIC PRINCIPLES
BASED ON ITERATIVE ERROR-CORRECTION

Miodrag J. Mihaljević and Jovan Dj. Golić

Institute of Applied Mathematics and Electronics, Belgrade
School of Electrical Engineering, University of Belgrade
Bulevar Revolucije 73, 11001 Beograd, Yugoslavia

ABSTRACT: A cryptanalytic problem of a linear feedback shift register initial state reconstruction using a noisy output sequence is considered. The main underlying principles of three recently proposed cryptanalytic procedures based on the iterative error-correction are pointed out and compared.

I. INTRODUCTION

A weakness of a class of running key generators for stream ciphers is demonstrated in [1], and fast algorithms for the cryptanalysis are proposed in [2]-[7] having origins in [8]. In this paper the main underlying principles for the algorithms [2]-[6] are analyzed. The following three principles are considered:

P.1: Error-correction is based on the number of satisfied parity-checks.

P.2: Error-correction is based on the estimation of the relevant posterior probabilities obtained by using the average posterior probability estimated in the previous iteration as the prior probability in the current iteration.

P.3: Error-correction is based on the estimation of the relevant posterior probabilities obtained by using the posterior probabilities estimated in the previous iteration as the prior probabilities in the current iteration.

II. ALGORITHMS

In this section three algorithms corresponding to the principles P.1-P.3 are specified. Algorithm P.1 is the algorithm proposed in [3]. Algorithm P.2 could be regarded as a simplification of the Algorithm [4]. Algorithm P.3 could be seen as a simplification/modification of the Algorithm B [2].

Denote by $\{x_n\}_{n=1}^{N}$ an output segment of a linear feedback shift register (LFSR) of length L with w feedback tapes. In a statistical model, a binary noise sequence $\{e_n\}_{n=1}^{N}$ is assumed to be a realization of a sequence of i.i.d. binary variables $\{E_n\}_{n=1}^{N}$ such that $Pr(E_n=1) = p$, $n=1,2,\ldots,N$. Let $\{z_n\}_{n=1}^{N}$ be a noisy version of $\{x_n\}_{n=1}^{N}$ defined by

$$z_n = x_n \oplus e_n \quad , \quad n=1,2,\ldots,N \quad . \tag{1}$$

The problem under consideration is a reconstruction of the LFSR initial state based on the principles P.1-P.3 assuming that the segment $\{z_n\}_{n=1}^{N}$, the LFSR characteristic polynomial, and the parameter p are known. For the comparison purposes we assume that all the algorithms are based on the parity-checks defined as follows.

Definition: $\Pi_n = \{\pi_k(n)\}_k$ is a set of orthogonal parity-checks related to the n-th bit that are generated according to the characteristic polynomial multiples as in [2]-[3], $n=1,2,\ldots,N$.

Let

$$c_k(n) = \sum_{\substack{mod2 \\ \ell \in \pi_k(n)}} z_\ell \quad , \quad k=1,2,\ldots,|\Pi_n| \quad , \quad n=1,2,\ldots,N \quad , \tag{2}$$

where $|\Pi_n|$ denotes the cardinality of Π_n. Assume that $c_k(n)$ is a realization of a binary random variable $C_k(n)$, $k=1,2,\ldots,|\Pi_n|$, $n=1,2,\ldots,N$. Let $Pr(E_n, \{C_k(n)\}_{k=1}^{|\Pi_n|})$ be the joint probability of the variables E_n and $C_k(n)$, $k=1,2,\ldots,|\Pi_n|$, and let $Pr(E_n| \{C_k(n)\}_{k=1}^{|\Pi_n|})$ be the corresponding posterior probability, $n=1,2,\ldots,N$.

The following steps are identical for all the algorithms:
Initialization: $i=0$, $I=const$, $p^{(0)}=p$.
Step 1: Set $i \rightarrow i+1$. If $i > I$ go to the last step.
Step 2: Calculate $c_k(n)$, $k=1,2,\ldots,|\Pi_n|$, $n=1,2,\ldots,N$.

ALGORITHM P.1 [3]:
Step 3: Calculate $t_n = |\Pi_n| - 2 \sum_{k=1}^{|\Pi_n|} c_k(n)$, $n=1,2,\ldots,N$.
Step 4: If $t_n < 0$, set $z_n \rightarrow z_n \oplus 1$, $n=1,2,\ldots,N$. Go to Step 1.
Step 5: Stop the procedure.

ALGORITHM P.2:
Step 3: For $n=1,2,\ldots,N$, calculate
$$p_n^{(i)} = Pr(E_n=1|\{C_k(n)\}_{k=1}^{|\Pi_n|}=\{c_k(n)\}_{k=1}^{|\Pi_n|}) =$$

$$\frac{p^{(i)} \; p_w^{s_n} \; (1-p_w)^{|\Pi_n|-s_n}}{p^{(i)} \; p_w^{s_n} \; (1-p_w)^{|\Pi_n|-s_n} + (1-p^{(i)}) \; (1-p_w)^{s_n} \; p_w^{|\Pi_n|-s_n}} \quad , \quad (3)$$

where

$$s_n = \Sigma_{k=1}^{|\Pi_n|} \; c_k(n) \quad , \quad p_w = [1-(1-2p^{(i)})^w] \; / \; 2 \quad . \tag{4}$$

Step 4: If $P_n^{(i)} > 0.5$, set $z_n \rightarrow z_n \oplus 1$, $P_n^{(i)} \rightarrow 1-P_n^{(i)}$, $n=1,2,\ldots,N$.

Step 5: Calculate $p^{(i)} = (1/N) \; \sum\limits_{n=1}^{N} P_n^{(i)}$. Go to Step 1.

Step 6: Stop the procedure.

ALGORITHM P.3:

Step 3: Calculate

$$P_n^{(i)} = Pr(E_n=1 \, | \, \{C_k(n)\}_{k=1}^{|\Pi_n|} = \{c_k(n)\}_{k=1}^{|\Pi_n|}) =$$

$$\frac{p_n^{(i)} \; \prod\limits_{\ell=1}^{|\Pi_n|} p_\ell(n)^{c_\ell(n)} \; [1-p_\ell(n)]^{\bar{c}_\ell(n)}}{p_n^{(i)} \; \prod\limits_{\ell=1}^{|\Pi_n|} p_\ell(n)^{c_\ell(n)} \; [1-p_\ell(n)]^{\bar{c}_\ell(n)} + (1-p_n^{(i)}) \; \prod\limits_{\ell=1}^{|\Pi_n|} [1-p_\ell(n)]^{c_\ell(n)} \; p_\ell(n)^{\bar{c}_\ell(n)}}$$

$$\tag{5}$$

where

$$\bar{c}_\ell(n) = 1 - c_\ell(n) \quad , \quad p_\ell(n) = [1 - \prod\limits_{j=1}^{w} (1 - 2 \, p_{m_j})] \; / \; 2 \quad , \tag{6}$$

and $\{m_j\}_{j=1}^{w}$ denotes the set of indices of the bits involved in the parity-check $\pi_\ell(n)$, for any $\ell=1,2,\ldots,|\Pi_n|$, $n=1,2,\ldots,N$.

Step 4: If $P_n^{(i)} > 0.5$, set $z_n \rightarrow z_n \oplus 1$, $P_n^{(i)} \rightarrow 1-P_n^{(i)}$, $n=1,2,\ldots,N$.

Step 5: Set $p_n^{(i)} \rightarrow P_n^{(i)}$, $n=1,2,\ldots,N$. Go to Step 1.

Step 6: Stop the procedure.

III. EXPERIMENTAL RESULTS

The experiments are realized using an LFSR of length 47 with 2 feedback tapes on the stages 5 and 47, when the observed sequence is of length $N=10^5$. The following self-explanatory table presents the experimental results. According to the experimental investigations, all the algorithms could work when the noise is under a limit which is a function of the observed sequence length. For higher noise, Algorithm P.1 is the first to fail, and Algorithm P3 is the last one to fail.

530

Table: The number of residual errors as a function of the iteration step for Algorithms P.1-P.3 and the noise $p = p_1 \cdot p_2 \cdot p_3$ where $p_1 = 0.400$, $p_2 = 0.425$ and $p_3 = 0.435$.

iteration   # of residual errors

i	Algorithm P.1			Algorithm P.2			Algorithm P.3		
	p_1	p_2	p_3	p_1	p_2	p_3	p_1	p_2	p_3
1	40357	44440	45774	37728	41693	43077	37728	41693	43077
2	40383	45868	47301	35734	41397	43015	34462	40943	42712
3	39343	46758	48388	33477	41002	42934	30249	40194	42397
4	36610	47147	48566	30400	40659	42814	24943	39270	42211
5	31750	47468	48763	26130	40259	42821	15333	38191	41977
6	23614	47779	48626	19808	39827	42657	5719	36618	41796
7	13714	47610	48699	11850	39214	42522	1484	34849	41376
8	6246	47530	48817	6315	38544	42423	117	32711	41133
9	1820	47736	48667	3184	38935	42359	2	30097	40768
10	230	47606	48699	717	38661	42335	0	26603	40515
11	0	47528	48704	13	38432	42347		22190	40156
12		47574	48820	0	38216	42346		16766	39918
13		47478	48962		38028	42326		11810	39579
14		47532	48854		37870	42337		8403	39307
15		47551	48878		37688	42315		6110	39033
16		47466	48822		37505	42344		4006	38755
17		47578	48852		37320	42344		2198	38420
18		47613	48623		37127	42358		831	38079
19		.	48790		36940	42348		139	37718
20		.	48704		36661	42340		0	37277
21		.	48800		36304	42338			36800
22		.	48776		35838	42340			36235
23		.	48785		35225	42343			35655
24		.	48763		34429	42349			35003
25		.	48862		33569	42351			34262
26		.	48762		32504	42356			32350
27		.	48835		31189	42350			31183
28		.	48818		29703	42353			29750
29		.	48893		28146	42355			28273
30		.	48805		26409	42352			25309
31		.	48833		24191	42352			23818
32		.	48816		21280	42352			22280
33		.	48835		18105	42358			20518
34		.	48789		15042	42360			18441
35		.	48801		12245	42360			15922
36		.	.		9443	42360			12801
37		.	.		7080	42360			9685
38		.	.		5197	42360			7140
39		.	.		3446	42360			5337
40		.	.		1910	42360			3837
41		.	.		745	42360			2604
42		.	.		122	42360			1317
43		.	.		0	.			329
44		.	.			.			3
45		.	.			.			0

IV. CONCLUSIONS

A cryptanalytic problem of an LFSR initial state reconstruction using the noisy output sequence is considered. The main underlying principles of the cryptanalytic algorithms based on the iterative error-correction, recently proposed in [2]-[6], are compared. The three corresponding algorithms, named Algorithms P.1-P.3, are specified and analyzed.

Let an iteration cost be an equivalent of the iteration cycle complexity and a reconstruction cost be a product of the iteration cost and the number of iterations needed for the reconstruction. The main complexity difference between the algorithms is in the third step. Note that, for a given $|\Pi_n|$, the probability (3) depends only on $s_n = \Sigma_{k=1}^{|\Pi_n|} c_k(n)$, instead of the individual parity-checks $c_k(n)$. Accordingly, it can be shown that the complexity of Algorithm P.3 is considerably greater than the complexities of both Algorithms P.1 or P.2.

According to the experimental results and the complexity analysis, we have the following heuristic conclusions:

- When the noise is lower than the limit below which all the algorithms work, Algorithm P.1 yields the minimum reconstruction cost.
- In the case of higher noise when Algorithm P.1 fails and both Algorithms P.2 and P.3 work, it is better to use Algorithm P.2 because of the lower reconstruction cost.
- Finally, when Algorithm P.3 works and Algorithms P.1 and P.2 both fail, in order to minimize the reconstruction cost the following procedure could be used: make the initial error-rate reduction using Algorithm P.3, and after the certain points change the running algorithm by Algorithms P.2 and P.1, respectively.

REFERENCES

[1] T.Siegenthaler, "Decrypting a Class of Stream Ciphers Using Ciphertext Only", IEEE Trans. Comput., vol. C-34, Jan. 1985, pp.81-85.
[2] W.Meier, O.Staffelbach, "Fast Correlation Attacks on Certain Stream Ciphers", Journal of Cryptology, vol.1, 1989., pp.159-176.
[3] K.Zeng, M.Huang, "On the Linear Syndrome Method in Cryptanalysis", Lecture Notes in Computer Science, Advances in Cryptology - CRYPTO '88, vol.405, pp.469-478. Springer-Verlag, 1990.
[4] M.Mihaljević, J.Golić, "A Fast Iterative Algorthm for a Shift Register Initial State Reconstruction Given the Noisy Output Sequence", Lecture Notes in Computer Science, Advances in Cryptology - AUSCRYPT '90, vol.453, pp.165-175. Springer-Verlag, 1990.
[5] K.Zeng, C.H.Yang, T.R.N.Rao, "An Improved Linear Syndrome Algorithm in Cryptanalysis with Applications", to appear in Lecture Notes in Computer Science, Advances in Cryptology - CRYPTO '90.
[6] V.Chepyzhov, B.Smeets, "On a Fast Correlation Attack on Stream Ciphers", EUROCRYPT '91.
[7] M.Živković, "An Analysis of Linear Recurrent Sequences over the Field GF(2)", Ph.D. thesis, University of Belgrade, 1990.
[8] R.G.Gallager, "Low-Density Parity-Check Codes", IRE Trans. Inform. Theory, vol. IT-8, Jan. 1962, pp.21-28.

Cryptanalysis of the Chaotic-Map Cryptosystem Suggested at EUROCRYPT'91

Eli Biham

The Weizmann Institute of Science
Department of Applied Mathematics and Computer Science
Rehovot 76100, Israel

Abstract

In this conference, Habutsu[1] suggested a cryptosystem based on iterating a chaotic map. In this paper several properties of this cryptosystem are studied and two cryptanalytic attacks are described.

1   Introduction

The cryptosystem based on iterating chaotic maps encrypts 64-bit plaintexts using a key α into a random 147-bit ciphertext out of the 2^{75} ciphertexts corresponding to the plaintext. The plaintexts and the ciphertexts are viewed as numbers between zero and one whose least significant bits are 2^{-64} and 2^{-147} respectively and the key α is between 0.4 and 0.6. The encryption process which contains 75 iterations using 75 random bits r_i is formulated by

$$a_{75} = P$$
$$a_{i-1} = \begin{cases} \alpha a_i, & \text{if } r_i = 0; \\ (\alpha - 1)a_i + 1, & \text{if } r_i = 1 \end{cases}$$
$$T = a_0$$

where P is the plaintext and T is the ciphertext. The decryption process is

$$a_0 = T$$
$$a_{i+1} = \begin{cases} a_i/\alpha, & \text{if } a_i \le \alpha; \\ (a_i - 1)/(\alpha - 1), & \text{if } a_i > \alpha \end{cases}$$
$$P = a_{75}.$$

2 Properties

The ciphertext size is much larger than the plaintext size. In the decryption process we find the plaintext along with the 75 random bits r_i used in the choice of a_{i-1}'s. In order to make the ciphertext size closer to the plaintext size we can change the encryption function to have 139-bit plaintexts, from which 64 bits enter as the plaintext of the original function and 75 bits enter in place of the random bits r_i.

This modification has several disadvantages which lead to several possible attacks. One of the chosen plaintext attacks fixes all the 75 "random" bits to zero. In this case the ciphertext is just $T = \alpha^{75}P$ and α is easily derivable from $\alpha^{75} = T/P$. A simple ciphertext only attack can easily predict r_1 which is now one bit of the plaintext. If $T \leq 0.4$ then $r_1 = 0$. If $T \geq 0.6$ then $r_1 = 1$. If $T \leq 0.4^2$ then the last two random bits can be predicted and if $T \leq 0.4^k$ then k random bits can be predicted.

Another observation is that for each fixed choice of the random bits r_i there is a linear relationship between the plaintexts and the ciphertexts. All the ciphertexts received using a fixed choice of the random bits are in a small range. Therefore, if we only find two ciphertext in such a range and their corresponding plaintexts we can find the linear relationship $T = c_r P + d_r$. The limits of the range are just $T_0 = c_r \cdot 0 + d_r = d_r$ and $T_1 = c_r + d_r$. We can easily decrypt any ciphertext in this range by this relationship and can encrypt any plaintext into this range.

In contrast to the remark in [1] that about 147 ciphertext bits (44 decimal digits) always suffice for a successful decryption, we observed that more than 164 ciphertext bits (about 50 decimal digits) are needed. For example, in the range near the zero ciphertext, where all the random bits are chosen as $r_i = 0$ and the key is taken as $\alpha = 0.4$, the 2^{64} possible plaintexts are encrypted into a range of size about $\alpha^{75} = 0.4^{75} \approx 2^{-100}$. Therefore, the difference between two consecutive ciphertexts in this range is about $2^{-100} \cdot 2^{-64} = 2^{-164}$. In the analysis in this paper we ignore this technical difficulty and assume that the ciphertext size suffices.

3 A Chosen Ciphertext Attack

The ciphertext range corresponding to the choice of all the 75 random bits to be zero ($r_i = 0$) is $[0, \alpha^{75}]$ ($2^{-100} < \alpha^{75} < 2^{-55}$). In this range every ciphertext corresponds to the plaintext $P = T/\alpha^{75}$. In particular, for any key α any ciphertext $T \leq 2^{-100}$ is in this range. Therefore, the following chosen ciphertext attack finds α:

1. Choose a ciphertext $T \leq 2^{-100}$.
2. Request the decrypted plaintext P of T.

3. Calculate $\alpha^{75} = T/P$ and derive α.

The attack uses only one chosen ciphertext and its corresponding plaintext.

4 A Known Plaintext Attack

We observed that each choice of the random bits r_i leads to a ciphertext range for which there is a linear correlation between the plaintexts and the ciphertexts $T = c_r P + d_r$, where c_r and d_r depend on the choice of the r_i's and the key α. The values of c_r and d_r are

$$c_r = \prod_{i=1}^{75} \alpha - r_i$$

$$d_r = \sum_{i=1}^{75} r_i \prod_{j=1}^{i-1} \alpha - r_j.$$

We can see that the value of c_r depends only on the number n_0 of the r_i's with values zero rather than on the actual values of the r_i's. Therefore, for a given α, there are only 76 possible values of c_r which are $c_r = \alpha^{n_0} \cdot (\alpha - 1)^{75-n_0}$, $n_0 \in \{0, \ldots, 75\}$. The 38 even values of n_0 cause negative values of c_r and the 38 odd values of n_0 cause positive values of c_r.

Given about 2^{38} known plaintexts and their corresponding ciphertexts, there is a high probability to have two plaintexts which are encrypted by the same choice of random bits. In such a pair the difference between the ciphertexts should be smaller than c_r, and in particular, smaller than 2^{-50} (since $c_r < 2^{-50}$). The average difference between two adjacent ciphertexts is much larger (about 2^{-38}).

In the attack, we search for the pairs of adjacent ciphertexts whose difference is sufficiently small, find the value of c_r they suggest by $c_r = \frac{T_2-T_1}{P_2-P_1}$ and solve the polynoms $c_r = \alpha^{n_0} \cdot (\alpha - 1)^{75-n_0}$ numerically for all the 38 choices of n_0 for which c_r has the calculated sign. Each such polynom has at most two solutions in the range $0.4 \leq \alpha \leq 0.6$ and every solution is verified by decrypting ciphertexts and comparing the result to the known plaintexts.

This attack needs about 2^{38} known plaintexts and has complexity about 2^{38}.

References

[1] Toshiki Habutsu, Yoshifumi Nishio, Iwao Sasase, Shinsaku Mori, *A Secret Key Cryptosystem by Iterating Chaotic Map*, Abstracts of EUROCRYPT 91, pp. 61–69, 1991.

How To Broadcast A Secret

Shimshon Berkovits

University of Lowell
and
The MITRE Corporation
Burlington Road
Bedford, MA 01730 USA

Abstract. A single transmitter wishes to broadcast a secret to some subset of his listeners. He does not wish to perform, for each of the intended recipients, a separate encryption either of the secret or of a single key with which to protect the secret. A general method for such a secret broadcasting scheme is proposed. It is based on "k out of n" secret sharing. An example using polynomial interpolation is presented as well as a related vector formulation.

INTRODUCTION AND HISTORY

A single transmitter (such as a key distribution center) wishes to broadcast a secret S which is an integer (and could represent a cryptographic key). However, the broadcaster does not wish the secret to be intelligible to all possible listeners. In fact, he wants only a certain, recently selected subset of subscribers to recover S. All other subscribers (and anyone else listening) should either compute nonsense or should be unable to complete the computations all together. We refer to the subscribers either as recipients or as non-recipients depending on whether they are to receive S or not. All other listeners are eavesdroppers.

Till now, the only technique available to the transmitter is the obvious one - with variations. He encrypts S in some random key R. Before he broadcasts the encrypted secret $E_R(S)$, he must send R to each recipient. To do this securely, the transmitter encrypts R individually and separately in the private key encryption key of each recipient. He then communicates the result of these encryptions individually to each recipient. There are several ways he can do this as part of the same message in which he broadcasts $E_R(S)$. He reserves a field in the message for each subscriber. In the field associated with a recipient, he places R encrypted under that subscriber's private key. In all other subscriber fields, he places some null sequence. Alternatively, if there are many subscribers but only a few who are to receive S, he enters the identification of each recipient followed by R encrypted for that subscriber. In either of these variations, the transmitter is using the broadcast message to reach each separate recipient "in series."

The broadcaster can, if he prefers, communicate with all the individual recipients "in parallel." First, each subscriber is given a unique integer n_i which is larger than the encryption of any key in that subscriber's private key encryption key. The transmitter computes a single integer R' that, modulo each n_i, is congruent to the appropriate encryption of R when the n_i belongs to a recipient and is congruent to a null otherwise([3]). The integer R' is of the same size as the product of all the n_i for all subscribers. The broadcaster can reduce its size and save on transmission if he does not send nulls to the non-recipients. Then R' is of the same magnitude as the product only of the n_i belonging to recipients. However, non-recipients will have no way of knowing that the key they compute is erroneous. Only if the secret has an expected meaning or an expected format can they tell that they were not to receive the secret.

All these schemes are variations on the same theme. The transmitter, for convenience, uses a single message to send information intended for and unique to each individual recipient. A true broadcast scheme, however, is one in which the broadcast message contains the same information for each and every listener. From it, the recipients each deduce the secret and all others derive nonsense or nothing. Such schemes are possible.

A true broadcast system can be created out of any "k out of n" secret sharing scheme (e. g., [1], [4]). This is not entirely surprising since the broadcaster wishes to share a secret with each individual recipient. The remainder of this paper describes how to create such a system. The ideas are made concrete by using a system derived from Shamir's polynomial interpolation secret sharing scheme. Finally, a vector based method related to Brickell's secret sharing is presented.

TRUE BROADCAST SCHEMES

In secret sharing schemes, each participant gets a share in the secret. For a "k out of n" scheme, any k of the n participants can pool their shares and reconstruct the secret. Shamir's method, which serves as our example, encodes the secret S into the coefficients of some polynomial P of degree $k - 1$. For simplicity, assume that S is the constant term of P. Each of the n shares is then a distinct point on the graph of P. Obviously, any k participants can pool their shares, interpolate P and recover S.

In a secret broadcasting system, participants are given pseudoshares which are shares in an, as yet, uncreated "k out of n" system. In our example, pseudoshares are points (x_i, y_i) with distinct values x_i. The broadcaster keeps some unassigned pseudoshares for his own use in order to introduce a degree of randomness into his messages. If he ever must resend a secret to a particular set of recipients, he can create a totally different message to do so.

To broadcast to k recipients:

1. Choose $j \geq 0$.
2. Create a $k + j + 1$ out of $2k + j + 1$ secret sharing system with
    a) Secret $= S$
    b) Pseudoshares of recipients as real shares
    c) Pseudoshares of non-recipients must not be real shares
    d) Broadcaster includes j randomly chosen, unassigned pseudoshares.
3. Broadcast $k + j$ randomly chosen shares - all different from those used in step 2.
4. Each subscriber adds his pseudo share as a possible share to the $k + j$ shares received
    a) If that pseudoshare is an actual share, as in 2b), he recovers S
    b) If not, as in 2c), he does not recover S.

For our polynomial example:

1. Choose j points (x_i, y_i) with unassigned x_i.
2. Find a polynomial P of degree $k + j$ passing through

   a) $(0, S)$

   b) (x_i, y_i) for the k real recipients and the j dummy recipients belonging to the broadcaster

   c) no (x_i, y_i) for any non-recipient.

3. Broadcast $k + j$ other points on the graph of P.

It is worth noting that, if all the y_i are equal to some fixed b, then Rolle's Theorem guarantees that 2c) is satisfied. By 2b), there are $k + j - 1$ intervals on which P has value b at the endpoints. Thus, there are $k + j - 1$ local extrema. Another point at which P has the value b would mean another local extreme point. But P has degree $k + j$ so it has at most $k + j - 1$ local extrema. Therefore, P cannot pass through any other pseudoshare with $y_i = b$. Of course, S cannot also equal b or P would just be a constant function. Also, each pseudoshare reduces to the value of x_i only. The broadcaster can change b daily or even from message to message but whether there is a security penalty for choosing all $y_i = b$ still needs examination.

A VECTOR BASED BROADCAST SYSTEM

The first $k + j$ equations each receiver uses in our polynomial example are the same for all participants. Only the $(k + j + 1)^{\text{st}}$ equation is unique to each subscriber. The broadcaster, who may have greater computing resources, can reduce those first $k + j$ equations and transmit only the result. This leads to a vector formulation which is related to Brickell's secret sharing scheme ([2]).

   1. Pseudoshares are pairs (v_i, y_i) where the set of all vectors v_i, including the broadcaster's dummy pseudoshares form an independent set.

   2. Pick a random vector P (equivalent to the coefficients of Shamir's polynomial) such that

      a) $P \cdot v_i = y_i$ for the k pseudoshares of the recipients and the j dummy pseudoshares of the broadcaster

      b) $P \cdot v_i \neq y_i$ for the pseudoshares of the non-recipients.

   3. Pick a random vector u with $u \cdot v_i \neq 0$ for any recipient.

   4. Broadcast u and the vector $Q = P + Su$.

   5. Each subscriber solves $(Q - Tu) \cdot v_i = y_i$ for T.

The last computation is

$$T = (Q \cdot v_i - y_i)(u \cdot v_i)^{-1} \tag{1}$$

Any recipient will recover $T = S$. Any non-recipient will compute a T which is different from S provided that $P \cdot v_i = y_i$ does not happen accidentally for a non-recipient. The broadcaster can assure that a non-recipient who does not accidentally recover S cannot complete the computation of T. He does this by choosing u with $u \cdot v_i = 0$ for all non-recipients. This is nice for it immediately informs the non-recipients they were not to get the secret. Unfortunately, there is an obvious computational cost to the broadcaster for choosing such a u.

The choice of the random vector u with $u \cdot v_i \neq 0$ for any recipient is quite easy   The broadcaster selects random, non-zero numbers r_i and solves $u \cdot v_i = r_i$ for each recipient at the same time he solves $P \cdot v_i = y_i$. There is an interesting variant of the scheme in which each pseudoshare consists of (v_i, y_i, z_i). The broadcaster solves, for each intended recipient, $P \cdot v_i = y_i$ and $u \cdot v_i = z_i^{-1}$. Then he need broadcasts only Q as each receiver uses his own z_i in place of the $(u \cdot v_i)^{-1}$ of equation (1). Of course, it no longer is useful to chose u so that $u \cdot v_i = 0$ for all non-recipients because everyone is using his own z_i and not computing any reciprocals.

There is another way the broadcaster can guarantee that no non-recipient can accidentally find S. As with Rolle's Theorem, he chooses all y_i equal to some fixed b. In the scheme which follows, truncation to length k means projection on the first k coordinates.

1. Pseudoshares are vectors v_i chosen so that any set of differences $\{v_1 - v_2, v_1 - v_3, \ldots, v_1 - v_k\}$, when truncated to length k, are independent and span a space containing no other similarly truncated $v_1 - v_r$.
2. If the v_i are truncated to length $k + j$, the broadcaster can find a P such that $(v_{i_1} - v_{i_m}) \cdot P = 0$ for k real recipients and for j dummy recipients. There is a one dimensional solution space. Choose P in it with $v_{i_1} \cdot P = b$. Then $v_{i_m} \cdot P = b$ for all k recipients.
3. The remainder of the scheme proceeds as before with all subscribers truncating their vectors to $k + j$ components.

Theorem 1: A non-recipient with vector v_r cannot recover S.

Proof: Assume $v_r \cdot P = b$ for a non-recipient. Then $(v_{i_1} - v_r) \cdot P = 0$ and the truncated vectors $v_{i_1} - v_{i_2}, v_{i_1} - v_{i_3}, \ldots, v_{i_1} - v_{i_{k+j}}$ and $v_{i_1} - v_r$ are a basis for the entire $k + j + 1$ dimensional space. So P must be 0. But $v_{i_1} \cdot P = b$. Contradiction! Hence, $v_r \cdot P \neq b$. ◆

The next theorem suggests a way to choose the vectors v_{i_m} so that they posses the property described in Step 1 of the last scheme. The polynomial origins of the scheme become more apparent.

Theorem 2: Choose a random n-vector A. Let $v_i = (x_i, x_i^2, x_i^3, \ldots, x_i^n) + A$ with distinct x_i. Then any set of differences $\{v_1 - v_2, v_1 - v_3, \ldots, v_1 - v_k\}$, when truncated to length k, will span a space which does not contain any other $v_1 - v_r$.

Proof: Consider the Vandermonde matrix formed by $x_1, x_2, x_3 \ldots, x_k, x_r$. Since the x_i are distinct, the determinant is non-zero. But

$$
\begin{vmatrix}
1 & 1 & 1 & \cdots & 1 & 1 \\
x_1 & x_2 & x_3 & \cdots & x_k & x_r \\
x_1^2 & x_2^2 & x_3^2 & \cdots & x_k^2 & x_r^2 \\
\cdot & \cdot & \cdot & & \cdot & \cdot \\
\cdot & \cdot & \cdot & & \cdot & \cdot \\
x_1^k & x_2^k & x_3^k & \cdots & x_k^k & x_r^k
\end{vmatrix}
=
\begin{vmatrix}
1 & 0 & 0 & \cdots & 0 & 0 \\
x_1 & x_2 - x_1 & x_3 - x_1 & \cdots & x_k - x_1 & x_r - x_1 \\
x_1^2 & x_2^2 - x_1^2 & x_3^2 - x_1^2 & \cdots & x_k^2 - x_1^2 & x_r^2 - x_1^2 \\
\cdot & \cdot & \cdot & & \cdot & \cdot \\
\cdot & \cdot & \cdot & & \cdot & \cdot \\
x_1^k & x_2^k - x_1^k & x_3^k - x_1^k & \cdots & x_k^k - x_1^k & x_r^k - x_1^k
\end{vmatrix}
$$

Expanding the second determinant by the first row yields a $k \times k$ non-zero determinant whose columns must be linearly independent. Obviously, these columns are exactly the truncated vectors $v_1 - v_2, v_1 - v_3, \ldots, v_1 - v_k$ and $v_1 - v_r$. ◆

Although this version assures that no non-recipient can accidentally compute the secret, all non-recipients do compute something. As before, with some additional computation, the broadcaster can choose u so that $u \cdot v_i = 0$ for all non-recipients. To do this, he cannot truncate the vectors to length any less than $n - k$, the number of non-recipients.

CONCLUSION

We have shown how to convert any "k out of n" secret sharing scheme into a secret broadcasting scheme. We have also developed a specific vector based broadcast scheme which allows several variations. At one extreme, vectors are truncated to save computational effort and transmission time while, at the other, an extra matrix reduction ensures that non-recipients know they are not to get the secret because they cannot complete the required computation.

Some examination of the security of these schemes is still necessary. One can think of $Q = P + Su$ and u as an encryption of the secret S with P and u chosen with somewhat randomly. However, P was not a completely random vector but is selected to satisfy certain conditions. Just how secure this encryption of S is must still be determined.

LIST OF REFERENCES

1. Blakley, G. R., "Safegaurding Cryptographic Keys," Proceedings of the. AFIPS 1979 National Computer Conference, Vol. 48, June 1979, pp. 313-317.

2. Brickell, E. F., "Some Ideal Secret Sharing Schemes," Third Carbondale Combinatorics Conference, Carbondale, IL, J. Combinatorial Mathematics and Combinatorial Computing, Vol. 6, 1989, pp. 105-113.

3. Chiou, G. C. and W. C. Chen, "Secure Broadcasting Using the Secure Lock," IEEE Transactions on Software Engineering, Vol. SE-15, No. 8, Aug. 1989, pp. 929-934.

4. Shamir, A., "How to Share a Secret," Communications of the ACM, Vol. 22, No. 11, November 1979, pp. 612-613.

Probabilistic Analysis
of
Elementary Randomizers

Josef Pieprzyk *

Department of Computer Science
University College
University of New South Wales
Australian Defence Force Academy
Canberra, ACT 2600, AUSTRALIA

Abstract

In the paper, elementary randomizers based on random functions and the DES structure are examined. First, it is proved that the randomizer with three different random functions produces the outputs which are independent and uniformly distributed random variables. Next, randomizers based on two different random functions are considered and it is shown that their statistical properties depend upon the order of the functions used in them. Finally, it is proved that the randomizer with a single random function gives outputs which are statistically related.

1 Introduction

Luby and Rackoff [1] introduced an elementary randomizer $\psi(f, g, h)$ based on three random functions f, g, h and the DES structure. They proved that such randomizer cannot be efficiently distinguished from a truly random permutation (function). Ohnishi [2] showed that it is possible to simplify the Luby-Rackoff randomizer to $\psi(f, f, g)$ without any significant deterioration of its quality - it cannot be distinguished from a truly random permutation as well. Schnorr [5] asked about the possibility of a further reduction of the number of random (or pseudorandom) functions to a single one. Pieprzyk [3] proved that $\psi(f, f, f, f^2)$ is indistinguishable from a truly random permutation, when f is a truly random or pseudorandom function.

The four elementary randomizers $\psi(f, g, h)$, $\psi(f, f, g)$, $\psi(g, f, f)$, and $\psi(f, f, f, f^2)$ are not distinguishable from a truly random permutation and in this paper, we will examine the statistical properties of their outputs.

---

*Support for this project was provided in part by TELECOM Australia under the contract number 7027 and by the Australian Research Council under the reference number A48830241.

2   Preliminaries

Let $I_n = \{0,1\}^n$ be the set of all 2^n binary strings of length n. For $a, b \in I_n$, $a \oplus b$ stands for bit-by-bit exclusive-or of a and b. The set of all functions from I_n to I_n is F_n, i.e., $F_n = \{f \mid f : I_n \to I_n\}$. If we have two functions $f, g \in F_n$, their composition $f \circ g$ is denoted as $f \circ g(x) = f(g(x))$ for all $x \in I_n$. For a function $f \in F_n$, we define the DES-like permutation associated with f as $D_{2n,f}(L,R) = (R, L \oplus f(R))$, where L and R are n-bit strings $(L, R \in I_n)$ and $D_{2n,f} \in F_{2n}$. Having a sequence of functions $f_1, f_2, \cdots, f_i \in F_n$, we can determine the composition of their DES-like permutations ψ and $\psi(f_1, f_2, \cdots, f_i) = D_{2n,f_i} \circ D_{2n,f_{i-1}} \circ \cdots \circ D_{2n,f_1}$ Of course, $\psi(f_1, f_2, \cdots, f_i) \in F_{2n}$.

Definition 2.1 *A random function $f \in_R F_n$ is a sequence $(f(0), f(1), \cdots, f(2^n - 1)\,)$ of random variables, where any random variable $f(x_i)$; $x_i \in I_n$, has a uniform and independent distribution so $P[f(x_i) = x_j] = \frac{1}{2^n}$ for all $x_i, x_j \in I_n$ ($f(x_i)$ and $f(x_j)$ are independent for $i \neq j$).*

The following properties of random variables and the exclusive-or operation are exploited in the paper:

P1. Let X and Y be independent random variables. The random variable $X \oplus Y$ may be described by its conditional probabilities

$$P[X \oplus Y = z_i \mid X = x_j] = P[X \oplus Y = z_i \mid x_j] = P[Y = y_k]$$

where $y_k = z_i \oplus x_j$.

P2. Let X and Y be independent random variables and one of them, say X, be uniformly distributed. Then $X \oplus Y$ is also a uniformly distributed random variable.

P3. Let X and Y be uniformly distributed independent random variables i.e., $P[X = x_i] = P[Y = y_i] = \frac{1}{2^n}$ for all $x_i, y_i \in I_n$. Then $X \oplus Y$ is a uniformly distributed random variable that is independent from both X and Y.

3   Analysis of elementary randomizers

In this section, elementary randomizers $\psi(f, g, h)$, $\psi(f, f, g)$, $\psi(g, f, f)$, and $\psi(f, f, f, f^2)$ are analysed. First, we consider the Luby-Rackoff randomizer.

Theorem 3.1 *Given the L-R randomizer $\psi(f, g, h)$, where $f, g, h \in_R F_n$ are three different random functions, then its outputs (β, γ) are represented by two independent random variables each of the uniform probability distribution.*

Proof: The following notations are used in the proof: $X = f(R)$, $\alpha = L \oplus X$, $Y = g(\alpha)$, $\beta = Y \oplus R$, $Z = h(\beta)$, and $\gamma = Z \oplus \alpha$. The input R specifies a single random variable $X = f(R)$ in the random function f. Clearly, $P[^{'}(R) = i] = \frac{1}{2^n}$, where $i \in I_n$ so the random variable X is uniformly distributed. The second random function g operates on values of the random variable $\alpha = X \oplus L$ (of the uniform distribution). The resulting variable $Y = g(\alpha)$ has the uniform distribution and because g is a collection of independent random variables, Y is independent from α (it is easy to check that $P[Y = i \mid \alpha = j] = P[Y = i] = \frac{1}{2^n}$ for all $i, j \in I_n$). As $\beta = Y \oplus R$ is permuted random variable Y (a deterministic transformation of Y), β is independent from α and has the uniform distribution. The application of the third random function h generates the random variable $Z = g(\beta)$ which is uniformly distributed and independent from β. As α and Z are independent and uniform, $\gamma = \alpha \oplus Z$ is the uniform random variable and independent from both β and Z (see the property P3). Thus, the outputs (β, γ) are independent and uniformly distributed random variables.

□

Theorem 3.2 *Given the elementary randomizer $\psi(f, f, g)$, where $f, g \in_R F_n$ are two different random functions, then its outputs (β, γ) are represented by two independent random variables and γ has the uniform distribution (β does not have the uniform distribution).*

Proof: Observe that if the random variable $X = f(R) = L \oplus R$ in the first call of f, then $\alpha = X \oplus R = R$ and in the second call of f, the same value must be used. Thus $P[Y = L \oplus R \mid f(R) = L \oplus R] = 1$. Other conditional probabilities are as follows: $P[Y = i \mid f(R) = j; j \neq L \oplus R] = \frac{1}{2^n}$ for all $i, j \in I_n$. It means that

$$P[Y = L \oplus R] = \frac{2^n - 1}{2^{2n}} + \frac{1}{2^n}$$

and for all $j \neq L \oplus R;\ j \in I_n$, we have

$$P[Y = j] = \frac{2^n - 1}{2^{2n}}$$

As $\beta = Y \oplus R$, β has the following probability distribution:

$$P[\beta = i] = \begin{cases} \frac{2^n-1}{2^{2n}} + \frac{1}{2^n} & \text{if } i = L \\[2mm] \frac{2^n-1}{2^{2n}} & \text{otherwise} \end{cases}$$

Clearly, the application of the second random function g generates a uniform random variable $Z = g(\beta)$ which is independent from β and according to the property P2, $\gamma = Z \oplus \alpha$ is uniformly distributed and independent from β.

□

Theorem 3.3 *Given the elementary randomizer $\psi(g, f, f)$, where $f, g \in_R F_n$ are two different random functions, then its outputs (β, γ) are represented by two independent random variables and the both have the uniform probability distribution.*

Proof: R assigns a random variable $X = g(R)$ from the random function g. Clearly, X has the uniform distribution. The input L permutes values of X, and the resulting random variable $\alpha = X \oplus L$ is also uniform. Values of α are arguments of the second random function f which is independent from g. As all random variables $f(\alpha_i);\ \alpha_i \in I_n$, are uniformly distributed, the random variable $Y = f(\alpha)$ is uniform and so is the random variable $\beta = Y \oplus R$. The probability distribution of $Z = f(\beta)$ is not uniform as it depends on $f(\alpha_i)$ and $P[Z = \alpha_i \oplus R \mid f(\alpha_i) = \alpha_i \oplus R] = 1$. In the rest of the cases (i.e., $j \neq \alpha_i \oplus R$), the probabilities are as follows: $P[Z = j \mid f(\alpha_i) \neq \alpha_i \oplus R] = \frac{1}{2^n}$. Therefore the probability distribution of Z is

$$P[Z = j] = \begin{cases} \frac{2^n-1}{2^{2n}} + \frac{1}{2^n} & \text{if } j = \alpha_i \oplus R \\[2mm] \frac{2^n-1}{2^{2n}} & \text{otherwise} \end{cases}$$

Obviously, α and Z are independent and according to the property P2, $\gamma = \alpha \oplus Z$ is uniformly distributed and independent from β.

□

Theorem 3.4 *Given $\psi(f, f, f, f^2)$ where $f \in_R F_n$. If the inputs $(L \neq R)$, then the outputs (γ, δ) are statistically related and their probability distributions are not uniform.*

Proof: We use the following notations: $X = f(R)$, $\alpha = L \oplus X$, $Y = f(\alpha)$, $\beta = Y \oplus R$, $Z = f(\beta)$, $\gamma = Z \oplus \alpha$ and $\delta = \beta \oplus f^2(\gamma)$. We are going to calculate conditional probabilities of variables Z and γ provided that $f(R)$ is fixed. There are two different cases: the first when $f(R) = i$ and $i \neq L \oplus R$ ($i \in I_n$), and the second when $f(R) = L \oplus R$.

1. $f(R) = i$ and $i \neq L \oplus R$. Observe that $f(R) = i$ implies that $\alpha = L \oplus f(R)$ becomes $i \oplus L$. The probability of attaining the points of Z can be found by starting from the point $\alpha = i \oplus L$ and counting all possible paths (there are 2^n of them) along with their probabilities. The probabilities are

$$P(Z = i \oplus L \oplus R \mid f(R) = i) = P(\gamma = R \mid f(R) = i) = \frac{2^n - 2}{2^{2n}} + \frac{1}{2^n}$$

$$P(Z = i \mid f(R) = i) = P(\gamma = L \mid f(R) = i) = \frac{2^n - 2}{2^{2n}} + \frac{1}{2^n}$$

$$P(Z = j \mid f(R) = i) = P(\gamma = j \oplus i \oplus L \mid f(R) = i) = \frac{2^n - 2}{2^{2n}}$$

where $j \in I_n$ and is different from i and $i \oplus L \oplus R$.

2. $f(R) = L \oplus R$. It means that $\alpha = R$ and Z has a uniform distribution thus

$$P(Z = j \mid f(R) = L \oplus R) = P(\gamma = j \oplus R \mid f(R) = L \oplus R) = \frac{1}{2^n}$$

for all $j \in I_n$.

The probability distribution of γ is as follows:

$$
\begin{aligned}
P(\gamma = L) &= \sum_{k \neq L \oplus R} P(\gamma = L \mid f(R) = k)P(f(R) = k) + \\
&\quad P(\gamma = L \mid f(R) = L \oplus R)P(f(R) = L \oplus R) = \\
&\quad \frac{(2^n - 1)(2^n - 2)}{2^{3n}} + \frac{1}{2^n} \\
P(\gamma = R) &= \sum_{k \neq L \oplus R} P(\gamma = R \mid f(R) = k)P(f(R) = k) + \\
&\quad P(\gamma = R \mid f(R) = L \oplus R)P(f(R) = L \oplus R) = \\
&\quad \frac{(2^n - 1)(2^n - 2)}{2^{3n}} + \frac{1}{2^n} \\
P(\gamma = j) &= \sum_{k \neq L \oplus R} P(\gamma = j \mid f(R) = k)P(f(R) = k) + \\
&\quad P(\gamma = j \mid f(R) = L \oplus R)P(f(R) = L \oplus R) = \\
&\quad \frac{(2^n - 1)(2^n - 2)}{2^{3n}} + \frac{1}{2^{2n}}
\end{aligned}
$$

where $j \in I_n$ and is different from L and R.

Clearly the second output variable $\delta = f^2(\gamma) \oplus \beta$ not only depends upon the random function f but also upon γ and its probability distribution is not uniform. $\square$

If the inputs to $\psi(f, f, f, f^2)$ are the same i.e., $L = R$, then the probability distribution of γ has a single point with bigger probability and

$$P(\gamma = R = L) = \frac{(2^n - 1)(2^n - 2)}{2^{3n}} + \frac{2(2^n - 1)}{2^{2n}} + \frac{1}{2^n}$$

$$P(\gamma = j) = \frac{(2^n - 1)(2^n - 2)}{2^{3n}}$$

where $j \in I_n$ and is different from L.

4 Conclusions

We can define a perfect randomizer as the one whose outputs are statistically independent for different inputs. It also means that oracle gates of a distinguisher evaluated by a perfect randomizer are not "transparent" for the input. From the analysis, we can conclude that the composition of randomizers $\psi(f, f, f, f^2)$ does not provide a perfect randomizer. Perhaps perfect randomizers can be built from $\psi(g, f, f)$. However, the direct composition of $\psi(f, f, g)$ does not yield perfect randomizers. The composition of $\psi(f, g, h)$ creates a perfect randomizer (see [4]).

ACKNOWLEDGMENT

I would like to thank Lawrie Brown and other members of the CCSR for their assistance.

References

[1] M. Luby and Ch. Rackoff. How to construct pseudorandom permutations from pseudorandom functions. *SIAM Journal on Computing*, 17(2):373–386, April 1988.

[2] Y. Ohnishi. A study on data security. Master Thesis, Tohoku University, Japan, 1988. (in Japanese).

[3] J.P. Pieprzyk. How to construct pseudorandom permutations from single pseudorandom functions. Abstracts of EUROCRYPT'90, May 1990.

[4] J.P. Pieprzyk and R. Safavi-Naini. Randomized authentication systems. In *EURO-CRYPT'91, Brighton, UK*, April 1991.

[5] C.P. Schnorr. On the construction of random number generators and random function generators. In *Proc. of Eurocrypt 88, Lecture Notes in Computer Science*, New York, 1988. Springer Verlag.

Race Integrity Primitives Evaluation (RIPE): A status report

B. Preneel*
ESAT Lab, K.U.Leuven

D. Chaum
C.W.I., Amsterdam

W. Fumy
Siemens AG, Erlangen

C.J.A. Jansen
Philips Crypto B.V., Eindhoven

P. Landrock
Århus University

G. Roelofsen
PTT Research, The Netherlands

Abstract

Early in 1989, a call for integrity primitives was disseminated within the cryptographic community by the RIPE consortium. The goal of this consortium is to put forward an ensemble of techniques to meet the anticipated requirements of the future Integrated Broadband Communication Network in the European Community. The aim of this paper is to describe the status of the RIPE project.

1 Integrated Broadband Communication for Europe

The European Community plans to set up a unified European market of about 300 million customers by 1993. In view of this market Integrated Broadband Communication (IBC) is planned for commercial use in 1996. This communication network will provide high speed channels and will support a broad spectrum of services. In order to pave the way towards commercial use of IBC, the Commission of the European Communities has launched the RACE program (Research and Development in Advanced Communications Technologies in Europe) [RACE88]. Under this RACE program pre-competitive and pre-normative work is going on.

---

*NFWO aspirant navorser, sponsored by the National Fund for Scientific Research (Belgium).

It is clear that the majority of the services offered as well as the management of the network are crucially dependent on the use of cryptographic techniques for their security.

Within RACE, the RIPE project (RACE Integrity Primitives Evaluation) will put forward a portfolio of techniques to meet the anticipated security requirements of IBC. Consensus on integrity primitives is essential for interoperability. The members of the RIPE project are: Centre for Mathematics and Computer Science, Amsterdam (prime contractor); Siemens AG; Philips Crypto BV; PTT Research, The Netherlands; Katholieke Universiteit Leuven and Århus Universitet.

2 An open call for integrity primitives

The project's motivation is the unique opportunity to attain consensus on openly available integrity primitives. In order to achieve wide acceptance for a collection of algorithms, the RIPE consortium decided to disseminate an open call [VdW89]. The scope of the project and the evaluation procedure were fixed after having reached consensus with the main parties involved.

The scope includes any digital integrity primitive, except data confidentiality. In this context it is important to note that in some documents (e.g. [ISO7498]) integrity is *not* the complement of confidentiality, but has a very restricted meaning.

In response to the call, that was announced at Eurocrypt'89 and Crypto'89 and was published in the Journal of Cryptology and the IACR Newsletter, fifteen submissions were received. Most types of primitives were represented, but three additional primitives were invited for more comprehensive coverage. In fact, many well known primitives were ultimately submitted, as well as proprietary submissions from major suppliers, thus demonstrating the widespread acceptance and perceived need for the project.

From the eighteen submissions, ten came from academic submitters and eight from industry. The division over different countries was as follows: West Germany 5; U.S.A. 4; Denmark 3; Canada and Japan 2; Belgium and Australia 1. In October 1989, many of the submitters attended special meetings to clarify the submissions.

3   Evaluation results

The evaluation was carried out following a fixed procedure. In view of the potential use in IBC the submissions were evaluated with respect to three aspects: functionality, modes of use, and performance. The evaluation comprised computer simulation, statistical verification and analysis of mathematical structures, particularly to verify the integrity properties. Because of the limited resources and time period, it was decided that if any flaw was identified, the submitter would not be allowed to patch the flaw, thus preventing a moving target.

The submissions can roughly be divided into four categories: identification protocols, digital signatures, hash functions and keyed hash functions. Note that a single submission can contain primitives in more than one category. Five submissions could be rejected in a preliminary screening. After the main phase of the evaluation and after taking into account deficiencies implied by work done in the cryptographic community (external work), seven submissions remained. The reader is referred to table 1 that indicates how the different categories evolved through the evaluation process.

	Identification Protocols	Digital Signatures	Hash Functions	Keyed Hash Functions
Total number	6	3	14	8
After first phase	6	3	9	3
After main phase	3	2	4	1
External work	3	2	2	0

Table 1: Evolution of the number of submissions in different categories.

The remaining submissions show significant potential, but each requires modification and/or further specification by the submitters. Five of these seven show minor functional problems. In most of the cases, it is clear how these problems can be avoided. It was however decided to stick to the agreed policy and perform further evaluation together with the new submissions from the second call. One primitive was incompletely specified and one primitive needs more analysis before it can be recommended. More details on the promising submissions are given in table 2.

For six submissions permission was obtained from the submitters to publish the

	Identification Protocols	Digital Signatures	Hash Functions	Keyed Hash Functions
Total remaining	3	2	2	0
Minor functional problems	3	1	1	0
Incomplete specification	0	1	0	0
More analysis required	0	0	1	0

Table 2: Problems concerning submissions showing significant potential.

evaluation or attack by the RIPE consortium. Preprints of the reports [RIPE91-1, RIPE91-2, RIPE91-3, RIPE91-4, RIPE91-5, dRo91] are available from:

Gert Roelofsen, PTT Research, P.O.Box 421, NL-2260 AK Leidschendam, The Netherlands. Telephone +31(70)332 64 10; Fax +31(70)332 64 77; Telex 311236 rnl nl; email g_roelofsen@pttrnl.nl. Note also that the version of MD4 submitted to the RIPE consortium differs in some details from the published version [Riv90].

4 Second call for integrity primitives

In 1989, it was already foreseen that some first round submissions would require fixing of functional problems. Moreover, the period of 9 months between announcement of the call and the deadline for submission was relatively short. A final argument for a second call is that work on functional specifications for security within RACE had started only in 1989.

In order to assure that the recommended integrity primitives result in a comprehensive coverage of IBC requirements, following sources for primitives will be taken into account in the second evaluation phase: the responses to the second call, the revised versions of the first round primitives believed to be promising after the first evaluation and other primitives proposed in open literature and in the international standards community. Finally, if necessary, some submissions might be invited.

5 Conclusion

The first call for primitives and the subsequent evaluation process was certainly successful. On one hand, important flaws were identified in several submitted schemes, and on the other hand a selection of seven submissions showing significant potential survived. The need for a second call for integrity primitives has been demonstrated. The results of the second evaluation phase will be available by July 1992.

References

[ISO7498]   *"Information Processing - OSI Reference Model - Part 2: Security architecture*, International Standard ISO 7498/2, International Organisation for Standardisation, 1988.

[VdW89]   J. Vandewalle, D. Chaum, W. Fumy, C.J.A. Jansen, P. Landrock and G. Roelofsen, "A European call for cryptographic algorithms: RIPE; Race Integrity Primitives Evaluation", *Proceedings Eurocrypt'89, Lecture Notes in Computer Science 434*, Springer Verlag, 1990, p. 267-271.

[RACE88]   *"RACE Workplan"*, Commission of the European Communities, 1988, Rue de la Loi 200, B-1049, Brussels, Belgium.

[RIPE91-1]   *"Evaluation of N-HASH"*, RIPE Internal Report 1991-1, 1991.

[RIPE91-2]   *"Evaluation of a hash function based on modular squaring"*, RIPE Internal Report 1991-2, 1991.

[RIPE91-3]   *"Evaluation of a hash function based on 32-bit arithmetic"*, RIPE Internal Report 1991-3, 1991 (can not be published before March 1992).

[RIPE91-4]   *"Evaluation of LOKI"*, RIPE Internal Report 1991-4, 1991.

[RIPE91-5]   *"Evaluation of MD4 (as submitted to RIPE)"*, RIPE Internal Report 1991-5, 1991.

[dRo91]   Peter J.N. de Rooij, "On the Security of the Schnorr scheme using preprocessing", *these proceedings*.

[Riv90]   R.L. Rivest, "The MD4 Message Digest Algorithm", *Abstracts Crypto'90*, pp. 281-291.

The Information Leakage through a Randomly Generated Function

Lennart Brynielsson

TSA

S-107 86 Stockholm, Sweden

Abstract: If a randomly filled memory is used to combine some ML-shift registers then the obtained mutual information between the output and a set of inputs will be a random variable. Its distribution is demonstrated to be approximately proportional to a χ^2-distribution.

In cryptographic systems several pseudo-random sources are often combined by means of a combining function. This is sometimes accomplished by a memory filled with random data, for instance derived from parts of the key. In order to evaluate the feasibility of a correlation attack, the statistical behaivor of such a combination function must be examined. [1]

If the arguments of the function are assumed to be independent and uniformly distributed random variables, then the correlation, or more generally the mutual information, between the output and some of the arguments can be computed. This gives, per output symbol, the maximal entropy loss of the source that controls those arguments. [1,2]

Without loss of generality we consider a function $w = F(u,v)$ of two variables, $u \in Z_m$ and $v \in Z_n$, with values $w \in Z_N$. Let the arguments U and V be independent and uniformly distributed random variables and consider the mutual information $I(U,W)$ between U and the output W. (In most applications m, n and N are powers of two). If the function values are independently drawn according to a distribution on Z_N then this information I will be a random variable. We here claim that I, if natural logarithms are used, has the approximate expectation:

$$E[I] \approx \frac{(m-1)(N-1)}{2mn}$$

Moreover, asymptotically for large n, the variable $2mn \cdot I$ is χ^2-distributed with $(m-1)(N-1)$ degrees of freedom.

Let X_{ij} be the frequency of j:s among the function values with $u=i$ and let $\bar{X}_j$ be the average frequency.

$$X_{ij} = \#\{ v \; ; F(i,v) = j \} \qquad \bar{X}_j = \frac{1}{m}\sum_{i=1}^{m} X_{ij}$$

The mutual information can now be expressed:

$$I(U,W) = H(W) - H_U(W) = H(W) - \frac{1}{m}\sum_{i=1}^{m} H(W \mid U=i) =$$

$$= \frac{1}{m}\sum_{i=1}^{m}\sum_{j=1}^{N} \frac{X_{ij}}{n} \log\frac{X_{ij}}{n} - \sum_{j=1}^{N} \frac{\bar{X}_j}{n} \log\frac{\bar{X}_j}{n} =$$

$$= \frac{1}{mn}\sum_{i=1}^{m}\sum_{j=1}^{N} X_{ij} \log(X_{ij}/\bar{X}_j) \approx \frac{1}{2mn}\sum_{i=1}^{m}\sum_{j=1}^{N} \frac{(X_{ij} - \bar{X}_j)^2}{\bar{X}_j}$$

where we for each j have used the series expansion around X_j. The last sum is however known from the statistical analysis of the homogenity of contingency tables. It is known to be approximately χ^2-distributed with $(m\text{-}1)(N\text{-}1)$ degrees of freedom. [3]

References:

[1] Siegenthaler T, "Methoden für den Entwurf von Stream Cipher Systemen", Ph.D Dissertation, ETH Zürich, 1987.

[2] Brynielsson L, "Radgeräte und ihre kritische Länge", Kryptologie Aufbauseminar, J. Kepler Universität Linz, 1984.

[3] Cramer H, "Mathematical Methods of Statistics", Princeton University Press, 1951.

Some Weaknesses of "Weaknesses of Undeniable Signatures"

David Chaum

CWI (Centre for Mathematics and Computer Science)
Kruislaan 413 1098 SJ Amsterdam

ABSTRACT: The weaknesses that are the subject of [DY 91] have already been addressed in the published literature [C 90 & CvA 89]. The main class of these weaknesses consists of ways of cheating undeniable signatures; but these ways are shown here to themselves be "weak." Specifically, a cheater using them can double-cross the other cheaters, to the extent that the original ways of cheating are rendered useless. The remaining cited weaknesses are re-statements of, or variations on, some previously observed blinding techniques [CvA 89]. These techniques allow advantages in some applications when desired, but are also easily excluded when not desired.

Introduction

The paper [DY 91] proposes two classes of "weaknesses" of undeniable signatures. It presents a main class in Section 3, which includes two "attack" protocols, and a minor class in Section 4, which comprises three more such protocols. Here, the discussion is similarly organized into two sections whose titles include those of the original.

On "Verification by multiple unknown verifiers is possible"

This first and main weakness class relates to the desirable property of undeniable signatures that requires cooperation of the signer for each verification of a signature. Thus, for example, the only way to be convinced that the signature on a piece of software is valid should be to pay for the software and then verify the signature by conducting a protocol with its author. The weakness perceived by [DY 91] takes the form of two specific attack protocols that are claimed to allow multiple cooperating cheating parties to be convinced while the software author believes he is convincing only a single paying customer. (This would of course still not allow any after-the-fact cheating or victimization of non-cheating customers.)

It has already been pointed out by [C 90] that such attacks can exist, and it was also claimed there that they could be prevented by special techniques for a very broad class of protocols, including known undeniable signature protocols (see [C 91] for details of how this is achieved). But none of these techniques are needed to prevent the attacks of [DY 91]; in fact, no preventive measures are needed at all. The two attack protocols simply have the feature that a cheating verifier can compute messages from exactly the same distribution as those issued by the genuine signer. This allows a cheater to double-cross all other cheaters into believing that the signer is participating. The double-crossing cheater can even convince the other cheaters that arbitrary values are valid signatures on chosen messages.

To see this, observe that knowing how the first message in the protocol is formed, i.e., knowing a and b, allows one to generate acceptable responses—even when $z \neq m^x$. Thus, in the first attack, which is just a set of cheaters who do a coin-flipping protocol to determine their challenge to the signer, any cheater can create false responses that are apparently valid responses from the signer. The second attack is a chain of "challenge and response blinding" [CvA 89] cheaters stretching from an honest customer to the signer. In this attack, the cheater nearest the customer can simply put the customer in communication with the signer and cheat all the other cheaters into believing a false signature. More generally, any chain segment is similarly cheated by those who control both its ends.

On "Vulnerability to on-line multiplicative attacks"

The second of the three attacks in this minor class seems to be simply a re-statement of the well-known basic blind signature protocol described in the context of undeniable signatures by [CvA 89]. It involves a set of valid messages, each of which the signer is willing to sign, but without knowing which one is being signed. An example use for this is where each valid signed message is the equivalent of an electronic coin [C 85]. The bank does not care which of the equivalent denomination coins it signs, so long as it can deduct the coin value from the recipient's account. If the signer does not wish to issue blind signatures, and hence wishes to prevent the attack, then the signer simply issues signatures only on valid messages.

The first and third attacks involve a cheater who interposes herself in the communication between the signer and a victimized receiver of a signature. These protocols are superfluous, since the same effect can always be achieved without interacting with the signer. To see this, notice that the assertion made at the end of Section 2 in [DY 91], that signatures on random messages cannot be forged (sometimes referred to as "existential forgery"), is incorrect: anyone can simply raise the public generator g and the public key g^x to the same random power r to obtain each message g^r and its corresponding signature g^{rx}. Of course such ease of obtaining signatures on random messages in no way compromises the security of systems that make a distinction between messages and valid messages, which distinction is a well-known component of blind signature systems.

These first and third attacks also suffer from an additional problem, similar to that of the second attack of this class. They both expect a receiver who is following protocol to accept a signature on a random message (i.e., an invalid message), which of course no receiver need do. Furthermore, the first attack also involves blinding of the challenge and response, as detailed in [CvA 89], which, while possibly useful in some applications, is easily thwarted in other applications by the signer confirming signatures only on valid messages.

Conclusion

No significant weakness of undeniable signatures is contained in [DY 91].

References

[C 85]   Chaum, David "Security without identification: Transaction systems to make big brother obsolete," Communications of the ACM, October 1985, pp. 1030–1044.

[C 90]   Chaum, David "Zero-knowledge undeniable signatures," Advances in Cryptology—Eurocrypt '90, Springer-Verlag, pp. 458–464.

[C 91]   Chaum, David "Provers *can* limit the number of verifiers," pre-print available from the author.

[CvA 89]   Chaum, David and Hans van Antwerpen, "Undeniable signatures," Advances in Cryptology—CRYPTO '89, Springer-Verlag, 1991, pp. 212–216.

[DY 91]   Desmedt, Yvo and Moti Yung "Weaknesses of undeniable signature schemes," Pre-Proceedings of Eurocrypt '91.